WJEC **GCSE**

Food and Nutrition

Alison Clough-Halstead
Fiona Dowling • Victoria Ellis
Jayne Hill • Bethan Jones

Illuminate Publishing

Published in 2016 by Illuminate Publishing Ltd, P.O Box 1160, Cheltenham, Gloucestershire GL50 9RW

Orders: Please visit www.illuminatepublishing.com
or email sales@illuminatepublishing.com

© Alison Clough-Halstead, Fiona Dowling, Victoria Ellis, Jayne Hill, Bethan Jones

The moral rights of the authors have been asserted.

All rights reserved. No part of this book may be reprinted, reproduced or utilised in any form or by any electronic, mechanical, or other means, now known or hereafter invented, including photocopying and recording, or in any information storage and retrieval system, without permission in writing from the publishers.

British Library Cataloguing in Publication Data

A catalogue record for this book is available from the British Library

ISBN 978-1-908682-93-2

Printed by Barley Print, Cuffley, Herts

05.16

The publisher's policy is to use papers that are natural, renewable and recyclable products made from wood grown in sustainable forests. The logging and manufacturing processes are expected to conform to the environmental regulations of the country of origin.

Every effort has been made to contact copyright holders of material reproduced in this book. If notified, the publishers will be pleased to rectify any errors or omissions at the earliest opportunity.

This material has been endorsed by WJEC and offers high quality support for the delivery of WJEC qualifications. While this material has been through a WJEC quality assurance process, all responsibility for the content remains with the publisher.

WJEC examination questions are reproduced by permission from WJEC.

Editor: Just Content
Cover Design: Nigel Harriss
Design & Layout: emc design ltd.

Acknowledgements

To Bea, my inspiration, my guide, gyda fi am byth. To Dan, ever patient and kind, thank you. To C and J, my blessings and to Bryan, love to you all. A big thank you to my students past, and present, for all your enthusiasm and dedication. **Fiona Dowling**

I would like to thanks my friends Jaqui Housley for her inspiration and Sue Ives for her support, my son Ben for being ... my son and most of all my husband Raymond for doing everything whilst I was on the computer. I would also like to "thank" the bit of mud in Cuba in which I fell, because without the broken leg and ankle that followed, I would not have had the opportunity to be involved in this great project.
Alison Clough-Halstead

The publisher wishes to thank Rachel Rogers for her support in the development of this book.

CONTENTS

INTRODUCTION — 4

SECTION 1: CORE KNOWLEDGE — 7

PRINCIPLES OF NUTRITION	8
DIET AND GOOD HEALTH	44
THE SCIENCE OF COOKING FOOD	68
FOOD SPOILAGE	84
FOOD PROVENANCE AND FOOD WASTE	96
CULTURES AND CUISINES	106
TECHNOLOGICAL DEVELOPMENTS	120
FACTORS AFFECTING FOOD CHOICE	134

SECTION 2: BASIC MIXTURES AND RECIPES — 157

Cake making	158	Whipped cream	165	Flaky pastry	171
Pastry making	160	Choux pastry	166	Tomato sauce	172
Sauces	162	Bread	168	Roux sauce and gelatinisation	173
Batters	164	Shortcrust pastry	170	Setting	174

SECTION 3: COMMODITIES — 175

CEREALS	176
FRUIT AND VEGETABLES	213
MILK, CHEESE AND YOGHURT	241
MEAT, POULTRY, FISH AND EGGS	261
BEANS, NUTS AND SEEDS, SOYA, TOFU AND MYCOPROTEIN	317
BUTTER, OIL, MARGARINE, SUGAR AND SYRUP	335

SECTION 4: ASSESSMENT — 362

PART ONE THE WRITTEN EXAM	362
PART TWO NON-EXAMINATION ASSESSMENTS (NEAs)	386

GLOSSARY — 428
INDEX — 443

INTRODUCTION

Welcome to our WJEC GCSE Food and Nutrition textbook. All the authors have collaborated throughout the writing process to deliver the course content in what we hope is a very informal and user-friendly way. You'll see that we've closely followed the content and structure of the exam specification to make sure all the topics have been covered fully. Our editorial team also worked closely with WJEC throughout the development process, and the book has been endorsed by the awarding body.

What's behind our thinking in writing the book?

Our course is divided into four clear sections, designed to help you access specific information easily and quickly. As a group of very experienced teachers we decided to use this approach because we know that this subject is vast, and so a logical route through all that content seemed sensible and important. Therefore we decided to split all the specification theory into two distinct sections – Core Knowledge and Commodities.

Our feeling was that it is unlikely that you will simply start at page 1 of the book and then work your way through to the end. We'd recommend the approach that after learning part of Section 1 you will then link this with a topic from another section – this should develop independent and holistic learning. We hope that by doing this your learning is made manageable, straightforward and enjoyable.

So what will I find in each section?

Section 1 is Core Knowledge

This covers eight core knowledge subjects which as authors we felt were vital to getting a good grip on the course. They are the nuts and bolts of food preparation and nutrition, which in our view you really need to understand as the basics. You can tackle them totally separately from Commodities, but they really do filter into the commodity topics found in Section 3. To help in this you will see 🔗 throughout these which indicates a link to the other topics. For example the Protein topic in Principles of Nutrition will indicate links to the alternative protein foods section found in the commodity: *Beans, Nuts and Seeds, Soya, Tofu and Mycoprotein*.

We've covered the following topics in Section 1, and they all match to the exam specification content:
- Principles of nutrition
- Diet and good health
- The science of cooking food
- Food spoilage
- Food provenance and food waste
- Cultures and cuisines
- Technological developments
- Factors affecting food choice

Section 2 is all about the cooking – Basic mixtures and recipes

We decided to include standard basic recipes. It wasn't a hard decision, because once you know how to make these basic recipes you can easily adapt them to suit different ingredient choices. You can easily link these recipes to the Commodities in Section 3, or in fact to every chapter in Section 1. All of your knowledge and understanding of the topics in Sections 1 and 3 can be illustrated through practical work using the recipes in Section 2.

The accompanying Digital Teacher Book has many more recipes available.

Section 3 is all about the foods – Commodities

As well as following the commodities listed in the exam specification, you can see from the groupings opposite that we have also loosely followed the Eatwell Guide.

The theory for each group of foods follows a similar format to reinforce your learning: normally each commodity starts with a discussion of where the food originates or comes from, then deals with the nutrition found in the food, how it is processed, how it must be stored, any safety and hygiene points and finally how it is used in cooking.

The commodities covered are:
- Cereals
- Fruit and Vegetables
- Milk, Cheese and Yoghurt
- Meat, Poultry, Fish and Eggs
- Beans, Nuts and Seeds, Soya, Tofu and Mycoprotein
- Butter, Oil, Margarine, Sugar and Syrup

Section 4 covers Assessment

There are two parts to this Section:
- Part 1 The written exam
- Part 2 The non-examination assessments

Part 1 describes the assessment objectives, the types of exam questions you are likely to come across, as well as giving sample exam-style questions, markschemes and possible model answers to those questions at two different levels.

Part 2 describes the way the non-examination assessment part of the GCSE works – the Food Investigation Assessment and the Food Preparation Assessment. As well as an explanation of what the exam board requires for each assessment type, there are examples and samples with helpful hints and tips that clearly show you what you need to be creating and presenting.

A helpful hint that we as authors have found useful – ask your teacher for, or download a copy of the specification course content that you can keep in your folders. As each topic is completed you can highlight the corresponding information on the course content sheets. It is a great visual aid!

You'll also find that we've provided some suggested exam-style questions for all Section 1 Core Knowledge topics and all Section 3 Commodities. There's also a list of suggested Food Investigations too.

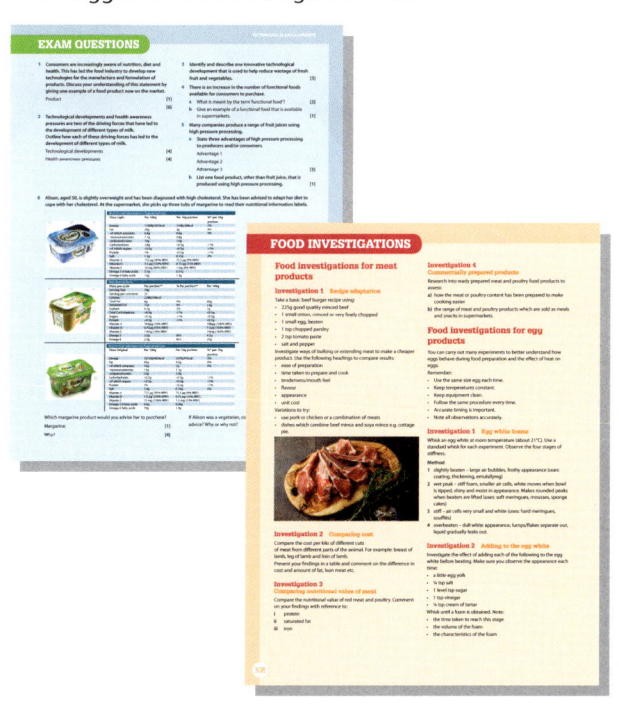

Finally there's a detailed glossary at the back of the book covering all the key terminology we think you will need to learn as you progress through the course.

That's it! We really hope that you enjoy using this book and that it supports, inspires and motivates you as you study GCSE Food and Nutrition.

Best wishes and good luck!

How is the book structured?

Each topic in each section follows a similar layout starting with the heading 'What will I learn?' which makes clear what needs to be learned by the end of each chapter. All the chapters are sprinkled with all sorts of helpful extra features which are there to help you to keep a check on your learning and to monitor your progress. These are:

Food Science or Nutrition flags

These remind you of the importance of the underlying Food Science or Nutrition information

[N] [FS]

Study tip

Advice or hints to help secure knowledge

> **Study tip**
> Are you able to explain what the term 'food provenance' means?

Activity

Slightly longer and more detailed solo, pair or group tasks

> **Activity**
> Produce a poster or leaflet that would encourage people to reduce food miles.

Key point

A simple summary of important facts that you really need to know

> **Key point**
> Convenience foods are useful for particular groups of people but should be used in conjunction with fresh ingredients to prepare dishes and meals.

Check it

Quick, short questions

> **Check it**
> What is the difference between advertising and marketing? Give examples of the types of advertising used to attract customers.

Key terms

that are important and we think you will need to know are highlighted throughout the book – terms in blue are defined at the end of each topic, and terms in black bold are defined in the Glossary at the back of the book.

> **Key terms**
> Origin – the place from which something is derived.

Link

Cross-refers you to related information or knowledge

Milk, Cheese and Yoghurt: Lactose intolerance p246

MEET THE TEAM!

Alison Clough-Halstead

Alison Clough-Halstead has worked as a Food teacher for over 30 years, firstly in Manchester and now in Lancashire where she is lead in Food for KS3, GCSE and post 16, as well as being an achievement leader. She has been a moderator and examiner for two awarding bodies for over 10 years. Alison has also written resources and has been involved in face-to-face professional development from Licence to Cook to Food Teachers Centre's guest presenter.

Outside the classroom Alison's life revolves around visiting different countries, especially the Far East, India and now the Caribbean. However after her last 'break' in Cuba – somehow breaking her ankle and leg – she is hoping to go back to see all the people who helped her… and finish her holiday properly!

Bethan Jones

Bethan has been a Food and Nutrition teacher for over 30 years, and during this time she's been involved with exam setting, delivering CPD and examining and moderating for various examination boards. She likes nothing better than eating out and singing in a ladies choir at competitions home and abroad and at local charity events.

Fiona Dowling

Fiona Dowling has worked in food and education for over 30 years and has been lead teacher in Food at KS3, GCSE and post 16. She has been moderating and examining for a major Awarding Body for over 10 years, as well as writing online resources and excelling at face to face professional development provision. She is a simple soul to please – her idea of fun includes eating Italian food, preferably served al fresco somewhere on the Italian Riviera!

Jayne Hill

Jayne qualified as a Home Economics teacher back in the late 1970s and so has seen many changes to the subject over the years. As well as teaching in the London Boroughs of Bexley and Greenwich and latterly in Plymouth, Jayne also owned a small catering business and a restaurant/tea room. However, the call of the classroom pulled her back into teaching! She was the Principle Examiner and a Senior Moderator for GCSE Catering for a major Awarding Body. Outside the classroom Jayne's life revolves around her two daughters and two Burmese cats – all of whom are lovely! She has also been a local Borough Councillor and Mayor and with what little free time is left she helps her daughters run an online business, chases the Northern Lights in the Arctic Circle and can usually be found planning her next holiday in the sun …

Victoria Ellis

Victoria is an examiner and moderator for Food and Nutrition and a published author in this field. She has been teaching for 14 years at Cwmtawe Community School, South Wales, but has recently taken a six month sabbatical to teach Home Economics in Lesotho. In her spare time (which is limited) she runs a Guide and Rainbow unit, and also enjoys going for long walks, especially ones that end in a coffee shop.

SECTION 1
CORE KNOWLEDGE

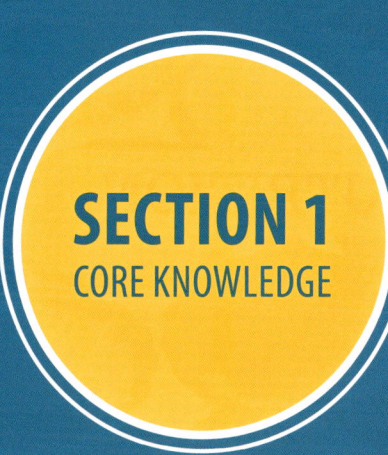

- **PRINCIPLES OF NUTRITION** 8
- **DIET AND GOOD HEALTH** 44
- **THE SCIENCE OF COOKING FOOD** 68
- **FOOD SPOILAGE** 84
- **FOOD PROVENANCE AND FOOD WASTE** 96
- **CULTURES AND CUISINES** 106
- **TECHNOLOGICAL DEVELOPMENTS** 120
- **FACTORS AFFECTING FOOD CHOICE** 134

SECTION 1
CORE KNOWLEDGE

PRINCIPLES OF NUTRITION

What will I learn?
- The key nutrients that are needed for good health
- Why the body needs nutrients
- The functions and sources of nutrients
- What happens if we have too many or too few nutrients
- The nutrients provided by different foods
- How water and fibre contribute to the diet

Key point
For good health it is important to have a wide range of nutrients in your diet. A **deficiency** is a lack of something that is needed in the diet. The **function** is what something does, or why it is needed.

Study tip
Remember the main nutrient groups and make sure you can give examples of food sources for each nutrient.

Be able to explain what happens if we have too much (excess) or not enough (**deficiency**) of each nutrient.

Check it
1. Explain the difference between the terms macronutrient and micronutrient.
2. List the 5 key nutrient groups.
3. What do the following terms mean?
   i Function
   ii Source
   iii Deficiency
   iv Excess

The key nutrients in the diet

Nutrients are chemicals found in food which give the body nourishment and are needed for the maintenance of life. The body needs nutrients to perform its daily **functions** properly. Health problems might occur if any one of these nutrients is lacking in a person's diet.

There are two main types of nutrients:

Macronutrients refer to carbohydrates, protein and **fat** which the body needs in large amounts. They are measured in grams.

Micronutrients refer to vitamins, minerals and trace elements which the body needs in small amounts. They are measured in mg (milligram) or μg (microgram).

The body also needs dietary fibre and water.

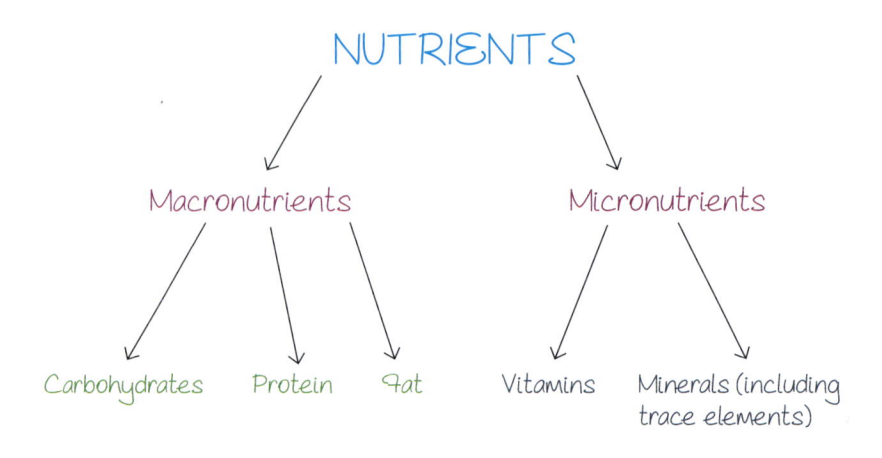

```
                    NUTRIENTS
                   /         \
            Macronutrients    Micronutrients
           /     |     \       /        \
   Carbohydrates Protein Fat  Vitamins  Minerals (including
                                         trace elements)
```

▲ Carbohydrates, protein, fat, vitamins and minerals are the key nutrients needed for a healthy diet

CORE KNOWLEDGE

PRINCIPLES OF NUTRITION

The role of nutrients

Throughout this chapter, you will gain knowledge and understanding of why the body needs nutrients and which foods provide them. The next three pages give you an overview of the key nutrients, their functions and sources.

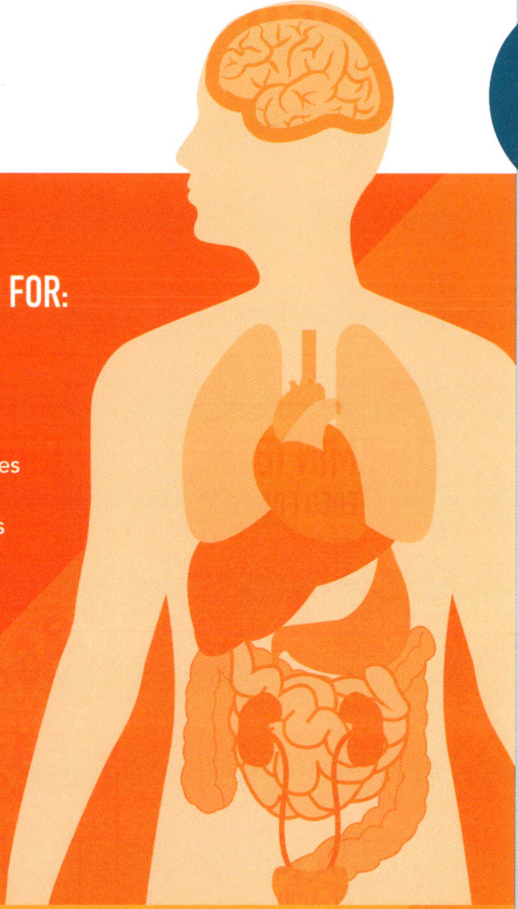

CARBOHYDRATE

NEEDED FOR:
energy

FOUND IN:
cereals   potatoes
bread   cakes
pasta   biscuits

PROTEIN

NEEDED FOR:
growth
repair
maintenance

FOUND IN:
meat   cereals
dairy products   pulses
fish   nuts
eggs   seeds

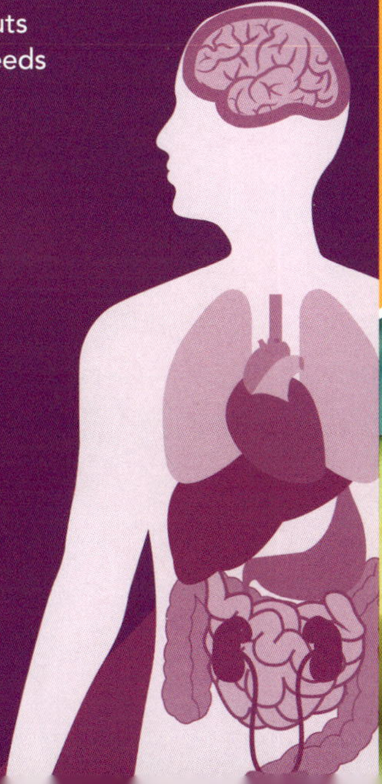

FAT

NEEDED FOR:
energy
warmth
protection of organs
source of fat soluble vitamins

FOUND IN:
sausages   nuts
bacon   seeds
lard   avocados
dairy products
oily fish

9

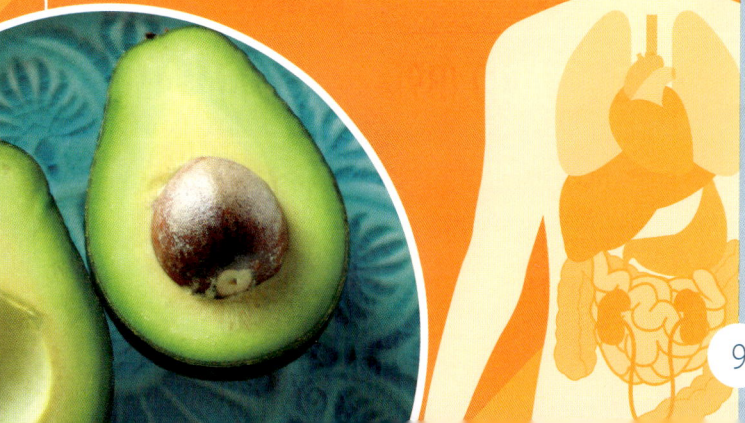

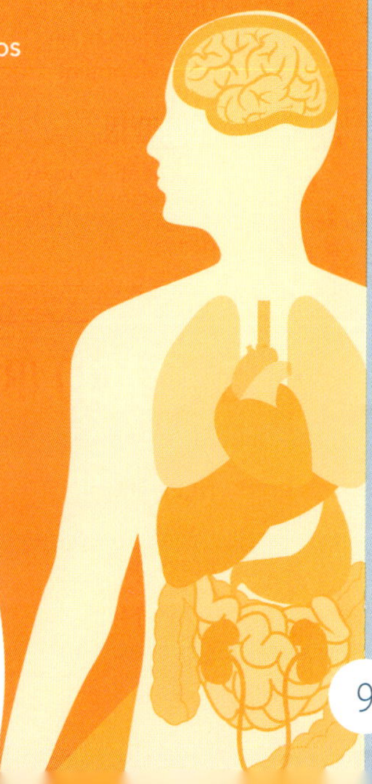

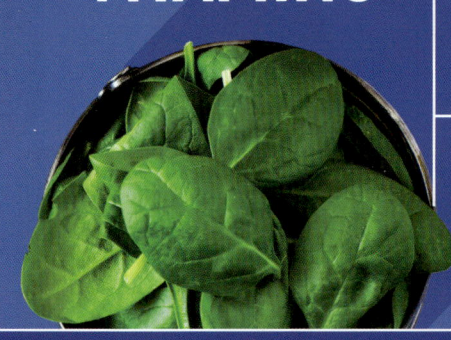

VITAMINS

A
- **NEEDED FOR:**
  healthy immune system; helps us to see in dim light
- **FOUND IN:**
  dairy, leafy vegetables, eggs, mango, oily fish, apricot

C
- **NEEDED FOR:**
  fights infection, heals wounds
- **FOUND IN:**
  oranges, kiwi fruit, blackcurrants, strawberries, Brussels sprouts

B GROUP

THIAMIN (B1)
- **NEEDED FOR:**
  energy release, healthy nervous system
- **FOUND IN:**
  eggs, dried fruit, liver, whole grain bread, peas, fortified breakfast cereals

RIBOFLAVIN (B2)
- **NEEDED FOR:**
  energy release, healthy nervous system
- **FOUND IN:**
  milk, eggs, rice, fortified breakfast cereals

D
- **NEEDED FOR:**
  healthy bones and teeth
- **FOUND IN:**
  oily fish, eggs, fortified margarines

  made by the body when exposed to sunlight

NIACIN (B3)
(NICOTINIC ACID)
- **NEEDED FOR:**
  energy release, healthy nervous system
- **FOUND IN:**
  meat, milk, fish, wheat, eggs

PANTOTHENIC ACID (B5)
- **NEEDED FOR:**
  metabolism of nutrients
- **FOUND IN:**
  meat, potatoes, tomatoes, broccoli, whole grains

E
- **NEEDED FOR:**
  healthy skin and eyes, strong immune system
- **FOUND IN:**
  plant oils, nuts, seeds, wheat germ

PYRIDOXINE (B6)
- **NEEDED FOR:**
  nerve and brain development
- **FOUND IN:**
  red meat, yeast, liver, nuts and beans, dairy, whole grain cereal

BIOTIN (B7)
- **NEEDED FOR:**
  energy production, protein metabolism
- **FOUND IN:**
  offal, nuts, milk, berries, vegetables

K
- **NEEDED FOR:**
  wound healing, blood clotting
- **FOUND IN:**
  broccolli, spinach, vegetable oils, cereal grains

FOLIC ACID (B9)
(FOLATE)
- **NEEDED FOR:**
  healthy red blood cells, prevents spina bifida
- **FOUND IN:**
  liver, cereals, milk, spinach, broccoli, asparagus

COBALAMIN (B12)
- **NEEDED FOR:**
  healthy red blood cells, energy release
- **FOUND IN:**
  meat, fish, cheese, eggs

MINERALS

CALCIUM
- **NEEDED FOR:**
  - bone formation
  - heart function
  - healthy red blood cells
- **FOUND IN:**
  - dairy foods
  - green leafy vegetables
  - soya beans
  - nuts
  - fish bones
  - bread (fortified)

IRON
- **NEEDED FOR:**
  - healthy red blood cells
- **FOUND IN:**
  - red meat
  - beans
  - nuts
  - soybean flour
  - dark-green leafy vegetables
  - apricots
  - cocoa
  - treacle

POTASSIUM
- **NEEDED FOR:**
  - controlling body fluids
  - heart function
- **FOUND IN:**
  - bananas
  - broccoli
  - parsnips
  - pulses
  - nuts and seeds
  - fish
  - meat

PHOSPHOROUS
- **NEEDED FOR:**
  - bone formation
  - energy release
- **FOUND IN:**
  - red meat
  - fish
  - dairy foods
  - brown rice
  - oats

MAGNESIUM
- **NEEDED FOR:**
  - energy release
  - bone health
- **FOUND IN:**
  - green leafy vegetables
  - nuts
  - brown rice
  - whole grain bread
  - fish
  - meat
  - dairy

SODIUM
- **NEEDED FOR:**
  - balancing bodily fluids
- **FOUND IN:**
  - salt
  - processed foods
  - cured meats
  - savoury snacks

TRACE ELEMENTS

IODINE
- **NEEDED FOR:**
  - hormone in thyroid
- **FOUND IN:**
  - sea fish
  - shellfish

FLUORIDE
- **NEEDED FOR:**
  - preventing tooth decay
- **FOUND IN:**
  - tea
  - fish

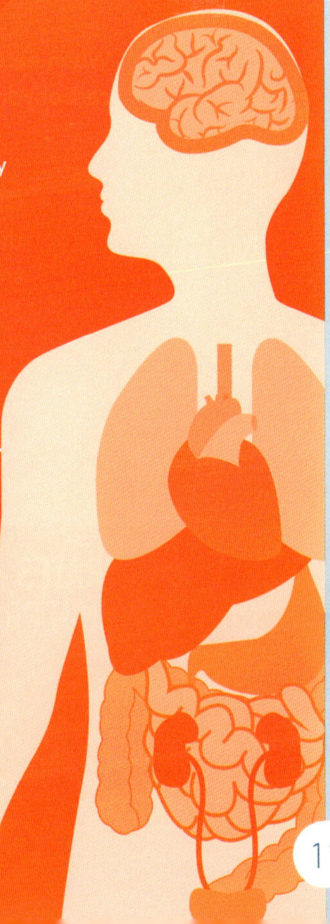

SELENIUM
- **NEEDED FOR:**
  - hormone in thyroid
  - healthy immune system
- **FOUND IN:**
  - meat
  - fish
  - cereal
  - nuts

ZINC
- **NEEDED FOR:**
  - healing
  - protecting against infection
- **FOUND IN:**
  - meat
  - dairy
  - shellfish
  - cereals

SECTION 1

CARBOHYDRATES

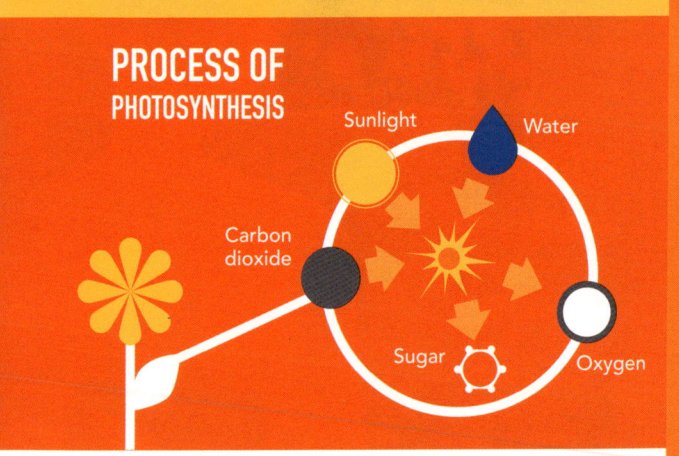

Key point
Sugar and starch are both carbohydrates.

COMPOSITION

H (Hydrogen) + **C** (Carbon) + **O** (Oxygen)

PROCESS OF PHOTOSYNTHESIS

Sunlight, Water, Carbon dioxide → Sugar, Oxygen

WHY WE NEED CARBS

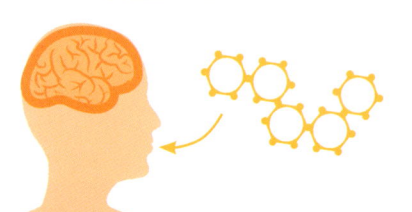

FOR ENERGY

When eaten, the body breaks down carbohydrate foods into glucose

Glucose is absorbed into the blood through the small intestine

The pancreas produces insulin to allow glucose to enter cells

SUGAR

MONOSACCHARIDES

Glucose:
- Fruits
- Vegetables
- Corn
- Cane/sugar beet
- Honey
- Animal blood

Fructose:
- Fruits
- Vegetables
- Corn
- Cane/sugar beet
- Honey

Galactose:
- Not in foods
- Produced when lactose is broken down in the body during digestion.

GLUCOSE ABSORBED DIRECTLY INTO THE BLOODSTREAM DURING DIGESTION

DISACCHARIDES

Sucrose: (the sugar we tend to use in cooking)
GLUCOSE + FRUCTOSE
Cane/sugar beet

Lactose:
GLUCOSE + GALACTOSE
Milk

Maltose:
GLUCOSE + GLUCOSE
- Sweet potatoes
- Soyabeans
- Barley
- Wheat

FORMED WHEN TWO MONOSACCHARIDE MOLECULES ARE JOINED

STARCH

POLYSACCHARIDES

Starch:
- Potatoes
- Wheat
- Barley
- Pulses
- Oats
- Corn
- Rice

Cellulose:
- Fruit
- Vegetables
- Whole grains

Pectin:
- Fruit
- Vegetables

STARCH IS A COMPLEX CARBOHYDRATE

CARBOHYDRATES ARE CONVERTED TO ENERGY QUICKER THAN PROTEIN AND FAT SOURCES

→ 1g carbohydrate = 16kJ / 3.75 kcal

carbohydrates are the main energy source for the body
starch provides the body with a slow and steady release of energy

1/3 OF THE DIET SHOULD COME FROM STARCHY FOODS

CORE KNOWLEDGE — Dietary fibre: Principles of Nutrition pp16–17

PRINCIPLES OF NUTRITION

As well as providing **energy**, starchy foods also supply other important nutrients to the body such as protein, calcium, iron, B vitamins and dietary fibre.

Sugar is another source of carbohydrate and it is also sometimes referred to as a simple carbohydrate. Sugar in food and drink can be present naturally, for example in fruit and dairy products. It can also be added during manufacturing and processing, for example in sweets, cakes, biscuits, sauces and fizzy drinks. Sugar is sometimes referred to as '**empty calories**' because apart from providing energy, sugar offers virtually no **nutritional value**.

There is a real concern about the amount of sugar consumed in the UK. A diet high in sugary foods can lead to serious health issues including **obesity**, type 2 diabetes, heart disease, some cancers and tooth decay.

▲ Foods and drinks high in sugar provide the body with a fast release of energy.

Striking a balance with carbohydrates in the diet

If your diet is low in sources of carbohydrate foods then your level of **blood sugar** (called glucose) may drop to below the normal range. The immediate effect of this is that you become hungry, but you may also feel weak and dizzy. Without carbohydrates your body then starts to burn stored fat and then protein in order to get its energy. However, if you consume more energy than your body needs the extra glucose from starch and sugar is stored in the liver and muscles as energy. This will be converted into fat and stored in the **adipose tissue**. This can lead to weight gain and over time, **obesity**. This can put you at risk of **heart disease** and **type 2 diabetes**. Too much sugar can also cause tooth decay (dental caries).

▲ A diet high in sugary foods can lead to tooth decay, often called dental caries. This is caused by acids produced from bacteria in the mouth.

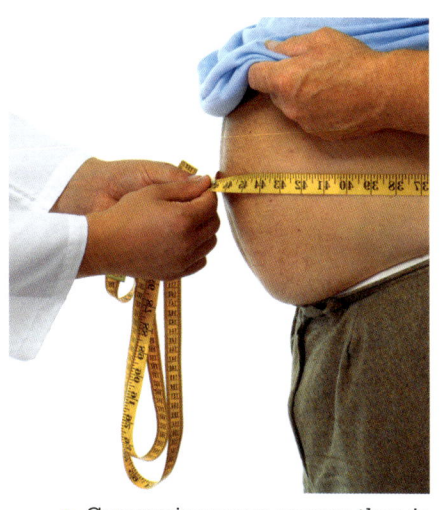

▲ Consuming more energy than is needed by the body will lead to weight gain and obesity.

▲ Diabetes type 2 can occur in later life; it is often associated with obesity and can cause serious long term health problems.

Check it

1. Give examples of food sources that contain:
   i Glucose
   ii Fructose
   iii Sucrose
2. Which two monosaccharide units is sucrose made from?

Key point

Foods containing sugar and starch both provide energy.

Sugary foods are simple carbohydrates that release energy quickly; they can cause uneven blood sugar levels.

Starchy foods are complex carbohydrates that provide slow release energy.

Starch-based carbohydrate foods should be consumed as a source of energy, not sugary foods.

Check it

1. Give the main function of carbohydrates in the diet.
2. List 3 foods that are good sources of starchy carbohydrate.
3. State which other important nutrients are often found in starchy foods.
4. Why is sugar sometimes referred to as 'empty calories'?
5. Suggest 3 health problems that could arise from having a high sugar diet.
6. Why should we include more starchy foods and fewer sugary foods in our diet?

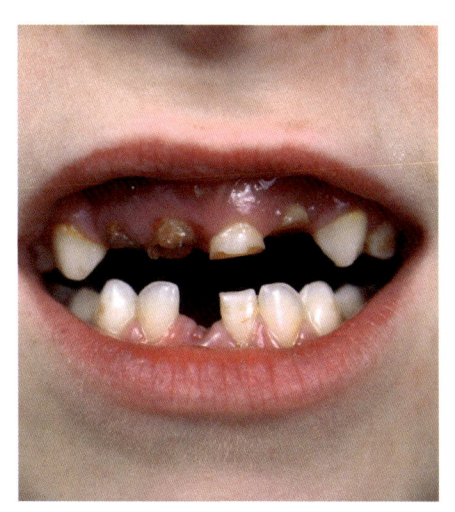

Diet and good health: Special diets pp58–61

▲ Eating sugary foods can raise blood sugar levels to a dangerous level.

Study tip
Be able to explain the health problems that can result due to a diet high in sugars.

Check it
Explain the terms intrinsic and extrinsic sugars.

Study tip
Learn to recognise the chemical names of 'hidden sugars' listed on food labels, e.g. dextrose, fructose, glucose, glucose syrup, hydrolysed starch, invert sugar, lactose and sucrose.

▼ Honey is a source of non-milk extrinsic sugar.

Slow release and fast release carbohydrates

Starchy foods are known as slow release carbohydrates because they provide a slow and steady release of glucose energy into the blood. In contrast, sugary foods are fast release carbohydrates. This means that glucose is released more quickly into the blood. This can cause highs and lows in blood sugar level and less stable energy levels in the body.

Sugar in the form of glucose is a key energy source, and the different sugars in our diets can be divided into two types, depending on how they are found in foods:

Intrinsic sugars (glucose, fructose, lactose and sucrose) occur naturally in foods such as fruit and some sweet vegetables.

Extrinsic sugars are added to food. The main one is sucrose (white sugar) which comes from sugar cane, sugar beet or corn (high fructose corn syrup). Other extrinsic sugars include honey and those used in soft drinks and artificial sweeteners. It also refers to sugars in milk.

▲ Fruits are a source of intrinsic sugar.   ▲ Sucrose is an extrinsic sugar.

What are Non-Milk Extrinsic Sugars (NMES)?

These are all extrinsic sugars not from milk. They are also called 'free sugars'. The term NMES is only used in the UK.

NMES consist largely of sucrose but also include honey, glucose, fructose and glucose syrups.

PRINCIPLES OF NUTRITION

SECTION 1

HOW MUCH SUGAR SHOULD WE CONSUME?

In July 2015 the SACN (Scientific Advisory Committee on Nutrition) Report on Carbohydrates and Health recommended a reduction of free sugars to 5% energy intake. It identified the maximum daily intake of sugar by age group as follows:

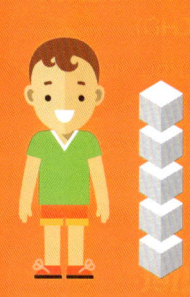

FOR CHILDREN AGED 4 TO 6:
19g of added sugar a day (approximately 5 sugar cubes)

FOR CHILDREN AGED 7 TO 10:
24g of added sugar a day (approximately 6 sugar cubes)

FOR ADULTS AND CHILDREN AGED 11 TO 18:
30g of added sugar a day (approximately 7 sugar cubes)

▲ The SACN recommended maximum intake of free sugars per day

What is the Glycaemic Index (GI)?

The **Glycaemic Index (GI)** is a ranking of carbohydrate foods based on their overall effect on blood glucose levels. Foods that are absorbed slowly have a low GI rating. Foods that are absorbed more quickly have a higher rating. GI ratings give people with diabetes important information to monitor their blood glucose levels.

Low GI foods (55 or less) include most fruits, non-starchy vegetables, carrots, 100% stone-ground whole wheat bread and legumes.

Medium GI (56-69) foods include brown rice, basmati rice and oats.

High GI (70 or more) foods include white bread, corn flakes, white rice, white pasta, pineapple and melon.

Study tip

Make sure you understand why it is important for diabetics to monitor blood glucose levels.

▲ Brown rice and oats have a medium GI index.

◀ A can of cola can have as much as 9 cubes of added sugar.

Butter, Oil, Margarine, Sugar and Syrup: The nutritional value of sugar in the diet p354

> **Key point**
>
> Dietary fibre can be either insoluble or soluble.
>
> Soluble fibre helps to lower blood cholesterol.

Dietary fibre

Dietary fibre is also referred to as roughage, cellulose and **non starch polysaccharide** (NSP).

Fibre is a type of carbohydrate that is found in plant-based foods, including fruit, vegetables and whole and unprocessed grains. Dietary fibre mostly refers to **insoluble fibre**, meaning that it is not easily broken down by the digestive system and most of it passes through the body unchanged. This fibre helps to keep healthy bowels and prevent digestive problems such as constipation and haemorrhoids (piles).

Soluble fibre is broken down by bacteria in the large bowel and can then be digested. This fibre may help to reduce the amount of **cholesterol** in the blood which can guard against **coronary heart disease** (CHD).

Oats are often recommended in a cholesterol-lowering diet because they contain a soluble fibre called oat **beta-glucan**.

Pectin is another form of soluble fibre. It is a complex carbohydrate, which is found both in the cell walls of plants such as apple, plums, pears and citrus fruits peel. It is used as a setting agent in jams and jellies.

Why we need dietary fibre in the diet

Fibre is important to keep your bowels healthy. When fibre passes through your bowels, it absorbs lots of water and increases the bulk of any waste material that leaves your body. This makes your stool (poo) softer and easier to pass.

A diet high in fibre will prevent constipation, haemorrhoids and diverticulitis (when the bowel wall becomes inflamed and damaged). It can also help to prevent type 2 diabetes, some cancers (such as cancer of the colon) and is believed to lower the risk of coronary heart disease.

When you eat foods which are high in fibre, you feel fuller for longer. This can reduce the temptation to snack in between meals and can help people maintain a healthy weight. It also slows down the absorption of carbohydrates in the blood, which helps to keep blood sugar levels constant. This can be useful for those who have diabetes.

When a diet is too low in fibre it is often as a result of eating refined foods, for example eating white bread instead of wholemeal bread or white rice instead of brown rice. It also means a general lack of fruit and vegetables in the diet. This can lead to a variety of conditions, such as constipation, haemorrhoids, diverticulitis and certain cancers.

Of course it is possible to eat too much fibre, which would leave you feeling bloated with stomach cramps, flatulence and in extreme cases diarrhoea. Too much fibre can also affect mineral absorption and your body may not take in vital minerals such as iron and calcium. Phytic acid is present in wheat, and too much causes phytates of calcium and iron to form, depriving the body of both these minerals.

▲ All of these foods are good sources of fibre – how many do you eat regularly?

DIVERTICULOSIS and DIVERTICULITIS

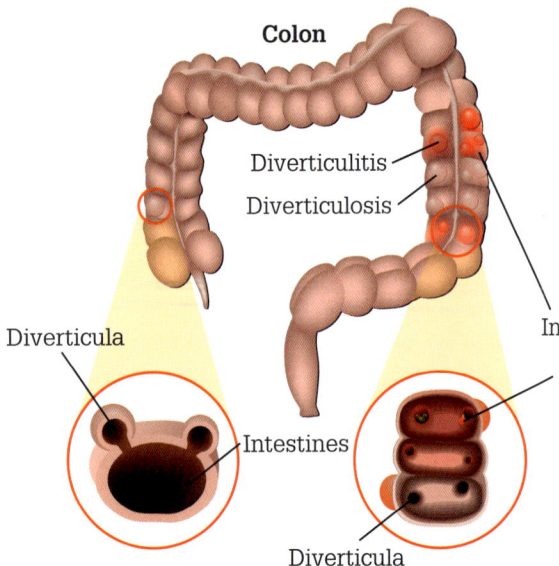

How much dietary fibre do we need?

The NHS recommended daily intake for dietary fibre is:

2–5-year olds, about 15g

5–11-year olds, about 20g

11–16-year olds, about 25g

16 year olds and older, about 30g

SACN recommends that the dietary fibre intake for adults should be 30g each day. However, if a person has a digestive disorder such as irritable bowel syndrome (IBS) then they may need to alter their fibre intake.

The sources of dietary fibre in the diet

Insoluble fibre: whole grain cereals, wholemeal bread, bran, nuts, corn, oats, fruit and vegetables (especially the skins).

Soluble fibre: oats, barley, rye, most beans and peas, fruit such as bananas and apples, and root vegetables such as carrots.

Check it

1. Explain the difference between insoluble fibre and soluble fibre.
2. Why are oats often recommended in a cholesterol lowering diet?

Key point

Irritable bowel syndrome (IBS) is a common, long-term condition of the digestive system. It can cause stomach cramps, bloating, diarrhoea and/or constipation.

Key point

A high fibre diet can reduce chances of some diseases, including those relating to the bowel.

A high fibre diet can help to regulate blood sugar levels.

Phytates in fibre rich foods can prevent the absorption of some essential nutrients such as calcium and iron.

Study tip

Be able to explain the difference between insoluble and soluble fibre and give examples of food sources for each.

Check that you know the dietary issues linked to a low fibre diet.

In your written examination, you may be asked about why fibre is an important factor in a healthy diet, make sure you can answer this!

▼ Dietary fibre content of common breakfast cereals and breads

BREAKFAST CEREALS

ALL-BRAN — 6 tbsp | 10.3g

SHREDDED WHEAT — 2 | 4.4g

BRAN FLAKES — 4 tbsp | 4.2g

WEETABIX — 2 | 3.9g

UNSWEETENED MUESLI — 3 tbsp | 3.4g

FRUIT 'N' FIBRE — 4 tbsp | 2.2g

PORRIDGE — 1 bowl | 1.3g

CORNFLAKES — 5 tbsp | 0.3g

NB: Serving sizes are based on medium portions
www.weightlossresources.co.uk

BREAD

WHOLEMEAL BREAD — 1 slice | 2.1g

GRANARY BREAD — 1 slice | 1.5g

BROWN BREAD — 1 slice | 1.3g

WHITE BREAD — 1 slice | 0.5g

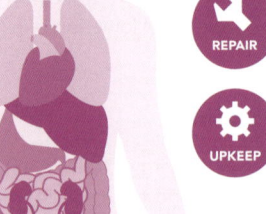

Protein

Why do we need protein?

Protein is a very important macronutrient in the diet. It is essential for the growth and repair of the body and for the maintenance of good health. It is also needed in the production of body chemicals such as enzymes and hormones.

Proteins are another energy source. For instance 1g of protein provides 17kJ / 4 kcal.

Protein can be obtained from both animal and plant sources. Animal sources are often referred to as high biological value (HBV) protein and the plant sources are often referred to as low biological value (LBV) protein.

ANIMAL SOURCES (HBV)

lean meat, poultry and fish

eggs

dairy products such as milk, yoghurt and cheese

*VEGETABLE SOURCES (LBV)

seeds and nuts

beans and legumes such as lentils and chickpeas

*grains e.g. such as wheat, oats, buckwheat and millet

**soya products like tofu and TVP

**mycoprotein such as Quorn

NOTE:

*Grain and cereal-based products are also sources of protein, but they are not as high in protein as meat and meat alternative products (TVP and the mycoprotein Quorn). The grain quinoa is an exception and is HBV.

**Meat alternative products (soya products such as tofu, TVP and the mycoprotein Quorn) are vegetable protein sources which are high biological value sources of protein.

CORE KNOWLEDGE — Beans, Nuts and Seeds, Soya, Tofu and Mycoprotein: Alternative protein foods pp326–334

PRINCIPLES OF NUTRITION

Amino acids

Proteins are made up of chains of smaller building blocks called amino acids. There are about 20 different amino acids that combine to make up the millions of proteins found in nature. A protein can consist of between 50 and tens of thousands of amino acids.

The body breaks down protein into amino acids. These amino acids are sometimes referred to as the building blocks of all proteins.

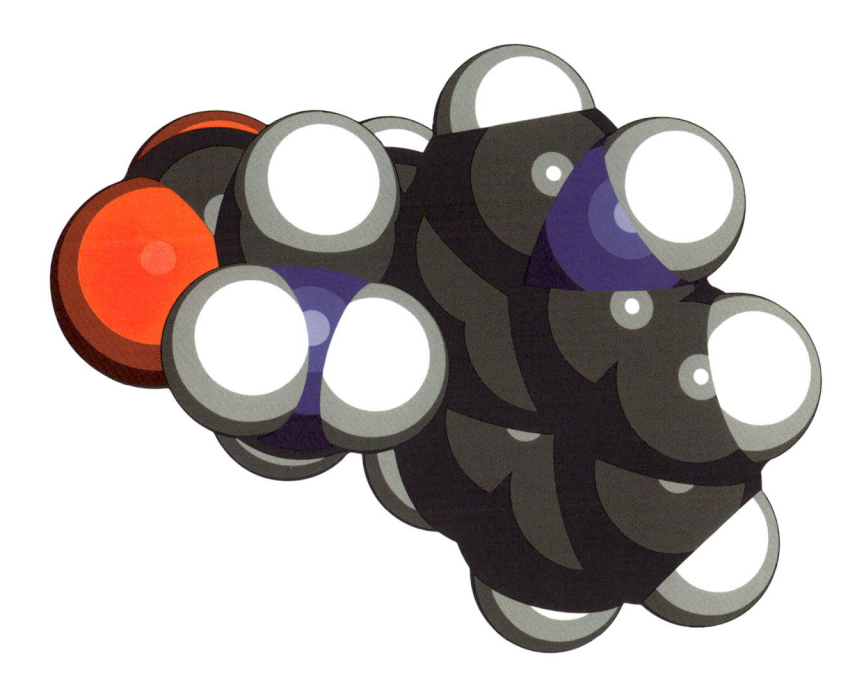

▲ Amino acids are the building blocks of protein.

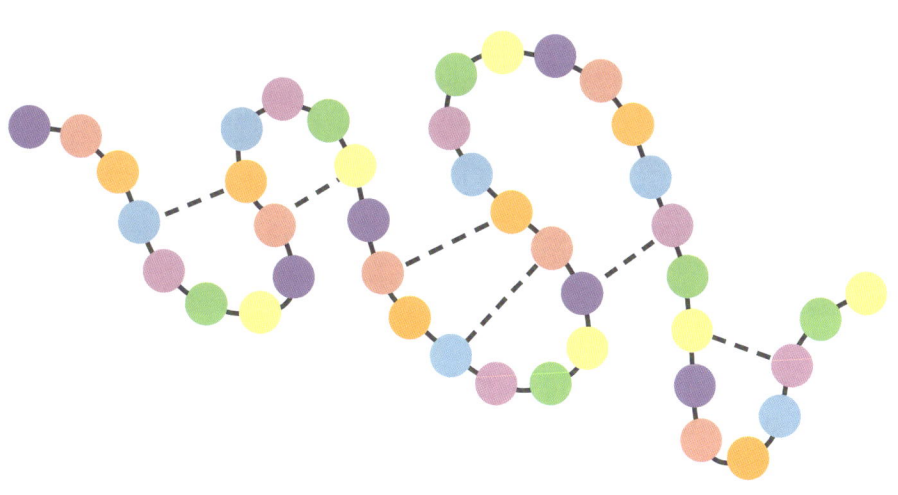

▲ A protein chain is made up of many amino acids.

Amino acids can be categorised as:

essential amino acids (indispensable) – these are amino acids that must be supplied to us through our diet (they cannot be made by the body).

non-essential amino acids (dispensable) – these are amino acids that can be made by the body.

Key point

Proteins are made from amino acid chains.

Animal protein sources are HBV.

Vegetable protein sources are LBV (vegetable sources from soya, Quorn and quinoa are exceptions and are HBV).

Activity

Look at the following photos of protein foods. Identify whether each food is a source of HBV or LBV

Extension

Using a nutritional database, plan a one day menu that will supply you with your RNI (reference nutritional intake) of protein. Make sure your diet includes sources of both HBV and LBV protein.

19

ESSENTIAL AMINO ACIDS

For adults, 8 amino acids have to be provided in the diet:

- Isoleucine
- Leucine
- Lysine
- Methionine
- Phenylalanine
- Threonine
- Tryptophan
- Valine

For children, the following amino acids are also considered essential:

- Arginine
- Cysteine
- Glutamine
- Glycine
- Histidine
- Proline
- Tyrosine

> **Study tip**
>
> Don't panic – you don't need to recall the names of all these amino acids. If you can, try to remember one or two. Just make sure you understand that some amino acids are 'essential' – meaning they have to be provided through the diet.

Children are unable to make enough of the above listed amino acids to meet their needs. These amino acids are also referred to as 'conditionally' essential. There may also be certain illnesses or diseases during adult life when a particular amino acid becomes 'conditionally' essential. The amino acid histidine is also an essential amino acid for the rapidly growing infant.

> **Study tip**
>
> Can you explain the differences in nutritional value between animal and vegetable protein sources? (Hint: talk about amino acids and biological values.)
>
> Be sure to know examples of vegetable protein sources that are high biological value (HBV).

High biological value (HBV) and low biological value (LBV) protein foods

The nutritional value of a protein is measured by the amount of essential amino acids that it provides. High biological value (HBV) protein foods contain all the essential amino acids whereas low biological value (LBV) protein foods are missing one or more of the essential amino acids. Different foods contain different amounts of amino acids. For instance:

Animal products (such as chicken, pork, beef, fish, etc.) contain all the essential amino acids.

Soya products, including soya milk, tofu and TVP, quinoa and the seed of a leafy green called amaranth, also contain all the essential amino acids.

Plant proteins usually lack at least one amino acid.

> **Activity**
>
> 1. What is the difference between the nutritional value of HBV and LBV protein foods?
> 2. Give examples of food products made from soya beans.

CORE KNOWLEDGE

PRINCIPLES OF NUTRITION

Essential amino acids are sometimes referred to as indispensable amino acids. These cannot be made by the body and must be obtained through the diet.

Non-essential amino acids are sometimes referred to as dispensable amino acids, these can be made by the body.

Conditionally essential amino acids need to be obtained from food sources at certain life stages because they cannot be produced in sufficient quantities to satisfy the needs of the body.

How much protein do we need?

CHILDREN		ADULTS	
1 to 3 years	15g	19 to 50 years	55g
4 to 6 years	20g	50 years +	53g
7 to 10 years	28g		
11 to 14 years	42g		
15 to 18 years	55g		

The amount of protein needed in a diet depends on a person's weight, age and health. As a rough guide, the RNI (Reference Nutrient Intake) for protein is:

Any surplus of protein our body does not need for growth, repair and maintenance will be used as energy. The most effective way to reach the daily protein requirement is to eat small amounts of protein at every meal. Most people in the developed world eat far more protein than they actually need, so **deficiencies** are rare.

Protein deficiency in the diet can cause:
- wasting and shrinkage of muscle tissue
- oedema – build-up of fluids, particularly in the feet and ankles
- anaemia – the blood's inability to deliver sufficient oxygen to the cells, usually caused by dietary deficiencies such as a lack of iron
- slow growth (in children).

In very severe cases, such as in the case of starvation during famine, a deficiency disease called kwashiorkor can occur. This is a form of malnutrition that most often affects children in developing areas of the world where there is a limited food supply or famine breaks out. Symptoms of kwashiorkor include an enlarged tummy ('pot belly') caused by oedema, a failure to grow and brittle hair. The child will die unless the protein deficiency is treated.

What are complementary proteins?

Combining two or more LBV protein foods creates complementary proteins. This is one way to ensure that the diet provides adequate amounts of all the essential amino acids. For example, a meal containing cereals and legumes, such as baked beans on toast, provides all the essential amino acids found in a typical meat dish. Other examples of complementary protein meals include dhal with rice and hummus with pitta bread.

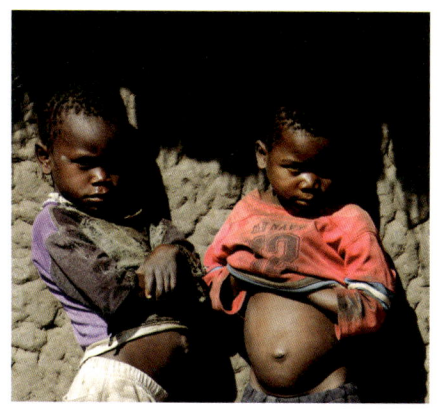

▲ Children with kwashiorkor

Key point

Excess protein from the diet will be used as an energy source.

Protein deficiency is rare in the Western world.

Check it

1. Why does the amount of protein needed in a diet vary with age?
2. What are the symptoms of an extreme protein deficiency?

Key point

To obtain the required balance of amino acids, strict vegetarians need to include a variety of protein sources from a combination of plant foods in their daily diet.

Check it

Suggest 3 snacks or meals which would be examples of complementary proteins.

FAT

Fats play an important part in our diet. They provide us with energy and essential vitamins and fatty acids. However, some people don't get the balance of nutrients right and consume more fat than is recommended. A diet that is too high in fat can lead to health problems including obesity, type 2 diabetes and heart disease.

As part of a healthy diet, we should try to cut down onw foods and drinks high in saturated fats and trans-fats and replace some of them with unsaturated fats.

Why do we need fat in our diet?

Fat is a macronutrient which provides energy, but in a more concentrated form than energy obtained from carbohydrate or protein based foods. The term fat also covers oils and lipids. For comparison 1g of fat provides 37kJ / 9 kcal.

As well as providing energy, foods containing fat also perform the following functions:

- **WARMTH** — Insulation and body warmth
- **PROTECT** — Protects the vital organs (e.g. heart, liver, kidneys and lungs)
- **TRANSIT** — As a carrier for the fat soluble vitamins: Vitamin A, D, E and K
- **HORMONES** — Important for hormone production
- **FATS** — Contain essential fats which the body is unable to make for itself

Fats can be divided into two main types:

FAT
→ Saturated
→ Unsaturated
  → Monosaturated
  → Polyunsaturated

CORE KNOWLEDGE — Diet and good health: Special diets p58–61

Saturated fats

Saturated fats are the least healthy fats as they can raise blood cholesterol levels and increase the risk of **coronary heart disease**.

Saturated fats often are from animal sources such as lard and butter, full fat dairy foods, fats visible on meat, processed meat products such as sausages and burgers and sweet foods such as pastries, cakes and biscuits. Some vegetable fats can also be saturated such as block margarine, palm oil and coconut oil.

Trans-fats (hydrogenated vegetable oils)

Trans-fats are vegetable oils which have been processed to make them hard. This is done by passing hydrogen through liquid oil. This process of **hydrogenation** turns the liquid oil into a solid or semi-solid fat, known as a trans-fat. Hydrogenation makes fats less healthy, like saturated fats. Trans-fats clog arteries and increase the risk of coronary heart disease. Food manufacturers use trans-fats in products such as cakes, biscuits and convenience foods as they increase the **shelf life** and improve the flavour foods. This results in greater profitability for the food manufacturers and retailers.

▲ Food manufacturers use trans-fats in the manufacture of cakes, biscuits and pastries.

◀ Marks and Spencer is the first UK food retailer to ban hydrogenated fat in all their foods.

Trans-fats not only raise the bad cholesterol (LDL), they also reduce the healthy cholesterol (HDL). They are found in many processed foods like cakes, pastries, biscuits, doughnuts and pizza. They may appear on the ingredients list as 'partially hydrogenated vegetable fats/oil' or '**shortening**'.

Trans-fats also occur naturally in meat and dairy products. Choosing low fat dairy and lean meats will reduce the amount of harmful trans- and saturated fats in the diet. To help customers reduce the amount of trans-fats they eat, some UK retailers are working hard to reduce and eventually eliminate trans-fats in their products.

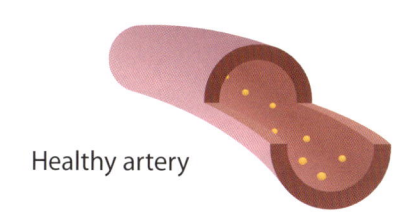

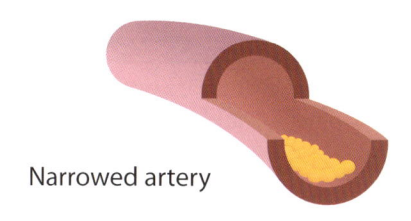

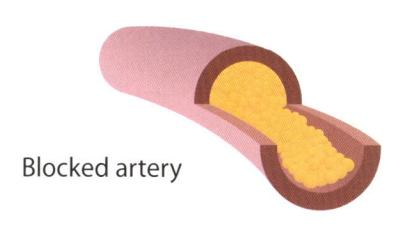

PRINCIPLES OF NUTRITION

Healthy artery

Narrowed artery

Blocked artery

▲ An image showing how a diet high in saturated fat can block arteries

Key point
Saturated fats come mostly from animal sources and are often referred to as the unhealthy fats.

Study tip
Try to remember at least three functions of fat in the diet.
Be able to explain why saturated fat is called the 'bad' fat.

Check it
1. How much energy does 1g of fat provide?
2. State 3 or more reasons as to why fat is needed by the body.

Key point
Oils are turned into solid fats by the process of hydrogenation. Hydrogenated fats are unhealthy.
Trans-fats are unhealthy.

Study tip
In your written examination, you may be asked to explain what trans-fats are, make sure you can!

Factors affecting food choice: Medical conditions p142

▲ Oily fish are good sources of omega-3 and vitamin D, which is found in very few foods.

▲ Canned tuna does not provide omega-3. To get good sources of omega-3 fresh oily fish should be eaten.

Key point

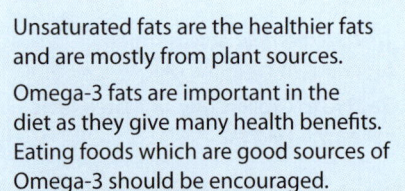

Unsaturated fats are the healthier fats and are mostly from plant sources.

Omega-3 fats are important in the diet as they give many health benefits. Eating foods which are good sources of Omega-3 should be encouraged.

▲ Foods containing invisible fats

Unsaturated fats

These are the more healthy fats and they are often liquid at room temperature. **Unsaturated fats** help to promote the healthier type of cholesterol in our blood (HDL). There are two main types:

Monounsaturated fats found in olive and rapeseed oils, almonds, hazelnuts, peanuts as well as avocados.

Polyunsaturated fats include the fats found in sunflower, soya, corn, and sesame oils, plus other plant food sources such as whole grains and seeds, nuts, fruits and vegetables.

Omega-3 and omega-6 are polyunsaturated fats and are classed as 'good fats' or 'essential fatty acids' as they cannot be made in the body in sufficient amounts. Omega-3 fats are important because they help prevent the blood from clotting, promote heart health by regulating heart rhythm, and improve survival chances after a heart attack. Advice suggests we should increase our omega-3 intake.

There is growing evidence that omega-3 offers many other health benefits too, including helping with depression and eye development in infants. Fish such as salmon, mackerel, trout, herring and sardines are all good sources of omega-3, and plant foods can provide them in small amounts.

Walnuts, soya and rapeseed oil are examples of plant foods that supply omega-3 fats.

Omega-6 can be found in poultry, eggs, cereals, nuts and vegetable oils.

Visible and invisible fats

Visible fats are the ones you can see such as butter, margarine, lard or vegetable oils plus the fat you can see on meat such as on the rind of bacon or marbling through a beef steak. Invisible fats are the fats within products such as milk, cheese, yogurt, ice cream, pork pies, burgers, nuts or avocados.

▲ Foods containing visible fats

Whichever fats are eaten, they can all cause weight gain if intake is not carefully monitored. Prolonged weight gain and obesity can lead to heart disease, stroke, type 2 diabetes, and certain cancers. So to have a healthy diet we should not eliminate all fat but instead try to replace bad fats with good ones that promote health and well-being.

CORE KNOWLEDGE   Diet and good health: **Dietary Reference Values (DRVs)** pp49–50, **Reference Nutrient Intakes (RNIs)** p51

PRINCIPLES OF NUTRITION

How much fat do we need?

The amount of fat needed in the diet may vary according to the stages of life. As a general guide, UK government advice based on the 1991 COMA Report on Dietary Reference Values for energy says that no more than about one third of our energy intake should come from fat.

A diet high in fat can result in too much energy being consumed leading to weight gain and obesity. The table below gives guidelines as to how much fat should be consumed daily.

Based on the COMA Report on Dietary Reference Values for Energy 1991	Men	Women
Total fat	95g	70g
Saturated fat	30g	20g

If you don't get enough fat in your diet you may develop vitamin deficiencies, particularly of the fat soluble vitamins A, D, E and K (see the *Vitamins* section in this chapter), symptoms of which include fatty food cravings, night blindness, dry and brittle hair and nails and depression.

So we do need some fat in our diet as a source of energy and as a carrier for essential fat soluble vitamins. However if our intake of energy is greater than is actually needed then the body will gain weight. The extra fat will be stored in adipose tissue, and if it is saturated fat, this can lead to increased risk of heart disease.

What is cholesterol?

Cholesterol is a waxy substance that circulates in the blood. It does not dissolve in the blood but instead it bonds to carriers called lipoproteins, which transport the cholesterol between cells. The two types of cholesterol are:

Low-density lipoproteins (LDL)

High-density lipoproteins (HDL)

Low-density lipoproteins (LDL) are also called 'bad cholesterol'. High levels of this can build up in your arteries (called atherosclerosis) leading to coronary heart disease. Fatty deposits form on the artery walls and this causes hardening and narrowing of the arteries. This can be dangerous as it causes restricted blood flow; this can damage organs and stop them functioning properly. If these fatty deposits come away from the artery wall it can cause a blood clot. This can block the blood supply to the heart and lead to a heart attack, or it can block the blood supply to the brain, causing a stroke.

High-density lipoproteins (HDL) are referred to as 'good cholesterol'. HDL cholesterol carries cholesterol from other parts of the body to the liver. The liver then processes the cholesterol out of the body. It's important to have healthy levels of both types of cholesterol.

What are plant sterols and stanols?

Plant sterols and stanols (phytosterols) are found naturally in plants and are similar in structure to cholesterol. Sterols and stanols have the effect of lowering the level of cholesterol in the body. They are added to foods such as milk, spreads and yoghurt, in a process known as fortification. High blood cholesterol levels in adults can be reduced when products fortified with plant sterols are included as part of a healthy diet.

Check it
What percentage of our energy intake should come from fat?

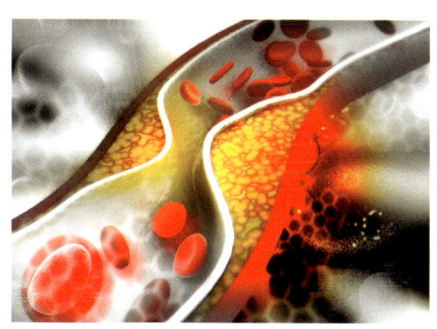

▲ Cholesterol plaque in arteries can cause atherosclerosis

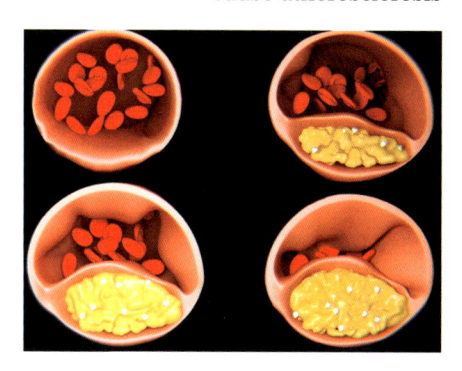

▲ Image showing how atherosclerosis can build up in an artery

▲ Spreads fortified with plant stenols can lower blood cholesterol levels

Key point
LDL is the 'bad cholesterol'. HDL is the 'good cholesterol'.

Check it
1 Name the 2 types of cholesterol and explain how cholesterol levels can affect our health.
2 What are the health benefits of foods fortified with plant sterols and stanols?

25

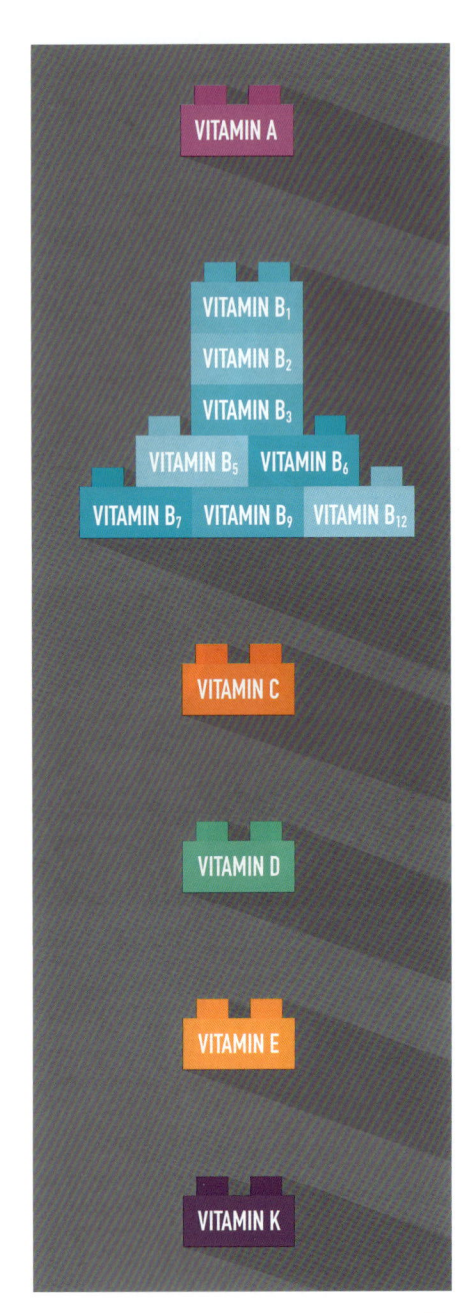

Vitamins

Vitamins are micronutrients and can be categorised into six main groups as shown by the six blocks on the left.

Vitamins are essential nutrients the body needs in tiny amounts, typically measured in milligrams (mg) or micrograms (μg). In order for the body to function properly it needs a range of vitamins. Vitamins can have many functions depending on the specific vitamin, but as a general idea, vitamins help the body:

- with the reactions that take place in the body for energy release
- by keeping the body healthy and preventing some diseases linked to a poor diet
- to regulate the function and repair of cells.

The body produces only two kinds of vitamins: Vitamin D and some B vitamins from amino acids. The body needs vitamins every day and if your diet is lacking in vitamins you can feel unwell and overtired. Lack of vitamins can slow down growth in childhood.

Fat soluble and water soluble vitamins

There are two types of vitamins:

Fat soluble vitamins (Vitamin A, D, E and K)

While the body needs these vitamins every day to work properly, foods containing fat soluble vitamins don't have to be eaten every day. This is because the body stores fat soluble vitamins in both the liver and fatty tissues. The body can use these stores when needed.

If you have more fat soluble vitamins than you need they can build up in the body and eventually cause harm. Sources of these vitamins are fatty foods and animal products, such as milk and dairy foods, eggs, liver, oily fish and vegetable oils.

Water soluble vitamins (The B group of vitamins and vitamin C)

Water soluble vitamins are not stored in the body so they need to be eaten in the diet. They are found in a wide range of foods, including fruits and vegetables, milk and dairy foods and grains.

They can be easily destroyed by heat or exposure to the **air**. To prevent the loss of water soluble vitamins, it is important to try to minimise the amount of cooking water used in food preparation. Steaming vegetables instead of simmering them in water is a good example of how more water soluble vitamins can be retained. So is reserving the cooking liquid to make a sauce or gravy. Even better would be to eat the vegetables raw as heat also destroys the vitamin content of food.

The body eliminates any excess of water soluble vitamins in the urine.

The tables on pages 27–31 highlight the functions and sources of each vitamin group and chart the effects of having too much or too little of these specific vitamins in the diet.

Key point
Most people should get all the vitamins they need by eating a varied and balanced diet.

Study tip
Make sure you can give a general explanation of why vitamins are important in the diet.

Key point
The body can store fat soluble vitamins but not water soluble vitamins.

▲ Steaming vegetables will retain more of their water soluble vitamins

VITAMINS
FAT SOLUBLE VITAMINS

PRINCIPLES OF NUTRITION

SECTION 1

VITAMIN A

- Also known as retinol
- Vitamin A is found in the liver of animals
- It can also be made in the body from beta carotene found in foods

FUNCTIONS
- Healthy immune system
- Produces 'visual purple', helping vision in dim light
- Keeps mucous membranes moist (e.g. linings of nose, mouth, eyelids, windpipe and lungs)
- For good health and development in children

WHICH FOOD SOURCES SUPPLY IT?
- dairy products; milk, butter, yoghurt, cheese
- egg yolk
- oily fish
- fortified low fat spreads
- liver
- yellow, red and green (leafy) vegetables; spinach, carrots, sweet potatoes, tomatoes, red peppers
- yellow fruit; mango, papaya, apricots

WHAT HAPPENS IF YOU DON'T HAVE ENOUGH?
- Vitamin A deficiency is rare in developed countries
- Can cause **night blindness**
- Reduces the ability to fight infections
- Can limit growth in children

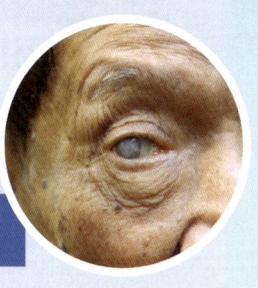

Severe lack of vitamin A can cause blindness

WHAT HAPPENS IF YOU HAVE TOO MUCH?
- Excess intake over years can affect bone health, increasing the risk of fracture in older age
- Pregnant women should avoid liver and liver-based foods such as pâté as they contain high concentrations of vitamin A which can cause birth defects

VITAMIN E

- Also known as tocopherol

FUNCTIONS
- Acts as an **antioxidant** which protects the body from diseases
- Strengthens the immune system
- Helps to maintain healthy skin, eyes

WHICH FOOD SOURCES SUPPLY IT?
- plant oils; soya, corn, olive oil
- nuts, seeds, wheat germ oil
- milk, egg yolk
- polyunsaturated spreads / oils

WHAT HAPPENS IF YOU DON'T HAVE ENOUGH?
- Vitamin E deficiency is unlikely

WHAT HAPPENS IF YOU HAVE TOO MUCH?
- Headaches, nausea
- Can affect blood coagulation

VITAMIN K

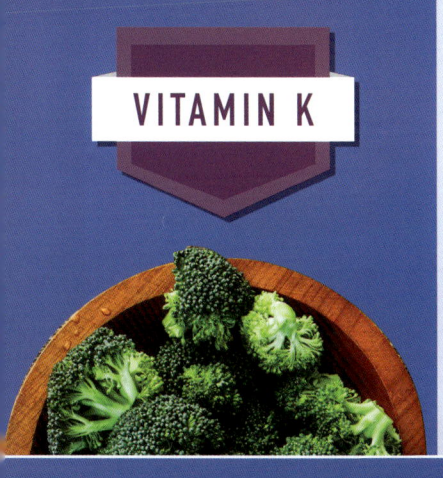

FUNCTIONS
- For blood clotting, which helps wounds to heal properly
- For good bone health

WHICH FOOD SOURCES SUPPLY IT?
- green leafy vegetables
- cauliflower
- liver, bacon
- cereals
- vegetable oils
- small amounts in meat / dairy foods

WHAT HAPPENS IF YOU DON'T HAVE ENOUGH?
- Vitamin K deficiency is unlikely

WHAT HAPPENS IF YOU HAVE TOO MUCH?
- Any vitamin K that the body doesn't need immediately is stored in the liver for future use

27

VITAMINS
FAT SOLUBLE VITAMINS

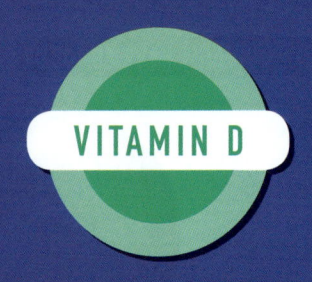

VITAMIN D

- Also known as cholecalciferol
- Sometimes called the 'sunshine' vitamin

FUNCTIONS
- For formation of strong bones and teeth, especially during childhood and adolescence when it is important that bones reach their 'peak bone mass'
- Helps control the amount of calcium absorbed from food

WHICH FOOD SOURCES SUPPLY IT?
- oily fish
- eggs
- liver
- fortified foods; breakfast cereals, margarines, dietary supplements
- Sunlight – where it is made under the skin and stored in the liver
- In the UK, cow's milk is generally not a good source of vitamin D because it isn't fortified as it is in other countries

WHAT HAPPENS IF YOU DON'T HAVE ENOUGH?
- Prevents absorption of calcium leading to weak teeth and bones. Can lead to rickets in children and osteomalacia in adults
- Extreme cases can cause heart failure
- Certain people are more at risk of not getting enough Vitamin D (pregnant and breastfeeding women, babies and children under 5 years, those over 65 years, people who cover up skin to sunlight, darker skinned people)

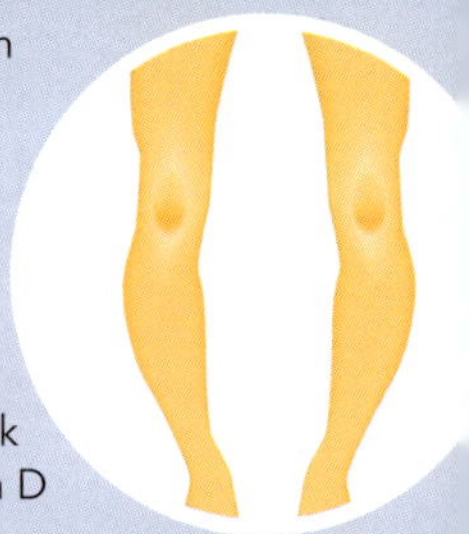

WHAT HAPPENS IF YOU HAVE TOO MUCH?
- Can cause kidney damage
- In infants can lead to hypercalcaemia

RICKETS: the most common cause of rickets is a lack of vitamin D and calcium. Any child whose diet does not contain enough vitamin D or calcium can develop rickets. Rickets is more common in children with dark skin, children born prematurely and children taking medication that interferes with vitamin D.

UK GOVERNMENT ADVICE IS THAT NO DIETARY INTAKE OF VITAMIN D IS NECESSARY FOR INDIVIDUALS LIVING A 'NORMAL LIFESTYLE'

WHICH GENERALLY MEANS:

ANYONE EATING A HEALTHY BALANCED DIET

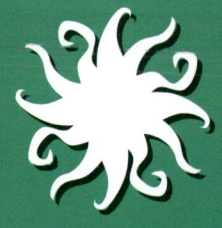

GETTING SOME SUMMER SUN

THOSE WHO ARE AT RISK OF VITAMIN D DEFICIENCY ARE ADVISED TO TAKE A DAILY SUPPLEMENT:

- Pregnant and breastfeeding women (10 μg)
- Infants and children aged under 4 years (7–8.5 μg) 
- Adults over 65 years (10 μg) 
- Those with limited exposure to the sun (e.g. if they cover their skin for cultural reasons or are housebound) (10 μg)  
- People with darker skin tones – e.g. those of Asian, African, Afro-Caribbean and Middle Eastern descent – living in the UK or other northern climates (10 μg).

CORE KNOWLEDGE

PRINCIPLES OF NUTRITION

VITAMINS
WATER SOLUBLE VITAMINS

SECTION 1

B GROUP VITAMINS

B1 THIAMIN
- Very soluble in water; destroyed in alkaline conditions

FUNCTIONS
- Releases energy from carbohydrate foods
- For a healthy nervous system
- Helps growth in childhood

WHICH FOOD SOURCES SUPPLY IT?
- red meat, liver
- whole grain cereals
- yeast / yeast extract products (e.g. Marmite)
- dairy products
- fresh and dried fruits
- eggs
- seeds, nuts, beans
- fortified breakfast cereals and wheat products

WHAT HAPPENS IF YOU DON'T HAVE ENOUGH?
- In extreme cases a muscle wasting disease called **beri beri** can occur – most likely in developing countries where white rice is a staple food
- Beri beri can also develop in alcoholics

WHAT HAPPENS IF YOU HAVE TOO MUCH?
- Can lead to headaches and insomnia

B2 RIBOFLAVIN
- Easily destroyed by sunlight and in alkaline conditions

FUNCTIONS
- Releases energy from food
- Helps growth in childhood
- Keeps the skin, eyes and the nervous system healthy

WHICH FOOD SOURCES SUPPLY IT?
- red meat
- yeast / yeast extract products
- dairy products
- eggs
- rice
- mushrooms
- fortified breakfast cereals and wheat products

WHAT HAPPENS IF YOU DON'T HAVE ENOUGH?
- Can cause swollen tongue, dry skin and sores around the corners of the mouth

WHAT HAPPENS IF YOU HAVE TOO MUCH?
- Very rare, but can increase the risk of kidney stones

B3 NIACIN
- Also known as nicotinic acid
- Soluble in water but more resistant to heat and alkali than the other B vitamins

FUNCTIONS
- Releases energy from food
- Keeps the skin and nervous system healthy
- Helps to lower the levels of fat in blood
- The amino acid tryptophan can be converted to niacin in the body

WHICH FOOD SOURCES SUPPLY IT?
- red meat, liver
- whole grain cereals
- yeast / yeast extract products
- dairy products
- eggs
- seeds, nuts, beans
- fortified breakfast cereals and wheat products

WHAT HAPPENS IF YOU DON'T HAVE ENOUGH?
- In extreme cases a deficiency disease called **pellagra** can occur – most likely where maize (corn) is a staple food. Pellagra can cause diarrhoea, rough, scaly and sore skin, confusion and memory loss

WHAT HAPPENS IF YOU HAVE TOO MUCH?
- High doses over a long time can lead to liver damage

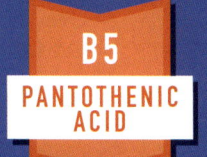

B5 PANTOTHENIC ACID
- Also known as tocopherol

FUNCTIONS
- Releases energy from fat and carbohydrate

WHICH FOOD SOURCES SUPPLY IT?
- beef, liver, kidney, chicken
- whole grains; brown rice, wholemeal bread, oats
- yeast
- potatoes
- broccoli
- tomatoes
- eggs

WHAT HAPPENS IF YOU DON'T HAVE ENOUGH?
- Vitamin B5 deficiency is unlikely as it is in so many food sources

WHAT HAPPENS IF YOU HAVE TOO MUCH?
- Very unlikely, but may lead to symptoms including diarrhoea, **dehydration**, heartburn and nausea

29

VITAMINS
WATER SOLUBLE VITAMINS

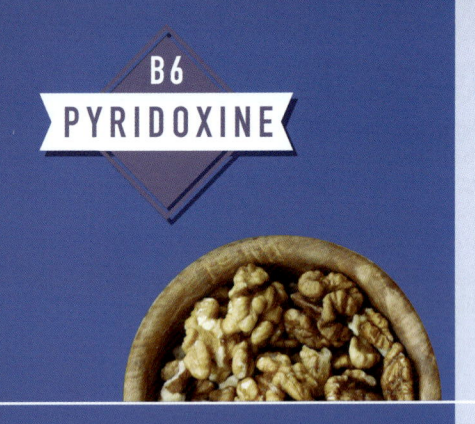

B6 PYRIDOXINE

FUNCTIONS
- Various body functions, including nerve function and brain development
- Helps the body use protein
- For the formation of **haemoglobin**

WHICH FOOD SOURCES SUPPLY IT?
- red meat, liver, kidney
- chicken, pork
- eggs
- soya beans
- yeast and yeast extract products
- whole grain cereal
- peanuts, walnuts

WHAT HAPPENS IF YOU DON'T HAVE ENOUGH?
- Unusual, but can lead to **anaemia**, headaches and general weakness

WHAT HAPPENS IF YOU HAVE TOO MUCH?
- High doses over a long time can lead to loss of feeling in arms and legs

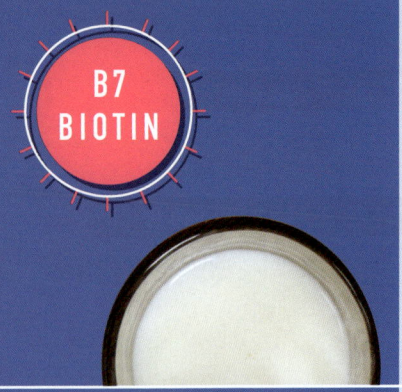

B7 BIOTIN

FUNCTIONS
- For the **metabolism** of fat
- Production of energy, protein metabolism, strengthening hair and nails

WHICH FOOD SOURCES SUPPLY IT?
- kidney, liver
- egg yolk
- dried fruit
- raspberries
- avocado
- cauliflower
- fish
- peanuts
- soya beans
- milk

WHAT HAPPENS IF YOU DON'T HAVE ENOUGH?
- If large quantities of raw egg white are eaten (unlikely) the avidin in the raw egg white combines with biotin, making it unavailable to the body

WHAT HAPPENS IF YOU HAVE TOO MUCH?
- No toxic side effects

B9 FOLATE
- Also known as folic acid
- Easily destroyed by cooking

FUNCTIONS
- To release energy from food, especially protein
- Works with vitamin B12 (cobalamin) to form healthy red blood cells
- Helps to reduce the formation of **spina bifida** in unborn babies

WHICH FOOD SOURCES SUPPLY IT?
- green leafy vegetables; spinach, broccoli, Brussels sprouts
- liver *
- potatoes
- beans, seeds, nuts
- whole grain cereals
- oranges, berry fruits
- yeast extract products

WHAT HAPPENS IF YOU DON'T HAVE ENOUGH?
- A type of anaemia called **megaloblastic anaemia** (enlarging of red blood cells), feeling sick with loss of appetite and diarrhoea
- Lack of folate can cause **spina bifida** in unborn babies. Women are advised to take folic acid supplements before conception and in the early stages of pregnancy
- * Pregnant women should avoid liver

WHAT HAPPENS IF YOU HAVE TOO MUCH?
- High doses can cause stomach problems, trouble sleeping and skin reactions

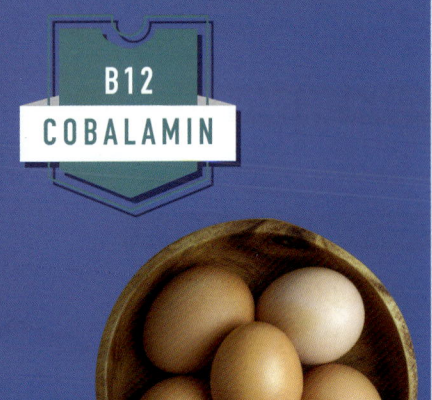

B12 COBALAMIN

FUNCTIONS
- Making red blood cells and keeping the nervous system healthy
- Releasing energy from food
- Processing folic acid

WHICH FOOD SOURCES SUPPLY IT?
- liver, meat
- fish
- milk, cheese
- eggs
- fortified breakfast cereal
- yeast

WHAT HAPPENS IF YOU DON'T HAVE ENOUGH?
- A type of anaemia called **pernicious anaemia**.
- Also causes fatigue and depression. Long term deficiency can cause damage to the brain and central nervous system.
- **Vegans** have to supplement their diet with fortified foods such as yeast extract products, soya products and breakfast cereals or supplements

WHAT HAPPENS IF YOU HAVE TOO MUCH?
- No toxic side effects

VITAMINS
WATER SOLUBLE VITAMINS

PRINCIPLES OF NUTRITION

SECTION 1

DISEASES CAUSED BY VITAMIN DEFICIENCY

Beri beri is a muscle wasting disease, most likely to occur in developing countries when diet is based on white rice. The person will lose weight and become tired they will experience weakening of muscles, especially in legs

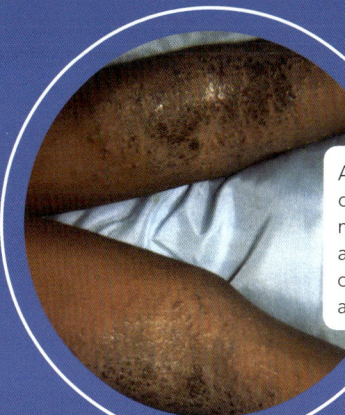

A person with pellagra, which can occur when diet is based on maize (corn). Pellagra is known as the disease of the 3 Ds – diarrhoea, dermatitis and dementia

Women are advised to take folic acid supplements before conception and in the early stages of pregnancy to help prevent birth defects known as neural tube defects, including spina bifida

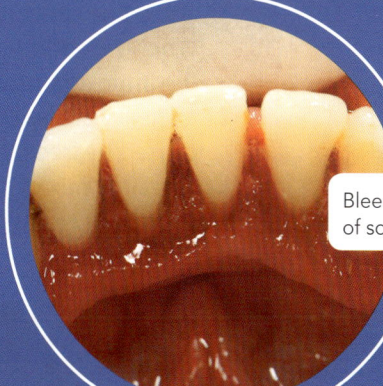

Bleeding gums could be a sign of scurvy

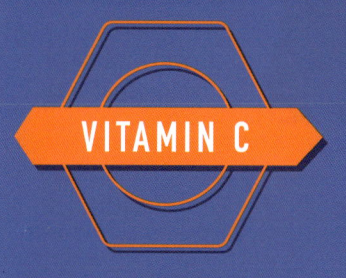

VITAMIN C

- Also known as ascorbic acid
- Easily destroyed by heat and by oxidation

FUNCTIONS
- Helps the body to absorb iron from foods
- Needed for the formation of **collagen** (the substance that holds the whole body together. It is found in the bones, muscles, skin and tendons. It forms a scaffold to provide strength and structure)
- Helps to resist infection
- Helps wounds to heal

WHICH FOOD SOURCES SUPPLY IT?
- fruits (especially citrus fruits); kiwi fruit, blackberries, tomatoes
- dark green vegetables; Brussels sprouts, broccoli, green peppers
- potatoes

WHAT HAPPENS IF YOU DON'T HAVE ENOUGH?
- Extreme deficiency can cause **scurvy** which is very rare nowadays. Symptoms include bleeding gums, wounds not healing, general tiredness
- Iron deficiency anaemia as iron needs Vitamin C for the efficient absorption of iron.

WHAT HAPPENS IF YOU HAVE TOO MUCH?
- Any extra Vitamin C is flushed out of the body with urine

31

Check it

1. List the 8 B vitamins.
2. Name the deficiency diseases associated with lack of B vitamins.
3. Which B vitamin should be taken as a supplement by women in the early stages of pregnancy?
4. Which vitamin helps the body to absorb iron from foods?
5. Which vitamin is sometimes called the 'sunshine' vitamin? Why is this?
6. Explain the term rickets.
7. Suggest factors that will affect how much of each vitamin we need each day.

Key point

The B group of vitamins and vitamin C are the most likely groups to be destroyed by heat, storage and processing.

Key point

A diet containing a 'rainbow' of colourful fruits and vegetables will provide antioxidants to protect the body from harmful free radicals.

▲ Nutritional supplements are not a substitute for a healthy diet.

How much of each vitamin do we need each day?

How much of each vitamin a person needs will depend on many factors, including age, gender and medical conditions – for instance if a woman is pregnant, or if a person is recovering from an illness.

See Appendix 1 at the end of this chapter.

Vitamin losses during food preparation and cooking

Some vitamins are more stable (less affected by processing) than others. Fat soluble vitamins (A, D, E and K) are more stable than water soluble vitamins (B group and C) during food processing and storage.

During the preparation and cooking of foods, it is likely that some vitamins will be 'lost' this is usually due to the foods being exposed to heat, light, the air or long storage. Preservation processes such as drying (dehydration), canning and pasteurisation will also affect the vitamin content of foods. (Note: the vitamin content of frozen foods, especially fruits and vegetables, is usually higher than fresh products. This is because they are usually processed and frozen within hours of picking).

What are free radicals?

Free radicals are chemicals which can harm cells in the body and cause conditions including high blood pressure, obesity, heart disease, stroke and some cancers (including mouth, throat, stomach and colon cancers). When we eat foods containing **antioxidants**, such as fruits and vegetables, the antioxidants will protect the body from these harmful free radicals. Antioxidants are natural substances that may stop or limit the damage caused by free radicals. To get the most antioxidants, a diet that includes a healthy mix of colourful fruits and vegetables and foods which are good sources of vitamins A, C and E should be eaten.

◀ Antioxidants will be increased by eating a wide range of colourful fruits and vegetables

What are nutritional supplements?

Nutritional supplements boost the intake of specific nutrients. They can be taken as pills, capsules, powders, liquids and gels. Some people with dietary restrictions or special diets need these supplements to achieve a balanced diet.

Nutritional supplements should be taken under medical advice and should not be used as a substitute for nutrients obtained from foods. Supplements can react with medication and can be dangerous, e.g. vitamin C supplements can affect the blood sugar levels of people with diabetes. Vitamin E supplements should be avoided by people with cardiovascular disease and vitamin A supplements should be avoided in pregnancy, post-menopausal women and the elderly as it affects bone density.

CORE KNOWLEDGE   Fruit and Vegetables: Different ways of cooking vegetables p224

Minerals

Minerals are micronutrients that the body needs in small amounts, typically measured in grams (g) and milligrams (mg). They are found in foods such as cereals, (including cereal products such as bread) meat, fish, milk and dairy foods, vegetables, fruit – especially dried fruit – and nuts.

Minerals have many functions and these vary depending on the specific mineral, but generally they are needed by the body to:

- turn the food we eat into energy
- build strong bones and teeth
- control body fluids.

Essential minerals include calcium and iron, although there are also many other minerals that are an important part of a healthy diet.

Check it
Give the general functions for minerals in the body.

MINERALS

Ca — Calcium

FUNCTIONS
- To form, strengthen and maintain bones and teeth
- For blood clotting
- To keep nerves and muscles working properly, including the heart
- To help with normal growth in children

WHICH FOOD SOURCES SUPPLY IT?
- dairy foods
- green leafy vegetables; broccoli, cabbage, okra
- whole grain cereals
- soya drinks with added calcium
- fish with edible bones; sardines, pilchards
- bread, food made with fortified flour

Note: Spinach, dried fruits, beans, seeds and nuts are not good sources of calcium. This is because they contain oxalates and/or phytates which reduce how much calcium the body can absorb from them

WHAT HAPPENS IF YOU DON'T HAVE ENOUGH?
- Can cause rickets in children and osteomalacia in adults
- Rickets and osteomalacia are most likely to occur when there is a deficiency in vitamin D, which means too little calcium is absorbed
- **Osteoporosis** – a condition which causes a reduction in bone density and strength which causes bones to become brittle and fracture easily
- You are more at risk of calcium deficiency if you:
  - are on a diet free from lactose or cow milk
  - have **coeliac disease**
  - have osteoporosis
  - are breastfeeding
  - are past the menopause

WHAT HAPPENS IF YOU HAVE TOO MUCH?
- Taking high doses of calcium (over 1,500mg a day) could lead to stomach pain and diarrhoea
- Calcium can build up in the kidneys and can be fatal

OSTEOPOROSIS occurs when the struts which make up the mesh-like structure within bones become thin, causing bones to become fragile and break easily. Brittle bones like in the hip joint may lead to surgery.

Diet and good health: Bone health and dental health pp60–61

MINERALS

Fe — Iron

Two types of iron:
- **Haem iron** (also called ferrous iron) is easily absorbed by the body
- **Non-haem iron** (also called ferric iron) is less easily absorbed in the body

FUNCTIONS
- Helps to make haemoglobin in the red blood cells which carry oxygen to the body cells

WHICH FOOD SOURCES SUPPLY IT?
Haem iron
- red meat, offal (liver, kidney, heart)

Non-haem iron
- whole grain cereals
- green leafy vegetable such as watercress, curly kale
- beans, nuts
- dried fruit; raisins, apricots
- fortified breakfast cereals
- curry powder
- blackstrap molasses
- cocoa
- all wheat flour (apart from wholemeal) is fortified with iron by law

IRON DEFICIENCY ANAEMIA – where there are fewer red blood cells than is normal, meaning that organs and tissues will not get as much oxygen as they usually would

WHAT HAPPENS IF YOU DON'T HAVE ENOUGH?
- **Iron deficiency anaemia** Symptoms include being tired, weak, lethargic (no energy), and having a pale complexion
- Teenage girls often need additional iron to compensate for iron depletion due to menstruation (monthly periods)
- Pregnant women and nursing mothers need additional iron to provide sufficient iron for both themselves and their growing baby
- Iron must be combined with vitamin C in order to be absorbed efficiently by the body

Anaemia

WHAT HAPPENS IF YOU HAVE TOO MUCH?
- The side effects of taking high doses (over 20mg) of iron include:
  - constipation
  - nausea
  - vomiting
  - stomach pain
- Very high doses of iron can be fatal, so iron supplements should be kept out of the reach of children

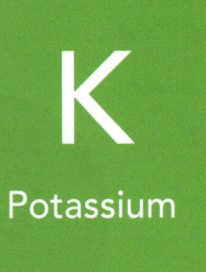

K — Potassium

FUNCTIONS
- Helps to balance body fluids
- Helps to lower blood pressure
- Needed to keep heart muscles healthy
- Improves bone health and helps to prevent muscle cramps
- Potassium works with sodium to balance body fluids and to control the nerves and muscles Potassium helps to remove excess sodium and may help to prevent high blood pressure

WHICH FOOD SOURCES SUPPLY IT?
- Fruit and vegetables bananas, potatoes, broccoli, parsnips, Brussels sprouts
- pulses, nuts, seeds
- fish, shellfish
- beef
- chicken, turkey
- coffee
- salt substitutes

WHAT HAPPENS IF YOU DON'T HAVE ENOUGH?
- Occurs in cases of malnutrition (kwashiorkor)
- Diarrhoea
- Can also cause heart failure

WHAT HAPPENS IF YOU HAVE TOO MUCH?
- Too much potassium can cause stomach pain, nausea and diarrhoea
- Any excess can be excreted through the kidneys

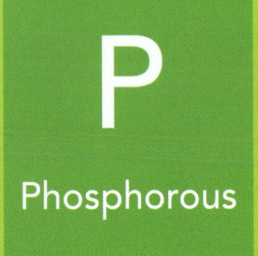

P — Phosphorous

FUNCTIONS
- Helps to build strong bones and teeth
- Works with calcium
- Important for energy release and other metabolic processes

WHICH FOOD SOURCES SUPPLY IT?
- a wide range of animal and plant foods
- red meat
- dairy foods
- fish
- poultry
- bread
- brown rice
- oats

WHAT HAPPENS IF YOU DON'T HAVE ENOUGH?
- Unlikely to happen as it is found in so many food sources

WHAT HAPPENS IF YOU HAVE TOO MUCH?
- Can trigger involuntary muscle convulsions
- High doses of phosphorus supplements for a short time can cause diarrhoea or stomach pain
- High doses for a long time can reduce the amount of calcium in the body, which means that bones are more likely to fracture

MINERALS

PRINCIPLES OF NUTRITION

Mg — Magnesium

FUNCTIONS
- For bone development
- Helps the nervous system to work properly
- Important for energy release

WHICH FOOD SOURCES SUPPLY IT?
- meat
- fish
- dairy foods
- whole grain cereals
- nuts, seeds
- green leafy vegetables such as spinach

WHAT HAPPENS IF YOU DON'T HAVE ENOUGH?
- Deficiency is rare, but symptoms may include loss of appetite, nausea, vomiting, fatigue, and weakness
- May cause high blood pressure and heart disease

WHAT HAPPENS IF YOU HAVE TOO MUCH?
- High doses of magnesium (more than 400mg) for a short time can cause diarrhoea
- There is not enough evidence to say what the effects might be of taking high doses of magnesium over a long time

Na — Sodium

FUNCTIONS
- Helps to control the amount of water in the body
- Helps the body to use energy
- Helps to control the nerves and muscles

WHICH FOOD SOURCES SUPPLY IT?
- salt
- processed foods; crisps, ready meals, bacon, ham, kippers, anchovies, sausages, beef burgers, pies
- some breakfast cereals
- yeast extracts
- stock cubes

WHAT HAPPENS IF YOU DON'T HAVE ENOUGH?
- Muscle cramps

WHAT HAPPENS IF YOU HAVE TOO MUCH?
- Can lead to high blood pressure, can damage heart and kidneys and can also lead to strokes

WHAT IS THE DIFFERENCE BETWEEN SALT AND SODIUM?

Salt is also called sodium chloride (formed by sodium and chlorine).
The sodium in salt can be bad for your health.
Since December 2014, however, sodium is no longer listed on food labels. They only list salt.

x 2.5 TO CONVERT SODIUM TO SALT, MULTIPLY THE SODIUM AMOUNT BY 2.5
so 1 gram of sodium = 2.5 grams of salt.

Guidelines for MAXIMUM sodium intake are as follows:
- Children aged one to three: 0.8g sodium (2g salt) a day
- Children aged four to six: 1.2g sodium (3g salt) a day
- Children aged seven to 10: 2g sodium (5g salt) a day
- Children aged 11 and over and adults : 2.4g sodium (6g salt) a day

BE AWARE OF HIDDEN SALT added to foods such as ready meals, ketchups, breakfast cereals, savoury snacks, soy sauce, baked beans

ONE 28.5g PACK of salted crisps contains 8% of the salt reference intake for an average adult

Note:

Vitamin D will help to improve the absorption of calcium in the body. Exercise will also help to improve the absorption of calcium in the body.

Calcium absorption will be reduced if:
- Phytic acid is present (e.g. from whole grain cereals and legumes)
- Oxalic acid is present (e.g. from spinach and rhubarb)

Foods rich in vitamin C should be eaten with foods rich in iron to improve the iron absorption in the body.

Iron absorption will be reduced if:
- Phytic acid is present (e.g. from whole grain cereals and legumes)
- Oxalic acid is present (e.g. from spinach and rhubarb)

Complementary actions of nutrients

Some nutrients work with each other to improve the way these nutrients are absorbed in the body.

Vitamin C and iron: foods which are good sources of vitamin C will improve the absorption of non-haem iron. Examples are a bowl of cereal topped with strawberries and kiwi fruit, a piece of wholemeal toast with lemon curd or lentil dhal speckled with sautéed red pepper.

Vitamin D helps your body absorb calcium for healthy bones and teeth. Even if you have a calcium-rich diet (for example from eating plenty of low fat dairy foods and green leafy vegetables), without enough vitamin D, your body will not be able to absorb the calcium into your bones and cells where it is needed.

Examples of dishes which contain both calcium and vitamin D include macaroni and cheese, and grilled herring with a watercress salad or sardines on toast.

Trace elements

Trace elements are micronutrients that the body needs to work properly, but in much smaller amounts than vitamins and minerals. They are measured in mg (milligram) or µg (microgram). Trace elements are found in a variety of foods such as meat, fish, cereals, milk and dairy foods, vegetables and nuts.

OTHER TRACE ELEMENTS INCLUDE COBALT, COPPER, CHROMIUM, MANGANESE, MOLYBDENUM, POTASSIUM, AND PHOSPHOROUS

Like vitamins, how much of each mineral and trace element a person needs will depend on many factors, including age, gender and medical conditions e.g. pregnancy, recovering from an illness, etc.

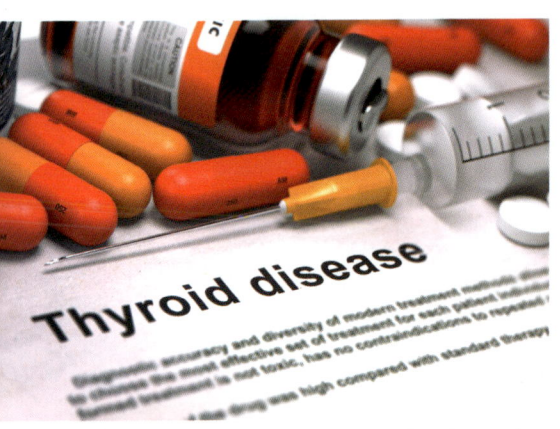

▲ Examples of dishes that work together to improve the way nutrients are absorbed in the body

▲ Fluoride toothpaste helps prevent tooth decay

▲ Iodine deficiency can lead to goitre (an enlargement of the thyroid)

CORE KNOWLEDGE

TRACE ELEMENTS

PRINCIPLES OF NUTRITION

I — Iodine

FUNCTIONS
- Helps to make the thyroid hormones (which help to keep cells and the metabolic rate healthy)

WHICH FOOD SOURCES SUPPLY IT?
- sea fish, shellfish, seaweed
- dairy products
- plant foods; cereals, grains (depends on iodine content in the soil)

WHAT HAPPENS IF YOU DON'T HAVE ENOUGH?
- The body will not be able to make enough thyroid hormone
- Can lead to enlargement of the thyroid (called **goitre**)
- In pregnancy, can result in the baby's brain not developing as well resulting in lower IQ or poorer reading ability
- Vegetarians, particularly vegans, are at risk of iodine deficiency as they do not eat foods rich in iodine (fish and/or dairy products)

WHAT HAPPENS IF YOU HAVE TOO MUCH?
- Can affect the way the thyroid gland works

Zn — Zinc

FUNCTIONS
- Helps the immune system to fight disease and infections
- Helps wounds to heal and blood to clot
- Keeps skin healthy and enables normal growth and development

WHICH FOOD SOURCES SUPPLY IT?
- meat
- dairy foods
- eggs
- shellfish
- pulses
- whole grain cereals
- white bread
- breakfast cereals
- fermented soya such as tempeh and miso

WHAT HAPPENS IF YOU DON'T HAVE ENOUGH?
- Evidence shows it can lead to poor growth in children
- Phytates are found in plant foods such as whole grains and beans
- Reduce zinc absorption, so it is important to eat good food sources of zinc

WHAT HAPPENS IF YOU HAVE TOO MUCH?
- High doses of zinc reduce the amount of copper the body can absorb. This can lead to anaemia and weakening of the bones

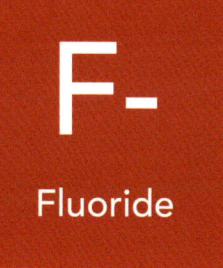

F- — Fluoride

FUNCTIONS
- Helps to harden tooth enamel and prevent tooth decay

WHICH FOOD SOURCES SUPPLY IT?
- tea
- sea fish (especially with edible bones)
- vegetables; endives,
- curly kale
- added to drinking water in some areas of the UK

WHAT HAPPENS IF YOU DON'T HAVE ENOUGH?
- Teeth may develop decay (Fluoride toothpaste and mouthwash has helped in the prevention of tooth decay as has the addition of fluoride to drinking water)

WHAT HAPPENS IF YOU HAVE TOO MUCH?
- Can cause discoloration or pitting of the teeth

Se — Selenium

FUNCTIONS
- Important in the control of thyroid hormone metabolism
- Makes sure the immune system is functioning properly
- As an antioxidant
- Helps to protect against heart disease

WHICH FOOD SOURCES SUPPLY IT?
- red meat
- fish
- cereals, Brazil nuts
- eggs

WHAT HAPPENS IF YOU DON'T HAVE ENOUGH?
- Depression

WHAT HAPPENS IF YOU HAVE TOO MUCH?
- Causes **selenosis** – can lead to loss of hair, skin and nails

Check it

1. Explain why spinach should not be relied on as a good source of calcium in the diet.
2. Which factors may put people more at risk of a calcium deficiency?
3. Explain the difference between haem iron and non-haem iron.
4. What symptoms might you experience when suffering from iron deficiency anaemia?
5. Which mineral works with calcium for the formation of strong bones and teeth?
6. Name 3 foods which have salt added to them when they are made.
7. Explain why the government recommends no more than 6g of salt per day per adult.
8. A lack of which trace element can lead to goitre (an enlargement of the thyroid)?
9. Why is fluoride often added to drinking water and toothpaste?

Activity

1. Create a Wikipedia page summarising the importance of minerals in the diet.
2. Create a Bingo game – write the key minerals and trace elements on the bingo cards. The bingo caller will call out the functions of each nutrient and players have to cross these off on the bingo cards when the nutrients are matched to the functions.

Key point

Fluids (including water) are needed by the body daily.

Check it

Why is water essential for life?

Activity

Create a fact sheet highlighting the importance of fluids and hydration to ensure good health.

Water

Water is essential for life. The human body is 50 to 75% water, and it is an important component of blood, digestive juices, urine and perspiration. It is also contained in lean muscle, fat and bones. As the body cannot store water, we need it daily to make up for losses from the lungs, skin, urine and stool (poo). The amount we need depends on our body size, metabolism, the climate we live in, the food we eat and our activity levels.

Fluids include fresh water and all other liquids like milk, coffee, tea, soup, juice and soft drinks.

ALL ABOUT WATER...

FUNCTIONS

- Transporting nutrients in blood
- Removing waste products that are then passed in to the urine and faeces
- Regulating body temperature (e.g. by sweating)
- Aiding digestion and prevents constipation
- Acting as a lubricant and shock absorber in joints

WHICH SOURCES SUPPLY IT?

- **Water:**
Fresh water is the best way to hydrate the body: it contains no energy, is sugar free and will not rot teeth.
- **Other fluids:**
Milk (particularly low fat milk) is an important fluid, especially for children, and is about 90% water (whole milk should be consumed until two years old as under 2 years they may not get the calories they need from lower-fat milks).
Tea can be an important source of fluid. It can help meet daily fluid recommendations, and is a source of antioxidants and polyphenols, which reportedly protect against heart disease and cancer. Caffeine drinks are stimulants and should be avoided as they cause the body to produce urine more quickly. Fruit and herbal teas are suggested instead of tea varieties that contain caffeine. Fresh fruit is preferable to fruit juice because it has more fibre and nutrients, and less sugar.

HOW MUCH IS NEEDED?

- In a typical UK diet, drinks provide 70-80% of water needs; the remaining 20-30% comes from food, e.g. soup, casseroles, fruits and vegetables.
- How much fluid a person needs will depend on factors such as: room temperature, room humidity, exercise.

WHAT HAPPENS IF YOU DON'T HAVE ENOUGH?

- Lack of fluids causes dehydration. Symptoms include thirstiness, a dry and sticky mouth, feeling tired, losing concentration, dizziness and headaches.
- Dehydration can increase the risk of kidney stones and urinary tract infections.

WHAT HAPPENS IF YOU HAVE TOO MUCH?

- Very rare – but can damage the body and cause hyponatremia (water intoxication). Hyponatremia occurs when sodium in the blood drops to a dangerously low level (sodium is needed for muscle contraction and for sending nerve impulses).

CORE KNOWLEDGE

Key terms

Adipose tissue – cells that store energy in the form of fat.

Amino acids – simpler units of protein, made up of long chains.

Anaemia – a condition where the body lacks enough healthy red blood cells or haemoglobin.

Antioxidants – chemicals in food which can prevent or slow down damage to our body which otherwise can lead to diseases such as heart disease and cancers. Antioxidants also improve our immune system.

Atherosclerosis – a build-up of fatty deposits in the arteries, sometimes called 'furring of the arteries'.

Beri beri – a muscle wasting disease due to a lack of vitamin B1 (thiamin) in the diet.

Beta-glucan – a form of soluble fibre.

Blood sugar – how much glucose is in the blood.

Cholesterol – a fatty substance found in our blood and the food we eat.

Coeliac disease – a chronic intestinal disorder caused by sensitivity to the protein gliadin contained in the gluten of cereals.

Collagen – protein in the connective tissue which holds cells together.

Composition – the different parts or substances that make up something.

Coronary heart disease (CHD) – a narrowing of the arteries that supply your heart with oxygen-rich blood, due to the build-up of fatty material within their walls.

Deficiency – a lack of something that is needed in the diet.

Dehydration – when the body loses more fluid than it takes in.

Digestion – the breaking down of food in the body to obtain nutrients.

Disaccharide – a carbohydrate made from two sugar molecules (*di* means two).

Empty calories – calories that are present in foods that have very little or no nutritive value.

Extrinsic sugar – added sugar.

Fat soluble vitamins – these vitamins (the A, D, E, and K groups) dissolve in fat.

Fortified food – a food product in which a nutrient is added to increase its nutritional value.

Free radicals – chemicals in food which can cause us harm. Antioxidants will protect the body from these harmful free radicals.

Free sugars – extrinsic sugars not from milk.

Function – what something does, or why it is needed.

Goitre – an enlargement of the thyroid gland seen as a neck swelling, from insufficient intake of iodine.

Haem iron – from animal sources.

Haemoglobin – the part of blood that contains iron, carries oxygen through the body, and gives blood its red colour.

High biological value (HBV) – protein foods containing all the essential amino acids.

Hydrogenation – the process of changing a liquid fat or oil to a solid one at room temperature by the addition of hydrogen.

Hypercalcaemia – an abnormally high level of calcium in the blood.

Insoluble fibre – fibre which the body cannot absorb.

Intrinsic sugar – natural sugar.

Iron deficiency anaemia – lack of iron in the body leads to a reduction in the number of red blood cells.

Kwashiorkor – a form of malnutrition linked to protein deficiency.

Low biological value (LBV) – protein foods lacking in one or more of the essential amino acids.

Macronutrients – a class of chemical compounds which humans consume in the largest quantities.

Megaloblastic anaemia – a type of anaemia caused by a lack of vitamin B9 (folate).

Metabolism - all the chemical processes in the body, especially those that cause food to be used for energy and growth.

Micronutrients – required in small quantities to facilitate a range of physiological functions.

Monosaccharide – a simple carbohydrate (mono means one; saccharide means sugar).

Mycoprotein – a food made from the fungi family which contains all the essential amino acids needed by the body. Suitable for lacto-ovo vegetarians.

Non- haem iron – from vegetable sources.

Non-Milk Extrinsic Sugars (NMES) – added sugar from non-milk sources.

Non starch polysaccharide – another term for insoluble fibre.

Nutrient – a substance that provides nourishment essential for growth and the maintenance of life.

Nutritional value – the nutrients in foods and how they impact on the body.

Obesity – when a person is carrying around so much extra weight that it is dangerous to their health.

Omega-3 – fatty acids that are important for a healthy heart.

Osteomalacia – softening of the bones in adults, results in bone pain and muscle weakness.

Key terms (continued)

Osteoporosis – a medical condition in which the bones become brittle and fragile.

Oxidation – exposure to the oxygen in the air.

Peak bone mass – refers to the largest amount of bone tissue that a person has at any point in life. Most people reach their peak bone mass by the age of 30.

Pellagra – a deficiency disease due to a lack of vitamin B3 (niacin) in the diet. Causes skin, nerve and mental health problems plus diarrhoea. Often occurs where maize is a staple food.

Pernicious anaemia – a type of anaemia caused by a lack of vitamin B12 (cobalamin).

Photosynthesis – the process used by a plant to obtain energy from sunlight. Starch is produced during photosynthesis.

Polysaccharide – a complex carbohydrate (*poly* means many).

Rickets – a disease caused by lack of calcium and vitamin D. The bones become soft and weak, leading to bone deformities.

Saturated fats – come mostly from animal sources and can be bad for our health.

Scurvy – a disease due to lack of vitamin C, causes swollen gums and bleeding and can be fatal if left untreated.

Shelf life – how long a food is fit to consume.

Shortening – a fat that is solid at room temperature.

Soluble fibre – fibre which can be absorbed by the body.

Sources – the specific foods that contain certain nutrients.

Spina bifida – a serious birth abnormality causing a defect of the spine.

Starch – a polysaccharide, a complex carbohydrate.

Sugar – a monosaccharide or disaccharide, a simple carbohydrate.

Trans-fats – occur naturally in meat and dairy products; most trans-fat is formed through the industrial process of hydrogenation.

TVP – textured vegetable protein, made from soya beans.

Unsaturated fat – a fat that comes from a vegetable source and is good for our health.

Vegan – a person who does not eat or use animal products.

Water soluble vitamins – these vitamins (the B group and vitamin C) dissolve in water.

Data is taken from the *Department of Health, Dietary Reference Values for Food Energy and Nutrients for the United Kingdom, HMSO, 1991*

APPENDIX 1

Reference nutrient intake per person per day

Children						Males				Females				Pregnant females
Age:		Under 1	1 to 3	4 to 6	7 to 10	11 to 14	15 to 18	19 to 50	50+	11 to 14	15 to 18	19 to 50	50+	16 to 50
Energy[a]	kcal	721	1197	1630	1855	2220	2755	2550	2340	1845	2110	1940	1877	2140
Protein	g	13.5	14.5	19.7	28.3	42.1	55.2	55.5	53.3	41.2	45.0	45.0	46.5	51.0
Calcium	mg	525	350	450	550	1000	1000	700	700	800	800	700	700	700
Iron	mg	5.4	6.9	6.1	8.7	11.3	11.3	8.7	8.7	14.8	14.8	14.8	8.7	14.8
Sodium[b]	g	0.3	0.5	0.7	1.2	1.6	1.6	1.6	1.6	1.6	1.6	1.6	1.6	1.6
Vitamin A	µg	350	400	500	500	600	700	700	700	600	600	600	600	700
Vitamin B1 (Thiamin)	mg	0.2	0.5	0.7	0.7	0.9	1.1	1.0	0.9	0.7	0.8	0.8	0.8	0.9
B2 (Riboflavin)	mg	0.4	0.6	0.8	1.0	1.2	1.3	1.3	1.3	1.1	1.1	1.1	1.1	1.4
B3 (Niacin (Nicotinic acid)	mg	4	8	11	12	15	18	17	16	12	14	13	12	13
B6 (Pyrodxine)	mg	0.3	0.7	0.9	1.0	1.2	1.5	1.4	1.4	1.0	1.2	1.2	1.2	1.2
B9 (Folic acid/Folate)	µg	50	70	100	150	200	200	200	200	200	200	200	200	300
B12 (Cobalamin)	µg	0.3	0.5	0.8	1.0	1.2	1.5	1.5	1.5	1.2	1.5	1.5	1.5	1.5
Vitamin C	mg	25	30	30	30	35	40	40	40	35	40	40	40	50

(a) Estimated Average Requirement

(b) The RNI for sodium is the amount that is sufficient for 97 per cent of the population. In May 2003 the Scientific Advisory Committee on Nutrition made recommendations about the maximum amount of salt that people should be eating, i.e. that the average salt intake for adults should be no more than 6 grams per day, equivalent to 2.4 grams of sodium per day.

APPENDIX 2

Average fat content of foods, uncooked (edible portion)

	Fat (g/100 g)
Milk, whole	3.9
Milk, semi-skimmed	1.7
Milk, 1%	1.0[c]
Milk, skimmed	0.2
Cream, double	53.7
Yogurt, low-fat, fruit	1.1
Ice cream, non-dairy, soft scoop[c]	7.7
Cheese, Cheddar	34.9
Cheese, Edam	26.0
Cheese, cottage, plain	4.3
Eggs	11.2
Beef, stewing steak	6.4
Lamb, leg, lean and fat	12.3
Pork, chop, lean and fat	21.7
Bacon, streaky	23.6
Sausages, pork	25.0
Ham	3.3
Beefburgers	24.7
Chicken, dark and light meat	2.1
Turkey, dark and light meat	1.6
Cod, filleted	0.7
Mackerel	16.1[d]
Tuna, canned in oil, drained	9.0
Tuna, canned in brine, drained	0.6
Butter	82.2
Fat spread (62–75% fat), not polyunsaturated[c]	73.2
Reduced-fat spread (41–62% fat), not polyunsaturated[c]	60.6
Low-fat spread (26–39% fat), polyunsaturated[c]	36.9
Vegetable oils	99.9
Lard and dripping	99.0
Ghee, made from vegetable oil[e]	100.0
Potatoes, old	0.2
Chips, takeaway	8.4[f]
Potato chips, oven-baked[c]	4.9
Peanut butter, smooth	51.8
Bread, white	1.6
Bread, wholemeal	2.5
Porridge oats	7.8
Biscuits, digestive, plain	21.3

This data is taken from the Department of Health, Manual of Nutrition, 12th edition.

The main sources of fat in the diet are meat and meat products, cereals and cereal products (including biscuits, buns, cakes and pastries), and milk and milk products.

Source: unless otherwise stated, *McCance and Widdowson's Composition of Foods Integrated Dataset* (COFIDS), published by the Food Standards Agency, 2008.

(c) Source: average from product's label information.

(d) Levels range from 6g to 23g fat per 100g

(e) Source: *Nutrient Analysis of a Range of Processed Foods with Particular Reference to Trans Fatty Acids – Summary Report*, Department of Health, 2011.

(f) Content variable and depends on a number of factors relating to preparation.

APPENDIX 3

Recommended adequate intakes of water from drinks

	Age	Adequate water intake from drinks (ml/day)
Infants	0–6 months	550 through milk
	7–12 months	640–800
Children	1–2 years	880–960
	2–3 years	1040
	4–8 years	1280
	9–13 years	Boys 1680
		Girls 1520
	14+	As adults
Adults (including older people)		Men 2000
		Women 1600
Pregnant women		As adults + 300ml per day
Lactating (breast feeding) women		As adults + 600–700ml per day

The values on this table are averages and an individual's requirement will depend on many factors including temperature and humidity and exercise. Warm and dry environments such as air-conditioned offices or centrally-heated homes increase the need for water as they speed up the evaporation of sweat on the skin.

Source: https://www.bda.uk.com/foodfacts/fluid.pdf

APPENDIX 4

Reference nutrient intakes for vitamins

	Age	Vitamin A µg/day	Thiamin Mg/day	Riboflavin Mg/day	Vitamin B$_{12}$ µg/day	Folate µg/day	Vitamin C Mg/day	Vitamin D µg/day
Infants	0–3 months	350	0.2	0.4	0.3	50	25	8.5
	4–6 months	350	0.2	0.4	0.3	50	25	8.5
	7–9 month	350	0.3	0.4	0.4	50	25	7
	10–12 months	350	0.5	0.4	0.4	50	25	7
Children	1–3 years	400	0.5	0.6	0.5	70	30	7
	4–6 years	500	0.7	0.8	0.8	100	30	*
	7–10 years	500	0.7	1.0	1.0	150	30	*
Males	11–14 years	600	0.9	1.2	1.2	200	35	*
	15–18 years	700	1.1	1.3	1.5	200	40	*
	19–50 years	700	1.0	1.3	1.5	200	40	*
	50+ years	700	0.9	1.3	1.5	200	40	*
Females	11–14 years	600	0.7	1.1	1.2	200	35	*
	15–18 years	600	0.8	1.1	1.5	200	40	*
	19–50 years	600	0.8	1.1	1.5	200	40	*
	50+ years	600	0.8	1.1	1.5	200	40	*
Pregnant women		+ extra 100	+ extra 0.1	+ extra 0.3	No increase	+ extra 100	+ extra 10	+ extra 10
Lactating (breast feeding) women		+ extra 100	+ extra 0.2	+ extra 0.5	+ extra 0.5	+ extra 60	+ extra 30	+ extra 10

Reference nutrient intakes for minerals and protein

	Age	Calcium mg/day	Sodium mg/day	Potassium mg/day	Iron mg/day	Protein g/day
Infants	0–3 months	325	210	600	1.7	12.5
	4–6 months	325	280	850	4.3	12.7
	7–9 month	325	320	700	7.8	13.7
	10–12 months	325	380	700	7.8	14.9
Children	1–3 years	350	500	800	6.9	14.5
	4–6 years	450	700	1100	6.1	19.7
	7–10 years	550	1200	2200	8.7	26.3
Males	11–14 years	1000	1600	3100	11.3	42.1
	15–18 years	1000	1600	3500	11.3	55.2
	19–50 years	700	1600	3500	8.7	55.5
	50+ years	700	1600	3500	8.7	53.3
Females	11–14 years	800	1600	3100	14.8	41.2
	15–18 years	800	1600	3500	14.8	45.0
	19–50 years	700	1600	3500	14.8	45.0
	50+ years	700	1600	3500	8.7	46.5
Pregnant women		No increase	No increase	No increase	No increase	+ extra 6g
Lactating (breast feeding) women		550	No increase	No increase	No increase	+ extra 11g

EXAM QUESTIONS

1. **Tick (✓)** the box next to each statement to show whether it is **true** or **false**. [3]

Statement	True	False
i Pulses, beans and lentils are a good source of dietary fibre		
ii Fruit and vegetable intake must come from fresh produce only		
iii Adults should consume no more than 6g of salt a day		

2. a Complete the chart using the words in the box. [3]

| To fight infection | Pasta | Strong teeth and bones | Liver |

Macro-nutrient	Function	Rich food Source
i Vitamin B1 (Thiamin)	To help the body use energy	
ii Vitamin C		Kiwi fruit
iii Iron	To help make red blood cells	

3. Complete the following chart on vitamins and minerals. [2]

Name of vitamin or mineral	Function	Food source
Vitamin A	Healthy development of skin and tissue	i
ii	Helps heal wounds and the absorption of iron	Oranges
Calcium	iii	Cheese

4. a Name **two** functions of protein in the diet. [2]

   b Different protein foods 'complement' each other. Explain why it can be beneficial to include a mixture of protein foods in the diet. [4]

5. It is important to reduce salt in the diet.

   a State **one** reason for reducing salt in the diet. [1]

   b Suggest **three** ways of reducing salt in the diet. [3]

   c Explain what is meant by **hidden salt** in food. [2]

6. a List **two** foods that are good sources of dietary fibre (NSP). [2]

   b Explain the difference between soluble and insoluble fibre and include a discussion on the health benefits of dietary fibre in your answer. [2]

TOTAL: 24

SECTION 1
CORE KNOWLEDGE

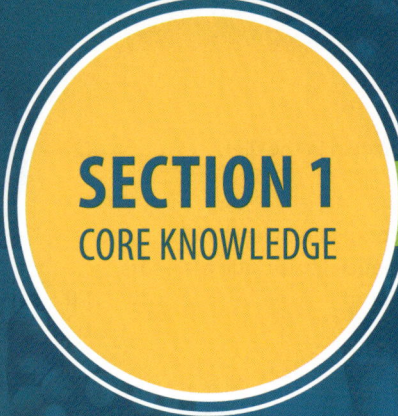

DIET AND GOOD HEALTH

What will I learn?

- What is meant by a 'healthy diet'
- Guidelines and recommendations for a healthy diet
- Nutritional needs which change during life and how to plan diets to suit these changing needs
- How to plan diets for people with specific dietary needs or deficiencies
- How lifestyle can affect food choice and diet

Diet is the term for the food and drink that we consume daily. A diet needs to be both healthy and sustainable.

A healthy diet is a balanced diet. It provides the necessary nutrients needed for healthy body functions and normal physical activity.

To keep a balanced diet is to eat a variety of foods to give the body the range of nutrients it needs to stay in top condition. Eating a balanced diet promotes good health and contributes to a healthy lifestyle.

To help people achieve a balanced diet, health experts and the Government have put together some dietary guidelines and calculated nutritional requirements for individual groups of people.

Dietary guidelines N

These include:

- the Eatwell guide
- the five-a-day campaign
- the eight tips for healthy eating

The Eatwell Guide

The Eatwell Guide is designed to help all those aged over two years of age to eat a healthy, balanced diet as it shows how much of what is eaten should come from each food group.

The four food groups are:

- potatoes, bread, rice, pasta and other starchy carbohydrates
- fruit and vegetables
- dairy and alternatives
- beans, pulses, fish, eggs, meat and other proteins

Key point

Potatoes belong to the starchy foods group, not to fruit and vegetables. That is why they do not count towards five-a-day.

44 CORE KNOWLEDGE

DIET AND GOOD HEALTH

Eatwell Guide

Use the Eatwell Guide to help you get a balance of healthier and more sustainable food. It shows how much of what you eat overall should come from each food group.

Check the label on packaged foods

Each 28.5g pack contains

ENERGY	FAT	SATURATES	SUGARS	SALT
626kJ 150kcal	8.6g	0.8g	1.1g	0.43g
8%	12%	4%	1%	8%

% of the Reference Intakes
Typical values per 100g: Energy 2195kJ/526kcal

Choose foods lower in fat, salt and sugars

Eat at least 5 portions of a variety of fruit and vegetables a day
Fruit and vegetables

Choose wholegrain or higher fibre versions with less added fat, salt and sugar
Potatoes, bread, rice, pasta and other starchy carbohydrates

6–8 a day

Water, lower fat milk, sugar-free drinks including tea and coffee all count.

Limit fruit juice and/or smoothies to a total of 150ml a day.

SECTION 1

Eat less often and in small amounts

Beans, nuts, eggs, fish, meat and other proteins
Eat more beans and pulses, 2 portions of sustainably sourced fish per week, one of which is oily. Eat less red and processed meat

Dairy and alternatives
Choose lower fat and lower sugar options

Oil and spreads
Choose unsaturated oils and use in small amounts

Per day ♀ 2000kcal ♂ 2500kcal = ALL FOOD + ALL DRINKS

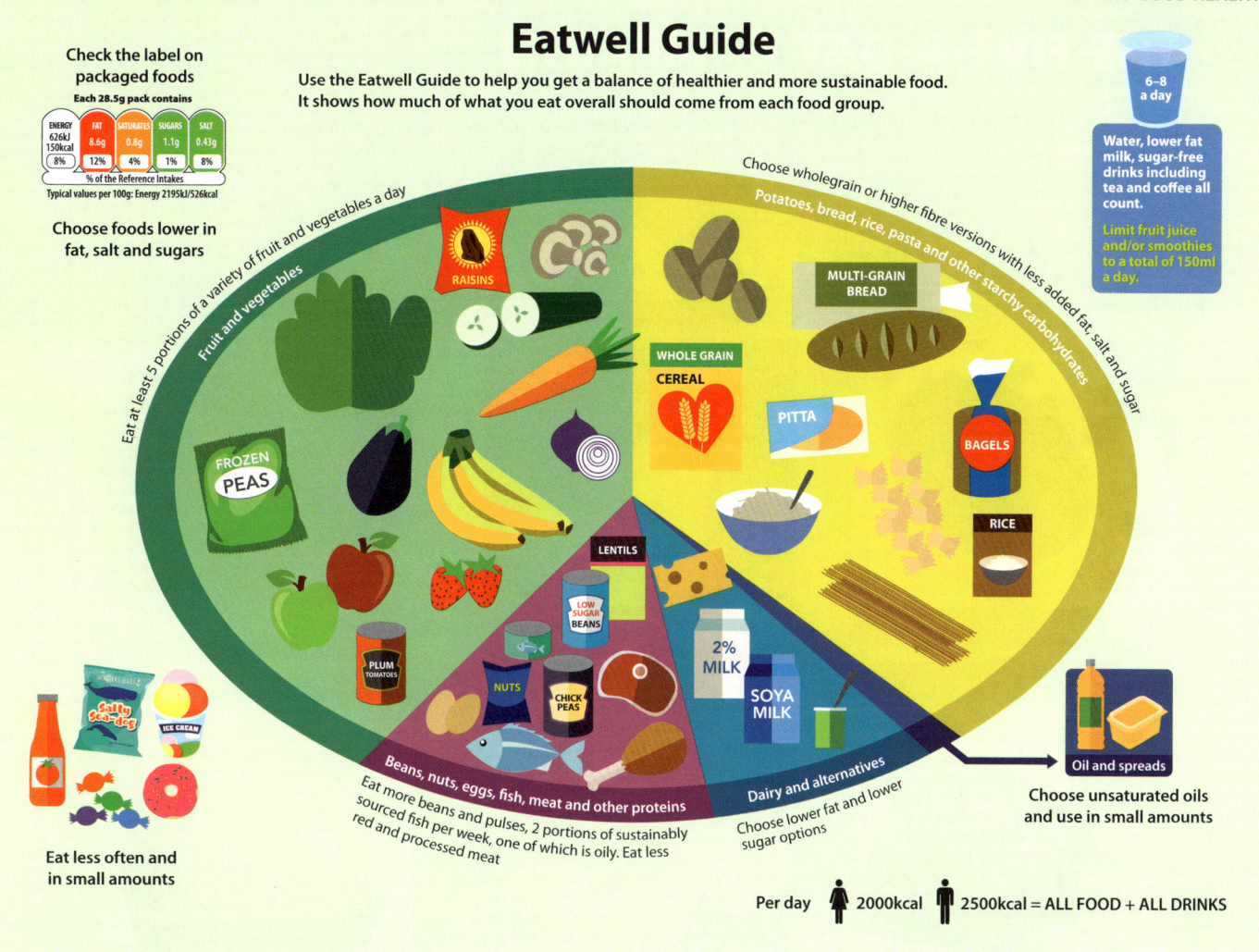

There is a fifth segment of the Eatwell Guide – oils and spreads – but this small section reflects the fact that our diet should have only small amounts of unsaturated fat and lower fat spreads.

The Eatwell Guide shows that we should eat some food from each of the four main food groups every day, with more foods from some than others. Our diet should be based on starchy carbohydrate foods such as bread, pasta, potatoes and rice as well as fruit and vegetables. A variety of foods from these two food groups should make up two thirds of the food we eat. The remaining third of the diet should be made up of milk and alternatives, beans, pulses, fish, eggs, meat and other proteins. Guidance is given on healthy hydration. Fruit juice is included in the hydration message. A front-of-pack label is included and average energy requirements for men and women are added. Some snacks or dishes are made up of ingredients from more than one of the food groups on the Eatwell Guide. These are called composite or **composition** foods. Examples include cottage pie, pizza, pasties and sandwiches.

- ham (meat)
- pineapple
- cheese
- base (mainly cereal)

Check it

1. What are the four main food groups on the Eatwell Guide?
2. Do you know the nutritional value each group contributes to the diet?

Study tip

Can you explain the benefits of following the Eatwell Guide guidelines?

Key point

Green and yellow include foods that contain all the essential nutrients and are low in fats and sugar. Eat more of those foods for a healthy balanced diet.

Purple contains unsaturated oils and fat spreads. Consume these foods in small amounts otherwise it's not a healthy balanced diet.

THE FIVE-A-DAY CAMPAIGN

Evidence shows that there are significant health benefits to consuming five 80g portions of fruit and vegetables every day. The World Health Organisation recommends eating a minimum of 400g of fruit and vegetables a day to lower the risk of serious health problems.

FIVE-A-DAY

▼ What counts as a portion?

- 1 tablespoon raisins
- 1 medium pear 
- 7 strawberries 
- 1 handful grapes 
- 3 whole dried apricots 
- 1 medium orange 
- 2 broccoli florets 
- 3 heaped tablespoons peas 
- 3 tablespoons cooked kidney beans 
- 1 medium glass orange juice 

CORE KNOWLEDGE

Government guidelines for healthy eating

These consist of eight tips:

1. Base your meals on starchy foods.

Most of the food on your plate should consist of starchy foods.

These foods will supply energy and also give us important vitamins and minerals and dietary fibre, particularly if whole grain or whole wheat varieties are chosen.

Eat plenty of rice, pasta, bread, potatoes (but not cooked in fat/oil), cassava, oats, quinoa or yam.

4. Cut down on saturated fat.

Eat few foods which contain a high amount of saturated fats*. There is 'hidden fat' in many processed foods.

Too much saturated fat contributes to an unhealthy diet.

- High in fat = foods containing more than 5g saturates per 100g.
- Low in fat = foods containing 1.5g or less saturates per 100g.

You should eat just a small amount every day.

7. Do not skip breakfast.

Breakfast is the most important meal of the day because the body needs energy and vital nutrients to set up for the day.

Eating breakfast means that we are less likely to snack on sugary, fatty foods mid-morning.

Nutritious breakfast foods include high fibre breakfast cereals, fruit juices and eggs.

2. Eat lots of fruit and vegetables.

Eat fresh fruit and vegetables. Canned, frozen and dried varieties as well as fruit juices, vegetable juices and smoothies also count.

All fresh fruit and vegetables contain vital vitamins, minerals and dietary fibre.

You should eat at least five portions a day.

5. Eat less salt.

There is 'hidden salt' in many processed foods.

Too much salt has a bad effect on the body. The chemical name for salt is sodium chloride; sodium can put extra strain on the kidneys and can raise blood pressure.

- High = more than 1.5g of salt per 100g food.
- Low = 0.3g or less salt per 100g food.

You shouldn't eat more than 6g a day (1 tsp) is recommended. Babies and very small children should ideally have a salt-free diet.

8. Get active and try to maintain a healthy weight.

Regular exercise such as walking, cycling, dancing or any sporting activity is important for health.

To maintain body weight, strengthen bones, the immune system and improve general well-being, 30 minutes of moderate activity several times a week is recommended.

3. Eat more fish.

Eat fish, both canned and frozen as well as fresh varieties, but avoid eating too much canned fish – it contains a lot of salt.

Oily fish contains omega-3 fatty acids which are important for good health. Fish is a good source of protein, vitamins and minerals.

You should eat at least two portions a week, one of which should be oily fish.

6. Drink plenty of water.

Often, we do not drink enough water.

Water helps with digestion, helps process waste, controls body temperature, prevents dehydration, and helps mental concentration.

You should drink at least 6–8 glasses a day, but more during hot weather.

In addition to the Eatwell Guide guidelines, the National Health Service recommends:

- matching the amount of calories with the level of activity, so that the energy obtained from food balances out the energy spent. Eating or drinking too much will mean putting on weight. Eating or drinking too little will mean losing weight.
- eating a wide range of foods.

*examples of foods high in saturated fats include cakes, biscuits, pies, fatty cuts of meat, sausages, bacon, cheese, cream

Study tip

Learn the eight guidelines and how they contribute to health and wellbeing.

Check it

Explain the meaning of a 'healthy, balanced diet'.

The benefits of a healthy diet

Eating a healthy diet and getting regular exercise is a way of preventing obesity. A healthy diet assists the brain and body to function at their optimum. A nutrient-rich diet and drinking plenty of fluid and water helps maintain a healthy body and organs, which also help towards building a stronger immune system.

In the UK, most people are fortunate enough to eat what they like when they like. In today's global food market, most foods are available all year round, for example, leeks in summer and strawberries at Christmas time.

There are, however, people in the world whose health and quality of life suffers through lack of food and lack of good quality food.

There are global challenges to be met:

- over one billion people worldwide are overweight or obese
- one billion others do not have access to adequate food
- an additional one billion have inadequate micronutrient intakes.

Three terms are often used to describe a person's state of health in relation to food intake:

- **undernutrition** – a condition where the body does not get enough food. It includes being underweight for one's age or deficient in particular micronutrients. Undernutrition can lead to health problems, e.g. anaemia.
- **overnutrition** – a condition where the body gets too much of a particular nutrient or nutrients.
- **malnutrition** – a condition linked to imperfect or bad nutrition when the body either gets too much or too little of a particular nutrient. Malnutrition describes both starvation (not eating enough of the right kind of food to meet dietary needs) and overeating (becoming obese).

Many organisations including government, the farming industry, the food industry and academia are working together to provide food using fewer resources such as fuel, land and water to feed a growing global population.

Looking ahead, we need to change our food consumption patterns.

Strategies on healthy eating in Wales

The Food Strategy for Wales 2010–2020 sets out a vision and an integrated approach to food and life. It was founded on the principles of sustainable development, which includes economic, social and environmental aspects of the production and consumption of food. It takes into consideration issues such as health, food culture, education, food security, environmental sustainability and community development.

In the UK there is evidence of both over and under consumption of dietary energy and nutrients. Despite more than 60% of adults currently classified as overweight or obese, many still have inadequate intakes of some micronutrients due to poor dietary choices.

Unhealthy diets can lead to health issues such as obesity, coronary heart disease, type 2 diabetes, high blood pressure, dental decay and some types of cancer.

Key point

Eating a balanced diet promotes good health and a healthy lifestyle.

CORE KNOWLEDGE — Factors affecting food choice: p134

Nutritional requirements [N]

A wealth of knowledge is now available on the role of nutrients in health and disease. We know that people need many different nutrients if they are to maintain health and reduce the risk of diet related illnesses. The amount of each nutrient needed is called the nutritional requirement.

It varies according to age, body size, health and level of activity carried out. It means that some individuals, in order to maintain health, may need more or less of a particular nutrient.

Nutritional requirements are based on information gained by health professionals in order to determine how much of each nutrient our bodies need.

The way that people absorb nutrients varies according to body type and age. Some people utilise nutrients less effectively than others and so will have higher than average nutritional requirements. For example, it is common amongst older people to have low levels of vitamin B12.

Pregnant women and women who breast-feed have different requirements.

Each nutrient fulfils particular functions in the body, and some are needed in larger quantities than others. For example, protein is needed in gram (g) quantities, vitamin C is needed in milligram (mg) quantities and vitamin B12 is needed in micromilligram (μ) quantities.

There are also special diets such as low fat, high fibre, low or high calorie, weight loss and low salt which are specific to individuals or groups of individuals.

The terminology used for diet and nutrients

Dietary Reference Values (DRVs) [N]

Dietary Reference Values (DRVs) are an estimate of the nutritional requirements of a healthy population. These guidelines are based on information gained by health professionals in order to determine how much of each nutrient our bodies need, i.e. someone who does not suffer from a health condition or illness.

DRVs were set by the Committee on Medical Aspects of Food and Nutrition Policy (COMA) in 1991. COMA has since been disbanded and replaced by the Scientific Advisory Committee on Nutrition (SACN) that advises the government on diet and health.

SACN revised energy requirements in 2011. Its report *Carbohydrates and Health 2015* made new recommendations for free sugars and fibre.

The new recommendations address how most people need to reduce the amount of free sugars and increase the amount of fibre they consume. It is expected that the new recommendations will help with obesity risk reduction and improve dental health.

Current average intakes of free sugars are at least twice the new 5% recommendation, and three times the 5% value in 11- to 18-year olds.

The main sources of free sugars are drinks, cereal products sweetened with sugars, confectionery, table sugar and fruit juice. The consumption of sugar-sweetened drinks should be minimised in children and adults.

'Free sugars' includes all monosaccharides and disaccharides added to foods by the manufacturer, cook or consumer, plus sugars naturally present in honey, syrups and unsweetened fruit juices. Under this definition, lactose (milk sugar) which is naturally present in milk and milk products and sugars contained within the cellular structure of foods (particularly fruits and vegetables) are excluded.

> **Study tip**
> Keep up to date on diet and healthy eating issues. It helps to support your answers.

> **Key point**
> DRVs apply to healthy people; they are guidelines only.

FREE SUGARS

FOOD PRODUCT	TOTAL SUGAR	FREE SUGARS	COMMENT
Plain yoghurt (low fat) 125g	9.9g	none	No free sugars – all of the sugar is lactose from milk.
Fruit yoghurt 125g	15.9g	11.25g	A mix of free sugars, sugars from the fruit (not 'free'), and lactose from the milk. Levels of free sugars vary and can be low when non-caloric sweeteners are used.
Regular cola 330ml	36.0g	36.0g	All free sugars.
Calorie-free cola 330ml	zero	zero	No sugars present.
Orange juice 150ml	12.9g	12.9g	All the sugars in juices from concentrates are classed as free sugars.
Semi-skimmed milk 200ml	9.4g	Zero	No free sugars; all of the sugar is lactose from milk.
Flavoured milk 200ml	28.0g	16.2g	A mix of added free sugars and lactose from milk. Flavoured milk is permitted within the School Food Standards if it does not contain more than 5% added sugars.

Key point

The definition of 'free sugars' excludes lactose (sugar from milk) and fructose (sugars naturally found in fruit and vegetables).

Activity

Collect labels from a range of drinks such as milk shakes, smoothies, yoghurt drinks, fruit juices.

Identify the ingredient which acts as a sweetener. Record your findings in a chart. Which ones contain free sugars?

To identify sources of free sugars, look for ingredients like brown sugar, high fructose corn syrup, fruit juice concentrate, corn syrup, fructose, sucrose, glucose, crystalline sucrose, nectars on food labels.

For most vitamins and minerals, DRVs are given as Reference Nutrient Intakes (RNI). This is a figure set by the Department of Health for the amount of a nutrient that is enough to meet the dietary needs of most people (97.5% of the population).

These nutrition requirements are reflected in the UK's food based guidelines and the Eatwell Guide. DRVs are used widely by schools, hospitals and residential homes to provide healthy balanced meals to the people in their care.

Reference Nutrient Intake (RNIs)

Reference Nutrient Intake (RNIs) provide an estimate for the amounts of protein, vitamins and minerals that meet the needs of the groups to which they apply.

Estimate Average Requirement (EARs)

Estimate Average Requirement (EAR) is used for energy. They are not targets but give a useful indication of how much energy the average person needs.

The energy value of foods is measured in kilocalories or kilojoules.

1 kilocalorie (kcal) = 1,000 calories

1 kilojoule (kJ) = 1,000 joules (J)

1 kilocalorie (kcal) = 4.2 kilojoules (kJ)

Kilojoules (kJ) and kilocalories (kcal) are units of energy referring to the energy value of food and drink, and the amount of energy for our bodies to burn.

Kilojoules are the accepted standard way of measuring energy, although calories (kcal) are still widely listed. Kilojoules are the metric equivalent of calories.

Individuals need enough energy to meet the demands of BMR and PAL.

BMR stands for **Basic Metabolic Rate**; the number of kilojoules the body uses to stay alive each day. It is determined by the amount of calories burnt each day based on sex, height, weight and level of activity.

PAL stands for **Physical Activity Level**; the number of kilojoules the body uses to fuel physical activity. In combination with BMR, it can be used to work out the amount of food energy a person needs to consume in order to suit a particular lifestyle.

BMR + PAL = your daily energy requirement. Energy balance is the relationship between the 'energy in' (food calories taken in) and the 'energy out' (calories used for daily energy requirements, that is, BMR + PAL).

Reference Intakes (RIs)

RIs are set by European law and are benchmarks for the amount of energy and key nutrients that can be eaten on a daily basis in order to maintain a healthy diet. As recommendations, they give a useful indication of how much energy the average person needs and how a particular nutrient fits into the daily diet.

The needs of individuals vary depending on age, gender and level of physical activity. There are currently no RIs that can be used specifically for children.

RIs are found on the nutrition labels of food products and give more detailed information on the nutrients needed.

RI daily recommendations for an average adult are:

Energy or nutrient	RI
Energy	8400kJ/2000kcal
Fat	70g
Saturates	20g
Carbohydrate	260g
Sugars	90g
Protein	50g
Salt	6g

	EARS MJ/DAY (KCAL/DAY)			
AGE	MALES		FEMALES	
0–3 months	2.28	545	2.16	(515)
4–6 months	2.89	690	2.69	(645)
7–9 months	3.44	825	3.20	(765)
10–12 months	3.85	920	3.61	(865)
1–3 years	5.15	1 230	4.86	(1 165)
4–6 years	7.16	1 715	6.46	(1 545)
7–10 years	8.24	1 970	7.28	(1 740)
11–14 years	9.27	2 220	7.72	(1 845)
15–18 years	11.51	2 755	8.83	(2 110)

▲ EARs energy for children

Study tip

Learn the definition of energy balance.

Key point

New recommendations for dietary fibre and salt were made by SACN in 2015 for the population aged 2 years and over:
The recommended dietary fibre intake for 11–16 year olds is 30g a day. The recommended salt intake for 11 years and above is no more than 6g a day.

Study tip

Learn nutritional terminology and understand how the various guidelines for energy requirement and intake are useful when planning diets in the UK.

Key point

Food labelling regulations determine the information consumers must have available when buying food.

Study tip

Can you list the information found on a food label?

Activity

Choose a range of readymade foods such as soup, sweet and sour meals, a pasta sauce, tomato ketchup, beef burgers, meatballs, curries, etc.

Study the labels and note the nutritional information per average portion, particularly the fat, saturated fat, salt and sugar content.

Present your results in a chart.

Prepare home-made versions of some of these products and use a nutritional programme to calculate their nutritional value per portion.

Food labelling

European regulations control all the information displayed on food labels. As of 2016 the following nutrition information has become compulsory:

- Energy provided per 100g and per portion, and as kJ and kcal
- Guideline Daily Amounts (GDAs) have been replaced by Reference Intakes (RIs)
- % RI is used for fat, saturates, sugars and salt
- The order of nutrients on the back labels has changed to the following, in descending order: energy, fat, saturates, carbohydrates, sugars, fibre (not required by law), protein
- On front labels in the UK, colour coding and high/medium/low labelling is used for fat, saturates, sugars and salt (but not energy)

The table below shows how high, medium and low levels of fat, saturates, total sugars and salt in foods are classified for front of pack labels.
These levels have been decided by the UK government. The 'per portion' in red is used where portions are 250g or more.

	COLOUR CODE	FAT	SATURATES	TOTAL SUGARS	SALT
LOW	green	up to 3.0g/100g	up to 1.5g/100g	up to 5.0g/100g	up to 0.3g/100g
MEDIUM	amber	3.0g/100g to 17.5g/100g	1.5g/100g to 5.0/100g	5.0g/100g to 22.5g/100g	0.3g/100g to 1.5g/100g
HIGH	red	more than 17.5g/100g 21g/portion	more than 5.0g/100g 6.0g/portion	more than 22.5g/100g 27g/portion	more than 1.5g/100g 1.56g/portion

Alongside these traffic light colours, the label also shows the amount of these nutrients in one portion of the food or drink, and the percentage of the Reference Intake (RI) provided in one portion.

Specific guidelines have been given on claims made on labels on food packaging, for example:

1. **Nutritional claims** which relate to what a product does or doesn't contain, or contains in a higher or lower amount. For example:
   - Sugar free (must contain less than 0.5g sugars per 100g)
   - Low fat (must contain less than 3g fat per 100g)
   - High in fibre (must contain at least 6g fibre per 100g)
   - Source of vitamin D (must contain at least 15% of the RI for vitamin D per 100g)

2. **Health claims** which suggest that there is a relationship between a product and health. For example:
   - Calcium is needed for the maintenance of normal bones
   - Plant sterols and plant stanol esters have been shown to lower/reduce blood cholesterol. High cholesterol is a risk factor in the development of coronary heart disease.

DIET AND GOOD HEALTH

DAILY NUTRITIONAL NEEDS CHANGE ACCORDING TO Ⓝ

AGE

BABIES are provided with all the nutrients they need in the right proportions until about six months when they are weaned on to solid food.

CHILDREN need to follow a varied, balanced diet so that they grow and stay healthy.

TEENAGERS grow faster than at any other life stage and their nutritional needs are high. Teenagers tend to be more active than those in later life.

ADULTS and ELDERLY PEOPLE need a well-balanced diet and should not eat more food than they require for their energy needs otherwise they will put on weight.

GENDER

For example, iron for women aged 19–50 years; RNI is 14.8mg/d, which is higher than for men (8.7 mg/d) to cover menstrual blood losses.

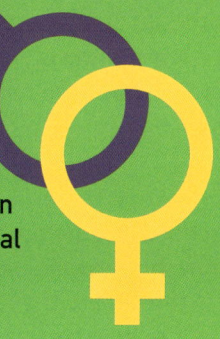

GROWTH

For example, adolescents have higher calcium requirements to cover their bone growth

Other factors include individual lifestyle and state of health.

Factors affecting nutritional requirements: Age Ⓝ
Babies

Newborn babies should only be on a milk diet for the first 4–6 months of their life. After 4–6 months, small amounts of soft foods are introduced. This is called weaning.

Department of Health guidelines suggest that solid food should be introduced to the baby's diet from 26 weeks. By this time, the baby's natural supply of iron will be running out and the diet will need to supplement the supply. A variety of raw and cooked foods need to be gradually introduced to allow the baby to adjust to new flavours and textures. Popular foods for weaning include baby rice, puréed fruit and vegetables.

From 7–9 months, the range and variety can be extended, progressing from soft purées to mash to more lumpy food.

From about 9 months onwards the baby will be able to cope with chewing and swallowing a range of new flavours and textures.

Babies' diet should contain a wide selection of fruit and vegetables, chicken, fish, eggs, pulse vegetables, dairy foods, pasta, rice and bread. Foods to avoid include whole nuts, fried foods, salt and added sugar. It is recommended that cow milk should be given as a drink from 12 months onwards. It can, however be used in small quantities to mix with other foods from an earlier age.

Study tip

Explain why milk is important for a baby.

Toddlers or pre-school children

It is essential to give growing toddlers a balanced diet in order to supply all the important nutrients they need.

Nutrient	Why it is needed	Examples of food sources
Protein	Children grow rapidly at this stage in life	Meat, poultry, fish, eggs, milk, cheese, soya
Carbohydrate (from starchy foods)	For energy	Bread, pasta, rice, potatoes
Thiamin	To enable the release of energy and to keep up with quick growth	Red meat, liver, milk, fortified breakfast cereals
Calcium	For good bone health and tooth development	Milk, cheese, green vegetables
Vitamin D	To combine with calcium for bone health	Fortified margarine, sunlight
Iron	For healthy blood and to keep up with level of activity	Meat, liver, green vegetables
Vitamin C	To work with iron	Citrus fruits, blackcurrants, green vegetables
Fat	For energy and fat soluble vitamins A, D, E and K	Oily fish, dairy foods

Children need to be taught good eating habits that they will hopefully maintain into adulthood. They should be given three balanced meals a day with healthy snacks in between if necessary. By the time they are 1 year old, children are able to eat the same food as the rest of the family.

Children normally develop their own likes and dislikes for food. Their tastes may vary over time. This should be respected by offering suitable alternatives. Many children eat a wide range of foods but go through periods of being fussy eaters. Healthy foods should be reintroduced in order to develop sound eating patterns.

> **Study tip**
>
> Explain why it is important to encourage children to eat a healthy balanced diet from an early age.

Children

When children start attending school they are normally very active. From five years onwards, children can follow the Eatwell Guide guidelines. Their food should be varied and balanced in terms of nutrients. They should be given regular meals and healthy snacks. Children have regular 'growth spurts' and may be hungrier than usual when this happens. A good supply of protein food and energy giving food is essential as well as the minerals required for good bone health. Regular exercise is also essential to develop bone strength.

Research shows that the average dietary intake of school children in the UK is low in fresh fruit and vegetables and high in snacks containing a significant amount of fat, sugar and salt.

The Welsh Government has initiated a number of programmes to address the problem of overweight and obesity in children. These include:

- The *Food and Fitness* five-year plan aims to improve access to healthier food and drink in a range of early years settings.
- *Change 4 life* is a campaign introduced by the government in 2010. It aims to help people make lifestyle changes through better nutrition and exercise.
- The *Appetite for Life Action Plan 2007* aims to improve the nutritional standards of food and drink provided to school children in Wales. It outlines the following measures:
    - no confectionery (chocolate and sweets) or salty savoury snacks to be served
    - increase fresh fruit and vegetables in meals
    - limit meat products and potatoes cooked in fat/oil to once a week
    - include more healthy drinks such as water and milk.
- The *Healthy Eating in Schools* measure was passed in 2009 to make the nutritional standards of school meals a statutory requirement.

Teenagers

Teenagers need a healthy varied diet, incorporating all the major food groups. In the short term this will help with general development of the body and energy levels, while in the long term, it will help prevent CHD, type 2 diabetes and osteoporosis.

Research shows that:

- intakes of saturated fatty acids, salt and added sugars (non-intrinsic) are too high amongst teenagers
- intakes of some vitamins and minerals, in particular vitamin A, riboflavin, iron, calcium, magnesium are low
- overweight and obesity is prevalent among British teenagers
- a large **proportion** of teenagers are inactive.

Encouraging a healthy lifestyle is of prime importance during the teenage years. Good habits adopted at that age are likely to carry health benefits through adulthood.

There is a tendency for teenagers, particularly girls, to try and control weight by adopting very low energy diets. A restricted diet can lead to nutrient deficiencies and problems later in life. Teenagers with weight problems may need specialist advice from health professionals.

Growth spurts usually happen around 10 years of age for girls and 12 years for boys. During that time, iron requirements increase to help with growth and muscle development. Girls need more iron than boys to replace iron loss when they begin to menstruate. Reference nutrient intake for girls 11–18 years old is 14.8mg while for boys of the same age it is 11.3mg of iron daily.

> **Study tip**
>
> Give advice to a teenager on healthy eating and the importance of exercise. Give reasons for your advice.

Adulthood and old age

The nutritional requirements of adults vary according to age, body size and level of activity. Body growth stops, metabolism slows down with age, and there may be a tendency for the body to lose muscle and gain weight.

A well balanced diet is required to maintain and repair body cells and to maintain health. People in very physical occupations need high energy foods whilst people in more sedentary occupations need less high energy foods.

Older people tend to eat less food but it is still essential to eat a well balanced, varied diet to get a supply of all the essential vitamins and minerals. Although body metabolism slows down with age, regular exercise is important as it offers health benefits. Physical activity can help prevent CHD, type 2 diabetes, promote good bone health and strengthen muscles.

As people grow older they require additional calcium and vitamin D rich foods in their diet to help prevent decalcification from the bones and teeth. Good sources of calcium rich foods include dairy products, canned fish, soya products and fortified breakfast cereals.

IRON AND VITAMIN C

Extra iron is needed to prevent anaemia. Iron from meat sources, such as liver, red meat and poultry, is known as haem iron. This type of iron is readily absorbed by the body.

Iron from other sources e.g. green leafy vegetables, nuts, whole grain cereals, pulses and dried fruit is known as non-haem iron, and is not as easily absorbed by the body. A vitamin C food should be consumed with an iron rich food to enable absorption of iron. Examples of vitamin C rich foods include all citrus fruit and all green vegetables and juices.

Pulses and cereals provide a cheaper alternative to meat and a good supply of vitamins B6, and B12, and folic acid which is important to help prevent coronary heart disease and memory loss.

Fish, poultry, green vegetables, whole grain cereals, dairy produce, eggs and soya milk are all good sources of the B vitamin group.

MEALS ON WHEELS

Elderly people living alone may need help with planning and preparing meals. Local authorities help arrange hot midday meals deliveries to the elderly people in need of this service, for example Meals on Wheels. Many private companies also provide frozen portion controlled ready meals to cater for those who cannot cook for themselves.

> **Key point**
>
> As people age their appetite decreases; smaller portions should be given to the elderly.

> **Study tip**
>
> Why does an elderly person need a balanced diet with diminishing amounts of sugary and fatty foods?

Dental problems are common in later life and can affect food choice. Nutritious foods that are hard to chew are often replaced by soft foods which may not be as high in nutrients. This can result in a low dietary fibre intake, increasing the risk of gut problems such as constipation and deficiency in important vitamins such as vitamin C.

For a number of reasons, elderly people are at a greater risk of dehydration than younger people, particularly those who are frail or who have a chronic illness. Long term mild dehydration increases the risk of kidney stones, urinary tract cancers and constipation.

DIET AND GOOD HEALTH

Factors affecting nutritional requirements:
Pregnancy and lactation

Normal healthy eating guidelines apply during pregnancy in addition to extra amounts of particular nutrients. As a rule, pregnant women do not need to eat for two but need to follow specific dietary advice with emphasis on the following nutrients:

Nutrient	Why it is needed	Sources
Starchy, fibre-rich foods	Energy needs increase a little in the last three months of pregnancy – an additional 200 kcalories per day should be consumed	Wholemeal bread and cereals
Vitamin D	To absorb calcium and to prevent low birth weight	Sunlight, oily fish and margarine
Folic acid (folate)	Reduces the risk of the foetus developing spina bifida, a defect in the spine	Breakfast cereals, bread, green vegetables
Calcium	Helps with bone and skeletal growth	Dairy foods, white bread, green vegetables
Iron	Helps with baby growth and prevents the mother becoming anaemic	Red meat, dark green vegetables
Dietary fibre	Prevents constipation and piles	Whole grain foods, vegetables
Protein	For baby growth	Meat, fish, eggs, milk cheese and soya
Vitamin C	Helps with absorption of iron	Citrus fruits

There are some foods that pregnant women should avoid, mainly because they could harm the baby. These foods contain food poisoning bacteria such as salmonella and listeria which could cause serious illness and may lead to a miscarriage.

Foods to avoid which may contain salmonella are;

- Uncooked meats
- Uncooked vegetables
- Unpasteurised milk and milk products such as yoghurt and cheese
- Some chilled ready meals.

Foods to avoid which may contain listeria are:

- Raw and lightly cooked meat and poultry
- Raw eggs and any food containing raw eggs such as home-made mayonnaise
- Soft and blue veined cheeses
- Pâté made from liver contains a high amount of vitamin A which is stored in the body; a build up of vitamin A can be toxic, and this toxicity can cause birth defects.

Some types of fish such as swordfish, marlin and shark contain high levels of mercury which can harm the baby's nervous system. Tuna also contains mercury and should be limited in a pregnant woman's diet.

Lactation

The mother produces milk after the birth of the baby. This is called lactation. During this period, her energy requirements will increase slightly to cope with the demands of a growing baby. A breastfeeding mother should ensure that her diet contains good sources of protein, calcium, zinc and vitamins. It is very important that she increases liquid intake to help produce breast milk for the baby.

▲ A pregnant woman should follow normal healthy eating guidelines and any special dietary advice

Study tip

List foods a pregnant woman should avoid during pregnancy. Why should these foods be avoided?

Principles of nutrition: p8

- Dairy free
- GM free
- Organic
- Low carb
- Eatwell apple
- Contains nuts
- Vegetarian
- Kosher
- Gluten-free
- Sugar free
- Vegan
- Halal

Special diets

In addition to dietary needs based on age, gender and growth, there are also special diets which are specific to individuals or groups of individuals.

Some health conditions, see panels below, may be also be diet related and may be specifically associated with a poor diet. Other health conditions can be hereditary but controlled by special diets. These health conditions include coeliac disease, type 2 diabetes, iron deficiency anaemia, cardiovascular disease (CVD), obesity and bone related health conditions, obesity, nut allergy and lactose intolerance.

COELIAC DISEASE

Coeliac disease is triggered by gluten (a collective term for protein found in cereals, wheat, rye and barley) and causes the body's immune system to attack its own tissues.

Foods that are naturally gluten-free such as rice, corn, maize, potato, buckwheat, polenta, soya and millet can be made into flours which can be used in gluten-free dishes.

All types of plain meat, fish, eggs, cheese, milk, most yoghurts, fruits, vegetables and pulses (peas, beans and lentils) are also naturally gluten-free and can be eaten freely on a gluten-free diet.

Foods such as bread, biscuits, cakes, couscous and pastas must be avoided.

Gluten can also be found in custard powders, thickening starch, some cheese spreads and sauces.

Gluten-free products are widely available and their packaging carries a special symbol.

IRON DEFICIENCY ANAEMIA

Iron deficiency anaemia is a condition where a lack of iron in the body leads to a reduction in the number of red blood cells. Iron is used to produce red blood cells, which help store and carry oxygen in the blood. A lack of iron in the body means that organs and tissues will not get as much oxygen as they normally would.

There are several different types of anaemia and each one has a different cause, although iron deficiency anaemia is the most common type.

An iron-rich diet includes the following foods:

- dark green leafy vegetables, such as watercress and curly kale
- iron-fortified cereals or bread
- brown rice
- pulses and beans
- nuts and seeds
- meat, fish and tofu
- eggs
- dried fruit, such as apricots, prunes and raisins

DIET AND GOOD HEALTH

DIABETES

TWO KINDS OF DIABETES

In type 1 diabetes, the body makes little or no **insulin** because beta cells that make insulin are destroyed by the immune system. So people with type 1 diabetes, usually children and young adults, must take insulin every day.

In type 2 diabetes, the body may produce too little insulin properly or become resistant to it. This kind of diabetes usually affects people who are older or overweight. In recent years more children and teens have been diagnosed with type 2 diabetes, most likely because of obesity and inactivity.

This means that glucose stays in the blood and is not used as fuel for energy.

Maintaining a healthy weight, eating a healthy, balanced diet and regular exercise are ways of preventing and managing diabetes. In addition, the following advice is given to people suffering from type 2 diabetes:

- Eat regular meals
- Include carbohydrates in the food you eat each day. Healthier sources include whole grain starchy foods, fruits and vegetables, pulses. All carbohydrates affect blood glucose levels.
- Cut back on saturated fats, which are found in foods that are made of animal products like butter and cheese, red and processed meats, palm oil, coconut oil, ghee, and cakes and pastries.
- Cut back on salt. Too much salt is associated with high blood pressure, which increases the risk of complications from diabetes. Choose lower salt options whenever possible.
- Try using artificial sweeteners when sweetening food and drinks at home.

CARDIOVASCULAR DISEASE N

Cardiovascular disease (CVD) is a general term that describes disease of the heart or blood vessels. Specific examples of CVD include coronary heart disease (CHD), stroke, and diseases where the arteries or vessels carrying blood around the body become blocked or damaged.

The flow of blood to the heart can become blocked or reduced by a build-up of fatty material (atheroma) in the arteries.

Most of the risk factors for CVD are related to diet and lifestyle. They include being overweight, high blood pressure, high blood cholesterol and a lack of exercise.

It is important to reduce the risks of developing CHD by looking at lifestyle as a whole. The following are dietary recommendations for the prevention of CHD:

- low in saturated fat
- higher in unsaturated fat such as oily fish, nuts and seeds, rapeseed oil, olive oil
- high fibre to include whole grains
- at least 5 portions of fruit and vegetables
- no more than 6g salt daily because of the risk of raising blood pressure.

In addition, it is important to maintain ideal body weight, limit alcohol intake, increase the amount of exercise taken and avoid smoking.

OBESITY [N]

Obese is a term used to describe somebody who is very overweight, with a lot of body fat. It is a common problem, estimated to affect one in every four adults and around one in every five children aged 10–11 in the UK.

The most widely used method of classifying a person's health in relation to their weight is body mass index (BMI).

BMI is a measure of whether individuals are a healthy weight for their height. It is worked out on an individual's age, height and weight:

- a BMI of 25 to 29.9 means you are considered overweight
- a BMI of 30 means you are considered obese
- a BMI of 40 or above means you are considered severely obese.

The best way to treat obesity is to eat a balanced, calorie-controlled diet and to exercise regularly. Activities such as fast walking, jogging, swimming or playing tennis for 150–300 minutes a week are recommended.

Calories are a measure of the amount of energy in food. Knowing the calorific value of food can help balance the energy taken by the body with the energy used by the body.

Obesity occurs when energy intake from food and drink consumption is greater than energy expended over a prolonged period of time. Given the high rates of obesity in the UK, aiming to reduce the overall population's energy intakes is likely to improve national health indicators.

It means cutting down the number of calories consumed every day. The general guidelines for people on a calorie controlled diet are to eat more starchy foods and cut down on fat and high sugar foods.

Obesity can affect quality of life as well as increasing the risk of developing other illnesses such as cardiovascular disease, strokes, diabetes and breathing problems.

Key point

1 calorie is the energy needed to raise the temperature of 1 gram of water by 1 °C.

BONE HEALTH AND DENTAL HEALTH [N]

Bone density increases with age until the early twenties when it is at its maximum.

From the age of about 40, bone density decreases. Excessive loss of bone density can lead to the natural development of **osteoporosis** in later life when the bones become weaker.

Women lose bone density rapidly in the first few years after the menopause, when their monthly periods stop and the ovaries stop releasing eggs.

Losing bone density is a normal part of the ageing process, but for some people it can lead to an increased risk of bone fractures. To prevent this, regular exercise is important. Adults aged 19–64 should do at least 150 minutes of moderate activity every week. As well as exercise, eating a healthy, balanced diet is recommended for everyone.

In addition to other nutrients, calcium is important for maintaining strong bones; calcium rich foods include leafy green vegetables, dried fruits, tofu and dairy foods.

Vitamin D is also important for healthy bones and teeth because it helps the body absorb calcium. Vitamin D can be found in eggs, milk and oily fish. However, most vitamin D is made in the skin in response to sunlight. Deficiency of vitamin D is prevalent in:

- people who are housebound or particularly frail
- people on a poor diet
- people who keep covered up in sunlight because they wear total sun block or who adhere to a certain dress code
- women who are pregnant or breastfeeding.

Calcium is a vital mineral for building strong bones and teeth. Calcium rich foods should be eaten daily, in conjunction with vitamin D rich foods.

Insufficient calcium or vitamin D in the diet can increase the risk of developing osteomalacia and a calcium deficiency disease, known as hypocalcaemia.

Dental caries (cavities) continue to be a widespread problem in the UK. The Adult Dental Health Survey found that 31% of adults in England, Wales and Northern Ireland experienced tooth decay in either the crown or root of the tooth.

In the Children's Dental Health Survey UK, 57% of eight-year-olds had some kind of tooth decay in their primary dentition. In permanent teeth, 14%, 34% and 49% of 8, 12 and 15-year-olds, respectively, had obvious tooth decay

FOOD ALLERGIES AND FOOD INTOLERANCES

A food allergy involves an immune system response.

A food intolerance is a term applied to a range of adverse responses to certain foods and does not involve an immune system response.

ALLERGIES

Some people are either born with or develop an allergy, which means they have to avoid certain foods or drastically reduce intake of these foods.

Allergy to peanuts and tree nuts is the most common food allergy in adults and children. Recent studies have shown that peanut allergy is on the increase.

People with nut allergies should avoid foods with peanuts and nuts altogether. Food labels need to be checked carefully for warnings about the possibility of nut traces.

Allergic reactions to peanuts include a rash, eczema and vomiting. However, some allergic reactions can be severe, causing difficulty in breathing due to asthma or throat swelling, or a drop in blood pressure. This is known as anaphylaxis, and can be life-threatening.

Other foods which can bring on allergic reactions include eggs and shellfish.

All pre-packed foods sold in the UK must clearly state on the label if they contain any of the 14 major food allergens. The food allergens are: peanuts, nuts, eggs, milk, celery, mustard, crustaceans (e.g. crab), molluscs (e.g. oysters), fish, sesame seeds, cereals containing gluten (wheat, barley, rue), soybeans, lupin and sulphur dioxide.

Allergens can be written in bold, italics, highlighted, contrasting colour, capitals and underlining on food labels. Allergen cross contamination risk warnings must also be used.

LACTOSE INTOLERANCE

Lactose intolerance means that the person must avoid cow milk. This can be replaced with other milks such as hazel, hemp, almond, rice or soya milk. Lactose-free products such as cheese are also available.

People with lactose intolerance cannot digest the milk sugar, lactose, because of an enzyme deficiency in the body. The body digests lactose using a substance called lactase to break down lactose into two sugars called glucose and galactose, which can then be easily absorbed into the bloodstream. People with lactose intolerance do not produce enough lactase, so lactose stays in the digestive system where it is fermented by bacteria, leading to the production of various gases, causing the symptoms associated with lactose intolerance.

Many processed foods contain lactose. Lactose intolerant people should read the labels to check.

> **Study tip**
> Name food-related disorders or illnesses. Outline the main causes of these disorders.

> **Key point**
> The UK Food Information Regulations 2014 came into force when the EU listed 14 allergens that need to be identified if they are used as ingredients in a dish. Allergenic ingredients must be indicated in the list of ingredients and the substance named clearly.

Diet and lifestyle

Specific lifestyle needs include vegetarians, vegan, lacto-ovo, lacto, and those with religious beliefs such as Hindus, Muslims and Jews.

Vegetarians

There are different types of vegetarians but all vegetarians avoid eating meat and fish for a variety of reasons, including:

- ethical beliefs: they object to the cruelty of killing animals, animal welfare issues
- religious beliefs
- medical reasons: cases of food poisoning, health scares such as BSE and Foot and Mouth disease are linked to meat consumption
- cost factor
- family influences, peer pressure, media pressure
- dislike the taste or texture of meat
- environmental concerns – they consider using land for rearing animals wasteful.

The majority of vegetarians do eat some animal products, mainly milk, cheese and eggs.

Types of vegetarians include:

- lacto-vegetarians eat dairy products but not eggs, poultry, meat, fish or seafood
- lacto-ovo vegetarians eat egg and dairy products but not poultry, meat, fish or seafood
- vegans do not eat any foods from animal origin. This includes meat, fish, dairy foods and honey.

▲ Examples of symbols on food products suitable for vegeterians

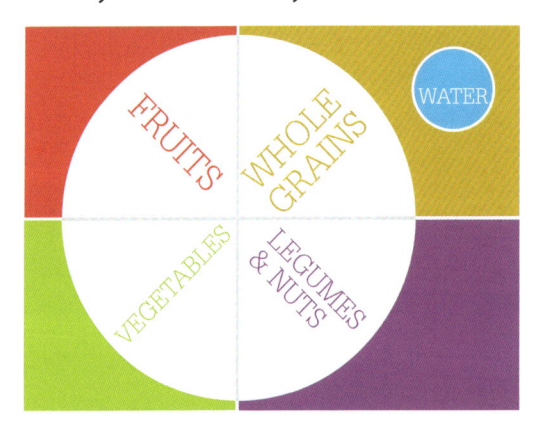

◀ Components of a balanced vegetarian or vegan diet

As long as a varied diet is consumed, vegetarian and vegan diets can provide all the nutrients needed to be healthy.

The main nutrients to consider for vegetarians and vegans are iron, selenium, vitamin B12 and omega-3 fatty acids.

Suitable sources of iron for vegetarians and vegans include:

- pulses
- wholemeal bread and flour
- breakfast cereals fortified with iron
- dark green leafy vegetables such as watercress, broccoli and spring greens and okra
- nuts
- dried fruits such as apricots, prunes and figs.

Key point

An allergy involves the body's immune system. An intolerance does not involve the immune system.

CORE KNOWLEDGE Milk, Cheese and Yoghurt: **Alternatives to cow milk** p246

The iron in these foods is not as well absorbed as it is from meat but absorption of the iron becomes easier if a food or drink that contains vitamin C is consumed as the same time.

Selenium is a mineral needed for the immune system to function properly. Meat, fish and nuts are the best sources of selenium; a vegan will need to make sure that nuts are included in the diet. Brazil nuts are a particularly good source of selenium. Bread and eggs also provide some selenium.

Vitamin B12 is needed to make red blood cells and to keep the nervous system healthy. It also helps release energy from the foods eaten. Dairy foods, fortified breakfast cereals, yeast extract and fortified soya drinks contain vitamin B12 but vegans may need to include vitamin B12 supplements in their diet.

Omega-3 fatty acids

The Eatwell Guide recommends eating at least one portion of oily fish a week because of its omega-3 fatty acid content. Alternative omega-3 sources for vegetarians include flaxseed and flaxseed oil (linseed), rapeseed oil, soya based foods such as tofu, walnuts and walnut oil, omega-3 fortified eggs.

Vegans need to ensure they are getting sufficient protein in their diet.

Eating a variety of foods is the key to achieving an adequate intake of protein in a vegetarian diet. This is because most plant food proteins have a low content of one or more of the essential amino acids needed by the body. It is important to get some of these essential amino acids at the same time.

The following are all good sources of protein:

- pulses (beans and lentils)
- nuts and seeds
- eggs
- soya and soya products such as tofu
- mycoproteins such as Quorn
- wheat proteins such as cereals, bread, rice and maize
- milk and dairy products

Soya and quinoa are the only vegetarian sources which contain good amounts of all the essential amino acids. Combining different types of protein foods at the same meal ensures a better intake of these essential amino acids. The following combinations give an optimum combination of essential amino acids in a vegetarian diet.

- beans on toast
- breakfast cereal with milk
- rice with lentil dhal
- bean chilli served with tortillas
- couscous with spicy chick pea stew
- houmous with pitta bread

Cheese is often a popular choice for people following vegetarian diets, but while it is a good source of protein, calcium and other nutrients, some varieties can be high in saturates and salt. Soya milk and products fortified with calcium are excellent sources of calcium in a vegetarian diet.

Good sources of calcium in vegan diets include:

- fortified soya, rice and oat drinks
- calcium-set tofu
- sesame seeds and tahini
- pulses
- brown and white bread (in the UK calcium is added to white and brown flour by law)
- dried fruit such as raisins, prunes, figs and dried apricots

Vegan sources of vitamin D include:

- exposure to summer sunshine
- fortified fat spreads, breakfast cereals and soya drinks (with vitamin D added)
- vitamin D supplements

> **Study tip**
>
> Learn the definitions of lacto vegetarian, lacto-ovo vegetarian and vegan.

RELIGIOUS BELIEFS

People choose to eat or avoid certain foods depending on their religious belief. Some beliefs have been followed for centuries and are well established as part of life.

BUDDHISTS

Many Buddhists are vegetarians, as the religion preaches against killing.

Buddhists believe they should not be responsible for the death of any other living organism. Therefore, most Buddhists follow a strict vegetarian, if not vegan diet.

Chinese Buddhists also avoid garlic and onions as they believe it makes meditation more difficult. All Buddhists avoid the consumption of alcohol.

HINDUS

The cow is a sacred animal, and cannot be eaten. Strict Hindus are vegetarians.

They do not eat beef or any beef products and all flesh except lamb, chicken and fish is prohibited.

Milk is permitted as no animal is killed during the collection.

Some devout Hindus observe fasting on special occasions as a mark of respect to personal Gods or as part of their penance.

CHRISTIANS

They do not have any restriction, but some denominations only eat fish on Fridays

Meat is not allowed on Ash Wednesday, Good Friday and all Fridays in Lent – and, for many Catholics, on any Friday. Animal products such as fat, eggs, dairy and broth are permissible, as is fish.

Fasts from solid food on Ash Wednesday and Good Friday are required of strict Catholics between the ages of 18 and 59.

JEWS

Jewish food must be kosher, meaning slaughtered according to strict Jewish laws. Kosher animals have a completely split hoof and chew cud e.g. cows, goats and sheep. Horses and pigs are not kosher animals.

Pork, birds of prey, eels, fish without scales are forbidden. Meat must not be cooked or eaten with dairy products because Jews do not eat mother and child together – so chicken and egg together or milk and beef together are not allowed.

Cheese must be made with vegetable rennet and meat must not be cooked with butter. Separate cooking utensils and storage must be used for meat and dairy products.

MUSLIMS

Food eaten by Muslims must be halal (lawful) which means animals are killed according to the Muslim law. Pork, fish without scales, shellfish and alcohol is forbidden

The Qur'an outlines halal, the foods which can be eaten, and haram, foods which are forbidden. Muslims only eat halal meat (which is killed in the same way as kosher).

RASTAFARIANS

Most will only eat Ital foods, which are seen as natural or pure, without the addition of artificial colours, flavourings or preservatives.

Many Rastafarians are vegetarians or vegans. Coffee and alcohol and other caffeinated drinks are avoided by some because these are considered to confuse the soul.

SEVENTH DAY ADVENTISTS

All animal flesh such as pork, beef and lamb are prohibited. Many Adventists are ovo-lacto vegetarian, which means that they do not consume animal flesh of any kind, but will consume dairy and egg products.

Some Adventists avoid food and drinks which contain caffeine, therefore they do not consume tea and coffee. They also avoid alcohol as they believe it corrupts the senses.

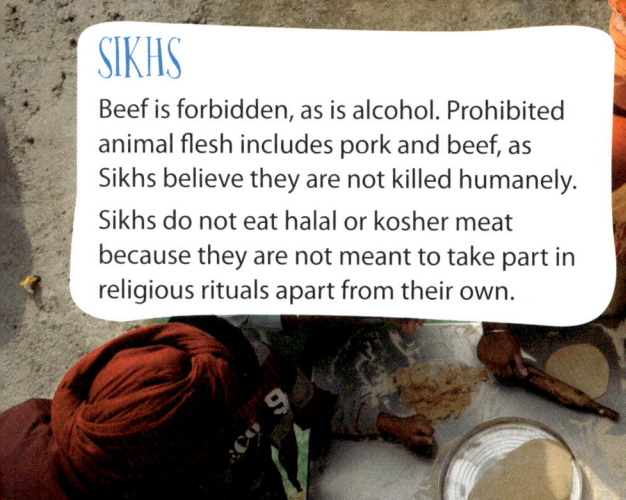

SIKHS

Beef is forbidden, as is alcohol. Prohibited animal flesh includes pork and beef, as Sikhs believe they are not killed humanely.

Sikhs do not eat halal or kosher meat because they are not meant to take part in religious rituals apart from their own.

	BEEF	PORK	POULTRY & GOAT	FISH/ SHELLFISH	EGGS	MILK	ALCOHOL
BUDDISM	✗	✗		some	✓	✓	
HINDUISM	✗	✗	Restricted/Avoided		?		✗
JUDAISM	Kosher	✗	Kosher	✗	Kosher	Not with meat	
ISLAM	Halal	✗	Halal	✗			✗
RASTAFARIANISM	✗	✗		no fish over 12"			✗
SEVENTH DAY ADVENTIST	✗	✗		✗	?		
SIKH	in some sects halal or kosher						✗

▲ Summary of religious based diets

🔑 Key terms

Diet – the type of food we eat or drink.
Balanced diet – a diet which provides all the necessary nutrients in the correct amount to meet the body's needs.
Undernutrition – eating too little food to meet the body's needs.
Overnutrition – a condition where the body gets too much of a particular nutrient or nutrients.
Metabolism – the chemical processes that occur within the body in order to maintain life.
Malnutrition – imperfect nutrition.
Dietary Reference Values (DRVs) – an estimate of the nutritional requirements of a healthy population
Estimate Average Requirement (EAR) – a useful indication of how much energy the average person needs.
Reference Nutrient Intake (RNIs) – an estimate of the amount of proteins, vitamins and minerals that should meet the needs of most of the group to which they apply.

Physical Activity Level (PAL) – the number of kilojoules the body uses to fuel physical activity.
Basic Metabolic Rate (BMR) – the number of kilojoules the body uses to stay alive each day.
Dietary guidelines – advice on diet.
Insulin – a hormone which controls blood sugar level.
Nutritional requirements – estimates of energy and nutrients needed by individuals or groups of people.
Decalcification – gradual removal of calcium from bones and teeth.
Primary dentition – first set of teeth, 20 in all.
Osteomalacia – a softening of the bones, through deficiency from calcium or vitamin D.
Osteoporosis – a medical condition in which the bones become brittle and fragile.
Calcium deficiency – also known as **hypocalcaemia**, where the body suffers from not having enough calcium for its needs.

CORE KNOWLEDGE

EXAM QUESTIONS

DIET AND GOOD HEALTH

1. True or false? Tick (✓) the correct box. [3]

Statement	True	False
A diet rich in fibre helps to prevent bowel disorders.		
Eat large amounts of food containing sugar and fat.		
Too much salt has a bad effect on the body.		

2. Match the acronyms of nutritional requirements with the correct description. The first one has been filled in for you. [3]

| PAL | EARs | RIs | DRVs |

	Description
EARs	Not targets but give a useful indication of how much energy the average person needs.
	The number of kilojoules the body uses to fuel physical activity.
	An estimate of the nutritional requirements of a healthy population.
	Benchmarks for the amount of energy and key nutrients that need to be taken in on a daily basis.

3. a State two factors which influence how much energy a person needs. [2]
   b Explain the importance of maintaining a correct energy balance. [4]

4. a Give general dietary advice to a friend who is trying to lose weight. [4]
   b Suggest a suitable food choice for your friend for the following meals:
      i breakfast   iii snacks
      ii midday meals   iv evening meal [4]

5. The Eatwell Guide is based on 4 food groups.
   a Complete the chart with the following information. The first one has been completed for you. [8]

Name of food group	Amount recommended each day	Main nutrients provided
potatoes, rice, pasta and other starchy carbohydrates	one third of our daily food intake or 5–6 portions	carbohydrate, calcium, iron, vitamin B and fibre

   b State additional advice given in the Eatwell Guide. [4]

6. Reference Intake (RI) is an example of how nutritional requirements are calculated.
   a Name two other methods of calculating nutritional requirements. [2]
   b Explain how RIs, as stated on food labels, give useful information to the consumer [4]

7. Children need to be encouraged to eat a healthy balanced diet from an early age.
   a Explain the benefits of a healthy, balanced diet. [4]
   b Outline recent measures which have been taken in Wales to ensure that school meals are healthy and balanced. [4]

8. Food labels often have claims about the product on the packaging.
   Explain the difference between a nutrition claim and a health claim, giving examples to support your answer. [6]

9. Outline the functions of the following nutrients and describe the changing nutritional needs of these nutrients from birth to adolescence: [9]
   a protein   b calcium   c iron

10. Lifestyle and beliefs can affect a person's choice of food and diet.
    Discuss this, giving examples of special diets to support your answer. [10]

TOTAL: 71

67

SECTION 1
CORE KNOWLEDGE

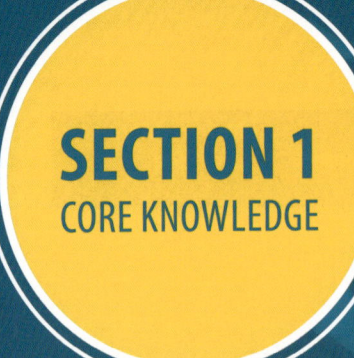

THE SCIENCE OF COOKING FOOD

What will I learn?

- Why foods are cooked
- How heat is transferred to foods
- The methods used for cooking foods
- How to maintain the nutritional value of foods through preparation
- The types and functions of raising agents
- The scientific principles behind preparing and cooking foods
- The basic terminology of food science

▲ A burger on the barbeque – what is going on as it cooks?

You may be asking yourself '*What has **science** got to do with my **food lessons***?' The answer is that many chemical and physical changes occur during the preparation and cooking of food, and you are unknowingly conducting basic scientific experiments in that great laboratory, the kitchen!

When things go wrong with our cooking we need to know why. If we have some knowledge of the underlying food science that goes on within recipes, then we can prevent errors from happening, for instance, how to stop sliced apple from turning brown, choux buns not expanding or a white sauce becoming lumpy.

REASONS WHY WE COOK FOOD

REASON FOR COOKING	EXAMPLES
To kill **pathogenic bacteria** and toxins making the food safe to eat	Meat, fish, kidney beans
To soften the food making it easier to chew and swallow	Tenderised meat, softened vegetables and fruit
To make the food more digestible	Animal protein foods, starchy foods
It improves and intensifies the flavour of food	Roasted vegetables, scrambled egg, ragù sauce
The food looks more attractive and appealing	Grilled bacon, poached egg, roast chicken
It reduces the 'bulk' of the food	Leafy vegetables – cooking reduces their volume, so more can be eaten
Provides variety to our meals	Roasting, grilling, frying, boiling, stewing all give different textures to food
To enable certain ingredients to work together	Starch for thickening sauces, melting gelatine and chocolate, raising agents in cakes
We eat hot food to keep warm in cold weather	Casseroles, soups and stews

Cooking food

Cooking can be defined as the transfer of heat energy (heat transfer) from one item to another, such as boiling water to carrots. The heat energy changes the molecular structure of the proteins, fat, starch, sugar and water and these transformations alter the texture, flavour, aroma and appearance of the food.

To cook foods successfully, you must first understand the ways in which heat energy is transferred: these are conduction, convection and radiation (radiant heat). Many dishes are cooked using two methods, for instance, roasting vegetables uses both convection and conduction. If you choose the wrong method of cooking, then the food will not have a good texture, colour or flavour.

A general rule of thumb is that hard or tough pieces of food need to be cooked slowly, in moisture, for a relatively long time. Take beef as an example: fillet or sirloin steaks are tender and so can be cooked very quickly on a hot griddle pan. By contrast, braising and stewing steak are much tougher and benefit from long, slow cooking in a casserole. If you pan-fried the stewing steak it would become very hard and inedible.

Check it
State four reasons why we cook our food.

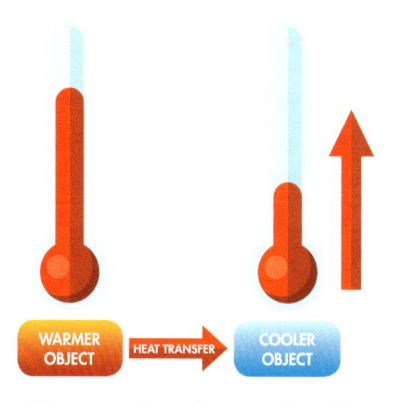

▲ Heat transfer: the transfer of heat energy between objects

CONDUCTION

DESCRIPTION: The transfer of heat by direct contact from a hot surface

This is a relatively slow method of heat transfer because there must be physical contact between the surfaces to transfer energy between molecules. Surfaces need to be good conductors of heat. That is why saucepans and frying pans are made of metal, but with plastic handles.

EXAMPLES: Lamb chops, bacon, sausages or Welsh cakes touching the hot surface of a frying pan

USES: Dry frying, griddling, searing, sautéing

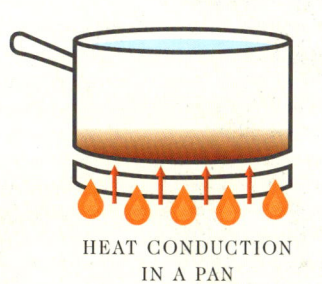

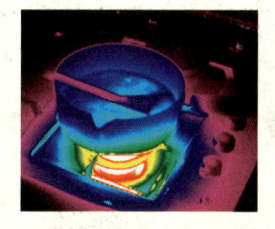

HEAT CONDUCTION IN A PAN

HEAT SENSITIVE VIEW OF PAN

CONVECTION

DESCRIPTION: The transfer of heat by the mass movement of heated particles into a cooler mass or area.

Natural convection uses the tendency of warm liquids or gases to rise and cooler ones to sink, leading to a constant circulation of heat.

Mechanical convection uses the fan in an oven to move heat around quickly and evenly. Food cooks evenly because the oven does not have hot or cold zones in it. Ovens without a fan rely on natural convection and food is heated from the outside – the inside heats up slowly.

EXAMPLES: Hot water, air or oil surrounding the food such as boiled potatoes, chicken stew, roast beef, poached eggs, deep-fried fish
Natural convection – making cheese or white sauce, gravy

USES: **Dry heat methods:** Baking, roasting and deep frying
Wet heat methods: Boiling, braising, simmering, poaching, steaming, pressure cooking

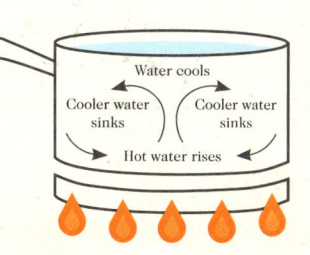

HEAT PROCESS SHOWING CONVECTION

HEAT PROCESS SHOWING CONVECTION IN FAN ASSISTED OVEN

RADIATION (INFRA-RED RADIANT HEAT)

DESCRIPTION: The heat is transferred using electromagnetic radiation: waves of heat or light strike the food.

There is no physical contact between the heat source and the food being cooked.

EXAMPLES: Waves of heat are directed at the food e.g. grilling sausages, bacon, Welsh rarebit, kebabs

USES: Toast, grilling and barbequed foods

RADIANT HEAT FROM GRILL

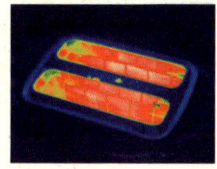

HEAT SENSITIVE VIEW OF TOASTER

RADIATION (MICROWAVE)

DESCRIPTION: The magnetron in the microwave oven converts electricity to radio waves called microwaves which penetrate the food

EXAMPLES: Ready meals, microwave-only meals or foods, scrambled eggs, burgers, bacon

USES: Heating up leftovers, quick defrosting of frozen food, ready meals such as lasagne

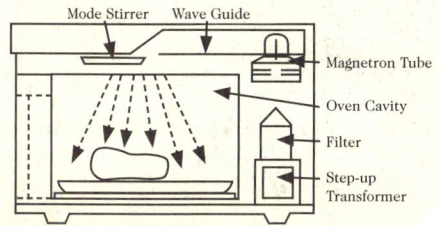

Check it

Describe the three methods of heat transfer. Give examples of foods cooked by each method.

Moist, dry and frying methods of cooking

There are many different ways of using the cooking methods listed above to cook your food. The one you choose will be determined by several factors:

- Individual preference, e.g. a person may prefer food steamed rather than boiled
- Time – how much preparation and cooking time is available
- The type of food to be cooked
- Equipment and facilities available
- Healthy eating choices, e.g. grill or bake rather than fry

DRY HEAT METHODS

BAKING
Food is cooked using the dry, hot air of the oven

EXAMPLES: Cakes, pastries, puddings, bread and biscuits, some fish

ADVANTAGES: Food has good colour and texture, several items can be cooked at once, exterior of food is browned and adds flavour

DISADVANTAGES: Needs very specific cooking times and temperatures

ROASTING
Food is cooked using the dry, hot air of the oven but is basted with hot fat to prevent it from drying out

EXAMPLES: Joints of meat, vegetables

ADVANTAGES: Good flavour, crisp texture and appearance, possible to bake another dish whilst roasting for fuel economy

DISADVANTAGES: Joints of meat take a long time to cook, the food has to be **basted** with extra fat, meat can become hard and chewy if cooked at a high temperature

TOASTING
Dry radiant heat is applied to food. May be direct but brief exposure to heat in an oven, or longer exposure to mild heat. It is NOT simply putting bread in a toaster.

EXAMPLES: Bread, nuts, seeds, whole spices

ADVANTAGES: Toasting bread lowers the Glycaemic Index, flavours are released and enhanced

DISADVANTAGES: Dry roasting of spices or herbs in a frying pan needs lots of attention to avoid burning

GRILLING
Small pieces of food are cooked by the **radiant heat** produced by a hot grill either above or below the food

EXAMPLES: Sausages, bacon, chops, Welsh rarebit

ADVANTAGES: It is a healthy method; fat drains out of food, quick method

DISADVANTAGES: Food needs careful supervision to prevent burning/undercooking, only tender cuts of meat can be grilled

FRYING METHODS

SHALLOW FRYING
Small pieces of food are cooked in a shallow amount of very hot fat/oil.

EXAMPLES: Chicken, steak, sausages, vegetables

ADVANTAGES: A quick method of cooking, uses minimal fat

DISADVANTAGES: Frying foods should not be left unattended, unhealthy method due to added fat/oil used, fat splashes caused by 'wet' foods being fried

DEEP FRYING
Foods are submerged into very hot fat/oil.

EXAMPLES: Chips, chicken pieces, fish fillets

ADVANTAGES: Gives food a golden and crunchy surface, very quick cooking method

DISADVANTAGES: Deep fat fryers should not be left unattended, very unhealthy method due to the fat/oil used, over-heated fat/oil can combust causing a fat fire

STIR FRYING
Very small pieces of meat and vegetables are cooked quickly in a minimal amount of hot oil. The food is kept moving during the cooking process.

EXAMPLES: Thin strips of tender meat, fish and vegetables

ADVANTAGES: Very quick cooking method, vegetables remain crunchy, healthier than frying, limited vitamin loss

DISADVANTAGES: Needs constant attention and stirring, requires fat or oil with high smoke point, some foods need preparing beforehand

CORE KNOWLEDGE

MOIST HEAT METHODS

BOILING
Starchy food is cooked in vigorously boiling water called a 'rolling boil'.

EXAMPLES: Potatoes, pasta and rice

ADVANTAGES: A quick method of cooking, healthy – no added fat

DISADVANTAGES: Water soluble vitamins are easily lost, food becomes soft (especially vegetables), less suitable for meat as it toughens proteins

SIMMERING
Food submerged in boiling water, stock, beer or juice that is gently bubbling.

EXAMPLES: Meat, fish, eggs, sauces, fruit and vegetables

ADVANTAGES: Ideal for tender pieces of food

DISADVANTAGES: Tender foods can fall apart if the simmer becomes a boil. Loss of water soluble vitamins, especially from fruits and green, leafy vegetables

POACHING
Food is cooked in a small amount of gently simmering liquid.

EXAMPLES: Meat, fish and eggs

ADVANTAGES: Small pieces of tender food (such as fish) are cooked very gently and quickly, a healthy way of cooking

DISADVANTAGES: Loss of water soluble vitamins, the food can break apart, some foods may taste bland when poached

STEWING
Food is submerged in liquid, cooked slowly to develop the flavours and tenderise tougher cuts of meat. If cooked on the hob it is a stew and if cooked in the oven it is a casserole.

EXAMPLES: Tough cuts of meat, fish, pulses, beans and vegetables

ADVANTAGES: Tough cuts of meat are tenderised, good flavour, water soluble vitamins are absorbed in the sauce/gravy

DISADVANTAGES: Need to plan ahead because stewing takes a long time; it can take up to 2 or 3 hours to tenderise the meat and develop the flavours

BRAISING
Usually cooked in the oven: the vegetables are surrounded by liquid with the seared meat cooking in the steam on top of the vegetables. The dish must have a well-fitting lid.

EXAMPLES: Tough cuts of meat, beans and vegetables

ADVANTAGES: Tough cuts of meat are tenderised, good flavour, water soluble vitamins are consumed in the sauce/gravy

DISADVANTAGES: Braised dishes take 1-2 hours to cook

PRESSURE COOKING
Food is cooked in a pressure cooker where the temperature of the boiling liquid can be increased from 100°C to 105–120°C allowing the food to cook very quickly.

EXAMPLES: Tough cuts of meat, vegetables, soup, rice, steamed puddings

ADVANTAGES: Food is cooked quickly (3 times faster than boiling), tough meat is made tender, less fuel is used, water soluble vitamins are not so easily lost

DISADVANTAGES: Food is easily overcooked, food can become very soft

STEAMING
Food is cooked in the steam of boiling water.

EXAMPLES: Tender meat, fish, vegetables, sponge puddings

ADVANTAGES: Water soluble vitamins are not lost, healthier method, food is easy to digest

DISADVANTAGES: Food can take longer to cook than boiling, the steamer has to be topped up with water, kitchen can fill with condensation

BLANCHING
Food is plunged briefly into boiling water or steamed, then removed and placed in chilled water.

EXAMPLES: Often used with leafy vegetables

ADVANTAGES: Healthy, can enhance the colour of green vegetables, the blanching process stops enzyme actions which otherwise would lead to loss of flavour, colour or texture

DISADVANTAGES: Vitamins and minerals may be lost, not suitable for all types of food

SOUS VIDE
Food is vacuum-packed and slowly heated in water at a precise temperature.

EXAMPLES: Meat and fish

ADVANTAGES: Little loss of moisture or weight, flavour and aroma of food are preserved, nutrients not lost into cooking water, consistent results every time a dish is cooked

DISADVANTAGES: The water-bath machine itself is expensive, foods do not brown

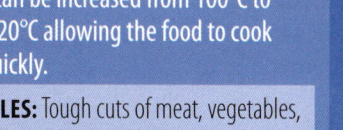

Check it

What is the difference between conduction, convection and radiation?

Study tip

Give examples of foods which are cooked using more than one method of heat transfer.

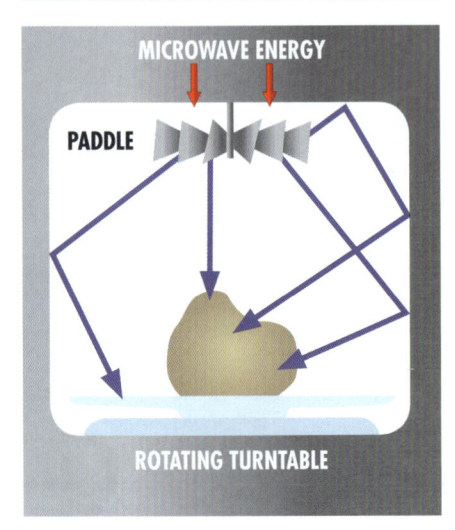

▲ How a microwave oven works

Check it

How is heat transferred in a microwave oven?

Study tip

Can you explain what happens when cooking a readymade chicken curry in a microwave oven?

▼ Visible protein coagulation

Cooking food using microwave energy

Microwave cooking relies on a form of radiation that penetrates only the top 1cm of the food surface. Microwave radiation **agitates** the water molecules in the food causing **friction** heat between the molecules. This causes the heat energy to spread gradually through the food by conduction (and also convection in liquid dishes). This is an uneven method of cooking leading to cold spots in the food and it is the reason why cooking instructions on readymade meal packaging advise to stir the contents half way through cooking or after cooking leave the food to stand for 2 minutes before eating. This allows the 'cold spots' to absorb the heat from the hotter areas.

To be cooked successfully in a microwave oven, foods need to have a fairly high water content which enables them to cook much faster than with traditional methods.

Microwave energy neither browns nor crisps food so it is unsuitable for cooking baked products. This is because only the water molecules in the food are heated, creating a soft or mushy texture. No heat is generated in the microwave oven so most china, glass and plastic dishes can be used. Food plates only become hot due to the heat of the food being conducted to the plate. However, heat resistant glass, china with gold paint designs, metal containers and foil cannot be used because the microwaves cannot penetrate the dish and will be deflected causing damage to the **magnetron** in the oven.

The effects of heat on food

Heat alters the flavour, texture, volume and appearance of foods due to the effects of the heat on the proteins, fats, starch and water found in the food.

What happens to proteins

During cooking proteins **denature** (unravel) and **coagulate**. The structure of each protein is irreversibly changed by heat, acid or alkali resulting in a loss of moisture, shrinkage and becoming firm. Some examples of what happens to proteins in cooking are:

- The skin formed on the top of heated milk is denatured protein. The nutritional value of denatured proteins is generally unchanged and most denatured proteins are more easily digested by the body.
- Egg whites changing from a clear liquid to a white solid
- Meat fibres become firm
- Wheat proteins (**gluten**) in bread change during baking.

Overcooked proteins become very hard, tough and dry. Most proteins coagulate between 71°C and 85°C.

CORE KNOWLEDGE

THE SCIENCE OF COOKING FOOD

Check it

The Maillard reaction should not be confused with caramelisation which occurs with sugars only.

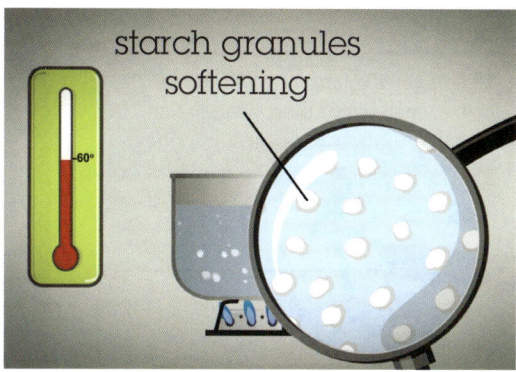

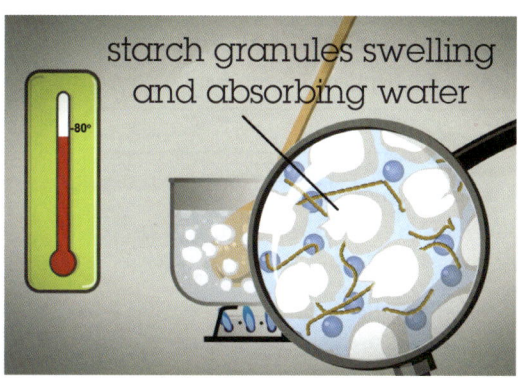

When proteins and a carbohydrate are heated with dry heat a **Maillard reaction** occurs and many different flavour compounds are created. Think for example about the flavours on the surface of roasted meat (see above).

What happens to fats

Because fats contain a small amount of water, they soften then liquefy when heated. This property is called **plasticity**, and it reflects the fact that fat cannot evaporate. The chemical make-up of fat determines its hardness at room temperature and how quickly it will soften or melt; for instance butter melts more slowly than a spreadable margarine. It is important to understand how easily a fat will melt before preparing or cooking food, for example a shortcrust pastry would need to be made using a hard fat. Fat, once heated, adds colour and flavour to foods.

What happens to carbohydrate

The change that starches undergo during cooking is called **gelatinisation**. When starch and liquid are heated together visible changes occur. The starch granules absorb water causing them to soften and swell up, and this makes the liquid mixture thicken. The thickness of a starch-based sauce is determined by the ratio of starch to liquid. It must be stirred continuously to prevent lumps from forming. Gelatinisation occurs at 66°C and above.

▲ Gelatinisation of starch

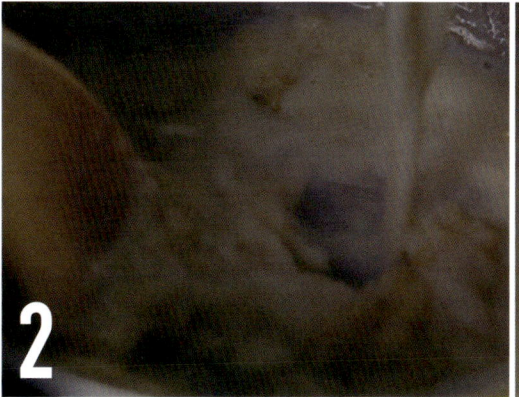

▲ The three stages of gelatinisation

▲ Dextrinisation on bread

Check it

1. Can you explain the differences between denaturing, coagulation, gelatinisation and dextrinisation?
2. Why don't fats evaporate?

Activity 1

Make a hot chocolate drink using boiling milk.
Leave it to cool for 15 minutes.
Describe the surface of the drink.
What has happened to the milk?

Activity 2

1. In groups make 4 roux sauces
   (See the roux sauce recipe, p. 173)
   Sauce 1: use the standard recipe
   Sauce 2: use ½ the amount of milk
   Sauce 3: use twice the amount of milk
   Sauce 4: use the standard recipe – stirring only occasionally as you bring it to the boil
2. Record your findings.
   a. What is the consistency of each sauce?
      Sauce 1: _____
      Sauce 2: _____
      Sauce 3: _____
      Sauce 4: _____
   b. Explain why you obtained different consistencies.

Starchy foods cooked in dry heat produce dextrins which are brown in colour and have a distinct flavour and consistency. This is known as **dextrinisation,** and it is a chemical change in the starch molecule caused by the breakdown of the sugar within it. Starch is also present in flour, so in a cake mixture the starch gelatinises by absorbing the liquid from the egg or milk.

Caramelisation happens when sugar is cooked; the food gradually turns brown and changes flavour. Caramelised sugar is partly responsible for the flavour and colour of baked products and the browning of meats and vegetables. Using dry heat methods of cooking allows high temperatures to be reached at which browning occurs. Moist heat methods of cooking cannot get food hot enough for caramelisation, as water cannot be heated above 100°C.

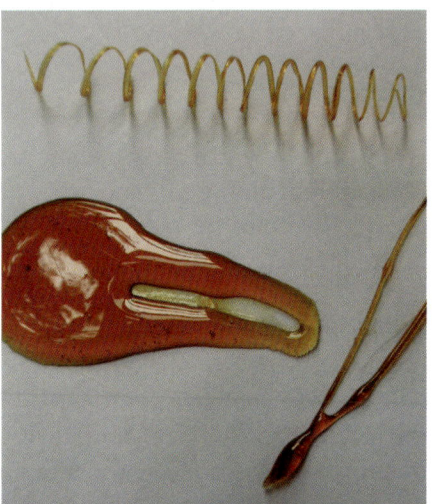

▲ Some examples of caramelisation

What happens to water

All foods contain water and some, such as milk or eggs, are almost entirely water. As the temperature of the food increases during cooking, the water molecules move faster and faster until the water turns to gas (steam) and evaporates. The evaporation of water molecules during cooking is responsible for the reduction in the food's volume and its becoming dry.

74 CORE KNOWLEDGE

The effects of changing the pH of food

Some foods, such as citrus fruits, are **acidic**. Others, like sodium bicarbonate, are **alkaline**. Foods that are neither acid nor alkaline are neutral and have a pH value of 7.

Acids

- Lemon juice, tomatoes and vinegar will help soften **connective tissue** in meat and cornflour based sauces.
- A drop of vinegar / lemon juice added to meringue mixture affects the protein giving it a soft, marshmallowy texture.
- Indian paneer and Italian ricotta cheese are made using acid to coagulate the proteins in the milk.
- Vinegar is used to preserve vegetables when pickling and chutney making.
- Vinegar, tomato juice, citrus juices, and yogurt are used in marinades to denature the proteins on the outer portion of the meat, so they open up and absorb the other flavours in the marinade.
- Fish can be 'cooked' in lime juice in traditional ceviche recipes, and eggs can be 'hard boiled' by pickling in vinegar.

Alkali

- Bicarbonate of soda (baking soda) is an alkali that is a very good raising agent. However, it gives the food a slightly soapy flavour. This can be avoided if it is mixed with cream of tartar. Together, these two ingredients form baking powder.
- Some nutrients such as the vitamin C found in green vegetables are destroyed if bicarbonate of soda is added to the water.

The effects of oxygen on food

Fruit and vegetables

Foods such as apples, pears, bananas, potatoes and parsnips all go brown when peeled or sliced. The oxygen in the air comes into contact with the food's damaged cells causing the surface to oxidise and go brown. This is known as enzymic browning.

To slow down enzymic browning, place the cut pieces of vegetable or fruit, such as parsnip or apple, into cold water. Sliced apples and pears brown very quickly, so in order to minimise discolouration, either add lemon juice to the cold water or toss the slices of fruit in a little neat lemon juice.

Meat, poultry and fish

The myoglobin in raw meat gives the flesh a bright red colour. However, once fresh meat has been stored for several days, chemical changes in the myoglobin cause it to turn brown. After cooking the meat is usually still safe to eat, but this discolouration makes people think otherwise.

White meat such as chicken and fish, contains less myoglobin so it doesn't turn dark brown like red meat. The level of myoglobin is one of the distinguishing factors between white meat from red meat.

Fats and oils

Fats and oils exposed to oxygen in the air will gradually turn rancid. They develop a very unpleasant smell or flavour and undergo changes in colour. All foods containing fats or oils can become rancid and must therefore be stored correctly to reduce exposure to oxygen in the open air.

▲ Oxidised apple

▲ Oxidised potato

Check it

How would you stop apple in a fruit salad from going brown?

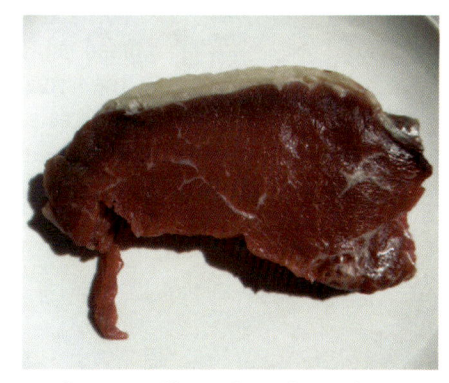

▲ Oxygen affects the colour of meat

Check it

State how enzymes can affect our food.

The effects of enzymes on food

The working properties of all cells are controlled by **enzymes** which can work together or singly. Heating food will stop enzyme activity.

Apples, bananas and tomatoes are picked when they are slightly under-ripe and still very firm, sour or tasteless. However they will continue to ripen due to enzymic action and become softer and sweeter. As the ripening process continues the food will become soft or slimy with unpleasant flavours developing.

Food technologists make it possible to control these changes so that fruits and vegetables are available out of season.

Food enzymes also work with oxygen to affect foods. Damaged fruit and vegetable cells will brown and soften, raw meat will go brown and raw fish will become soft and slimy.

Animal carcasses are not butchered immediately after slaughter. Butchers hang beef carcasses in cold storage for up to 28 days to let the enzymes do their work. The muscle fibres soften and the meat flavour improves. When meats are cured, salt is used to reduce enzymic activity.

Enzymes are found in the human digestive system and they help to break down foods into protein, fat and starch molecules. Without these enzymes food cannot be digested nor the nutrients absorbed.

The use of microorganisms in food production

Yeasts, moulds and non-pathogenic bacteria are **microorganisms** which have been used since ancient times to make bread, cheese, yoghurt and wine. Food manufacturers use these microorganisms and a fermentation process to change and improve the flavour, texture and shelf life of food products.

THE USES OF MICROORGANISMS

- Mushrooms are the edible fruiting bodies of fungi.
- Yeasts are used in bread manufacture, the fermentation of cereals in beer making and fruit to produce wine.
- Lactic acid bacteria is fermented in milk to produce yoghurt, lassi milk drinks and cheese.
- Probiotic microorganisms are used in yoghurt to aid digestion, the immune system, and keep the body's intestinal flora in balance.
- Blue and Roquefort cheese use moulds to create creamy textures, sharp, tangy flavours and some protection from more harmful bacteria.
- Lactic acid and yeasts can be used to ferment soft drinks such as ginger beer, kefir and kombucha.
- Moulds are used to ripen the surface of sausages, preserving the product and controlling flavour development.
- Sauerkraut is made from fermented cabbage and soy sauce from fermented soya beans.
- Lactic acid bacteria is used to make salami, pepperoni, chorizo and dried ham.

Cereals: Bread pp185–191
Milk, Cheese and Yoghurt: How is cheese made? pp248–249, How is yoghurt made? pp252–253

RAISING AGENTS

What will I learn?
- Why raising agents are used in baking and how they work
- The different types of raising agents
- What happens if too much raising agent is used

Why raising agents are used in baking

Raising agents are added to most baked products during the making process using gas, air or steam which, when heated, expands causing the food to swell and rise up. Raising agents produce a risen, light and airy texture in the food. Unleavened products don't use a raising agent.

Types of raising agent
Mechanical raising agents
Air will expand when heated is incorporated into the recipe through:
- **Sieving** flour will trap air. Used in pastry, cakes or batters.
- **Whisking** eggs. Whole egg plus caster sugar or egg whites, when whisked, will trap a large volume of air creating a foam. The mixture must be cooked immediately to set and stabilise the foam. Egg whites create a stiff foam and will be stabilised by the addition of a drop of lemon juice (acid) or some sugar. The foam is formed due to the unravelling and stretching of the protein, ovalbumin, creating the increased volume. Unstable foams lose the air particles very easily and become liquid again. Whisked eggs are used in meringue, mousse, sponge cake to give a very light texture.
- **Rubbing** fat into flour will incorporate a little air.
- **Creaming** fat and sugar together traps minute air bubbles. The fat becomes pale in colour and the mixture looks creamy.
- **Lamination** – air is trapped each time flaky and rough puff dough is rolled and folded to create the layers.

> **Experiment to trap air**
> 1. Place 200g flour in a measuring jug.
> 2. Mark the level of flour on the jug.
> 3. Sieve the flour onto a piece of greaseproof paper.
> 4. Carefully pour the flour back into the jug.
> 5. Mark the level of flour on the jug.
> 6. Repeat steps 3, 4 and 5.
>
> Has the volume of flour appeared to increase?
>
> Explain your findings.

Physical raising agent
Steam is created in products such as Yorkshire pudding and choux pastry which contain large quantities of water. The high temperature of the oven turns the water to steam forcing it through the mixture, pushing or raising it upwards. The heat of the oven then sets the egg and flour creating a hollow, risen food. The oven must be hot for the steam to be created quickly before the egg and flour 'set'. Opening the oven repeatedly during cooking or removing the food too early will cause the food to collapse.

THE SCIENCE OF COOKING FOOD

Check it
Make sure you understand how air, steam and baking powder raise a baked product.

▲ Whisked egg white foam

▲ Yorkshire puddings

▲ Choux pastry

Check it
Make sure you understand how steam raises a baked product.

77

Chemical raising agents

Most cakes and some biscuits need Carbon dioxide (CO_2) to create the baked light, airy texture.

- Bicarbonate of soda + moisture + heat will create bubbles of CO_2 to raise the food. However, the food can have a slightly 'soapy' flavour so only use bicarbonate of soda in strong flavoured foods such as chocolate cake and ginger bread or biscuits.
- Baking powder is a commercially made mixture of bicarbonate of soda + cream of tartar. Baking powder works the same as bicarbonate of soda, needing both moisture and heat to produce CO_2. The inclusion of the cream of tartar stops the food having the 'soapy' flavour. The majority of the CO_2 gas is released once the mixture is heated. Baking powder is used in the 'all-in-one' cake method because it is quicker than using the traditional, lengthy creaming method.
- Self-raising flour is plain flour with baking powder added in a correct quantity to suit most cake making recipes.

> **Chemical raising agent experiment**
> 1. Place 100ml cold water in a glass.
> 2. Stir in 1 tsp bicarbonate of soda.
> 3. State what happens.
> 4. Repeat steps 1, 2 and 3 using bicarbonate of soda and warm water.
> 5. Repeat steps 1, 2 and 3 using bicarbonate of soda and very hot water.
>
> Repeat the experiment using baking powder.

Biological raising agent

Yeast is a living organism grown commercially for bread making and alcohol production. Yeast can bought either fresh or dried.

Yeast + moisture + oxygen + food + time will produce masses of carbon dioxide gas bubbles. Bread needs lots of gas bubbles to raise the dough so yeast is the perfect raising agent when bread making.

To make bread the yeast is added to strong flour and water to form a dough. After kneading the dough must be left to rise or '**prove**' in a **warm** environment allowing the yeast to do its work. The yeast is activated by the warmth, oxygen and moisture found in the dough and it feeds on the natural sugars in the flour creating the carbon dioxide gas bubbles. This process is called **fermentation**.

As the dough rises the gluten strands in the flour form a complex mesh trapping the gas bubbles which creates a soft, spongy doubled in size dough. Traditional bakers **knock back** the risen dough and give it a second proving. This helps give a better flavour and creates a uniform, finer texture to the finished bread.

> **Yeast experiments**
>
> You will need:
> 6 test tubes labelled A-F   6 x ½ tsp dried yeast
> 6 balloons – to seal each test tube 2 x ½ tsp sugar
> 1 test tube rack   1 x ½ tsp salt
>
> | | ½ tsp yeast in each test tube | Observations after 10 mins / 20 mins |
> |---|---|---|
> | A | Add 4cm cold water | |
> | B | Add 4cm warm water | |
> | C | Add 4 cm very hot water | |
> | D | Add 4 cm cold water + ½ tsp sugar | |
> | E | Add 4 cm warm water + ½ tsp sugar | |
> | F | Add 4 cm warm water + ½ tsp salt | |

Check it

Make sure you understand how baking powder raises a baked product.

▲ Fresh and dried yeast

▲ Fermenting yeast

Check it

Make sure you understand how yeast raises a baked product.

Activity

Yeast experiment: Look at the liquid in the test tubes after 10 minutes – make notes on what you see.

Look at the liquid in the test tubes after 20 minutes – make notes on what you see.

After 20 minutes look at the balloons:

Which balloon/s has inflated the most?

Why do you think this is?

Which balloon/s has not inflated?

Can you explain why?

CORE KNOWLEDGE   Cereals: **The importance of yeast** p190

THE SCIENCE OF COOKING FOOD

Sourdough

Sourdough uses the natural yeasts in flour as a raising agent and is made using a 'starter' rather than commercially produced yeast. Sourdough bread tends to have a dense texture and a slightly tangy flavour.

Gluten

Gluten is a mixture of two proteins, gliadin and glutenin, found in wheat, rye, spelt and barley grains, and it is responsible for the elastic texture and structure of all doughs. When flour is mixed with water, the two proteins combine to create gluten particles, which come together to create stretchy gluten strands in the dough. The gluten strands in the flour need to be worked during kneading to become stronger and able to stretch.

Gluten forms the structure of many different foods such as pasta, pastries, cakes and bread.

Yeast-raised doughs and pasta use 'strong' flour with gluten levels of about 12%+, so the dough can be stretched and expanded during kneading. Chemically risen baked goods such as cakes, biscuits, and scones use 'soft' flour with 7-10% gluten levels because the mixtures do not need stretching and the mixtures should be handled gently to prevent gluten development. Over-worked gluten makes biscuits and pastry heavy and tough and batters rubbery.

Emulsions

We all know that oil and water do not mix. Some dishes we make need to have the oil and water permanently mixed together. To do this we create an emulsion.

If you place olive oil and vinegar into a jar and shake it vigorously, a salad dressing is made. However, if the liquids are left in the jar to settle, the oil and vinegar will separate. This is called an unstable emulsion.

By gradually beating egg yolk into the oil and vinegar solution mayonnaise is made which is classed as a stable emulsion. The egg yolk contains lecithin which is a good emulsifier. The oil and vinegar now cannot separate.

Other emulsions are homogenised milk, butter and creamed cake mixtures.

Foams

A foam is a food that has been aerated, which means that a gas has been added to a liquid. Foaming denatures the proteins causing the food to become light and airy. Whisked egg white, whipped cream, marshmallow and soft scoop ice cream are very good examples of foams. Under-whisked egg white and cream become unstable and cannot hold the required shape. Over-whisked egg white protein denatures causing the food structure to lose volume and break down making the mixture very dry. Over-whisked cream 'splits' because the fat globules clump together forming butter.

How to stop things going wrong

At the start of this chapter we stated that having some food science knowledge can help us prevent errors from happening. It is best to understand what is happening when you are cooking rather than to rely on luck. There are a number of points that need to be learned to prevent your cooking from failing.

Check it

Make sure you understand the differences between soft and strong flour and their uses.

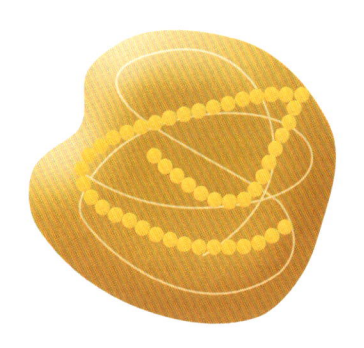

▲ Gluten ball

▲ Olive oil and vinegar in a jar – an unstable emulsion

Check it

How well do you understand the terms 'aerated', 'denatured' and 'globules'?

▲ These egg whites have been aerated and the proteins denatured, making them stiff

Cereals: Gluten formation p184, What are sourdoughs and starters? p191

Activity

Make a mayonnaise

You will need

1 mixing bowl
1 teaspoon
1 tablespoon
1 jug
1 mixer

- 125ml oil
- 1 egg yolk
- ½ tsp powdered mustard
- ½ level tsp salt
- black pepper
- 1 tblsp white wine vinegar

Method

Place the oil in a jug.

Place the rest of the ingredients in a mixing bowl and stir well.

Beat the oil into the mixing bowl one drop at a time.

Once half the oil has been added drop by drop the rest of the oil can be added in a thin stream.

Taste and season the mayonnaise.

Understanding how ingredients work

FLOUR	provides bulk and volume in baked products and, through gelatinisation, will thicken liquids.
FAT	gives food products flavour, moisture, colour and traps air.
EGGS	add colour, flavour, will set a liquid and aerate cake and some dessert mixtures.
SUGAR	adds flavour, colour and texture to food. A biscuit will not be crisp if sugar is not used in the mix.
BAKING POWDER	with moisture and heat will produce carbon dioxide bubbles causing a cake/biscuit mixture to rise.
YEAST	given food, moisture, warmth and time produces carbon dioxide bubbles enabling bread dough to rise.

Measuring

Accurate measuring is vital especially with core ingredients such as flour, fat, sugar, eggs, raising agents and liquid. Recipes are simple science experiments: follow the instructions accurately and you should be successful. Many recipes are based on the ratio of one ingredient to another. If the ratios are altered because too much liquid is added and then more flour needs to be used, the consistency or texture of the final dish will be affected.

An example is when too much water is added to shortcrust pastry. More flour needs to be worked into the wet, sticky paste. As a result the ratio of ½ fat to flour has been altered creating a hard, chewy and dry finished pastry. The final consistency will not be right because good shortcrust pastry should crumble and melt in the mouth.

Faults due to inaccurate measuring of ingredients ▼

Too much flour	Cake, bread, biscuit, pastry	Stodgy, dry and stiff mixtures
Too little flour	Baked products and sauces	Lacks bulk, volume and may be too soft or runny
Too much fat	All food products	May be greasy and have a rubbery or crunchy texture
Too little fat	Baked product	Dishes will be dry and lacking some flavour
Too much sugar	Baked products	Food will be too brown and sweet, crisp, brittle and risk burning
Too little sugar	Baked products and desserts	Affects flavour creating a dry product lacking volume
Too much egg	Baked products	Will taste 'eggy' or similar to an omelette and have a dense texture
Too little egg	Cake, custard, quiche	The coagulation process will be compromised
Too much liquid	Baked products and sauces	The correct batter and dough consistencies will not be formed
Too little liquid	Baked products and sauces	Will result in very dry mixtures
Too much raising agent	Bread, biscuit and cake	Cracked cake surface, cake spilled over the sides of the tin
Too little raising agent	Bread, biscuit and cake	Baked product unrisen, dense/close texture

CORE KNOWLEDGE

THE SCIENCE OF COOKING FOOD

Accurate heat control

The need for accurate heat control sounds fairly obvious but this is often overlooked! Having the oven, hob or grill setting on very high heat does not cook foods faster; it simply burns them.

- **Oven** – always use the oven temperature stated in the recipe. Cakes are easily spoiled if cooked at the wrong temperature or if the oven door is opened before the mixture sets, causing the cake to sink. If the food browns too quickly **turn the oven temperature down** by 1 gas mark (10°C) or place it on a lower oven shelf.
- **Hob** – water boils at 100°C. Using the highest heat on the hob will not make the boiling water any hotter. All that will happen is the water will quickly evaporate burning the food in the pan.

  Care needs to be taken when frying in oil or fat. If the oil/fat becomes too hot it will smoke and can spontaneously ignite at temperatures between 180°C and 250°C (depends on the type of oil/fat)
- **Grill** – the heating element should be glowing red before placing food under the grill. Food must be checked regularly to prevent burning. The grill pan can be lowered away from the heat source to control the cooking.

▲ The top of this cake has sunk

▲ Different oils have different smoke points

COOKING MISTAKES AND HOW TO RECTIFY THEM

Make sure you read and understand the recipe and weigh ingredients accurately. Ask yourself why is each ingredient in the recipe and what function does it play? By understanding this you are likely to be successful. However, occasionally things do go wrong and the art of the cook is to be able to rectify these errors. Here are a few simple tips:

Don't overcrowd pans and baking tins with food because it will need room to move and expand as it cooks.

Pasta and rice should be added to a pan full of vigorously boiling water and cooked on a rolling boil. If not the food becomes squidgy, starchy and wet.

Use lids on pans to stop the liquid from evaporating and prevent the food from burning.

Beat sauces vigorously *before* they come to the boil and thicken. Make sure the edges and base of the pan are scraped clean during beating to prevent the starch in the sauce from becoming lumpy, sticking and burning. If a sauce does become lumpy, try liquidising it or passing it through a sieve.

Food should be fried in hot fat/oil. If it is not hot enough, the food absorbs excess fat/oil making the end product very greasy.

A cake will sink in the middle if it has not been cooked for long enough; a cracked surface is due to the oven being too hot or too much raising agent added. If the cake is too thin it is because the tin is too big or no raising agent was used.

If shortcrust pastry is stretched or too wet it will be tough and shrink from the sides of the dish. If it is over-kneaded it will become hard and 'leathery' due to the gluten development. Flat puff pastry is due to opening the oven door during cooking or the oven not being hot enough.

81

Key terms

Heat transfer – the way heat moves from one area to another through conduction, convection and radiation.

Denaturation – the process of altering a protein's molecular characteristics or properties by heat, enzyme action, or chemicals.

Composition – the different parts or substances that make up something.

Conduction – heat is transferred between two surfaces by direct contact, and molecules in each surface pass heat to each other.

Convection – heat is transferred by the circulation of either a heated liquid or gas.

Coagulation – an irreversible change to proteins from a liquid or semi-liquid state to a solid state.

Emulsion – a fine dispersion of minute droplets of one liquid in another.

Maillard reaction – a chemical reaction between a protein and a carbohydrate in the presence of dry heat.

Sear – to scorch the surface of food with a sudden, intense heat.

Radiant heat – in the form of infra-red waves, can be applied above or below the food with the heat transferring to the surface of the food.

Agitate – to stir, shake or disturb a liquid.

Friction – the action of one surface or object rubbing against another.

Magnetron – the part of the microwave oven that generates the microwave radiation.

Gelatinisation – the process where starch and water are heated causing the starch granules to swell. The water is gradually absorbed in an irreversible manner. This produces a viscous texture to food.

pH value – the measure of the acidity or alkalinity of a liquid substance.

Dextrinisation – the browning that occurs when foods containing starch are cooked, or exposed to an alkali, acid or enzyme.

Caramelisation – a change in the food's molecular structure due to the removal of water resulting in a nutty flavour and brown colour.

Enzymic browning – a chemical process where oxygen and enzymes in the food react to cause the cut surface to become brown. This process cannot be reversed.

Oxidise – to undergo a chemical reaction with oxygen resulting in food losing freshness and colour.

Myoglobin – a protein that stores oxygen in muscle cells of animals.

Rancid – refers to foods which develop an unpleasant flavour or smell as a result of decomposition or chemical change to the fat or oil within the food.

Enzymes – proteins that make the chemical reactions in a cell possible.

Microorganism – usually single cell microscopic organisms such as bacteria, moulds and fungi.

Fermentation – the chemical breakdown of sugar to acid, gas or alcohol by bacteria, yeasts or other microorganisms.

Aeration – incorporating air into the mixture.

Unleavened – refers to bread, cake and biscuits made without raising agent.

Plasticity – the ability of fat to hold its shape.

Prove – refers to a specific rest period during fermentation.

Gluten – formed from two proteins found in flour, gliadin and glutenin.

Knock back – to re-knead the dough which knocks out some of the CO_2 allowing the yeast to produce more CO_2.

Strong flour – flour with a higher level of gluten, e.g. durum wheat flour.

Soft flour – flour with a slightly lower level of gluten.

Over-worked gluten – the dough has been over handled/rolled/beaten.

EXAM QUESTIONS

THE SCIENCE OF COOKING FOOD

1 Name the three methods of heat transfer. [3]
2 a What is meant by 'denaturing'? [2]
  b Give one example of denaturing. [1]
3 Explain two differences between roasting and boiling. [2]
4 List 3 foods that MUST be cooked before they are eaten. [3]
5 Give reasons why the outside of a barbecued steak is burnt, but the inside is still raw. [4]
6 Give one advantage and one disadvantage of deep frying. [2]
7 Why should an oven be preheated before the food is placed inside? [3]
8 We are being encouraged to reduce the amounts of energy we use when cooking meals. Discuss how this can be done in the home. [4]
9 Name 3 methods of cooking in an oven. [3]
10 Describe 5 ways to cook potatoes and explain the effect that each form has on the product. [10]
11 Describe how heat passes into food when cooked by the following methods.
   a in an oven
   b in a toaster
   c in a steamer
   d in a microwave [8]
12 Compare how cooking methods affect the nutritional values of the following foods:
   a Roast potatoes and baked jacket potatoes
   b Steamed broccoli and boiled broccoli [4]
13 State one advantage and one disadvantage of the following methods of cooking.
   a Boiling vegetables
   b Roasting vegetables
   c Grilled vegetables [6]
14 Complete the table. [6]

Description	Method of heat transference	Example of cooking method
	Convection	
		Metal pan on a hob – frying, boiling etc
		Baking tins, trays etc in oven, baking/roasting
Heat travels directly onto food by infra-red rays		

15 Define the following terms and give two examples of how each is used when cooking
   a coagulation [3]
   b caramelisation [3]
   c dextrinisation [3]
16 Discuss two scientific principles that occur when a sauce thickens. [5]
17 The chart below shows a range of cooking equipment. [6]
   Name TWO different foods that can be cooked in each piece of equipment

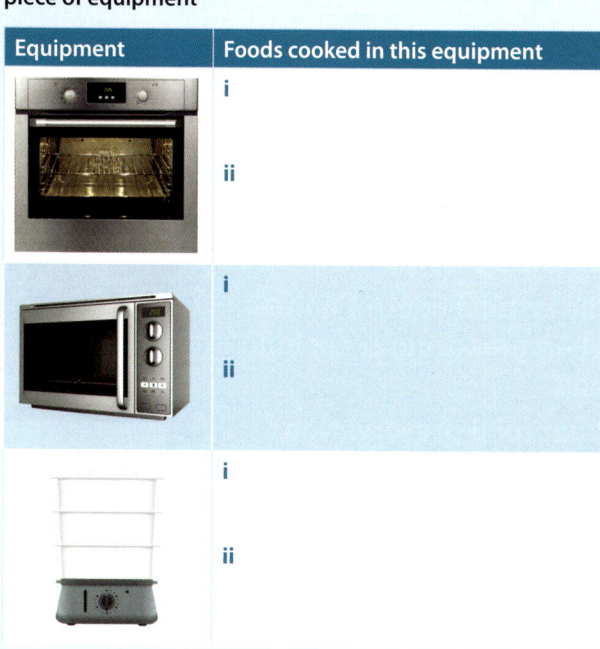

Equipment	Foods cooked in this equipment
(oven)	i
	ii
(microwave)	i
	ii
(steamer)	i
	ii

18 State two ways of making tough meat tender by cooking. [2]
19 Name one gas that raises a baked product. [1]
20 Give TWO reasons why scones might fail to rise. [2]
21 Frying is a popular method of cooking. [4]

State TWO advantages for frying food	State TWO disadvantages for frying food
i	i
ii	ii

TOTAL: 90

SECTION 1

83

SECTION 1
CORE KNOWLEDGE

FOOD SPOILAGE

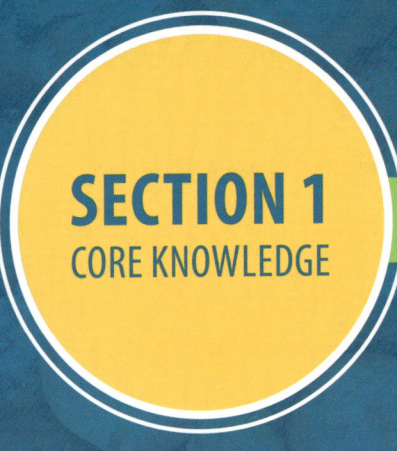

What will I learn?

- How to recognise signs of food spoilage and prevent it
- How to safely handle foods
- What pathogenic bacteria are and how to prevent food poisoning
- The critical control points when preparing & cooking food
- What food preservation methods exist
- The environmental and financial effects of food wastage

Food safety

Food handlers must understand the reasons why food hygiene and safety is vital when buying, storing, preparing and cooking food ingredients. Everyone has a duty of care to make sure that food has not become hazardous through any kind of contamination.

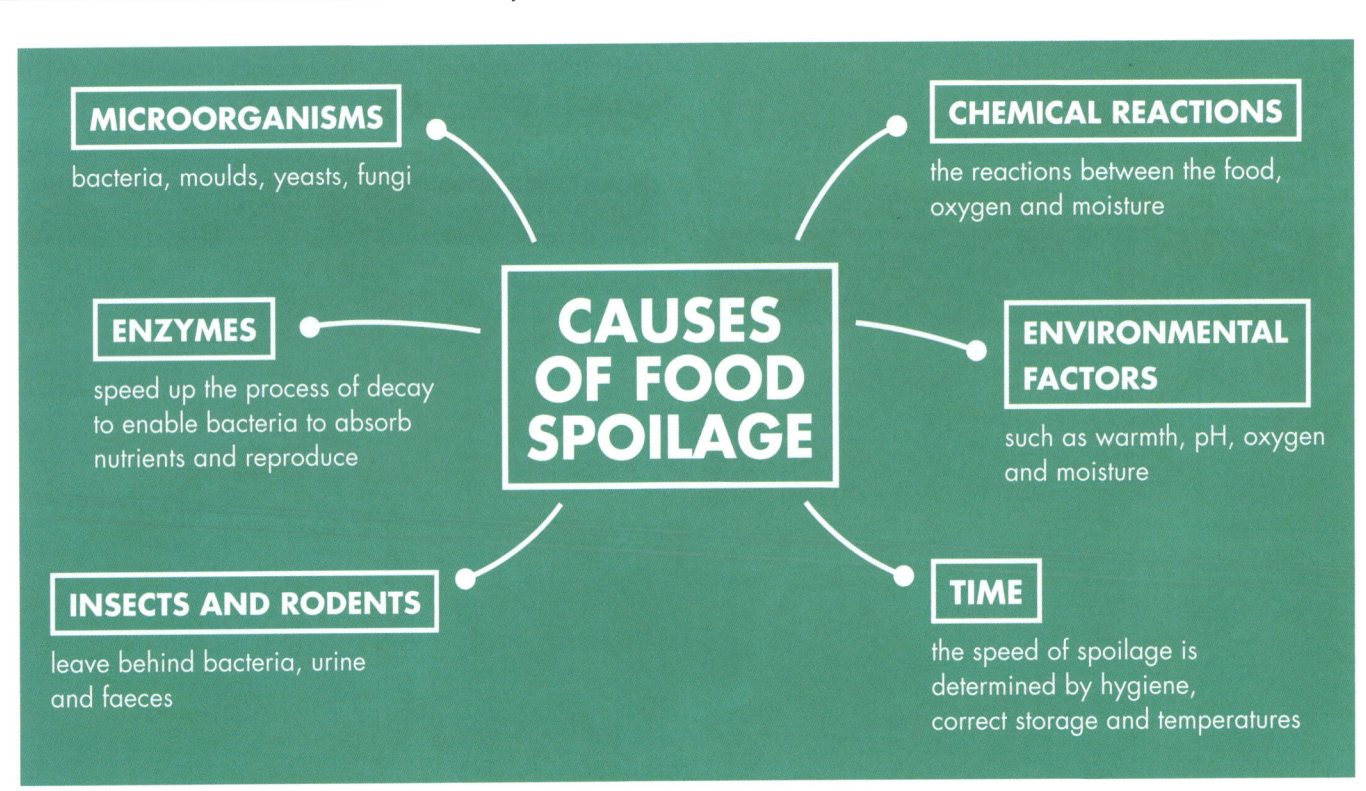

CAUSES OF FOOD SPOILAGE

MICROORGANISMS
bacteria, moulds, yeasts, fungi

CHEMICAL REACTIONS
the reactions between the food, oxygen and moisture

ENZYMES
speed up the process of decay to enable bacteria to absorb nutrients and reproduce

ENVIRONMENTAL FACTORS
such as warmth, pH, oxygen and moisture

INSECTS AND RODENTS
leave behind bacteria, urine and faeces

TIME
the speed of spoilage is determined by hygiene, correct storage and temperatures

Food spoilage is a natural process caused by bacteria, mould, fungi and yeasts. Once a food item is picked, harvested, slaughtered, stored or cooked, microorganisms will start a gradual decay process, eventually making the food unsafe to eat. Food spoilage happens more quickly when warmth, oxygen and moisture are present, and in the case of **perishable foods**, for example raw and cooked meats and fish, dairy foods, fruit and vegetables. How quickly a food will spoil determines its '**use-by date**'.

It is important to be able to identify the signs of food spoilage which are:

- Discolouration
- Changes in texture – wrinkly, slimy, lumpy, hard, sloppy
- Visible mould
- Unpleasant odour – often sour, bitter, sharp
- Changes in flavour – sour, **rancid**, acidic, unpleasant
- 'Blown' cans and jar lids – spoilage microorganisms have produced gas causing the can or jar lid to 'blow'.

Safe storage of food

To maintain food safety all foods must be stored in correct storage areas.

- **Ambient foods** are stored at room temperature on shelves or in cupboards. The packaging must be tightly closed or stored in air tight containers.
- Chilled foods must be stored in a refrigerator. The core temperature of the chilled food must be 8°c or colder so keep the refrigerator at 4°c–5°c to achieve this.
- Frozen foods must be stored in a freezer and not be allowed to defrost until it is required. The recommended freezer temperature is -18°c.
- Carvery and buffet 'hot held foods' core temperature must be above 63°c when put out on display and, if not used, must be discarded after four hours.
- Check that food packaging is not split or damaged allowing bacteria to enter.
- Consume pre-made foods before the '**use-by date**' mark. Food eaten after this date may not be safe to eat.

Study tip
Make sure you can explain the causes of food spoilage.

Check it
1. State two microorganisms.
2. What does perishable mean?

Study tip
Do you understand what 'ambient temperature' means?

▲ Visible signs of food spoilage

▲ Physical contamination

▲ Chemical contamination

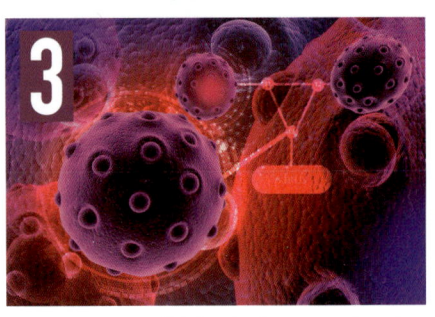

▲ Biological contamination

Check it

Name four different types of contamination.

Key point

High risk foods are those more likely to cause food poisoning than other foods.

Study tip

Learn a range of high risk foods.

Check it

State why gravy, ham and pasta salad are high risk.

Sources of food contamination

Foods can be contaminated in three ways:

1 Physical contamination – something (a foreign object) has dropped into the food such as hair, jewellery, finger nails, flies, plasters, grit, bone and metal components from machinery screws which can cause choking, broken teeth and internal cuts/bleeding.

2 Chemical contamination – cleaning products and pesticides which can cause liver damage, internal burns and nerve damage.

3 Biological contamination – bacteria, viruses, moulds and fungi which can cause food poisoning.

Bacterial contamination

Bacteria are microscopic, single cell organisms that are found everywhere and are very hard to detect.

Most bacteria are harmless to humans and some are beneficial such as those found in both intestinal flora and the 'blue' in blue cheese.

Some bacteria are known to cause illness or death if ingested. These bacteria are classed as pathogenic bacteria. Generally, large colonies of pathogenic bacteria are needed in order to develop food poisoning but there are some exceptions such as E. coli and campylobacter which can cause serious illness from just a few bacteria.

Sources of pathogenic bacteria

- Human beings – poor hygiene
- Raw meat and poultry – pathogenic bacteria live harmlessly in the gut of all animals but can contaminate the meat when the animal is slaughtered
- All animal protein foods / high risk foods
- Pests – rats, mice, cockroaches, flies, birds, etc.
- Dust, dirty bins and waste food
- Contaminated water

High risk foods

Foods with high protein content are classed as high risk.

These foods are rich in both nutrients and moisture and provide an excellent breeding ground for bacteria. High risk foods can be harmful to the consumer if not stored or handled correctly. These include:

- Any dish made using milk, cheese, eggs, meat and fish
- Shellfish
- Gravies, soups and stocks
- Cooked rice and pasta
- Readymade meals, cook-chill meals, prepared salads

CORE KNOWLEDGE

How pathogenic bacteria affects us

Eating or drinking food contaminated with pathogenic bacteria can cause mild to severe illness and could result in death. The following pathogenic bacteria are very common causes of food poisoning:

- Campylobacter
- Salmonella
- Staphylococcus Aureus (Staph A)
- E. coli 0157.

These bacteria can make us ill, producing symptoms such as fever, headache, vomiting and diarrhoea. These symptoms are the body's way of, very quickly, trying to get rid of the poison.

Pathogenic bacterium	Where it is found	Typical symptoms	Average onset time
Campylobacter	Raw poultry, meat, milk, sewage	Abdominal pain, diarrhoea (bloody), nausea, fever	48-60 hours
Salmonella	Intestines of humans and animals. Raw poultry and meat eggs, milk	Abdominal pain, diarrhoea, nausea, vomiting	12-36 hours
Staphylococcus A	Humans – skin, hair, nose, mouth, throat, cuts, spots	Abdominal pain/cramps, vomiting, chills	1-6 hours
E. coli 0157	Human and animal sewage, water, raw meat, muddy vegetables	Abdominal pain, fever, diarrhoea, vomiting, kidney damage/failure	12-24 hours

To reproduce, bacteria need to be given ideal conditions which are:

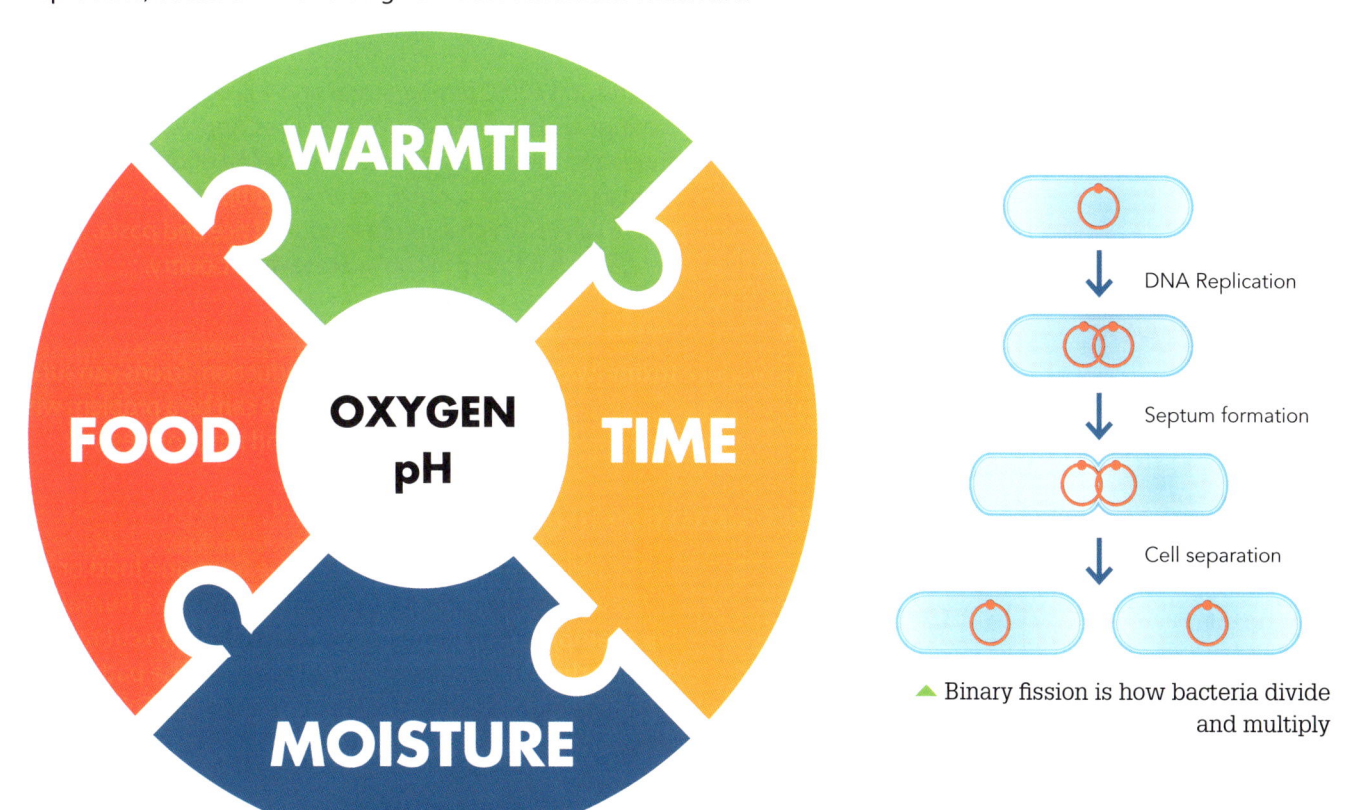

WARMTH · FOOD · OXYGEN pH · TIME · MOISTURE

▲ Binary fission is how bacteria divide and multiply

Given ideal conditions, bacteria will reproduce through **binary fission** where one bacterium splits into two bacteria, two into four, four into eight and so on every 10 to 20 minutes. Binary fission will happen more quickly in warm foods and high risk foods left in a warm area. Some bacteria, classed as **anaerobic** bacteria, are able to reproduce without the presence of oxygen.

> **Activity**
>
> Food handlers must control conditions to minimise bacterial growth.
>
> State four rules of personal hygiene that all food handlers must follow.

If one or more of the conditions is removed bacteria cannot grow. Once that condition is re-introduced to the food the bacteria will be able to start reproducing again, e.g. dried milk is fresh milk with the water removed and can be safely stored in a cupboard for up to a year. Bacteria cannot grow in this 'waterless' condition but as soon as the dried milk is **reconstituted** the bacteria will start reproducing and the milk must be treated the same as fresh milk.

Condition	How to control bacterial growth	Examples
Food	Bacteria will use the nutrients from the food on which it lives.	Mainly protein based foods
Moisture	Drying the food will remove the water and moisture content.	Milk, noodles, soup, gravy
Warmth	Food MUST be kept out of the **danger zone** 8°C – 63°C. Store chilled foods at 8°C and below or frozen foods at -18°C or colder. Foods should be heated to a core temperature of 75°C. Reheated food should reach at least 75°C for 2 minutes at its core. Foods that are hot held should not drop below 63°C.	All protein based dishes. Hot buffet and carvery foods
Time	If left in the danger zone bacteria reproduce every 10-20 minutes. At the end of the cooking time, cooked foods must be cooled to 8°C within 90 minutes and stored in a fridge.	Chilli con carne, curry, lasagne, soups, gravies, meat pies
Oxygen	Remove the air surrounding food.	Vacuum-packing, MAP, canning
pH	Alter the acidity/alkalinity levels.	Pickling, jam making, chutneys

▲ How bacterial growth can be controlled

▲ Bacillus cereus

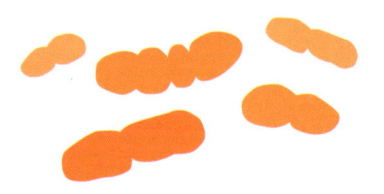

▲ Clostridium perfringens

Spores

Some bacteria can withstand 100°C temperatures and will go on to form strong, protective, outer coatings and become known as **spores**. Spores can survive very high temperatures and the drying process. They will lie dormant until the ideal conditions return allowing the spore to resume multiplying. Spore-forming bacteria include *bacillus cereus,* which is found in cooked rice and pasta, and *clostridium perfringens,* which is found in cooked meat and poultry.

Toxins

Bacteria produce **toxins** (waste material) during reproduction. Toxins can survive high temperatures, causing serious food poisoning. This can be a problem when reheating pre-cooked foods, particularly cooked rice and pasta dishes.

> **Check it**
>
> What is the difference between a bacterium and a toxin?

> **Key point**
>
> Remember: to grow and reproduce, bacteria need the same conditions as humans.

Cross-contamination

Bacteria have neither wings nor legs and cannot move from one food or surface to another. They need a 'vehicle' for this which is usually a human, insect or animal. For example, if someone uses the same knife to cut raw chicken then without washing it cuts cheese for a sandwich, the pathogenic bacteria will be transferred from the raw chicken to the cheese. This is called **cross-contamination**.

How to prevent cross-contamination

There are a number of precautions that need to be observed to prevent cross-contamination of food.

A pest infestation must be dealt with immediately.

Even domestic animals present a risk. Pets such as cats and dogs can bring pathogenic bacteria into the home, so always wash your hands after touching your pet.

> **Activity**
>
> 1 One bacterium divides into two every 20 minutes. Calculate how many bacteria will be produced in 4 hours.
>
> 2 Research the name of one anaerobic bacterium and state where it is found.

CORE KNOWLEDGE   The science of cooking food: The effects of changing the pH of food p75

FOOD SPOILAGE

1 Personal hygiene – dirty hands are the main source of cross-contamination

- Wash hands in hot, soapy water for 30 seconds before handling any foods.
- Cover cuts with a clean blue plaster.
- Keep nails clean and short.
- Shower daily to minimise bacteria found on the skin.
- Do not cough and sneeze near foods and wash hands after using a tissue.
- Do not handle food if you have an upset stomach/diarrhoea.
- Tie long hair back / wear a hat or hair net.
- Do not wear rings or bracelets when cooking. They harbour bacteria and pieces of the jewellery could fall, unseen, into the food.
- Wear clean clothes when preparing and cooking food.

2 Correct food safety

- Keep all chilled foods in the fridge until they are needed. If they are taken out too soon, bacterial growth speeds up.
- Fridges should be kept at, or below, 5°C to slow down the rate of bacterial growth.
- When chilling foods keep raw and cooked foods separate. Raw food **must** be stored below all cooked foods to prevent spillage.
- Keep all foods stored in sealed containers or wrapped in foil or cling film to prevent the risk of cross-contamination.
- Freezer temperature should be at −18°C or below to stop bacterial growth.
- Defrost all frozen foods in a covered container at the bottom of the fridge. When frozen foods are defrosted bacteria will resume reproducing.
- All ambient foods should be stored in sealed containers and in cupboards to prevent contamination from moisture and pests.

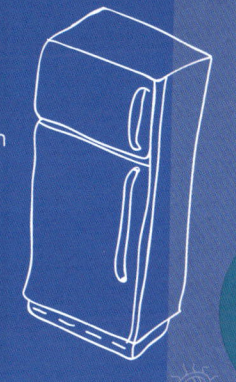

3 Correct use of equipment

- Use colour-coded cutting boards and knives, if possible.
- Equipment used on raw foods MUST be cleaned thoroughly before being used on other foods, in particular knives, spoons and boards.
- Clean and sanitise surfaces between uses.
- Use a temperature probe to check the core temperature of high risk dishes.
- Wash all equipment thoroughly using hot, soapy water or use a dishwasher.
- Cupboards, fridges and freezers must be washed regularly.
- Always use a clean spoon each time food is tasted.
- Bins should have tight fitting lids.

4

Pests which live in and around 'dirty' places such as sewers, rubbish tips or bins and come into contact with animal droppings will contaminate food areas by spreading pathogenic bacteria. Pests include:
- Flies and other insects
- Mice and rats marking their territory with urine and faeces
- Birds

HACCP

All food businesses have in place a **Hazard Analysis Critical Control Point** (HACCP) assessment to ensure that all food is safe to eat and no items have been contaminated. Every aspect of food hygiene and safety will be monitored for hazards from how the raw ingredients are produced, to how they are transported, prepared and cooked through to selling the final product.

What is classed as a hazard?

In food products, a hazard is anything that can cause harm to a customer. A hazard will be:

Biological: such as salmonella or campylobacter found in chicken

Chemical: such as cleaning chemicals finding their way into food products

Physical: such as pieces of glass or a fingernail found in food.

Check it

Learn what HACCP stands for.

Activity

A business has ordered a variety of fresh and frozen fish. Using the HACCP system, explain the hazards with actions you would take for handling these products at each of the following stages:

a Accepting the delivery
b Storing the fresh and frozen fish
c Preparing and cooking the fish

> **Key point**
>
> Hazard Analysis Critical Control Point (HACCP) is a recognised system for assessing food hazards and controlling the hazards to keep all foods safe.

What is a critical control point?

A critical control point is identifying any hazards that must be controlled. This step has to be carried out correctly to make sure that the hazard is either removed or reduced to a safe level.

STAGE	HAZARD	CONTROL
Accepting delivery of the minced beef	Minced beef temperature is not cold enough The packaging could be damaged	The supplier is reputable Check core temperature 8°C maximum Packaging not damaged
Storing the minced beef	Not stored at correct temperature allowing bacterial growth Storing incorrectly	Place in the fridge at 5°C Bottom shelf of fridge Place minced beef in a sealed container
Making the burgers	Removing raw meat from the fridge too early Unclean surfaces, hands and equipment Incorrect cleaning procedures Burgers left out in kitchen	Remove from the fridge only when needed Clean and sanitise all surfaces, equipment and hands before and after handling the raw meat Shape the burgers on a red board Immediately cook burgers or place them back in the fridge
Cooking the burgers	Burgers incorrectly cooked Very pink in the middle	Burgers must have a core temperature of 75°C when cooked Use a food probe
Serving the burgers	Cooked burgers left on the kitchen 'side'	Serve burgers immediately Do not allow the burger core temperature to fall into the danger zone

▲ Beef burgers HACCP

> **Study tip**
>
> Learn the different methods of food preservation and, for each one, identify two foods that can be preserved in that way.

Food preservation

It is possible to slow down the rate of food spoilage and decay by minimising most bacteria and enzyme activity, removing the moisture and/or oxygen, reducing the temperature or changing the pH levels. These steps are known as food preservation.

Food waste

Annually, approximately one million tonnes of edible food and drink is going to waste from our kitchens. Half of all food that ends up being thrown away is unopened or still whole. The reasons for the waste are that we prepare and cook too much food or the consumer is influenced by the 'best before'/'display until' dates rather than the use-by date. The foods we waste the most are fresh vegetables and salad, fresh fruit, bread and cakes.

Food waste costs the average household between £470 and £700 a year, meaning that approximately £40 to £60 a month is simply thrown away.

By reducing food waste you will save yourself money and 'help the planet' because fewer items will have to go to landfill sites. You can reduce food waste by:

- checking the cupboards and fridge before going shopping
- planning the week's meals in advance
- using a shopping list to buy only what you need to avoid buying excess food
- keeping an eye on the packaging 'use-by' dates and eat the food by that date

FOOD SPOILAGE

METHOD OF PRESERVATION	SIMPLE EXPLANATION	EXAMPLES
HEAT	Heat kills most microorganisms and it stops any enzyme activity.	Pasteurisation of milk, all cooked foods, canned foods
FREEZING	The microorganisms become inactive at very cold temperatures but will start reproducing during defrosting.	Frozen meat, fish, readymade meals, desserts
DRYING	Microorganisms need moisture to reproduce.	Pot noodles, coffee, milk, soups, gravy granules, pulses
REMOVING AIR (O_2)	Most microorganisms need oxygen to reproduce. Food items are sealed in cans, jars, MAP, vacuum packaging.	Foods in cans and jars, meat, cheese, fish, sandwiches, crisps
CHEMICALS – SALT, SUGAR, VINEGAR, SMOKE	The pH levels needed for bacterial growth and enzymic action are changed.	Salted meat and fish, pickles, chutneys, jams, smoked fish
IRRADIATION	Food is exposed to low doses of radiation which kills all microorganisms.	Herbs, spices, some vegetables and fruit

▲ Different methods of food preservation

- ignoring the 'best before', 'sell by' and 'display until' dates. These are supermarket dates and have nothing to do with **food safety**
- incorporating left over foods into the next day's meals
- freezing leftovers. Most foods will freeze successfully but remember to label and date the leftovers.

SECTION 1

91

Check it

Which packaging date identifies that food is safe to eat?

Study tip

Learn three reasons why food is packaged.

Packaging

Packaging is used:
- To protect food items from damage
- To minimise bacterial contamination
- To make the product easier to transport and store
- To provide information for the consumer such as contact details, ingredients list, allergy / intolerance warning, nutritional information, storage and cooking instructions
- For the convenience of the supplier, supermarket and customer.

PACKAGING FOOD LABELLING

The Food Labelling Regulations 1996 state the legal information that must be on all food packaging and is designed to protect the consumer.

- Manufacturer's contact details
- Place of origin
- Name and description of the product
- Weight of the product
- Ingredients list – in descending order
- Allergy / dietary information
- Storage instructions
- Cooking / reheating instructions
- Shelf life / use-by date
- Nutritional information
- Batch code

The product price, picture, recycling logo, customer guarantee and opening instructions do not have to be included on packaging.

Study tip

Research the traffic light nutrition system.

Check it

Make sure you can explain MAP packaging.

Types of packaging

There is a wide range of food packaging available. The factors to consider for food packaging include the type of food to be packaged, how protective it is, does it help increase the food shelf life, and is it recyclable?

Modified atmosphere packaging (MAP) is used extensively to extend the shelf life of raw and cooked meats and fish, cheese and some fruits. Air is removed from sealed plastic containers and replaced with carbon dioxide and/or nitrogen, which slows down the natural decaying process of the foods. Strawberries spoil and decay very quickly but by using MAP the strawberries' shelf life is increased by up to a week. However, once the MAP is opened, the bacteria on the foods will become active again.

FOOD SPOILAGE

▼ Various types of food packaging

PAPER BAGS / CLING FILM

BENEFITS
- Lightweight
- Can be 'shaped' to the food
- Recyclable

USES
- To wrap food items taken from home
- Sandwiches and baked products from a baker's shop

PAPERBOARD

BENEFITS
- Lightweight
- Easily printed on
- Inexpensive
- Biodegradable/recyclable

USES
- Pizza and take-away food boxes
- Drinks cartons
- Egg boxes

PLASTIC
[Including MAP and vacuum packaging]

BENEFITS
- Lightweight
- Made into shapes
- Flexible or rigid
- Can be made air tight
- Resistant to acids in foods
- Clear to see the food

USES
- Some fruit and vegetables
- Raw and cooked meat and fish
- Cheese, yoghurts and milk
- Readymade meals / products

METAL

BENEFITS
- Foil and foil trays are lightweight
- Easily printed on
- Cans are sealed to provide a long shelf life
- Recyclable

USES
- Readymade meal products
- 'Oven ready' products
- Canned fruit, vegetables and soups

GLASS

BENEFITS
- Provides a long shelf life
- Jars are reusable/recyclable

USES
- Jars of jam, sauces, pickles, baby foods

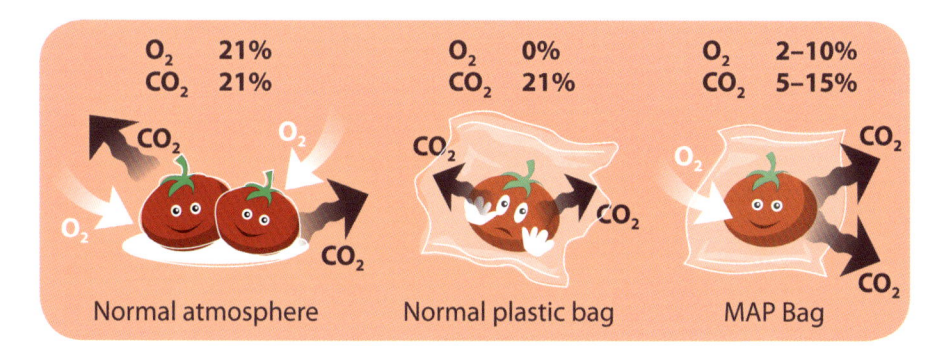

Normal atmosphere: O_2 21%, CO_2 21%

Normal plastic bag: O_2 0%, CO_2 21%

MAP Bag: O_2 2–10%, CO_2 5–15%

◀ How modified atmosphere packaging works in bagged salad

93

Vacuum packaging is where perishable foods such as bacon, cheese and fresh pasta are wrapped in plastic film and all the air is removed, creating a vacuum. Because there is no air in the packaging most bacteria cannot reproduce. Once the packaging is opened bacterial activity will resume.

Packaging waste

The food industry relies on using various types of plastic, paperboard, cans and jars packaging to give food items the longest shelf life possible. This makes it hard for the consumer to cut down on the use of packaging. Some packaging materials are biodegradable such as paper and paperboard and others can be recycled such as foil, cans, glass and some plastics. However, many people still throw these items into landfill bins which, long term, will have a negative environmental impact.

To minimise the waste impact of packaging, we could:

- recycle as much packaging as we can using the correct bins
- reuse packaging containers for storage e.g. ice cream containers, yoghurt pots, jam jars
- use traditional shopping bags or 'bags for life'
- buy perishable foods from independent retailers who use less packaging than supermarkets, e.g. meat will be in a plastic bag rather than a large, rigid plastic box
- buy 'loose' fruit and vegetables rather than prepacked items.

Date marks found on packaging

All pre-made foods must, by law, have a '**use-by**' date printed clearly on the packaging. This date informs the consumer of the **shelf life** of the food. High risk foods generally have a short shelf life of between 3 and 7 days whereas ambient foods may have a shelf life ranging from 1–12 months.

If the food is eaten after the use-by date, the manufacturers cannot guarantee that it will be safe to eat.

Packaging may also have a 'best before' date which informs the consumer that after this date the food is perfectly safe to eat but the quality of the food may have changed ie changes to the food's texture such as being harder, softer, less crisp, drier, or **syneresis** may have occurred.

Check it

1. List the main food packaging materials.
2. State the advantages and disadvantages of each.

🔖 Key terms

Perishable foods – foods that will decay or 'go bad' quickly.

Use-by date – indicates the date after which there is no guarantee that the food is safe to eat.

Rancidity – the unpleasant taste or odour that fats and oils develop over time.

Ambient foods – foods that can be stored, at room temperature, in a sealed container. All foods found on supermarket shelves are 'ambient' foods.

Onset time – the time it takes for the pathogenic bacteria to produce symptoms.

Binary fission – the reproduction of one cell splitting into two genetically identical cells.

Anaerobic – being able to exist without oxygen.

Reconstituted – dried food that is restored to its original form by adding water.

Danger zone – the temperature range within which bacteria multiply rapidly.

Spore – a bacterium that has formed a strong, protective outer coating.

Toxins – bacterial poisons.

Syneresis – moisture which slowly 'leaks' out of cooked egg mixtures.

EXAM QUESTIONS

1. Correct food storage is essential.
   Indicate on the picture below where the following foods should be stored. [3]

   | Milk | Cheesecake | Raw chicken |

2. One way of preventing cross-contamination is to use colour coded chopping boards.
   a. Complete the chart below. [3]

Colour of chopping board	Food to be prepared
i Red	
ii	Raw fish
iii Green	

   b. Explain the benefits of using different coloured boards for different foods. [5]
   c. State two other ways of preventing cross-contamination. [2]

3. Identify, on the thermometer below, what happens at each temperature. [4]

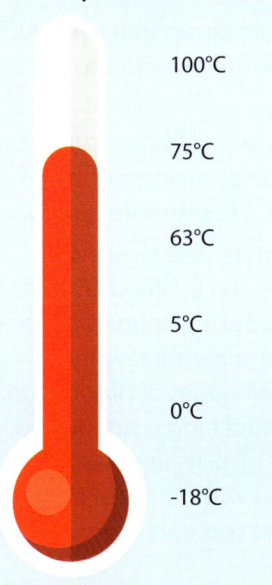

   100°C
   75°C
   63°C
   5°C
   0°C
   -18°C

4. Name 2 pathogenic bacteria. [2]

5. What is meant by 'use-by' date? [1]

6. State 4 ways in which to reduce the risk of food poisoning when storing, preparing and cooking meat. [4]

7. Food spoilage can be minimised by using food preservation methods. Complete the chart below. [6]

Method of preservation	Foods preserved this way
a	i
	ii
b	iii
	iv

8. What does HACCP stand for? [1]

9. Name 3 foods from the list below that are classed as high risk foods. [3]

   | banana | cod | roast chicken | raisins |
   | yoghurt | peanuts | leeks | rice salad |

10. Explain the food safety and hygiene procedures a carvery chef should follow when preparing, cooking and serving food. [9]

TOTAL: 43

SECTION 1
CORE KNOWLEDGE

FOOD PROVENANCE AND FOOD WASTE

What will I learn?
- What food provenance means
- The impact of food miles on the environment
- The importance of packaging
- The impact of packaging on the environment
- The sustainability of food and food waste
- That food security can provide access to safe sufficient food for all

▲ Do most consumers know – or even care – where their food comes from?

Food provenance

'Food provenance' refers to where food comes from – where it is grown, raised or reared, i.e. its point of origin. In many cases the food we eat can come from many different sources. Food provenance tells us what we are eating as well as where it comes from.

When consumers buy food from the supermarket they are not always aware of its provenance or the food chain involved in getting it there. Buying food from primary producers at local markets is the shortest of food chains because they grow it, rear it, or make it themselves.

Highlighting the provenance of food is important in allowing consumers to make decisions about which food to choose:

- Some people feel that buying locally produced food means that it is fresher, of a better quality and can be trusted.
- Locally produced food has a better carbon footprint.
- Fairtrade labelling on foods is a guarantee to consumers that a product was produced using ethical methods and supporting workers in the developing world.

The food industry has recognised the importance of making consumers aware of the provenance of food, how it is produced, transported, and delivered to us. It uses these product characteristics to promote quality.

Food provenance is also a useful way for governments and regulatory bodies to trace food products. Regulations, such as the EU Food law, makes traceability a requirement for food, feed, food-producing animals and any other substance intended to be, or expected to be, incorporated into a food or feed. Traceability must be established for all stages of production, processing and distribution. Whenever contaminated food is discovered, the ability to trace the suppliers or manufacturers of all its ingredients is critical to preventing health risks and to allow swift withdrawal of products. This process has been used to deal with many food scandals and outbreaks, including the BSE crisis.

▲ Farmers' markets have grown hugely in popularity over the last decade

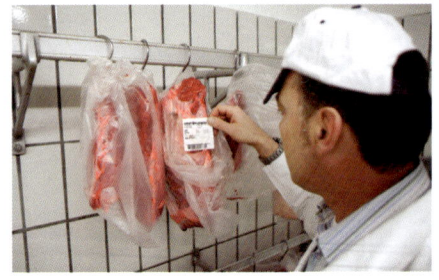

▲ Traceability labels being applied to meat products

Study tip
Are you able to explain what the term 'food provenance' means?

Origins of food products

Understanding the origins of products is important, especially when making choices about food. This can be the difference between choosing free range products like chicken or eggs, deciding between line-caught fish or a farmed variety, or buying New Zealand lamb rather than Welsh lamb. The products are basically the same, but aspects like the farming methods used can alter the quality, cost and environmental impact of the food.

Consumers often consider traditional products to be quality products. When the authenticity and origin of a traditional product can be guaranteed, it can be certified by the EU under a protected food name scheme designed to recognise regional and traditional foods. This is the case with various foods produced throughout the UK.

There are three protection marks producers can apply to the EU for:

Protected geographical indication (PGI)

To protect a product under PGI, it must be produced, processed or prepared within the geographical area it is associated with, e.g. Yorkshire Wensleydale cheese or Welsh lamb.

Protected designation of origin (PDO)

To protect a product under PDO, it must be produced, processed and prepared in one geographic area and have distinct characteristics from this area, e.g. Stilton blue cheese and Halen môn sea salt. PDO differs from PGI in that all three processes must take place within the area that gives the product its name and it must be made with distinct local knowledge.

Traditional speciality guaranteed (TSG)

To protect a product under TSG, it must have a traditional name and characteristics that make it different from similar products, e.g. traditionally farmed Gloucester Old Spot pigs.

A named food or drink registered with the EU will be given legal protection against imitation throughout the European Union. This means that consumers who are keen on traditionally produced products will be able to look out for the associated logos.

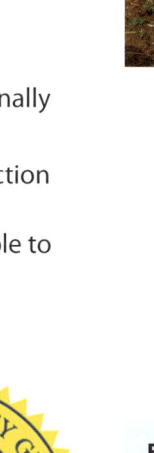

▲ Wensleydale cheese

▲ Halen môn sea salt

▲ Gloucester Old Spots, a purely English breed of pig

▲ The three EU protection logos denoting PGI, PDO and TSG

Fact: From 4 January 2016, use of the EU scheme logos will be compulsory for products marketed as registered PDO/PGI/TSGs. The logo must appear in the same field of vision as the registered name.

Check it

1. Explain how understanding the origin of food allows consumers to make food choices.
2. Describe each of the following protection marks:
   a Protected geographical indication
   b Protected designation of origin
   c Traditional speciality guarantee.
3. Give a reason why a consumer would chose a product displaying one of these logos?

Activity

Investigate products in your local area that display PGI, PDO or TSG protection marks. Try and find at least one product for each logo.

Food miles

Food miles are the distance that food travels from field to plate. The means of transport, as well as the distance, is an important consideration when choosing which foods to buy. For example a longer journey by boat has less environmental impact than a shorter one by road.

Carbon footprint

Food miles also lead us to consider the **carbon footprint** of a product. This involves looking at the entire production chain, including all the processes involved in the product's creation and transportation, to calculate the total emissions of carbon dioxide and other greenhouse gases that it is responsible for.

If we choose to buy products that are grown and produced in the UK, it is possible to reduce the amount of unnecessary food miles. However this is not always the case; reports show that even though it reduces food miles, it is less environmentally friendly to grow tomatoes in the UK under glass than it is to import tomatoes from Spain. The reason for this is that Spain's warm climate does not require heated glass houses, meaning the energy used in transporting tomatoes from Spain is less than the energy it would take to heat glass houses for growing tomatoes in the UK.

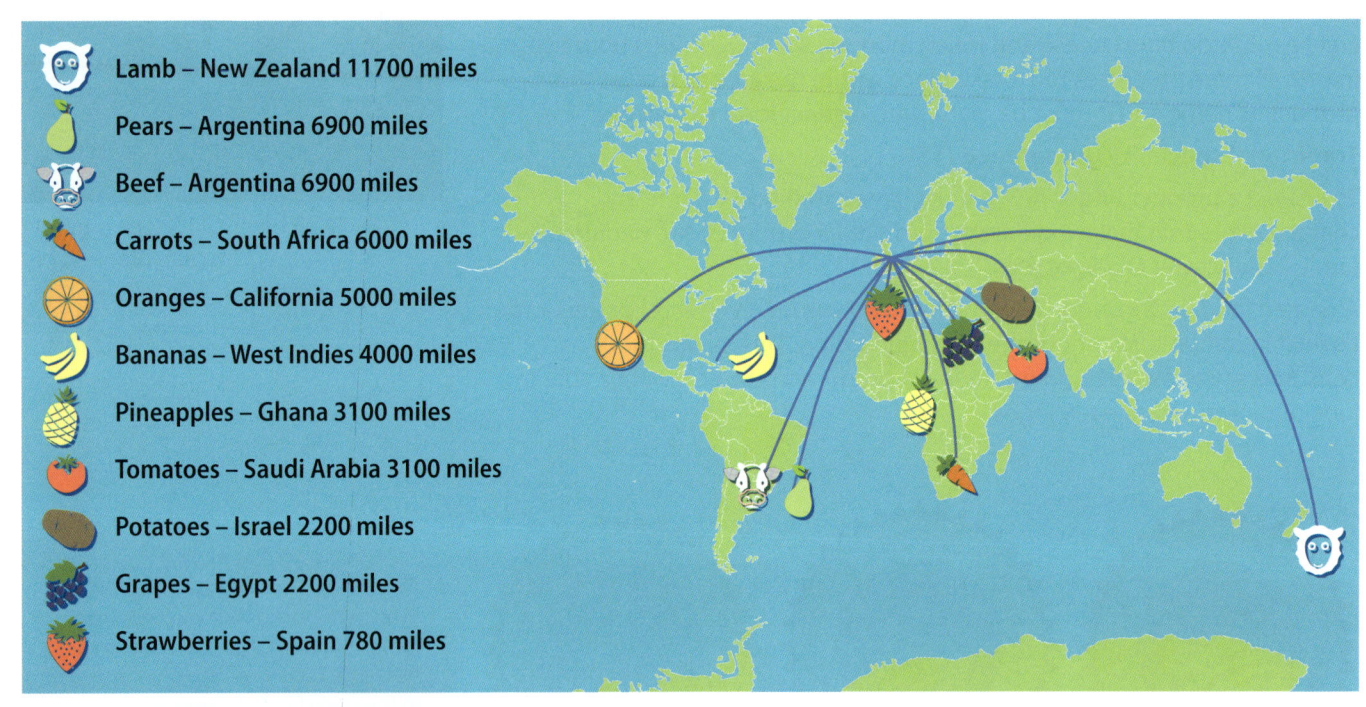

- Lamb – New Zealand 11700 miles
- Pears – Argentina 6900 miles
- Beef – Argentina 6900 miles
- Carrots – South Africa 6000 miles
- Oranges – California 5000 miles
- Bananas – West Indies 4000 miles
- Pineapples – Ghana 3100 miles
- Tomatoes – Saudi Arabia 3100 miles
- Potatoes – Israel 2200 miles
- Grapes – Egypt 2200 miles
- Strawberries – Spain 780 miles

▲ Amount of miles food travels to the UK

Consumers also increase food miles through the distance they travel to buy food. In the UK we travel further and use the car more often to do our shopping, compared to the past when shoppers were more likely to walk to local shops. On average someone in the UK travels about 135 miles a year by car to shop for food, frequently making trips to large, out-of-town supermarkets.

◀ Global transportation of food to the UK

CORE KNOWLEDGE

FOOD PROVENANCE AND FOOD WASTE

8 WAYS TO REDUCE FOOD MILES

1 BUY LOCAL – choosing locally produced food can make the biggest impact on food miles so it is important to read food labels. Buying food from your local area is the best way to reduce food miles, followed by food from the region. Even choosing food from anywhere within the UK is helpful in reducing food miles.

3 GROW YOUR OWN VEGETABLES – having a vegetable patch, no matter how large or small means that you can produce meals that have not created any food miles.

2 SHOP AT FARMERS MARKETS – a great place to source local seasonal foods is at farmers and organic markets.

4 EAT SEASONALLY – this ensures that you are eating foods that are produced locally for your area, e.g. strawberries in the summer. Plan your meals around what is being harvested around you at the time.

5 PICK YOUR OWN – go to local farms where you can pick anything from raspberries to asparagus.

6 LEARN TO COOK FROM SCRATCH – a lot of convenience foods are not made locally. They come from national food producers and are then packaged for the individual stores.

7 WALK OR CYCLE TO THE SHOP – if you only have a couple of things to buy and a shop within walking or cycling distance, consider a walk rather than going by car.

8 SHOP LESS FREQUENTLY – go once a month or less by making use of stockpiling techniques so that you are never without the things you use most and can create meals from scratch.

SECTION 1

The concept of food miles also includes the waste generated from the product, which must be transported from a home to a landfill site. The average household throws away more than three kilograms of food and 14 kilograms of food packaging per week. Buying food with as little packaging as possible and composting organic waste can also make a difference.

Check it

1 Explain the following terms:
   a Food miles
   b Carbon footprint
2 Why is it not always better for the environment to grow food in the UK rather than importing it from other countries?

Activity

Produce a poster or leaflet that would encourage people to reduce food miles.

99

Food packaging

As well as for marketing and promotional reasons, food is packaged:
- to preserve the freshness of the product
- to prevent contamination of the product
- to protect the product from damage
- to make the product easier to transport.

There is no doubt that food packaging is a necessity for some products, but it is important to consider the types of packaging material that is used and the impact that this has on the environment.

TYPES OF PACKAGING MATERIALS

PAPER AND CARDBOARD

Cartons and bags, e.g. egg boxes, juice cartons, pizza boxes

Paper and cardboard are a good choice environmentally: they can be recycled and can **biodegrade**. They are also cheap to produce, strong but lightweight, and can be printed on. However they are not water resistant and can be easily damaged.

PLASTIC

Bottles, trays and pots, e.g. ready meal containers, water bottles and yoghurt pots

Plastic can be easily shaped into a number of products. It can be recycled, but it causes a problem with litter due to the fact that it does not biodegrade.

GLASS

Jars and bottles, e.g. jams, baby food and sauces

Glass presents environmental advantages: it is reusable and easily recycled. It is also rigid and moisture proof. Unfortunately it is easily broken which makes it dangerous to handle.

METAL

Aluminium and steel, e.g. cans and foil trays

Packing food in metal containers is one of the oldest methods of food preservation. It can be used with a variety of food and drink items, allowing them to be stored for long periods of time. Both steel and aluminium can be recycled.

CORE KNOWLEDGE

FOOD PROVENANCE AND FOOD WASTE

Recycling food packaging

Packaging accounts for 25% of waste in the UK, it is therefore an important environmental consideration for manufacturers. Many are trying to reduce the amount of packaging they produce by using only that which is essential.

There has also been an improvement in the way that waste is recycled in the UK, with local authorities operating schemes to collect waste suitable for recycling alongside general waste. In 2010 Wales became the first country within the UK to make recycling a legal requirement. In most areas it is possible to recycle plastic, paper and cardboard, metal and glass, as well as organic waste. This increase in recycling and composting is an attempt by Wales to become a zero waste nation by 2050.

Biodegradable packaging

Biodegradable packaging reduces the amount of waste going to landfill as it can completely decompose with the aid of microorganisms. Additional benefits include the fact that it consists of renewable resources or can be harvested directly from nature, e.g. corn, used to make carrier bags.

How can waste be reduced?

As consumers it is important to apply the **3 R's** principle when considering packaging:

Reduce: Choose products which have the least amount of packaging and take reusable bags when shopping to avoid using too many plastic bags.

Reuse: Look out for products that are available in refill packs such as cleaning products and coffee. Glass milk bottles are returnable and jars can be reused for storage or home preservation e.g. pickled onions.

Recycle: Products such as paper, cardboard, metal, glass and plastic can be taken to recycling banks or collected weekly or fortnightly.

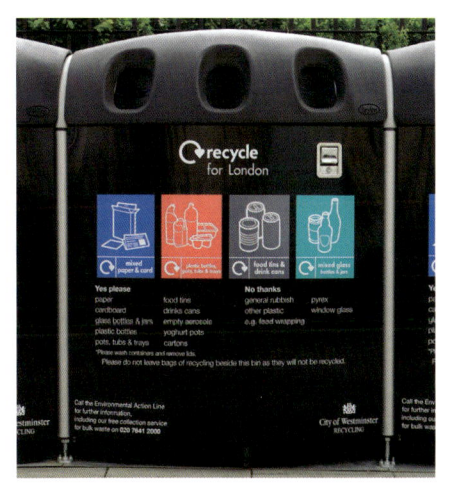

▲ A recycling point

Check it

1. Explain the 4 main reasons why food is packaged.
2. What are the 4 different materials used for food packaging. Give the advantages and disadvantages of each?
3. Give 3 ways in which recycling and biodegradable packaging is better for the environment
4. Give one example each for the way consumers can reduce, reuse and recycle food packaging waste.

Activity

Using the Internet, research the different types of biodegradable packaging available and produce a PowerPoint or poster to show your findings.

Fact: In October 2011, the Welsh Government introduced a 5p charge on plastic bags which led to a drop of between 70 and 96% in the use of plastic bags in food shops. Public support for the charge rose from 59% before its introduction to 70% afterwards, with 82% of people using their own bag instead. In April 2013 and October 2014 respectively, Northern Ireland and Scotland followed suit with a minimum 5p charge on single use carrier bags. In October 2015, England also introduced a 5p charge for carrier bags in large shops.

> **Study tip**
>
> Explain what is meant by sustainable food and what it requires of producers and consumers.

Sustainability of food

Food sustainability looks at the impact of producing and consuming food on the world's economy. Sustainability means that the resources we use should not exceed the earth's capacity to replace them. Sustainable food should be produced, processed, bought, sold and eaten with consideration to the following principles:

1 Aiming to be waste-free by reducing food waste and packaging. Food should have the minimum packaging and where possible be produced from materials that are reusable or recyclable.

2 Buying local and seasonal foods minimises the energy used in food production, transport and storage, and helps protect the local economy.

3 Eating a healthy diet and reducing foods of animal origin. Meat and dairy products are the most energy and greenhouse gas intensive food products. Consuming more vegetables and fruit, grains and pulses.

4 Choosing Fairtrade certified products. This scheme ensures workers are paid fairly for their work.

5 Selecting fish only from sustainable sources, such as wild-caught fish certified by the Marine Stewardship Council (MSC). Overfishing is the biggest threat to marine wildlife and their habitats.

6 Getting the balance right. Cut down on sugar, salt and fat, and include five portions of fruit and vegetables in the diet. Poor diet in the UK is leading to illnesses such as obesity, whilst 15% of the global population go hungry.

7 Growing our own, and buying the rest from a wide range of outlets rather than relying on large companies who lower prices at the expense of farmers, local communities and the environment.

(Source: www.sustainweb.org, Sustain Guide to Good Food, June 2013)

▲ Where does food waste come from?

▲ Over-consumption of food – a problem in many developed countries

Food waste

It is impossible to separate sustainability of food from the issue of food waste.

Every year in the UK 18 million tonnes of food end up in landfill – the chart alongside shows where it all comes from. Food waste from homes is estimated to cost each family around £700 a year or almost £60 a month.

We are wasting about a third of all food produced and a significant amount of this could have been eaten. It is not just the food that is being wasted but also the valuable resources used to produce and package it. However, the UK is making progress: between 2007 and 2012 the amount of avoidable food waste decreased by 21%, and by 2012 the amount of food waste being composted had risen to 43%.

The impact of food waste

Estimates suggest that by 2050 food production will need to increase by 60% on 2005 levels to feed a growing global population. Yet according to the UN, if the amount of food waste was reduced by just 25% there would be enough food to feed all the people in the world who are malnourished.

The impact of food waste has far-reaching global effects in developing countries. Poor equipment, transportation and infrastructure result in 'food loss' which is unintentional waste, whereas in the developed world unintentional loss is at a low level. Here food waste is actually caused by consumers overbuying and companies rejecting food that does not meet specific aesthetic standards.

Ways to reduce food waste

There are many ways that consumers can minimise the amount of food waste they produce.

- Plan your food shopping - this helps to avoid buying food already in the house, or being tempted to buy too much.
- Store food in the correct place at the correct temperature – a cool cupboard, the fridge or the freezer – to avoid it going off prematurely.
- Be waste-free by using up leftovers, for example in soups and smoothies.
- Understand the difference between 'use-by' and 'best before' dates. Food that is eaten after the 'best before' date will not be of such good quality but will not be harmful to eat.
- Compost food that cannot be eaten such as vegetable peelings and teabags.

Food poverty

Food poverty can be defined as the inability to obtain healthy, affordable food. According to figures from the Joseph Rowntree Foundation, despite the UK being the sixth richest country in the world, 4 million people are affected by food poverty.

The **four** main factors that influence food poverty are:

1. Accessibility – Lack of private or public transport means that some families are limited in the types of shops they have access to.
2. Availability – Many people who are living on a low income lack shops in their area, giving them less access to a variety of healthy, fresh foods.
3. Affordability – Food is often the most flexible part of a household budget, resulting in less money being available to spend on food if other bills increase. There is a perception that healthy food is more expensive, so when money is reduced, the quality of food purchased also reduces.
4. Awareness – Many people lack the skills and knowledge needed to create healthy meals.

Due to these factors, people on low incomes have the lowest intakes of fruit and vegetables and are far more likely to suffer from diet-related diseases such as cancer, diabetes, obesity and coronary heart disease. People who are living in food poverty often consume a diet filled with 'junk food', which results in poor diet.

Food banks are increasingly taking the brunt of food poverty, but they are only a short term solution. Food banks provide an emergency food distribution service, where people are referred and provided with a voucher that can be exchanged for food. In 2015 the amount of people using food banks in the UK rose to over 1 million.

Whilst food banks deal with the short term needs of people facing food poverty, community food projects work to tackle food poverty in their local areas. They give control to the community and allow for specific local needs to be identified and addressed.

Projects include:

Food co-ops – food distribution outlets organised by the local community where decisions regarding the production and distribution of its food is chosen by its members.

Community cafés – run by the community for the community; money that is made is reinvested into the café.

Cooking and nutrition programmes and courses – these initiatives allow people to be hands-on with food preparation skills, and show them that making healthy meals can be economical and improve their diet.

Check it

1. What is food sustainability?
2. Suggest 4 ways of producing sustainable food.
3. Why is food waste such a global problem?
4. Explain the difference between 'food loss' and 'food waste'.

Activity

Produce a list of ways to help families reduce the amount of food waste they produce.

Facts: Reviewing 'Best before' labelling could save around 370,000 tonnes per year.

Eliminating household food waste would deliver greenhouse gas benefits equivalent to taking one in five cars off the road – a reduction of 18M tonnes of CO2.

Fact: Diet-related ill health is responsible for about 10 per cent of deaths in the UK, and is estimated to cost the NHS some £6 billion every year.

▲ The UK is in the top 10 of the world's richest countries, and yet over 1 million people depend on foodbanks to make ends meet

Check it

1. Explain what is meant by 'food poverty'.
2. What initiatives are being used in the UK to try to tackle food poverty?
3. Why do you think there has been such a rise in people needing to use food banks? You may want to use the Internet to find out more information.

Study tip

Learn the main factors that contribute to food insecurity.

Check it

1. What is meant by the term food security?
2. What does the World Health Organisation (WHO) see as the basic pillars of food security?
3. What is the global effect of food insecurity?

Key terms

Origin – the place from which something is derived.

Food chain – a series of processes by which food is grown, produced, and eventually consumed.

Carbon footprint – a carbon footprint measures the total carbon dioxide emissions caused directly and indirectly by a person, organisation, event or product.

BSE (Bovine Spongiform Encephalopathy) – commonly referred to as mad cow disease, a slow developing disease affecting the nervous system of cattle. It is often fatal.

Traceability – the ability to track any food through all stages of production, processing and distribution.

Traditional products – foods made in a specific way according to their gastronomic heritage and transmitted from one generation to the next. Food is associated with a certain local area, region or country.

Biodegradeable – decomposed by bacteria or other living organisms.

Breakfast or lunch clubs – these offer the opportunity to have an affordably priced meal in a social setting, and can be for the community in general or specific groups, e.g. older people.

School tuck shops – school tuck shops provide fruit and vegetables to children. This is especially important for children from low income families who may not otherwise have access to fresh fruit and vegetables.

These initiatives are about more than providing food. They build confidence and allow communities to take charge of what is available to them, increase knowledge and skills, and help promote good health.

FOOD SECURITY

The World Food Summit of 1996 defined food security as existing 'when all people at all times have access to sufficient, safe, nutritious food to maintain a healthy and active life'.

According to the World Health Organisation (WHO), food security is built on three pillars:

- Food availability: sufficient quantities of food available on a consistent basis.
- Food access: having sufficient resources to obtain appropriate foods for a nutritious diet.
- Food use: appropriate use based on knowledge of basic nutrition and care, as well as adequate water and sanitation.

WHAT IS THE IMPACT OF FOOD INSECURITY?

Unfortunately globally there is not safe sufficient food for all. According to 2015 figures from the World Food Programme, 795 million people in the world do not get enough healthy food regularly. Ill health and a shorter life expectancy are real risks. Children who suffer from food insecurity will most likely be smaller and less able physically and intellectually.

The demand for food is increasing at a faster rate than the ability to produce it. There is a danger that this will lead to increased damage to soils and overuse of water, which in turn would lead to reduced capacity of agricultural land.

WHY IS THERE FOOD INSECURITY?
- HEALTH
- WATER AND THE ENVIRONMENT
- POVERTY
- TRADE
- GENDER INEQUALITY
- POPULATION AND URBANISATION
- DISASTERS AND CONFLICTS

CORE KNOWLEDGE

EXAM QUESTIONS

1. Explain the term 'food provenance'. [2]

2. Give three ways that food manufacturers can reduce the amount of packaging waste from their food products. [3]

3. Explain what is meant by biodegradable packaging. [2]

4. Explain how EU food protection marks help protect products against imitation. [3]

5. Give 3 ways food miles can be reduced. [3]

6. Explain how food waste can be reduced when buying and cooking food. [6]

7. Give one environmental advantage and one environmental disadvantage of the following types of packaging. [6]

	Advantages	Disadvantages
Plastic		
Paper/Cardboard		
Metal		

8.
   a. Explain the difference between 'food loss' and 'food waste' [4]
   b. How can each of the issues be addressed? [6]

9. Food packaging is changing in order to reduce the effect on the environment.
   a. Discuss the importance of packaging to the food industry. [6]
   b. Evaluate how food packaging has been developed to reduce its impact on the environment. [6]

10. The number of people using food banks is increasing. Discuss the possible reasons for this and suggest ways that food poverty can be addressed. [10]

TOTAL: 57

SECTION 1
CORE KNOWLEDGE

CULTURES AND CUISINES

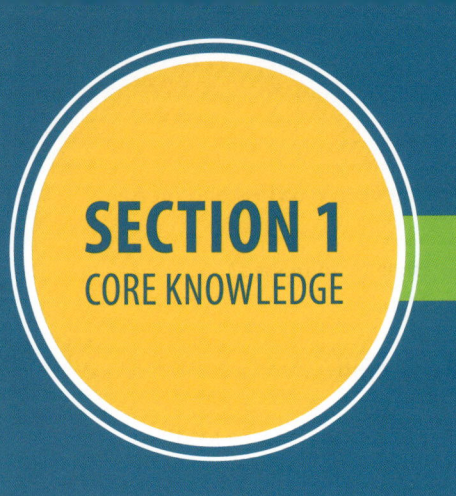

What will I learn?
- The different types of cuisine available throughout the world
- The key ingredients and popular dishes from each cuisine

World **cuisines** are influenced by factors such as the **terrain** and **climate** of the land, the history and **culture** of its people, the faith and religion of the population, as well as the economic situation of the country.

The foods eaten across the world evolve and change over time. Technology, together with improved transport and communication links, has made a significant impact on how ingredients are grown and distributed across the world, giving consumers greater access to and a wider knowledge of types of ingredients and how to cook with them.

Foods are often described as **fusion**. Influences include European, Asian, Chinese and Japanese cookery in particular.

The influences that shape world cuisines
Geography and climate
The way food is grown and reared is influenced by the terrain and climatic conditions, including the weather and changing seasons. For example, in areas where the land is **fertile** and the weather is warm and humid, such as in southeast Asia, rice may grow easily. In colder climates such as northern Europe cereals such as rye and wheat may be grown more successfully. If the land cannot be farmed productively, people may rely on grazing animals for their **sustenance**.

People migrations
Throughout history people have **migrated** between countries, sometimes out of necessity, or sometimes in search of a better **standard of living**. As people travel they take with them their food culture – their familiar recipes and cooking utensils; they often take their ingredients too.

Faith and religion
Religion can have a significant impact on the diet of the population. For example the vegetarian **traditions** of India and many parts of southeast Asia have evolved because of dietary requirements of the Hindu and Buddhist faiths.

Restrictions on other ingredients in addition to meats often occur, for example strict Hindus will avoid mushrooms, garlic, onions, alcohol and caffeinated drinks.

Economy
The economic wealth of a nation will influence the diet of the population. In developing countries people may have less **disposable income** and may rely more heavily on **staple foods** to satisfy hunger and meet their nutritional needs.

Wealthier nations may have a greater choice of ingredients and educational awareness of foods, although this does not always lead to a healthier diet.

> **Key point**
>
> The climate and terrain of a land will determine which foods can be grown or reared.
>
> Religious beliefs influence the choice of ingredients used in cooking and their preparation.
>
> How much money people have to spend on food will affect the types of ingredients they can afford to buy and the types of dishes they will cook.

CORE KNOWLEDGE Factors affecting food choice : Culture and religion p137

THE UNITED KINGDOM

CULTURES AND CUISINES

United Kingdom

People from all around the world have come to live in the UK, and have brought with them their culinary traditions. In the past, people from British colonies such as India and the Caribbean arrived in the UK to join the workforce for an expanding economy. More recently, the population has grown due to the arrival of EU citizens.

The growing immigrant population, together with increased awareness and availability of new ingredients and cuisines continues to fuel our desire to try new foods.

This section focuses on the more typical and historical *regional foods* within the UK. These are typically British foods that have been established for centuries and *signature dishes* that are made with locally produced ingredients.

> **Check it**
>
> Make sure you understand the meaning of **regional food**.
>
> Give examples of regional dishes from around the UK.

England

Many typically English dishes are found throughout the country as a whole, such as roast beef and Yorkshire pudding, fish and chips and steak and kidney pie. Others come from specific areas of England and are known as regional foods.

Some typical ingredients

Vegetables – potato, swede, leek, onion, root vegetables such as carrot and parsnip

Fruit – apples, pears, rhubarb, soft fruits, e.g. raspberries, gooseberries and blackberries

Fish – haddock, mackerel, herring, eels

Seafood – oysters, prawns and shrimps

Cheese – a large range of regional cheeses from the famous Cheddar, Cheshire and Stilton to the less well known Stinking Bishop and Garstang Blue

Poultry and game – chicken, turkey, duck, venison, guinea fowl, hare, rabbit, pheasant

Meats – beef, lamb and pork: made into hams, bacon, sausages, offal including liver and kidneys and black pudding

English signature dishes

Cumberland sausage – a pork sausage rolled into a coil

Morecambe bay shrimps – shrimps cooked and sealed in butter

Cromer crab – tender cooked crab

Lancashire hotpot – oven baked lamb or mutton and onion, topped with sliced potatoes

Glazed gammon and cider – cooked cured pork in cider

Fidget Pie – a savoury pie containing onions, apples, bacon, and sometimes potatoes

Cornish pasty – a pastry snack containing seasoned beef and vegetables (potato, swede and onion) formed into a D shape and crimped

Jellied eels – chopped cooked eels set in a jelly

Jugged hare – hare, cooked with red wine and juniper berries in a tall jug that stands in a pan of water

Yorkshire pudding – an egg, flour and milk batter, oven baked, often served as an accompaniment to roast beef

Eccles cakes – small, round pastries filled with currants

Bath buns – a sweet roll made from milk based yeast dough

Devonshire cream tea – a type of afternoon tea with scones, clotted cream and jam

Devonshire splits – a type of yeast bun split open and served with whipped cream or butter and jam

Bread pudding – rich, heavy cake or pudding made from pieces of bread soaked in milk and baked with eggs, sugar, dried fruit, and spices

Canterbury pudding – a dry pastry filled pudding made from breadcrumbs, brandy, milk and lemon juice

Bakewell tart – a shortcrust pastry shell with layers of jam, frangipane, and a topping of flaked almonds

Parkin – a gingerbread cake traditionally made with oatmeal and black treacle

Stottie cake – a leavened bread with an indent in the middle produced by the baker.

THE UNITED KINGDOM

Wales

Traditional Welsh cooking has its origins in the diet of the working people of Wales – farmers, labourers, fisherman, coal miners and steel workers. Welsh foods and recipes are ones that have evolved from using home grown fruits and vegetables, fish caught from the rivers, lakes or sea, using the rugged land for sheep and beef farming, **foraging** (often for cockles, laverbread, mushrooms) and meat reared from the family pig.

Geography

- a small country, the land and surrounding sea is lush and fertile
- the sea, rivers and lakes give us a range of fish and seafood such as mackerel, sole, skate, turbot, salmon, brown trout, sewin (Welsh sea trout) crab, lobster, mussels, scallops, cockles and laverbread; the land is farmed to produce cereals such as wheat, oats, barley and to grow vegetables such as leeks, root vegetables and cabbages
- good for rearing sheep and cattle
- pigs are raised and their meat cured to make bacon and ham
- contour of land means large scale farming is less popular

Welsh signature dishes

Wales has many dishes that are well known and quoted as being examples of Welsh cuisine. Many of these famous Welsh dishes are simply made, often using one pot, pan or griddle, as would have been used traditionally in the kitchens of the working people. Here are examples of dishes that are well known throughout Wales.

Cawl – a hearty soup with lamb and vegetables

Faggots – a kind of meatball made from offal and wrapped in caul fat served with mushy peas and onion gravy

Lavercakes with bacon and eggs – small laverbread patties with bacon rashers and a fried egg

Welsh rarebit – a posh 'cheese on toast' made from mixing up Welsh cheese, ale and mustard

Glamorgan sausages – vegetarian sausage made with Caerphilly cheese, leek and mustard rolled in breadcrumbs

Welsh cakes – sweet, biscuit-like product, flavoured with spice and dried fruit, baked on a griddle

Bara Brith – 'speckled bread', a rich spiced fruit loaf made with tea

Anglesey

- mild climate and low rainfall
- leeks, potatoes, brassicas and root vegetables
- sheep, cattle, pigs and poultry are all reared successfully
- lobster fishing and scallop and mussel dredging
- sea salt is also produced

History

Welsh cuisine and culture has been influenced by industrialisation during the last two centuries. The trading of Welsh coal resulted in a growth in population to support this trade, many people came from abroad, bringing with them their cultures and traditions.

One significant influence on Welsh cuisine that must be mentioned is the influence of Italian foods, since many Italian families moved to Wales in both the 19th and 20th centuries. Pasta, coffee and gelato are amongst the Italian influences on Welsh food and culture.

CULTURES AND CUISINES

Llŷn Peninsula
- harsh coastline
- fish such as bass, plaice, sole and skate
- Bangor is known for producing mussels
- cockles, winkles and mussels are foraged as are berries in summer time
- livestock farming includes dairy, Welsh Black beef and salt marsh lamb

Snowdonia
- wild, mountainous and rugged
- rainfall is heavy
- mountainous regions and salt marshes can only be inhabited by sheep
- lakes and reservoirs supply locals with a source of fish

Denbigh and Flint
- land is lush and green
- good for dairy and livestock farming
- wild and farmed game
- Moorland lamb is popular
- dairy products such as milk drinks, yoghurts and cheeses
- foraging of mushrooms and berries is popular
- this area of Wales has a number of large food manufacturing units

Ceredigion
- green and fertile land
- farming smaller scale
- lamb from Cambrian mountains
- area is well known for artisan cheeses using milk from cows, sheep and goats
- lobster and crab are fished on a small scale
- plaice, sole, turbot, bass and mackerel
- samphire and sea beet grown

Pembrokeshire
- natural harbours
- small fishing fleets trawl for fish and seafood including mackerel, bass, sole, plaice, turbot, skate, lobster and crab
- laverbread is still gathered, cockles and mussels, crabs, prawns are all foraged
- Pembrokeshire potatoes which are harvested early
- Preseli mountain lamb and Welsh Black beef

Camarthenshire
- lush fields used for dairy farming and livestock
- the rivers are well stocked with salmon, brown trout and sewin
- sheep flourish in Cambrian and Black mountains
- pigs are reared and Carmarthen ham
- cockles are also in good supply in estuaries
- high quality of cow milk

Monmouthshire
- generally drier
- suitable for growing grains
- trout and salmon are fished from the rivers, and game such as venison, pheasant, partridge and even hare are hunted
- speciality cheeses are produced
- foraged elderflowers, wild garlic, fungi, nuts and berries

Montgomery
- many rivers especially good for trout
- mountainous area is ideal for sheep grazing
- pheasants are reared
- pork is processed into ham and bacon, as well as made into speciality sausages
- foraging for fungi and many varieties of mushrooms

Brecon and Radnor
- large area
- mostly mountainous
- main rivers are the Usk and Wye
- sources of salmon and trout
- game and deer
- The distinctive Radnorshire lamb, Welsh Black Beef and venison are all farmed
- vegetables and fruits grow well

West Glamorgan
- cattle and sheep are now reared on what was previously waste land. Gower salt marsh lamb and Welsh Black beef are popular food sources
- well known for fishing and mackerel, bass, sole, brill, turbot, skate, crab and lobster
- foraging for cockles, winkles and laverbread is well known around the Gower

Glamorgan Vale
- terrain varies
- lush green fields ideal for farming further south
- polluted rivers and land used for waste from coal mining all now regenerated
- land suitable for livestock and arable farming
- lamb, beef, pig and poultry production
- cheese, wine and beer are also made

Modern classics

Here are suggestions of Welsh inspired modern dishes that can be made using Welsh ingredients, the emphasis is using seasonal and local produce:

Starters:
Conwy mussels cooked in Gwynt y Ddraig cider with tender leeks
Menai oysters
Cothi Valley goats cheese grilled on a red onion marmalade croute with a carpaccio of beetroot and celeriac
Penclawdd cockles and laverbread with pan fried dry cured crispy bacon rashers
Mains:
Welsh Black beef fillet steak with sea beets and horseradish potatoes with an oxtail sauce
Roasted Welsh Preseli rack of lamb, with a rosemary and garlic crust and caramelised onion jus
Fillet of Wye sewin poached and served with beurre blanc, Pembrokeshire new potatoes and courgette spaghetti
Roasted quail with pan fried bubble and squeak with foraged mushrooms and a red wine reduction
Desserts:
Salted caramel tart with Halen Môn and vanilla custard
Monmouth pudding, with hedgerow berries and served with Caernarfon cream
Blackberry panacotta with an Anglesey shortbread biscuit
Welsh Cheese Platter - a selection of cheeses from around the Welsh coast and valleys, served with Welsh oat crackers, chutney, celery, apple and grapes

Welsh food markets

Food markets provide a real sense of community and give local people the opportunity to buy foods direct from the producers and suppliers. Most products can be bought with minimal packaging. Food markets give us the chance to talk to the producers, to find out more about the provenance of the ingredients.

Farm shops

Farm shops give farmers the opportunity to sell their produce direct to the customer, this helps to make the products more economical for the customer and means that the farmer has more control over pricing and profitability. Many farm shops also sell goods made by a range of local producers.

Food festivals

Local producers are given the opportunity to show their produce to the public and give visitors the opportunity to learn more about how the food is produced, as well as tasting and buying the foods. Abergavenny Food Festival is one of the most well know Welsh food festivals. Others include the Anglesey Oyster Festival and Llangollen Food Festival.

Agricultural Shows

Agricultural shows are a popular way for farmers and food producers to meet and show their livestock and food produce. Such events enable food lovers to sample and buy directly from the producers. The Royal Welsh Agricultural Show in Builth Wells is one of the most well known shows, others include the Pembrokeshire County Show.

SECTION 1

109

EUROPE

Scotland

Like Wales and England, cuisine from Scotland has evolved from the use of local ingredients, including game, fish, dairy, fruit and vegetables.

Some typical ingredients

- Vegetables – potato, swede, turnip, onion and cabbage
- Cereals – oats and barley
- Fruit – berry fruits
- Fish – haddock, mackerel, herring and salmon
- Seafood – including cockles and mussels
- Poultry and game
- Meats – Aberdeen Angus beef, cuts of offal
- Cheeses – many locally produced, including Lanark Blue and Caboc

Scottish signature dishes

- Scotch broth – a hearty soup with pearl barley, root vegetables, cabbage and meat (lamb)
- Haggis – a savoury pudding made from animal organs with onion, suet, oatmeal and seasoning
- Lorne sausage – a square shaped sausage
- Cullen Skink – a hearty soup made from smoked haddock, potatoes, onions and milk
- Arbroath smokies – hot smoked haddock
- Cranachan – a dessert made with whipped cream, whisky, oatmeal, honey and raspberries
- Shortbread – a buttery and crumbly biscuit made with butter, flour and sugar
- Porridge – oats that have been cooked in water or milk, sometimes with flavourings, can be sweet or savoury

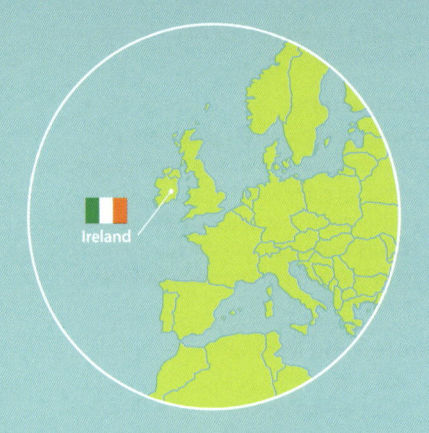

Ireland

Irish cuisine has evolved from centuries of social and political change. One of the biggest influences on Irish cuisine was the introduction of the potato in the 16th century.

Some typical ingredients

- Vegetables – cabbage, potatoes, root vegetables, such as carrots and parsnips, onions and scallions (spring onion)
- Cereals – oats and wheat
- Bacon
- Corned beef
- Salmon
- Seaweed
- Buttermilk

Irish signature dishes

- Ardglass potted herring – herring marinated in vinegar, rolled with bay leaf and baked with breadcrumbs
- Colcannon – a dish made from mashed potatoes and kale (or cabbage). It can contain other ingredients such as spring onions, leeks, onions and chives
- Crubeens – a snack made from boiled pig's feet, coated in breadcrumbs and deep fried
- Dublin coddle – a filling stew-like dish made from salty bacon, pork sausages and potatoes
- Irish stew – a hearty casserole made with meat, potatoes, carrots and onions
- Potato bread farl – a dense flat bread made with potatoes, flour and buttermilk, cooked on a griddle. Used as part of the Ulster Fry breakfast
- Soda bread – chunky soft bread, using the raising agent of bicarbonate of soda rather than yeast
- Ulster Fry – a version of a cooked breakfast (bacon, sausage, fried egg, white pudding, black pudding, tomato and sometimes mushrooms), with the addition of soda bread and potato farls

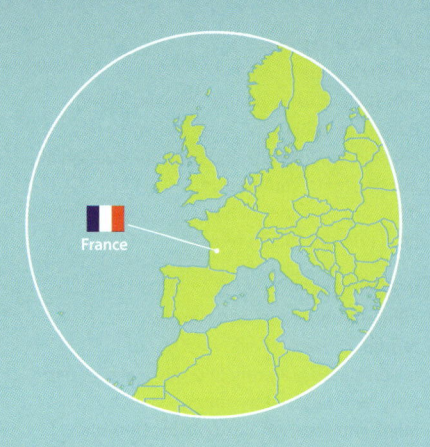

France

Some typical ingredients

- Vegetables – onions and shallots, garlic, mushrooms, haricot verts (a type of French green bean), leeks
- Speciality vegetables – such as globe artichokes, asparagus, chicory
- Fruit – including peaches, pears and plums
- Fresh herbs – tarragon, chervil and parsley
- Foie gras (duck or goose liver)
- Fish and shellfish – oysters, scallops, langoustines, mussels
- Escargot (snails)
- Frog legs
- Dairy products, e.g. butter, milk, cream, regional cheeses
- Truffles

French signature dishes

- French onion soup – made with meat stock and onions, served gratinéed with cheese
- Pâté – forcemeat mixture cooked and served in a terrine
- Bouillabaisse – a fish stew from Marseille
- Galettes – savoury crepes made with buckwheat flour
- Cassoulet – from southern France, a rich, slow cooked stew containing meats such as sausage and duck, or haricot beans
- Coq au vin – chicken cooked in red wine (traditionally was a cockerel)
- Tarte tatin – an upside down pastry in which the fruit (usually apples) are caramelised in butter and sugar before the tart is baked
- Pastries – croissant, pain au chocolat
- Breads – pain de campagne, fougasse and baguettes

CORE KNOWLEDGE

CULTURES AND CUISINES

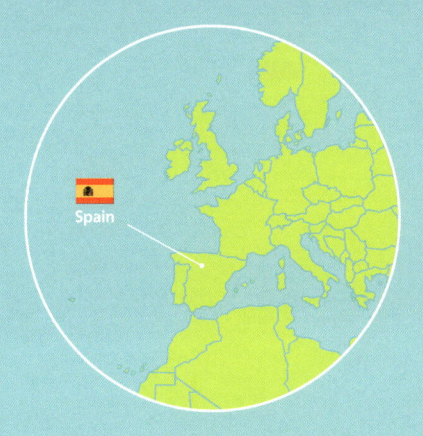

Spain

Some typical ingredients

Vegetables – onion, garlic, tomatoes, peppers and olives
Fruits – oranges, lemons, figs, pomegranates, grapes
Spices and herbs – saffron, pepper, coriander, cumin, nutmeg
Pork, including suckling pig, mountain ham (jamón serrano), chorizo
Chicken
Fish and seafood – anchovies, salt cod, squid
Speciality cheeses
Pulses – including butter beans, haricot beans
Almonds
Olive oil
Olives
Sherry vinegar

Spanish signature dishes

Tapas – hot or cold snacks
Gazpacho – iced tomato soup with peppers, cucumber and bread
Tortilla española – a potato omelette
Bacalao en samfaina – salt cod with aubergines, peppers and onion
Patatas bravas – cubes of fried potatoes, served warm with a sauce such as a spicy tomato sauce or an aioli
Paella – a rice dish cooked in a wide flat pan with rabbit or chicken, and often seafood, coloured with saffron
Crema Catalana – also called flan, this is the Spanish version of crème brulée. It has a base of rich custard and is topped with hard caramel
Churros – a fried-dough pastry

Specialist equipment

Paella pan

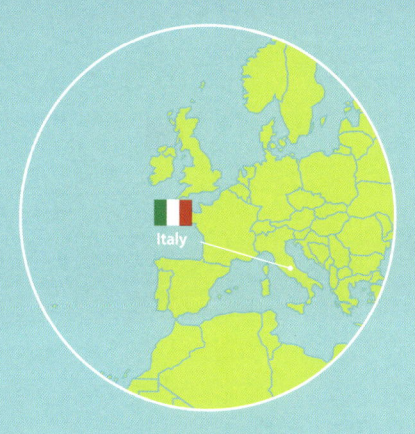

Italy

Some typical ingredients

Vegetables – onion, garlic, aubergines, courgettes, mushrooms, spinach, peppers, fennel, artichokes, asparagus
Salad leaves – endive, radicchio
Fruits – figs, lemons, oranges, pears, peaches, berries, melon, tomatoes
Herbs – basil, parsley, sage, thyme and marjoram
Beef, veal, including offal and air dried beef (bresaola)
Cured pork and game
Fish and seafood – sardines, tuna, anchovy, octopus and squid
Regional cheeses – ricotta, mascarpone, mozzarella, Parmesan
Wheat – made into fresh and dried pasta and breads
Pasta – spaghetti, tagliatelle, pappardelle, penne, farfalle
Pulses – cannellini, broad and haricot beans
Balsamic vinegar, olive oil

Italian signature dishes

Anti pasti – starter with a selection of products such as cured meats, olives, artichoke hearts, cheeses and vegetables in oil or vinegar
Minestrone soup – chunky soup with pieces of vegetables and pasta
Crostini – small pieces of toasted bread served with a topping
Foccacia – a dimpled flat bread, sometimes topped with herbs and olive oil
Lasagne al forno – layers of lasagne sheets, meat ragù and white sauce, oven baked
Gnocchi – potato dumplings
Risotto – a north Italian rice dish cooked in a stock to a creamy consistency
Pizza – a bread base topped with tomato sauce and cheese and baked. Toppings often include meats, vegetables and different cheeses
Polenta – a mash made from cornmeal, can be served hot or allowed to cool and solidify into a loaf, which is then baked, fried, or grilled
Cannoli – Sicilian fried pastry cylinders filled with ricotta cheese and chocolate or candied fruits
Tiramisu – a dessert made with sponge, mascarpone cheese, chocolate and espresso coffee

Central and Eastern Europe

Some typical ingredients

Vegetables – potatoes, cabbage, turnip
Fruits – apples
Spices and herbs – paprika, dill, junipers, caraway seeds
Meat – wild boar, pork, beef
Sausage from Germany, e.g. bratwurst, knackwurst, bockwurst
Wheat, barley, oats and rye flours (to make breads)

Central and Eastern European signature dishes

Schnitzel – a thin, boneless cutlet of meat, coated in breadcrumbs and fried
Wurst – German sausage
Sauerkraut – salted and fermented cabbage
Apfelstrudel – (apple strudel) thin pastry filled with apples, sugar, cinnamon, raisins and breadcrumbs
Black Forest gateau – layers of chocolate cake, cherries and whipped cream
Rösti – flat round potato patties sautéed in oil
Sacher torte – a luxurious chocolate cake from Austria
Pierogi – Polish dumplings

▲ Crostini

▲ Wurst

SECTION 1

111

EUROPE AND RUSSIA

Greece

Some typical ingredients

Vegetables – aubergines, courgettes, onion, garlic, peppers, artichokes, cucumber
Fruits – cherries, plums, peaches, figs, grapes, apricots, melons and lemons
Spices and herbs – cinnamon, allspice, mint, thyme, parsley, fennel, dill
Meat – lamb and goat
Fish – sardines, anchovies, mackerel, swordfish, cuttlefish, squid, octopus
Sheep and goat milk – made into yoghurt and feta cheese
Filo pastry
Olive oil
Olives

Greek signature dishes

Mezedes – small savoury dishes eaten in tavernas and cafés
Tzatziki – mezze dish of yoghurt, garlic, cucumber and dill
Hummus – a dip made from cooked, mashed chickpeas
Taramasalata – dip made from fish roe
Dolmades – vine leaves stuffed with rice and vegetables; sometimes with meat
Horiatiki – traditional Greek salad
Keftedes – lamb or beef meatballs
Pitta bread – round pocket bread dipped in spreads or used with meat dishes
Moussaka – aubergine based dish with spiced lamb and béchamel sauce
Souvlaki – small pieces of meat and sometimes vegetables on a skewer
Spanokopita – savoury pie made with spinach and cheese
Loukoumi – Greek version of the sweet delicacy 'Turkish delight'

▲ Dolmades

Turkey

Some typical ingredients

Vegetables – garlic, onion, aubergine, peppers, potatoes
Fruits – plums, apricots, pears, quince, sour cherries, pomegranates, tomatoes, apples, figs, citrus fruits
Dried fruit – apricot and currants
Spices and herbs – parsley, mint, oregano, thyme, cumin, black pepper, paprika, pul biber (red pepper), allspice
Meat – lamb, sheep tail fat (kuyrukya)
Yoghurt
Beyaz peynir (white cow milk cheese)
Nuts – pistachios, chestnuts, almonds, hazelnuts, and walnuts
Olives

Turkish signature dishes

Kofte – meatballs
Kebabi – meat grilled on skewers
Imam bayildi – stewed aubergine
Corek – sweet buns
Lokum – Turkish delight
Borek – filled pastries
Patlican receli – sweet aubergine jam
Baklava – layers of filo pastry with nuts and a sugar syrup

Check it

Write down the key foods used as sources of starchy carbohydrate across Europe.

▲ Baklava

Russia

Some typical ingredients

Vegetables – garlic, onions, cabbage, turnips, carrots, cucumber, potatoes, beetroot, horseradish
Fruits – berries e.g. cranberries, lingonberries, gooseberries
Spices and herbs – dill, poppy seeds
Dried and pickled fish
Smoked salmon
Ikra (caviar) – sturgeon roe (very much a luxury food)
Soured cream
Pearl barley
Rye and wheat – bread, including sourdough
Chestnuts
Honey

Russian signature dishes

Borsch – beetroot soup
Golubtsy – stuffed cabbage rolls
Russian salad – diced potato, peas, egg and mayonnaise / sour cream
Cucumber salad
Pelmeni – Russian dumplings filled with meat
Kasha – grain porridge from buckwheat groats
Chornyi khleb – sticky Russian black bread made from rye and molasses
Kisel – apple pudding
Blinis – small yeasted pancakes

112 CORE KNOWLEDGE

AMERICAS

CULTURES AND CUISINES

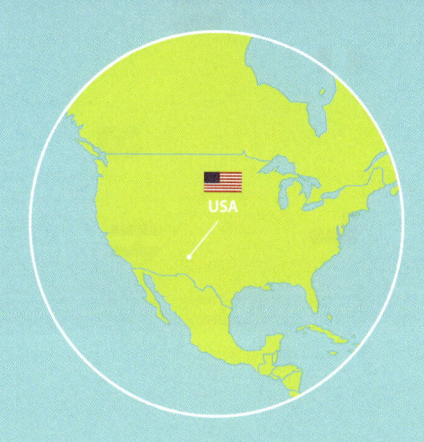

USA

Historically, the foods which originated in the USA have included corn, beans, squash, nuts, berries, fruits, fish, small game (such as rabbits), wild turkey, maple syrup and buffalo.

Many of the dishes we associate with the USA originate from other countries. Dishes such as hot dogs, pizza, pasta, apple pie, ice cream and tacos have been introduced as people settled in America.

Some typical ingredients
Vegetables – potatoes, pumpkins, squashes, cranberries, blueberries, beans, okra, yams, sweet potatoes
Fruits – grapes, apples, melons, citrus fruits, cherries, apricots, avocados, tomatoes
Meat – pork, beef, deer, buffalo, bacon
Poultry – chicken and turkey
Fish and seafood – lobster, crayfish, prawns, mussels, salt cod
Peanuts
Maple syrup

American (USA) signature dishes
New England clam chowder – a chunky and thick clam soup
Meatloaf – minced meat and other ingredients, formed into a loaf and baked
Southern fried chicken
Jambalaya – a Cajun rice stew from New Orleans, made with sausage and seafood
Gumbo – a southern stew made with meat or shellfish and vegetables
Boston baked beans – baked beans with salt pork and molasses
Succotash – contains lima beans, carrots and sweetcorn, can include cured meat or fish
Grits – coarsely ground corn boiled with water or milk
Hash browns
Fruit pies, e.g. apple, cherry, blueberry
Key lime pie – made from condensed milk and limes
Pumpkin pie – a sweet dessert with pumpkin
Devil's food cake – a rich chocolate layer cake

Canada

Canadian cuisine has its origins in European **pioneer** cooking (particularly influenced by the British and French cuisines). The Canadian population in the 21st century is a mix of many cultures and ethnicities, which influences the foods found in Canada today.

Native ingredients from Canada still influence signature dishes, including fish and seafood, game, berries and maple syrup.

Some typical ingredients
Vegetables – potatoes
Sea vegetables – seaweed
Fruits – blueberries, cloudberries, partridgeberries, cranberries, saskatoons, peaches, plums, pears and cherries
Meat – beef, pork, bacon
Game – moose, deer, caribou meat, snow geese
Fish and seafood – salmon, trout, salt cod, lobster
Wheat
Maple syrup

Canadian signature dishes
Fish and shellfish chowders
Fish and brewis – a regional dish from Newfoundland, made from salt cod, hardtack (dried bread), potatoes, onions and pork fat
Poutine – a savoury dish made with French fries and cheese curds topped with light brown gravy
Fiddlehead fern – pickled before it unfurls and served boiled with butter
Bannocks – griddle baked oat cakes
Pancakes with maple syrup
Muktuk – made of whale skin and blubber, eaten by the indigenous population

Mexico

Some typical ingredients
Vegetables – onions, garlic
Fruits – tomatoes, tropical fruits e.g. avocado, bananas, pineapples, limes, papaya, tomatillo (a small green husk coloured fruit)
Spices and herbs – cinnamon, allspice, cloves, bay, vanilla, coriander, thyme, oregano, chillies (many varieties, with varying degrees of heat), chipotle – smoked and dried jalapeño chilli
Meat – pork, beef, sheep, goat
Corn
Beans – black, red kidney, pinto
Nuts and seeds
Sugar cane
Lard
Chocolate

Mexican signature dishes
Huevos rancheros – a breakfast dish of fried eggs served with a tomato chilli hot sauce
Sopa de tortilla – a chicken soup topped with dried chillis, lime juice and cheese
Moles, pipians and adobos – types of thickened chilli sauces
Ceviche – raw fish 'cooked' in lemon or lime juice
Tortilla – can be made from wheat or corn
Frijoles refritos – refried beans
Quesadilla – a tortilla with a filling, cooked on a griddle
Empanada – a stuffed bread or pastry baked or fried
Guacamole – a spicy avocado-based dip
Doughnuts and churros

Specialist equipment
Tortillero – tortilla press
Comal – griddle

SECTION 1

113

AMERICAS

The Caribbean

Some typical ingredients

Vegetables – sweet potatoes, okra, breadfruit, cassava, plantains, yams, peppers, christophene (also called chayote), chilli peppers

Fruits – mangoes, coconuts, avocados, papaya, guavas, ackee, soursop, coconut, bananas

Spices and herbs – thyme, bay, nutmeg, mace, ginger, cloves, cinnamon, allspice

Meat – pork, chicken and goat

Fish and shellfish – red snapper, salt cod, lobster, crayfish and conch (sea snail)

Rice

Achiote (annatto seeds)

Sugar cane and molasses

Cassareep – a thick brown syrup made by boiling down the juice of grated cassava with sugar and spices

Caribbean signature dishes

Calaloo – a thick soup made from okra and greens such as spinach or amaranth

Pepper pot – stewed meat or fish with vegetables, typically flavoured with cassareep

Salt cod and ackee

Curried goat

Jerk pork and chicken

Run down – a Jamaican dish of preserved fish in coconut milk, served with plantains

Metagee – a thick stew containing vegetables, fish, salted meat, and coconut milk, with a distinctive grey colour

Rice and peas (the peas are actually beans or lentils)

Patties – a savoury and spicy pastry snack

▲ Jerk pork

Central America

Includes Belize, Costa Rica, El Salvador, Guatemala, Honduras, Nicaragua, and Panama; ingredients are often similar to those used in Mexico.

Some typical ingredients

Vegetables – onions, garlic, squash, cassava, plantains

Fruits – tomatoes, avocado, coconut, bananas and limes

Chillies (many varieties, with varying degrees of heat)

Meat – beef, turkey

Corn (maize)

Rice

Beans (black, red kidney, pinto)

Achiote

Sugar cane

Chocolate

Central American signature dishes

Nicaragua

Nacatamal – a parcel filled with meat or vegetables, wrapped in a corn husk and cooked by steaming

El Salvador

Pupusa – stuffed corn tortillas

Guatemala

Pepián – a thick, hearty stew of vegetables with chicken, pork (or both) in a broth

▲ Pepian

▲ Ceviche

South America

Some typical ingredients

Vegetables – potatoes (fresh as well as dehydrated and freeze dried), peppers, cassava, pumpkin, okra, squash, plantains

Fruits – coconut, avocados, oranges, bananas, tomatoes

Chillies (many varieties, with varying degrees of heat)

Meat – beef, mutton and lamb, llama, alpaca, guinea pig

Fish and shellfish – scallops, sea bass, sea urchins and abalone

Quinoa

Beans

Sugar cane

Chocolate

Palm oil

South American signature dishes

Tamales – called different names in each country, a corn filled snack wrapped in a banana leaf

Peru

Ceviche – raw fish marinated in lemon or lime juice

Chile

Pastel de choclo – a meat (beef or chicken) and corn pie

Paraguay

Bori-bori – meat broth with dumplings, corn meal and cheese

Argentina

Carbonada criolla – beef stew made with squash and vegetables, often baked in a pumpkin

Brazil

Feijoada – Brazilian black bean and meat stew served with rice and orange slices

Colombia

Papas chorreadas – boiled potatoes with a sauce of spring onion, tomatoes, cheese coriander, chillies and cream

CORE KNOWLEDGE

ASIA

CULTURES AND CUISINES

Foods from Asia are as varied as the countries within this continent. There are often ingredients and cooking methods that you will see shared between different cultures and countries. Asian cooking uses lots of fruits and vegetables and there is often use of locally grown spices to give dishes a particular flavour and aroma.

India and the Indian sub-continent

The cuisine from the Indian sub-continent (Pakistan, Bangladesh, Sri Lanka) is varied and diverse, and is influenced by the terrain and climate as well as by religion and faith. Religions that impact considerably are Buddhism, Hinduism, Sikhism, Christianity, Jainism and the Muslim faith. This sometimes means that certain ingredients are not permitted – and indeed some areas of this continent focus greatly on vegetarian foods made from locally grown ingredients.

Some typical ingredients

Vegetables – onions, garlic, aubergines, okra, cucumber, coconut, drumsticks, peas, cauliflower, spinach, bitter gourd, jackfruit, yam, plantain

Fruits – bananas, mango, lemon, lime, pomegranate, melons, apricot, guava

Spices and herbs – cumin seeds, nutmeg, ginger, cloves, coriander, curry leaves, turmeric, mustard seeds, cardamom, cinnamon, star anise, chillies, asafoetida, fennel, tamarind, saffron, fenugreek seeds

Meat – lamb, mutton, goat or chicken are popular choices but not eaten in large quantities (beef and pork are often forbidden for religious reasons)

Fish and shellfish – in coastal areas, including scallops, prawns, crab

Dairy products – milk, yoghurt, buttermilk, paneer (a type of cheese), ghee (clarified butter)

Rice – basmati

Pulses and beans (dried) – red split lentils, whole green lentils, black eyed beans, chickpeas, red kidney beans

Nuts – peanuts, cashew nuts, almonds

Sugar cane – jaggery (unrefined sugar made from sugar cane juice that is reduced and set into blocks)

Indian signature dishes

Samosas – stuffed deep fried pastries

Pakoras – piece of vegetable or meat, coated in seasoned batter and deep-fried

Bhajis – small flat cake or ball of vegetables, often onion, fried in batter

Curry – dish of meat, vegetables, etc., cooked in an Indian style sauce of strong spices (examples include: rogan josh, vindaloo, korma, dopiaza, pasanda)

Chana masala – a chickpea curry

Saag aloo – spinach with potatoes

Dhal – pureed legumes

Raitas – yoghurt salads

Breads (roti) – Poppadums, poori, naan, paratha, chapati

Rice dishes – Biryani, pilau (or pilaf)

Chutneys and pickles – eg tomato chutney, mango chutney; lime pickle

Kulfi – a type of Indian ice cream with subtle spice flavouring

Specialist equipment

Tandoor – a clay oven

Karhai – a deep bowl shaped frying pan

Chapatti tava – a flat pan on which chapatti bread is cooked

▲ Samosa

▲ Dhal

▲ Poppadums

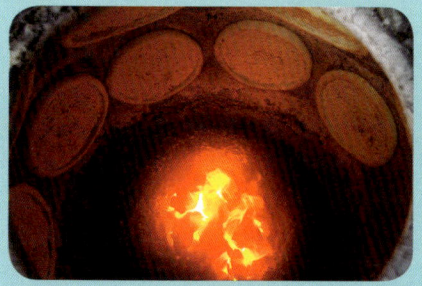

▲ Tandoor

Factors affecting food choice Culture and religion, p137

115

ASIA

Southeast Asia

Some typical ingredients

Vegetables – carrots, cucumber, lettuce, beansprouts, sweet potatoes, yams, onions, garlic, mushrooms, water chestnut, bamboo shoots, pandan leaf, long beans, potatoes

Fruits – coconut, rambutans, mangosteens, banana, papaya, pineapple, citrus fruits, durian, star fruit, jackfruit, lychee, sour plums

Spices and herbs – kaffir lime leaves, lemongrass, galangal, curry leaves, chilli, cardamom, cinnamon, cloves, pepper, ginger, nutmeg, mace, turmeric, coriander, cumin, caraway, dill, fennel, Thai basil

Meat – beef, pork, buffalo, chicken

Fish and shellfish – fresh and salt water sources

Eggs

Tofu

Tempeh (fermented soya bean cake)

Rice

Cassava

Corn

Noodles – rice, wheat

Beans – black, yellow, soya

Peanuts, candlenuts

Sesame seeds

Lard

Flavourings:

Spicy shrimp paste (various names such as Belacan or Rojak)

Rempah – an aromatic paste used to flavour foods (can contain herbs spices, shrimps, nuts)

Tamarind

Soy sauce

Fish sauce

Check it

Write a list of the most popular herbs and spices used in Asian cookery.

Southeast Asian signature dishes

Indonesia

Satay – strips of meat or fish on skewers coated in spices and grilled, served with a peanut sauce

Gado gado – vegetable salad arranged in layers with peanut sauce

Nasi goreng – rice fried in spices and served with vegetables and sometimes meat

Beef rendang – a dry, spicy beef curry, cooked slowly for hours in coconut milk

Tempeh – fermented soya bean cakes

Sambal – a relish

Malaysia

Bubur (also called congee) – a porridge using coconut milk with vegetables and meats

Laksa – a spicy noodle soup with vegetables and often fish

Nasi lemak – coconut rice with chilli, fried anchovies, peanuts, hard boiled egg and cucumber

Char koay teow – flat rice noodles, stir fried over very high heat with beansprouts, vegetables and prawns

Roti chanai – a thin griddle bread often served with vegetable curry or lentil dhal

Roti jala (net bread) – a type of lacy pancake made on a griddle

Cendol – green, chewy, jelly like noodles mixed with coconut cream, palm syrup and pieces of ice

Thailand

Tom yum – hot and sour soup

Som tum – spicy green papaya salad

Pad thai – rice noodles with egg, beansprouts, tofu and peanuts

Gaeng keow wan gai – green chicken curry, cooked in coconut milk

Khao phat – Thai fried rice with added ingredients such as meat, egg, onions, garlic and flavourings such as soy sauce, chilli sauce, fish sauce

Vietnam

Hu tieu (Saigon soup) – chicken broth with rice vermicelli

Bot chien – fried rice flour dough balls served with slices of papaya, shallots and green onions, pickled chilli sauce and rice vinegar

Cha gio – rice paper spring rolls with noodles and vegetables

Cuon diep – lettuce rolls filled with protein and noodles

Cao lau – a pork noodle dish with thick noodles

Xoi – savoury sticky rice

Cambobia

Samlor kako – a traditional soup with spice paste, fish paste, fish, pork or chicken and vegetables

Khmer red curry – a spiced coconut milk curry, with lemongrass, beef, chicken or fish, aubergine, green beans, potatoes

Laos

Pho – rice noodle soup

Khao poon – rice vermicelli served with accompaniments and sauces

Khao niaow – sticky rice

Singapore

Hokkien mee – a noodle dish with seafood

Chilli crab – crab, sir fried in its shell with a sweet and sour tomato sauce

Hainanese chicken rice – poached chicken served with aromatic rice, broth, Chinese vegetables and dipping sauces

Specialist equipment

Pestle and mortar – for pounding spices and herbs, making pastes

Wok

Bamboo steamer

▲ Satay

▲ Som tum

▲ Pho

CORE KNOWLEDGE

ASIA

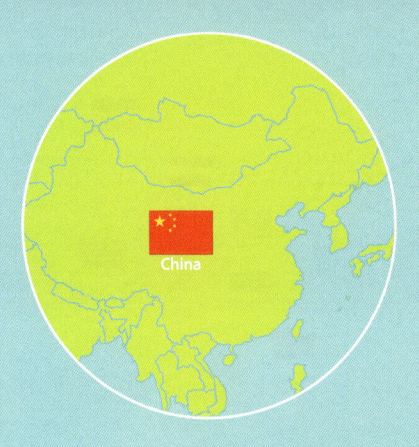

CULTURES AND CUISINES

China

Some typical ingredients

Vegetables – onion, garlic, chilli, spring onion, mushrooms, edamame beans, choi sum, bamboo shoots, water chestnuts, bitter melon, bok choi, Chinese broccoli, long beans, mooli, aubergine, lotus root, mange-tout, squash, taro

Fruits – lychee, apples, pears

Spices and herbs – five-spice powder, Sichuan peppercorns, ginger, fennel, cloves, star anise, coriander

Meat – pork, lamb, duck, chicken (all parts of the animal are eaten)

Fish and shellfish

Soya beans and by-products – milk, soy sauce (light and dark), tofu (curd), miso (paste)

Eggs

Rice, rice paper

Noodles (rice and wheat)

Nuts – cashew, peanut

Fermented black beans

Flavourings – Shaohsing rice wine, toasted sesame oil, oyster sauce, hoisin sauce, yellow bean sauce

Chinese signature dishes

Baozi – steamed filled buns

Dim sum – bite sized portions of food served in small steamer baskets or on small plates

Vegetable spring rolls

Sesame toast – bread brushed with egg and coated with minced prawn and sesame seeds, fried or baked

Peking duck – crispy skinned shredded duck with thinly sliced spring onion and cucumber, with a plum sauce, wrapped in thin steamed pancakes

Fried rice

Chow mein – stir fried egg noodles with vegetables and meat

Beef in oyster sauce

Dan dan noodles – a spicy sauce with vegetables and noodles

Spicy Sichuan-style prawns – stir fried prawns with a spicy tomato, ginger and chilli bean sauce

Specialist equipment

Wok

Bamboo steamer

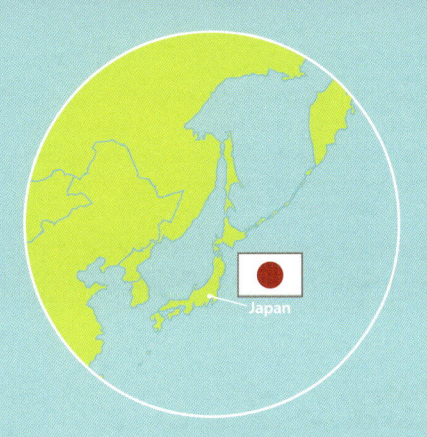

Japan

Some typical ingredients

Vegetables and fruits – yams, lotus root, red plums, cucumber, mushrooms (e.g. shiitake), mooli, bamboo shoots, aubergine, lotus root, cabbage, spinach, potato, carrot, onion, pumpkin, bitter melon, edamame beans

Herbs and spices – ginger, Japanese mint (shiso)

Kobe beef

Fish and shellfish – bonito tuna (often using dried flakes), eel

Egg

Rice – short grain sushi rice

Soba – buckwheat noodles

Udon – wheat noodles

Soya beans and by-products – milk, soy sauce, tofu (curd), miso (paste)

Sesame seeds – white and black

Panko – a type of breadcrumb

Flavourings – rice wine vinegar, shoyu (soy sauce), mirin, sake, wasabi (horseradish)

Seaweed – wakame, nori, kombu

Japanese signature dishes

Sushi – slices of raw fish, mixed with, wrapped in or atop cooked sushi rice (flavoured with vinegar)

Norimaki – cooked and vinegared sushi rice rolled in a sheet of nori (seaweed), often with fillings – served in a cylinder shape

California rolls – vinegared sushi rice rolled in a nori cone, with additional ingredients added, such as cucumber, crab, avocado

Sashimi – thin slices of raw fish (without rice)

Gyoza (pan fried dumplings)

Yakitori – seasoned chicken on skewers

Shabu-shabu – meat and vegetable one pot with dipping sauces

Miso soup

Vegetable tempura – pieces of vegetables in a light batter, deep fried

Teriyaki – a glaze of soy sauce, mirin, and sugar

Teppanyaki – the use of an iron griddle to cook food

Specialist equipment

Bamboo mat – for rolling sushi

Activity

Find out more about the different types of chilli. How is the heat from chilli measured?

▲ Peking duck

▲ Sushi

▲ Gyoza

SECTION 1

117

AFRICA

Africa

The African continent covers a large land mass, and contains over fifty countries. Many unique grains and vegetables originate from Africa, many found nowhere else in the world. African cuisine has many influences, such as from Arab traders, European colonisers and Asian immigrants. The foods cooked and served in Africa vary from country to country.

Many African meals are based around a starchy dish which is served with a meat or a vegetable stew or a soup. In some parts, grilled meats and smoked fish are also popular.

Some typical ingredients

Vegetables – cassava, yams, sweet potatoes, potatoes, onions, garlic, carrots, peas, okra, yams, plantain
Fruits – banana, pineapples, oranges, lemons, coconut, mangoes, dates, figs, apricots, quinces, plums, guava, tomatoes
Dried fruits – apricots, sultanas, raisins, prunes
Spices and herbs – saffron, nutmeg, cinnamon, cumin, cloves, paprika, cayenne pepper, ginger, aniseed, mint
Harissa – a hot sauce or paste of chilli peppers, paprika, and olive oil, used in North Africa
Meat – beef, lamb, goat and pork (in non-Islamic areas), chicken
Chicken
Fresh fish – red mullet, pilchards and anchovies
Salt fish
Grains – corn, wheat, sorghum, millet, barley, rice
Beans – red kidney beans, black eyed beans, broad beans, chickpeas and lentils
Peanuts, almonds, pistachio
Olives
Sugar cane
Palm oil, argan oil
Floral essences (rose, orange, geranium water)
Cocoa

▲ Couscous

African signature dishes

Flatbreads
Fufu – mash made with a starchy carbohydrate such as yam, maize, cassava, millet or potato

North Africa

Couscous – small particles of grain (can be semolina, sorghum, millet or barley), cooked by steaming, traditionally served with a meat or vegetable stew
Gueddid – mutton jerky
Tagine – a slowly simmered stew
Slata mechouia – salad with sweet, hot grilled peppers, tomatoes and onion
Kefta – spiced sausage shape meatballs, grilled on skewers
Zaalouk – aubergine salad
Kab el ghzal – almond paste-filled pastries

South Africa (Cape Malay cooking – a combination of Dutch and Malaysian cooking)

Bobotie – a savoury dish containing minced beef, nuts and curry powder
Biltong – sun dried meat
Peanut bread
Karkelinge – figure of eight cookies
Mealie meal – coarsely ground corn cooked to form a type of porridge

Mozambique
Fish and shrimp stew

East Africa
Steamed papaya

Egypt Injera
Ful Medames – fava beans served with oil, garlic and lemon juice
Mulukhiya – vegetable leaves, garlic and coriander and cooked in a meat based stock
Kunafa – sweet made of a very thin noodle-like pastry

Ethiopia
Injera – thick pancake-like sourdough bread with a spongy texture, often eaten with wat (a meat stew with red pepper)

Kenya
Cassava chips
Maandazi – fried bread, similar to doughnuts

Tanzania
Kashata – sweet peanut and coconut snack

Specialist equipment

Cast iron pot balanced on stones, or hung above, the fire. Cooking usually takes place outside.

▲ Kefta

▲ Biltong

▲ Kunafa

THE MIDDLE EAST

CULTURES AND CUISINES

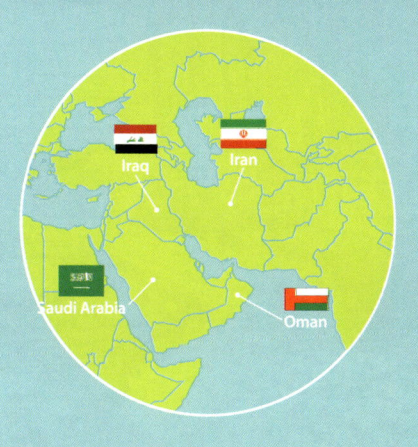

The Middle East

Some typical ingredients

Vegetables – courgette, onions, garlic, aubergines, radishes, peppers, squash, cucumber, okra
Fruits – figs, citrus fruits, grapes, pomegranates, tomatoes, avocado
Dried fruits – dates, apricots, sultanas
Spices and herbs – cinnamon, cumin, allspice, ginger, cardamom, cloves, mahlab, sumak, turmeric, saffron, coriander, mint, parsley, dill
Meat – lamb and mutton, goat (including offal)
Eggs
Yoghurt and cheese (lamb and goat)
Wheat (including a cracked wheat called burghul)
Filo pastry
Rice
Beans and pulses – chickpeas, yellow split peas and lentils
Nuts – almonds, pistachios, walnuts, pine nuts
Floral essences (rose, orange water)
Olives
Olive oil
Tahini (sesame seed paste)
Honey

Middle Eastern signature dishes

Mezze style dishes (snacks)
  Tabouli – salad made from cracked wheat, chopped herbs and fresh vegetables
  Baba ganoush – a dip made from pureed, grilled aubergine and tahini
  Hummus – a smooth garlicky dip made from chickpeas and tahini
  Āsh – thick main course soups that combine meats, vegetables, beans, herbs and spices
Kibbeh – meat and wheat paste balls filled with minced meat, spices and nuts
Khoresh – type of Iranian stew
Kofte – ground meat balls or sausage shapes
Shish kebab – meat cooked on a skewer
Fattoush – bread based salad, pitta bread combined with mixed greens and other vegetables and herbs
Falafel – bean or chickpea croquettes or balls, deep fried
Shawarma – roasted lamb cooked on a rotisserie
Breads (flatbreads) – naan, lavash, simit, pitta bread
Chelou – an Iranian rice dish, cooked with butter, saffron and yoghurt
Kookoos – Iranian omelette; thick and fluffy filled with meat or vegetables
Khoshaf – fruit salad made up of dried fruit
Halva – a popular sweet dish, made from a variety of ingredients, sometimes with dates and nuts
Sheer berenj – a milky rice pudding
Muhallabia – a creamy pudding, often served with flavourings such as pistachios and date syrup

Check it

What does the term 'mezze' mean? How is this similar to the Spanish term 'tapas'?

Key terms

Cuisine – a style of cooking.
Terrain – a stretch of land, typically referred to in reference to the characteristics of that land. For example, rough terrain.
Climate – the weather conditions typical to an area in general or at any specific time.
Culture – the way of life, the general customs and beliefs of a particular group of people at a particular time.
Fertile land – land or soil that is able to produce plentiful crops.
Migrate – when people or animals move from one geographical area to another
Standard of living – The measure of wealth, comfort and material goods typical of people in a community or region.
Traditions – customs, ways of living or beliefs that are recognised as very long established and typically passed from one generation to another over time.
Disposable income – the portion of income that a household or individual has left after tax has been deducted and that they are able to spend as they please.
Sustenance – food or drink that provides nourishment to sustain the body and life.
Staple food – food that forms a large part of the diet, usually from starchy foods.

SECTION 1

SECTION 1
CORE KNOWLEDGE

TECHNOLOGICAL DEVELOPMENTS

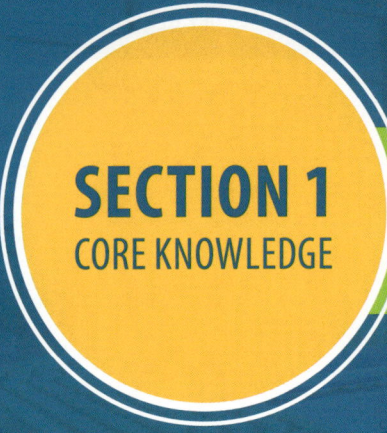

What will I learn?
- The factors affecting food technology
- The importance of new technologies on food production and processing
- The effects of food processing on food and drink
- The positive and negative health impacts of technological developments

▼ Technological developments within the food industry

Check it
What are the factors that affect the food we eat? Give examples of each.

Study tip
Know examples of different types of new technological developments within the food industry.

The factors affecting technological developments in food [FS]

New technologies in food production and processing are driven by:
- knowledge and new techniques gained from research
- attempts to increase efficiency
- attempts to reduce the effect of production on the environment
- competition between food companies
- consumer demand.

Innovation in food production, processing and new product development can offer benefits for consumers and the environment.

There have also been many technological developments in recent years that are now commonplace in the home, from refrigerators in the 1950s, domestic freezers in the 1970s to microwave ovens in the 1980s. Frozen and microwavable food and ready meals followed these developments. New technologies have given us a greater range of methods to package and store foods. This enables the preservation of nutrients and the extension of food product shelf life.

Today, factors affecting technological developments in food include:
- Population increase
- Transport and travel
- Preservation methods
- Media
- Environmental factors
- Economic understanding and trade
- Scientific advancements
- Consumer demand
- Changes in work / leisure time
- Wider understanding of nutrition, diet and health

120 CORE KNOWLEDGE

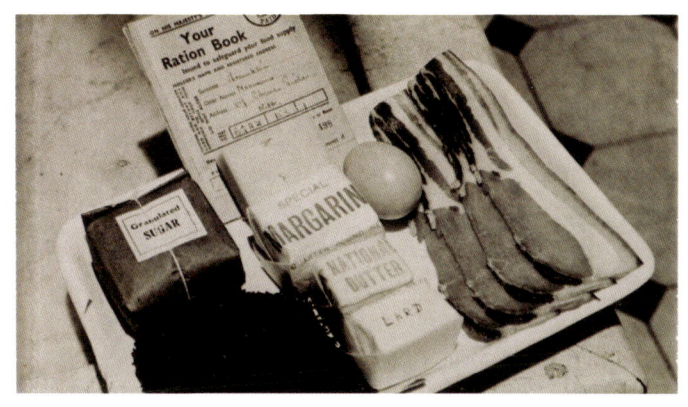

TECHNOLOGICAL DEVELOPMENTS

In many parts of the world, eating habits have changed dramatically during the twentieth century. Food was seen simply as a source of **energy**. However, these days people want food to be a sensory, cultural and social experience, and not just fuel our bodies but to enhance our health and well-being.

Innovation in food production, processing and new product development can offer benefits for consumers and the environment. However, fewer resources, population growth and **climate change** are all putting pressure on the world's food supply.

Population increase

A country's ability to feed itself depends on three factors: availability of arable land, accessible water and population pressures. The more people there are, especially in poor countries with limited amounts of land and water, the more resources are needed.

The population of the UK is increasing with migration being a key factor. The change in **demographics** of the UK means immigrant communities have dramatically changed the kinds of food we eat. In almost every UK town or city you will see global food influences. For instance, you will see shops and restaurants offering foods from China, India, Italy, Korea, Japan, USA or Mexico. Some of this food comes from chain restaurants with global domination, but mostly it is the product of small restaurants and food shops run by first- or second-generation immigrant families that have come to the UK to set up.

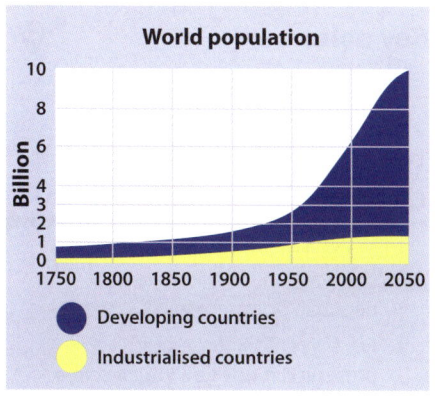

▲ How does the weekly food ration from the Second World War compare to many families' food habits today?

Check it
Name 4 technological developments that you can find in a home kitchen. How have these impacted on the foods we eat?

▲ Global population increases

Key point
Changes on the high street mirror the changing demographics of the UK.

Activity
Look at your local high street, and using a map or diagram show how the food shops/takeaways have changed over the past 5 years (size, type, nationality, chain or privately owned). Give 5 reasons why you think this change has occurred.

▲ Global food influences in the UK

Check it

Large scale food distribution lowers the overall cost of products, but it can have negative effects on the foods we buy. How many can you mention?

▲ Large scale distribution

Key point

Preservation extends the shelf life of a product, but it can also change its flavour, colour or texture.

Check it

1. Name 4 different preservation methods and list positive and negative points for each.
2. Fresh vs cold (refrigerated) vs preserved food? Can you describe each method in terms of price, availability, and its impact on the environment?

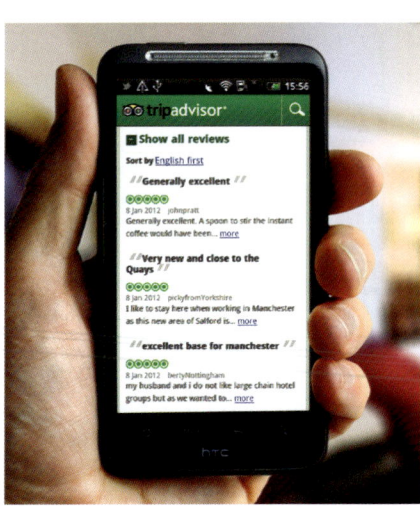

▲ Customers can read or write reviews on hotels and restaurants using their phone or tablet

Transport and travel

Changes in food processing and distribution, such as freezing and refrigerated transport, contribute to the longer distances over which foods can be transported and still remain fresh. Food distribution is now dominated by a few large groups, who have the buying power to be able to set the price of many products.

In recent years, however, consumer concern about **food miles** and CO_2 production has boosted interest in local food production. Consumers also value the opportunity to support their local economy by buying local.

New technologies do have the potential to make our roads and transport systems greener and efficient, for instance using new biofuels or drones to deliver food parcels.

Improvements in travel have helped the transport of food as well as people. It is now possible to travel all over the world and try different food. Immigrants who come to the UK bring with them foreign foods and traditions to be absorbed into our way of life.

Preservation methods [FS]

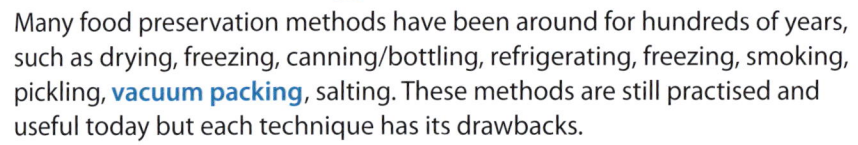

Many food preservation methods have been around for hundreds of years, such as drying, freezing, canning/bottling, refrigerating, freezing, smoking, pickling, **vacuum packing**, salting. These methods are still practised and useful today but each technique has its drawbacks.

In recent years demand has increased for minimally processed foods which retain their freshness. New techniques have replaced methods that rely on heating and drying.

Modified atmosphere packaging (MAP) is a way of extending the shelf life of fresh food products. The technology substitutes the air inside a package with a protective gas mix. The gas in the package helps ensure that the product will stay fresh for longer.

High Pressure Processing (HPP) is a cold **pasteurisation** technique by which products already sealed in a package are subjected to a high level of pressure transmitted by water. HPP is a natural, environmentally friendly process that respects the ingredients and helps maintain the fresh food characteristics like its natural flavours, colours and textures. It improves nutrient retention and extends the shelf life of products.

Media

Consumers obtain their information from adverts on these forms or media, provided by the manufacturer or supplier. The traditional media (television, radio, newspapers and magazines) used to play a crucial role in conveying information and influencing consumers. However, with the rise of social media and the use of tablets and smartphones, companies are switching to personal conversation with the customer. Consumers access personal technology 24/7 and have the ability to directly influence food retailers, restaurants and even product manufacturers. Social media has changed food advertising and purchasing patterns.

Apps and barcodes

Applications (apps) are having a huge impact on food production and consumption. For example a user rating function on such sites as TripAdvisor® allows consumers to pass on their personal views to other users. Consumers are willing to search for information and best deals rather than rely entirely on what manufacturers and suppliers tell them in their adverts.

TECHNOLOGICAL DEVELOPMENTS

Most food outlets have a web page where customers can order or rate products and services. This can have a substantial influence on businesses: as much as 50% of all retail is influenced by digital in some way. Many organisations are capitalising on the power of social media to interact directly with consumers and get their message across. For instance, Public Health England have developed their Sugar Smart app, allowing you to find out how much sugar a particular food contains.

Modern technology allows for better information capture and transfer in other areas. **Barcodes**, the machine-readable codes consisting of numbers and a pattern of parallel lines of varying thickness, printed on a commodity are used especially for stock control. **Quick response codes (QR codes)** placed on products can be scanned with a smartphone. This then links directly to information or the product's website. QR codes are used primarily for the marketing and advertising of products, brands, and services.

Ordering a takeaway via an app is now becoming common place, and recent innovations have taken this a stage further. For instance, customers can now choose their meal but order it in the form of pre-weighed ingredients and a recipe that they can then follow to cook the meal themselves.

Programmes influence consumers

Television is still a great medium for passing information, influencing consumers to buy advertised products and launching trends. Programmes such as The Great British Bake Off, Come Dine with Me, Saturday Kitchen, and celebrity chefs such as Jamie Oliver and many more have had a tremendous impact on the nation's food knowledge. In some cases they have even had a positive influence on legislation, for instance in 2009 Jamie Oliver successfully campaigned against childhood obesity by improving school meals standards.

However, there is growing concern over the possible negative effect that adverts on television could have on children's choices, leading them to choose the unhealthy option. This has led to some foods not being advertised during children's programmes, but with the rise of TV on demand and changing viewing habits, how effective might those advert bans really be? (For more on advertising, see p.144.)

Environmental factors

Increased food production is one of the greatest causes of environmental degradation worldwide. Basically we need to produce more food with less environmental impact. In meat production for instance, current methods to rear animals directly raises water and air pollution. These processes increase carbon dioxide emissions. Crop production for animal feed and the use of land for grazing threatens biodiversity and wildlife species.

Crop production negatively affects the environment as the use of pesticides, artificial fertilizers and other chemicals pollutes the environment and threatens wildlife species.

Progressive climate change will gradually reduce the amount of land available for habitation, as some regions experience desertification and others permanent flooding from rising sea levels. This will only increase the pressure on what land there is available to produce even more food.

The overall aim should be to produce more food with less environmental impact. **Sustainability** is the term used to describe food production that aims to preserve the world's natural resources for future generations.

▲ QR code being scanned using a smartphone app

Study tip

Summarise how customer demand has changed school meals in recent years.

▲ Popular apps such as JustEat allow customers to use their phone to easily and quickly order from a massive range of different menus.

▲ Over-farming can have a massive impact on the environment

Key point

Large scale food production has a major impact on the environment. Responsible and sustainable practices offset that impact.

Study tip

Learn the definitions of 'organic', 'climate change' and 'sustainability'.

Make sure you can explain how the environment is affected by food production (small scale or mass production).

Check it

1. Can you discuss the advantages and disadvantages of locally produced foods and globally sourced foods?
2. Why are organic foods seen to be good for the environment?

Fewer resources, population growth and climate change are all putting pressure on the world's food supply. Challenges include:

- sustainable, affordable food supply and demand
- stability in food supplies
- achieving global access to food and ending hunger
- reducing the impact of food production on the world's ecosystems.

Solutions to the problem with food production and its effects on the environment may be choosing locally produced food (as less fossil fuel is used for its transportation) or choosing organic over non-organic food. **Organic foods** are those produced without the use of chemicals. The benefits are that it dramatically reduces water use and decreases soil and air pollution.

New technologies have enabled the development of new farming methods to help increase food production. **Hydroponics** is a method of growing plants in a soil-less medium or an aquatic based environment. It uses mineral nutrient solutions to feed the plants in water. Some of the positive aspects of hydroponics include: [FS]

- the ability to produce higher yields than traditional, soil-based agriculture
- allowing food to be grown and consumed in areas of the world that cannot support crops in the soil
- eliminating the need for large scale use of pesticides.

Lettuce hydroponic ▶

Research and development of food ingredients

Food developers and food scientists alter the genetic makeup of foods to develop plants that are resistant to diseases and produce a bigger yield. Genetically modified (GM) foods are derived from organisms whose genetic material (DNA) has been modified through the introduction of a gene from a different organism.

Most existing genetically modified crops have been developed so:

- Consumers benefit from improved nutritional value, non-allergenic foods and cheaper foods, etc.
- Farmers benefit financially from improved yields.
- Food distributors, such as supermarkets, benefit financially from the longer shelf life of products.
- Less developed countries benefit from higher crop yields and crops which can grow in normally barren soil.

GMO and GMF [FS]

Genetically modified organisms (GMO) are organisms (i.e. plants, animals or microorganisms) in which the genetic material (DNA) has been altered in a way that does not occur naturally by mating and/or natural recombination. The technology is often called 'modern biotechnology' or 'genetic engineering'.

CORE KNOWLEDGE

Genetically modified foods (GMF) are developed to produce a product with a lower price, greater benefit (in terms of durability or nutritional value) or both. GM foods currently available on the international market have passed safety assessments and are not likely to present risks for human health.

In the future, genetic modification could be aimed at altering the nutrient content of food, reducing its allergenic potential, or improving the efficiency of food production systems. For example scientists are developing a breed of cows that produce lactose-free milk for lactose intolerant consumers.

There are however three main concerns:

1 Genetic engineering raises many moral issues, particularly involving religion, which questions whether man has the right to manipulate the laws and course of nature. Some religions object to the intervention of mankind in an otherwise 'natural' process of evolution.

2 Consumers worry that the results of genetic modification could harm the environment and pose a danger to humans.

3 Nature is a fragile and complex system which links many species in the food chain. Some scientists believe that introducing genetically modified genes may have an irreversible effect with consequences yet unknown. For example, if genes 'escaped', we could end up with fast growing insects and 'super weeds'.

Food labelling alerts consumers to the presence of genetically modified ingredients that might cause concern to some people on ethical grounds.

Labelling of GMF is not required for foods in which the inserted gene has been destroyed by processing, and is therefore absent from the final product. However, food from genetically modified organisms must be clearly labelled if:

- it contains a copy gene originally derived from a human being
- it contains a copy gene originally derived from an animal which is forbidden by some religions, e.g. pigs for Muslims or Jews
- it is a plant or microbial food containing a copy gene originally derived from any animal.

New foods

Technology has also allowed manufacturers to develop and introduce 'new' food ingredients, such as **Textured Vegetable Protein (TVP)** and **mycoprotein**. The use of **biotechnology** and **nanotechnology** is increasing too, and increases in the use of biotechnology by the food industry are due to:

- competition between food companies for an increased market share
- attempts to increase efficiency and reduce the environmental impact of production
- consumer demand for convenient, high quality products at reasonable cost.

Manufacturers also look at products that are available now but have not yet fulfilled their full potential. For example, food developers have worked with **soya beans** as they are a low fat source of protein. They are free from cholesterol and soya protein can lower a person's overall cholesterol levels. Soya beans, which grow in pods, are an equal source of protein to animal foods and can be used in many ways – whole beans, soya sprouts, soya milk, soya sauce, tofu and miso.

TECHNOLOGICAL DEVELOPMENTS

Facts and figures about GM crops

- In the UK and Ireland, most people have probably eaten some GM food products as ingredients.
- Of the 2.6m tonnes of soya imported into the UK last year, nearly two-thirds was genetically modified (Royal Society UK, 2009).
- No GM crops have been grown in the UK or Ireland, except for research purposes.

▲ How would you like your tomato? Enhanced, or as nature intended it?

▲ Fried-bamboo-caterpillar

▲ Functional foods provide additional or enhanced benefits in the diet

▲ Blueberries contain phytochemicals shown in their blue colouring

Unusual new foods N

Food developers are looking at expanding the protein found in **insects** for the food market outside Asia (where they are commonly eaten). Insects are full of protein and rich in essential micronutrients, such as iron and zinc. They don't need as much space as livestock, emit lower levels of greenhouse gases, and have a high feed conversion rate: a single kilogram of feed yields 12 times more edible cricket protein than beef protein. Insect meal could also replace some of the expensive ingredients (e.g. soya beans and fishmeal) that are fed to farm animals, potentially lowering the cost of livestock products and freeing up feed crops for human consumption.

Food manufacturers also process **seaweeds** as ingredients in many foods as they are one of the most nutritionally dense plants, and also the most abundant source of minerals. This is because as seaweeds grow they have access to all the nutrients in the ocean.

Functional foods N FS

Functional foods deliver additional or enhanced benefits over and above their basic nutritional value. Some functional foods are generated around a particular functional ingredient, for example foods containing probiotics, prebiotics, or plant stanols and sterols. Functional foods and drinks may provide benefits in health terms, but should not be seen as an alternative to a varied and balanced diet and a healthy lifestyle.

Examples of functional foods include:

Probiotics are live bacteria and yeasts promoted as having various health benefits. They are usually eaten in yoghurts or taken as food supplements, and are often described as 'good' or 'friendly' bacteria.

Prebiotics are a source of food for probiotics to grow, multiply and survive in the gut. Prebiotics are fibres which cannot be absorbed or broken down by the body and therefore serve as a great food source for probiotics to increase in numbers. Prebiotics by nature do not stimulate the growth of bad bacteria or other pathogens.

Stanols and **sterols** are found in a range of plant foods such as cereals, vegetable oils, seeds and nuts. They work to reduce the absorption of cholesterol in the gut so more of it is eliminated through digestion. This in turn helps to lower total cholesterol levels in the blood, and in particular LDL-cholesterol (the bad cholesterol).

A range of dairy foods fortified with plant stanols and sterols is available to help reach the amount needed to lower cholesterol. These include fortified milk, spreads, yoghurts and yoghurt drinks. These products are generally more expensive, however.

Phytochemicals are natural compounds found in plants (vegetables, fruits, and legumes) which contribute to the plant's aroma, taste and other characteristics. For instance they give onions their distinct flavour, blueberries and tomatoes their distinct colour, and chilli peppers their burning hot taste. They do not contribute nutrients, but contain biologically active components that affect our bodies in healthy ways. They also act as antioxidants.

Phytochemicals may reduce the risk of a wide range of ailments. They are thought to be largely responsible for the protective health benefits of plant-based foods and beverages, beyond that of their vitamin and mineral contents. This dietary approach to health appeals to many because it is a natural alternative to medication. Consumers want these products to be more readily available.

TECHNOLOGICAL DEVELOPMENTS

Fortification involves the addition of nutrients to foods including some that were originally present in the food.

They might be added to:

- replace nutrients lost during food processing
- produce a substitute product with similar nutritive value
- bring in extra nutrients that would not normally be there, e.g. added fibre in yoghurt or folic acid in breakfast cereals.

Adding nutrients to foods, particularly staple foods, can increase intakes among most of the population. In countries where intakes of certain nutrients are very low, fortification can help to reduce nutrient deficiency diseases. There may also be some technical benefits such as increasing the shelf life of the product.

In the kitchen **molecular gastronomy** blends physics and chemistry to transform the tastes and textures of food. The result can be a new and innovative dining experience. The term molecular gastronomy is commonly used to describe a style of cuisine in which chefs explore culinary possibilities by borrowing tools from the science lab and ingredients from the food industry. [FS]

▲ Heston Blumenthal, a leading chef in molecular gastronomy techniques: bacon and egg ice-cream, anyone?

Key point

Functional and fortified foods have a higher nutritional value than the original products.

Check it

1. List the key nutrients added to fortify breakfast cereals.
2. Name 2 diseases that eating fortified cereals may help to reduce.
3. What is molecular gastronomy? Give an example.

Study tip

You need to know the difference between functional and fortified foods.

Can you discuss the health benefits of a diet containing fortified or functional products?

Activity

1. Summarise the health benefits of fortifying breakfast cereals.
2. Research recipe ideas that can be adapted using TVP or mycoprotein. Assess the cost difference.
3. Collect a label from a fortified food product and highlight the fortification and explain its requirement in the diet.

Check it

Compare and contrast Fairtrade products with products that have low food miles. What are the positive and negatives aspects of buying either one?

Key point

The economy of many communities depends upon their trade in food commodities.

Activity

1. What is meant by the provenance or traceability of food? Why is it important?
2. Compare and contrast the positive and negatives or buying a product which is fair trade to a product which has low food miles.

▲ Nanotechnology used within plastic food containers

Economic understanding and trade

Economic understanding and trade can affect the varieties and the quality of foods available for purchase, the prices consumers pay, the information consumers receive about a product, and consumer confidence in the food supply.

For instance, when a customer decides to buy a **Fairtrade** item, they are making a statement supporting better wages, decent working conditions and fair terms of trade for farmers and workers. In the UK other schemes have been set up to assure consumers of the quality of products, such as Farm Assured, Soil Association or RSPCA Assured.

▲ Economic trade using quality assurance.

Buying from local farmers markets or local independent producers puts money back into the local economy. Customers know the **provenance** or traceability of their food. In addition, food miles decrease and less CO_2 is produced in transporting the food to the end consumer.

Scientific advancements

Innovation in food production, processing and new product development can offer benefits for consumers and the environment. The availability of new techniques in biotechnology and genetic research provides an opportunity to control cell metabolism and breeding. This makes it possible for developers to meet more specific requirements, e.g. to increase a specific nutrient in a food.

Scientific advancements in nanotechnology are leading the way in the preservation of food products. Nano particles of silver have anti-bacterial properties and were first used in medical settings. However they have been adapted to the food industry and are used on:

- kitchen tools and tableware
- preparation surfaces
- plastic food storage containers
- plastic wrap
- dish clothes to kill bacteria
- to extend the shelf life of food.

Nanotechnology is also used to produce active and intelligent packaging which features temperature and time gauges that show the consumer if an item is stored correctly and if the product is within its use-by date and safe to eat.

Automation

Automation in the food industry has moved far beyond simple labelling machines or conveyor belts. Thanks to significant developments in areas such as gripper technology, hygienic design and intelligent image processing, there is now huge potential for the use of robots in food processing, production and handling. The benefits of using robots is that they work fast and reliably and actually improve efficiency and product consistency.

One example of this comes from China, where a café in Ningbo has invested in robot waiters that cost £7000 each, and has them waiting on tables. The robots navigate their way around the restaurant using advanced optical sensing systems, and are very popular with diners, especially children, who want to be served by them.

Vending machines that dispense food and drink have been around for years. New generation vending machines can do much more, for example they can serve up fresh pizza: the machine kneads the dough, sauces the pizza, adds toppings (from a choice of three), and heats the pizza in an oven, all in less than three minutes. Another new vending machine on the market dispenses French fries. It stores frozen fries and when an order comes in, it will flash fry them for two minutes then season them before serving.

Activity

1 Compare and contrast the positive and negative points of GM foods.
2 How can robotic technology improve food production?

▲ Automation in the food industry

Consumer demand

'Necessity is the mother of invention' and so it is in the food industry. As consumers' expectations and tastes change, they make new demands that the food industry must answer. So if in the past customers might have been satisfied with cheap, convenient foods, now they still insist on convenience but also want foods that are fresh (less processed and less packaged), healthy and all natural (no preservatives), without a perceived negative (no high fat, high salt, and high sugar content). And they are willing to pay for this.

Consumers are also becoming more concerned about the amount of waste in the food supply chain. New packaging and developments in food technologies are aimed at extending the shelf life and quality of food. For example, there is a new type of packaging film that is bio-degradable compostable film. It is designed to significantly increase the shelf life of fresh produce, including sensitive, high respiration products like strawberries and potatoes. It could save consumers money by significantly reducing the amount of food they throw away. It could also save the fruit and vegetable industry large sums of money in wastage costs by extending the amount of time products stay fresh on shelves.

▲ About 33% of all food produced ends up being wasted.

Check it

List the 6 changes large food chains have made in response to customer demand.

Concerns for the welfare of animals and humans in food production have also influenced the types of foods available and how they are produced.

Requests from consumers for specific product characteristics like grass-fed or organic

Retailers pass on request to packers to meet customer demands

Packers ask producers for livestock with desired characteristics of a specific stock

Producers raise animals to satisfy customer and consumer needs for a specific stock

▲ A typical kitchen in the 1960s

Changes in work and leisure time

Many of us are no longer willing to spend scarce leisure time preparing elaborate meals. Our food has to be quick and convenient to prepare, as well as healthy and tasty. Finally, we expect our food to be reasonably priced. In short, our demands include: tasty, safe, cheap, healthy, available all year round, 'as natural as possible', varied, and sometimes elegant or exotic foods!

In the 1960s, households prepared most of their own food and consumed it at home. Today, more preparation is being performed by food manufacturers and less at home. This development has been facilitated by the use of technological innovations in preservation, packaging, freezing, artificial flavourings and ingredients, and by the use of microwaves.

OTHER FACTORS THAT HAVE LED TO THE POPULARITY OF CONVENIENCE FOODS INCLUDE:

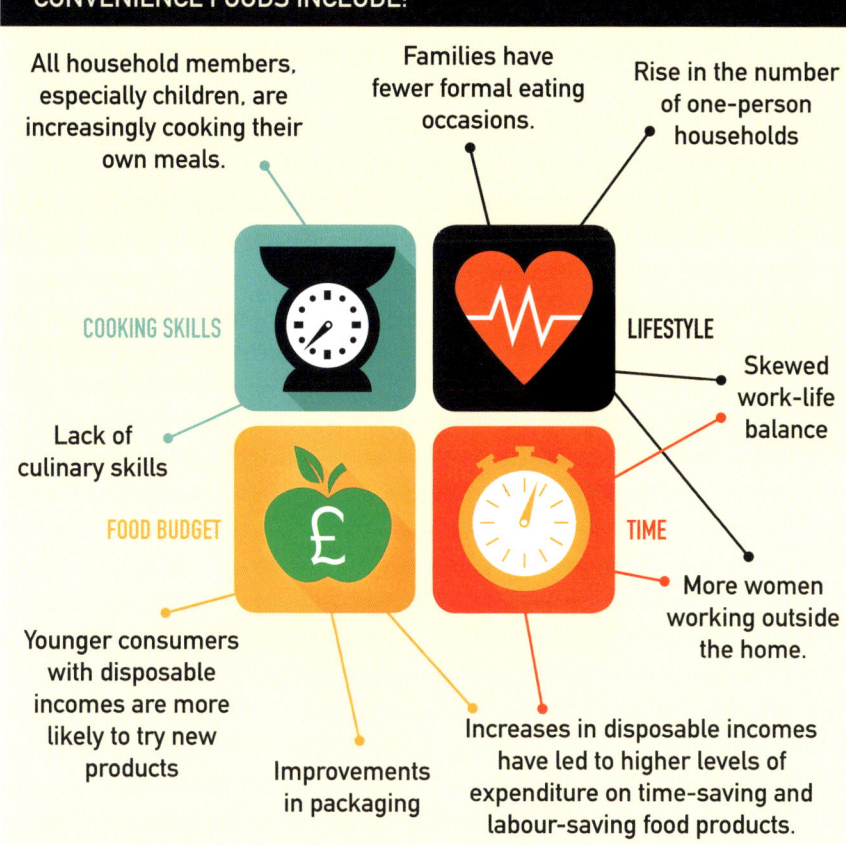

- All household members, especially children, are increasingly cooking their own meals.
- Families have fewer formal eating occasions.
- Rise in the number of one-person households

COOKING SKILLS
- Lack of culinary skills

LIFESTYLE
- Skewed work-life balance

FOOD BUDGET
- Younger consumers with disposable incomes are more likely to try new products
- Improvements in packaging

TIME
- More women working outside the home.
- Increases in disposable incomes have led to higher levels of expenditure on time-saving and labour-saving food products.

Convenience foods offer many benefits, including less time spent planning meals and grocery shopping, less preparation time, fewer leftovers (with single-portion foods), and generally being easier to clean up. Convenience foods also provide options for those who don't like to cook, have limited cooking skills or ability, or have poor or no kitchen facilities. However, processed convenience foods generally have a low nutritional quality compared to other foods. This is because of the sodium, fat, and/or added sugars they contain, along with low amounts of essential nutrients.

Wider understanding of nutrition, diet and health

Greater consumer awareness of nutrition, diet and health has led to new areas of food manufacture and the creation of food products with modified nutritional composition. One example of this is low fat products: low fat spreads, low fat dairy products and low calorie drinks.

The government has run campaigns and initiatives to encourage and enlighten consumers about healthy eating. These include:

- Eatwell Guide
- Change4Life – Eat Well, Move More, Live Longer
- Be food smart
- 5-a-day
- Healthy school meals
- Livewell – NHS Choices
- Eat Better Feel Better
- New labelling guidelines on packaged food

▲ Government initiatives to help promote and educate a healthy lifestyle

---

TECHNOLOGICAL DEVELOPMENTS

Check it
1. Why have convenience foods become popular over the past few years?
2. How has the change in working/leisure time changed the eating habits of families?

Activity
Many food products are convenience foods, not just microwave dishes. Look in your cupboards at home or in a supermarket and make an inventory. Discuss your findings.

Check it
1. List the key reasons for technological developments within the food industry.
2. Identify factors which have affected the development of food technology.

Activity
1. Discuss how new technological developments have changed the food we eat.
2. Look online to find images showing how food was produced 50 years ago and in the present day and discuss the pros and cons for each method.
3. Is bigger better? Discuss the advantages and disadvantages of buying food from:
   a Large supermarkets
   b Farmers markets
   c Online retailers

Key terms

Climate change – a large-scale, long-term shift in the planet's weather patterns or average temperatures.

Sustainability – describes human activity that is not harmful to the environment and does not deplete natural resources, thereby supporting long-term ecological balance.

Preservation – keeping something in its present state or preventing it from being damaged.

Environmental factors – the impact of human activities on the natural environment.

Demographics – the statistical data on a population.

Food miles – a measure of the distance food travels between the place where it is produced and the place where it is consumed.

Vacuum packing – a preservation method that removes all the air from a food container or package before sealing, particularly oxygen which causes degradation.

High Pressure Processing (HPP) – a processing method that subjects food to elevated pressures (with or without the addition of heat) to render bacteria inactive.

Pasteurisation – the process of heating a food to a specific temperature for a specific period of time in order to kill microorganisms that could cause disease, spoilage or undesired fermentation.

Application (app) – a self-contained program or piece of software designed to fulfil a particular purpose, especially as downloaded by a user to a mobile device.

Barcode – a small image of lines (bars) and spaces on retail store items, identification cards and postal mail to identify a particular product number, person, or location.

Quick response code (QR Code) – a two-dimensional barcode that can be read by smartphones and links directly to text, emails, websites, or phone numbers.

Organic food – any food that is grown or made without the use of chemicals.

Hydroponics – the growing of plants in a soil-less medium, or an aquatic based environment.

Genetically modified organisms (GMO) – organisms whose genetic material (DNA) has been altered by mating and/or natural recombination.

Genetically modified foods (GMF) – foods derived from organisms whose genetic material has been modified.

Textured Vegetable Protein (TVP) – vegetable protein, especially from soya beans, that is used as a substitute for meat, or is added to it.

Modified Atmospheric Packaging (MAP) – food packaging that changes the internal atmosphere of the packet, normally reducing the amount of oxygen present to slow down food decay.

Mycoprotein – protein derived from fungi, especially as produced for human consumption.

Nanotechnology – the science of manipulating materials on an atomic or molecular scale.

Biotechnology – the manipulation (as through genetic engineering) of living organisms or their components to produce useful usually commercial products, e.g. pest resistant crops.

Soya bean – an Asian bean plant.

Insect – any small arthropod animal that has six legs and generally one or two pairs of wings.

Seaweeds – large algae growing in the sea or on rocks below the high-water mark.

Functional foods – foods that have a positive effect beyond basic nutrition, such as boosting optimal health or reducing the risk of disease.

Probiotics – live microorganisms which when taken in adequate amounts confer a health benefit.

Prebiotics – promote the growth of particular bacteria in the large intestine that are beneficial to intestinal health and also inhibit the growth of bacteria that are potentially harmful to intestinal health.

Fortification – adding an ingredient to a food that fortifies or protects it.

Molecular gastronomy – the scientific study of the physical and chemical processes that occur while cooking.

Fairtrade – a partnership between producers and consumers: selling on Fairtrade terms provides farmers with a better deal and more income. This allows them the opportunity to improve their lives and plan for their future.

Provenance – the place where food originates, i.e. where is it grown, raised or reared.

Convenience food – food that needs little preparation, especially food that has been pre-prepared and preserved for long-term storage.

Phytochemicals – a group of plant-derived compounds supposedly responsible for disease protection.

EXAM QUESTIONS

1. Consumers are increasingly aware of nutrition, diet and health. This has led the food industry to develop new technologies for the manufacture and formulation of products. Discuss your understanding of this statement by giving one example of a food product now on the market.
   Product [1]
   [6]

2. Technological developments and health awareness pressures are two of the driving forces that have led to the development of different types of milk.
   Outline how each of these driving forces has led to the development of different types of milk:
   Technological developments [4]
   Health awareness pressures [4]

3. Identify and describe one innovative technological development that is used to help reduce wastage of fresh fruit and vegetables. [3]

4. There is an increase in the number of functional foods available for consumers to purchase.
   a. What is meant by the term 'functional food'? [2]
   b. Give an example of a functional food that is available in supermarkets. [1]

5. Many companies produce a range of fruit juices using high pressure processing.
   a. State three advantages of high pressure processing to producers and/or consumers.
   Advantage 1
   Advantage 2
   Advantage 3 [3]
   b. List one food product, other than fruit juice, that is produced using high pressure processing. [1]

6. Alison, aged 50, is slightly overweight and has been diagnosed with high cholesterol. She has been advised to adapt her diet to cope with her cholesterol. At the supermarket, she picks up three tubs of margarine to read their nutritional information labels.

Nutritional Information (Typical Values)

Flora Light	Per 100g	Per 10g portion	% per 10g portion
Energy	1158kj/281kcal	116kj/28kcal	1%
Fat	30g	3g	4%
-of which saturates	6.4g	0.6g	3%
-monounsaturates	7.7g	0.8g	
-polyunsaturates	16g	1.6g	
Carbohydrates	2.8g	<0.5g	<1%
-of which sugars	<0.5g	<0.5g	<1%
Protein	1%	<0.5g	<1%
Salt	1.3g	0.13g	2%
Vitamin A	753 µg (90% NRV)	75.3 µg (9% NRV)	
Vitamin D	7.5 µg (150% NRV)	0.75 µg (15% NRV)	
Vitamin E	10 mg (80% NRV)	1 mg (8% NRV)	
Omega-3	3.1g	0.31g	
Omega-6	12g	1.2g	

Nutritional Facts

Flora pro-activ	Per 100g	Per 10g portion	% per 10g portion
Serving Size		10g	
Serving per container		25	
Calories		224kj/54kcal	
Total Fat	60g	6g	9%
Saturated Fat	12g	12g	6%
Sodium	1g	0.1g	2%
Total Carbohydrate	<0.5g	<0.5g	<1%
Sugars	<0.5g	<0.5g	<1%
Protein	<0.5g	<0.5g	<1%
Vitamin A	788µg (100% NRV)	78.8µg (10% NRV)	
Vitamin D	7.5µg (150% NRV)	0.75µg (15% NRV)	
Vitamin E	19mg (160% NRV)	1.9mg (16% NRV)	
Omega-3	4.7g	3.1g	N/A
Omega-6	25g	2.5g	N/A

Nutritional Information (Typical Values)

Flora Original	Per 100g	Per 10g portion	% per 10g portion
Energy	1672kj/405kcal	167kj/41kcal	2%
Fat	45g	4.5g	6%
-of which saturates	10g	1g	5%
-monounsaturates	11g	1.1g	
-polyunsaturates	23g	2.3g	
Carbohydrates	<0.5g	<0.5g	<1%
-of which sugars	<0.5g	<0.5g	<1%
Protein	1%	<0.5g	<1%
Salt	1.4g	0.14g	2%
Vitamin A	753 µg (90% NRV)	75.3 µg (9% NRV)	
Vitamin D	7.5 µg (150% NRV)	0.75 µg (15% NRV)	
Vitamin E	15 mg (130% NRV)	1.5 mg (13% NRV)	
Omega-3	4.6g	0.46g	
Omega-6	19g	1.9g	

Which margarine product would you advise her to purchase?
Margarine: [1]
Why? [4]

If Alison was a vegetarian, could you give her the same advice? Why or why not? [3]

TOTAL: 33

SECTION 1
CORE KNOWLEDGE

FACTORS AFFECTING FOOD CHOICE

What will I learn?

- The range of factors that influence food choice
- The choices that people make about foods according to culture, religion, ethical beliefs, or for medical reasons
- How to make informed choices to achieve a varied and balanced diet

▲ Supermarket (top picture) and smaller independent store

Check it

1. How does food availability vary for different people in different parts of the UK?
2. What effect does food availability have on the consumer?

What makes us choose the foods we do?

In the UK we are fortunate to have a wide variety of foods available to us: we do not all choose to eat the same food and the reasons for this are varied. The main factors that affect food choice are:

- Availability
- Cost
- Culture
- Religious beliefs
- Ethical food choices
- Seasonal food
- Medical conditions
- Marketing and advertising
- Labelling

Food choice is influenced by a range of factors including time of day, enjoyment of particular foods or the occasion being celebrated. Individual dietary needs will also be significant as people's food choice will depend on gender, age group and activity level.

Not everyone enjoys the same food and one of the most important factors for food choice is personal preference. Some of the main ways in which this can be influenced are through opportunities to try foods from a young age, the family culture you grow up in, where you live and your (or your family's) religious beliefs.

Availability

Not everyone has the same access to food. It can depend on a number of factors such as:

- whether the food is grown locally or whether it needs to be imported.
- the climate and terrain available for food to be grown.
- the types of shops that are available.

134 CORE KNOWLEDGE

Towns and cities will have a wide variety of large supermarkets offering a range of products, often at competitive prices. By comparison, people living in more rural areas may have to drive long distances to access these facilities or instead, must rely on smaller shops where stock is limited and often sold at a premium price.

Cost

Food prices in the UK are linked to global prices and the following factors can cause food prices to rise:

- Increase in global population
- Increase in agricultural costs
- Increase in fuel costs, affecting production and transport
- Political unrest, e.g. wars
- Change in the weather and climate
- Change in buying habits

There is often speculation about rising food costs, and there are many reasons for changing food prices such as those listed above. Even though media concern has highlighted rising food costs, families in the UK actually spend approximately 15% of their income on food compared to about 33% in 1957. According to the Office of National Statistics Family Food Survey 2014, the average spend per person per week is £9.14 on eating out and getting takeaways. That's on top of the £26.27 spent on weekly groceries, including drinks.

Despite worries about a rise in the cost of living and food costs in particular, modern Britain has a firm culture of choosing to eat outside of the home, a cost that wasn't even measured in the 1957 Food Survey, due to eating out being considered a luxury at that time.

▲ Small scale food production cannot cope with global pressures on food

Food poverty

For some, rising food costs are more than a passing concern: 4 million people in the UK are affected by food poverty. **Food poverty** means that an individual or household isn't able to obtain healthy, nutritious food, or can't access the food they would like to eat. Despite the increasing choice and affordability of food in the UK, many people eat what they can afford, not what they want.

What are the effects of food poverty?

- Restricted food choice resulting in poor diet.
- Diet related diseases such as heart disease, obesity, diabetes and cancer.
- Inadequate levels of many vitamins and minerals.
- Rise in malnutrition.
- Children from poorer families experiencing hunger and problems accessing food during school holidays.

The role of food banks

Food banks are meeting a very real need in the UK. A 2014 report by Oxfam UK, the Trussell Trust and Church Action on Poverty revealed that 350,000 food parcels were provided to people in the UK who could not afford to feed themselves – more than double the number from the previous year. However, food banks are only a short term solution, providing food to families in times of need. They provide a minimum of 3 days nutritionally balanced, non-perishable food in exchange for food vouchers.

Milk (UHT or powdered)
Sugar (500g)
Fruit juice (carton)
Soup
Pasta sauces
Sponge pudding (tinned)
Tomatoes (tinned)
Cereals
Rice pudding (tinned)
Tea bags/instant coffee
Instant mashed potato
Rice/pasta
Tinned meat/fish
Tinned vegetables
Tinned fruit
Jam
Biscuits or snack bar

▲ Foods provided to Trussell Trust food bank users

▼ A leading UK low-cost supermarket; coupons and vouchers

Study tip

Know how food costs can be reduced through smart choice of ingredients and cooking methods.

▲ Microwave ovens reduce the amount of time needed to cook food, so less energy is used

Activity

Meat is a popular ingredient in many family meals. However, it can increase the cost of a recipe. Research the price of different cuts of meat and produce a recipe that could be used to feed a family of four on a limited budget. Explain why you have chosen the recipe.

How can we save money when buying food?

Many people on a limited budget have to plan the amount of money they are going to spend on food carefully. Often this leads them to buy cheaper products which are highly processed and contain higher quantities of fat and sugar. There is a common misconception that healthy foods are more expensive, but good planning and food knowledge can ensure that even those shopping on a limited budget can still eat nutritious meals.

How to food-shop economically:

- Compare food prices on the Internet, e.g. mysupermarket.com.
- Buy foods from low-cost supermarkets.
- Choose supermarket own brands or value lines which are cheaper than other brands.
- Take careful advantage of 'special offers' in the shops, e.g. buy one get one free or half price. These are especially good for fruit and vegetables and encourage people to include a greater variety in their diet. However, don't be tempted to buy products you don't need – or that you know you can't consume within the use-by date – as these will be wasted, making the deal less cost-effective.
- Use coupons, vouchers or collect loyalty points from shops.
- Plan your meals before you go shopping, and stick to the list.
- Avoid buying more food than you need, check dates on food and eat by the 'use-by' or 'best before' date to avoid waste.
- Buy foods that are in season locally, when they are cheaper, because they are plentiful and have lower transport costs.

How can we save money when cooking food?

- Plan meals so that leftovers from making one meal can be used for another, e.g. use leftover carrots from a casserole to make carrot and coriander soup.
- Use cheaper cuts of meat and offal such as liver, belly pork, breast of lamb and beef brisket.
- Use quick methods of cooking, e.g. microwave, to reduce the amount of energy used.
- Make food in large batches to avoid ingredients being wasted and then freeze for use at a later date, e.g. chilli con carne or Bolognese.
- Use leftover food to create meals, e.g. mashed potato to make the filling for a corned beef pie or fish cakes.
- Make meals at home rather than buying takeaway foods and ready meals, which can be more expensive, especially if cooking for a family.

CORE KNOWLEDGE

Culture and religion

Culture refers to the ideas, customs, and social behaviour of a particular people or society. The type of food we eat, how we prepare the ingredients to make a certain dish and how we consume and share it, reflects the culture of who we are and where we are from.

Culture and religion are often linked. Some religions have dietary food laws that limit food choices or forbid eating certain foods. Some rules are limited to certain celebrations and festivals, whilst others are continually observed.

Christianity
The Christian religion does not forbid any foods; however, there is a tradition that fish is eaten on Fridays instead of meat.

Judaism
In order to meet Jewish dietary laws, food must be **kosher**, meaning 'clean' or 'proper'. Kosher rules ensure that:
- Meat and poultry has been slaughtered in a special way.
- Pork and shellfish are forbidden.
- Meat and dairy products must not be prepared or eaten together. Separate cooking equipment should also be used.

Islam
Food must be **halal**, which means that animals have been slaughtered in the Islamic way, according to the rules set out in the Qur'an.

Muslims are not permitted to eat pork, pork products, lard or gelatine. They are also forbidden from drinking alcohol or eating food which contains alcohol.

Hinduism
Beef is a forbidden food, as Hindus believe the cow is sacred. Although other meat is allowed, many Hindus follow a vegetarian diet. Strict Hindus will avoid onions, mushrooms, garlic, tea and coffee.

Buddhist
As Buddhist teaching preaches against killing, many Buddhists are vegetarian, although some will eat fish.

Sikh
The food laws for Sikhs are less strict than those of Hindus and Muslims. Beef is the only forbidden meat and they must avoid alcohol.

Rastafarian
Rastafarians must eat foods that are natural and clean, and some choose to follow a vegetarian or vegan diet. They will eat fish but it cannot be more than 30cm long, and food is prepared without salt and usually cooked in coconut oil. Rastafarians do not drink alcohol.

Check it
1. What global factors affect the price of food?
2. Suggest 3 reasons for the increased popularity in eating out and getting takeaway?
3. How can a family reduce the amount they spend on food through:
   a Smart shopping?
   b Cooking meals at home?

Check it
1. How are culture and food choice linked?
2. What foods are forbidden in the following religions?
   a Judaism
   b Islam
   c Hinduism
3. Are there any similarities between the food rules followed by the main religions?

Extension
Identify a culture of your choice and investigate the importance of food within that culture. Suggest reasons why the foods you have identified are part of that culture. You could also try making a dish that you have found in your research.

Carry out a survey of the meals available at your favourite restaurant to identify the dishes that would be suitable for people with religious dietary restrictions.

ETHICAL FOOD CHOICES

Intensive farming or **factory farming** is a way of meeting consumer demands for reasonably priced food in plentiful supply. Food production by this method has been increased by growing high-yield crops, removing other plants and pests and adding fertiliser to the soil. Other intensive farming practices include keeping animals indoors, often in restricted spaces, e.g. hens in battery cages. Many of these practices have unwelcome side effects such as increased risk of disease, lower quality products and ethical concerns over the welfare of animals.

Free range (picture above) is a production method associated with eggs and meat, and it means that unlike intensive methods of farming, the animals are not confined to an enclosure for 24 hours each day, having at least some time each day when they can roam freely outdoors.

Organic farming is an alternative way to produce food without the use of fertilisers, herbicides or pesticides. These are replaced with more 'natural' methods. 'Organic' also means that foods are free from **trans-fats**, GM food and most additives.

Advantages of organic production:

- Some believe this produces higher quality food with greater nutritional benefits such as vitamins and minerals.
- Many people think that it tastes better.
- It doesn't raise as many ethical concerns, as animals have more space.
- There is less environmental impact, as organic food tends to travel less distance.
- It relies on crop rotation, a more sustainable method of production than intensive farming. Alternating crops every year prevents the different pests and diseases that affect certain plants from getting established in the same location, therefore avoiding the need for pesticides.

Disadvantages of organic production:

- Food produced organically tends to be more expensive as the yield is lower than with intensively produced food.
- Organic food is more labour intensive to produce.

How is food produced?
Farm assured

Farm Assured means that the farms have met robust standards of food safety and hygiene, animal health and welfare and environmental protection and are inspected annually to ensure those standards are being met. In the UK, foods display the Red Tractor logo as a sign of farm assurance. The logo also means that the product has met strict standards through the whole of the food chain and products can be traced back to the farms they came from. It is used by major UK retailers, many branded manufacturers and food service operators. Red Tractor was established in 2000 and is the largest farm and food assurance scheme in the UK.

FACTORS AFFECTING FOOD CHOICE

Genetically modified

Genetically modified or GM food involves scientists pinpointing the individual gene which produces a desired outcome, then extracting it, copying it and inserting it into another organism. It is used in crops such as tomatoes and maize, and it is thought that it will be introduced into animal products in the future.

Advantages of GM foods:

- ✔ More plentiful food supplies – most existing GM crops have been developed to increase yield, through the introduction of genes that are resistant to plant diseases or are more tolerant of herbicides.
- ✔ Plants are able to grow in more hostile environments than normal.
- ✔ Food can be grown more cheaply.
- ✔ In the future, genetic modification could be aimed at altering the nutrient content of food such as reducing its allergenic potential.
- ✔ Products can be produced with a longer shelf life, which aids transportation.

Disadvantages of GM foods:

- ✘ Altering the DNA of plants has been very controversial with some people feeling that we shouldn't be tampering with nature.
- ✘ It is not possible to identify GM food and labelling of this information is not always clear.
- ✘ There is concern it will lead to new allergy outbreaks and other health risks.
- ✘ Cross-pollination, leading to a mix of non-GM and GM crops.

▲ A genetically modified tomato

Ethical food choices

Our food comes from a wide range of sources and due to the rise in global population levels the amount of food that needs to be produced has also risen. For many years changing production methods have been developed to cope with the increasing demand. However, many consumers are now taking an interest in the way their food products have been produced and are paying attention to the ethical considerations of the way they shop.

Fairtrade

Fairtrade changes the way trade works through better prices, decent working conditions and a fairer deal for farmers and workers in developing and **lower economically developed countries (LEDC)**. This enables them to have more control over their lives and decide how to invest in their future, and maintain their livelihood.

There is a wide range of food products that are certified as being Fairtrade such as coffee, cocoa, bananas, rice and sugar. By choosing Fairtrade products the purchaser makes a decision to try and support not only farmers and their families, but also the communities that they live in. The premium attached to Fairtrade products means that the additional money raised from products can be invested, by the farmers themselves, into community development such as schools, health care, transport and sanitation.

▲ Fairtrade bananas

Activity

Investigate the range of Fairtrade products available in the UK, and compare their prices to the non-Fairtrade alternatives.

Check it

1. How does intensive farming differ from free range farming?
2. List three advantages and three disadvantages of organic farming
3. What is genetically modified food? What are the concerns about it?
4. How might genetically modified food benefit food production?
5. List 5 Fairtrade food products available in UK supermarkets.
6. How does Fairtrade help farmers in LEDC?
7. What are food miles?
8. How can we reduce the number of food miles our food travels?

Extension

According to projections by the National Farmers Union, on current trends the UK will reach a tipping point in about 25 years, beyond which a majority of our food will have to be imported, unless governments take strong action to improve food production and protect consumers from a future of relying on food brought from abroad.

Self-sufficiency in food in the UK has been eroding since the 1980s: about 60% of food currently consumed here is grown in the UK, down from nearly 80% in the mid-1980s, even though more varieties of food previously thought exotic are now grown in the UK.

Source: *The Guardian*, 24 February 2015

1. Discuss why you think the UK is becoming less self-sufficient in food production.
2. How could consumers be encouraged to eat more locally produced food?

Food miles

Food miles is the phrase used to describe a way of calculating how far food has travelled to get to the consumer. It encompasses other terms such as 'from farm to fork' or 'field to plate', and makes us think about where the food we eat really comes from.

In the UK our food travels 30 billion miles a year. Food miles not only include the distance that food travels to reach the UK, but also transportation to the factory, from the factory to the shop, from the shop to our homes and even removing the waste foods away from homes and to landfill. Food can travel to the UK by plane, boat or road and all of these methods can cause pollution, so measuring food miles allows us to consider the environmental impact of our food choices and their effects on the environment.

▲ Carbon footprint symbol

It is possible to reduce the amount of food miles our food travels by buying food locally. Walking to the local shop or getting the bus rather than driving can also help to reduce the 'food mileage' effect. Composting and recycling packaging, where possible, is another way of reducing the environmental impact of our food. This reduces the amount of waste that needs to be taken to the landfill sites and again helps to cut pollution.

Reducing food waste can have a dramatic effect on reducing the **carbon footprint** of our food – i.e. the amount of carbon dioxide produced by all aspects of the product's production and consumption.

Seasonal food

When we visit the supermarket we often take for granted the range of products available to us. However, we don't often stop to think about where the foods come from and whether or not they are in season. Seasonal food means the foods that are available at different times of the year in the UK, according to their growing season. When considering seasonal foods we most often think of fruits and vegetables, although meat and fish also have seasons.

There are a number of benefits to eating more local, seasonal food:

- To reduce the energy needed to grow and transport the food we eat, which also reduces carbon emissions.
- To avoid paying more for food that has had to travel further.
- To support the local economy.
- Seasonal food is fresher and so tends to be tastier and more nutritious.

CORE KNOWLEDGE

FACTORS AFFECTING FOOD CHOICE

SEASONAL FOOD

Fruit and vegetables that are grown in the UK throughout the year

Spring

March: Spring greens

May: Asparagus, Rhubarb

April: Cauliflower

Summer

July: Cucumber, Curly lettuce Cherries

June: Peas, Broad beans Strawberries

August: Raspberries, Kos lettuce, Plums

Autumn

September: Courgettes, Blackberries, Runner beans

October: Sweetcorn Cox's apples

November: Potatoes Red cabbage

Winter

December: White cabbage Brussels Sprouts

January: Carrots, Kale

February: Leeks, Savoy cabbage

Check it

1. What is seasonal food?
2. List three benefits of choosing seasonal food.
3. Produce a recipe for each season that includes at least one seasonal ingredient.

SECTION 1

141

▲ Pulses and beans are a good source of iron

▲ Foods high in saturated fat increase the risk of coronary heart disease

Medical conditions

Some people need to control their diet due to a medical condition. This has to be taken into consideration when planning meals for the following diets:

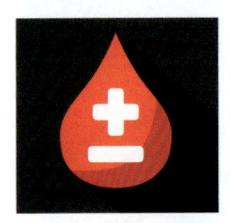

Diabetics should follow the same healthy eating guidelines as recommended for the general UK population; ensuring their diet is high in starchy carbohydrates and fibre-rich foods, and low in fat and sugar. Non-insulin-dependent (type 2) diabetics must follow a healthy diet to control their blood sugar levels.

Coronary heart disease (CHD) is a preventable disease caused by the coronary arteries, which supply blood to the heart, becoming blocked. This can be caused by eating too much saturated fat, especially from animal sources, which increases the cholesterol in the blood stream.

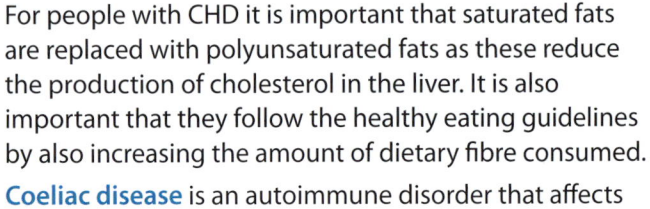

For people with CHD it is important that saturated fats are replaced with polyunsaturated fats as these reduce the production of cholesterol in the liver. It is also important that they follow the healthy eating guidelines by also increasing the amount of dietary fibre consumed.

Coeliac disease is an autoimmune disorder that affects the lining of the gastrointestinal tract. It is important that someone who is coeliac avoids eating the protein gluten which is found in wheat, and some other cereals like rye and barley. Eating these foods causes damage to the villi in the small intestine and can prevent nutrients from being absorbed.

Gluten-free alternatives to a range of products are now available, e.g. bread, biscuits and cakes. They are able to include alternative starches such as rice, potatoes, millet, corn and quinoa.

As with other **allergies** and **intolerances** it is important that food labelling is checked before consuming any foods that may include potentially harmful ingredients.

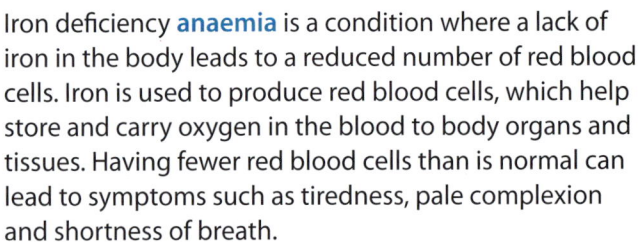

Iron deficiency **anaemia** is a condition where a lack of iron in the body leads to a reduced number of red blood cells. Iron is used to produce red blood cells, which help store and carry oxygen in the blood to body organs and tissues. Having fewer red blood cells than is normal can lead to symptoms such as tiredness, pale complexion and shortness of breath.

Including the following foods in the diet can boost low iron levels.

- Dark green leafy vegetables, such as watercress and curly kale
- iron-fortified cereals or bread
- brown rice
- pulses and beans
- nuts and seeds
- meat, fish and tofu
- eggs
- dried fruit, such as apricots, prunes and raisins.

FACTORS AFFECTING FOOD CHOICE

Calcium deficiency is a condition in which there is inadequate calcium intake, which can lead to depleted calcium stores in the bones, thinning and weakening of the bones, and osteoporosis. The body also needs calcium to keep the heart beating and the brain functioning. When we don't have enough of it in our diets, the body takes it from our bones. Unfortunately, most people do not know how it feels to be deficient in calcium so the first they will know about a calcium deficiency is when they suffer an unexpected bone fracture.

To prevent conditions such as osteoporosis it is important to eat a diet that includes foods high in calcium such as dairy products like milk, yogurt and cheese. Calcium is also found in fortified soy and rice drinks, fortified juice, and fish like sardines, where you eat the bones. While some vegetables like leafy greens have calcium in them, this form of calcium is not well absorbed by the body.

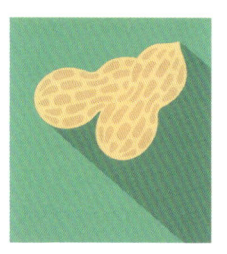

Nut allergies, like other food allergies, can cause a reaction when the food is eaten or touched. A reaction can happen in minutes or develop over a number of hours. Reactions to peanuts or nuts can result in **anaphylactic shock**, which can be life threatening. Once diagnosed it is important that nuts and all traces of nuts are excluded from the diet at all times.

Dairy intolerances can be caused by either the protein in dairy products or specifically the milk sugar (lactose). Lactase is needed by the body to break down lactose found in dairy foods. People with lactose intolerance don't produce enough lactase, so lactose stays in the digestive system where it is fermented by bacteria, leading to the production of various gases, which cause symptoms such as a bloated stomach and diarrhoea. Someone suffering from a dairy intolerance should avoid milk and milk products and choose alternative dairy products like soya milk.

Study tip

You need to know what medical conditions call for a special diet.

Make sure you know what foods should be avoided.

Check it

1. What changes should a diabetic make to their diet?
2. What foods should someone suffering with coronary heart disease reduce in their diet?
3. What is coeliac disease? What foods should someone who is coeliac avoid eating?

Extension

Choose one of the medical conditions discussed and produce a day's meal plan. Explain why you have chosen each of the dishes and discuss any changes you made to ensure it suits the medical condition chosen.

Diet and good health: Special diets pp58–59

MARKETING AND ADVERTISING

What will I learn?

- What information is available to consumers about food choice
- How marketing and food labelling influence food choice

Marketing

The food industry invests large amounts on advertising its products, and supermarkets alone spent over £450 million on advertising in 2014. **Advertising** highlights the range of products available to consumers, whilst **marketing** covers the strategies companies use to sell their products.

To ensure that the products made are going to be popular, companies will carry out **market research**. This can involve finding out the range of food products being produced by rival companies and identifying the target market for the product.

Market research can include:

- Primary research – this is research carried out directly for the development of a product, and can include tasting sessions, questionnaires and telephone surveys.
- Secondary research – this research is gathered from existing information available on websites and from research reports.

Marketing techniques are also employed within supermarkets to ensure that products are highlighted to customers. This is called **product placement**, and it can involve techniques such as placing products on prominent display such as on the end of an aisle or at the entrance to the store.

Other ways of increasing customer interest in a particular product include the distribution of money off coupons, in store tasting sessions and special offers such as buy one get one free (BOGOF) and three for two.

Advertising

Advertising is big business – wherever you go you will see adverts for a variety of products and services. Ways of advertising include:

- Television
- Internet
- Billboards
- Shop windows
- Buses and trains
- Newspapers and magazines
- Cinemas
- Leaflets
- Using celebrities to endorse products.

A large proportion of these adverts are for food and drink items and most are designed to target the group or groups of people who are most likely to buy these products. Advertising is regularly aimed at children, as through '**pester power**' they often have the ability to influence food and drink purchases made by the family.

However, since 2007 new rules have been introduced to prevent the advertisement of food and drinks classified as being high in fat, sugar and salt during television programmes aimed at any young person under the age of 16. This is in response to concerns about the rise in childhood obesity.

Activities

1. Explain how companies can use primary and secondary research to help develop new products.
2. Discuss ways that supermarkets could use marketing and advertising to increase sales of healthy option foods.

Extension

Collect a range of advertisements for foods. Discuss who they are aimed at and what techniques have been used to encourage consumers to buy the product.

Check it

Make a list of different ways that foods can be advertised.

How is advertising controlled?

The rules surrounding advertising are covered by the Advertising Standards Agency (ASA). This is an independent body which monitors and regulates the advertising industry. The ASA investigates any complaints about adverts in many different formats that include billboard posters, cinema adverts, adverts on television and radio or in magazines, newspapers and leaflets. It states that all advertising should be legal, decent, honest and truthful.

Action by the ASA

August 2012
"Cola Capers", part of an online game produced by Swizzels Matlow sweet manufacturers, was banned for encouraging poor nutritional habits.

February 2013
A Weetabix app was banned on grounds of it exploiting children's naivety and vulnerability.

May 2014
TV advert for Benecol yoghurt drinks were found to be misleading and had made unauthorised health claims.

▲ Colourful advertising attracts children

Check it
What is the difference between advertising and marketing?

Activities
Describe how effective the following are in encouraging people to make food choices that will improve their health:
1. Current government-led campaigns
2. In-store supermarket advertising

Labelling

Food labelling information can be a useful tool for consumers when they are choosing between different products. The aesthetic appeal of the label and packaging is also important and can attract customers to choose a particular product.

How does labelling affect food choice?

- It can provide consumers with nutritional information to allow them to make choices based on the fat, sugar, salt or fibre content. This is especially helpful for consumers who have health conditions and need to monitor their nutritional intake.
- People who have food allergies rely on food labelling to ensure they choose foods that are safe for them to eat.
- It provides information on how to store and cook the product to ensure the food can be prepared as intended, e.g. 'This product is not suitable for microwave cooking.'
- It helps consumers make decisions about which product is the best value for money'.
- It provides information on animal welfare and environmental issues so that consumers can choose products that meet their ethical beliefs.
- It allows people to avoid certain foods or ingredients based on their cultural or religious beliefs.
- It provides information on the food's origin so that consumers who want to choose local or British products are able to make an informed choice.
- It gives information about volume or quantity, so that when choosing ingredients for a recipe customers know they are buying the correct amount.

WHAT DOES LABELLING SHOW?

The Food Labelling Regulations 1996 require certain information to be given on all pre-packed foods. The following information must appear on the front of packaged food:

The **name** of the food

Quantity information; weight or volume

Country of origin

A 'BEST BEFORE' OR 'USE-BY' DATE

'Best before' dates are used for products that have quite a long shelf life e.g. breakfast cereals. After this date the product is still safe to eat, though its quality may deteriorate.

Vs

'Use-by' dates are generally used on perishable foods which will go off after the date stated. 'Use-by' indicates the food must be eaten by that date.

ANY SPECIAL STORAGE CONDITIONS

These tell you what is the best way of storing the food and whether it should be kept in the fridge or freezer.

ANY NECESSARY WARNINGS E.G. ALLERGIES

There are 14 main allergens which, from 2014, must be labelled on pre-packaged food when used as ingredients. These are celery, cereals containing gluten, crustaceans (including prawns, crabs and lobsters), eggs, fish, lupin, milk, molluscs (including mussels and oysters), mustard, nuts, peanuts, sesame seeds, soya beans, sulphur dioxide and sulphites.

The **lot number**

A LIST OF INGREDIENTS

If there are more than 2 ingredients they should be listed in descending order of weight, i.e. largest amount first.

Instructions for use or cooking, if necessary

The **name and address** of the manufacturer, packer or seller

Quantitative Ingredient Declaration (QUID)

This can be useful to the consumer as it requires the quantity of an ingredient used in a food product to be shown as percentage, which can help when comparing products, for example:

	Cheese and bacon quiche	Cheese and bacon quiche (economy)	Cheese and bacon quiche (luxury)
FILLING	75%	70%	78%
PASTRY	25%	30%	22%

146 CORE KNOWLEDGE

FACTORS AFFECTING FOOD CHOICE

NUTRITION LABELLING

Nutritional information on the label can help you make healthier eating choices. Since 2014 there have been new European regulations on food labeling, controlling all the information on food labels from nutrition labelling and the ingredients list, to the size of the writing used.

What do nutrition labels on food include now?

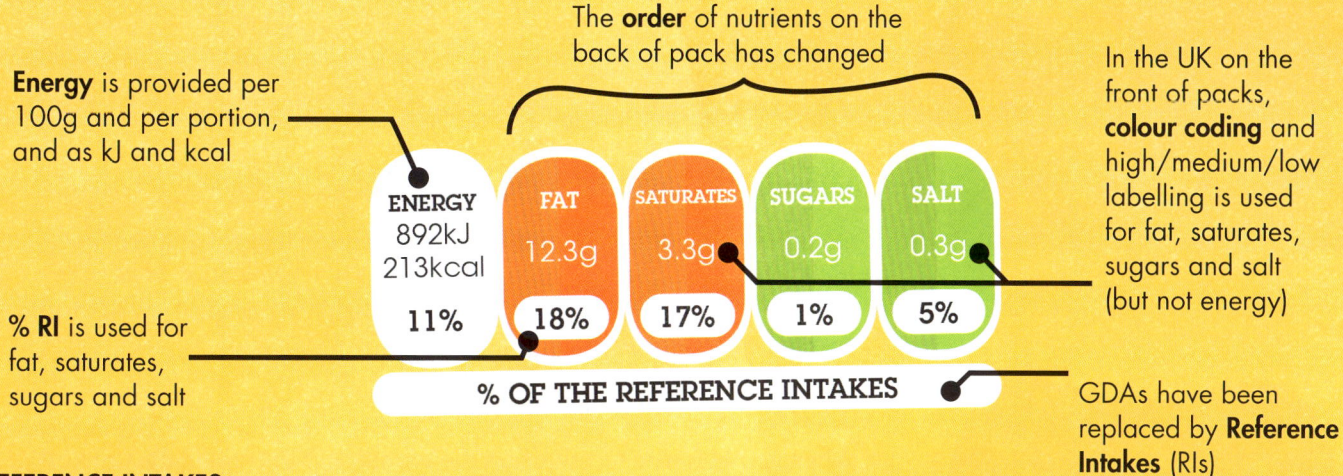

Energy is provided per 100g and per portion, and as kJ and kcal

The **order** of nutrients on the back of pack has changed

In the UK on the front of packs, **colour coding** and high/medium/low labelling is used for fat, saturates, sugars and salt (but not energy)

ENERGY	FAT	SATURATES	SUGARS	SALT
892kJ 213kcal	12.3g	3.3g	0.2g	0.3g
11%	18%	17%	1%	5%

% OF THE REFERENCE INTAKES

% RI is used for fat, saturates, sugars and salt

GDAs have been replaced by **Reference Intakes** (RIs)

REFERENCE INTAKES

The term 'Reference Intakes' (or RIs) has replaced 'guideline daily amounts' (GDAs), which used to appear on food labels.

Unless the label says otherwise, RI values are based on an average-sized woman doing an average amount of physical activity. The values are maximum amounts. They are not individual recommendations and your needs may be different to the RI, depending on your age, gender and how physically active you are.

These are useful guidelines based on the approximate amount of nutrients and energy you need for a healthy, balanced diet each day.

REFERENCE INTAKES FOR ENERGY AND SELECTED NUTRIENTS (ADULTS)

Energy or nutrient	Reference Intake
ENERGY	8400kJ / 2000kcal
TOTAL FAT	70g
SATURATES	20g
CARBOHYDRATES	260g
SUGARS	90g
PROTEIN	50g
SALT	6g

The RI for total sugars includes sugars from milk and sugars contained in fruit, as well as added sugar.

This information can be expressed as a percentage of the Reference intake for that nutrient. Percentage Reference Intakes (%RIs) can be given:

by weight (per 100g)   by volume (per 100ml)   and/or by portion

If the percentage RIs are provided on a 'per 100g/ml' basis, food manufacturers have to include the statement 'Reference intake of an average adult (8400kJ/2000kcal)'

USING THE e MARK

Putting the e mark on labels allows food companies to export their products to other European Economic Area (EEA) countries without having to meet the weights and measures requirements of those countries.

Activities

1. List 5 pieces of information that must be included on a food label.
2. Why do companies often include nutritional information on labelling even though it is not compulsory?
3. Evaluate the importance of information given on food labelling.

SENSORY ANALYSIS AND TESTING

What will I learn?

- How sensory perception guides the choices that people make
- How taste receptors and the olfactory system work
- The sensory qualities of a range of foods and dishes
- How to set up preference taste testing panels

What is sensory perception?

Our experience of food is multi-sensory. We often take for granted that a food will look or taste a particular way, but it is a culmination of all of the senses and the signals that are sent to the brain that result in our **sensory perception** of the food.

Taste

When you eat, taste receptors on the tongue and the roof of your mouth send neural impulses which give your brain signals about taste. The four main tastes are sweet, salty, sour or bitter. Although in recent years a fifth taste has been identified called umami. Umami is a savoury taste; it is a subtle taste and blends well with other tastes. Most people do not recognise this taste unless attention is drawn to it. After eating Cheddar cheese or tomatoes, there may be a 'savoury' taste lingering – this is umami.

The average person has about 10,000 taste buds and they're replaced every 2 weeks or so. But as a person ages, some of those taste buds don't get replaced. An older person may only have 5,000 working taste buds. That's why certain foods may taste stronger to children and teenagers than they do to adults. Smoking also can reduce the number of taste buds a person has.

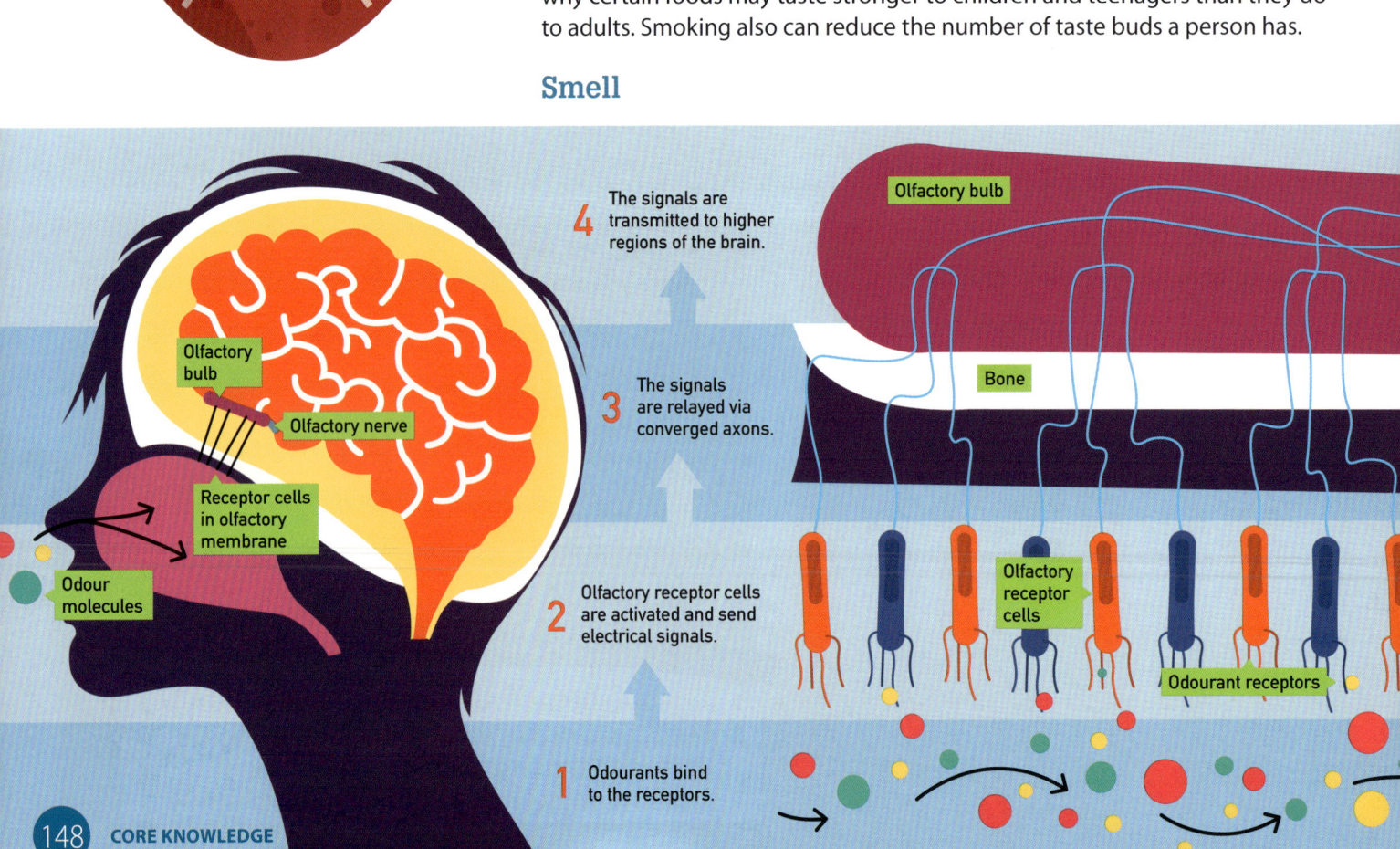

Smell

1. Odourants bind to the receptors.
2. Olfactory receptor cells are activated and send electrical signals.
3. The signals are relayed via converged axons.
4. The signals are transmitted to higher regions of the brain.

FACTORS AFFECTING FOOD CHOICE

You cannot however give taste buds all the credit for your favourite flavours, it's important to thank your nose. **Olfactory receptors** inside the uppermost part of the nose contain special cells that also send messages to the brain and help you smell. While you're chewing, the food releases chemicals that immediately travel up into your nose. These chemicals trigger your olfactory receptors. They work together with your taste buds to create the true flavour of that slice of pizza by telling the brain all about it.

When you have a cold or allergies, and your nose is blocked, you might notice that your food doesn't seem to have much flavour. That's because the upper part of your nose isn't clear to receive the chemicals that trigger the olfactory receptors (that inform the brain and create the sensation of flavour).

If you hold your nose when you eat something, you'll notice that your taste buds are able to tell your brain something about what you're eating – that it's sour, for instance – but you won't be able to pick the exact flavour until you let go of your nose.

Although the senses play an important role in determining our food preferences, and helping us to evaluate food, other factors are also involved. These include:

- previous experiences with food
- hunger and **satiety**
- mood
- where you eat, e.g. home, canteen, picnic
- beliefs and values, e.g. religion, culture and traditions
- social aspects, e.g. special occasions, events

Check it

Explain how taste receptors work.

Activity

1. What is meant by sensory perception?
2. Explain how olfactory receptors work.
3. What other factors affect food preference?

Extension

Find out about who discovered umami and produce a PowerPoint or leaflet to explain what umami is, giving examples of foods that have the umami taste.

Sensory descriptors

When analysing food products we use a range of vocabulary to describe each of the sensory qualities. Often these descriptors can be used to describe more than one of the food's attributes. This is because the senses are closely linked.

▲ Appearance and colour    ▲ Taste and texture    ▲ Smell or aroma 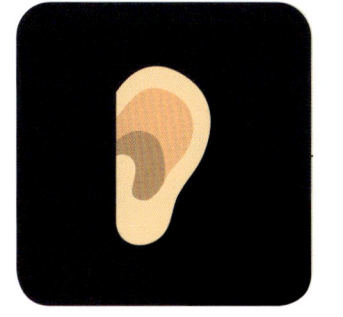   ▲ Sound

Below are some examples of sensory descriptors.

Taste	Texture	Aroma	Appearance	Sound
Spicy	Moist	Sweet	Colourful	Crunchy
Bland	Soft	Yeasty	Dull	Sizzling
Sour	Juicy	Spicy	Shiny	Bubbling
Sweet	Crunchy	Citrus	Smooth	Popping
Salty	Chewy	Savoury	Rough	Fizzy
Fruity	Crisp	Buttery	Uniform	
Bitter	Smooth	Cheesy	Size	

SECTION 1

149

Activity

1. Thinking about all the senses, make a list of the words that you could use to describe the following products:
   a Vegetable lasagne
   b Jam doughnut
   c Strawberry trifle
   d Chocolate biscuit
   e Salt and vinegar crisps
2. Explain why you think the sensory qualities of a food product are so important when making food choices.

Check it

1. Can you explain the term sensory analysis?
2. Can you explain the different sensory analysis tests?

Extension
Use the Internet to research how food companies use sensory analysis to help them develop new products.

Study tip
Can you explain how to set up a tasting panel?

What is sensory analysis?

Sensory analysis is a way of evaluating the taste of a product. The senses play an important part in evaluating the quality of a food product, so it is important that food tastes, looks and smells good and has the correct texture. When we develop food products by changing and improving these aspects, we do so using **sensory analysis**.

▲ Tasters carrying out sensory analysis

How is sensory analysis used?

Food companies use sensory analysis to find out if people will like the products they are developing. People have different tastes so food companies need to make changes to the ingredients they use in their products so that they appeal to more people. As they make changes they will carry out more sensory analysis until they produce a satisfactory product.

We can use sensory analysis in a similar way in school if we want to change and develop a product. We can ask people to taste the products we make and give their opinions. For example, you may want to develop a new vegetarian product so you may try using a variety of meat replacements and ask people to give their opinion about which one is best.

When developing a new product it is important that you get the views of your chosen target group, e.g. children, teenagers or adults, so you will need to test your dishes on people who belong to the correct specific group.

Setting up a sensory analysis tasting session

When carrying out sensory analysis it is important to make your tasters aware of what it is they will taste, what is expected of them, and how to fill in the charts.

You must:

- Set up in a quiet area where tasters cannot talk to one another.
- Serve small portions of food in identical, plain containers.
- Serve all samples at the same temperature.
- Allow the tasters to have a drink of water / lime water between each sample to cleanse their palates.
- Do not give too many samples at once as tasters become less able to discriminate. The amount of samples given can depend on the product, but on average 6 is a suitable amount.
- Use random codes for the products to avoid the tasters being influenced by a brand name, this is called a **blind tasting test**.

CORE KNOWLEDGE

What test?

When carrying out sensory analysis it is important to choose the test that helps you get the information you are looking for.

Tests can be used to determine how much a product is liked or disliked or to evaluate a specific quality, e.g. saltiness.

Ranking tests

This type of test allows food to be put into a rank order, either according to how much a product is liked or according to a specific quality such as sweetness. Tasters could be asked to rank order different flavours of cupcakes, and their findings used to discover the most popular flavour and determine which one will be produced.

Sample	Rank Order
■	3
●	1
▲	2

Triangle tests

Triangle tests are carried out to see if tasters can identify the odd one out where two products are the same and one is different. This can be used to see if one product is significantly different from the others. Companies who want to develop a product similar to others on the market use this type of test.

Rating tests

Rating tests allow tasters to give samples or qualities a mark on a five or seven point scale from 'extreme like' to 'extreme dislike'.

	Tick a statement for each sample		
	BTR	TRZ	XTE
Like extremely	✓		
Like a lot			
Like a little		✓	
Neither like nor dislike			
Dislike a little			✓
Dislike a lot			
Dislike extremely			

Profiling tests

This type of test is similar to a rating test, but instead of using one quality or overall preference, tasters rate different sensory aspects of the product. The results of profiling tests are usually shown as a star diagram; the star can have six or eight points depending on the sensory characteristics chosen. Each taster rates the characteristics on a scale of 1 to 5 (1 being the lowest and 5 being the highest). Results from all tasters are averaged and then displayed on the star diagram to give a visual profile.

Activity

Now you can try out some of the tests above:

a Use a ranking test to compare 3 flavours of crisps and find out which one was most popular in your class.

b Conduct a profiling test in your class with a cake of your choice. Average the results for each characteristic and produce a visual profile of your class in a star diagram.

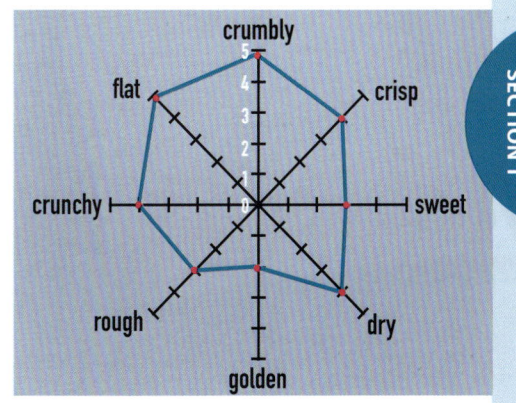

▲ Star diagram for biscuit tasting

CONVENIENCE FOODS

What will I learn?

- Types of convenience foods available to the consumer
- The role of convenience foods in food preparation
- The advantages and disadvantages of convenience foods

The term convenience foods applies to foods which have been pre-prepared and preserved commercially. Such food is usually ready to eat and requires minimum further preparation.

They shorten meal preparation time, save effort, have a long storage life and are often 'portion controlled'.

Examples include:

- Canned foods
- Frozen foods and meals
- Cartons
- Jars and bottles
- Packets of dried foods and packet mixes
- Chilled ready prepared foods and cook chill ready meals

There has been an increase in recent years both in the choice of convenience foods available to the consumer and in the popularity of convenience foods. There is, however, some concern over the possible impact on health of consuming too many convenience foods.

The advantages and disadvantages of convenience foods:

ADVANTAGES +	DISADVANTAGES −
save time and effort	the quality may not be as good as the fresh equivalent
make meal preparation easier	some are highly processed and contain low amounts of dietary fibre
have a long shelf life	some contain high amounts of salt, sugar and saturated fat
useful for people who have limited food preparation and cooking skills	they are often more expensive
useful for people with limited cooking equipment and space in the kitchen	they contain additives such as preservatives, artificial colour and flavours
useful for people who find difficulty in using kitchen equipment, for example people with physical disabilities	they use a great deal of packaging which in turn can have a negative impact on the environment
useful for people who find shopping difficult	
the range available allows individual preferences or special diets to be catered for at meal times	
some are portion controlled and contain nutritional information so that consumers can make informed choices	

Activity

Examples of convenience foods include dried, canned, dehydrated (instant) and fresh.

List examples for each of the following foods:

a sauces
b pastry
c bread
d vegetables

Key point

Convenience foods are useful for particular groups of people but should be used in conjunction with fresh ingredients to prepare dishes and meals.

Check it

Name types of convenience food with examples.

Study tip

Evaluate the role of convenience foods when planning family meals.

Give examples of how convenience foods can be used with fresh foods to make sweet and savoury dishes.

CORE KNOWLEDGE

ADDITIVES

What will I learn?
- What are additives
- Types and role of additives in food manufacture
- Issues concerning use of additives

Food additives are substances added to products to perform a specific function. The functions include adding colour, adding flavour or preserving by inhibiting microbial growth of increasing shelf life.

All additives are thoroughly tested before being allowed for use. The ones approved by the EU are given an 'E' number.

Additives may be:

Natural – obtained from natural sources such as extracts

Synthetic – man-made copies of natural substances

Artificial – produced chemically and not copies of substances found naturally.

Study tip
Evaluate the role of additives in food processing.

Check it
Can you name at least 4 types of additives and explain why they are used in food processing?

Key point
Additives are widely used in food processing to improve colour and texture and extend shelf life.

There are arguments for and against the use of additives in food processing.

Types of additives

Preservatives
They prevent microbial growth which causes food spoilage and reduces shelf life.

Examples are nitrite (E249) and nitrate (E252) added to cured meats, bacon and ham.

▲ Packed bacon contains a preservative

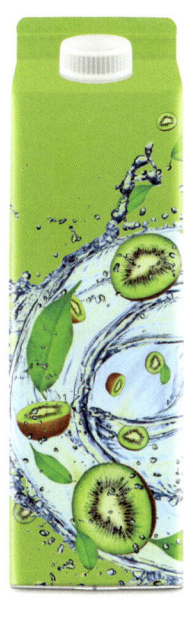

▲ Cartons of fruit juice contain antioxidants

Antioxidants
They prevent *rancidity* and the browning of cut fruit caused by *oxidation*.

An example is ascorbic acid (E300).

Colours
They restore the original colour of a food lost through processing or storage. This is done to ensure quality control and obtain a unified colour for each batch during production. It also helps to enrich or intensify an existing colour or give additional colour to food which would otherwise be unattractive. There has been concern over the use of particular colours which have proved to contribute towards behavioural problems associated with hyperactivity in children.

▲ Colour is added to tinned vegetables to restore the natural colour lost during processing

Flavour enhancers

They bring out the natural flavour in some processed foods.
An example is monosodium glutamate (E612).

Sweeteners

These are used in small amounts to intensify the sweetness of a product. They are used in cordial drinks and diet foods. Examples are sorbitol and sucralose.

Anti-caking agents

They allow for free movement of dried foodstuffs.

▲ Dried snack products and soups often contain a flavour enhancer

Most pre-packed powdered ingredients contain anti-caking agents ▶

Emulsifiers, stabilisers, gelling agents and thickeners

Emulsifiers help mix ingredients together that would otherwise normally separate. An example is lecithin (E322).

Stabilisers prevent ingredients from separating again. An example is locust bean gum (E410).

Both emulsifiers and stabilisers give foodstuffs an improved consistent texture.

Gelling agents are used to change the consistency of a food product. An example is pectin (E440) which is commonly used in commercial jam making. Thickeners improve viscosity and help to give more 'body' to the product.

Examples of foods containing emulsifiers, stabilisers, gelling agents and thickeners ▼

Key terms

Intensive farming – farming that aims to produce as much as possible, usually with the use of chemicals.

Factory farming – a farm in which animals are bred and fattened using modern industrial methods.

Carbon footprint – a carbon footprint measures the total carbon dioxide emissions caused directly and indirectly by a person, organisation, event or product.

Diabetic – a person who suffers from diabetes, a condition that occurs when the body can't use glucose normally.

Coronary heart disease – any heart disorder caused by disease of the coronary arteries.

Coeliac disease – a chronic intestinal disorder caused by sensitivity to the protein gliadin contained in the gluten of cereals.

Allergies – an immune system reaction that occurs soon after eating a certain food.

Intolerances – individual elements of certain foods cannot be properly processed and absorbed by our digestive system.

Organic farming – farming that produces food without the use of chemicals, fertilizers and pesticides.

Trans-fats – unsaturated fatty acids formed by the partial hydrogenation of vegetable oil, believed to raise blood cholesterol level.

Farm assured – a British organisation that promotes and regulates food quality.

Free range – a method of farming, where for at least part of the day, animals can roam freely outdoors.

GM food – genetically modified food

Fairtrade – trade between companies in developed countries and producers in developing countries in which fair prices are paid to the producers.

Food miles – the distance the food travels from field to plate.

Deficiency – a lack of something that is needed in the diet.

Advertising – providing information to consumers about a product or service.

Marketing – the activities involved in encouraging consumers to buy a product or service.

Market research – the gathering and studying of data relating to consumer opinions and preferences, purchasing power, etc., especially prior to introducing a product on the market.

Product placement – placing a product in a prominent position to encourage people to buy it.

Pester power – the ability of a child to nag a parent relentlessly until the parent succumbs and agrees to buy something they would not usually buy.

Rancidity – having an unpleasant smell or taste.

Oxidation – when oxygen combines with an element, changing the appearance of the element.

EXAM QUESTIONS

1. Give 4 factors that affect food choice. [4]

2. List 3 factors which affect the cost of food. [3]

3. Medical conditions affect the food choices of some consumers. Explain what is meant by the following conditions and suggest ways they can be controlled through diet.

   Coeliac disease [2]

   Iron-deficiency anaemia [2]

   Dairy intolerance [2]

4. What food laws are followed by the religions shown below?

Islam	
Judaism	
Hinduism	

5. Name the following food label symbols and explain their meaning. [6]

6. Discuss the ethical issues that affect food choice. [6]

7. Discuss the role of the following factors in affecting food choice:
   a. marketing and advertising [6]
   b. food labelling [6]

8. How can families save money when
   a. shopping for food? [6]
   b. preparing and cooking food? [6]

9. Food choice has been increased by current developments such as ethical, organic and GM foods.
   a. Discuss the range of foods available as a result of current developments. [6]
   b. Assess the factors that could influence the inclusion of these foods in family meals. [6]

   TOTAL: 61

SECTION 2
BASIC MIXTURES AND RECIPES

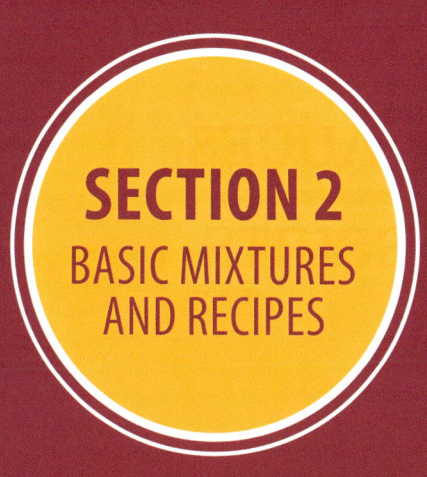

- **CAKE MAKING** 158
- **PASTRY MAKING** 160
- **SAUCES** 162
- **WHIPPED CREAM** 165
- **CHOUX PASTRY** 166
- **BREAD** 168
- **SHORTCRUST PASTRY** 170
- **FLAKY PASTRY** 171
- **TOMATO SAUCE** 172
- **ROUX SAUCE AND GELATINISATION** 173
- **SETTING** 174

SECTION 2
BASIC MIXTURES AND RECIPES

CAKES, PASTRY, SAUCES, BATTERS AND BISCUITS

What will I learn?

- Which ingredients are needed for basic mixtures
- Proportions of ingredients used in basic mixtures
- How basic mixtures are made

Key point

The basic ingredients used to make cakes are the same but each method of making displays different techniques.

Study tip

Learn the methods of cake making with examples.

Check it

List the basic steps to follow making the following mixtures:
- rubbing
- creaming
- melting
- whisking

Cake making

The basic ingredients used in cake making are:

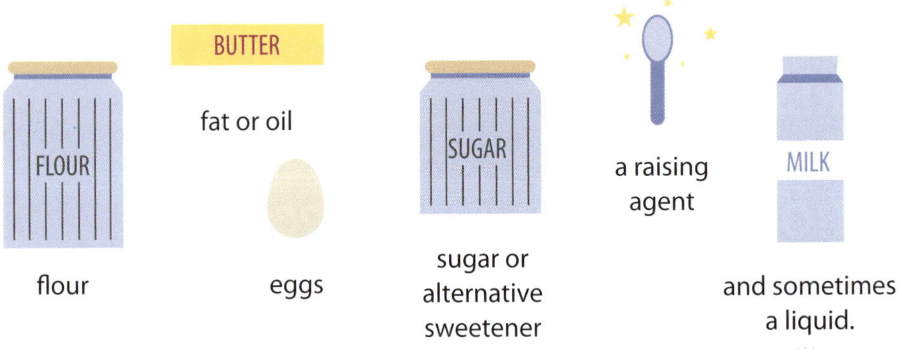

- flour
- fat or oil (BUTTER)
- eggs
- sugar or alternative sweetener
- a raising agent
- MILK and sometimes a liquid.

Other ingredients such as dried fruit, spices, chocolate or nuts may be added for extra flavour and texture

The quantity and proportion of ingredients used depends upon the method of cake making, and variation in the processes and techniques used to make the cakes will produce a different end product.

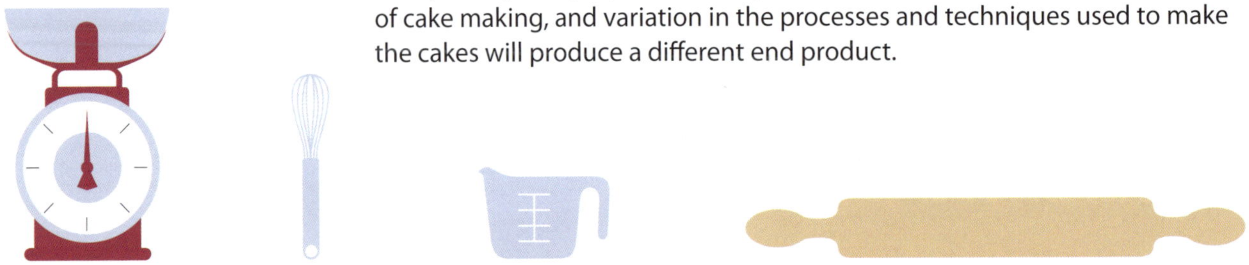

158 BASIC MIXTURES AND RECIPES

CAKES, PASTRY, SAUCES, BATTERS AND BISCUITS

There are five main methods of cake making:

RUBBED IN

PROPORTION OF FAT TO FLOUR: ½ or less
PROPORTION OF SUGAR TO FLOUR: ½ or less

EXAMPLES:
Rock cakes, raspberry buns, fruit cake, Welsh cakes

TECHNIQUE USED TO MAKE:
Fat rubbed into flour, sugar and other dry ingredients added, egg and liquid (if used) added

CREAMING

PROPORTION OF FAT TO FLOUR: equal
PROPORTION OF SUGAR TO FLOUR: equal

EXAMPLES:
Queen cakes, fairy cakes, Victoria sandwich, Madeira, cherry, Dundee

TECHNIQUE USED TO MAKE:
Fat and sugar are mixed, egg added and flour folded in with any other ingredients

WHISKING

PROPORTION OF FAT TO FLOUR: no fat used
PROPORTION OF SUGAR TO FLOUR: equal

EXAMPLES:
Swiss roll, Genoese sponge cake

TECHNIQUE USED TO MAKE:
Eggs and sugar are whisked, flour folded in

MELTING

PROPORTION OF FAT TO FLOUR: ½ or less
PROPORTION OF SUGAR TO FLOUR: equal

EXAMPLES:
Gingerbread, parkin, brownies

TECHNIQUE USED TO MAKE:
Fat melted with sugar and syrup or treacle, egg added with the flour and other ingredients

ALL-IN-ONE

PROPORTION OF FAT TO FLOUR: equal
PROPORTION OF SUGAR TO FLOUR: equal

EXAMPLES:
Small cakes, muffins

TECHNIQUE USED TO MAKE:
All ingredients mixed together at the same time

The science of cooking food p68   Cereals p175, Meat, Poultry, Fish and Eggs p261, Butter, Oil, Margarine, Sugar and Syrup p335

Pastry making

The basic ingredients in pastry are:

- flour
- fat (BUTTER OR OTHER FAT)
- salt
- water.

The quantity or proportion of ingredients vary according to the type of pastry and the techniques used to make the pastries also vary.

Basic techniques used in all pastry

Sieving flour and salt

Mixing the fat and flour according to type of pastry

Adding liquid – use sufficient cold water and mix thoroughly into the dough

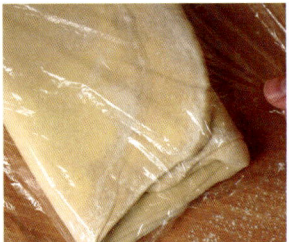

Resting – allow shortcrust, flaky and rough puff pastries to rest before rolling

Rolling out – use a little flour to roll out and handle the pastry as little as possible

Cooking – all pastry dishes are cooked in a hot oven (190°C- 200°C)

Study tip

Name each type of pastry and give examples.

Check it

Can you list at least 4 important techniques when making pastry?

Key point

The gluten content of flour is an important factor in making successful pastry.

Shortcrust and suet require a soft, low gluten flour to keep the pastry short and crumbly.

Choux, flaky and rough puff require a strong, high gluten flour to enable the pastry to stretch and form layers during cooking.

Laminating pastry dough

1. fat / dough — fold
2. fold
3. chill
4. rotate 90°
5. roll out
6. fold to centre
7. fold

(BOOK FOLD)

Repeat steps 3–7 three times, chilling for 20 minutes after each turn. The pastry is now ready to be used.

---

160   BASIC MIXTURES AND RECIPES   Recipes: Making Shortcrust pastry, Making Flaky pastry pp170–171

CAKES, PASTRY, SAUCES, BATTERS AND BISCUITS

The six main types of pastry are:

1

SHORTCRUST* / ALL-IN-ONE

RECOMMENDED FAT TO USE:	½ lard or cooking fat, ½ margarine or butter	soft margarine or cooking oil
PROPORTION OF FAT TO FLOUR:	½ fat to flour	⅔ fat to flour
TYPE OF FLOUR:	soft plain	soft plain
TECHNIQUE USED TO MAKE:	fat cut into cubes and rubbed in to the flour, liquid added	fat, flour and liquid mixed together with a fork

*for a richer pastry, egg yolk and sugar are added

2

SUET

RECOMMENDED FAT TO USE:	shredded suet
PROPORTION OF FAT TO FLOUR:	½ fat to flour
TYPE OF FLOUR:	self-raising
TECHNIQUE USED TO MAKE:	suet and flour mixed with liquid

3, 4, 5

FLAKY, PUFF / ROUGH PUFF

RECOMMENDED FAT TO USE:	a mixture of lard or cooking fat and block margarine or butter	
PROPORTION OF FAT TO FLOUR:	¾ fat to flour	
TYPE OF FLOUR:	strong flour	
TECHNIQUE USED TO MAKE:	¼ of the fat rubbed in, liquid added to form a dough. Dough rolled out and fat added (see diagram above)	fat cut up into cubes, stirred into the flour and liquid added

6

CHOUX

RECOMMENDED FAT TO USE:	margarine, butter or cooking fat
PROPORTION OF FAT TO FLOUR:	¾ fat to flour
TYPE OF FLOUR:	strong flour
TECHNIQUE USED TO MAKE:	fat and liquid heated in a pan, flour worked in, eggs added to the paste

The science of cooking food p68   Cereals p175, Meat, Poultry, Fish and Eggs p261, Butter, Oil, Margarine, Sugar and Syrup p335

Sauces

Sauces are either used as part of a dish - for example a pasta bake – or may be served as an accompaniment to a food - for example pepper sauce with a steak. The main point to consider is how the sauce will complement the dish. For example, a delicate lemon sauce might complement a grilled sole but would be unsuitable served with a grilled steak.

What can a good sauce add to a food or a dish?

- flavour
- colour
- moisture
- nutritional value.

▲ Sauces add flavour, colour and interest to a dish

Types of sauces commonly used include:

- Roux based, all-in-one or infused sauces such as béchamel and velouté
- Blended sauces such as a custard or cornflour sauce
- Reduction sauces such as tomato, a jus or gravy
- Emulsions such as mayonnaise, a hollandaise sauce or salad dressing.

A good quality roux based sauce has the following characteristics:

- an acceptable flavour
- smooth
- glossy
- desired consistency.

CAKES, PASTRY, SAUCES, BATTERS AND BISCUITS

Roux based sauces

A roux is a combination of fat and flour cooked for a particular length of time, depending on the colour of the sauce required. The example on page 173 uses a white roux sauce with milk as the liquid. To make an infused sauce, ingredients such as herbs, carrot, peppercorns and onion are gently heated in milk and or stock in order to flavour the liquid. The flavoured liquid is then used to make the roux.

Basic ingredients in white roux sauces include fat, flour, liquid and seasoning. Other ingredients such as cheese, parsley and mushrooms may be added for flavouring.

The proportion of liquid to flour depends upon the desired consistency of the sauce. If too much liquid is used the sauce will not be as thick as required; if too little is used the sauce will be too thick.

A white sauce can be made using the one-stage method. All the weighed and measured ingredients are placed in a pan and brought to the boil until thickened, or alternatively placed in a jug and cooked in a microwave oven.

There are three consistencies:

Pouring – to 250ml liquid, use 15g fat and 15g flour.
Uses: to serve as an accompaniment.

Coating – to 250ml liquid, use 25g fat and 25g flour.
Uses: to coat food in dishes such as cauliflower cheese.

Panada – to 250g liquid, use 50g fat and 25g flour.
Uses: to bind ingredients together such as in a recipe for croquettes.

Blended sauces

Milk and cornflour are mixed together and heated until the sauce thickens. There is no fat in a blended sauce.

Reduction sauces

Sauces made from the meat's own juices. It is usually boiled to reduce the liquid, to intensify the flavour and to thicken the consistency of the sauce. A jus is a reduced sauce made from concentrated stock.

Emulsions

Sauces made with oil and vinegar which are shaken together with an added emulsifying agent to stabilise the mixture.

The basic ingredients are:

flour

fat

salt pepper

liquid

Activity

List at least 10 sweet and savoury dishes where a sauce forms part of the dish, for example cauliflower cheese.

Study tip

Learn the different types of sauce with examples.

Check it

1. What is a roux?
2. What are the qualities of a good roux sauce?

Key point

Sauces are used to complement other ingredients or foods by adding colour, texture and moistness. They can also add nutritional value to a dish.

The basic ingredients are:

flour a liquid eggs

Batters

A batter is a mixture of flour, egg and liquid such as milk. There are two main types and consistencies – thin or pouring, and thick or coating.

Thin batter is used to make pancakes, toad in the hole and Yorkshire pudding.

Thick batter is used to make fritters and to coat pieces of raw fish before deep fat frying.

A tempura is a light Japanese batter made from cornflour, flour, sea salt and sparkling water. It is used to coat vegetables before frying in hot oil.

▲ Uses of a coating batter

The basic ingredients are:

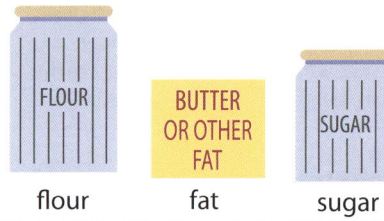

flour fat sugar

Biscuits

Biscuits are made using the same basic methods as for cakes – rubbing in, creaming, whisking and melting. The basic ingredients in biscuit mixtures include flour, sugar and fat.

Method of making	Rubbed in	Creaming	Whisking	Melting
Examples	Shortbread	Viennese, Shrewsbury	Sponge fingers	Ginger nuts, flapjacks

Key terms

Ingredients – the foods or substances needed to make a particular dish.

Raising agent – a substance added to a food product that makes them rise when cooked.

Proportion – a part or amount to be considered in relation to the whole.

Gluten – formed from the two wheat proteins gliadin and glutenin, in presence of water. Gluten is developed by kneading.

Consistency – thickness or viscosity.

Accompaniment – things that accompany something else in a complementary way, for example, table sauces, or foods that work well with other foods or drinks.

BASIC MIXTURES AND RECIPES

WHIPPED CREAM

1. Place the cream into a bowl.

2. Use an electric whisk and put it on the medium speed setting.

3. The cream will be very frothy and bubbly to start but as you continue to whisk it will become frothy and lighter in colour.

4. Keep whisking; when there are trails in the cream you will have reached the soft plop stage.

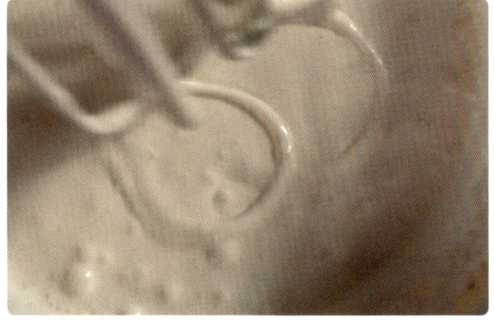

5. When the trails in the cream become more solid you will have reached the soft peak stage.

6. You should now reduce the speed of the whisk and continue until the trails in the cream have become stiffer.

7. Serve it immediately or cover well and store it in the refrigerator for a few hours.

CHOUX

1 Pre-heat the oven to gas mark 6, 200°C or 190°C for fan oven.

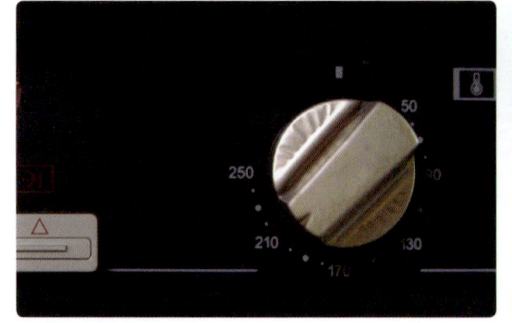

2 Grease a baking tray and sprinkle with water.

Ingredients:
150g strong flour
100g unsalted butter
250ml cold water
4 eggs

3 Sift 80g flour and salt onto kitchen paper.

4 Put 50g of chopped-up butter in a medium-sized saucepan – add 150ml of cold water.

5 Stir with a wooden spoon over a moderate heat until butter has melted and the mixture comes to the boil. Turn the heat off.

6 Tip in all the flour and mix thoroughly with the wooden spoon to form a roux.

7 Beat the mixture vigorously using a wooden spoon / electric whisk. Continue for a minute until you have a smooth ball of choux paste.

8 Thoroughly beat the eggs in a jug – then add them to the mixture a tablespoonful at a time.

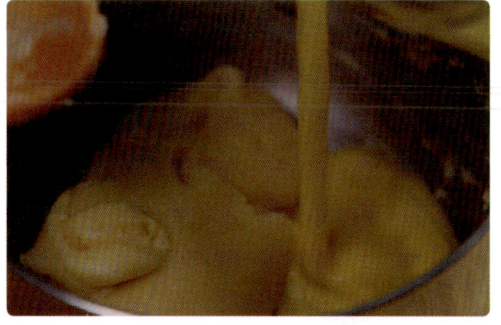

166 BASIC RECIPES

9 Beat vigorously until you have a smooth glossy paste.

10 Insert a plain piping nozzle and carefully fill the piping bag with the mixture. Pipe into even-sized sausage shapes to make éclairs.

11 Bake the éclairs for 15 mins, then reduce temperature to gas mark 5 / 190°C (180°C fan) for a further 10 mins.

12 Make a slit along the length of each éclair at the side. Allow to cool.

13 Fill with whipped cream and top with melted chocolate.

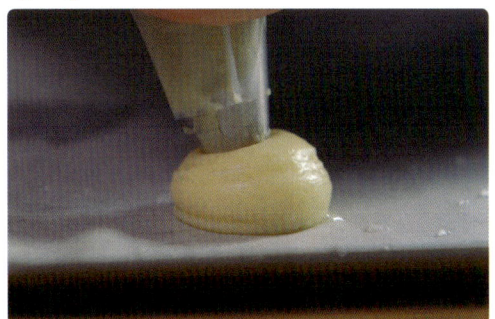

14 To make profiteroles, pipe the mixture into small, even-sized balls

15 Wet your finger and smooth down any points on each ball.

16 Bake for 10–15 mins

BREAD

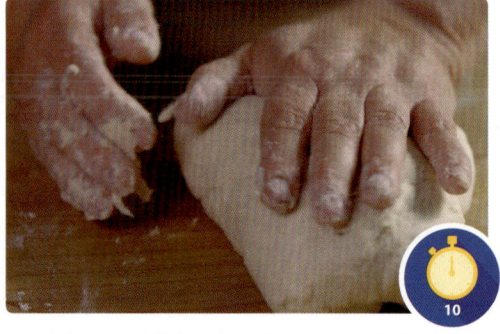

Ingredients:
- 450g strong flour
- 2 tsp fast action dried yeast
- 270ml warm water
- salt
- sugar

1 Preheat the oven to 220°C or gas mark 7.

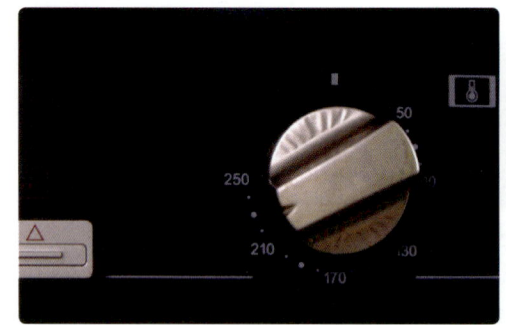

2 Combine 450g of strong plain flour and a sachet of fast action yeast - mix well.

3 Add 1 teaspoon of sugar and half a teaspoonful of salt and mix thoroughly.

4 Make a well in the centre and pour in most of the warm water (25-37 °C).

5 Use a wooden spoon to mix the flour and water together.

6 Add more water if necessary, to produce an elastic pliable dough.

7 Use your hand to bring the dough together. Tip out onto a floured surface.

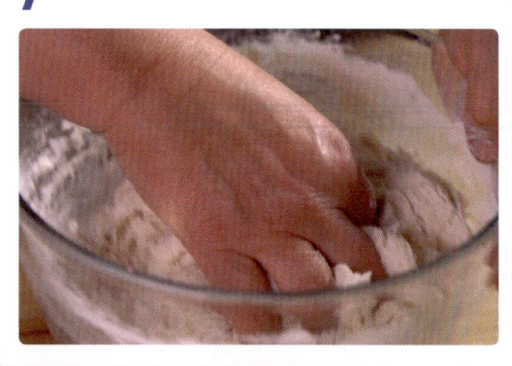

8 Knead for at least 10 mins until smooth and elastic.

BASIC RECIPES

9 Put dough into a warm place to prove.

10 Once the dough has doubled in size re-knead (knock back).

11 Cut and shape into 8 equal sized rolls.

12 Place rolls on a baking tray covered with baking parchment. Leave to rise until doubled in size.

13 Brush the rolls with water, oil, milk or beaten egg depending on the type of crust required.

14 Place into the pre-heated oven at 220°C, gas mark 7, for 10–15 mins.

15 Remove rolls from the oven and place them on a wire rack to cool.

SHORTCRUST PASTRY

1 Sieve flour and salt into a bowl.

2 Cut the fat into cubes and add to the flour.

3 Rub the fat into the flour using fingertips.

4 Initially the pastry will be large clumps.

5 With further rubbing the mixture will eventually resemble breadcrumbs.

6 Add sufficient cold water to make a stiff dough. Mix with a metal knife.

7 Knead pastry very lightly to bring together.

8 Wrap in cling film and chill.

Ingredients:

125g plain flour

55g butter

salt

30–45ml cold water

FLAKY PASTRY

1. Mix the fats together on a plate so that they are evenly distributed. Shape the fat into a block and divide into four equal pieces.

2. Sieve the flour and salt, and rub in one quarter of the fat until it resembles breadcrumbs.

3. Add enough water to mix to a soft, elastic dough.

4. Roll the pastry to a rectangle, three times as long as it is wide. Mark into three squares.

5. Place the fat in small lumps on the pastry to cover two of the three sections. Lots of air gaps are formed in between the lumps. This helps form the layered flakiness associated with this type of pastry.

6. Fold the bottom third to the middle and the top third to the bottom. Seal the edges. Refrigerate for at least 5 minutes to harden.

7. Repeat steps 4–6 three times with the remaining fat, giving the pastry a quarter turn before rolling each time.

8. Repeat the rolling, folding and sealing one more time without fat. Leave the pastry to rest for at least 10 minutes.

Ingredients:

225g strong flour

80g lard

80g butter

salt

30–45ml cold water

TOMATO SAUCE

1 Crush the garlic and chop it.

2 Heat two tablespoons of oil in a saucepan and fry the garlic until it softens.

3 Add the tomatoes, seasoning, and pepper flakes.

4 Cook over a medium low heat for 10 mins. Add the chopped basil, and mix well.

5 Cook over a low heat for an additional 3 minutes.

6 The sauce can be blended to make it smooth or left with texture.

Ingredients:

- 1 clove garlic
- cooking oil
- 1x400g tinned plum tomatoes
- seasoning
- 1 bunch basil leaves

ROUX SAUCE AND GELATINISATION

Ingredients:
- 20g flour
- 20g butter
- 600ml liquid (milk or stock)
- salt
- pepper

1. Melt the butter in a saucepan and add the plain flour.

2. Stir continuously over a moderate heat with a wooden spoon to form a sticky ball (roux) – don't allow it to brown.

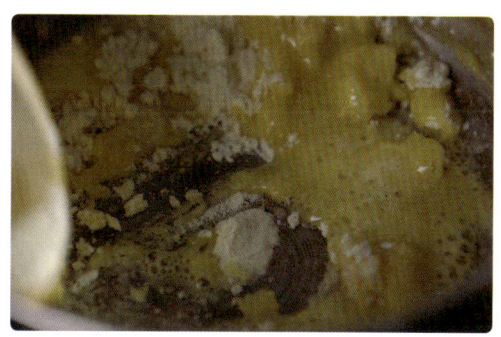

3. Stir the roux in a figure of 8 to prevent it from burning.

4. Remove pan from the heat and add a small amount of the milk and stir well.

5. Add the milk a little at a time stirring well to avoid lumps. Keep doing this until all the milk has been added.

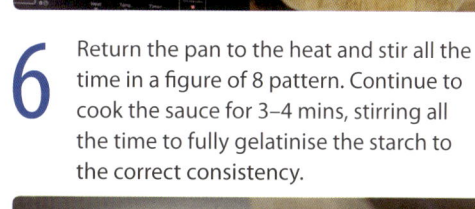

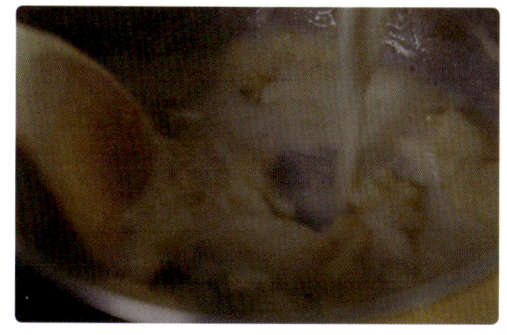

6. Return the pan to the heat and stir all the time in a figure of 8 pattern. Continue to cook the sauce for 3–4 mins, stirring all the time to fully gelatinise the starch to the correct consistency.

Milk can be infused with an onion, carrot, celery and bouquet garni. This mixture is strained and used with the rest of this roux sauce recipe, and the result is béchamel sauce.

SETTING

1. Melt the butter gently. Brush the base and sides of a 23cm spring-form cake tin with a little melted butter.

2. Mix crushed biscuits into the melted butter. Spoon the mixture into the tin and press down to line the base. Chill.

3. Soak the gelatine leaves in a bowl of water until soft, about 10 minutes.

4. Fold the mascarpone, lemon zest, whipped cream and caster sugar in a bowl.

5. Gently heat the lemon juice and water in a saucepan. Squeeze the excess water from the gelatine then add it to the warmed lemon juice, stirring to dissolve.

6. Fold the gelatine mixture into the mascarpone mixture.

7. Marble through the lemon curd a spoonful at a time.

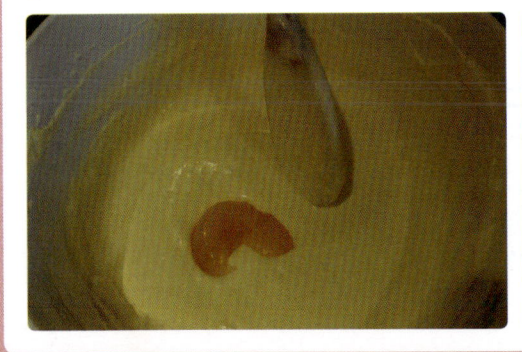

8. Pour the mixture on top of the base, smoothing with a palette knife. Cover and leave to set in the refrigerator.

Ingredients:

- 100g butter
- 300g gingernut biscuits
- 3 sheets gelatine
- 500g mascarpone
- 1 lemon, zest and juice
- 250ml whipping cream
- 175g caster sugar
- 4 tbsp lemon curd

174 BASIC RECIPES

SECTION 3
COMMODITIES

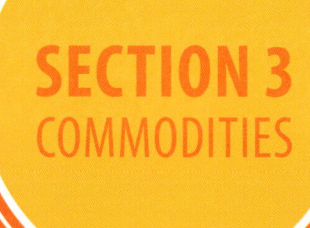

CEREALS

- WHAT ARE CEREALS? 176
- WHEAT 177
- BREAD 185
- PASTA 192
- BREAKFAST CEREALS 195
- RICE 196
- MAIZE 200
- OATS, BARLEY AND RYE 202
- OTHER GRAINS 206
- PREVENT FOOD POISONING IN CEREALS 207
- EXAM QUESTIONS 208
- FOOD INVESTIGATIONS 209
- RECIPES 210

SECTION 3
COMMODITIES

CEREALS

What will I learn?
- What cereals are
- The variety of cereals available
- The importance of staple foods in the diet

Check it
1. What are cereals? Give examples of three cereals grown and processed in the UK.
2. What is a staple food? Explain the importance of a staple food in a developing country.

Key point
Whole grain cereals have a higher nutritional value than processed cereals.

Check it
1. List the key nutrients found in cereals.
2. Name two diseases that eating whole grains may help to reduce.

Study tip
You need to know the key nutrients provided in cereals.

Make sure you can explain how the nutritional value can be affected when cereal is processed.

Can you discuss the health benefits of a diet containing whole grain cereals?

What are cereals?

The word **cereal** is used to describe many different edible grasses; these grasses are grown and harvested for their grain. The **endosperm**, the **germ** (sometimes called the embryo) and the **bran** have a particular interest and importance to those interested in cooking, nutrition and food science.

The most popular cereals consumed in the UK include: wheat, rice, maize (corn), oats and barley. Other cereals such as rye, millet, buckwheat, quinoa, sorghum and amaranth are growing in popularity.

wheat   rice   oats   maize   barley

Staple foods

Cereals are often referred to as **staple foods**. They are especially important in developing countries where there is a greater reliance on staple foods amongst the poorest people. Staple foods are usually starchy foods that grow well and can be stored for consumption throughout the year.

Nutritional value of cereals

When a cereal is left in its natural form (called **whole grain**) it is a rich source of nutrients, primarily starchy carbohydrate and protein. Fat is also found in whole grain as is a range of the B vitamins and vitamin E. Fibre is also present in the bran.

The nutritional value of cereals may change after the grain is processed.

Grains are an essential element in a healthy diet and eating high-fibre whole grains may help to reduce the risk of heart disease and type 2 diabetes and control blood cholesterol.

CEREALS

WHEAT

What will I learn?

- The basic structure of a wheat grain
- How wheat is grown and harvested
- The primary processing of wheat into flour
- The importance of protein content in flour
- Secondary processing of wheat
- The functional properties of wheat flour

Wheat is amongst the main cereal crops grown in the UK. Wheat is used in food production, primarily flour, bread, biscuits, cake, pastry, pizza and breakfast cereals.

Wheat grows well in a wide variety of soils.

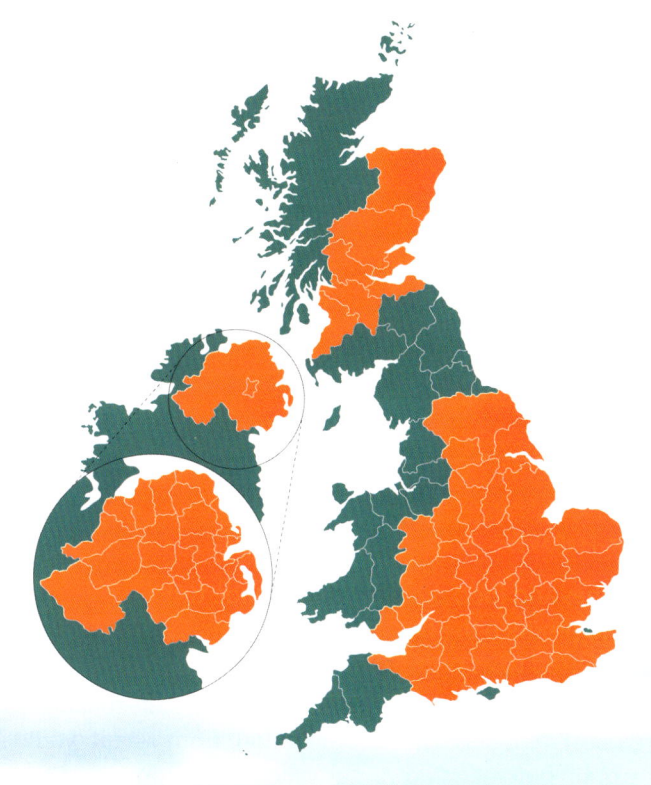

▲ Areas coloured orange on this map are the main wheat growing areas of the UK

Key point
Starch is found in the endosperm.

Check it
Draw a wheat grain and label the parts.

Study tip
Make sure you are able to explain the three main parts of a cereal grain (endosperm, germ and bran).

Wheat grain
- endosperm
- bran
- germ

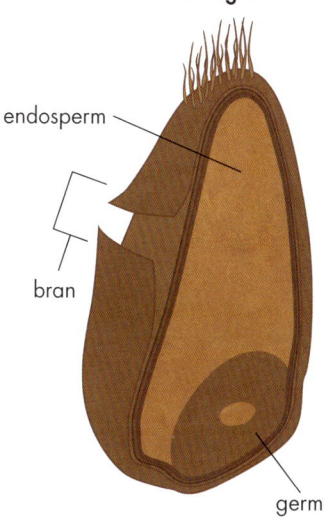

⌐ Key terms

Cereal – an edible grass.

Grain – the edible part of the cereal.

Endosperm – the main part of the grain, a starch and protein supply.

Germ – source of fat and B vitamins, it is where the new plant grows.

Staple food – forms a large part of the diet, usually from starchy foods.

Whole grain – 100% of the grain, nothing has been removed.

◄ Wheat crop growing in a field

> **Key point**
>
> The endosperm from wheat provides starch and protein.
> Dietary fibre is found in wheat bran.

▲ Planted seeds

How is wheat grown and processed?

Before wheat can be planted the ground firstly has to be prepared by ploughing. This involves turning over the top soil using a tractor and plough for the creation of a seedbed.

Wheat can be sown in either the autumn or the spring, the crop from both sowing times being harvested in August. In the UK, autumn **sowing** is most common. When the wheat crop is ready to be harvested UK farmers will do this using a combine harvester.

▲ Wheat harvesting using a combine harvester

Using wheat: primary processing to produce flour

In order for dishes and food products to be made using wheat, it first has to be processed to produce the flour and extract the wheat bran and wheat germ. This is referred to as **primary processing**.

Before the introduction of machinery and the large scale milling of flour, one of the earliest methods used to obtain flour from wheat would involve grinding the grain between two stones called a millstone.

While millstones are still used in **artisan** milling, large scale flour milling uses the process of rollers to grind wheat into flour.

The large scale modern production of wheat into flour can be summarised as the processes of grinding, sifting, separating and regrinding. These steps are repeated to extract the endosperm.

▲ Wheat is still ground using a millstone in small scale milling

COMMODITIES

THE KEY PROCESSES OF WHEAT MILLING

SAMPLING AND GRADING THE WHEAT — Laboratory checking wheat is to the required standard and storing wheat of same grades together in silos.

CLEANING THE WHEAT — Using a range of equipment the wheat is cleaned – large sieves, suction machines, spinners, scourers and metal detectors are all examples of ways that the wheat is cleaned.

CONDITIONING THE WHEAT — The cleaned wheat is washed in water and spun dry. The moisture content is monitored and controlled.

GRISTING THE WHEAT — The cleaned and conditioned wheat is blended with other types of wheat of different grades and moistures.

GRINDING THE WHEAT — The wheat moves between two large metal rollers known as break rolls. This is the process that turns the wheat into flour. The finest flour is called middlings or farina.

PROCESSING THE FLOUR (STREAMING) — Bran and wheatgerm are streamed into the middlings to make brown or wholemeal flour.

The flour is treated with improvers and fortified.

Baking powder (raising agent) will be added to make self-raising flour.

CEREALS

Key point
Milling wheat grain into flour is an example of primary processing.

By law, the nutrients calcium, iron and the B vitamins (niacin and thiamin) must be added to flour.

Check it
1. List the key stages required to turn wheat into flour.
2. Draw a flow diagram summarising how wheat is milled commercially.

Study tip
For the written examination you don't have to learn everything 'parrot fashion'.

If you search the Internet for videos it will give you a clear visual picture on how wheat is processed from the planting of the seed to milling the grain into flour.

Key terms
Primary processing – the conversion of raw materials into food commodities e.g. milling of wheat grain into flour.

Fortification – vitamins and minerals are added to foods.

SECTION 3

179

Activity

Write a summary or create a storyboard illustrating the stages in wheat production – from planting to harvesting.

Processing the flour after milling

After the milling process, different grades of flour are produced by sifting, separating and regrinding the flour several times. These grades are combined as needed to produce different types of flour.

Small amounts of bleaching agents (to make the flour more white) and oxidizing agents (to enhance the baking quality of the flour) are usually added to the flour after milling. The nutrients calcium, iron and the B vitamins (niacin and thiamin), which are legally required in all white and brown flours, are also added. This is called **fortification**. (Wholemeal flour already contains these nutrients, although it is lower in calcium.)

Baking powder (raising agent) will be added to make self-raising flour.

Types of wheat flour

▲ A range of flours produced from wheat

◀ The Soil Association logo is often used to show flour is organically produced

Wholemeal – This is made from the whole wheat grain, nothing is added or taken away. It is referred to as having a 100% **extraction rate**. It is a good source of dietary fibre, NSP (**non starch polysaccharide**). It is also called whole wheat flour.

Brown – This usually contains about 85% of the original grain. Some bran and germ have been removed.

White – This usually contains around 70–72% of the wheat grain (endosperm). Most of the bran and wheat germ have been removed during the milling process.

Granary flour – This flour is made by adding malted wheat (which has been toasted and flaked), to any type of flour but usually it is added to wholemeal or brown flour.

Stoneground – This is wholemeal flour ground in a traditional way between two stones.

Organic – This is made from grain that has been grown to organic standards. Growers and millers must be registered and are subject to regular inspections.

Study tip

Make sure that you can give examples of the different types of flour produced from wheat.

Key point

Wholemeal flour is made from the whole wheat grain, nothing is removed.
White flour has most of the bran and wheat germ removed.

Check it

What does the term 'extraction rate of flour' mean?

COMMODITIES   Factors affecting food choice: Ethical food choices p138

Nutritional value of wheat

Wheat is a good source of starchy carbohydrate, found in the endosperm. Wheat is also a source of protein and provides us with a range of vitamins and minerals. If the wheat still has the bran it will provide dietary fibre in the form of non starch polysaccharide (NSP). B vitamins are found in the bran layers. Flour sold in the UK is fortified with calcium, iron and B vitamins.

Wholemeal flour and the effect on iron and calcium absorption

Wheat will store the mineral phosphorus in a form known as **phytic acid**. This phytic acid is present in the bran of wheat. The phytic acid will bind with both calcium and iron to form phytates and this then limits the absorption of these minerals in the body.

Should we be avoiding foods containing phytates?

Some people do, especially if they have health issues relating to iron deficiency anaemia or osteoporosis. However, for most people, it is not necessary to avoid foods containing phytates; what is important is that we have a balanced diet. Research has shown that consuming foods that contain phytic acid can help to reduce the risk of breast and prostate cancer and prevent hardening of the arteries.

How important is the protein content in flour?

Wheat flour is available with different protein levels. To get the best results when cooking it is important to make sure that the correct type of flour, with the correct **protein content**, is used.

- *Strong flour* (high protein content) – used for bread making, some chefs also prefer to use strong white flour for puff, flaky and choux pastry. Strong flour is made from **hard wheat** varieties and produces a strong elastic dough because it is high in protein.
- *All purpose flour* – used for cakes and biscuits. Milled from softer wheat varieties, there should be a lower protein content than strong flour. It is used when a light, short, crumbly texture is desired.
- *Self-raising flour* – this is all purpose flour with added raising agent.

You can also buy cake flour and sauce flour – these have been made to produce the best results when making cakes and sauces.

What is gluten-free flour?

Flour that is free from wheat, barley, oats and rye and is usually a blend of gluten-free flours such as rice, potato, tapioca, maize and buckwheat flours.

Is it possible for oat flour to be gluten-free?

Gluten is a protein found in wheat, rye and barley. Oats contain a similar protein called avenin which most people with coeliac disease can tolerate. The reason that oats are included in the list of gluten-containing grains is that they are commonly cross-contaminated in the manufacturing process. If the oats are pure and uncontaminated then it is possible to label them gluten-free. There are several gluten-free oat flours on the market at the moment, many of which are Crossed Grain symbol certified.

◀ Coeliac UK Crossed Grain certification symbol for gluten-free foods

▶ Gluten-free flour is a popular alternative to wheat flour for coeliacs

Key point

Wheat provides energy in the form of starch.

Wheat bran provides dietary fibre and is a source of B vitamins.

Check it

1. Which nutrients are found in the following parts of a wheat grain:
   i Bran?
   ii Endosperm?
   iii Germ?
2. Explain what is meant by the phrase 'fortification of flour'.

Key point

The absorption of calcium and iron are affected by the presence of phytic acid.

Study tip

Can you explain the nutritional differences between a food product made with wholemeal flour and one made with white flour?

Key terms

Extraction rate – how much of the original wheat grain is in the flour. 100% means that it contains all the grain.

NSP (non starch polysaccharide) – indigestible carbohydrates found in plant food, often called dietary fibre.

Phytic acid – a form of phosphorous which limits absorption of calcium and iron in the body.

What other ways are there to process wheat?

We have already discussed the primary processing of wheat into flour, here are other ways that the wheat grain can be processed and used in cooking:

WHEAT BRAN

Wheat bran and **wheat germ** – added to biscuits, cakes, muffins, breads and breakfast cereals to increase the dietary fibre content. Also sprinkled onto yoghurt, breakfast cereal or fruit dishes.

PUFFED WHEAT

Flaked, **puffed** and **extruded wheat** – used to manufacture breakfast cereals and cereal snack bars.

KIBBLED WHEAT

Kibbled wheat – grains are cracked or broken into smaller particles and then moistened or steamed and dried. Used as an ingredient in mixed grain bread or cooked as a side dish.

SEMOLINA

Semolina – mainly used for making pasta. The preferred variety of wheat for pasta is durum wheat due to its high protein content. It can also be used in cakes and cooked in milk to make semolina pudding.

COUSCOUS

Couscous – made from semolina grains, is a popular starchy carbohydrate accompaniment in North African cuisine.

BURGHUL

Burghul (also known as bulgur or cracked wheat) – made by parboiling wheat, drying it and then coarsely grinding it. It is a key ingredient in tabouli and kibbeh, and can be used in soup, stuffings, burgers and casseroles.

Secondary processing of wheat

Wheat is used to make many different types of food products. This production is referred to as **secondary processing**.

- Pizza
- Cakes
- Waffles
- Crumpets
- Biscuits
- Pastries
- Muffins
- Doughnuts
- Sauces
- Pies
- Ice cream cones
- Pancakes
- Noodles
- Pasta
- Crackers
- Bread
- Crisp breads
- Breakfast cereals
- Cereal bars

Key point

Secondary processing of wheat uses flour to make food products such as biscuits, cakes, sauces, breads, pasta and breakfast cereals.

Check it

Can you name 2 dishes that you could make using the following types of flour?

i   Stoneground wholemeal flour
ii Plain white flour
iii Self-raising flour

Study tip

Make sure you are able to explain the difference between primary and secondary processing and give examples of food products.

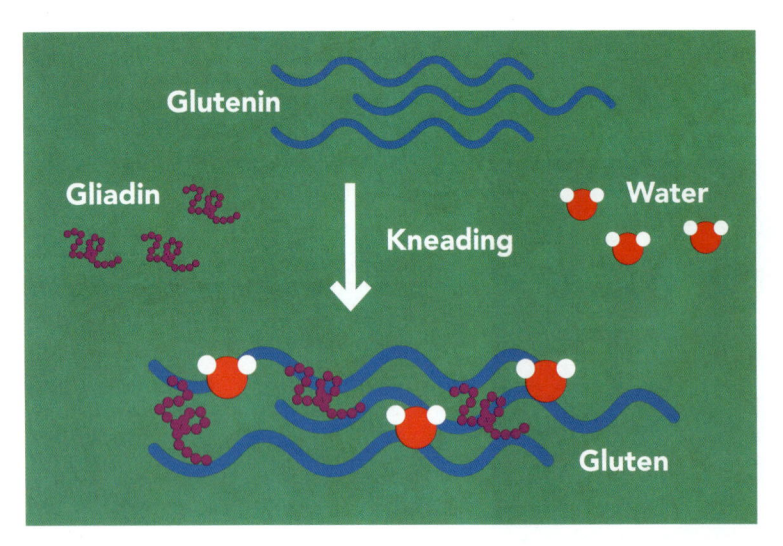

Functional properties of wheat flour

Gluten formation [FS]

Wheat flour contains two proteins called **gliadin and glutenin**. When moisture such as water is added to wheat flour the protein **gluten** is formed. Strong flour contains a higher percentage of protein than softer flours.

Some food products require gluten development for strength and structure such as in the making of bread, also in puff, flaky and choux pastry. Softer flour should be used in products such as cakes, batters and muffins where gluten development is to be avoided, as strong flours will result in an undesirable tougher and chewy texture.

Key point

The more you knead dough or beat a mixture containing wheat flour, the more gluten will be formed.

Check it

1 Name two proteins found in wheat flour.
2 Which protein is developed during the kneading process of bread making.

The effect of heat

Coagulation

In the case of a dough (such as bread) or a cake mix, heat will cause the protein present in the flour to coagulate. This will help to set the mix.

Gelatinisation

When starch is mixed with water it forms a suspension, and with heat, the starch granules absorb moisture and swell. A matrix is formed and this results in a thickening of the liquid. This results in a **gel**. The presence of sugar and acidic ingredients (e.g. lemon juice) will affect gelatinisation

Dextrinisation

When starch is exposed to dry heat the colour will change to brown. Dextrin causes the characteristic brown crust of baked products and toast.

The effect of freezing

Retrogradation

Chilling and freezing products thickened by wheat flour, such as sauces, can cause the sauce to 'weep' when defrosted. An example of this is with the freezing and defrosting of a béchamel sauce. The moisture escapes when the sauce is defrosted. The appearance and texture of the defrosted sauce is spongy and grainy. This is why corn starches and chemically modified starches are used in the manufacture of frozen foods as these starches do not have the same 'weeping' effect when frozen.

Check it

State the term used to describe 'weeping' of a frozen and defrosted white sauce thickened with wheat flour.

Study tip

The NEA and the written examination will test your knowledge and understanding of the science of food.

Think of a way to make sure that you understand the processes of **coagulation**, **gelatinisation**, **dextrinisation** and **retrogradation**. You could use your imagination and try to visualise the process or maybe write notes on each process and read them through several times. How will you make sure you understand these key scientific principles?

Key terms

Secondary processing – converting primary processed foods into other food products, e.g. flour into biscuits.

Gluten – formed from the two wheat proteins gliadin and glutenin, in the presence of water. Gluten is developed by kneading.

Coagulation – the setting of protein, in presence of heat.

Gelatinisation – the thickening of a mixture, in presence of heat, due to swelling of starch grains.

Gel – liquid which is dispersed in a solid.

Dextrinisation – the brown colour in starchy foods with the application of dry heat.

Retrogradation – when a gel 'leaks' liquid after solidifying.

CEREALS

SECTION 3

The secondary processing of wheat: bread, pasta and breakfast cereals

BREAD

What will I learn?

- The varieties of bread products available
- The key ingredients and their functions in bread making
- How bread is made
- The difference between unleavened and leavened bread
- The importance of yeast
- What are sourdoughs and starters?

Bread is a staple food in the UK. There are many varieties of bread: e.g. wholemeal, granary, white, spelt and rye. These can be shaped in a variety of ways.

Bread dough can be enriched with ingredients such as dried fruit, sugar, milk, butter and eggs to produce baked items like Chelsea buns, bara brith, Danish pastries, croissants and brioche.

Nutritional value of bread

Bread is a good source of starchy carbohydrate, protein, B vitamins, calcium and iron. Bread which is made with wholemeal flour is also a good source of dietary fibre.

Ingredients used in bread making

The four key ingredients used in bread making are: wheat flour, liquid, **yeast** and salt. Fat is sometimes used and will extend the keeping qualities of freshly baked bread.

▲ Key ingredients used in bread making

Check it

What does the term 'enriched bread dough' mean?

Key point

Bread is a staple food in the UK.

An enriched dough contains additional ingredients such as butter, eggs, milk, sugar and dried fruit.

▲ Bread varieties and shapes

▲ Bakery items made using enriched sweet doughs

Check it

List the key ingredients needed for bread making.

185

WHAT DO THE INGREDIENTS IN BREAD ACTUALLY DO?

WHEAT FLOUR

- **Bulk** – it gives bulk to the bread.
- **Taste** – different types of flour give different flavours to bread.
- **Absorbs moisture** – flour can absorb a lot of water to make a dough.
- **Strong flour** – has high protein content so will produce a good quality loaf that does not collapse.
- **Nutrients** – provides starchy carbohydrate, protein and is fortified with vitamins and minerals.

LIQUID

- **Moisture** – it helps to create the right conditions for the yeast to grow. Liquid hydrates the flour, helping with gluten formation.
- **Warmth** – just the right temperature to encourage the yeast to grow. The ideal temperature is 37°C.
- **Steam** – when the dough is baked, water turns to steam and helps it to rise.
- **Structure** – liquid binds everything together to make the dough.

Check it
Why is strong flour recommended when making bread?

Bread making

Bread can be made in bakeries in batches and on a much larger scale of production in factories.

▲ Small scale bread making in a bakery

▲ Mass production in a bread factory

The key stages to traditional bread making are:

- Mixing
- Kneading
- Proving
- Knocking back
- Shaping
- Proving
- Baking

This traditional method of bread making is often called **bulk fermentation**.

186 COMMODITIES

YEAST

- Raising agent – yeast is a living microorganism. When it has the ideal conditions for growth, it **respires** and produces carbon dioxide.

The ideal conditions for growth are:
- **Warmth** – ideally about body temperature (37°C)
- **Moisture** – water is added to the dough
- **Food** – sugar is an ideal food for the yeast
- **Time** – for the yeast to ferment

SALT

- **Structure** – helps with gluten formation.
- **Taste** – a small amount of salt improves the flavour of the bread.
- **Too much** – will stop the yeast from fermenting.

OTHER INGREDIENTS IN BREAD MAKING

Fat
- **Lubrication** – fat allows the other ingredients to slide over each other so the bread can rise.
- **Shortening** – fat coats the particles of flour and stops it absorbing water, so only a small amount should be used.
- **Taste** – enhances the flavour.
- **Shelf life** – fat improves the texture of the bread, keeping it moist and preventing it from going stale quickly.

Sugar
- **Food for the yeast** – sugar provides food energy for the yeast so that it can respire and grow.
- **Browning** – sugar turns to caramel when it is cooked and makes the crust brown.
- **Taste** – sugar adds sweetness to the bread.

Ascorbic acid
- Added mainly in the commercial manufacture of bread, it speeds up the time it takes to make the bread.

What is the Chorleywood bread making process?

This process was developed in 1961 to reduce the time taken using the traditional method. It is still used today in large bakeries where bread is mass-produced.

The Chorleywood process enables bakers to use lower protein wheat to produce bread. This means the bakeries can use UK-grown wheat.

Ascorbic acid (vitamin C) is added as an improver. Fast and vigorous **kneading** of the dough using high speed mixers develops the gluten structure more quickly and gives the dough its elasticity. The whole process from flour to a ready loaf can be done in approximately 3 ½ hours.

◀ Mass production of bread

> **Study tip**
> Gluten formation in bread making is particularly important. You must be able to know and understand the function of ingredients in bread making. Create a mind map to show the functions of the key ingredients in bread making.

> **Check it**
> List the key stages for traditional bread making.

THE SCIENCE OF BREAD MAKING

The simplest and quickest method to make bread at home is using fast-action dried yeast. Here is a summary of the key stages for bread making and the food science relating to the physical and chemical reactions taking place in the bread.

SIFTING THE FLOUR

The sifting process introduces air which acts as a raising agent and helps bread to rise in the oven.

ADDING WARM LIQUID

Water hydrates the flour. At 37°C the liquid provides the optimum temperature for the yeast to ferment and produce the raising agent CO_2. Moisture is needed for a soft dough.

Sugars are produced by this fermentation, which the yeast consumes. As it does so it creates alcohol and carbon dioxide gas as waste products.

MIXING AND KNEADING DOUGH

During mixing and kneading, two of the proteins present in flour (gliadin and glutenin) become hydrated and when the dough is kneaded an elastic protein complex called gluten is formed. This gluten gives bread its structure and prevents it collapsing.

PROVING DOUGH

During this step some of the starch present in flour is broken down and is fermented by the yeast.

CO_2 is produced which causes the gluten network to expand and therefore makes the dough rise; the gas produced is trapped in pockets.

The quality of gluten is important – if it is too weak bubbles can burst causing a lack of volume, if it is too strong the dough won't stretch enough.

'KNOCKING BACK' PROVED DOUGH
(THEN GO ON TO SHAPE AND GIVE A FINAL PROVE)

The dough is 'knocked back' to remove the large CO_2 bubbles produced by the yeast. This ensures a more even texture and a better rise.

Large bubbles of gas would make large holes in the finished bread.

BAKING

The bread dough rises as the CO_2 produced by fermentation of yeast expands with heat.

Yeast activity increases at first, but as the temperature of the dough rises it slows down until eventually the heat will kill the yeast.

The water is absorbed by the starch granules in the flour, the starch grains swell and gelatinise; this supports the firm structure of the loaf.

A gluten network forms a sort of skeleton which traps the CO_2 gas. During baking the gluten strands are stretched as the CO_2 gas (plus steam and air which are also present) expands, this together with the coagulation of the gluten protein results in the finished bread structure.

Steam, CO_2 and alcohol are released during baking.

Dextrin is formed on the outer parts of the bread, giving it its colour.

Common problems in bread making – and how to avoid them

Loaf is small and heavy
- Yeast is not active or not enough CO_2 is produced
- Not enough liquid so the dough cannot expand with steam
- Proving time too short
- Protein content in flour too low

Poorly risen bread showing a hard, open texture
- Bread has overproved, so that the gas pockets in the dough have collapsed. The gases (steam, CO_2) have escaped and dough has formed large uneven holes
- Yeast has died and failed to provide CO_2 as a raising agent
- Oven temperature too low (make sure it's pre-heated)
- Dough not kneaded long enough (poor gluten formation).

Bread rose but collapsed in oven
- Protein content in flour too low
- Dough overproved
- Oven temperature too low.

🔖 Key terms
Kneading – stretching the dough by hand or mechanically.
Proving – allowing time for the dough to rise; to prove that the yeast is alive.
Knocking back – a second kneading to remove large bubbles of gas.

CEREALS

Key point
Bread made on a small scale is made by bulk fermentation.
The **Chorleywood bread making process** is used when making bread in factories.

Check it
Describe the difference between making bread using the process of bulk fermentation and the Chorleywood process.

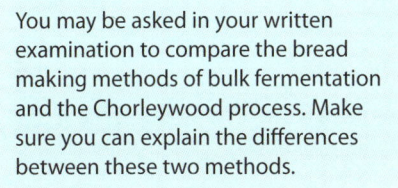

Study tip
You may be asked in your written examination to compare the bread making methods of bulk fermentation and the Chorleywood process. Make sure you can explain the differences between these two methods.

Check it
List the four ideal conditions needed for yeast to respire and produce carbon dioxide.

Key point
The raising agents in bread making are air, steam and carbon dioxide (CO_2).
The proteins gliadin and glutenin will form the protein gluten.
Gluten gives bread its structure and prevents it collapsing.
Proving shows that the yeast is alive and producing CO_2.

Check it
1 Name the gas produced by the fermentation of yeast.
2 Why is the formation of the protein gluten important in bread making?
3 What does the term 'knocking back' mean? Why is this process necessary?

Basic mixtures and recipes: Bread p168

> **Key point**
>
> Unleavened bread is free from raising agent.

> **Check it**
>
> 1 Explain the term 'unleavened bread'.
> 2 Give examples of unleavened bread.

> **Key point**
>
> As yeast ferments it produces the raising agent CO_2.

> **Check it**
>
> What are the benefits of fast-action dried yeast to a baker?

The difference between unleavened and leavened bread

Unleavened

Unleavened bread has no raising agent and consists of flour and water. Other ingredients can be added such as fat, herbs, spices etc. to improve the flavour. Examples include tortillas, roti, matzo.

Leavened bread

A basic **leavened bread** is made from flour, water, salt and yeast. It has a honeycomb structure that is often referred to as being a solid foam. This honeycomb structure is due to the formation of carbon dioxide gas, due to the yeast fermentation.

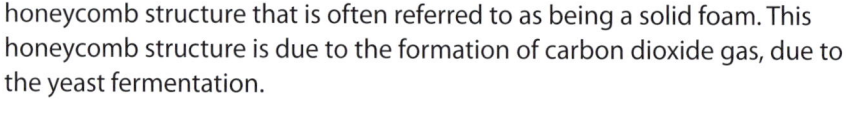

The importance of yeast [FS]

Yeast is a biological raising agent. As it grows it converts its food (in the form of sugar or starch) into alcohol and carbon dioxide CO_2 through the process of fermentation.

Yeast is available both as fresh yeast and as dried yeast.

Fresh yeast should be firm and moist with a cream colour. Dark, dry or crumbly yeast should be avoided. When using fresh yeast additional time is required to allow it to ferment with water and a food source (sugar) before it can be added to the flour.

Dried yeast keeps longer and is more convenient than fresh yeast.

Fast-action dried yeast does not need fermenting before adding to the flour, it can be added directly to the dough mix. This saves the baker time.

▲ Fresh and dried yeast

COMMODITIES — The science of cooking food: Raising agents p77

What are sourdoughs and starters? [FS]

Sourdough bread is a bread that is leavened with a **sourdough starter**. The starter is made from wild yeasts which are obtained from natural sources (such as the air and flour). A portion of the starter is mixed with the flour and other ingredients while the remainder is kept and 'fed' with more flour and water to use in future batches.

▲ Sourdough starter (left) and sourdough loaf

Bread makers

Bread makers can be used for making small batches of bread at home. Bread makers have a series of pre-set programmes which can be used to knead, prove, shape and bake bread. They can be set to work overnight resulting in freshly baked bread in the morning.

▲ Bread makers are used to save time and require little skill

Study tip

What is meant by the term 'sourdough starter'?

Activity

In class, conduct a taste testing of breads made with different flours (rye bread, granary bread, pumpernickel, spelt bread, soda bread, pitta bread, sourdough bread, corn bread, etc). Compare the appearance, texture, aroma and flavour of each bread. Which are the most popular breads and why?

⤶ Key terms

Unleavened bread – bread without a raising agent.

Leavened bread – bread with a raising agent.

Sourdough starter – a mix of flour and water which is allowed to sit for several days to develop natural yeasts.

▲ Different pasta shapes are made in different regions of Italy

Check it
Why is pasta unsuitable for coeliacs?

Key point
Three-dimensional pasta shapes are produced using machinery with a die. The pasta shape is extruded from the machine.

▲ tipo '00' flour is another way that semolina pasta flour is labelled ▶

PASTA

What will I learn?
- What pasta is
- The process of making pasta
- The variety of pasta available
- How to cook pasta
- How to store pasta

Pasta is a staple food of Italy and together with bread, rice and potatoes, it forms part of the staple food range in the UK. Pasta is usually bought fresh or dried and is available in a variety of shapes, flavours and colours. It can be filled or unfilled and can be served with a variety of sauces. Pasta is a **convenience food** as it is quick to cook.

Pasta is made from **durum wheat**; durum wheat has a higher protein content than other wheat varieties. It produces a grainy, yellow coloured semolina on milling. Durum wheat makes good quality pasta because it requires less water to make the dough, making it easier to dry the pasta. Pasta flour is sometimes labelled as **tipo '00' flour**.

Nutritional value of pasta
Pasta is a good source of starchy carbohydrate, protein and B vitamins. Whole wheat pasta also provides dietary fibre. Pasta is not suitable for coeliacs as it contains wheat flour.

COMMODITIES

CEREALS

How do we make PASTA?

Making pasta

Pasta can be:
- made in small batches by hand.
- prepared in semi-automatic machines when it needs to be made in larger quantities, such as in restaurants.
- mass-produced in large factories.

The four stages for making pasta are:
Forming a dough
Kneading and rolling the dough
Shaping
Drying

Pasta rolling using a table top pasta machine

	SMALL SCALE At home and some restaurants	**MEDIUM SCALE** Restaurants where pasta is made in large volume	**LARGE SCALE** Factories to sell to retailers, caterers and food manufacturers
Forming a dough	Wheat semolina is mixed with salt and egg or water to form a crumbly mixture.		
Kneading and rolling (also called laminating) the dough	Kneaded by hand on a table and dough is rolled out using a rolling pin or a table top pasta machine.	Kneaded by machine with some operator involvement.	Kneading and rolling is done by machinery – fully automated.
Shaping	All done by hand, small attachment to pasta machine can cut into strips such as tagliatelle and angel hair pasta, other shapes have to be cut and shaped by hand (e.g. papardelle, ravioli and fusilli).	Pasta shapes can be cut by hand or by using a pasta making machine with a selection of dies for different shapes.	Pasta shapes are obtained by using machinery with a die (to get the desired shape). The pasta shape is extruded from the machine and cut to the length wanted.
Drying	Hung or left out in the kitchen to dry – tagliatelle often seen hanging on coat hangers, clothes airers or over the backs of chairs.	Specialist wooden trays are used, stacked to allow air circulation for drying. Pasta is often used quickly after production so extending shelf life is not always needed.	Pasta shapes are taken to a specialist drying room to remove the moisture – which will give the dried pasta an extended shelf life.

Coloured pasta drying in the air.

Cutting tagliatelle through a table top pasta machine.

The process of making ravioli parcels in a factory

193

The variety of pasta available

There are many different shapes, flavours and colours available. Popular shapes include spaghetti, tagliatelle, vermicelli, macaroni, lasagne sheets, cannelloni and fusilli.

Flavours

Basic pasta can be made with flour and water although egg is usually added. Fresh herbs such as basil and parsley can be added to enhance the flavour.

Colours

Coloured pasta can be obtained by adding ingredients such as:

spinach - verdi (green)

tomato puree - pomodori (red)

beetroot - barbabietola rossa (purple)

squid ink - nero (black).

▲ Pasta can be coloured with a range of ingredients

Check it

Name two ingredients that can be used to colour pasta.

Study tip

Watch online videos on pasta making and read cookery books and online recipes to remind yourself of the different pasta shapes and colours. The best way to become knowledgeable about pasta is to make it, cook with it and of course taste it!

Study tip

Make sure you can give examples of sauces that work best with specific pasta varieties.

Activity

Research and then list as many different pasta shapes as you can. Ask your classmates to do the same and see who can research the most varieties.

Cooking pasta

Pasta needs to be cooked in boiling salted water, and in a large pan, to allow the starch to wash off the pasta, this will prevent the pasta being sticky. Pasta is said to be ready when it is '**al dente**' – this literally means 'to the tooth'. This means that the cooked pasta still has a little 'bite' or firmness in the middle.

Storage

Dried pasta can be stored in a cool, dry cupboard and has a long shelf life. Fresh pasta should be kept chilled. Packing should be clearly labelled with details of 'best before' or 'use-by' dates and storage instructions.

↳ Key terms

Convenience food – where some or all the preparation has been done in advance.

Durum wheat – high protein wheat used to make pasta.

Laminating – rolling out pasta into thin sheets.

Dies – machinery attachments used to make special pasta shapes that cannot be made by hand.

Extruded – pasta is forced through a die to achieve a special pasta shape, e.g. spaghetti, macaroni.

BREAKFAST CEREALS

What will I learn?

- The uses of cereal crops as breakfast cereals
- The correct way to store cereal products

▲ A selection of breakfast cereals

Many cereals are processed and made into breakfast cereals. The most common cereal crops used in the manufacturing of breakfast cereals include wheat, maize (corn), oats and rice.

The cereals are processed in different ways, such as puffed, shredded, flaked or rolled. They are often mixed with other ingredients, such as nuts, dried fruit and honey to improve their flavour, texture and nutritional value. Breakfast cereals are also fortified with vitamins and minerals to add to their nutritional value.

Some breakfast cereals have sugar and salt added to them, which makes them less healthy.

How should cereal products be stored?

Cereals should be stored in an airtight container in a cool, dry and well ventilated cupboard. If they are stored in a **humid** environment they will become **mouldy**. They will also lose their crisp texture and can even pick up flavours from other ingredients.

Whole grain cereals will deteriorate more quickly than processed cereals because they have a higher fat content; this is because the germ is still present (the germ is where the fat is stored in the cereal).

For best results cereals should be consumed well within the 'best before' dates indicated on the packaging.

Cereals which are stored incorrectly can become infested with insects such as weevils or beetles.

Key point

Breakfast cereals are fortified to improve their nutritional value.

Whole grain cereals will deteriorate more quickly than processed cereals.

Activity

Do a poll to find out which breakfast cereals your classmates eat. Which are the most popular breakfast cereals? Why do you think that is? Discuss the advantages and disadvantages of the most popular breakfast cereals; are they healthy?

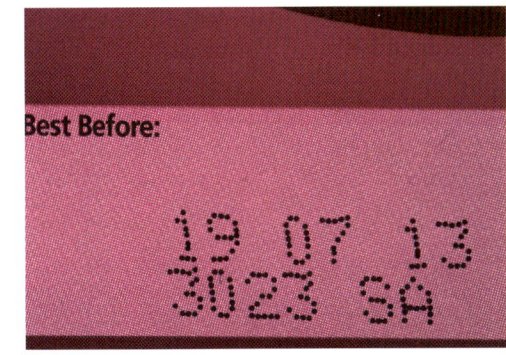

▲ Cereal packet label showing its 'best before' date

Check it

Describe how breakfast cereals should be stored. Explain why careful storage of breakfast cereals is important.

Diet and good health: p44
Food spoilage: p84

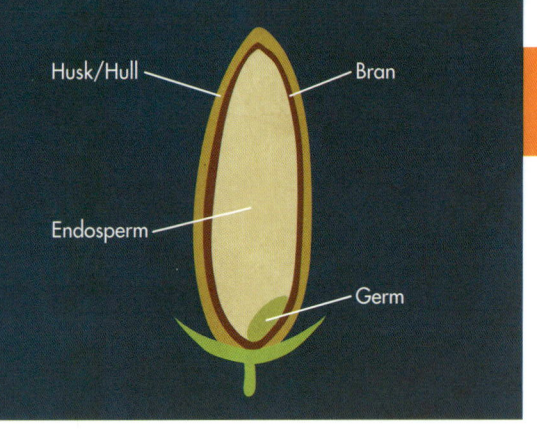

▲ A grain of rice

RICE

What will I learn?

- How rice is grown and harvested
- The primary processing of rice
- The types of rice available
- The secondary processing of rice into rice products

Rice is the most widely consumed staple food for a large part of the world's human population, especially in Asia. Rice grows well in hot and humid conditions in flooded fields called **paddies**. Rice is processed in a similar way to wheat.

Areas coloured orange/red on this map are the main rice growing areas of the world. The darker the area, the more rice produced. ▼

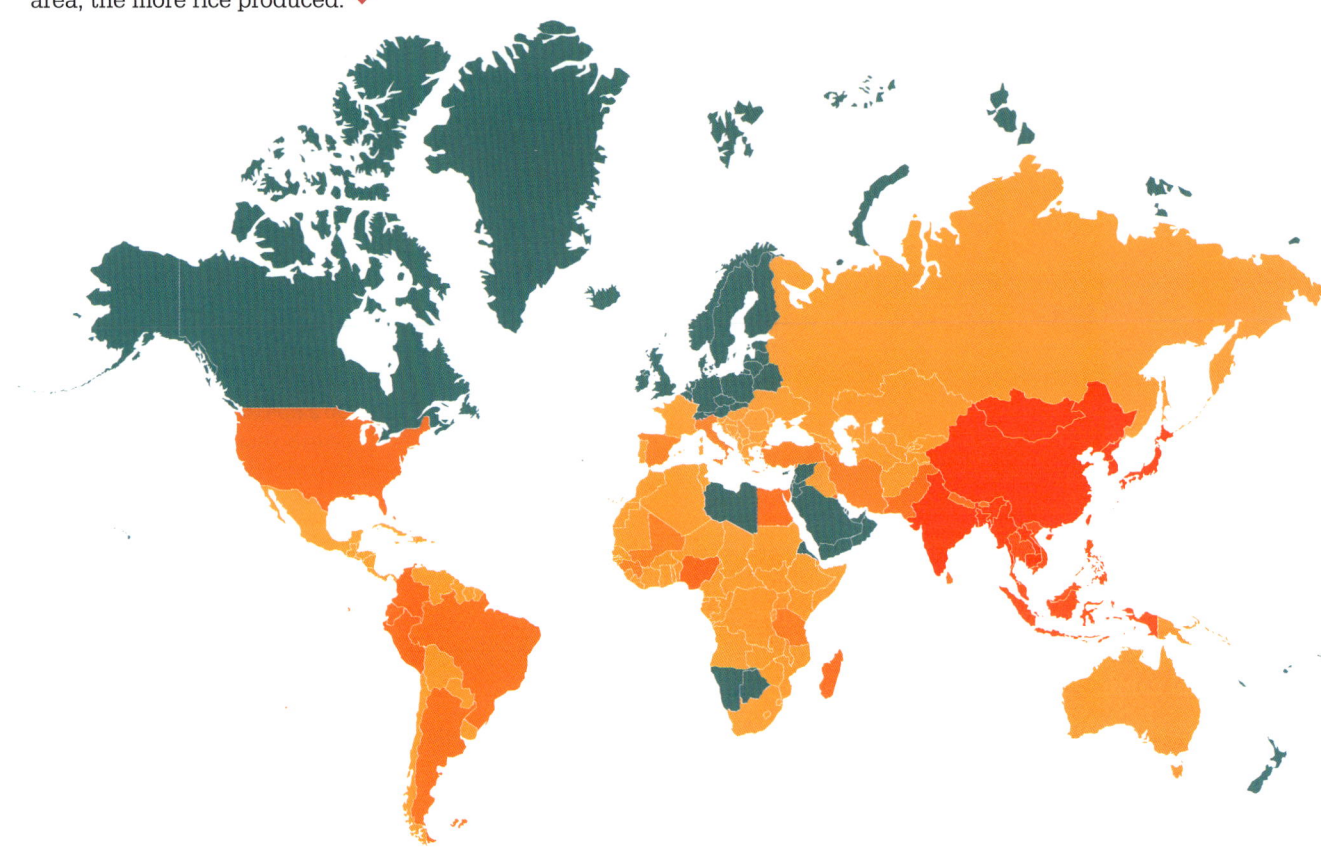

How rice is grown and processed

Many different types of rice are grown and used in cooking. In order to grow rice the land is firstly ploughed to 'till' or dig up, mix and level the soil. In most Asian countries the ancestral methods for cultivating and harvesting are still practised. The fields are often ploughed using water buffalo. Rice seedlings are planted by hand in the fields which have been flooded by rain or river water.

Hand planting rice in a paddy field ▶

196 COMMODITIES

CEREALS

The fields are drained before cutting of the crop commences. **Harvesting** can be done manually (by hand) or mechanically (using machinery). Manual harvesting is common across Asia; it is labour intensive and involves cutting the rice stalks with simple hand tools like sickles and knives.

Harvesting rice by hand ▶

Mechanical harvesting using reapers or combine harvesters is the other option for harvesting. In some regions, the availability and cost of machinery can determine whether harvesting is done by hand or machine.

Harvesting rice using a combine harvester in the USA ▶

◀ Threshing rice by hand in Thailand

Key point

Brown rice contains bran.
White rice has the bran removed.

Check it

What is the difference between brown and white rice?

Using rice: primary processing of rice

Once the rice is harvested it must be threshed to separate the grain from the stalk and then cleaned. These processes can be done by hand or machine.

After threshing, the rice is screened to remove stones, loose chaff and paddy stalks (parts of the plant). The rice is then slowly dried by warm air to reduce any moisture. Then the rice is screened again to remove dust particles.

The outer husk is removed next and if the bran layer is left intact, this then forms brown rice. The rice is then cleaned and graded. If the rice is to be sold as white rice it then undergoes milling, an abrasive action which removes the bran layer surrounding the rice grain.

Study tip

The primary processing of rice is similar to that of wheat, so if you can summarise how wheat is processed, you can describe the process for rice!

Have a look online for videos that will give you a clear visual picture of how rice is grown and harvested – this will reinforce your knowledge and understanding.

> **Key point**
>
> Cooked long grain rice should be fluffy and the individual grains will be visible.
> Cooked short grain rice will be sticky and starchier.

Types of rice

Rice is often categorised as either long or short grain.

Long grain rice is a thin grain which is 4-5 times as long as it is wide. It is sometimes called 'all purpose' rice. It is one of the most popular types of rice for everyday cooking in many cultures.

> **Check it**
>
> 1. List 3 varieties of rice.
> 2. Give the name of a dish that can be made with each rice variety.

> **Study tip**
>
> Make sure you know the different varieties of rice. You will need to be able to suggest recipes that use these rice varieties.

TYPES OF LONG GRAIN RICE

BROWN LONG GRAIN RICE (WHOLE GRAIN RICE)
This rice has a nutty flavour and is nutritionally the most complete rice available as it retains more vitamin, mineral and fibre content. Brown rice takes longer to cook than white rice and the cooked grains have a chewy texture.

WHITE LONG GRAIN RICE
This is white in colour and cooks much more quickly than brown rice.

BASMATI RICE
A long and thin-grained rice with a fragrant flavour and aroma, Basmati can be white or brown. It is the preferred rice in Indian cuisine.

JASMINE RICE (THAI FRAGRANT RICE)
This is an aromatic rice, often associated with Thai cooking. It has a soft and slightly sticky texture when cooked.

WILD RICE
Technically wild rice is not a variety of rice but an aquatic wild grass. It takes around 45 minutes to cook, a lot longer than ordinary rice. It is used for its a nutty flavour, texture and dark colour. It is often sold in rice mixes.

TYPES OF SHORT GRAIN RICE

Short grain rice is plump and absorbs water very easily resulting in the cooked rice being soft and a little sticky.

ARBORIO RICE
An Italian variety of rice which is used to make risotto.

PUDDING RICE
Most often used for desserts such as rice pudding where its starchy qualities make for a smooth and creamy finish.

GLUTINOUS RICE
Usually sold as a white rice and has a high starch content which, when cooked properly, makes the rice very sticky and the grains hold together. It is used in various Asian cuisines.

SUSHI RICE
A Japanese short grain sticky rice with a much higher ratio of the starch amylopectin to the starch amylose than longer grain varieties. This makes the rice much stickier when cooked.

Using rice: secondary processing

RICE
Rice can be processed into many different products, including:

- RICE BRAN
- RICE BRAN OIL
- RICE MILK
- RICE VINEGAR
- RICE FLOUR
- RICE CAKES
- RICE WINE
- RICE NOODLES
- RICE STARCH
- RICE TEA

CEREALS

Key point
Rice can be made into many different products including wine, vinegar, milk, noodles and tea.

Check it
Give 5 examples of products obtained from the secondary processing of rice. For each one, suggest one way that it can be used in cooking.

Nutritional value of rice
White rice is about 90% carbohydrate, 8% protein and 2% fat, and is a good source of iron and B vitamins. It is low in fibre.

Brown rice is a whole grain. It is about 85% carbohydrate, 8% protein and 7% fat, and contains as much as four times the amount of fibre and more minerals than white rice. It is a good source of B vitamins.

Nutritional deficiencies caused by a diet with rice as the staple food
In developing countries where white rice is the main source of starchy carbohydrate, a deficiency disease called **beri beri** may occur. This is caused by a lack of thiamin (vitamin B1). Brown rice is actually a good source of thiamin, but much of it is found in the outer layers of the rice grain which are removed during the polishing to make it into white rice.

Other B vitamins found in rice are also lost when rice is washed and during cooking.

Key term
Beri beri – a muscle wasting disease occurring in places where white rice is a staple food. The diet is deficient in thiamin (vitamin B1).

Nutrition: Water soluble vitamins B and C, Beriberi pp29–31

MAIZE

What will I learn?
- What maize and corn are
- The secondary processing of maize and corn into products

Maize – sometimes called corn – is now the third largest human staple food crop in the world after wheat and rice. It is grown and consumed in large quantities in South America, Asia, and Africa.

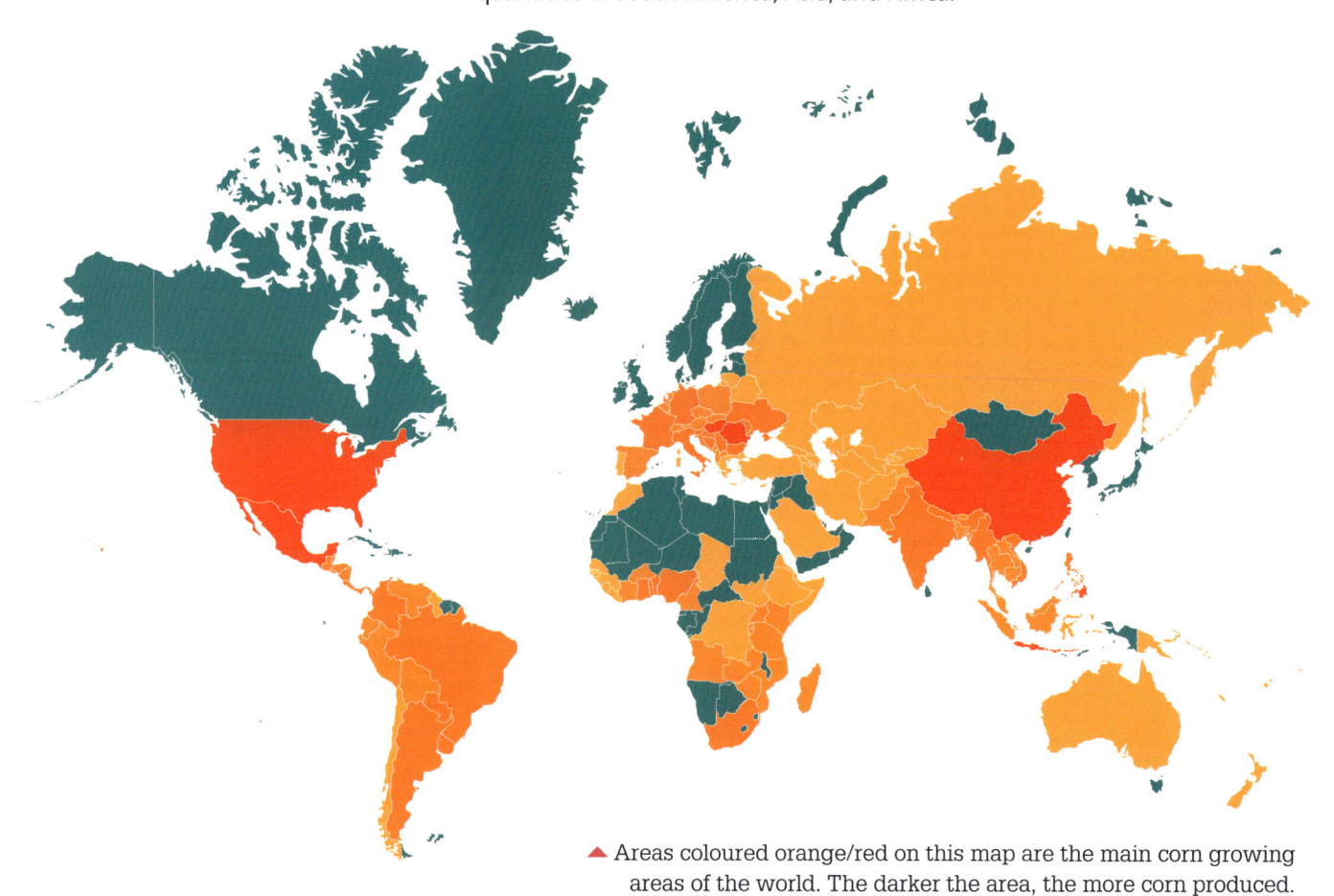

▲ Corn on the cob and corn kernels

▲ Areas coloured orange/red on this map are the main corn growing areas of the world. The darker the area, the more corn produced.

Check it
Give 3 examples of food products made from maize or corn.

It is often too cold to grow maize as a grain in the UK, although sweetcorn, a type of maize with a sweet grain, can be grown in Southern England. Corn on the cob is a popular snack and sweetcorn kernels are often used as a vegetable accompaniment in salads, chunky soups, sauces and casseroles.

CEREALS

Using maize and corn: secondary processing

Beyond the popularity of corn on the cob and sweet corn kernels, maize is processed into other food products and ingredients:

- CORNFLOUR
- CORN SYRUP
- CORNFLAKES
- POPCORN
- CORN OIL
- CORN MEAL

Check it

1. Give the name of the deficiency disease caused by a lack of niacin (vitamin B3) where maize (corn) is used as a staple food.
2. Give 3 examples of food products made from maize or corn.

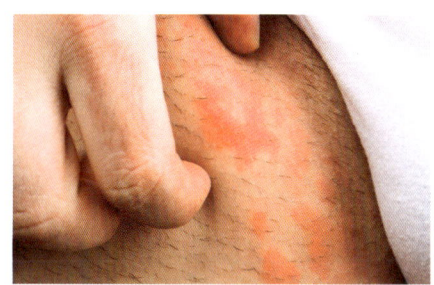

▲ A person suffering from pellagra

▲ Masa harina is used to make corn tortillas

Nutritional value of maize (corn)

Maize has a similar nutrient content to other cereals and is a good source of starchy carbohydrate and vegetable protein. Yellow varieties of maize (corn) also contain carotene which is converted in the body to vitamin A.

Maize also contains vitamin B3 (niacin) which helps to convert the food we eat into energy.

The niacin in maize is present in a form that cannot be easily absorbed in the body. This can cause the deficiency disease **pellagra**, which occurs in countries where maize is a primary source of nutrition.

In Mexico, Central and South America, where corn tortillas are a staple food, pellagra is avoided as the maize flour used (called **masa harina**) has been treated in a solution of lime and water, also called slaked lime.

🔑 Key terms

Pellagra – a deficiency disease where maize is a staple food. Diet is deficient in niacin (vitamin B3).

Masa harina – finely ground corn flour treated with slaked lime; main ingredient in corn tortillas.

Nutrition: Water soluble vitamins B, Pellagra pp 29–31

▲ Oats growing

OATS, BARLEY AND RYE

What will I learn?

- What oats, barley and rye are
- The primary processing of oats
- The secondary processing of oats, barley and rye into products

Oats

Oats are grown in cold temperate climates, such as in Scotland. Their popularity as a breakfast cereal has slowed down due to growth in the variety of breakfast cereals available in the UK. Oats are still a popular healthy breakfast cereal choice.

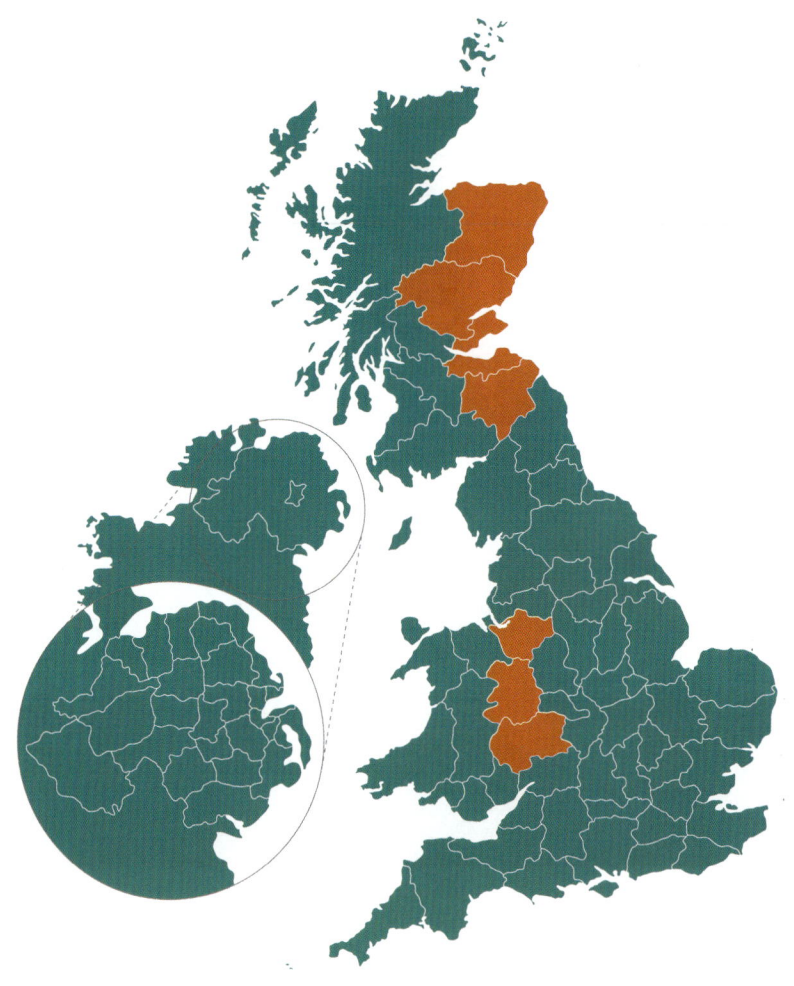

▲ Areas coloured orange on this map are the main oat growing areas of the UK

Using oats: primary processing of oats

Oats are rolled rather than crushed and are partially cooked during this process. After harvesting the oats are heated to develop the flavour and reduce their water content. The outer husks are removed by hullers and the remaining grains (called groats) are sieved to make sure the husks and groats are separated. These groats are then rolled into fine, medium or ground oatmeal.

▲ Hulling machine

Secondary processing of oats

Oats can be further processed to make them cook more quickly: one example is instant oatmeal, rolled oats cut into smaller pieces and then steamed.

How do we use oats?

Oats are used in the making of many products and dishes such as breakfast granola, biscuits, cakes, flapjacks, crumbles and herring coated in oatmeal.

▲ Examples of the many ways oats can be used in cooking

Nutritional value of oats

Oats are also a good source of starchy carbohydrate, protein and fat.

Oats are high in fibre, containing both soluble and insoluble fibre. **Insoluble fibre** will help with the speedy removal of waste products from the body (promoting healthy bowel movements). **Soluble fibre** has been proven to lower blood cholesterol due to the presence of beta-glucan in the oats.

A diet that includes a high intake of foods providing both soluble and insoluble fibre may help prevent obesity, stroke, high blood pressure and coronary heart disease.

Are oats gluten-free?

Pure oats do not contain gluten. However, most oat brands on the market today are not pure – they contain oats that have been cross-contaminated with wheat, barley and/or rye. Since those grains do have gluten in them, this cross-contamination makes most oatmeal brands unsafe on a gluten-free diet.

Check it

Name a popular breakfast cereal made from oats.

Check it

Explain the difference between soluble and insoluble fibre.

Key point

Oats are a good source of both soluble and insoluble fibre.
Soluble fibre helps to lower blood cholesterol.

Study tip

When discussing the health benefits of dietary fibre make sure you cover the importance of both soluble and insoluble fibre. This will increase your chances of higher marks.

▲ Pearl barley, barley flour

▲ Barley growing in field

▲ Orzotto, a risotto style dish made from pearl barley

Barley

Barley is the second most widely grown arable crop in the UK (after wheat). In the UK the most common way for processing barley is into pearl barley and barley flour. Other available forms include: flakes, malt, and whole grain.

Pearl barley is often used for thickening soups. Barley is also an important ingredient in beer making.

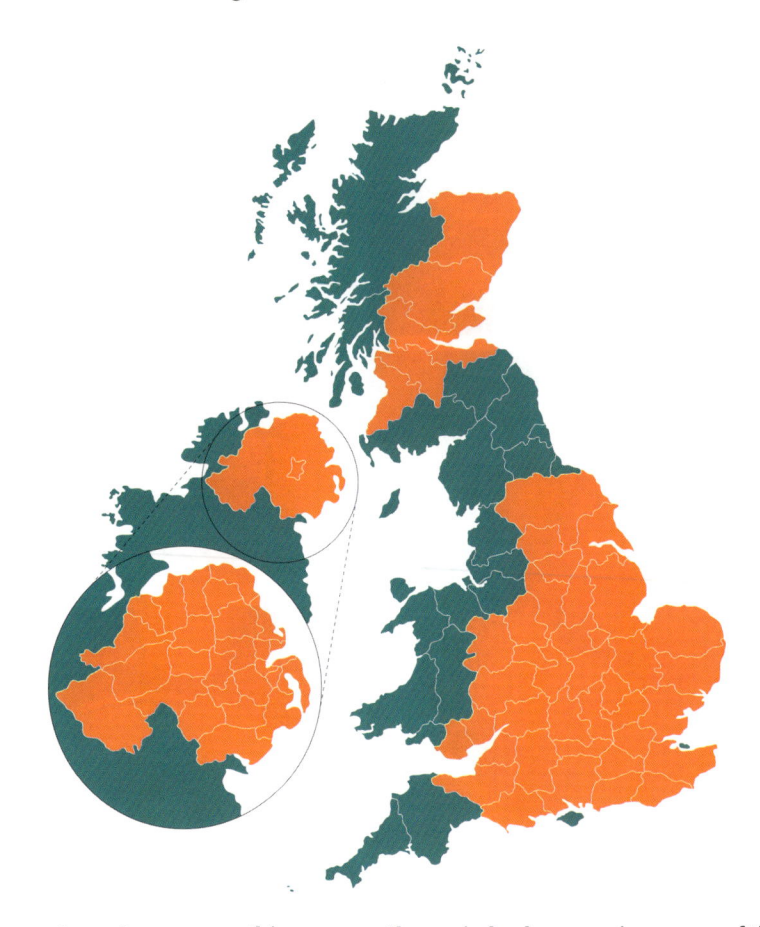

▲ Areas coloured orange on this map are the main barley growing areas of the UK

Using barley

Barley can be used whole, in the form of pearl barley, in both savoury and sweet dishes. Barley is often added as a thickener or to provide bulk and texture to soups and casseroles; it can also be used in orzotto (as an alternative to rice based risotto), as a breakfast porridge (as an alternative to oats) or as the main ingredient in salads.

Barley can also be ground to produce flour suitable for baking; it is often added as part of a blend with other flours for added health benefits and to add texture. Due to its low gluten content you should not substitute barley flour entirely for wheat flour.

Nutritional value of barley

Barley is a good source of starchy carbohydrate, iron, vitamin B3 (niacin) and vitamin B6 (pyridoxin). It is also high in fibre, providing both soluble and insoluble fibre. Barley contains the same type of soluble fibre as oats (beta-glucan), which can help to fill you up so you eat less; it also improves your blood cholesterol levels.

Barley contains gluten and is therefore not suitable for those with coeliac disease.

COMMODITIES

CEREALS

Rye

Rye is grown mainly in the north and east of Europe, e.g. Scandinavia, Russia, Poland. It is a hardy crop and grows well in climates that are cold and wet and not suitable for wheat cultivation.

Areas coloured orange/red on this map are the main rye growing areas of the world. The darker the area, the more rye produced. ▼

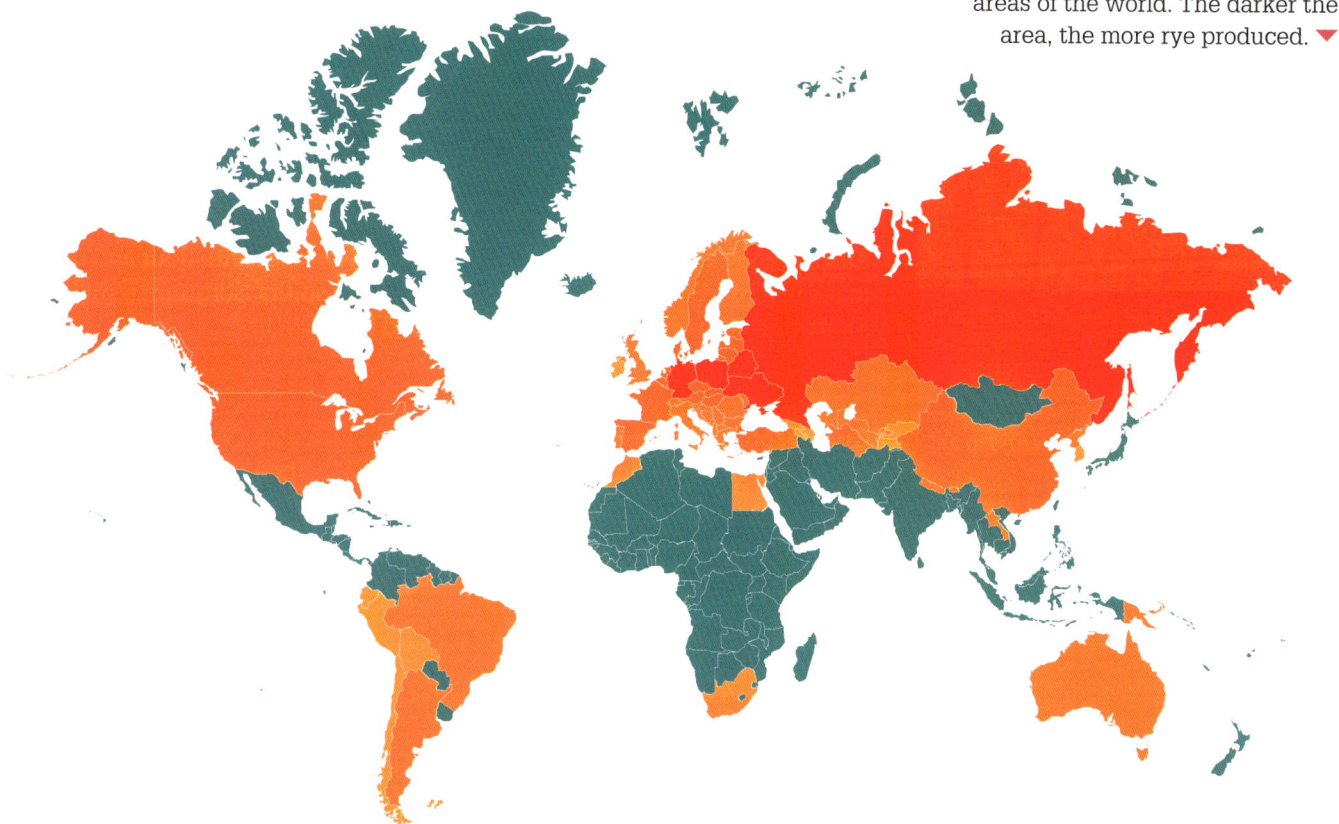

Using rye

Rye grain produces dense, close textured breads (such as pumpernickel) with strong flavours which are very popular in Germany and Scandinavia. Rye flour is often combined with wheat flour so that the dough is not too heavy or sticky.

Light and medium rye is produced from the endosperm while dark rye includes all the grain, which gives a coarser flour, resulting in a heavier bread.

Rye flour is used most often for breads and bread rolls. It gives a slightly sour flavour to the dough. Breads made with rye flour have a longer **shelf life** and taste fresh longer than breads made with wheat flours. Rye flour is high in the protein gliadin but low in the protein glutenin. This means that the dough will not develop as much gluten as dough made with wheat flour. This is why rye flour is often combined with other flours of a higher protein content. It is also made into crispbreads, sometimes flavoured with caraway seeds for a distinctive flavour.

Rye is also used to make alcoholic drinks, like rye whiskey and rye beer.

Nutritional value of rye

Rye is a good source of starchy carbohydrate, fibre, minerals and vitamin B1 (thiamin).

▼ Rye is a popular cereal in the north and east of Europe

Check it

Why is rye flour often combined with other flours when making bread?

↳ Key terms

Beta-glucan – a soluble fibre, helps to boost heart health.

Coeliac disease – an auto-immune condition where a person has an adverse reaction to gluten.

▲ Sorghum before it is processed

OTHER GRAINS

What will I learn?
- Find out about other less common cereals and grains
- Use of plants as thickening agents

Sorghum

Sorghum is the world's fifth most important cereal crop after rice, wheat, maize and barley. Sorghum is a cereal grain grown in many parts of Asia and Africa and often forms the staple food there. It is milled into flour and used to make flatbreads. It is also used in China to make spirits. Sorghum is milled to a soft, fine flour, it imparts a nutty taste and is gluten free.

Quinoa

Quinoa (pronounced keen - wah) is sometimes called a superfood; it is talked about as a whole grain, but it is actually a seed. Quinoa is a good source of protein – providing all the essential amino acids, making it a high biological value protein. Quinoa is a gluten free and cholesterol free whole grain. It is also high in dietary fibre, containing almost twice as much dietary fibre as most other grains.

There are three main types of quinoa: red, white and black, and it can be prepared in a similar way to rice or barley.

▲ Quinoa seeds     ▲ Millet and amaranth are alternative grains available for cooking

Arrowroot, sago and tapioca

Although these three ingredients are not true cereals, they are used as thickeners as they contain mostly starch.

Arrowroot comes from the maranta plant and is used to thicken sauces and as a glaze for fruits when a smooth and clear opaque gel is needed.

Sago comes from sago palm and is used for milky puddings.

Tapioca comes from a tuber called cassava and is also used for milky puddings as well as a thickener in soups and stews.

▲ Arrowroot, sago and tapioca are used as thickening agents

Check it

Why is quinoa sometimes referred to as a *superfood*?

Activities

1. Search online for nutritional information about cereals, or use nutritional software, to complete the following table:

	Per 100g				
	Wheat	Rice	Maize	Oats	Barley
Energy (kcal)					
Fat (g)					
Carbohydrate (g)					
Protein (g)					
Fibre (g)					

Write a summary paragraph based on your findings. Are you surprised with any data you obtained?

2. Find out which cereals the following food products are made from:
   wholemeal bread   porridge
   couscous   cornflakes
   dried spaghetti   popcorn

COMMODITIES

PREVENT FOOD POISONING IN CEREALS

What will I learn?
- The importance of storing cereal crops correctly
- The sources of food poisoning contamination in cereal crops
- Food poisoning risks in cooked rice and fresh egg pasta

To ensure cereal crops do not become a source of food poisoning bacteria, it is important that the harvested crops are stored in suitable conditions.

Storage areas must be:
- dry and cool to reduce the likelihood of yeasts, moulds and fungi contaminating the crop
- clean and free from rodents, birds, insects or pests.

Sources of contamination

Fungi may produce **mycotoxins**, which are toxic to humans.

Rodents and birds can transfer diseases such as Weil's disease, salmonella, cryptosporidium, toxoplasmosis and listeria.

Mites can carry fungal spores and bacteria such as salmonella. This can be controlled by using insecticides during the cultivation of the crop.

Cooked rice

Bacillus cereus is able to form spores that are very resistant to low or high temperatures, it can easily survive cooking and refrigeration temperatures. It is recommended that rice is cooked and consumed immediately rather than stored; this will reduce the risk of food poisoning.

Use of fresh egg in pasta making

Raw egg can contain the food poisoning bacteria **salmonella.** When making pasta using fresh egg, salmonella can be avoided by using eggs known to be salmonella free such as eggs with a British Lion Quality mark or by using pasteurised egg.

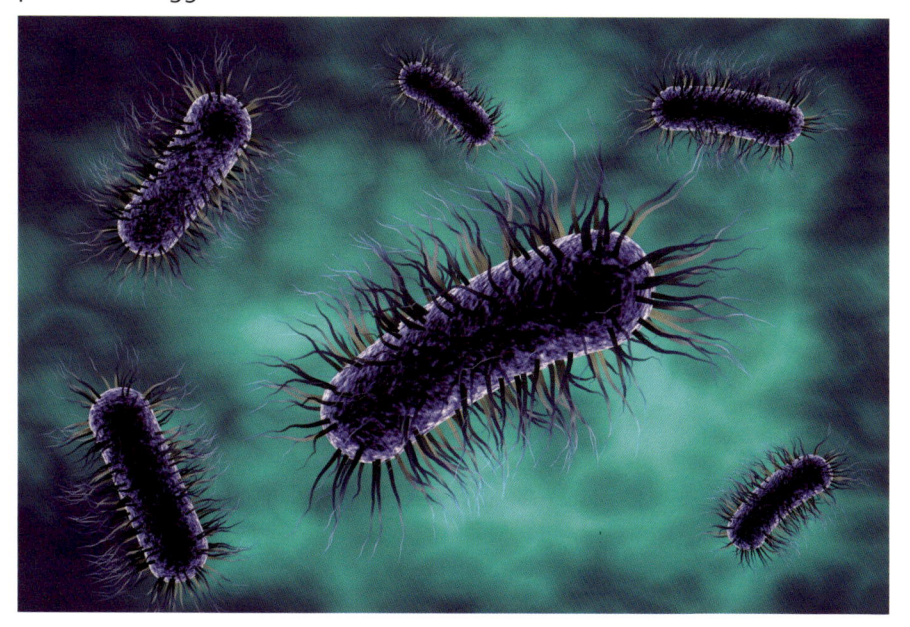

▲ Bacteria

Check it
1. What are the most likely contaminants that can affect the quality of cereal crops?
2. Give examples of pathogenic bacteria that can be passed to humans from poorly stored cereal crops.

Key point
Bacillus cereus is the pathogenic food poisoning bacteria associated with poorly stored cooked rice.

Key point
To reduce the risk of salmonella food poisoning, eggs should be either pasteurised or have the British Lion Quality mark.

Key terms

Bacillus cereus – a type of pathogenic bacteria that produces toxins, associated with poor hygiene in cooked rice.

Salmonella – pathogenic bacteria found in raw egg.

EXAM QUESTIONS

1. **a** The table below compares the nutritional values of both wholemeal bread and white bread.

	Wholemeal Bread, Medium Sliced		White Bread, Medium Sliced	
	Per 100g	Per 40g slice	Per 100g	Per 40g slice
Energy	221Kcal	88kcal	223kcal	93kcal
Protein	10g	4g	8.7g	3.5g
Fat	1.8g	0.7g	1.7g	0.7g
Carbohydrate	37.8g	15.1g	44.6g	17.9g
Fibre	6.8g	2.7g	2.4g	1.0g
Salt	0.90g	0.36g	0.90g	0.36g

Using the information given in the table, answer the following questions:
   - **i** Which bread has the most energy value per slice? [1]
   - **ii** Which bread type has the most protein content per 100g? [1]
   - **iii** State why 100g wholemeal bread has more fibre content than 100g white bread. [1]

   b Mass production of bread uses the Chorleywood method.
   Give two reasons why a large scale bakery uses the Chorleywood bread making process. [2]

   c Explain why kneading bread dough is an important process when making bread. [2]

   d A baker has produced a batch of bread rolls which are small and heavy.
   Give two reasons why this might have happened and suggest ways this can be avoided in the future. [4]

2. Pasta is a popular staple food and is made from wheat flour.
   a Give the name of the wheat type that is recommended when making pasta.
   b Match the image with the correct pasta name. [5]

spaghetti papadelle tagliatelle conchiglie fusilli lasagne sheets orzo farfalle

   c Pasta should be cooked to 'al dente'. State what the term 'al dente' means. [1]
   d Lasagne is a popular pasta dish and uses béchamel sauce as a component of the dish.
   Explain what is happening during the sauce thickening process. [4]

3. **a** Complete the table below stating the correct flour type used to make each product [3]

Food product	Type of flour used
Victoria sandwich	
White bread rolls	
Jam tarts	

   b Sandwiches are a popular lunchtime snack.

	Per pack
Energy	253kcal
Protein	10g
Fat	4.5g
Carbohydrate	36.6g
Fibre	2.3g
Salt	1.5g

   Each pack contains

ENERGY	FAT	SATURATES	SUGARS	SALT
1058kJ 253kcal	4.5g	2.0g	0g	1.5g
13%	6%	10%	0%	25%

   % of the Reference Intakes

   Typical values per 100g: Energy 854kJ/204kcal

   Use the nutritional information from the ham sandwich packaging above to answer the following questions:
   - **i** The energy content for the pack is 253kcals, what is this as a percentage of the reference intake? [1]
   - **ii** The protein content for the pack is 10g. State the main protein source. [1]
   - **iii** The salt content is 25% of the reference intake. What is the recommended daily salt intake, in grams, for an adult? [1]
   - **iv** The sandwich uses white bread and contains ham only. Suggest how the fibre content for the sandwich can be increased? [2]
   - **v** Sandwiches are referred to as 'high risk foods'. Give three good hygiene and food safety points to include when making fresh sandwiches. [3]

   c Food wastage in the UK is increasing. Suggest two ways in which bread wastage can be reduced. [2]

   TOTAL: 34

FOOD INVESTIGATIONS

CEREALS

Investigation 1 — Determine the suitability of flours in bread making

Some flours are recommended for bread making as they have a high protein content. Conduct an experiment to determine the suitability of the following flours for bread making:
- Strong plain flour
- Strong wholemeal flour
- Self-raising flour
- Plain white flour
- Rye flour

(you may alter the flour types depending on availability).

Method
Take a beaker or straight sided glass. Add 40g of one flour type, add 2g fast action dried yeast and 60ml water to the beaker. Mix until it forms a paste. Measure the volume or height of the mix (so that you know the volume or height at the start of the experiment).

Repeat the experiment with other flours using the same style of beaker/glass. (Keep the test fair.)

Place the beakers into a warm area (37°C is the optimum temperature) and observe what happens to the dough. Record your findings over regular time periods.

Note the volume/height achieved by each variation. Which flour would be most suitable for bread making? Think about the elasticity of the dough and its ability to retain gas.

> **Optional task**
> Repeat the experiment with the addition of a pinch of ascorbic acid powder and compare your findings.

Investigation 2 — Gluten formation in different flours

Investigate the amounts of gluten formed from dough made from the following flours:
- Strong plain white flour
- Plain white flour
- Cornflour
- Rice flour
- Rye flour

(you may alter the flour types depending on availability).

Method
Mix 50g of each flour with enough water to form a dough and knead it until the dough is smooth.

Weigh each dough ball and record the weight.

Wrap each ball of dough in a J cloth / muslin cloth. Hold each ball under cold running water and allow the water to wash over the dough to wash away the starch. Keep washing the dough until all the starch is washed away and the water turns from cloudy to clear.

What you are left with is the gluten that is present in the flour.

Remove the J cloth / muslin cloth and examine what is remaining. Are there any dough balls that have disappeared? If so – why do you think this is?

Weigh the gluten samples and calculate the percentage of gluten in each of the flour types.

Stretch the gluten samples by hand and observe how far they stretch.

> **Optional task**
> Bake the gluten balls at 220°C until each ball is puffed up and golden brown.
> Compare each cooked dough ball. Which flour do you think would produce the best bread?

Investigation 3 — Thickening properties of flour

Investigate flours for thickening.

Use:
- Plain white flour
- Cornflour
- Arrowroot

(you may alter the flour types depending on availability).

Method
Place 25g of the starch into a small saucepan and gently add 250ml cold water. Stir.

Place the saucepan onto the hob and stir constantly. Note the temperature at which the mixture begins to thicken. Keep stirring until the mix reaches 95°C. Transfer the mix (called a gel) while still hot into a bowl and allow to cool.

Repeat the experiment with other starches, ensuring your testing is fair.

When the gels formed are cool, turn them out onto a plate. If you have a viscosity mat use this.

Compare the cooled gels, what can you see and feel? Consider how the different starches can be used in cooking. Explain which starch would be suitable to use in a white sauce? Which starch would be most suitable as a glaze and why? Which starch would be suitable to use as part of a fruit pie filling? Explain why.

> **Optional task**
> Repeat the experiment, this time freeze the cooled gels. Once frozen, allow to defrost and examine the defrosted gels. Compare against gels made with the same starch which have not been frozen. Again, what can you see and feel? Consider the implications of using starches in frozen foods.

HOW TO MAKE FRESH PASTA

Portion size: 1 **Difficulty rating:** ★★★

INGREDIENTS:

- 70g strong white bread flour / Tipo '00' flour
- 30g fine semolina
- ¼ tsp salt
- ½ dessertspoon olive oil
- 1 whole egg
- Extra flour and semolina for kneading and rolling out

EQUIPMENT LIST:

digital scales	teaspoon	pasta machine (a rolling pin can be used if you don't have a pasta machine)
mixing bowl	dessertspoon	
wooden spoon	small knife	

METHOD:

1. Weigh the flour and semolina into the mixing bowl.
2. Add the salt and sprinkle over the oil, and stir.
3. Make a well in the centre of the mix and crack in the egg.
4. Using the wooden spoon, mix the dough together (you may need a little more egg if the dough is dry; you may need a little more flour if the dough is a little sticky).
5. Transfer to a lightly floured surface and knead for 2 to 3 minutes. The dough should become smooth and pliable.
6. Wrap the dough in clingfilm. Allow to rest (in the refrigerator) for at least 15 minutes.
7. Begin to roll the dough, do this by:
8. Dividing the dough in half and rolling each half separately
9. Push the dough through the widest setting of the rollers of the pasta machine, turning the handle. Repeat, again and again, each time adjusting the machine to make the rollers closer together, so that the pasta sheet gets thinner and longer (this is called laminating).
10. Dust the pasta rollers with semolina to prevent the dough from sticking to the rollers.
11. Cover the rolled out dough with a damp teatowel, to prevent it drying out. Cut it into the required shape quickly, as it will dry out.
12. Use the pasta as instructed in the recipe.

NUTRITION:	Recipe	100g	Portion	Reference Intake Men	Women	Children
Energy (kJ)	1986	1204	1986			
Energy (kcal)	470	285	470	19%	24%	26%
Fat (g)	12	7	12	13%	17%	17%
Saturates (g)	3	2	3	10%	15%	15%
Carbohydrate (g)	76	46	76	25%	33%	35%
Sugars (g)	1	2	1	1%	1%	1%
Salt (g)	1	1	1	17%	17%	25%

EATWELL GUIDE:

SUCCESS CRITERIA

- Pasta dough should be smooth and pliable after kneading.
- Cover the pasta dough with cling film to stop it drying out.

SKILLS / TECHNIQUES

- Weighing and measuring
- Mixing (by hand)
- Kneading
- Laminating

RECIPE MODIFICATION

- Coloured pasta can be made using the following ingredients: spinach, tomato purée, beetroot, squid ink
- Incorporate into the laminating process tender fresh herb leaves such as basil and parsley – this will add flavour as well as give a colourful appearance
- As well as lasagne sheets you can make interesting pasta shapes including tagliatelle and papardelle; filled parcels including ravioli can also be made.

SCIENCE INVOLVED

- Using a high protein flour will develop the gluten and give the pasta the elasticity needed during laminating.

COOK'S TIPS

- The traditional Italian way of making pasta is directly on the table. Try it, it's fun!
- You can also make fresh pasta in a food processor
- You may need a little more egg (it depends on the size of the egg and the flour that you use)
- The semolina gives the finished pasta a lovely yellow colour and improves the texture – but if you don't have any just replace with flour.

ALLERGENS

Wheat flour, egg

MUSHROOM RISOTTO

Portion size: 4 **Difficulty rating:** ★★★

CEREALS

INGREDIENTS:

- 1 tbsp dried porcini mushrooms
- 1 onion, diced
- 2 garlic cloves, crushed
- 225g sliced chestnut mushrooms
- 1.35 litres hot vegetable stock
- Big handful of fresh parsley, chopped
- 50g Parmesan cheese, grated
- 2 tbsp. olive oil
- 350g Arborio rice
- 25g butter
- salt and freshly ground black pepper

EQUIPMENT LIST:

kettle	garlic crusher	wooden spatula
2 x heatproof mixing bowl	measuring jug	sieve
dessertspoon	grater	ladle
chopping board	deep sided frying pan / saucepan	
chef's knife		

METHOD:

1. Fill a kettle with water and bring to the boil.
2. Place the dried porcini mushrooms in a heatproof bowl. Pour over 250ml of just boiled water and leave to stand (you want to use both the mushrooms and the stock in this recipe).
3. Make the stock (by pouring boiling water over the stock cube/powder).
4. When all the above is done you can start cooking:
5. Heat the oil in the pan and add the onion and garlic.
6. Sauté over a gentle heat for 2-3 minutes, until softened.
7. Add the sliced chestnut mushrooms and gently sauté for a further 2-3 minutes, until browned.
8. Whilst the mushrooms are sautéing, drain the soaked mushrooms and keep the mushroom water safe as you will need this. Roughly chop the mushrooms.
9. Add the rice to the pan. Stir in the rice and coat in the oil.
10. Add the mushroom stock and sliced chestnut mushrooms to the pan. Bring to a simmer, stirring, until the liquid has been absorbed.
11. Add a ladleful of the stock and simmer, stirring again, until the liquid has been absorbed. Continue adding the stock in this way, until all the liquid has been absorbed and the rice is plump and tender. This can take up to 35 mins.
12. Test the rice – it should have a little bite in the centre ('al dente'). Turn off the heat and stir in the chopped parsley, grated Parmesan cheese and butter. Taste and season. Serve.

NUTRITION:

				Reference Intake		
	Recipe	100g	Portion	Men	Women	Children
Energy (kJ)	8679	1017	1986			
Energy (kcal)	2061	242	515	21%	26%	29%
Fat (g)	73	9	18	19%	26%	26%
Saturates (g)	27	3	7	23%	34%	34%
Carbohydrate (g)	318	37	80	27%	35%	36%
Sugars (g)	9	1	2	2%	3%	3%
Salt (g)	11	1	3	46%	46%	69%

EATWELL PLATE:

SUCCESS CRITERIA

- Make sure the hot stock is added in gradually and stir the risotto regularly during cooking.
- The best results are with risotto rice such as arborio, vialone nano and carnaroli.

SKILLS / TECHNIQUES

- Knife skills – dicing, slicing, crushing, chopping
- Grating
- Sautéing
- Simmering
- Cooking the rice to the required texture and achieving the expected creaminess of the final risotto
- Control of hob

RECIPE MODIFICATION

- Use a selection of different and more exotic mushroom varieties e.g., Oyster, Portabello, Shiitake, Shimeji
- Mushrooms can be substituted with other vegetables – e.g., sliced peppers, diced courgettes, butternut squash, sweet potato
- Add cooked bacon, prawns, chicken
- Flavour with other herbs such as thyme, basil, sage

SCIENCE INVOLVED

- Stirring the risotto regularly during cooking releases starch from the rice grains, the starch gelatinises and thickens the dish.

COOK'S TIPS

Don't wash the mushrooms – this makes them spongy, a wipe over with kitchen roll is sufficient

Make sure the stock is really hot, heat in a small pan if you need to.

ALLERGENS

Milk

WELSH CAKES

Portion size: 12 individual cakes **Difficulty rating:** ★★★

INGREDIENTS:

- 225g self-raising flour (plus extra for rolling out)
- ¼ tsp mixed spice
- 110g salted butter (plus extra for griddling)
- 85g caster sugar, plus extra for dusting
- 50g currants
- 1 egg, beaten
- milk, if needed
- extra butter, for greasing

EQUIPMENT LIST:

- digital scales
- small knife
- measuring jug
- fork
- mixing bowl
- sieve
- rolling pin
- plain edged pastry cutter (7.5–10cm in diameter)
- bakestone or griddle (if you don't have one of these use a heavy frying pan)
- palette knife

METHOD:

1. Cut the butter into small even cubes.
2. Crack the egg into a measuring jug and beat with a fork.
3. Sift the flour and mixed spice into a mixing bowl and add the cubed butter.
4. Rub with your fingertips until the mixture resembles breadcrumbs.
5. Add the sugar, currants and beaten egg and mix well to form a ball of dough, using a splash of milk if needed.
6. Gently roll the dough out on a floured surface to a thickness of between 5mm to 10mm.
7. Cut into rounds with a 7.5–10cm plain cutter.
8. Rub a bakestone or heavy iron griddle with butter, wipe away the excess and place on the hob until it is heated through.
9. Cook the Welsh cakes a few at a time for 2–3 minutes on each side, or until golden-brown.
10. Remove from the griddle and dust with caster sugar while still warm.

NUTRITION:	Recipe	100g	Portion	Reference Intake Men	Women	Children
Energy (kJ)	8904	1677	1986			
Energy (kcal)	2120	399	177	7%	9%	10%
Fat (g)	100	19	8	9%	12%	12%
Saturates (g)	60	11	5	17%	25%	25%
Carbohydrate (g)	294	55	25	8%	11%	11%
Sugars (g)	127	24	11	9%	12%	12%
Salt (g)	4	1	Trace	6%	6%	8%

EATWELL GUIDE:

SUCCESS CRITERIA

- All Welsh cakes are rolled to the same thickness and cut to the same diameter.
- Surface colour is even and golden brown.
- Moist in the centre.

SKILLS / TECHNIQUES

- Sifting
- Mixing (by hand, gently)
- Shaping
- Rolling out and cutting
- Griddling
- Weighing and measuring
- Making the dough to the right consistency (not too dry)
- Controlling the heat from the griddling process

RECIPE MODIFICATION

- Replace currants with sultanas, raisins or even a tropical fruit mix
- Add zest of a citrus fruit (e.g., lemon, orange, lime) for an added zing!

SCIENCE INVOLVED

The baking powder in the self-raising flour acts as a raising agent.

COOK'S TIPS

- Cook the dough as soon as the dough is made
- They are best eaten on the day they are made.

ALLERGENS

Wheat flour, milk, egg, sulphur dioxide (in dried fruit)

SECTION 3
COMMODITIES

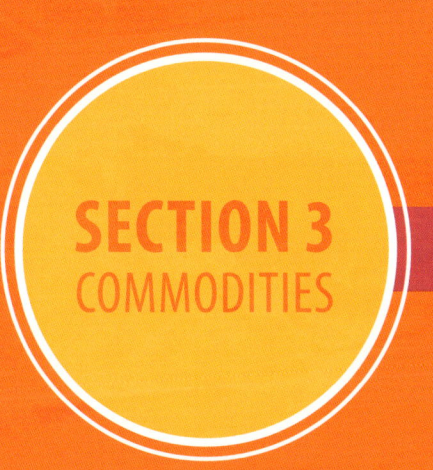

FRUIT AND VEGETABLES

- **VARIETY OF FRUIT AND VEGETABLES** 214
- **IMPORTANCE OF FRUIT AND VEGETABLES IN THE DIET** 216
- **CHOOSING, STORING AND USING FRUIT AND VEGETABLES** 220
- **POTATOES** 227
- **HERBS AND SPICES** 229
- **PRESERVING FRUITS AND VEGETABLES** 234
- **EXAM QUESTIONS** 236
- **FOOD INVESTIGATIONS** 237
- **RECIPES** 238

SECTION 3
COMMODITIES

FRUIT AND VEGETABLES

What will I learn?

- The variety of fruit and vegetables available
- The importance of fruit and vegetables in the diet [N]
- The nutritional value of fruit and vegetables [N]
- The characteristics and uses of herbs and spices

Study tip

Can you explain the meaning of seasonal fruit and vegetables?

What are the benefits of using seasonal fruit and vegetables in the diet?

▲ Parts of the plant growing above and below ground

A wide variety of fruit and vegetables are available, many of which are imported from all over the world. Fruit and vegetables are grown on farms and in gardens and allotments in the UK, and they ripen at certain seasons in the year. When they are in season, they are naturally at their best nutritionally, are in peak condition and have a very good flavour. When in season they are generally in plentiful supply and are also cheaper to buy.

However, as the UK now produces hundreds of varieties of fruit and vegetables – and many more are imported all year round – the seasonality of fruit and vegetables can lose its meaning.

All fruit and vegetables can be **organically produced**, that is, grown using natural fertilizers and pesticides. They can also be locally sourced.

Variety of fruit and vegetables

Fruit and vegetables can be classified (or grouped) according to the part of the plant from which they are obtained.

Fruits are generally described as the part of the plant that carries the seeds for future generations of plants.

Vegetables			Fruit
in the soil	above the ground	in water	
root	leaves	sea vegetables	stoned
tubers	flower heads		citrus
bulbs	stems		hard
	fungi		soft berry
	seeds and pods		currants

214 COMMODITIES

FRUIT AND VEGETABLES

Different types of vegetables

ROOT
beetroot, carrots, celeriac, parsnips, radishes, swede, turnips, cassava, galangal

TUBERS
potato, sweet potato, Jerusalem artichokes

BULBS
onions, leeks, shallots, garlic, fennel

FLOWER HEADS
broccoli, cauliflower, brassica, Brussels sprouts, cabbage, kale, Chinese cabbage, pak choi

SEA VEGETABLE
kelp, nori, samphire, agar-agar

STEMS
asparagus, celery, rhubarb, chicory, globe artichokes, kohlrabi, sea kale, endives

FUNGI
mushrooms (chestnut, chanterelle, shiitake, oyster, morels, ceps, portabello, open)

SEEDS AND PODS
beans, peas, lentils, runner beans, bean sprouts, okra, sweetcorn, sugar snap peas, mange tout

LEAVES
cabbage, Brussels sprouts, lettuce, spinach, watercress, pak choi, kale

VEGETABLE FRUITS
aubergines, tomatoes, courgettes, marrow, peppers, pumpkin, squash, avocado, cucumber

Different types of fruit

STONED
apricots, cherries, damsons, greengages, nectarines, peaches, plums

CITRUS
clementines, grapefruit, kumquats, lemons, limes, mandarins, pomelo, oranges, tangerines

HARD
apples, pears, quince

NUTS
Brazil, cashew, peanut, almond, walnut, hazelnut, pecan, pistachio, macadamia

SOFT BERRY
blackberries, blueberries, bilberries, cranberries, gooseberries, raspberries, strawberries

MISCELLANEOUS
banana, dates, passion fruit, figs, grapes, guavas, kiwi fruit, mangoes, melons, lychees, Sharon fruit, pineapple, pomegranate

DRIED FRUIT
banana, pineapple, prunes, figs, raisins, currants, sultanas, apricots

TROPICAL
acerola, cape gooseberries, jack fruit, avocado, water melon, guava, dragon fruit, lychee, mango, passion fruit, tamarind, coconut

Nuts are actually a type of fruit that are made up of hard shells and seeds. Some fruits can be eaten as vegetables. These include tomatoes, avocado pears, aubergines, peppers, sweetcorn, marrows, courgettes and butternut squash.

Importance of fruit and vegetables in the diet N

Fruit and vegetables contain a range of nutrients and are therefore an important part of the diet. We are advised to eat at least five **portions** a day as they are known to be beneficial to our health. They also provide a variety of flavour, colour and texture to meals.

> **Activity**
>
> Fruit and vegetables are imported to the UK from all over the world. Find out where different fruits and vegetables come from and complete a table with your findings under the following headings:
>
> **a** name of fruit or vegetable
> **b** country of origin
> **c** cost (per 100g or kg)
> **d** example of dish

5 EAT AT LEAST FIVE PORTIONS A DAY

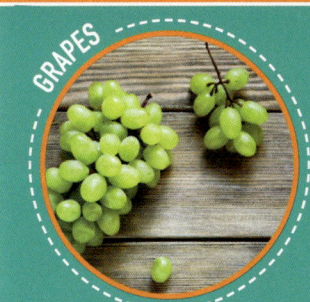

GRAPES

16 GRAPES = 1 PORTION

Black and red grapes contain more resveratrol, which is linked to a lower risk of prostate cancer, and may boost the immune system.

PEPPERS

HALF A PEPPER = 1 PORTION

Green ones are lowest in calories and natural sugars. Red ones contain more lycopene, a nutrient that helps prevent cancer.

BAKED BEANS

HALF OF A 400G CAN = 1 PORTION

The beans can count as one of your daily vegetable intake, and the sauce can count as another.

FRUIT LOLLIES

TWO LOLLIES = 1 PORTION

As long as it just contains fruit juice, then it is the same as having one glass of juice, but it's best to have it as a treat and not as a regular replacement for fruit.

AVOCADO

HALF AN AVOCADO = 1 PORTION

Avocado is rich in monounsaturated fatty acids as well as being a good source of vitamin K.

COMMODITIES

Beans, Nuts and Seeds, Soya, Tofu and Mycoprotein: **Legumes** p318

FRUIT AND VEGETABLES

What counts as a portion?

You will have seen by now that the word 'portion' is used a lot in meal and nutrition planning. A portion can be:

- fresh, frozen, tinned and dried varieties of fruit and vegetables
- fruit and vegetables cooked in dishes such as soups, stews or pasta dishes
- a glass of pure, unsweetened fruit or vegetable juice. However, juice counts as a maximum of one portion a day. This is because juice lacks fibre, compared to fruit or vegetables in other forms
- smoothies containing at least 80g of pulped fruit and/or vegetables and 150ml juice can count as up to two portions a day
- beans and pulses count as one portion a day no matter how many you eat. This is because they do not contain the same mixture of vitamins and minerals and other nutrients as fruit and vegetables. They do, however, provide a low fat source of protein as well as iron and dietary fibre.

> **Key point**
>
> A portion could be:
> - adding a handful of dried fruit to your breakfast cereal
> - drinking a glass of fruit juice
> - eating a banana sandwich
> - having a bowl of home-made tomato soup
> - eating a raw carrot.

> **Study tip**
>
> A portion = 80g or 3 tablespoons, or as much as you can fit onto the palm of your hand!

Unsweetened fruit juice is an important source of vitamin C, especially in children's diets. The National Diet and Nutrition Survey shows that on average for 4–18 year olds unsweetened fruit juice provides around 20% of their total daily vitamin C intake.

A 150ml glass of unsweetened orange juice can provide all the vitamin C requirements for a child as well as folate and potassium.

However fruit juice contains free sugars which are naturally present in the whole fruit, and so a practical tip recommended by public health organisations is to dilute unsweetened orange juice with water.

> **Activity**
>
> Research the ways fruit and vegetables can be used in meal planning. Record your findings under the headings of breakfast, snacks, main dishes and desserts.

Using fruit and vegetables

Fruit and vegetables can be used in a variety of ways:

- on their own as snacks
- as ingredients in a range of dishes
- vegetables can be an accompaniment to a meal, fruit can be eaten as a dessert or as part of a dessert.

Fruit and vegetables are an important part of the Eatwell Guide ▶

Nutritional value of fruit and vegetables

FRUIT AND VEGETABLES CONTAIN:

CARBOHYDRATE

Starch is stored in the roots and tubers of vegetables. Some of the starch is converted to sugar in vegetables such as beetroot, onions, peas and tomatoes. Fruit contains natural sugar in varying amounts depending on type.

VITAMIN A

Fat-soluble vitamin A **beta carotene** is found in dark green vegetables and in red, orange and yellow coloured fruits. Beta carotene can be converted to vitamin A by the body.

VITAMIN C

All citrus fruit, berry fruits, blackcurrants and rosehips are rich sources of vitamin C. Green vegetables, peppers and tomatoes are also good sources. As one of the staple foods in the UK diet, potatoes, particularly new potatoes, are a useful source.

B GROUP VITAMINS

Mainly riboflavin and nicotinic acid. Pulses are a good source of thiamine.

VITAMINS E AND K

Green vegetables and peas contain only a little vitamin E and K.

CALCIUM AND IRON

Found in various vegetables such as watercress, lentils and spinach but the presence of cellulose and oxalic acid reduces their availability to the body. Both cellulose and oxalic acid are naturally components within the plant structure, particularly dark green vegetables.

DIETARY FIBRE

Found in the skin, seeds, pith and fibrous parts of fruit and vegetables. It forms the part of the plant that gives it strength and structure, for example, the stringy bits in celery and cabbage and in the skin of potatoes.

Principles of Nutrition: Vitamins and Minerals pp10–11

FRUIT AND VEGETABLES

Key point

Fruits and vegetables are HIGH in vitamins, minerals and dietary fibre.
They are LOW in fat and calories.
They contain a HIGH amount of water.
Fruit and vegetables should make up approximately one third of total daily food intake.

Check it

1. What is 5 a day and why is it important?
2. Give examples of 5 a day.

What are the benefits of eating fruit and vegetables?

They contain:
- vitamin A, for maintenance of normal vision
- folate, for the formation of healthy blood cells and for the nervous system
- fibre, to help maintain a healthy gut
- potassium, to help maintain healthy blood pressure and nervous system functions
- magnesium, to help maintain healthy bones and teeth
- vitamin C, which acts as an antioxidant and is important for maintaining and healing body tissue. It also helps to absorb iron from plant sources.

How to include fruit and vegetables in the diet

- If you don't like eating vegetables on their own, try grating them into dishes that you do like. For example, grate carrot or courgette into Bolognese to add more flavour and texture.
- Use frozen fruit and vegetables – they can contain just as many nutrients as fresh produce. As they are frozen very soon after picking, their vitamin content is often higher than fresh fruit and vegetables that are a few days old. They are also useful to reduce waste as they keep much longer and are more economical as you can cook just the amount you need.
- Try a new vegetable each week to increase variety in meals and snacks.
- Pick seasonal fruit and vegetables - these are often cheaper and they taste better.
- Choose tinned fruit in natural juice with no added sugar, choose tinned vegetables with no added salt.
- A good way to have 5 a day is to have 1 portion at breakfast, 2 with lunch and 2 with dinner. More can be added in snacks.

Study tips

Learn the nutritional value of fruits and vegetables with examples.
Learn the benefits of including fruit and vegetables in the diet.

Activity

1. List examples of a portion of fruit and vegetables.
2. List ways in which 5 a day can be included in meals and snacks.
3. Find recipes which use fruit and vegetables that are in season.

▲ Try and include fruit from the full range of colour groups in your diet

CHOOSING, STORING AND USING FRUIT AND VEGETABLES

What will I learn?

- The factors to consider when choosing fruit and vegetables
- How storage and cooking affect the nutritional value of fruits and vegetables
- Uses of fruit and vegetables in cooking

The colour of fruit and vegetables

The green colour of leafy vegetables is due to the presence of **chlorophyll**. Chlorophyll responds to pH, so in acidic conditions it changes to olive green, whereas in alkaline conditions it becomes bright green. Some of the acids in chlorophyll are released in steam when vegetables are cooked.

The yellow/orange colour in fruit and vegetables is due to pigments (or colours) called **carotenoids** which are not affected by normal cooking methods or changes in pH.

The red/blue colour of some fruits and vegetables is due to water-soluble pigments called **anthocyanins**. These are also sensitive to pH, and in neutral pH conditions they will be purple. At acid pH they are red and at alkaline pH they are blue. They are very soluble in water.

Plants produce starch during **photosynthesis** and in unripe fruits most of the carbohydrate is in the form of starch. As fruit ripens, the starch is converted to sucrose and then to glucose and fructose. Fruit then becomes sweeter to the taste.

Choosing fruit and vegetables

When buying fruit and vegetables for menu planning, they should be chosen carefully. The following points should be considered:

- Choose ripe, fresh looking fruit with no blemishes, mould or bruising.
- Choose crisp, firm vegetables. Avoid vegetables that look damaged, mouldy or wilted.
- All fruits and vegetables should be a good colour.
- Fresh fruit should be used very quickly after it is picked or bought. This is because all fruit continues to ripen after it has been picked. During the ripening process, fruit takes in oxygen, gives off carbon dioxide and warms up.
- Keep fruit and vegetables in a cool, dark place until used.

Storing fruit and vegetables

Fruit and vegetables should ideally be consumed within a few days of purchase because they will be at their freshest and most nutritious.

All vegetables should be stored in a cool, dark place. Leaves such as spinach, cabbage, spring greens and broccoli should be kept in the salad drawer in a fridge. They should be eaten within two or three days of picking or purchase.

Root vegetables, bulbs and tubers will keep for several months in a dry, airy place. Try and store root vegetables separately in a dark, dry place.

Activity

Fruit and vegetables are imported to the UK from all over the world. Find out where different fruits and vegetables come from and complete a table with your findings under the following headings:

a name of fruit or vegetable
b country of origin
c cost (per 100g or kg)
d example of dish

▲ Potatoes sprouting if left in wrong storage conditions

Processing fruit and vegetables

Processed fruit and vegetables are useful alternatives to fresh. They are available in many forms:

- pre-prepared fresh
- canned
- frozen.
- dried
- juiced

There are several reasons why fruit and vegetables are processed:

- convenience
- all year round availability
- increased shelf life.

Chopped fruit and chopped vegetable salads are available pre-prepared and packed and ready to eat or use.

Frozen and canned fruits and vegetables can also be a good choice. They are generally processed and packaged within hours of being picked, ensuring that most vitamins are retained. Canning and freezing also help protect food from organisms that cause food spoilage.

Common frozen vegetables include carrots, peas, beans, corn and vegetable mixes.

Common canned fruits include pineapple, peaches, apricots, pears and mixed fruits. Choose varieties with no added sugar, or those canned in natural juice. Common canned vegetables include tomatoes, corn, baked beans, beetroot and baby carrots. Choose varieties with no added salt or fat.

Canned fruit and vegetables are sterilised by heating during the canning process, and can be kept on the shelf for two to four years. Fruits and vegetables packaged in glass jars, plastic tubs and flexible pouches are generally as good as canned, as they undergo the same kind of processing.

Fruit and vegetable juices are made by mechanically squeezing fruit or vegetable flesh without applying heat or a solvent. Many are then filtered to remove the fibre or pulp. Common methods for preservation and processing of fruit and vegetable juices include canning, pasteurisation, concentration, freezing, evaporating and spray drying.

Fruits are dried by removing the moisture content with hot air. They have a long shelf life, as long as the packaging is unopened and not damaged.

▲ Examples of fruits, vegetables and salads which have been prepared and are ready to eat or use

▲ Fruit and vegetables which have been processed by freezing, canning and bottling make a useful contribution to meal planning as they are convenient.

▲ A selection of dried fruits

▲ Cartons of fruit juices

TYPICAL FRESH-CUT PROCESS FOR FRUIT AND VEGETABLES

HARVEST AND TRANSPORTING TO THE PROCESSING PLANT

The instant a crop is removed from the ground, or separated from its parent plant, it begins to deteriorate. Post-harvest treatment largely determines final quality, whether a crop is sold for fresh consumption, or used as an ingredient in a processed food product.

RECEIVING

After the field, post-harvest processing is usually continued in a packing house. This can be a simple shed, providing shade and running water, or a large scale, sophisticated, mechanized facility, with conveyor belts, automated sorting and packing stations, walk-in coolers and the like. In mechanized harvesting, processing may also begin as part of the actual harvest process, with initial cleaning and sorting performed by the harvesting machinery.

WASHING TO REMOVE DIRT AND DISINFECTION TO REDUCE MICROBIAL CONTAMINATION

Sanitation is also an important factor, to reduce the possibility of pathogens that could be carried by fresh produce, for example, as residue from contaminated washing water.

PRE-COOLING

The most important goal of post-harvest handling is keeping the product cool, to avoid moisture loss and slow down undesirable chemical changes, and avoiding physical damage such as bruising, to delay spoilage.

PEELING, TRIMMING, DESEEDING; CUTTING INTO SPECIFIC SIZE

These are normally automated, production-line processes.

SORTING DEFECTS

A visual inspection of size, shape and quality of produce.

DIPPING IN ANTI-BROWNING, ANTI-MICROBIAL AND PRESERVING AGENTS

STORAGE AND DISTRIBUTION

The fruit or vegetables are stored and distributed in a temperature-controlled environment to prevent any deterioration, eventually ending up on the shelves.

PACKAGING AND LABELLING

The fruit or vegetables are weighed or counted into standard pack sizes and placed in the packaging. A label with all of the required information about origin and best before date as well as company branding (if applicable) is added.

Preparation of fruit and vegetables

All fruits and vegetables need to be washed to remove insecticide sprays, dirt, soil or insects. Before cooking or eating any fruit or vegetables it is generally a good idea to wash them carefully in cold water. Take care not to soak them.

If fruit or vegetables need peeling, peel as thinly as possible because there are vitamins and minerals in the flesh that are very close to the skin which could easily be removed. Young vegetables such as potatoes and carrots do not really need peeling.

Prepare green vegetables just before cooking to prevent destruction of vitamins by enzyme action released during chopping.

Once vegetables have been washed, peeled or seeded, they can be cut into a variety of specialist cuts to meet cooking and presentation requirements.

These are some of the common vegetable cuts:

▲ Strips (batons)　　▲ Shreds (chiffonade)　　▲ Diced (macedoine)

Fruits such as melon or strawberries can be cut with a knife to give a fanned effect and oranges can be segmented for enhancing presentation

▲ Segmenting an orange

Most fruits can be eaten raw. Plants produce starch during photosynthesis. As fruit ripens, the starch is converted to sucrose and then to glucose and fructose. Fruit then becomes sweeter to the taste and can therefore be eaten raw.

Some vegetables such as carrots, celery and peppers can be eaten raw as long as they are ripe.

▲ Fanning a strawberry

DIFFERENT WAYS OF COOKING VEGETABLES

BAKING
Potatoes should be scored or pricked before baking to allow the water inside to escape as steam, otherwise the skin will split during cooking.

BOILING
All root vegetables can be cooked by boiling. The vegetable must be fully covered with cold water in the pan before cooking, and then it can be brought to the boil and simmered until tender.

Green vegetables need to be cooked by plunging them into the minimum amount possible of boiling salted water. Boil for as little time as necessary to preserve as much colour, flavour and texture as possible. Use a tight fitting lid on the pan. Placing the green vegetables in boiling water will minimize loss of nutrients.

BRAISING
Braised vegetables are cooked in a stock inside a covered pan in a **mirepoix**, which is a mixture of sautéed, chopped vegetables. The whole pan – as long as it is ovenproof – can be put in a moderate oven. Celery, leeks, onions and red cabbage can be braised.

FRYING
Vegetables such as onions, potatoes and cauliflower florets can be fried in butter or oil to add colour and flavour.

Stir frying is also a popular method of cooking vegetables, often associated with Chinese methods of cooking. Usually a circular wok is used, which is heated to a high temperature before any oil is added and then the vegetables in order of cooking time. The cooking time is kept short in order to retain the crunchy texture associated with this method of cooking.

GRILLING
Vegetables such as peppers, mushrooms and peppers can be brushed with oil and placed under a grill to give a charred flavour and appearance.

Serve immediately; do not keep hot as there will be further loss of vitamin C.

ROASTING
Potatoes, butternut squash, peppers and root vegetables are examples of vegetables suitable for roasting. A roasting tray containing oil is heated before adding the prepared vegetables. Potatoes and root vegetables are often **parboiled** prior to roasting.

STEAMING
Vegetables are placed directly into perforated steamer trays, which allows moisture to build up and allow an even flow of steam to cook the vegetables.

Steaming is a method of cooking which retains the maximum amount of colour, flavour and texture in vegetables.

Serve immediately; do not keep hot as there will be further loss of vitamin C.

Any vegetables cooked in liquid will lose most of their vitamin content. Cooking in steam preserves most of the vitamins, and high pressure cooking, which is very fast, is one of the healthiest methods of cooking green vegetables.

Vegetables should be prepared, cooked and eaten straight away to maximise their goodness.

224 COMMODITIES The science of cooking food: p68

Cooking fruit and vegetables

It is important to cut vegetables to the same size to ensure that they cook evenly. Cooking makes vegetables more digestible because the cooking process breaks down the starch they contain and reduces their bulk. If cooked in water, however, some vegetables – such as potatoes – may increase in bulk as they absorb water.

There are many different ways of cooking fruit and vegetables.

Fruit is often stewed by cooking it gently in a little water, made into compote or baked.

Vegetables can be cooked by a range of methods depending on the texture and flavour required. These methods include baking, boiling, braising, frying, grilling, roasting and steaming.

Microwaving is also a popular method of cooking fruit and vegetables in order to retain colour, flavour and texture.

Green vegetables need careful cooking as the vitamins and minerals they contain are destroyed by over-heating. It is important to keep such losses to a minimum by choosing methods of cooking which use little additional water or if possible no extra water at all.

> **Key point**
>
> Fruit and vegetables add nutritional value, colour, texture to dishes.

> **Key point**
>
> Prepare vegetables just before cooking to maintain freshness and nutritional value.

Changes that take place during cooking of fruits and vegetables [N] [FS]

When fruit and vegetables are cooked, their flavour, colour, texture and nutritional value change. The same golden rule applies to both – use minimum cooking time and water.

Flavour

Cooking intensifies the flavour in some vegetables. For example, the taste of root vegetables such as parsnips and carrots becomes sweeter. The natural chemicals in vegetables such as onions are released when fried in oil or butter. This causes the natural sugars in onions to be released and changed to enable caramelisation to take place. Roast vegetables have a very characteristic taste because the cooking process reduces their water content making the resulting flavour more intense.

Colour

Cooking green vegetables in boiling water causes them to change colours. They first become very bright green, then the colour changes to olive green and finally to a grey green colour. In order to preserve as much colour as possible, boil quickly in as little water as necessary.

Yellow and orange coloured vegetables do not change colours when cooked.

Red and purple coloured vegetables are affected by acids and alkalis in the water when cooked. Acids such as vinegar will turn the vegetables bright red and alkalis such as bicarbonate of soda will turn the vegetables blue. Vegetables which are affected in this way include red cabbage, red onions and beetroot.

> **Activity**
>
> List one sweet and one savoury dish where fruit and/or vegetables add:
>
> a nutritional value
> b texture
> c flavour
> d appearance
>
> Give as much detail as possible to support your choice of dishes.

Fruit and vegetables can used in combination with other ingredients to produce main dishes, snacks and desserts. They can also be used to improve the flavour and appearance of many products ▶

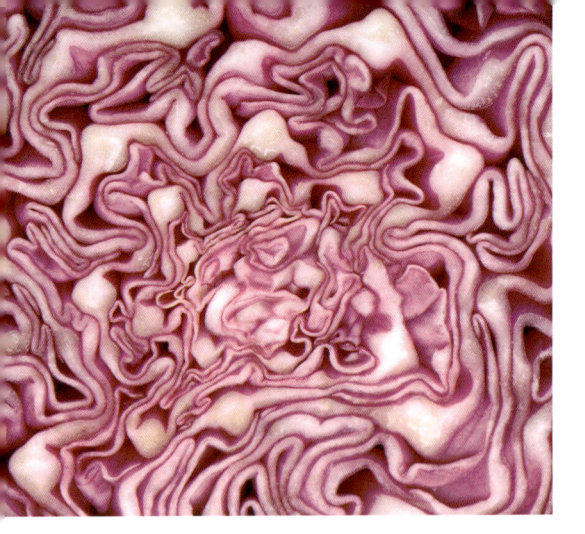

▲ When fruit or vegetables are cut, chopped or shredded, the cell walls are broken. This allows the enzyme in the cell walls to mix with and destroy the vitamin C

Texture

Cooking affects texture by softening the walls of cells in plant tissue. This releases the water inside the cells and softens the texture. Boiling vegetables reduces bulk; the higher the water content, the more the bulk is reduced. Spinach is a good example of a vegetable with a high water content which needs no additional water in cooking.

Overcooking enables the walls of cells to separate and makes vegetables very soft and mushy. Starchy vegetables such as potato absorb water and the granules swell which makes the vegetable soft and digestible to eat.

Nutritional value

Cutting and bruising causes damage to the plant cells. Exposure to the oxygen in the air and to light releases enzymes that destroy vitamin C and antioxidants present in the vegetables. To minimize this damage, vegetables should be prepared just before cooking and chopping or cutting kept to a minimum. Vitamin C, being water soluble, is released into the cooking liquid. Use very little cooking water and use the cooking liquid for gravy or a sauce. Keep cooking times to a minimum in order to retain vitamin C as well as colour and texture.

Beta carotene is found in yellow, orange and red vegetables and is released during cooking. When eaten our bodies are able to convert it to vitamin A.

Using fruits and vegetables

> **Study tip**
>
> Learn how to prepare and cook green vegetables in order to retain their colour, flavour, texture and nutritional value.

> **Study tip**
>
> Learn cooking methods with examples of suitable fruit and vegetables and/or dishes cooked using those methods.

> **Key point**
>
> All fresh, frozen, tinned or dried fruits and vegetable are suitable for vegetarians – aim for 5 portions a day. Some fruit and vegetables which are part of a ready meal or prepared in a sauce may not be suitable for vegetarians and vegans. Check the label.

FRUITS

- Raw, with or without skin
- Stewed
- Baked
- Dried, for example apricots, bananas, raisins, currants, sultanas
- Canned, bottled in syrup or preserved as jam or chutney
- Preserved in sugar as crystallised or candied fruit, for example pineapple, cherries, orange and lemon
- Added to jellies and mousses
- Served with meat, for example apple sauce with pork, cranberry sauce with turkey, mango with curries
- In recipes such as curries, sweet and sour dishes

VEGETABLES

- Raw, with or without skin
- Combined with other ingredients in salads and as side dishes
- In soups and to flavour stock
- Roasted, baked, fried, stir fried, barbequed, boiled, steamed, braised or cooked in a microwave
- Canned, though the heating process destroys some of the vitamins
- Dried
- Preserved in vinegar, for example onions, cucumber and pickles
- In chutneys and relishes
- As an accompaniment in a meal
- In recipes such as risottos, casseroles, sauces, pasta dishes
- Stuffed with fillings, for example peppers, courgettes, potatoes

POTATOES

What will I learn?

- The importance of potatoes as a staple food
- The varieties of potatoes available in season
- Storage of potatoes
- The nutritional value of potatoes [N]
- The effect of heat on cooking potatoes [N]
- Uses of potatoes in cooking

Potatoes are considered to be one of the most important staple foods in the UK. They are often eaten as the main vegetable accompaniment to a meal. Because of the frequency and amounts eaten, potatoes are a good source of vitamin C in the UK diet, even though they are not themselves a rich source of the vitamin.

Potato crops

There is a wide range of potato varieties available from UK supermarkets and greengrocers. Some are available at the beginning of the potato season in May, June and July. These are generally called new or early crop potatoes and include varieties such as Arran Pilot, Home Guard, Irish Cobbler, Pentland Javelin and Yukon Gold.

Early crop potatoes have a firm, waxy type flesh which will keep its shape on cooking. Because of this, however, they do not mash or cream easily.

Main crop potatoes appear from August onwards and are harvested at the end of the season in September and October. Varieties of main crop potatoes include Craig's Royal, Wilja, Home Guard, Desiree, Maris Piper, Cara, King Edward and Pentland Crown. Main crop potatoes will keep until the following year if they are stored in proper conditions.

▲ Varieties of potatoes are grown to suit different cooking methods

Varieties of potatoes are grown to suit different cooking methods. Some are better for mashing, others are more suitable for frying as chipped potatoes and there are varieties which make a good baked potato. Depending on the variety, potatoes can be granular and waxy, floury or sticky.

Cooking method	Suitable varieties of potato
Salad	Arran Pilot, Golden Wonder, Desiree
Baking	King Edward, Maris Piper, Wilja
Mashing	Desiree, Golden Wonder, King Edward
Frying	Majestic, Maris Piper, Croft
Boiling	Maris Piper, Epicure, Craig's Royal, Wilja

▼ Potato starch **gelatinisation**

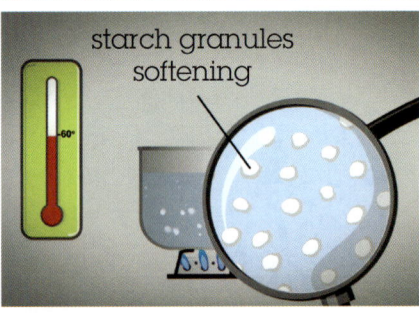

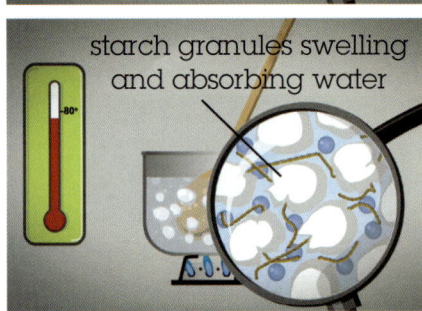

starch granules

starch granules softening

starch granules swelling and absorbing water

Changes during cooking

During cooking, the cells of the potato change in different ways. If the cells separate from each other during cooking, the cooked potato will be floury. If the cells stick to each other, the cooked potato will be waxy. [FS]

The cooking process also causes the potato starch grains to absorb water. This makes them swell into a tender mass. The starch gelatinises during the cooking process and if the potato is not cooked for long enough for all the starch to gelatinise, it will be hard in texture and taste starchy.

When cooked in fat or oil, potatoes absorb the fat. The smaller the pieces of potato, the more fat they absorb. This is because in proportion to its mass, the surface area exposed to the fat or oil is larger. That's why thin matchstick chips – such as you typically get from fast-food outlets – contain more fat than thick cut chips.

Potato starch makes an excellent thickener for soups and stews. The starch absorbs liquid, gelatinises and produces a gel which thickens the mixture. This gel does not break up if frozen and then thawed, so products thickened with potatoes can be frozen successfully.

Potatoes can be combined with most savoury ingredients. For example, they can be:

- creamed to make a topping for shepherd's pie or fish pie
- sliced on top of a casserole or hot pot
- grated or creamed to produce a rosti cake or latkes
- boiled or mashed and mixed with fish, meat, vegetables or nuts to make fish cakes, veggie burgers or rissoles
- mashed and mixed with flour to make potato cakes, pastry and bread.

Storing potatoes

Early and second crop potatoes do not keep for long but main crop potatoes have a long shelf life if kept under the right conditions. They will remain fresh and in good quality for many months.

Main crop potatoes will keep over the winter months in a cool, dry, dark place. Their shelf life will be longer if stored in paper bags or in racks than in polythene bags where they tend to sweat and rot.

Sunlight spoils potatoes by turning them green. The green part is toxic (poisonous) and should be removed before cooking.

HERBS AND SPICES

What will I learn?
- The variety of herbs and spices available
- The characteristics and uses of herbs and spices

Herbs

Herbs and spices have influenced multicultural cooking over the years. Many have both medicinal and culinary uses.

Herbs are actually the leaves, stems and roots of plants that are used to flavour foods. When cut, chopped, crushed or heated, they release aromatic oils which add flavour to other foods or dishes. Herbs are available as fresh plants, chopped or ground (powdered) and either dried, frozen or freeze-dried.

Pot-grown herbs, some of which can be grown in the UK, are available throughout the year. Fresh herbs are imported all year round, especially in winter. They come from many countries including Cyprus, Portugal, Spain, Holland and France. Dried herbs are imported from countries such as Egypt, Turkey and Algeria.

Fresh herbs generally give better results in cooking than dried varieties. However, dried herbs are generally stronger in flavour because the water content has been removed and they are more concentrated as a result. The odour and flavour of herbs come from their volatile oils.

▲ Herbs and spices commonly used in food preparation and cooking

Spices

Spices are dried flowers, seeds, leaves, bark and roots of aromatic plants. They are available whole or ground (powdered). Spices were first used in China, India and South East Asia to flavour foods which would otherwise be bland and uninteresting such as rice, fish and poultry. They were also used because their strong **pungent** flavour or aroma could mask that of meat if it was slightly off.

Spices do not have a long shelf life which means that they lose their flavour quickly. Therefore you should buy them in small quantities and store them in airtight containers. Whole spices have more flavour and aroma than ground spices. This is because the aromatic oils disappear quickly when the spice is ground.

Spices are generally ground in either a pestle and mortar, or using a specific grater.

Activity
Choose three commonly used herbs such as parsley, mint, basil, thyme, coriander.

Suggest products to illustrate each of the following for each herb:
a as a garnish
b as the main flavouring ingredients
c combined with other ingredients as part of a mixture.

▼ A pestle and mortar is useful for making spices into a powder or paste

▼ A nutmeg grater and nutmeg

Examples of HERBS and their uses

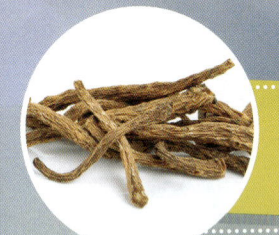

Angelica
Stem of the plant which when preserved in sugar is used as cake decoration.

Bay
Leaves are used to make a bouquet garni which is used to flavour meat, poultry and vegetables. Used on its own, it combines well with meat and poultry.

Basil
A popular flavouring in Italian dishes that combines well with tomato. The leaves have a strong flavour, so only small amounts are required; too much gives a bitter flavour.

Chives
The leaves are dark green, hollow stems which have a delicate flavour and can be chopped or snipped with scissors to make a good addition to salads, rice and pasta dishes.

Coriander
A member of the carrot family. The seeds are used whole or ground for both sweet and savoury dishes (whole seeds in casseroles and stews and ground seeds in cakes and puddings). The leaves are bright green and are chopped and added to or sprinkled over spicy food. The flavour is lemony with a touch of sage.

Dill
The stalks and seeds are used in pickle recipes. The leaves are used with many fish dishes.

Horseradish
The root is grated and used for making horseradish sauce to serve with beef or for flavouring other dishes such as stews, soups and salad dressings. It combines well with beetroot, cheese, fish such as mackerel and all types of smoked fish.

Lemongrass
The citric oils in the stalks give a lemony flavour which combines well with fish and lightly spiced ingredients.

Marjoram

The leaves are used to add flavour to potato, eggs and tomatoes and are good in stews and casseroles. They have a sweet, spicy flavour.

Mint

There are many varieties, the most common being spearmint. Apple mint has a finer, more delicate flavour and large white, hairy leaves. The leaves combine well with vinegar or other acid to make mint sauce or to make a mint jelly. Both mint sauce and mint jelly combine well with meat, particularly lamb. Mint leaves can be added during the cooking of new potatoes and peas to add flavour. Mint tea is popular as a refreshing drink.

Parsley

There are many varieties of parsley, including broad leaf, curly and Hamburg. The leaves and stalks can be tied in a bundle with celery, a strip of carrot and lemon rind and used to flavour soups and stews. Parsley is also used, with other herbs, to make a bouquet garni. The leaves are chopped to give a stronger flavour and used in stuffing, sauces or parsley-flavoured butter. Parsley makes a good garnish and combines well with many ingredients.

Rosemary

The taste and smell of rosemary comes from the oil the narrow needle-like leaves contain. This oil is called camphor. Rosemary combines well with lamb and garlic dishes.

Sage

The leaves are strong in flavour so sage should be used in small amounts. It combines well with onion and bread in stuffing. It goes well with pork, bacon, poultry and cheese dishes. The flavour can overpower other ingredients with a more delicate flavour such as fish.

Tarragon

The stem and leaves are delicate in flavour. It combines well with fish, poultry and eggs. The leaves are used to flavour vinegar, which can then be used to make a salad dressing. It is an essential flavouring ingredient in béarnaise and hollandaise sauces.

Thyme

The stem with leaves can be tied in a bundle with parsley, strips of carrot, celery and lemon rind to flavour strong meats such as beef and some cheese dishes. The leaves are small and need little chopping. They are added to stuffing, often combined with parsley.

Examples of spices and their uses

Allspice
Allspice is a mixture of nutmeg, cloves and cinnamon used in baking, pickling and for flavouring savoury dishes such as red cabbage.

Anise-pepper
This is the dried berry of a tree. It is used in Chinese five-spice powder and has a peppery flavour.

Caraway
This has a strong liquorice flavour and aroma. It is popular in Jewish cooking and used in seed cake recipes.

Cardamom
This is a pod containing the small black seeds of the plant which smell of camphor. They are used mainly in rice and curry dishes to give a scented aroma.

Cinnamon
This is the bark of the laurel tree which is available in sticks or ground into powder. It combines well with fruit, rice, fish, chicken and ham, egg and milk dishes. Ground cinnamon is combined with dried fruit in some types of rich cake recipes.

Chinese five-spice powder
This has a liquorice flavour and is used in many Chinese savoury dishes. It consists of a blend of spices.

Cayenne pepper
Cayenne pepper is extremely hot and must be used in very small quantities. It brings out the flavour of other ingredients such as fish. It can also be used in tiny amounts to sprinkle over savoury dishes as a garnish.

Cloves
Cloves are the flower buds of the clove tree which are picked before they open and then dried in the sun. They are used in baking and contain very strong essential oils.

Chilli
Chilli is available either whole, dried or ground in a variety of colours and taste, ranging from mild to very hot. They can be used whole, chopped and added to salads such as salsa, or when ground, combined with meat to make dishes such as chilli con carne.

FRUIT AND VEGETABLES

Fenugreek
The seeds are available as a spice and the leaves as a herb. It is used in curry recipes.

Ginger
Ginger is the root (or rhizome) of a plant and is available whole, sliced or ground. Crystallized ginger is the root stem preserved in syrup. All varieties have a sharp aroma and a strong taste. Ginger combines well with citrus fruits and in mild curries. Ground ginger gives gingerbread and parkin their characteristic flavour, combining well with the sweetness of syrup and treacle. Ginger root and ground ginger are used in savoury dishes such as stir fry mixtures and curries. Preserved ginger is often included in rich cake recipes.

Mustard seed
Mustard seeds vary in taste from mild to very hot. There are a number of varieties which are used mainly to make different types of mustard.

Pepper
There are two main varieties – black and white, both are the dried berries of the pepper plant. Black pepper is greenish-black in colour with a wrinkled skin and a strong 'hot' taste. White pepper is milder in taste and does not colour dishes, so it is best for white sauces. Both types are available ground.

Saffron
This is thought to be one of the most expensive spices in the world. It is the dried stigma of a particular crocus plant available as 'strands' or ground. It is used as a colouring and flavouring in cake and bread mixtures and in rice dishes such as paella and risotto. It has a slightly bitter taste and a bright yellow colour.

Poppy seed
These are small black seeds obtained from the poppy plant. They have a spicy, sweetish taste and a hard texture. They are used in curries and for sprinkling on top of cakes and bread. Poppy seeds are used widely in Jewish cookery.

Mace and nutmeg
Both come from the myrtle tree, an evergreen growing in Indonesia and have a similar taste.

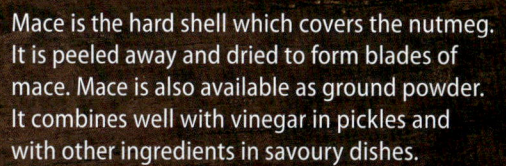

Mace is the hard shell which covers the nutmeg. It is peeled away and dried to form blades of mace. Mace is also available as ground powder. It combines well with vinegar in pickles and with other ingredients in savoury dishes.

Nutmeg is the nut or dried seed of the mace, available whole or ground. It gives the best result if grated or ground just before use and combines well with milk and egg dishes such as custards and milk puddings.

Turmeric
Available whole or ground, turmeric is made from the dried root or rhizomes of a plant of the lily family. It is a cheap alternative to saffron. It is bright yellow in colour, has a very spicy taste and combines well with vinegar to make pickle such as piccalilli. It is used to make curry powder and as flavouring in savoury rice dishes.

Sesame seed
These are the dried fruits of the sesame plant. The seeds are crushed to make oil which has a slightly nutty flavour. They are also available whole and can be sprinkled on breads, cakes and used in salad. Sesame seeds are crushed and made into a paste called tahina.

Cumin
This has a strong flavour and combines well with meat. It is used with other spices to make curries.

Paprika
A bright red powder made from a variety of pepper that grows in South America. The powder varies in taste from mildly hot to mildly sweet. It is used a lot in Hungarian cooking, for example to make a goulash. It combines well with meat, chicken and cheese.

SECTION 3

233

Fruit and vegetables in vegetarian diets

Fruit and vegetables play an important part in vegetarian and vegan diets. In such diets they supply the following nutrients:

Protein from soya beans, which contain a good range of essential amino acids. Beans and pulses such as chickpeas, kidney beans and lentils are other good sources of amino acids. Nuts such as peanuts, almonds and cashews also contribute valuable protein to a vegetarian or vegan diet.

Omega-3 is normally obtained from oily fish. In a vegetarian diet good sources of omega-3 include some seeds, walnuts and soya beans.

Iron is found in green leafy vegetables, dried apricots and figs, sesame and pumpkin seeds, pulses.

Calcium is obtained from leafy greens such as kale, rocket and watercress.

Vitamin B2 is found in nuts and seeds, such as almonds.

Selenium comes from nuts and seeds especially Brazil, cashew and sunflower seeds.

Iodine, from nori (seaweed used as a wrap) and kelp.

Potassium, from bananas, pulses, nuts and seeds.

Activity

Suggest different ways of preserving the following fruit and vegetables in the home:
- Strawberries
- Onions

Making jams, chutneys, jellies, curds and marmalade are methods of preserving fruit and vegetables in the home ▼

Fruit and vegetables can also be frozen when plentiful and in season ▼

Herbs can be dried to extend their shelf life ▼

Preserving fruit and vegetables

Preserving fruit with sugar and/or vinegar extends its shelf life. It is the method used to produce jams, marmalade, chutneys and pickles. Preserving with sugar increases the overall sugar content which helps reduce or prevent the growth of microorganisms. If, however, there is any evaporation of moisture on the surface of the product, moulds and yeasts may grow and cause spoilage.

There are many ways of preserving fruit and vegetables in the home:

- Jam and jelly making
- Pickling
- Making chutney
- Freezing
- Bottling
- Drying.

Key terms

Organically produced – grown using natural fertilizers and pesticides.
Portion – size and/or weight of a typical amount of food.
Cellulose – an insoluble substance which is the main constituent of plant cell walls. It is a polysaccharide.
Oxalic acid – a naturally occurring component of plants, particularly dark green vegetables.
Pectin – a soluble polysaccharide which is present in ripe fruits and used as a setting agent in jams and jellies.
Carotenoids – pigment or colour found in plants.
Anthocyanins – water soluble pigment or colour found in red, purple or blue plants.
Mirepoix – a mixture of sautéed chopped vegetables.

FRUIT AND VEGETABLES

Jam-making

Jam-making is a method of preserving fruit using high temperature and sugar. Fruit is first stewed – usually in a large pan sometimes called a jam kettle – to soften it and to break down the cellulose. Lots of sugar is then added and the mixture boiled. The combination of heat, sugar and pectin in the fruit enables the jam to form a gel and set on cooling.

Freezing

Freezing is a method of preserving vegetables and fruits as well as other foods such as meat, fish, baked goods and ready meals. The temperature of the freezer should be at -18°C or below. By freezing food, the water inside turns into ice and this stops the growth of microorganisms.

Fruits and vegetables for freezing must be absolutely fresh and frozen quickly to prevent large ice crystals from forming and damaging the structure of the food.

Most vegetables can be frozen successfully; some need to be blanched to stop enzymic activity.

Most fruits can be frozen. Freezing is especially successful with soft and berried fruits, particularly raspberries and currants.

Pickling

Pickling is a method of preserving vegetables and onions. An acid called acetic acid, which is naturally found in vinegar, is used. The vegetables are prepared and packed into clean jars with spices, the vinegar is poured on top to cover the vegetables and the jars are sealed. Making chutney also uses the acetic acid found in vinegar to preserve the vegetables and fruits.

Bottling

Bottling is when fruit and vegetables are prepared and placed in special glass jars with sugar syrup or brine. The jars are sealed and heated to a very high temperature to sterilise the contents. The sterilisation process will destroy the microorganisms and bottled fruit and vegetables will keep for several months.

Drying

Drying is a useful method of preservation for some fruits and herbs.

Examples of dried fruit are prunes, figs, raisins, currants and apricots. Currants, sultanas and raisins are usually sold washed and ready for use. Dried apricots, prunes and figs may need to be soaked before use. Peas, beans and lentils are examples of dried vegetables.

Fruit and vegetables are also commercially available in preserved form as frozen, canned and dried.

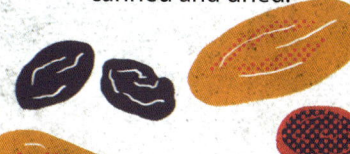

Canning

Canned fruits include pineapple, peaches, mandarins, plums. They are usually in a liquid such as natural juice or sugar syrup. Canned vegetables have a much softer texture than fresh vegetables due to the high temperature used in the canning process.

Food spoilage p84

EXAM QUESTIONS

1. Match the name of the fruit with the photograph. [5]

   peach   cherry   melon   lemon   pineapple   kiwi fruit

2. a Name two examples for each of the following
   - i citrus fruits [2]
   - ii root vegetables [2]
   - iii fruit rich in vitamin A [2]
   - iv leafy green vegetables: [2]

   b Explain why it is important to include a variety of fruit and vegetables in the diet. [4]

3. Explain how to prepare and cook broccoli in order to conserve the vitamin C content. [6]

4. Green vegetables can be cooked using a variety of cooking methods.
   - a Suggest suitable methods of cooking for green vegetables. [2]
   - b Evaluate the effect of each method of cooking on:
     - i appearance [2]
     - ii texture [2]
     - iii nutritive value [2]

5. a Describe steaming as a method of cooking. [3]
   b Discuss the benefits of steaming as a method of cooking vegetables. [4]

6. a Explain why it is important to include a variety of fruit and vegetables in the diet. [6]
   b Suggest ways of encouraging young people to eat more fruit and vegetables. [4]

7. Describe the following cooking methods and give an example of a vegetable that can be cooked that way. [12]

Cooking method	Description	Example
Boiling		
Steaming		
Braising		
Roasting		

8. Fruit can be preserved in many ways.
   Discuss how a family can preserve fruit to save money and minimise waste. [8]

9. Study the following table showing vitamin C content of 100g quantities of fresh, frozen, fried blueberries and blueberry juice.

	Vitamin C content
Fresh blueberries	14.4mg
Frozen blueberries	3.9mg
Blueberry juice	4mg
Dried blueberries	1.2mg

   Answer the questions

   a
   - i Identify the blueberries which have the highest vitamin C content per 100g. [1]
   - ii Identify the blueberries which have the lowest vitamin C content per 100g. [1]
   - iii State the Reference Intake for vitamin C. [1]
   - iv State two functions of vitamin C. [2]

   b Give an explanation for the difference in vitamin C content of the blueberries shown in the table. [5]

10. Correct storage, preparation techniques and cooking methods are important in maintaining the nutritional value of fruit and vegetables.
    Discuss this statement, giving examples to support your answer. [10]

    TOTAL: 88

FOOD INVESTIGATIONS

Investigation 1 Enzymatic browning of fruit

Some fruits become discoloured when peeled or cut. Conduct an experiment to determine which fruits discolour easily and which conditions speed up or delay this process.

Method

Cut equal sized slices of banana, apple and pear. You may use other fruits such as orange or kiwi to extend the experiment. Treat each as follows:

(a) expose to the air
(b) wrap in cling film
(c) sprinkle with lemon juice
(d) sprinkle with bicarbonate of soda
(e) dip in boiling water for few seconds, then remove.

Note the colour of each fruit at regular time intervals.

How does the enzymatic browning of fruit affect preparation, cooking and serving of apples, pears and bananas?

Investigation 2 Effect of heat on vegetables

Cooking and pH level can change the colour, texture and nutritional value of green vegetables. Conduct an experiment to determine the effect of heat and pH on the cooking of green vegetables.

Method

Take five 50g samples of a green leafy vegetable such as cabbage. Shred finely. Place in 150ml boiling water with the following variations:

(a) control sample – nothing added
(b) add ¼ tsp salt
(c) 1 tsp vinegar
(d) add a pinch bicarbonate soda
(e) soak in water for 10 minutes before cooking.

Simmer for 5 minutes, drain and reserve the water in a glass beaker.

Observe the amount and colour of the cooking water.

Repeat the steps above using red cabbage.

> **Optional task**
> Repeat the preparation steps above and boil for 30 minutes. Observe colour, texture and appearance.

Investigation 3 Cooking potatoes

Peel four potatoes of equal size.

(a) leave one whole
(b) cut one in half
(c) cut one into four equal pieces
(d) dice one.

Cook all the samples in boiling water for 5 minutes, test with a skewer.

Which is the softest and why?

Continue cooking for a further 20 minutes and observe the texture of each.

Investigation 4 Comparing different varieties of potato in food preparation

Use different varieties of potato to make simple potato rosti cakes. Compare each variety for:

- ease of grating and handling
- success criteria – does the potato 'hold' together or fall apart during cooking?
- sensory attributes – appearance, flavour, texture.

Basic recipe

1 large potato	1–2 tbsp. sunflower oil
1–2 tbsp. butter	salt and pepper

Method

1. Grate the potato coarsely into a clean tea towel.
2. Fold the towel and squeeze as much moisture as possible from the potato.
3. Season with salt and pepper and divide into two portions.
4. Heat a frying pan, add the butter and oil. Place 2 metal rings in the frying pan and fill each with a portion of potato. Push the mixture down gently to make a cake and remove the ring.
5. Fry for 3–4 minutes on both sides until golden brown.
6. Drain on kitchen paper.

Additional investigations Potatoes

Group investigation to find out the suitability of a variety of potatoes for different dishes.

Choose four different varieties of potato, for example, Desiree, Wilja, Maris Piper and King Edward.

Use the four varieties for:
- boiling
- baking
- making potato wedges
- making potato cakes.

Compare each variety for:
- ease of preparation,
- cooking
- suitability for the dish
- sensory qualities
- cost.

Compile a list of dishes where potatoes are a main ingredient and suggest a suitable variety of potato for each dish giving reasons for your choice of potato.

Investigation to find out the enzymic effect of pineapple on the setting of a jelly

Make up a quantity of jelly, divide in half, place in separate dishes and allow to cool.

To one half add two slices of chopped, fresh pineapple.

To the other half add two slices of drained, chopped, tinned pineapple.

Allow the jellies to set overnight.

Observe the results. Explain why one of the jellies has set and one has remained liquid.

> **Fact**
> Fresh pineapple contains an enzyme called bromelin. Heat destroys bromelin.

STUFFED BAKED APPLES

Portion size: 2   Difficulty rating: ★★

INGREDIENTS
- 2 large Bramley cooking apples
- 50g soft brown sugar
- 2 tbsps mincemeat
- 25g flaked almonds
- ½ tsp ground cinnamon
- 1 tbsp raisins
- 25g unsalted butter

EQUIPMENT
weighing scales	small sharp knife	teaspoon
ovenproof dish	mixing bowl	tablespoon

METHOD
1. Pre-heat the oven to 190°C/Gas mark 5
2. Wash apples, remove the cores and score around the middle. Place apples in the ovenproof dish.
3. Mix the sugar, mincemeat, flaked almonds, raisins and butter together and spoon into the cavities of the apples.
4. Place any excess filling in the bottom of the baking dish.
5. Dot with butter and bake for 45–60 minutes until tender.

NUTRITION:	Recipe	100g	Portion	Reference Intake Men	Women	Children
Energy (kJ)	3914	571	652			
Energy (kcal)	927	135	155	19%	23%	26%
Fat (g)	38	6	6	20%	27%	27%
Saturates (g)	14	2	2	23%	35%	35%
Carbohydrate (g)	152	22	25	25%	33%	35%
Sugars (g)	151	22	25	63%	84%	89%
Salt (g)	1	Trace	Trace	8%	8%	13%

EATWELL GUIDE:

SUCCESS CRITERIA
- Cooked apples have retained their shape
- Evenly browned with a firm texture

SKILLS / TECHNIQUES
- Weighing
- Preparation of fruit
- Baking

RECIPE MODIFICATION
- Filling can be varied – any combination of dried fruit and / or nuts.
- Replace sugar with honey or syrup
- Add grated rind of orange or lemon

SCIENCE INVOLVED
- Heat transfer
- Effect of heat on fruit
- Caramelisation of sugar

COOK'S TIPS
- Choose even sized apples for even cooking
- Cover apples with foil if they are browning too quickly

ALLERGENS
Almonds

RATATOUILLE

Portion size: 3   Difficulty rating: ★★

INGREDIENTS

800g tomatoes	3 cloves garlic
1 aubergine	Herbes de Provence (basil, thyme, parsley)
1 courgette	olive oil
1 large red bell pepper	salt and pepper
500g onion	70g tomato purée

EQUIPMENT

weighing scales	chopping board	spoon for stirring
chopping knife	large saucepan	

METHOD

1. Peel and cut the tomatoes in half.
2. Peel and chop the onion and garlic.
3. Wash, dry and cut the bell pepper into small strips.
4. Cut the eggplant (aubergine) into rondelles. Cut the un-peeled courgette into rondelles.
5. In a large heavy-based saucepan, put in olive oil, onions and chopped garlic.
6. Add in the bell pepper. Cover to keep in the moisture.
7. Cook on the hob for 20 minutes, stirring frequently, and add olive oil as necessary to prevent burning.
8. Add the peeled tomatoes, herbs de Provence and tomato purée. Stir well and cook for another 15 minutes.
9. Add the aubergine and courgette to the pot.
10. Cook for about 30 minutes.

NUTRITION:	Recipe	100g	Portion	Reference Intake Men	Women	Children
Energy (kJ)	3083	155	1028			
Energy (kcal)	737	37	246	10%	11%	12%
Fat (g)	31	2	10	11%	23%	23%
Saturates (g)	5	Trace	2	6%	50%	50%
Carbohydrate (g)	96	5	32	11%	5%	5%
Sugars (g)	79	4	26	22%	4%	5%
Salt (g)	6	Trace	2	33%	8%	13%

EATWELL GUIDE:

SUCCESS CRITERIA

- Even sized pieces of chunky courgettes and aubergines
- Good rich tomato flavour, well seasoned
- Soft vegetables yet retaining their shape

SKILLS / TECHNIQUES

- Vegetable preparation
- Boiling and simmering

RECIPE MODIFICATION

- Ratatouille is a traditional dish from France
- Use fresh tomatoes when in season, otherwise tinned tomatoes may be used

SCIENCE INVOLVED

- How cooking affects cell walls of fruit to change texture and colour

COOK'S TIPS

- Ratatouille can be cooked in a casserole in the oven for about an hour.
- Courgettes and aubergines can be sprinkled with salt after preparing and left for an hour before cooking. Salt removes the water content and the ratatouille is less watery.

ALLERGENS

None

VEGETABLE ROSTI CAKES

Portion size: 4 medium sized or 6 small   Difficulty rating: ★★★

INGREDIENTS

2 potatoes, peeled and halved
1 carrot halved lengthways
½ swede cut into chunks
1 courgette, grated
4 spring onions
2 level tbsps of plain flour
1 lightly beaten egg
sunflower oil

EQUIPMENT

peeler	basin	frying pan
chopping knife	fork	fish slice
chopping board	large mixing bowl	serving dish
saucepan	saucepan	
coarse grater	tablespoon	

METHOD

1. Wash and peel potatoes, carrots and parsnips or swede. Leave whole.
2. Place root vegetables and potatoes into pan. Just cover with boiling water and par boil for 10 minutes
3. Drain them through a colander, then place back in cool pan and cover with cold water and leave to cool.
4. Beat the egg in a jug.
5. Wash courgettes and spring onions. Coarsely grate the courgettes and chop the spring onions. Place in a large bowl.
6. Coarsely grate the par-cooked vegetables into the large bowl and stir all vegetables together with the flour, egg and seasoning. Divide the mixture into 4-6 portions.
7. Lightly oil a frying pan and cook the rosti until crisp and golden on both sides. Flatten with a fish slice as they cook. They will need about 3–4 minutes on each side.

NUTRITION:	Recipe	100g	Portion	Reference Intake Men	Women	Children
Energy (kJ)	4041	321	1010			
Energy (kcal)	962	76	241	10%	12%	13%
Fat (g)	31	2	8	8%	11%	11%
Saturates (g)	5	Trace	1	4%	6%	6%
Carbohydrate (g)	151	12	38	13%	16%	17%
Sugars (g)	29	2	7	6%	8%	9%
Salt (g)	1	Trace	Trace	4%	4%	6%

EATWELL GUIDE:

SUCCESS CRITERIA
- Firm, texture, well seasoned rosti cakes
- Even browning
- Even shape, size and thickness

SKILLS / TECHNIQUES
- Vegetables preparation
- Grating
- Boiling, frying
- Assembling rosti cakes – mixing and shaping

RECIPE MODIFICATION
- Vary the vegetables – any combination
- Pack mixture into a loose bottomed cake tin and bake at 190ºC/Gas 5 for 20–25 minutes.

SCIENCE INVOLVED
- Effect of heat on cooking of vegetables – changes in colour and texture
- Coagulation of egg to bind ingredients together

COOK'S TIPS
- Use a plain cutter in the pan to retain cake shape if the mixture appears to be falling apart
- Use the grater attachment on a food processor to save time

ALLERGENS
Plain flour, egg

RECIPES

240 COMMODITIES

SECTION 3
COMMODITIES

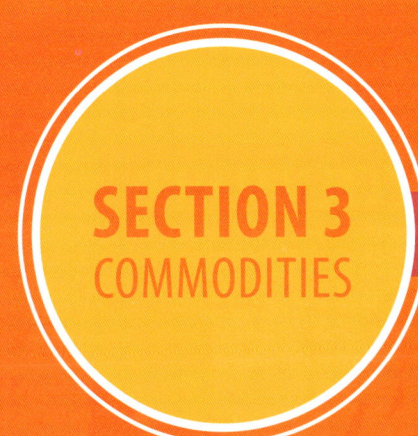

MILK, CHEESE AND YOGHURT

MILK 242

CHEESE 247

YOGHURT 251

CREAM 254

EXAM QUESTIONS 256

FOOD INVESTIGATIONS 257

RECIPES 258

SECTION 3
COMMODITIES

MILK, CHEESE & YOGHURT

What will I learn?

- The different types of dairy foods available
- How milk is processed to make it safe to use
- How milk is made into other dairy products
- Nutritional values of dairy foods
- How these foods are used in the diet

▼ A selection of dairy foods

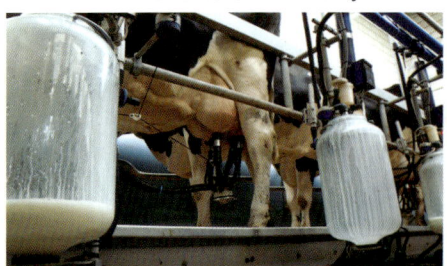

Milk

The source of *all* dairy foods is **milk** which is produced by female mammals for feeding their young. In the UK cow milk is used more than any other. The flavour, fat content and colour of cow milk is determined by:

- the breed of the cows
- the season when the milk was produced
- the type of grass or 'meal' eaten by the cows
- the age and general health of the cows.

Milk can also be obtained from goats and ewes (female sheep). Consumers may choose to use goat and sheep milk due to personal preferences or dietary needs. From milk we can produce butter, cream, cheese and yoghurt.

MILK, CHEESE AND YOGHURT

The nutritional values of milk

Milk is often called a 'complete food' because it contains all the indispensable amino acids and many of the essential nutrients that the body requires for bone health. These nutrients are easily absorbed by most people. Milk is an emulsion, meaning it has tiny globules of fat floating around in water.

Milk is about 85% water with the remaining 15% made up of the following nutrients:

- High biological protein (3.5%)
- Calcium
- Fat (3.5 - 5%)
- Carbohydrate in the form of lactose (4.8%)
- Water soluble B vitamins
- Vitamins A and D – depending on the fat levels
- Phosphorus
- Sodium
- Potassium
- Iron and vitamin C (in very low levels).

Primary processing of milk

Dairy cows need to have given birth to calves before they can start producing milk. Cows are then milked every morning and evening to keep the milk production going. Most cows can produce milk for about three years before being slaughtered for their meat.

Cows graze on outdoor pasture where they eat grass, except in the winter when they will be housed in sheds and fed on grass silage, maize and special cattle food.

Cows must be milked daily. A dairy cow produces on average 20 litres a day. The milk is collected and stored in holding tanks before being taken to the milk processing plant. All cattle herds are routinely and regularly tested to ensure they are free from disease such as tuberculosis.

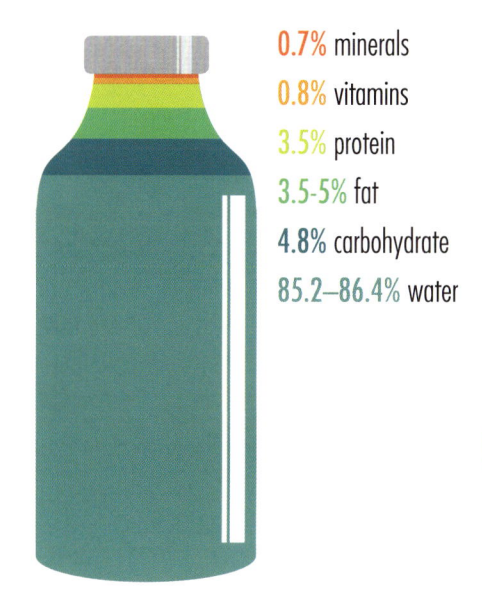

0.7% minerals
0.8% vitamins
3.5% protein
3.5-5% fat
4.8% carbohydrate
85.2–86.4% water

▲ The average composition of cow milk

Key point

There is no fibre in milk. Remember - fibre is not found in any animal product.

Activity

Draw a pie chart to show the percentages of each nutrient found in milk.

▼ Cow milk is the most popular milk in the UK

Milk Yields and Dairy Cow Numbers

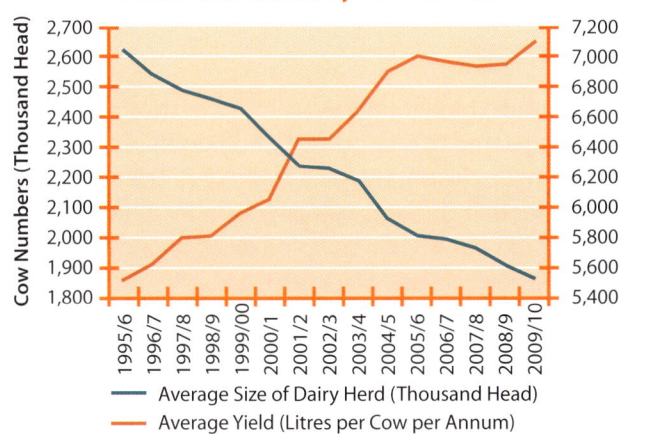

Producer Numbers - England & Wales

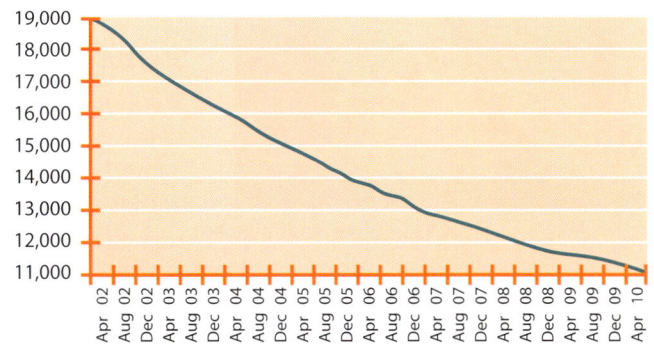

Milk Type	Fat % per 100g
Channel Island Milk	5.10%
Whole Milk	3.9%
Semi-skimmed Milk	1.7%
1% Milk	1%
Skimmed Milk	0% - 0.5%
Filtered milk	0% - 3.9%

▲ The fat content of different types of milk

Key point
Cream is the fat element of milk.

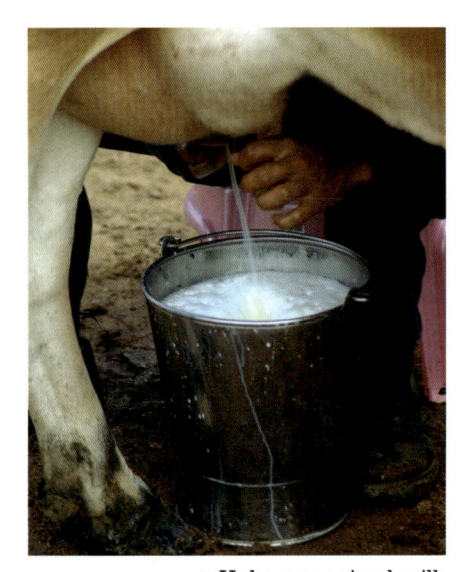

▲ Unhomogenised milk

▲ Homogenised milk

Check it
What is pasteurisation?

Types of milk

Milk is bottled according to its **fat (cream)** content. Most milk has a fat content of about 4%. However, during processing the fat may be reduced or removed.

Channel Island milk comes from the Jersey or Guernsey breed of cows. Their milk has a higher fat content compared to other cattle breeds.

Secondary processing of milk

By law all milk must be heat treated to destroy any pathogenic bacteria and ensure that it is safe to drink. This heat treatment takes place at the milk processing plant and is called 'pasteurisation'.

Pasteurised milk

'Raw' (untreated) milk must be pasteurised. Pasteurisation is the process of heating the milk to 75 °C for 25 seconds and rapidly cooling it to 5 °C. This level of heating is enough to destroy most pathogenic bacteria, making the milk safe to drink without affecting its overall flavour and giving it a longer shelf life. The pasteurised milk is then sealed into containers ready for sale. Pasteurised milk, if left to settle, will form a cream layer at the surface. To prevent this from happening milk can be **homogenised**.

Homogenised milk

Homogenisation is a process that forces pasteurised milk under pressure through a very fine mesh. This action breaks up the large fat (cream) globules into smaller particles so that the cream is evenly distributed throughout the milk. This gives a uniform consistency and creaminess.

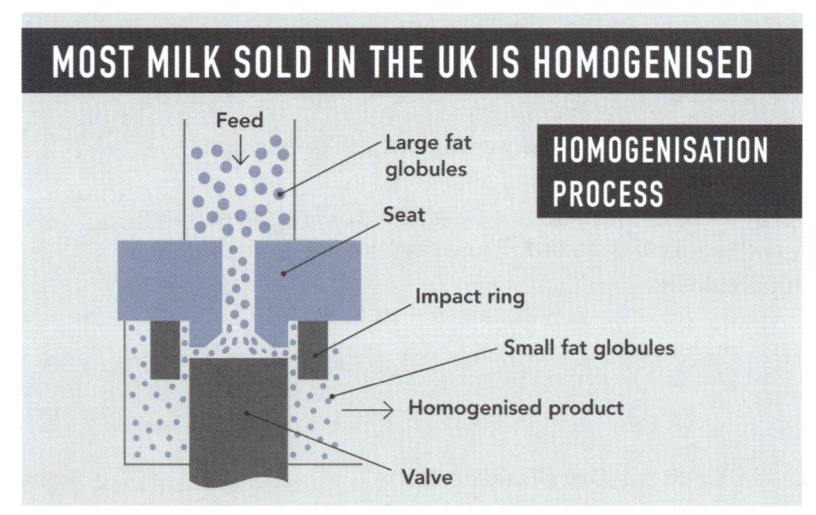

MOST MILK SOLD IN THE UK IS HOMOGENISED

HOMOGENISATION PROCESS

- Feed
- Large fat globules
- Seat
- Impact ring
- Small fat globules
- Homogenised product
- Valve

Sterilised milk

Sterilised milk is treated with much higher temperatures to destroy nearly all the bacteria in it. The milk is heated to around 50 °C, homogenised, then poured into glass bottles which are closed with an airtight seal. The filled bottles are carried on a conveyor belt through a steam chamber where they are heated to a temperature of between 110-130 °C for approximately 10-30 minutes. The bottles are then cooled and are then ready for sale.

Unopened bottles or cartons of sterilised milk will keep for approximately six months without the need for refrigeration. Once opened, sterilised milk must be treated as fresh milk and used within five days.

The sterilisation process causes a change to both taste and colour and also slightly reduces the nutritional value of the milk. The heat destroys some of the water soluble B and C vitamins.

MILK, CHEESE AND YOGHURT

Ultra heat treated milk (UHT)

UHT milk is heated to a temperature of at least 135 °C for one second in order to kill off any harmful bacteria it may contain. The milk is then packaged into sterile containers which can be stored, unopened, at room temperature for up to six months. Once opened, UHT milk must be treated the same as fresh milk.

Processed milks

Evaporated milk

50% of the water is evaporated from the milk which is then homogenised to prevent the fat from separating out. The evaporated milk is poured into cans, which are then sealed. The cans are heated for 10 minutes at a high temperature. Processing gives evaporated milk its slight caramel flavour and richer colour.

The shelf life of evaporated milk is generally 12 months. Once opened, it must be kept refrigerated at 5 °C.

▲ Evaporated milk

Condensed milk

To obtain condensed milk, fresh milk is heated to a temperature of 110–115 °C for one to two minutes, homogenised, and sweetened with sugar. It is then evaporated at a temperature of 55–60 °C. The milk is then cooled rapidly to 30 °C and canned.

Condensed milk is three times more concentrated than fresh milk. It is very sweet and has a thick, syrupy consistency. It is commonly used in the confectionary industry to make toffee, caramel and fudge. It is often used in very hot countries to replace fresh milk or where there is no access to a refrigerator.

▲ Condensed milk

Dried milk

Dried milk is produced by evaporating the water in milk. The milk is homogenised, heat treated and pre-concentrated before drying. The concentrated milk is sprayed into a chamber of circulating hot air causing the droplets of milk to lose their water content and fall to the floor of the chamber as fine, dried milk powder.

Dried milk powder can be stored at an ambient temperature for up to one year. Once it is reconstituted with water it can be used just like fresh milk. Dried skimmed milk powder mixes very easily with water, whereas dried whole milk powder tends to form small lumps when reconstituting. Reconstituted milk must be treated and stored like fresh milk.

▲ Dried milk

Comparing the fat contents in processed milks

EVAPORATED MILK 4–10% FAT CONTENT

CONDENSED MILK 10% + FAT CONTENT

DRIED MILK 0–3% FAT CONTENT

Alternatives to cow milk

Many people are **lactose intolerant**, meaning that they are unable to digest the lactose (natural sugar) found in cow milk. The bacteria in the gut will feed on this unabsorbed lactose causing varying degrees of abdominal symptoms. Most large supermarkets tend to stock a limited amount of sheep or goat milk; both are possible alternatives for the lactose intolerant. A small minority of people can be allergic to the proteins in milk so will have to follow a 'dairy free' diet to avoid serious allergic reactions.

Soya beans, oats, rice, almonds and coconuts can all be processed to produce a white liquid that can be used as a substitute for animal milk. These alternative 'milks' are fortified with extra vitamins and minerals to improve nutritional values. These products are now widely available in most supermarkets and are used due to health reasons, lactose intolerance or by vegetarians.

How is milk used?

Milk is very versatile and forms the 'liquid' part of many recipes.

Milk type	Recipes that use milk
All fresh, UHT and sterilised milk	In hot drinks, smoothies, white/cheese sauce, custard, panna cotta, batters, rice pudding
Evaporated milk	Pour over desserts, tarte au chocolat, add to coffee
Condensed milk	Fudge, caramel, millionaire shortbread
Dried milk	Add water to the dried milk and use as fresh

How should milk be stored?

- Fresh milk should always be stored in a refrigerator at 5 °C. The milk bottle should have a tight fitting lid and be stored away from strong smelling foods.
- Milk should not be kept in sunlight.
- Do not mix old and new milk together.
- Sterilised and UHT milk can be stored unopened at room temperature. However, once the bottle/pack has been opened it must be stored in a cold refrigerator.
- Evaporated milk has a long shelf life and can be stored, unopened, in a kitchen cupboard. Once opened, evaporated milk must be treated like fresh milk and kept in a cold refrigerator.
- Condensed milk once opened should ideally be stored in a cold refrigerator. However, because it has been treated at a high temperature and is high in sugar, it can be stored for a day or two at room temperature in a lidded container.
- Dried milk can be stored for a very long time, at room temperature, in a lidded container. Once the dried milk is reconstituted it MUST be treated like fresh milk and stored in a cold refrigerator.

Check it

1. Lactose is found in milk. What is lactose?
2. Explain what is meant by 'food intolerance'.
3. Explain what is meant by 'food allergy'.

Check it

State four rules for the safe storage of milk in the home.

Key terms

Emulsion – a fine dispersion of minute droplets of one liquid in another.

Lactose – the natural sugar found in milk.

Tuberculosis – a serious bacterial infection found in cattle.

Pasteurisation – a specific heat treatment applied to some foods.

Homogenisation – the breaking down of large milk fat globules into much smaller fat globules.

Pathogenic bacteria – disease causing bacteria.

Reconstituted – liquid or water has been added to a dried food.

CHEESE

MILK, CHEESE AND YOGHURT

What will I learn?
- The nutritional values of cheese [N]
- How cheese is made
- How cheese is stored
- How cheese is used in the diet

Cheese can be made from all types of milk but the most commonly used ones are cow, goat, sheep and buffalo milk. Cheese is a composition of coagulated milk proteins and fats.

The nutritional value of cheese

The nutrients found in milk will also be found in cheese, but in greater quantities due to the reduced water content.

Cheese is particularly high in:
- high biological protein
- calcium
- fat.

It also provides:
- Vitamins A and D
- some B group vitamins
- phosphorous
- zinc.

Cheese contains neither vitamin C nor dietary fibre.

▲ Assorted cheeses

Key point
A way to remember that cheese is higher in nutrients is to think of it as milk without most of its water!

▼ A large range of dishes use cheese

247

Cheese is made from fat, protein and water

COTTAGE CHEESE — 4g of fat per 100g

FROMAGE FRAIS (PLAIN) — 6g of fat per 100g

FETA — 16–23g of fat per 100g

RICOTTA — 10g of fat per 100g

MOZZARELLA — 22g of fat per 100g

EDAM — 25g of fat per 100g

PARMESAN — 28g of fat per 100g

BRIE — 28g of fat per 100g

CHEDDAR — 34g of fat per 100g

CHESHIRE — 31g of fat per 100g

BLUE STILTON — 36g of fat per 100g

MASCARPONE — 42g of fat per 100g

Extension

Soft cheeses such as Brie, feta and Camembert may be contaminated with the bacteria listeria monocytogenes. Listeria will grow to harmful levels even when the cheese is correctly stored in a cold fridge. Women are advised to avoid eating soft cheeses during pregnancy because they are approximately 20 times more likely than other healthy women to develop listeriosis, the illness caused by listeria. A listeriosis infection resembles a mild, flu-like illness but it can cause septicaemia, miscarriages, infection of the newborn baby and, possibly, stillbirths. Listeria is killed by high heat.

How is cheese made?

Fresh milk has to go through various processing stages before it becomes cheese.

Certain cheeses are commonly called 'blue cheese'. These usually have a strong flavour and smell. In fact the 'blue' is formed by adding **mould** to the cheese, either at the start of the cheese production or it can be sprayed onto the set **curds**. The curds are then pierced with stainless steel needles. The holes allow air into the cheese which activates the mould to form the cheese's familiar blue/green streaks.

There are many different types of cheese and they can be categorised into 'types':

Categories	Examples
Fresh	cottage cheese, cream cheese, fromage frais, ricotta, mozzarella
Soft	Brie, Camembert, feta
Semi-hard	Edam, St Paulin, Port Salut
Hard	Cheddar, Red Leicester, Parmesan, Emmental, Manchego
Blue	Stilton, Danish Blue, Gorgonzola, Roquefort
Processed	cheese slices, Cheese Strings, spreadable cheese

HOW IS CHEESE MADE?

MILK, CHEESE AND YOGHURT

1. Specific bacteria referred to as a '**starter culture**' is added to **pasteurised** milk. This culture 'ripens' the milk by **fermenting** the lactose into lactic acid which helps to develop the flavour and aroma of the cheese.

2. Once enough lactic acid has been produced **rennet** is added to the milk which helps it to coagulate forming the **curds** and **whey**. Rennet is an **enzyme** produced from vegetarian sources.

3. The whey is drained from the curds.

4. The curds are then 'scalded' by heating to encourage **syneresis**.

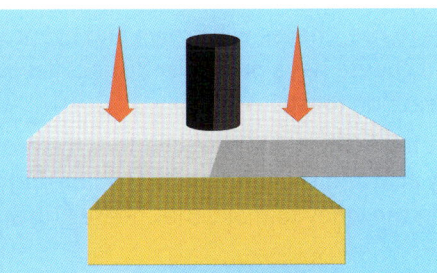

5. The cheese is pressed to force out any remaining whey and to form its final shape.

6. The more whey that is squeezed out the **harder** the cheese will be.

7. The cheese is cut into blocks and left to mature for up to 24 months.

8. The longer the cheese is left in storage the stronger the flavour becomes.

The appearance, colour, texture and flavour of the final cheese product depends on:
- the cheesemaker's recipe and manufacturing method
- the type of milk used
- how much water is removed from the curds and whey
- additional flavourings and colourings such as salt, herbs, fruit, moulds.

249

Key point

Cheese can be set using either rennet or an acid.

Study tip

Being able to correctly use these key terms in your written work will show your knowledge and understanding.

Check it

1. State 2 types of milk from which cheese can be made.
2. Give an example of
   (i) a soft cheese
   (ii) a blue cheese
   (iii) a hard cheese.
3. Cheese is a versatile commodity. Describe how it can be used in the kitchen.
4. Explain why vegetarians should monitor their cheese intake.

Key terms

Starter culture – a bacteria mix used to ripen milk and help start the cheese making process.

Rennet – an **enzyme** that used to be taken from calves' stomachs, but is mostly now produced from vegetarian sources.

Curd – a soft, white substance formed when milk sours, used as the basis for cheese.

Whey – the watery part of milk that remains after the formation of curds.

Enzymes – molecules (proteins) that act as **catalysts** and help complex reactions occur – helping to curdle the milk.

Syneresis – the sudden release of moisture from protein molecules.

Mould – a fungus that grows in filaments creating a fuzzy appearance on food. It is a soft, green or grey growth that develops on old food. May give some cheeses their characteristic colours and flavours.

Viscous – when a liquid is thick and sticky.

Silage – grass grown in the summer and preserved to feed cattle in the winter months.

The uses of cheese

Cheese can be eaten in its natural state, for instance on crackers, in sandwiches or in a salad. It can be added to foods to add flavour and texture – examples are broccoli and Stilton soup, cheesecake, cauliflower cheese and pizza.

All cheeses have varying colours, textures and strengths of flavour which must be considered when deciding which cheese to use when preparing food. Soft, creamy cheeses, such as Brie or ricotta, have a more gentle flavour than hard cheeses like Parmesan or Gruyère.

The effect of heat on cheese

The fat component of cheese melts at about 65 °C making it spreadable or stringy and it will 'dissolve' into food cooked at high temperatures. However, too much heat will 'burn' both the protein (caseinogen) and the fat in the cheese, making it bitter, hard and tough.

▼ Melting cheese on pizza and toast

Cheese is usually grated or diced before cooking and is often mixed with a starchy ingredient which will absorb the fat released from the cheese by the heat.

Cooked cheese is more easily digested than uncooked cheese. As the cooking temperature continues to rise, cheese will brown and eventually burn. Browned, partially burned cheese has a particular distinct flavour found in an au gratin topping and cheese on toast.

When cheese is made the curds are heated. The heat changes the proteins that were already denatured by acid and the rennet enzyme, making them bunch closer together, expelling the whey to make the cheese firm and less likely to spoil.

Most rennet-set cheeses melt easily and when enough protein bonds are broken, the cheese turns from a solid to a viscous liquid.

Acid-set cheeses, such as halloumi, paneer, some whey cheeses and fresh goat cheese have a protein structure that remains intact at high temperatures. When cooked, these cheeses just get firmer due to water evaporation. All melted cheese eventually turns solid again once enough moisture is driven off.

How to store cheese

All cheese should be covered or wrapped to prevent drying out and cross-contamination and then stored in a refrigerator at around 5°C. Softer, creamier cheese tends to have a very short shelf life. Hard cheese will last for several weeks if stored correctly. Cheese can be frozen but the texture may be affected once defrosted.

Cheese has an improved flavour if it is removed from the fridge 30 minutes before serving.

YOGHURT

What will I learn?
- The nutritional values of yoghurt
- How yoghurt is made
- The use of yoghurt in our diet

Yoghurt is made from treated fresh milk and is widely available in all supermarkets.

The nutritional value of yoghurt

Yoghurt has very similar nutrients to milk and is an excellent source of:
- High biological protein
- Calcium
- Vitamins A, D and the B group.

The fat content of the milk used to make the yoghurt will determine the fat content of the yoghurt. So, yoghurt made with skimmed milk is 'fat free' and yoghurt made using full fat milk or with extra cream added will have a rich, creamy texture and flavour. Note that fruit or fruit-flavoured yoghurt can be high in added sugar.

Types of yoghurt

There is now a vast choice of yoghurts available and they can be consumed as a snack or as part of a sweet or savoury meal.

They come in a range of:
- **textures** e.g. liquid, set, smooth,
- **fat content** e.g. luxury, creamy, low-fat, fat-free
- **flavours** e.g. natural, fruit, chocolate, fudge, nut

MILK, CHEESE AND YOGHURT

SECTION 3

251

How is yoghurt made?

The milk is heat-treated, homogenised and cooled.

Yoghurt is made from different types of milk, including skimmed, semi-skimmed, whole, evaporated or powdered forms.

The bacteria will ferment the milk sugar (lactose) to produce lactic acid.

A starter culture is usually added to the milk.

PROCESS

SOME TYPES OF YOGHURT ARE PROCESSED TO GIVE EXTRA HEALTH BENEFITS:

LIVE YOGHURTS contain harmless bacteria that are added to the milk and are still present and alive after processing.

PROBIOTIC YOGHURTS contain live probiotic microorganisms which are thought to be beneficial to health by assisting the 'good bacteria' found in the digestive system.

BIO YOGHURTS are made using bacteria such as *bifido bacterium bifidum* (bifidobacteria) and/or *lactobacillus acidophilius*. Bio yoghurt has a milder, creamier flavour and is less acidic than some other varieties. It has been shown to aid digestion and is thought to promote good health.

Activity

Lesson 1 - In pairs make 200ml natural yoghurt. Each pair make yoghurt with milk of different temperatures: 5 °C, 15 °C, 30 °C, 60 °C, 80 °C, 100 °C.

Lesson 2 - Describe and record the flavour and texture of each yoghurt using the chart opposite. Which do you think is the best starting milk temperature and why?

COMMODITIES

MILK, CHEESE AND YOGHURT

Sugar, sweetener, pieces of fruit and/or fruit flavouring are added to the yoghurt either before or after the fermentation stage.

Yoghurt is then packaged and chilled.

The fermentation process allows the milk proteins to coagulate and set producing sharp, tangy flavoured 'natural' yoghurt.

How is yoghurt used?

Yoghurt can be consumed as a snack or as part of a sweet or savoury meal. It can be used in numerous ways, such as:

- on desserts, as a healthy alternative to cream
- an alternative to milk on breakfast cereals
- a substitute for cream in cheesecakes
- an extra ingredient to give savoury dishes a creamy texture
- an ingredient in smoothies
- an alternative to mayonnaise.

Storage of yoghurt

Yoghurt should be stored in the refrigerator at 5 °C. Commercially made yoghurt has a shelf life of up to two weeks. The yoghurt will contain bacteria which will continue to slowly multiply.

Milk temp	Texture	Flavour
5 °C		
15 °C		
30 °C		
45 °C		
80 °C		
100 °C		

Activities

1. **Lesson 1** - Produce homemade natural yoghurt.
2. **Lesson 2** - Compare the flavour and texture of your homemade yoghurt with
   a) a value/basic natural yoghurt
   b) a brand named natural yoghurt.
3. Using a food nutritional program (there are several online), research the fat and sugar content per 100ml for the homemade, basic and branded natural yoghurts. What do you find? How can you explain it?

Key terms

Ferment – where bacteria produces lactic acid, which acts on the milk protein to give yoghurt its texture and characteristic tang.

Sterilise – to use boiling water or a very hot oven to kill bacteria that may be on the surface of equipment.

CREAM

What will I learn?
- The nutritional values of cream
- How cream is produced
- The different types of cream

Cream is derived from the fat found in all fresh milk.

The nutritional value of cream

Cream has a **high fat** content ranging from 18-55% fat depending on the production process used. The levels of saturated fat in cream are the reason why it should really not be eaten too frequently because of its links with coronary heart disease and raised cholesterol levels.

Cream also contains:
- Low levels of high biological protein
- Low levels of calcium
- Low levels of Vitamins A and D

The different types of cream available in the UK are legally defined by the **percentage of fat** that they contain.

▲ Piped double cream

Type of cream	Fat %/100g
Single	18%
Crème fraîche	30%
Whipping	35%
Double	48%
Clotted	55-64%

▲ Fat levels in cream

How is CREAM produced?

The production process involves separation of the fat from the milk which is done through centrifugation. **Centrifugation** involves spinning the milk at high speed; the force of this process causes the milk-fat globules to separate from the watery liquid to produce **single cream**. This process is continued to produce **double cream**. All cream is then pasteurised to destroy any harmful bacteria.

Clotted cream

According to the traditional method, fresh cow milk is placed in a shallow pan and left for 6–14 hours to allow the cream to float to the surface of the milk. This mixture is then heated (scalded) in the pan over a water bath at a temperature of 80-90°C for 40-50 minutes. It is cooled for 24 hours during which time 'clots' of cream with a firm yellow crust are formed. This cream is removed, 'potted' up and sold as clotted cream. The liquid left over is skimmed milk.

Clotted cream originated from Devon and Cornwall. It has a rich, buttery flavour, a thick, creamy consistency.

Whipping cream

This is made by mixing cream with air to roughly double its volume. The air bubbles are captured in a network of fat droplets.

MILK, CHEESE AND YOGHURT

Uses of cream

Cream is used to add a creamy texture and flavour to dishes. The correct cream must be used for specific tasks because different types of cream have different properties – for instance single and clotted creams cannot be whisked for piping, whereas whipping and double cream will aerate when whisked.

The different uses of cream

Type of cream	Uses
Single	Pouring over desserts or in coffee. Cannot be whisked.
Whipping	Pouring or whisked for piping onto cakes and desserts.
Double	Whisked into and piped onto desserts. Can be used for pouring.
Clotted	Formed into quenelles on scones and desserts. It must not be stirred or beaten.

How should cream be stored?

All fresh cream must be stored in a refrigerator at 5 °C. Sterilised/long life/UHT cream has a long shelf life and can be stored, unopened, in a kitchen cupboard. However, once opened this cream must be treated the same as fresh cream.

> **Study tip**
>
> Make certain that you can show your understanding of why long life cream, once opened, needs to be chilled and used quickly.

> **Study tip**
>
> **Butter**
> Butter is made from the fat found in the cream of milk.

🔑 Key terms

Centrifugation – the separation of two liquids such as the fatty cream from the watery liquid of the milk.

Lactic acid – an acid formed in sour milk.

Quenelle – soft food formed into a rugby ball shape between two spoons.

Long Life cream

Long life or UHT cream is produced from UHT milk. The high temperatures used during UHT processing give the cream a slightly caramelised flavour. The heat treatment allows the unopened cream to be stored at ambient temperatures for several months. Once opened the cream must be stored in a refrigerator at 5°C.

Soured cream

This cream has had a bacterial culture added resulting in the production of lactic acid, which sours and thickens the product.

Crème fraîche

Originally developed in France, it is now produced and widely available throughout the world. Crème fraîche is made by adding bacterial culture to cream which produces a slightly soured product, however it is less sour than soured cream.

Butter, Oil, Margarine, Sugar and Syrup p335

EXAM QUESTIONS

1. State how fresh milk should be stored. [1]
2. Name two types of milk that can stored in a cupboard. [2]
3. Other than cow milk, state 2 types of milk from which cheese can be made. [2]
4. Cheese is very rich in several nutrients. Identify the 2 missing nutrients:

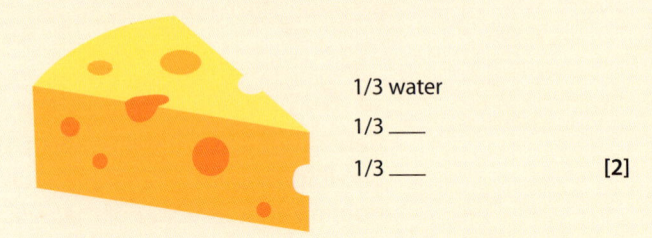

   1/3 water
   1/3 ____
   1/3 ____ [2]

5. Describe, with examples, the ways that cheese can be used in cooking. [6]
6. Discuss the choice and use of dairy foods when preparing and cooking meals. [8]
7. What does 'pasteurisation' mean? [1]
8. Explain why milk is pasteurised. [3]

TOTAL: 25

FOOD INVESTIGATIONS

Food investigations for dairy products

Investigation 1 Fresh curd cheese

This has a similar taste, texture and flavour to ricotta cheese and can be used in both sweet and savoury dishes.

You will need:
- stainless steel saucepan
- teaspoon
- food thermometer
- colander
- muslin
- sieve

And for the recipe:
- 1l whole milk – ideally unhomogenised
- a pinch of salt
- 1 tsp rennet

Method
1. Pour the milk and salt into a clean stainless steel saucepan.
2. Heat the milk gently to 38°C and immediately remove it from the heat.
3. Stir in the rennet until it's well combined, then leave for 15 minutes, for the milk to separate into curds and whey.
4. Line a colander with a double-layered piece of clean muslin.
5. Use a sieve to collect the curds in as large pieces as possible and put into the muslin.
6. Tie up the corners of the muslin and hang to drip above a bowl or sink for about three hours.
7. Unwrap the muslin, place the cheese into a covered bowl and store in the fridge.

Day 1-3 the curd cheese will be slightly sweet so better suited for use in desserts.
Day 3-6 the curd cheese will become tangy and cheesy so will be better suited for savoury dishes. It must be used within a week.

Investigate further by
- Using different types of milk
- Using yoghurt in place of milk
- Adding flavourings before heating the milk.

Investigation 2 Mozzarella

Making mozzarella is more difficult than making fresh curd cheese. To make two balls of mozzarella, about 200g, you will need:
- stainless steel saucepan
- food thermometer
- slotted spoon
- tablespoon
- teaspoon
- measuring jug
- chopping board
- sharp knife
- mixing bowl
- iced water

And for the recipe:
- ½ tsp citric acid
- 1 litre whole milk – ideally unhomogenised
- ¼ tsp rennet
- 1 tbsp salt

Method
1. Pour the milk into a saucepan and heat gently to about 13°C.
2. Dissolve the citric acid in 60ml warm water.
3. Add it to the warm milk increasing the heat to 30°C, stirring gently – it will start to curdle.
4. Dilute the rennet in a tablespoon of boiled, cooled water and add it to the milk.
5. Increase the heat to 38–39°C, stirring from time to time – the milk will begin to separate.
6. Remove from the heat and leave to stand for 15 minutes.
7. The curds will set and separate from the whey.
8. Carefully scoop the curds from the pan using a slotted spoon and place them in a sieve – leave the hot whey in the pan.
9. Carefully press the curds gently to remove some of the whey – you want them to be dripping a little, and if you remove too much the mozzarella will be tough.
10. Add the salt to the whey in the pan and heat to 80°C.
11. Put the curds on a chopping board and cut them into thick slices, about 2 cm.
12. Have a bowl of iced water ready.
13. One at a time, dip the curds into the hot whey for a minute or until they begin to soften and stretch.
14. Remove the curds from the hot whey using a slotted spoon.
15. Chill your hands in the iced water and gently stretch out the hot cheese, folding it back on itself and working it just until it's stretchy, shiny and smooth. Don't overwork it.
16. Mould and shape the cheese into a ball about 3cm wide and store in a bowl of chilled water.
17. Repeat with the remaining curds, refrigerate and use within two days.

Investigate further by trying different types of milk.

Investigation 3 Homemade yoghurt

- 1l whole milk
- 1 heaped tbsp powdered milk
- 60g natural full-fat yoghurt

Method
1. Wash and sterilise a 1l jar or several small jars.
2. Place the milk in a saucepan and heat it to 80°C – do not let it boil.
3. Remove from the heat and stir in the milk powder.
4. Once the temperature drops to 45°C, stir in the yoghurt.
5. Pour the milky mixture into the jar and seal with the lid.
6. Place somewhere slightly warm such as an airing cupboard, near an oven, wrapped in a towel to keep the heat in, for 4-6 hours – the longer the fermentation, the more 'tart' the yoghurt will taste.
7. Place yoghurt in the fridge for at least three hours to chill and firm it up.

Further investigation
- Compare yoghurts made with cow, goat, dried and soya milk.
- Divide the batch of yoghurt into three portions.
- Place yoghurt 1 in the fridge after 4 hours of fermentation, yoghurt 2 after 5 hours of fermentation and yoghurt 3 after 6 hours of fermentation. Compare the textures and flavours.
- Compare the flavour and texture of homemade natural yoghurt with a supermarket 'basic' yoghurt and a brand name yoghurt.

CHOCOLATE ORANGE MOUSSE

Portion size: 4   Difficulty rating: ★★★

INGREDIENTS:

150g good quality cooking chocolate
4 eggs – separated
40g butter (not margarine)
250ml double cream
1 orange – juice and zest
Decorations – chocolate buttons, cherries, nuts, grated chocolate

EQUIPMENT:

3 mixing bowls	plate	grater (for orange)
saucepan	whisk or electric mixer	spatula

METHOD:

1. Place chocolate into a bain-marie (mixing bowl over a pan of simmering water).
2. Leave over a low heat to melt the chocolate.
3. Separate the eggs.
4. Whisk the egg whites to a stiff foam.
5. Whisk the cream – to a thick mayonnaise consistency.
6. Zest and juice the orange.
7. Once the chocolate has melted, remove bowl from heat and add the butter.
8. Once butter has melted beat in the egg yolk, zest and 1 tbsp juice (chocolate must not be hot).
9. Add 1 tbsp cream to the chocolate and beat well – this slackens the mixture
10. Pour the chocolate and the whisked egg white into the cream and FOLD in gently.
11. Pour mousse carefully into dishes and chill until set.
12. Decorate the top with a swirl of whipped cream and a chocolate button/flake/cherry/nuts.

NUTRITION:	Recipe	100g	Portion	Reference Intake Men	Women	Children
Energy (kJ)	14177	1417	2869			
Energy (kcal)	2722	342	693	28%	35%	39%
Fat (g)	246	30	62	65%	88%	88%
Saturates (g)	154	19	39	128%	193%	193%
Carbohydrate (g)	102	13	26	9%	11%	12%
Sugars (g)	99	12	25	21%	28%	29%
Salt (g)	2	Trace	1	8%	8%	13%

EATWELL GUIDE:

SUCCESS CRITERIA
- The mousse will be light and airy.
- There will be a hint of orange flavour.
- It will be attractively and appropriately decorated.

SKILLS / TECHNIQUES
- Whisking
- Melting
- Piping
- Portion control
- Melting chocolate
- Slackening the chocolate mix
- Piping cream whirls

RECIPE MODIFICATION
- Use white chocolate instead of dark
- Use vanilla extract to flavour instead of the orange
- Make a Mocha mousse by dissolving 2-3 tsp coffee in a little boiling water and adding this to the melted chocolate mixture
- Stir pieces of fresh fruit into the mousse before stage 11

SCIENCE INVOLVED
- Shows how egg white can hold lots of air
- denaturing of egg proteins

COOK'S TIPS
- Dark chocolate gives a much better flavour than milk chocolate
- Do not 'beat' at stage 10. The mixture will lose volume and go syrupy if the mixture is beaten

ALLERGENS
Egg

COMMODITIES

HOMEMADE CUSTARD (CRÈME ANGLAISE)

Portion size: 2–3   Difficulty rating: ★ ★ ★

INGREDIENTS:

250ml Jersey milk or whole milk
1 split vanilla pod or 2 tsp vanilla extract
3 eggs
40g sugar

EQUIPMENT:

measuring jug	paring knife	saucepan
plate	large mixing bowl	sieve
cutting board	whisk	

METHOD:

1. Place milk and split vanilla pod (or extract) in a pan and slowly bring to the boil.
2. In a mixing bowl whisk together the eggs and caster sugar.
3. Take the pan of milk off the heat.
4. Slowly whisk the eggs into the milk.
5. Pour this mixture back into the mixing bowl.
6. Wash the saucepan and ¼ fill it with hot water.
7. Bring the water to the boil and reduce to a simmer.
8. Place the bowl of custard over the pan of simmer water (bain-marie) and keep stirring until the sauce has thickened.
9. Sieve the sauce to remove the vanilla pod.
10. Taste and adjust sweetness if required.

NUTRITION:	Recipe	100g	Portion	Reference Intake Men	Women	Children
Energy (kJ)	2486	529	1243			
Energy (kcal)	594	126	297	12%	15%	17%
Fat (g)	30	6	15	16%	21%	21%
Saturates (g)	12	3	6	20%	30%	30%
Carbohydrate (g)	53	11	27	9%	12%	12%
Sugars (g)	53	11	27	22%	29	31%
Salt (g)	1	Trace	1	8%	8%	13%

EATWELL GUIDE:

MILK, CHEESE AND YOGHURT

SECTION 3

SUCCESS CRITERIA
- The sauce will be smooth and thickened to a pouring consistency.
- The sauce will have the right level of vanilla flavouring and sweetness.

SKILLS / TECHNIQUES
- Pouring custard sauce
- Using the bain-marie method
- Producing a pouring sauce
- If using cornflour – slaking and blending

RECIPE MODIFICATION
- Use vanilla extract instead of a vanilla pod
- Chocolate custard – use cocoa instead of vanilla. Blend 1 tbsp cocoa powder with 1–2 tbsp milk and add to the milk after adding the eggs.
- Use other flavouring extracts in place of vanilla pods/extract.

SCIENCE INVOLVED
- The coagulation of eggs

COOK'S TIPS
- Slake 1 tbsp of cornflour with 1-2 tbsp milk. Stir into the custard at stage 4, after adding the egg. Place the custard onto the heat and gently heat until the sauce thickens. Be careful to NOT scramble the eggs
- Control the heat to prevent the eggs scrambling
- Use full fat milk / Jersey milk – it gives a creamier flavour
- Place cling film directly onto the surface of the custard to prevent a skin forming

ALLERGENS
Lactose intolerance (milk), egg

POTATO DAUPHINOISE

Portion size: 6 **Difficulty rating:** ★★

INGREDIENTS:
500g floury potatoes (e.g. King Edwards)
1 small red onion
200ml milk (or 100ml milk + 100ml cream)
50g Gruyère cheese (or Cheddar)
Salt and pepper

EQUIPMENT:
cutting board	large mixing bowl	baking dish
vegetable peeler	plate	baking tray
paring or chef's knife	measuring jug	

METHOD:
1. Peel the potatoes and place in a large bowl of cold water.
2. Slice onion thinly.
3. Dice the cheese into 0.5cm cubes.
4. Slice potatoes into slices approx. 3-4mm wide (do not wash or rinse the slices).
5. Layer 1/3 potato in the baking dish.
6. Cover the potato with half the onion.
7. Layer the second 1/3 of potato over the onion layer.
8. Cover the second potato layer with the rest of the onion.
9. Arrange the final 1/3 potato neatly and attractively over the final layer of onion.
10. Season the potato with a sprinkle of salt and freshly ground black pepper.
11. Pour the milk (or milk and cream mix) over the surface of the potato slices.
12. Sprinkle the diced cheese over the potato surface.
13. Place the baking dish on a baking tray.
14. Bake for 45 mins at gas mark 5 or 190°c – until the potato has softened.

NUTRITION:	Recipe	100g	Portion	Reference intake Men	Women	Children
Energy (kJ)	3106	365	518			
Energy (kcal)	738	87	123	5%	6%	7%
Fat (g)	26	3	4	5%	6%	6%
Saturates (g)	15	2	3	8%	13%	13%
Carbohydrate (g)	101	12	17	6%	7%	8%
Sugars (g)	17	2	3	2%	3%	3%
Salt (g)	2	Trace	Trace	6%	6%	8%

EATWELL GUIDE:

SUCCESS CRITERIA
- Potatoes will be evenly sliced.
- The dish will have balanced layers.
- The surface will be golden brown.

SKILLS / TECHNIQUES
- Vegetable preparation
- Knife skills
- Peeling
- Slicing
- Dicing
- Baking

RECIPE MODIFICATION
- Replace the milk with 200ml stock
- Use a different type of cheese
- Change the seasoning to fresh herbs or a few chilli flakes

SCIENCE INVOLVED
- the sauce is thickened by the starch in the potatoe
- denatured protein in cheese creates a stringy or crispy topping

COOK'S TIPS:
- Use a mandolin or food processor slicing attachment to speed up the preparation of the potatoes and onion
- A little grated nutmeg works well in this dish

ALLERGENS
Lactose (milk and cheese)

COMMODITIES

SECTION 3
COMMODITIES

MEAT, POULTRY, FISH AND EGGS

- MEAT 262
- POULTRY 266
- PREPARATION AND COOKING OF MEAT AND POULTRY 275
- STORAGE OF MEAT AND POULTRY 280
- FISH 283
- EGGS 294
- HOW DO WE USE EGGS? 299
- STORING EGGS 304
- EXAM QUESTIONS 306
- FOOD INVESTIGATIONS 308
- RECIPES 310

SECTION 3
COMMODITIES

MEAT, POULTRY, FISH, AND EGGS

What will I learn?

- The choice of meat, poultry and offal available to the consumer
- Information to help the consumer make a choice
- The value of meat and poultry in the diet
- The choice of cuts available when buying meat and poultry
- What to look for when buying meat and poultry
- How to handle, store and cook meat to prevent food poisoning

▲ Labelling on British produced meat and poultry

Meat

Meat is sourced from animals. **Poultry** is the name given to domestic fowl reared on farms for their meat. Examples are chicken and turkey. **Offal** is the name given to edible internal organs of the animal or bird. **Game** refers to meat sourced usually from wild animals, for example rabbit, but it can also mean meat from birds such as pheasant, pigeon, partridge, grouse and woodcock.

Meat and poultry labelled 'British' must come from animals and birds born, reared and slaughtered within the UK. If you are not buying direct from a farmer you might find it helpful to look for a quality mark. These mean that all stages of the food supply chain have been independently checked to ensure that they meet the required standards.

Under EU law, all meat and poultry for human consumption has to show traceability. Under the law, traceability means the ability to track any food, feed, food-producing animal or substance that will be used for consumption through all stages of production, processing and distribution.

Animal welfare

There are symbols on packaging to show that meat and poultry have met welfare standards. Animal welfare refers to the well-being of animals and covers areas such as the animals' access to fresh water and a diet to maintain full health. It also gives assurance that animals are reared free of any discomfort, pain, injury or disease, and are provided with adequate shelter and a comfortable resting area.

Key point

Tracing food through the production and distribution chain can identify and address risks and protect public health. Outbreaks of disease in animals that could be transmitted to humans or the presence of chemicals above acceptable limits in feed and food, can threaten both the quality and safety of products.

Check it

What is traceability? What are the benefits of traceability to the consumer?

262 COMMODITIES

RSPCA Assured

RSPCA Assured, previously Freedom Food, is the RSPCA's ethical food label dedicated to animal welfare. The RSPCA Assured label makes it easy to recognise products from animals that have had a better life. It is found on the packaging of meat and dairy products which have met animal welfare standards.

Check it

Can you explain the meaning of poultry, game and offal?

Red Tractor

The Red Tractor logo gives information on where the food has been farmed, processed and packed. Food given to animals on farms displaying the Red Tractor logo is safe for them to eat with no risk of contamination to the meat or milk produced. The animals' health and welfare is regularly checked. Farmers under the Red Tractor scheme must also use responsible farming methods not to pollute land and minimise the impact of their farming methods on wildlife, fauna and flowers.

Choice of meat and poultry available to the consumer

Beef, lamb, pork, veal, rabbit, venison, horsemeat and goat meat are examples of the types of meat available to the consumer.

Beef

British-reared breeds, such as Aberdeen Angus, Longhorn and Hereford have traditionally been considered to be among the best beef in the world. However the reputation of other premium breeds such as Wagyu, which originated in Japan, is on the rise.

Organic beef, and beef from rare breeds, is the most expensive to buy as the highest farming standards will have been needed at all stages of the animal's life. The length of time for which beef has been hung will also determine how flavoursome and tender it is; 10–14 days is a good length of time, though some super-premium beef is hung for up to six weeks.

When choosing any cut of beef, look for firm, fine-grained meat; it should be moist, rather than dry, but not slimy. A light marbling (thin streaks) of fat running through the meat is a good sign – this gives succulence and flavour and, without it, the meat will be dry once cooked. Any fat on the outside of the beef should be creamy-coloured (fat that is yellow might well be rancid). Properly hung beef should be deep burgundy in colour, rather than bright red. Go for cleanly cut, neatly trimmed pieces of beef, with no fragments of shattered bone.

▲ Labelling on organic produce

Activity

In recent years, meat has often been given bad press because of food poisoning outbreaks and other issues.

Carry out research and identify what these issues are.

Wagyu

Wagyu meat comes from a group of Japanese breeds whose meat is renowned for its high level of fat marbling. Where the best Western beef has white streaks running through it, Japanese wagyu has more fat than flesh and looks white with a splattering of pink.

The meat is extremely delicate: the soft fat has a low melting point, due in part to its high proportion of monounsaturated fats, to go along with high levels of omega-3 and 6. Fat is where the flavour of meat resides. The taste of wagyu is smooth, velvety and sweet. Many consider it to be the juiciest, richest steak in the world.

▲ Wagyu beef

Veal

In many countries, including the UK, veal production is closely linked to the dairy industry. Veal meat comes from the male calves of cows bred for dairy, slaughtered when they are a few months old.

For years, veal was shunned by British consumers on welfare issue grounds. However, Freedom Food laws and improved welfare standards for rearing calves have enabled veal to regain its popularity in supermarkets and on restaurant menus in recent years.

▲ Veal

Meat from sheep

- Lamb is a sheep under one year old.
- Hogget is a lamb older than one year.
- Mutton is the meat of older sheep.

Meat from pigs

Pork is all the meat that comes from a pig. If the meat is called 'pork' then it is raw.

To add extra choice and variety, pork can be cured and smoked.

Ham is a specific cut from the thigh part of the pig and has been cured (or salted).

Bacon is produced by curing pork with salt or in a brine solution. After maturing it is sold as unsmoked bacon, but it can also be smoked to give the bacon a darker colour and distinctive flavour.

Gammon is the cured whole leg of pork. It is often cut into easy to cook slices and eaten hot as gammon steaks. It is also sold cooked and cold as ham. Some hams may be cured and cooked to a special recipe to give distinctive flavours, such as 'honey roast'.

▲ Lamb

Key point

The name 'Wagyu' refers to all Japanese beef cattle, where 'Wa' means Japanese and 'gyu' means cow.

▲ Bacon

▲ Gammon

MEAT, POULTRY, FISH AND EGGS

Horsemeat

Horsemeat is one of our more controversial meats, because for many people the killing of horses for meat is still an emotive subject. The facts remain that it is a healthy meat choice: it has a lower fat content and more omega-3 than to beef, is high protein and provides lots of iron. Horsemeat is very similar in taste to beef but with a slightly sweeter or subtle game flavour.

Goat

Going under the names Cabrito or Chevon you will also find goat referred to simply as kid or goat. Whilst it is believed that up to 80% of the world's population have goat in their diet, it is considerably under-consumed in the UK. It is typically found in 'ethnic' butcher's shops, particularly those serving the Caribbean community, where goat curry is a staple. Increasingly, goat meat is appearing on restaurant menus around the country.

Rabbit

Rabbit was very popular in the UK in the 1940s and 1950s when meat was rationed during and after World War Two. It was available free to people who could catch wild rabbits for the table. The meat is low in fat, cholesterol free, high in protein with a taste similar to chicken.

Venison

Venison refers to the meat of a deer. Three species are commonly used for food in the UK: the red deer (largely from the Scottish Highlands); the fallow; and the roe (the smallest and considered the best by many cooks).

It is classed as game and can either be farm-reared (methods vary from free range to intensive) or park-reared (reared in herds that roam parklands). Venison is a red meat, similar to beef but leaner and with a slightly richer taste. It is increasingly popular in the UK for its distinctive flavour and high protein content, becoming widely available in supermarkets and butchers.

Meat products are also used in 'made-up' commodities such as sausages, salami, burgers and rissoles. They all contain meat mixed with other ingredients.

▼ Venison may be eaten as steak. It has a low fat content

▲ Goat meat is low in fat and cholesterol

▲ Rabbit meat is making a comeback on restaurant menus

Activity

Investigate the varieties and cost of meat, poultry, game and offal available locally.

Choose one type of offal or game, for example sausages or pâté, and set up a tasting panel. Present your results in a graph, histogram or pie chart.

Check it

Name three meat products.

Study tip

Meat is sourced from different animals and birds. For example, beef comes from cattle.

Can you name at least five animal and bird sources?

Check it

Give four examples of meat from game animals or birds.

Give reasons why chicken is a popular consumer choice in the UK.

Poultry

Poultry is a very popular food in the UK and is common on restaurant and takeaway menus. Examples of poultry include chicken, turkey, goose, duck, guinea fowl, poussin (young chicken), quail and ostrich. Partridge, pigeon and pheasant tend to be referred to as game.

Poultry is reared in different ways:

- indoors in large numbers – a standard chicken is about 40 days old when it is slaughtered
- free range – chickens are allowed outside and reared in large sheds; they are 56 days old when they are slaughtered
- organic – chickens are allowed to roam the fields and are given organic food to eat. They are 80 days old when slaughtered and their meat is usually more expensive to buy.

▲ Examples of poultry; poussin, goose, turkey

Chicken is the most widely eaten poultry in the world. It has both white and dark meats and has much less fat than other poultry. Through generations of genetic selection, specialized breeds have been developed for meat (broilers) and eggs (layers). Chickens have a squat and rounded appearance. They stand less than 70 cm (27.6 inches) tall and weigh 2.6 kg (5.7 pounds) on average. Male chickens are called cocks or roosters and females are hens.

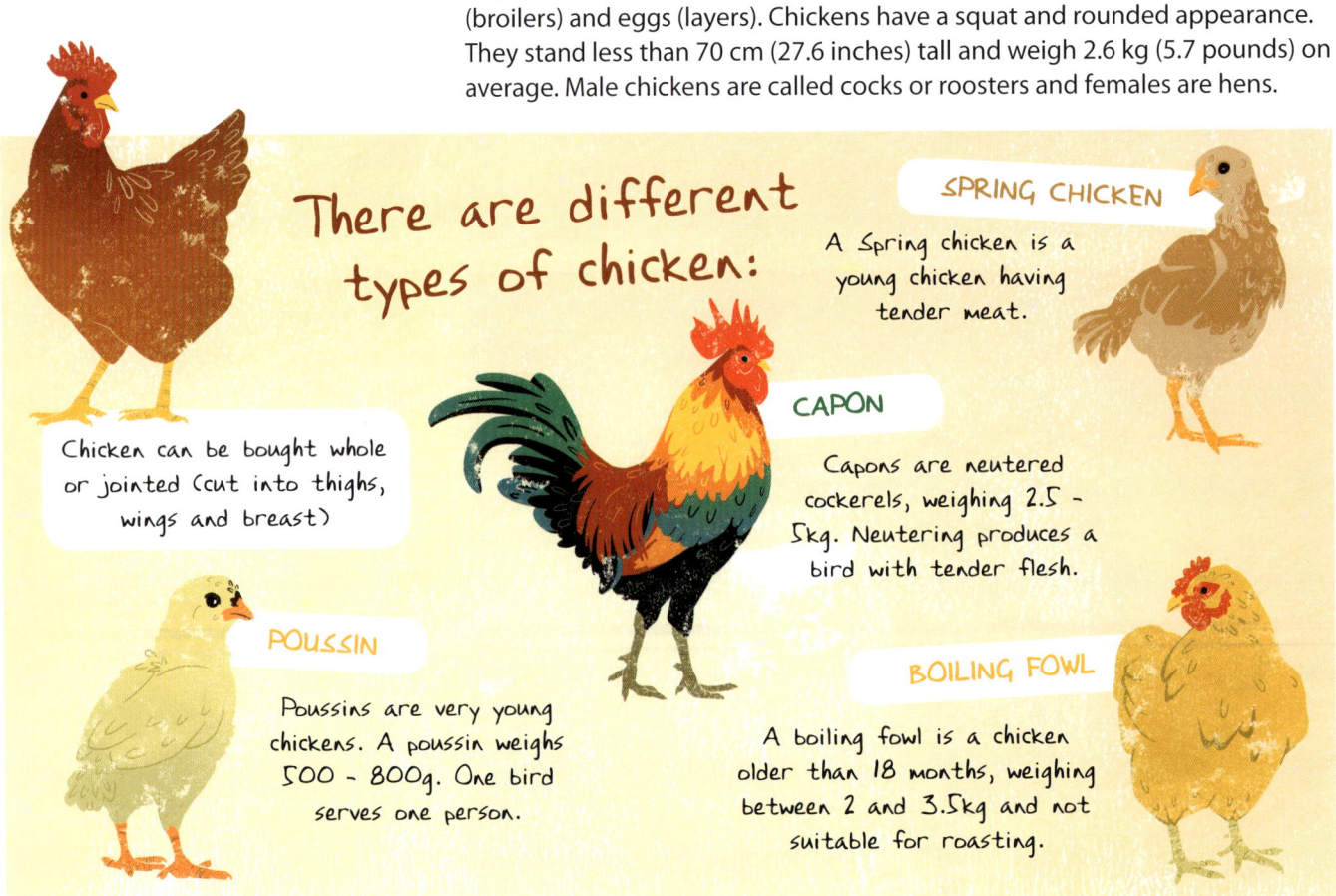

There are different types of chicken:

Chicken can be bought whole or jointed (cut into thighs, wings and breast)

SPRING CHICKEN
A Spring chicken is a young chicken having tender meat.

CAPON
Capons are neutered cockerels, weighing 2.5 – 5kg. Neutering produces a bird with tender flesh.

POUSSIN
Poussins are very young chickens. A poussin weighs 500 – 800g. One bird serves one person.

BOILING FOWL
A boiling fowl is a chicken older than 18 months, weighing between 2 and 3.5kg and not suitable for roasting.

MEAT, POULTRY, FISH AND EGGS

TYPES OF POULTRY

TURKEY

A turkey weighs anywhere from 3–12 kg.

Fresh turkey should have firm white flesh, supple, bendy feet and smooth legs.

Large turkeys tend to have more flavour but need careful cooking as the flesh can become dry.

DUCK

Ducks vary in weight from 800 g to 2.5 kg.

A large duck will serve four people.

The flesh is rich and fatty.

GOOSE

Geese are bigger birds weighing 6–12 kg.

Geese have very rich, dark flesh which is usually tender.

The meat is rich and fatty.

GUINEA FOWL

A breed similar to chicken.

The flesh tends to be tougher than chicken.

One bird serves one person.

WOOD PIGEON

Weighs around 450g.

A meaty bird with a distinctive gamey flavour and rich, deep-coloured meat.

Most of the meat comes from the breast and these are best quickly pan-fried and served pink.

Good source of protein and iron.

PHEASANT

The flesh is pale, lean and firm, with a subtle gamey flavour.

The breast meat is more delicate in flavour and tender than the legs, which tend to be darker in colour and more sinewy.

A pheasant will serve two to three people.

QUAIL

A domesticated game bird, bred for the table in the UK.

It has a good proportion of lean, meaty flesh to bone and a delicate flavour.

When eating quail it is common to eat the bones as well, as they are soft and the meat does not come off easily.

OSTRICH

Ostrich is a 'red meat' similar in colour and taste to beef.

It is lower in fat grams per serving compared to chicken and turkey, and much lower in fat and cholesterol than beef. Most all of the meat from an ostrich comes from the leg, thigh, and back. Ostrich has no breast meat.

SECTION 3

267

Offal

Offal literally means 'off fall', or the pieces which fall from a carcass when an animal is butchered. Originally the word applied principally to the animal's entrails. It now covers:

- insides including the heart, liver, lungs, kidney, sweetbreads (pancreas and thymus glands), tongue and tripe
- extremities such as tails and feet (pig's trotters)
- the head, including the brain and tongue.

Many people unwittingly tuck into offal every time they eat a sausage (the skins are usually made from sheep, pig or ox intestines), or spread chicken liver pâté on toast, yet shudder at the thought of eating heart or brain. In fact, the less popular cuts can be delicious, as well as nutritious.

> **Activity**
>
> Use a basic pâté recipe using different types of liver such pig's liver, lamb's liver, chicken liver, duck liver.
>
> Prepare each pâté in the same way and set up a tasting panel to compare appearance, flavour, texture and cost.
>
> Which type of liver would you choose to make a pâté and why?

Liver

FACTS
An important component of the Scottish national dish, haggis, and often used in Italian cooking, where they are valued for their spongy texture.

Liver is an excellent source of iron and Vitamin A.

COOKING
Cook quickly, so that the liver remains a little pink in the centre.

Liver can also be cooked and minced to make pâté.

Ox liver

Lamb liver

Heart

FACTS
Can be very chewy in texture.

Heart meat is high in protein, iron, selenium, phosphorus and zinc.

COOKING
Must be tenderised by a long, slow method of cooking. Heart can be stuffed and braised or casseroled.

Kidney

FACTS
Kidneys are particularly popular as food in European nations such as England, France, Spain, and Sweden

COOKING
The most common cooking method is grilling. The strong flavour is often concealed beneath sauces made with mustard and sherry. Chinese cooks stirfry them with other powerfully flavoured ingredients.

MEAT, POULTRY, FISH AND EGGS

As with meat, the taste and texture of offal depends on the particular organ, and on the species and age of animal from which it came. So offal from calves is said to be the best.

Lamb offal is also good, but sheep, pig, and ox offal tends to be coarse in flavour and texture.

Offal does not keep well so must either be prepared and cooked soon after slaughter or turned into products which have a longer shelf life such as brawn, haslet, pâté and some types of sausage.

Offal is a good source of protein. Some organs, notably the liver and kidneys, are very valuable nutritionally.

Traditional dishes made with offal include:

Haggis, brawn, liver and onions, braised ox cheeks, faggots, black pudding, steak and kidney pudding, tripe and onions, pâté.

Check it

Can you explain why offal is considered to be such a nutritious food? Can you give examples to support your answer?

Tail

FACTS: The bony ones from the ox and pig have rich meat on them. The fatty ones from the fat-tail sheep have no bone and are highly valued in the Middle East.

COOKING: Oxtails and pig's tails need long, slow cooking and are used in stews and soups, while the fat from the fat-tail sheep is eaten raw.

Produces animal gelatine when boiled.

Tongue

FACTS: Calf's and lamb's tongues need to be soaked then boiled to rid them of the blood and then peeled.

COOKING: It can be jellied and sliced thin as in beef tongue, which retains its bouncy and somewhat tough quality.

It can be simmered into oblivion in chilli sauce as is done in Mexican cuisine with goat and beef tongues;

It can be stir-fried in Chinese cuisine.

Tripe

FACTS: Tripe is stomach lining and it resembles a honeycomb.

COOKING: When thoroughly soaked before cooking, often in milk, it achieves a sparkling white appearance. Tripe has a neutral flavour that takes to many sauces. Can be eaten in soups or cold with vinegar.

Sweetbread

FACTS: Obtained from calves and lambs. It is a highly prized ingredient in French cooking. Sweetbreads are an organ meat from the thymus gland and pancreas.

COOKING: They are high in fat and can usually be sautéed with no extra oil once the exterior membrane has been removed. Most often they are breaded and fried or grilled over charcoal.

269

▲ Which type of mince shall I choose?

The nutritional value of meat and poultry N

Meat and poultry contain the following important nutrients:

Protein

Meat and poultry are excellent sources of high biological value protein.

Used for growth of the body, reproduction, hormones, nutrition and the immune system (the body's natural defences). Proteins are made up of amino acids which are essential for our body.

Fat

The amount of fat in meat and poultry varies. The fat is visible, found in between muscle fibre and beneath the skin. Red meat has a higher fat content than poultry and approximately half the fat in lean red meat is unsaturated fat (i.e. monounsaturated and polyunsaturated). Meat provides one of the major sources of monounsaturated fat in the British diet.

Red meat and meat products contribute to less than one quarter of the total fat intake of all food eaten at home. Beef and lamb usually contain a higher level of saturated fatty acids than pork. Advances in food processing technology, breeding programmes, changes in animal feeds and modern butchery techniques have led to a lower fat content of carcass meat. In the UK, fat content has been lowered by 30% for pork, 15% for beef, and 10% for lamb over the past 15 years.

Minerals

▼ The difference in fat content (per 100g) between three grades of mince beef.

100g beef	Traditional mince	Lean mince	Extra lean mince
grams fat	16.2	11.8	4.5
grams saturated fat	7.1	5.6	1.9

The main minerals supplied in meat are iron, magnesium, potassium, selenium and zinc.

Iron is a component of haemoglobin which gives blood cells their red colour. Haemoglobin carries oxygen around the body to all cells for the production of energy and the maintenance of cells. Red meat is an important source of iron.

Magnesium keeps the heart and liver healthy. It is essential for strong bones and good muscle function.

Potassium maintains fluid and electrolyte balance in the body.

Selenium plays a role in regulating the thyroid gland and has antioxidant properties.

Zinc is essential for healthy skin, bones and teeth, the immune and reproductive systems, liver function and our sense of smell and taste. It is important for brain development in the young.

MEAT, POULTRY, FISH AND EGGS

Vitamins

Meat contains the fat soluble vitamins A and D.

Meat is a good source of the B group of vitamins, especially B12.

The table below compares the nutritional value of chicken with and without skin. However, the skin gives flavour to the chicken when cooked.

100g chicken	energy (kcal)	fat (grams)	protein (grams)
skinless raw chicken	106	1.1	24
raw chicken with skin	201	4	19.1

How much meat should we eat? [N]

A portion of meat = 80g (roughly the size of a pack of cards). It is recommended not to eat more than 500g per week (around 6 portions).

Key point

Chicken is lower in fat and slightly higher in protein than red meat. It contains vitamin B6 and B12 and the mineral selenium, an **antioxidant** which helps protect against heart disease. To lower the fat in chicken, remove the skin.

REDUCING THE FAT YOU EAT

- Choose lean cuts of meat and meat products that are lower in fat such as sausage, burgers and pâté. Choose lean cubes of beef, lamb or pork for casseroles or kebabs.
- Cut visible fat off meat during preparation or at the table.
- Try healthier cooking methods such as dry frying, grilling, roasting on a rack or stirfrying.
- Drain and discard fat from the pan before making gravy/sauce with the remaining juices.
- Skim fat from casseroles and stews before serving.
- Drain any grilled or fried food on absorbent kitchen paper before serving.

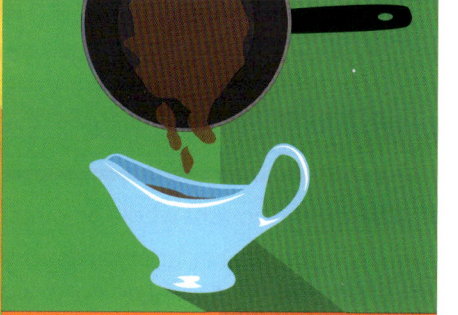

Key point

Meat is a particularly good source of vitamin B12, which is not found naturally in foods of plant origin.

Offal is high in protein, vitamin A and thiamin; liver is an important source of iron.

Key point

Women are advised against eating liver too often during the early stages of pregnancy as the build-up of retinol (a type of vitamin A in the liver) can be harmful to the foetus. Eating liver once or twice a month is considered to be 'safe'.

Activity

Suggest a recipe which uses the different cuts of meat in the table below.

Meat cut	Beef	Lamb	Pork
boneless cuts			
boned and rolled meat			
cubes			
lean mince			
thin strips			

Activity

Investigate the variety of choice available when purchasing:

a bacon
b chicken
c mince

Record your findings in a chart including cost per kilo.

Check it

1. Why are some cuts of meat more suitable for grilling or roasting?
2. Why are some cuts of meat more suitable for braising, casseroling or stewing?

▼ Customers can buy a wide range of meats and cuts

Study tip

State factors which would influence your choice of meat for a family lunch.

Choosing meat and poultry

Cuts of meat are prepared by butchers in shops or supermarkets to meet the different needs of consumers.

Today the consumer is looking for meat that:

- can be used in different ways
- is cut into convenient portion sizes, e.g. chops, steaks
- is convenient to prepare
- is simple to store
- is easy and quick to cook
- is low in fat.

A wide range of different cuts are available, giving greater choice and variety. They include cuts, joints and mince.

A carcass of beef, pork or lamb is divided into different cuts which may vary in weight and quality according to the carcass. Therefore cuts of meat vary in energy and nutrients, composition, weight and fat level.

THE CHOICE AVAILABLE TO THE CONSUMER COULD INCLUDE THE FOLLOWING:

Boneless cuts (beef, pork and lamb) – economical and suitable for quick and easy methods of cooking, e.g. grilling.

Boned and rolled joints of meat – smaller joints to reduce cooking time and making it easier to carve.

Lean and extra lean cuts – trimmed cuts of meat which are lower in fat.

Cubes of meat – sold cut into cubes, ready for making stews, kebabs and casseroles.

Lean minced meat – meat is trimmed of fat and minced.

Thin strips – meat is pre-cut into strips, suitable for quick cooking methods, e.g. stirfrying.

Poultry can be bought whole or jointed (cut into thighs, wings and breast).

Each type of meat has its own particular characteristics and consumers need to be aware of the quality points to look for when buying meat. Meats vary in colour according to the animal they come from. Beef is usually much darker than pork or lamb. Meat from a younger animal is usually lighter in colour than that from an older animal.

In general terms the front half (forequarter) of a carcass has more muscles (per cut of meat) which have worked harder, contain more connective tissue and therefore give less tender meat. Cuts of meat from the neck and shoulder muscles, in particular, have long thick fibres and contain a lot of connective tissue.

The back half (hindquarters) of a carcass contains fewer muscles (per cut of meat), which have done less work, have less connective tissue, and therefore produces the most tender cuts of meat. Cuts of meat from the loin and rump muscles have done the least work and have shorter, finer muscle fibres with less connective tissue. These are prime tender cuts.

COMMODITIES

MEAT, POULTRY, FISH AND EGGS

Cuts of meat: what to look for:

Lamb cuts: NECK, SHOULDER, LOIN, BREAST, CHUMP, LEG, SHANK

Beef cuts: TOP SIDE, RUMP, SIRLOIN, RIBS, CHUCK, NECK, THICK FLANK, FLANK, BRISKET, LEG, SHIN

Pork cuts: NECK, SHOULDER, LOIN, RIBS, CHUMP, BELLY, LEG, CHEEK, HOCK, TROTTER

Lamb

- Lean meat should be firm, dull red, with a fine texture/grain.
- Surface fat should be hard, brittle, flaky, a clear white colour and evenly distributed.
- In a young animal, the bones should be pink and porous, so that, when cut, a degree of blood is shown in their structure. Older bones become hard, dense, white and are inclined to splinter when chopped.

Beef

- Lean meat should be darkish red in colour, with small flecks of white fat (marbling).
- Fat should be firm, creamy white in colour and dry.
- Fat from older animals and dairy breeds is a deeper yellow.

Pork

- Lean meat should be pinkish, with small flecks of white fat (marbling).
- Fat should be firm, brittle in texture, creamy white in colour and odourless.

TO ADD EXTRA CHOICE AND VARIETY, PORK CAN BE CURED AND SMOKED.

Bacon
Bacon is produced by curing pork with salt or in a brine solution. After maturing it is sold as unsmoked bacon. It can also be smoked to give the bacon a darker colour and a distinctive flavour.

Gammon
Gammon is the cured whole leg of pork. It is often cut into easy to cook slices and eaten hot as gammon steaks. It is also cooked and sold as cold ham. Some hams may be cured and cooked to a special recipe to give distinctive flavours, such as 'honey roast'.

What to look for (bacon/ham):
- Good-quality bacon should have no smell. If it has an odour, then it's not fresh.
- Bacon should be slightly damp to the touch, but not wet or slimy.
- The fat should be firm and white – not yellow at all, unless it is smoked.
- There should be no yellow or green stains on the meat; these stains are a sign that the meat is past its best.
- The rind should be smooth and elastic, but the colour will depend on the curing process it has undergone. Some will be darker than others.
- The meat should be firm (not wet and floppy), lean, and with a deep pink colour.

SECTION 3

Key point

The tenderness and quality of meat depend on:
- the amount and type of connective tissue
- the length and thickness of the fibres
- how much 'marbling' it has to separate the fibres and make the meat tender.

Check it

Define 'marbling' in meat.

Key terms

Connective tissue – tissue which binds together, connects or surrounds body parts.

Collagen – the most abundant protein in the meat and the substance that holds the whole body together.

Composition of meat

The **flavour** of meat is determined by a combination of factors:
- The breed of the animal
- The diet of the animal

The **colour** of the meat varies according to:
- The type and breed of the animal (beef – red, pork – pink)
- The diet of the animal
- The welfare of the animal during rearing

The **texture** and taste of meat depends on
- the amount of water and fat in the meat
- the particular kinds of protein in the meat.

Meat is muscle with connective tissue. Muscle is made up of bundles of fibres which are very small tubes filled with water containing dissolved muscle proteins (myosin and actin) and mineral salts. Myosin and actin make it possible for the muscle to connect (i.e. shorten its length) and create movement in the body. This information is useful because when the muscles have worked hard, the resulting meat can be tough and needs careful cooking to make it tender.

Meat has several types of connective tissues. One type is **collagen** which
- surrounds the fibres to make a bundle
- wraps the bundles together to make the muscle
- lays a thin covering over the muscle called a sheath.

Two other types of connective tissues are **elastin** and **reticulin**.

Elastin is contained mainly in blood vessel walls and the elastin ligaments which attach the muscle to bone. It is yellow in raw meat and can stretch rather like elastic.

Reticulin is contained in the spaces between the muscle cells.

Fat surrounds the muscle tissues and is also contained within the muscle. It can be seen as flecks of white in raw meat. This effect is called 'marbling'.

The red colour of meat is due to muscle cell pigment called myoglobin and to haemoglobin in the blood.

Poultry has a similar structure to other meats. It has muscle fibres and connective tissue. The muscle fibres tend to be shorter which makes the meat more tender than, for example, beef and lamb.

When the cut surface of any raw meat is exposed to oxygen in the air the colour changes to a brighter red. When left standing the meat changes colour again, this time to a browny red.

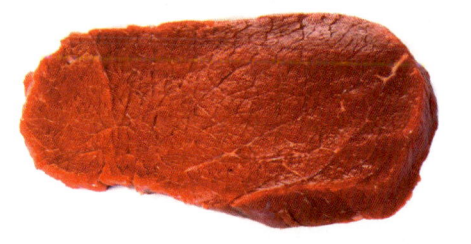

▲ Pork chops

▲ Lamb chops

▲ Lean beef steak

▲ Marbled beef steak

COMMODITIES   The science of cooking food: p68

PREPARATION AND COOKING OF MEAT AND POULTRY

What will I learn?

- Reasons for cooking meat
- What happens during cooking
- Suitable methods of preparation and cooking for meat and poultry
- Uses of meat and poultry in dishes and meals

Why is meat cooked?

- to kill bacteria and make the meat safe to eat, which prevents food poisoning
- to make the meat tender and easier to eat, and to improve texture
- to improve flavour and taste of meat
- to improve colour and appearance
- to help the meat keep for longer

During the process of cooking many chemical changes occur, affecting the appearance, taste and texture of meat:

- muscle proteins shrink and moisture is lost
- changes in colour occur, e.g. browning
- the connective tissue softens
- the fat melts
- the flavour develops.

Cooking decreases the nutritional value of meat as the heat destroys some vitamins and water soluble protein. A combination of high temperature and water converts collagen to gelatine. This increases the tenderness of meat and makes it more digestible.

Meat changes colour (beef/lamb red to brown, pork pink to white) at temperatures above 65°C as heat changes the pigment in myoglobin.

The Maillard or non-enzymic browning reaction between sugars and amino acids or proteins also produces brown pigments. The protein reacts with the simple sugars on the meat's surface. Savoury substances are released which produce characteristic smells.

Loss of juices causes meat to shrink and lose weight. If meat is overcooked it becomes tough and indigestible.

Key point
Meat must be cooked by a method suited to its structure.

Study tip
Give the main reasons for cooking meat.

▼ Meat cooked at a high temperature on a rotisserie causes a Maillard reaction. This creates flavour and browning

> **Activity**
>
> Look for recipes for meat dishes where the meat is tenderised by:
> - mixing with an acid such as lemon juice or vinegar before cooking
> - using a marinade
> - a commercial meat tenderiser mechanically beating or cutting the meat.
>
> Try out some of these recipes to compare texture and eating quality.

Preparing meat before cooking

All meats should be prepared separately from other ingredients being used in the meal, ideally using a chopping board set aside for the preparation of raw meat.

There are different preparation methods relating to a range of meat and poultry.

TENDERISING

Meats are tenderised to make them easier to digest and more enjoyable to eat. Tenderising can be done by **marinading**, ageing, hammering or adding artificial substances.

BONING

This involves the removal of bones in certain joints to make the carving and the portion control easier, for example, a leg of lamb.

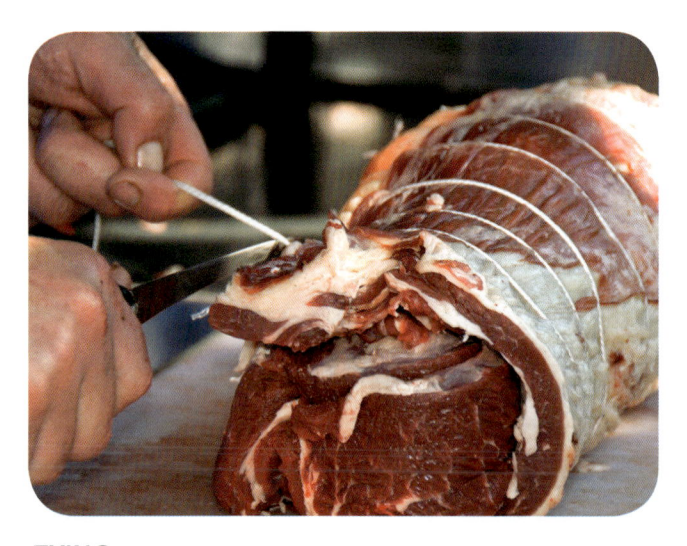

TYING

You can secure a joint for roasting with string, using a series of loops. This allows the meat to stay in place during cooking and helps to keep stuffing within the joint.

BATTING

You can use a meat hammer to flatten a small piece of poultry or meat. This has the effect of breaking down the connective tissue and tenderising the meat.

COMMODITIES

MEAT, POULTRY, FISH AND EGGS

Cooking methods suitable for and *meat* and *poultry*

boiling – suitable for larger cuts of meat and whole poultry. The cooking liquid is usually used to produce a nutritious broth, sauce or soup.

poaching – small pieces of meat and poultry can be poached using the shallow method, usually enhanced by the addition of aromatic vegetable and herbs. The cooking liquid is then used to make a sauce.

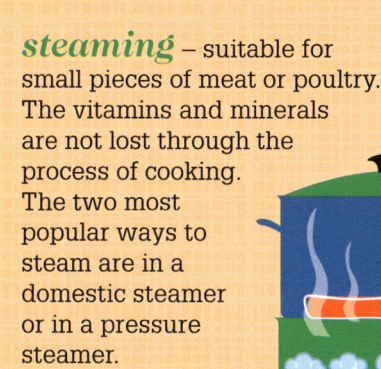

steaming – suitable for small pieces of meat or poultry. The vitamins and minerals are not lost through the process of cooking. The two most popular ways to steam are in a domestic steamer or in a pressure steamer.

stewing – similar to braising except the pieces of meat or poultry are quite small and the resulting cooking juices are served as part of the dish. Stewing can be done on the hob or in a casserole dish in the oven.

braising – a combination of moist and dry heat whereby a piece of meat is first sealed in hot fat or oil and then cooked slowly in a sauce or stock.

roasting – a term applied to meat or poultry cooked in the oven without extra fat or oil or with just a small quantity of fat or oil.

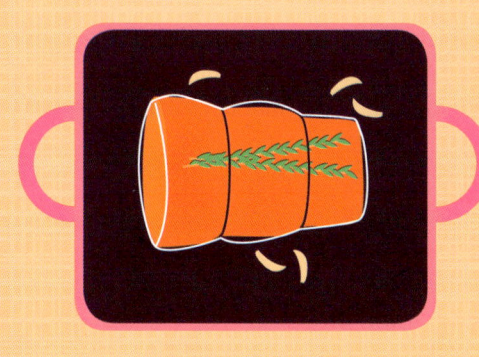

spit roasting – where a whole carcass is cooked over an open flame with a rotating centre spit.

pot roasting – where the meat or poultry is placed in a pot, generally on a bed of vegetables and the lid removed during the final stage of cooking to brown the surface.

chargrill – where meat or poultry is placed on metal bars over flames to create a lined effect on the product being cooked and a distinctive grilled flavour.

barbeque – a similar effect to chargrilling with a whole range of different barbeques available on the market.

grilling – where small, thin pieces of meat and poultry are cooked above or below a direct, radiant heat source. Catering establishments use a **salamander**.

SECTION 3

277

> **Study tip**
>
> Some processed meat products contain very little meat. Read the ingredients list on the packaging for more information on meat content.

▲ A plate of cured-raw meats

> **Activity**
>
> Choose a range of beef burgers such as frozen, supermarket brand, butchers and homemade. Try to ensure that all the burgers are of similar thickness.
>
> Measure the diameter of each burger before cooking each using a contact grill.
>
> Observe the amount of fat which drips out and measure again once cooked to see if there has been any shrinkage.

▲ Biltong

Meat products

A variety of meat products are available and are very popular with the consumer. These include:

Processed meats

These products are meat mixes composed of muscle meat with varying quantities of animal fat. Processed products are salted only. Examples are burgers, nuggets.

Cured meats

Cuts are made entirely of muscle meat. The meat pieces are treated with small amounts of nitrite, either as dry salt or as salt solution in water. There are two groups of cured meats:

- Cured-raw meats do not undergo any heat treatment during their manufacture. Examples are parma ham, prosciutto.
- Cured-cooked meats, after the curing process of the raw muscle meat, always undergo heat treatment to achieve the desired palatability, e.g. hams.

Raw-cooked meat

The product components are muscle meat, fat and non-meat ingredients which are processed raw, i.e. uncooked, shaped then cooked e.g. frankfurter sausages.

Precooked-cooked meat

They contain mixes of lower-grade muscle trimmings, fatty tissues, head meat, animal feet, animal skin, blood, liver and other edible slaughter by-products. There are two heat treatment procedures involved in the manufacture of precooked-cooked products. The first heat treatment is the precooking of raw meat materials and the second heat treatment the cooking of the finished product mix at the end of the processing stage. e.g. black pudding, liver pâté, corned beef.

Raw-fermented sausages

Raw-fermented sausages are uncooked meat products and consist of more or less coarse mixtures of lean meats and fatty tissues combined with salts, nitrite (curing agent), sugars and spices and other non-meat ingredients filled into casing e.g. fermented sausages. It is then left to dry and ferment to develop flavour.

Dried meat products

Dried meat products are the result of the simple dehydration or drying of lean meat in natural conditions or in an artificially created environment. Biltong is a variety of dried, cured meat that originated in South Africa.

Meat extracts such as stock cubes and pastes e.g. Bovril are also derived from meat.

It is traditional in the UK to serve **accompaniments** with roast meat and poultry. These are some of the most popular:

- beef – Yorkshire pudding, horseradish sauce or mustard
- chicken – chipolata sausage, bacon roll, bread sauce
- lamb – mint sauce
- pork – apple sauce
- turkey – chipolata sausage, bacon roll, cranberry sauce.

The effect of cooking on meat

Meat proteins coagulate (harden) on heating. At around 60°C the proteins begin to change. This process is called **denaturation**, which means that the proteins change in composition and structure.

As a result of denaturation, the muscle fibres become firmer.

Beyond 60°C the fibres shrink and the meat juices are squeezed out. Water-soluble vitamins, mineral salts and the substances that give meat its taste dissolve in the meat juices.

Dry heat or moist heat

Dry heat
- Grilling/roasting means the juices are lost from the surface of the meat and the 'taste' substances remain on the surface.
- Meat cuts with a small amount of connective tissue are the only ones that can be successfully cooked quickly at high temperatures in dry heat.

Moist heat
- When meat is cooked using moist methods (stewing, braising) the squeezed out juices are collected in the cooking liquid. Cooking by these methods produces moist meat with a good taste, unless it is overcooked, when it becomes dry, tasteless and 'stringy'.
- **Collagen** becomes water soluble more easily when there is some liquid with the meat, therefore meat cuts which have a lot of collagen are best cooked by a moist heat method.

The fat on the outside and on the inside of the meat melts during cooking. This means that more of the collagen is exposed to the heat which helps the meat to become tender.

Poultry must be thoroughly cooked. Care must be taken that it is cooked all the way through. The temperature must be high enough to destroy bacteria. Cooking meat, poultry in particular, until the core temperature is at 75°C or above will ensure that harmful bacteria are destroyed.

▲ Roasted meat and braised meat

> **Check it**
>
> List various moist heat and dry heat methods of cooking meat.

Tenderising meat

Aromatic herbs, spices, acids such as lemon juice or tomatoes, wine and vinegar are ingredients used to produce a marinade. Given time, the marinade tenderises and gives flavour to selected cuts of meat. By **marinading**, the tougher collagen is changed to gelatine. This allows meat to hold more water, which makes it more tender when cooked.

> **Check it**
>
> 1. How does the use of a marinade help to tenderise meat?
> 2. Explain how a tough cut of meat becomes tender during stewing.

🔑 Key terms

Gelatine – a natural protein substance present in the tendon, ligaments and tissues of animals. It is translucent and colourless.

Maillard reaction or non-enzymic browning – a reaction which occurs between a food containing protein and carbohydrate together are heated by dry heat.

Denaturation – A process whereby the proteins are changed in structure.

Marinading – a process of soaking foods in a liquid mixture, usually wine, vinegar or lemon juice with various spices and herbs, prior to cooking.

Salamander – a high intensity grill used in the catering industry.

The science of cooking food p68

STORAGE OF MEAT AND POULTRY

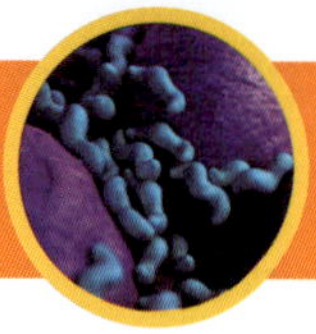

What will I learn?
- The correct storage of meat and poultry
- How to safely handle meat and poultry during food preparation and cooking

Meat and poultry are perishable foods. Poultry, in particular, is a high risk food because it contains bacteria that can cause food poisoning, such as salmonella, campylobacter, E. coli and staphylococcus aureus.

Poisoning with campylobacter is the most common cause of foodborne illness in the UK, with chicken being the prime culprit. Campylobacter causes more cases of food poisoning than E. coli, listeria and salmonella put together.

Campylobacter bacteria cannot be seen; it has no bad taste or smell but can have serious effects. Campylobacter poisoning usually develops a few days after consuming contaminated food and leads to symptoms that include abdominal pain, severe diarrhoea and, sometimes, vomiting. It can last for between 2 and 10 days and can be particularly severe in small children and the elderly.

Campylobacter and salmonella bacteria live in the intestines of poultry and other livestock found on farms. These bacteria are transmitted via the animals' faeces. They can pass into the human food chain during handling after the bird or animal has been slaughtered.

The following guidelines should be followed when buying, storing, preparing and cooking meat and poultry.

Buying
- Buy from reputable butchers and supermarkets.
- Check that packaging is not damaged or open.
- If buying pre-packed meat, check 'use-by date' on the packaging.
- Offal should smell fresh without a stale or strong odour.

Storage
- All meat and poultry should be stored at a temperature of 0-5°C.
- Raw and cooked meat and poultry should be stored separately.
- Raw meat should be stored at the bottom of the refrigerator so that the juices do not drip on to other foods and contaminate them with bacteria.
- If purchased in plastic packaging, the packaging should be removed and the meat or poultry placed on a plate, covered or in a container with a lid. If there are giblets inside raw poultry when purchased, remove and store separately
- Poultry should be stored well away from other meats because of the risk of salmonella cross-contamination.
- The shelf life of offal is short and ideally it should be used on the day of purchase. When buying loose from a butcher or meat counter it should look fresh, clean and moist with no dry patches and have an even colour and texture.
- Always leave pre-packed offal in its original packaging until required for cooking and adhere to any 'use-by' dates.
- As with all raw meat, store offal covered at the bottom of the refrigerator and away from cooked foods.

Check it

Name three potentially harmful bacteria found in poultry.

COMMON BACTERIA INFECTING HUMANS

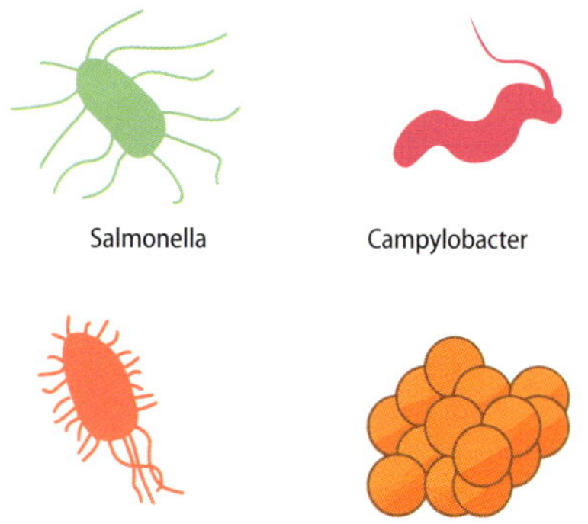

Salmonella Campylobacter

Escherichia Coli Staphylococcus Aureus

▲ Meat is a high risk food. Keep it cool, clean and covered

▲ Minced meat is a particularly high risk food because the surface area of the meat has been increased through the mincing process. As a result, the possibility of contamination is greater.

MEAT, POULTRY, FISH AND EGGS

Freezing

Raw meat can be frozen providing you do the following things:

- Freeze it before the 'use-by' date.
- Follow any freezing or thawing instructions on the label.
- Defrost it in a microwave if you intend to cook it as soon as it's defrosted, otherwise thaw it in the fridge so that it doesn't get too warm.
- Try to use the meat within two days of defrosting – it will go off in the same way as fresh meat.
- Cook food all the way through.

When meat thaws, lots of liquid can come out of it. This liquid will spread bacteria to any food, plates or surfaces that it touches. Keep the meat in a sealed container at the bottom of the fridge, so that it can't touch or drip onto other foods.

Always clean plates, utensils, surfaces and hands thoroughly after they have touched raw or thawing meat, to stop bacteria from spreading.

If you defrost raw meat and then cook it thoroughly, you can freeze it again, but remember never to reheat foods more than once.

▲ Meat handling in an abbatoir

Preparation

- It is important that food handlers follow personal hygiene rules and that food preparation areas are clean and hygienic.
- Use different chopping boards and knives for preparing raw and cooked meat and poultry.
- Wash hands thoroughly after preparing raw meat and, in particular, raw poultry.
- Frozen poultry should be thoroughly defrosted before cooking.

▼ Use different chopping boards to keep raw and cooked foods apart during preparation

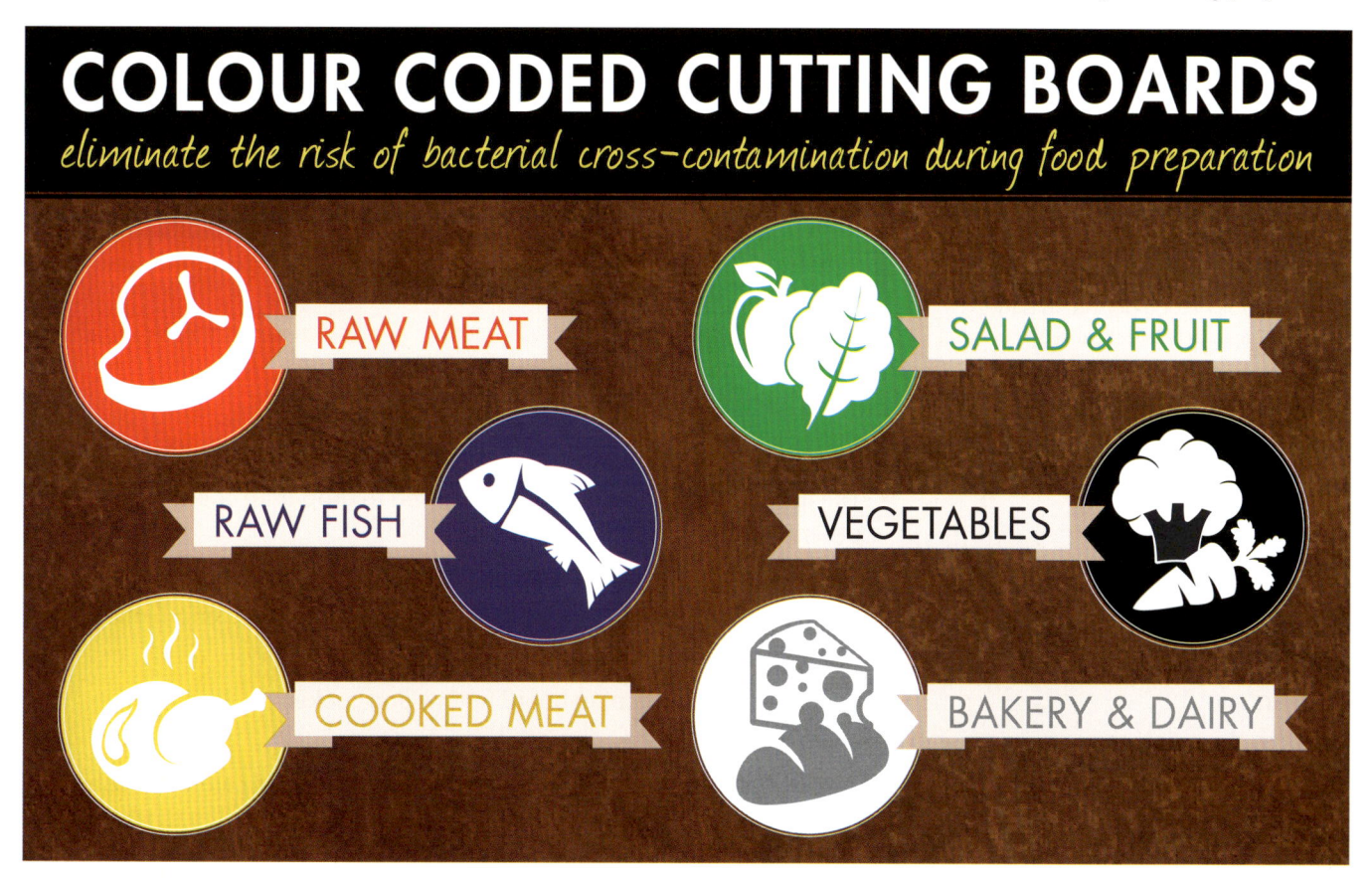

COLOUR CODED CUTTING BOARDS
eliminate the risk of bacterial cross-contamination during food preparation

- RAW MEAT
- SALAD & FRUIT
- RAW FISH
- VEGETABLES
- COOKED MEAT
- BAKERY & DAIRY

Key point

Food poisoning can occur as a result of:
- incorrect storage
- insufficient thawing
- cross-contamination
- incorrect cooking temperature or insufficient cooking time.

Study tip

Learn the names of food poisoning bacteria.

Study tip

State the importance of using hygienic practices when preparing poultry.

Learn the causes of food poisoning.

State the importance of following food hygiene guidelines when cooking poultry.

Activity

Read the following article adapted from a newspaper headline.

Food poisoning rise linked to undercooked offal

Campylobacter contamination has risen significantly in the last four years after reductions in the early part of this decade.

People have been warned by government agencies not to leave pink meat in livers and other offal when they prepare pâté or other dishes.

The food agency said liver, kidneys and other offal should be handled hygienically to avoid cross-contamination and cooked through until 'piping hot'.

What type of food poisoning is the newspaper article describing?

What foods caused the food poisoning?

How can this rise in food poisoning be prevented?

Key terms

Cross-contamination – the transfer of bacteria from one food to another, from humans, other food or equipment.

Giblets – the edible offal of poultry, typically including gizzard, heart and liver.

Cooking

It is very important to cook meat and poultry properly to make sure that any harmful bacteria have been killed.

Poultry in particular needs thorough cooking. If it's not cooked all the way through, bacteria may survive and cause food poisoning.

Cooking times are usually measured in minutes per kg of the bird's weight. For example, the Food Standards Agency gives the general guide below on cooking times for a turkey:

- Allow 45 minutes per kg, plus 20 minutes extra, for a turkey under 4.5kg.
- Allow 40 minutes per kg for a turkey weighing between 4.5kg and 6.5kg.
- Allow 35 minutes per kg for a turkey over 6.5kg.

To check if it's cooked, pierce the thickest part of the bird's legs with a clean skewer or knife. The thickest part is usually between the drumstick and the thigh. Check the colour of the juices that come out. If the bird is cooked, the juices will be clear, not red or pink.

1. Wash everything that has been in touch with raw chicken. Use soap and hot water on hands and utensils

2. Store raw chicken separately from other cooked food, covered and chilled on the bottom shelf of the fridge

3. Check chicken is cooked thoroughly – not pink inside, steaming hot and juices run clear

Food poisoning

This occurs as a result of poor food preparation and/or hygiene. For example:

- The juices from raw poultry being allowed to drop onto cooked poultry or other types of foods
- Poultry which has not been cooked at the correct temperature
- Poultry which has not been allowed to cook for the right length of time
- Failure to allow poultry to defrost thoroughly
- Using the same chopping board for raw and cooked poultry
- Eating poultry after the use-by date.

All offal should be eaten within 24 hours of purchase and carefully washed and prepared before cooking. Thorough cooking is essential to tenderize the offal and prevent food poisoning.

COMMODITIES

FISH

MEAT, POULTRY, FISH AND EGGS

What will I learn?
- The choice of fish available to the consumer
- The importance of sustainability for fish stocks
- The nutritional value of fish in the diet
- The things to consider when buying fish
- The composition of fish
- The storage, preparation and cooking fish

Choice of fish

There are a great variety of fish and at one time they were all profusely available. After the Second World War there was an increase in fishing, partly to feed the population and partly to feed animals reared for food. Gradually this has given rise to concern over the dwindling of fish stocks. Some countries impose fishing limits around their shores to regulate the amount of fish caught.

Today, many of our fish stocks are shrinking because:
- too many fish are being harvested from our seas and oceans
- too much rubbish is being thrown in the sea and too little is done to protect wildlife. Many fish become entangled in nets and are injured or die.

Sustainability

Many people prefer to eat fish that comes from a **sustainable source**, that is, from managed stocks farmed and caught in a way that causes minimal damage to the environment and to wildlife.

All UK fisheries and anglers have to operate under strict management regimes. Many stocks are currently very healthy. Many of the most plentiful species are exported, so there is scope to increase UK consumption of these fish stocks.

The Fish Environmental Stewardship logo means that the fish are caught with minimal impact on stocks, ecosystems and the environment, which helps ensure that the fish we eat today will still be available in the future.

The main source of omega-3 oil we need in our diet is marine fish but fish stocks are declining, particularly for some species such as wild salmon and trout. Therefore it is a good idea to choose fish from sustainable sources where possible. You can do this by looking for Marine Stewardship Council (MSC) certified products, or consulting *The Good Fish Guide* from the Marine Conservation Society.

▲ Fish caught at sea are usually processed and frozen before the trawler returns to land

▼ The fish environmental stewardship logo

TYPES OF FISH

SALT · FRESH · SHELL · SCALES

Fish can be classified according to their origin. Fish live in fresh or salt water, have fins and backbones. Shellfish have shells instead of backbones.

- Freshwater fish include trout, carp and salmon.
- Salt water fish (sea fish) include cod, haddock, plaice, sole, whiting, bream, tuna, mackerel and herring.
- Shellfish include crabs, prawns, shrimps, lobster, crayfish, langoustines, mussels, scallops, cockles, clams and oysters.

Cod

Haddock

Salmon

Plaice

Trout

Herring

Lobster

Crab

Prawn

284 COMMODITIES

MEAT, POULTRY, FISH AND EGGS

Fish can also be classified into oily fish, white fish and shellfish according to colour, fat content and body type.

Oily fish

The flesh of oily fish is more than 5% fat and is therefore dark in colour. They can be fresh water or sea fish, or, in the case of salmon, live in the sea but return to the river to mate and lay eggs and then return to the sea again. Examples are mackerel, herring, tuna, salmon, sardine and trout.

Trout is considered to be a fresh water fish, though it can be sea caught or, very often these days, farmed.

White fish

The flesh of white fish is less than 5% fat and as a result it is white. The oil/fat is found in the liver. White fish live in the sea. Examples are cod, haddock, sole, coley, hake, tilapia, whiting and sea bass.

Fresh fish has the following characteristics: firm flesh, clear and shiny eyes, red gills and a clean smell.

It is possible to further sub-divide white fish into two main types:
- round fish such as cod, mullet and hake
- flat fish such as sole (Dover and lemon), turbot, halibut and brill.

▲ Hake (top) and turbot

Shellfish

Shellfish are divided into:
- molluscs – small soft bodied sea animals which live inside a soft shell.
  Examples are cockles, winkles and mussels, whelks.
  Squid and octopus are also classed as molluscs – even though their shell is inside.
- crustaceans – soft bodied, jointed sea animals which are covered by a hard, protective shell. Examples are lobster, crayfish, crab and shrimp.

Check it

Explain the difference between oily fish and white fish in:
- appearance
- nutritional value

State the difference between a mollusc and a crustacean.

Study tip

Learn about white fish, oily fish and shellfish. Can you name examples of each type?

▲ Although they look quite different, each of these animals is actually a shellfish

285

Fillet

Steak

Cutlet

▲ Popular choices of fish cuts are fillets, steaks and cutlets

Key point

Fresh fish deteriorates very quickly. Use it as soon as possible after purchase.

Check it

Fillet, steak and cutlet are cuts of fish. Describe the difference between each of these cuts.

Study tip

Make sure you know all the signs of quality and freshness to look for when buying fresh fish.

Buying fresh fish

Most fish is hauled from trawl nets, gutted, filleted and frozen. Most of the fish we buy is bought in this way. Alternatively, fresh fish is also cleaned, left whole, chilled and transported to fishmongers on a daily basis.

Fish should always be bought as fresh as possible from a reputable fishmonger. The best ways to spot quality and freshness in fish are through looking and smelling. Fish of all types spoil very rapidly and can become unsafe to eat. They should be consumed as soon as possible after purchase because they are common carriers of food poisoning bacteria.

Fresh fish displayed at fishmongers and in supermarkets should ideally be stored on ice.

The following cuts of fish are available at most fishmongers and supermarkets. Some are boneless and some are bone-in.

- Round fish fillet – usually comes from a large round fish, such as cod. It is quite thick and long. The flesh is cut from the length of the fish.
- Flat fish fillet – usually comes from a large flat fish, such as Dover sole or plaice. This tends to be less thick and the fish is leaner than a round fish.
- Fish steak – these cuts come from the width of a round fish only. They are usually cut from the middle of the body.
- Fish cutlet – these are slightly thinner than the steaks and come from between the head and the mid body of the round fish.

Small fish such as herring, mackerel and trout are usually sold whole. Larger fish is usually filleted or sold as cutlets.

Storing and preparing fresh fish

Fish should be stored at a temperature of 0-5°C, away from other products. Fish is often packed in ice to keep it fresh. When bought it should be well wrapped to prevent the strong smell from contaminating other foods.

It is important that all fish is washed under cold running water before preparation. This will ensure that the fish is clean and free from any blood or innards prior to cooking. Scales and fins should be removed and, in most cases, the head. Some small fish, such as trout and lemon sole, can be cooked whole and large ones, such as turbot and salmon, are often cooked whole for special occasions.

However, most large fish is cut into portions, usually steaks or fillets.

MEAT, POULTRY, FISH AND EGGS

When selecting fresh fish, the following points should be considered:

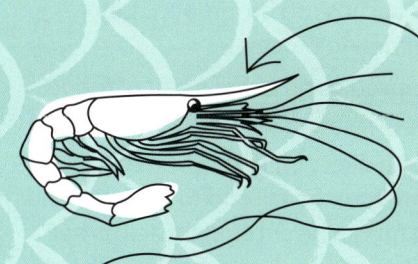

Prawns and shrimps should be **pink** or **greyish** in colour depending on variety.

Shellfish must have **tightly** closed shells or they must close tightly when tapped. Lobsters, crabs and prawns must have shells that are bright and hard.

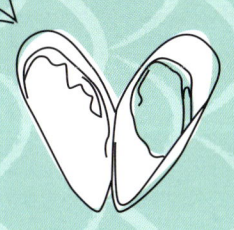

The fish should smell **pleasantly** of the sea or seaweed, it should not smell 'fishy' or strong which is a sign that it is past its best.

The fish should look **bright** and **shiny**, either through the presence of slime (flat fish in particular) or through plenty of **bright scales** (round oily fish in particular).

The eyes should be clear, full and shiny – almost **glistening** and not sunken.

SECTION 3

The **gills** should be **red** in colour, indicating that a good amount of **oxygen** is still present in the blood.

Any fish that has distinctive markings should **clearly show** these markings, for example, **orange** spots on plaice. There should be bright lateral lines on round white fish and bright stripes on mackerel.

It should be **firm** to the touch. Fish that has just been caught and killed will be in a state of rigor mortis (firm and stiff) for up to **24 hours**. As the fish becomes older it becomes softer and pliable, the '**bendier**' the fish the more likely it is to be an older fish.

When buying crab, **tap** it gently to make sure it doesn't contain water. Lobsters and crabs should have all their limbs and feel heavy relative to their size. They should be purchased **live** and should **move** their claws. Lobsters should flap their tails tightly against their chests or curl them under their shells. If they have been refrigerated, they will not be very active.

287

Filleting flat fish

Always wash the fish before trimming or filleting to remove surface slime which makes it difficult to hold the fish and keep it secure.

If required, the side and tail fins can be removed before filleting as part of the trimming process.

The side fins can be removed using either a pair of fish scissors or a chef's knife.

Always cut in the opposite direction that the fins naturally lie, this will mean cutting from the tail end to the head end for the side fins. The tail fin can be cut straight across but be careful that you do not cut into the flesh of the fillet at the tail.

A filleting knife is used to remove the actual fillets. It has a sharp point and a flexible sharp blade which is ideal for bending under the flesh and separating the flesh from the bone.

It is not necessary to cut off the head from flat fish before filleting as two of the fillets run right up alongside the head and there is the possibility of removing some of the flesh with the head. The head can be cut off using a chef's knife once the long fillets have been removed.

Filleting round fish

When filleting round fish it is necessary to cut the head off in order to be able to run the blade along the back bone.

Use a chef's knife for this task as it is heavier and the blade is firmer.

Removing pin bones

Once fillets have been removed from larger fish it is necessary to remove the bones left in the flesh. To do this we use fish pliers or tweezers. Pull the bones out at an angle of 45° towards the head end of the fillet to prevent unsightly holes appearing in the flesh.

Remove any rib bones with a filleting knife.

Skinning fish

Once fish has been filleted it is usually skinned although a number of fish are now cooked with the skin on.

Some fish can be skinned before filleting, notably Dover sole which is simply skinned by freeing the skin at the tail end then pulling it away towards the head by hand.

Other fish need to be skinned using a flexible sharp filleting knife in order to cut between the skin and the flesh without leaving any flesh remaining on the skin or vice versa.

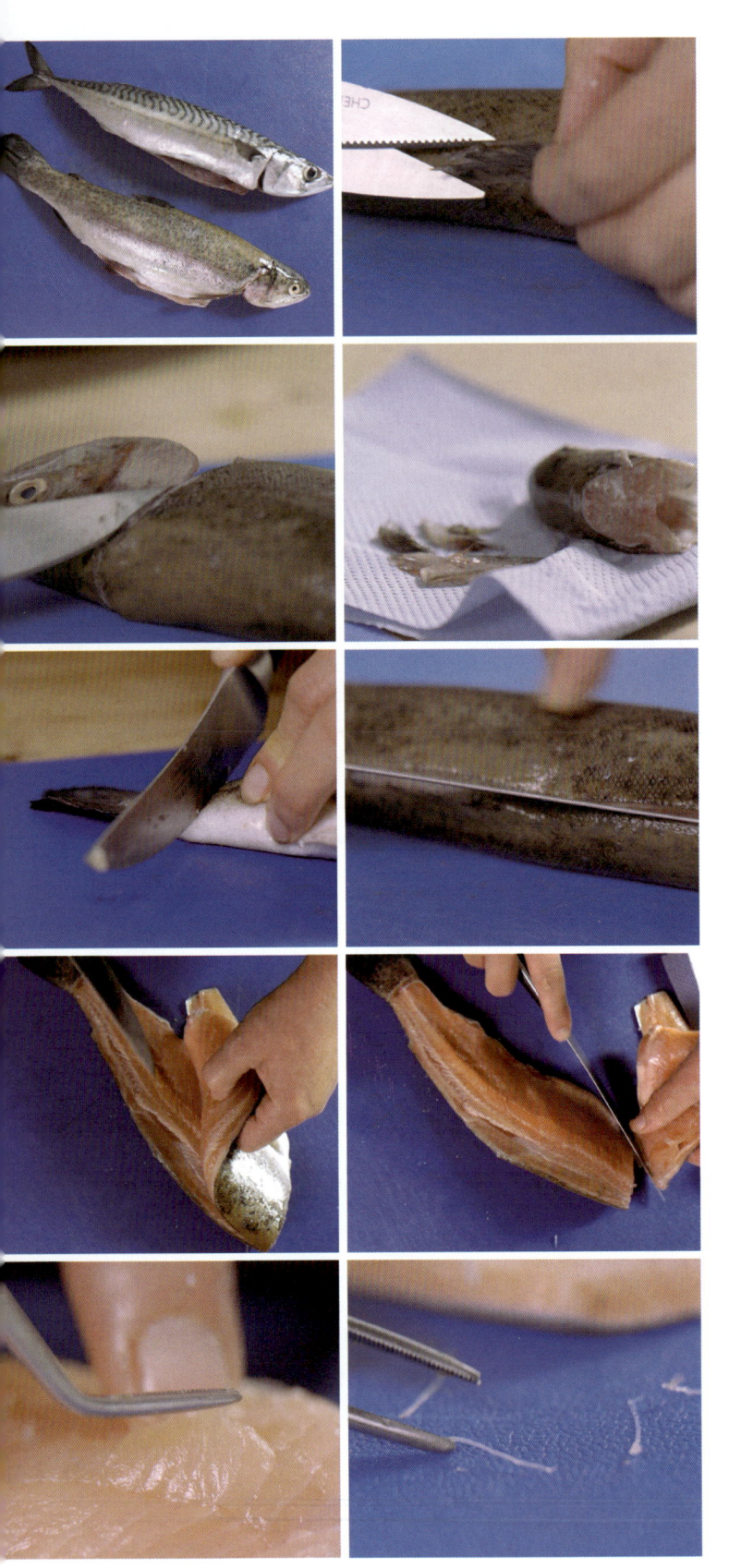

▲ Filleting a fish

Study tip

Learn at least 4 types of fresh fish cuts, naming suitable fish for each type. Explain how to prepare each cut.

Cooking fish

The choice of cooking method can have an effect on the nutritional value of the fish. Suitable cooking methods include steaming, poaching, grilling, frying, baking and microwaving.

Fish can be used in many dishes. In the UK it is most popular fried either in batter or coated in breadcrumbs. It can be cooked and served with a sauce as a starter or main course or used in soups and salads. It can be marinaded, stuffed, coated or wrapped in pastry before cooking.

Any liquid left behind after cooking fish can be used in a sauce to serve with the fish. This will replace any moisture squeezed out during cooking and can help to add flavour to the sauce.

Preparation of fish before cooking

Marinading fish

The purpose of a marinade is to impart additional flavour into the fish before cooking.

The structure and texture of fish means that the marinade ingredients quickly soak into the flesh and the marinading time is relatively short.

Marinades include an acidic ingredient such as lemon or orange juice. This acid can have the effect of 'cooking' the flesh of the fish so remember not to leave the fish in the marinade for too long (up to 24 hours).

There are many types of marinades but they all require the ingredients to be evenly distributed over the food item to be flavoured.

Dry marinades which are herb and spice based can also be used. The fish is dusted with the marinade, mixed to ensure all pieces are evenly coated and then transferred to a clean bowl or tray.

Coating fish

If the coating of the fish is only flour then this should be done just before cooking, otherwise the moistness of the fish will cause the flour to form lumps and clump together which will spoil the finished appearance. If the coating is batter-based for deep frying then this also needs to be done just before cooking for the same reason.

Fish to be coated in breadcrumbs goes through the system known as pané. This simply means passing items through seasoned flour, egg and breadcrumbs in that order to fully coat the items.

When the coated fish is placed into hot fat the coating immediately seals and protects the fish which then cooks as heat is conducted through the coating.

Cooking crustacean shellfish at home requires a bit of preparation. Alternatively, they can be purchased already cooked and 'dressed'.

Mollusc shellfish have shells but they are not multi-jointed. Some molluscs are eaten raw, such as oysters, but most need very little in the way of cooking through. Too much cooking will affect their texture and taste.

▲ The ingredients to coat fish – flour, breadcrumbs, egg and batter

Check it

Three different ways of cooking cod are:
- steamed and served with a sauce
- coated in egg and breadcrumbs and fried
- baked with a herb crust topping.

1. Can you analyse each dish with reference to the expected appearance and texture?
2. Can you evaluate the three methods of cooking and justify your comments?

Study tip

Learn 3 techniques for preparing fish before cooking.

Grilling

White fish should be brushed lightly with a little oil before grilling, but oily fish needs nothing adding. Make sure the grill is hot before the fish is inserted. Turn the fish over carefully once.

Shallow frying

Shallow frying is the best way to fry fish. The fish should be dried with kitchen paper, coated with beaten egg and dusted with flour. The oil in the frying pan should be hot enough for the fish to sizzle immediately when it is added.

Deep frying

Deep frying is usually done with battered fish. The batter is made from flour, milk, water and/or beer. The oil has to be hot enough for the fish to sizzle immediately when it is added otherwise the batter will become soggy and greasy.

Deep frying fish adds considerably to its calorific value.

Steaming

Steaming is a very healthy option. The fish is placed in a steamer that sits on top of a saucepan of boiling water. Steaming retains the flavour of the fish.

Poaching

Poaching is an excellent way to gently cook tender and delicate fish. Many liquid flavours are used, the most popular one being white wine. The cooking liquid is used to make an accompanying sauce.

Baking

Baking is a good way to cook fish as much of the flavour is retained. When cooked in parcels with herbs and a little wine, the flavours develop and enhance the taste of the fish. This method of baking fish is perfect for barbequing.

Microwaving

Easy and very quick, this method is usually reserved for fish poached in liquid. Milk works very well with salmon, as does white wine, cider or lemon juice. Precise timing is essential as the fish can quite easily become dry and overcooked.

▲ Fish that has been cooked by different methods: grilled, poached and shallow fried

Key point

100g raw fish contains 0.7g fat.

100g cod in batter, deep fried, contains 15.4g fat

Frying fish increases the fat content and adds to the calorific value of the fish.

Study tip

Learn suitable cooking methods for fish and the advantages and disadvantages of each one. Give examples of fish that can be cooked by each method.

Activity

Weigh out four equal portions of the same fish and cook as follows:

a grill   b steam   c fry

d bake wrapped in foil

Note the changes in appearance, size and texture. Account for any difference you see.

Nutrition value of 100g of fish						
	energy (kcal)	protein (g)	fat (g)	calcium (mg)	vitamin A (µg)	vitamin D (µg)
Cod, grilled	85	21	1.3	10	2	1
Mackerel, grilled	239	21	17.3	12	48	8.8
Salmon, grilled	215	24	13	25	16	7.1
Salmon, canned	153	24	6.6	91	31	9.2

MEAT, POULTRY, FISH AND EGGS

Fish products

There are several ways to preserve fish for long term storage:

WAYS OF PRESERVING FISH

CANNING
Produces a moist, flaky product and makes the bones edible. Oily fish and shellfish such as tuna, salmon, and prawns can be canned in brine, tomato sauce or oil which adds flavour to the fish.

SALTING
If enough salt is used the fish may keep for up to a year.

DRYING
Fish are laid out to be dried.

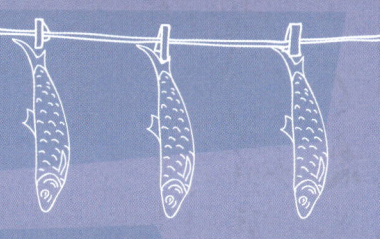

SMOKING
Fish can be smoked using different techniques. Hot smoked fish are moist, lightly salted and fully cooked. They can be eaten without further cooking. Cold smoked fish are generally more salty in flavour and have less moisture. Cold smoking does not cook the fish; it merely adds a smoked flavour. Smoked fish and salted fish such as kippers and bloaters should have have a firm flesh, shiny skin and a good 'smoky' smell.

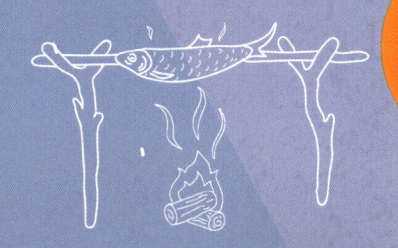

PICKLING
Pickling fish was originally conceived as a way to preserve it. It is a common technique in Scandinavia. Pickling is now used widely to add flavour and sharpness.

FREEZING
Package in blocks or freeze in water brushing glaze on top.

Processing of fish

Fish fingers were a resounding success when they were first launched in the UK in 1955. More than 60 years later, the frozen brick of fish is as popular as ever.

The fish arrives at the factory as frozen blocks and is X-rayed to check for large bones / foreign bodies. The product moves along a conveyer (mesh) which has a series of cutting blades. These blades cut the fish into logs, then into planks and then into fish fingers. The product is sprayed with beaten egg and passes through a breadcrumb curtain coating. The product emerges as coated fish fingers.

The fish fingers are heat treated for 30 seconds to seal the breadcrumb coating. They travel along a vibrating conveyor to remove any excess coating. Then they are blast frozen and and packaged in multiples of 6, 10, 16 or bags of 36 or 60.

They are mechanically guided into open boxes or bags, sealed and coded. They pass through weight checker and metal detectors before being packed into cardboard boxes and stacked for dispatch to supermarkets.

The process is known commercially as enrobing or coating.

▲ Manufacturing process of the fish finger

Activity

Suggest dishes which would be suitable for main meals using the following fish:
- tinned salmon
- fresh cod steak
- fresh mackerel
- frozen prawns

Suggest suitable accompaniments for each main dish.

Study tip

List the various ways of preserving fresh fish.

▶ The short connective tissues within fish flesh

Key point

Fish cooks quickly because of its short connective tissue. Fast methods of cooking such as grilling and microwaving are suitable.

▲ Fish is a key part of the Inuit diet

Key point

Two portions of fish per week is the recommended amount. One of these portions should be oily fish.

The composition of fish

The composition of fish muscle is similar to meat but with far less connective tissue. Fish muscle is made up of short fibres separated by very thin connective tissue which makes it much easier to tenderise and quicker to cook.

During cooking, fish muscle shrinks and moisture escapes. The connective tissue, called collagen, changes to gelatine.

It is important not to overcook fish as the proteins easily become tough and the flesh dry. The connective tissue weakens and dissolves, the muscle flakes and separates on cooking. Moderate temperatures and fast cooking methods are recommended.

In oily fish, the fat content helps to keep the flesh moist and prevents it from drying out.

The nutritional value of fish

Fish is made up of water, protein, fat, vitamins and minerals.

Protein

Fish is a good source of quality protein, essential for body building and repair of tissues. Like meat, the protein in fish has high biological value. Fish is the main source of protein in the diet of many countries.

White fish is very easily digested and creates little waste, so it is a recommendable food for people with digestive disorders.

Fat

Unlike meat, the fat in fish consists mostly of oils containing **unsaturated fatty acids**. Oily fish in particular provide essential fatty acids such as **omega-3** which are known to help reduce **cholesterol** levels and reduce the risk of heart disease.

Oil-rich fish such as mackerel, sardines, salmon, tuna, herring, kippers, swordfish and sprats are rich in unsaturated fats containing omega-3. Omega-3 is necessary for human health and cannot be produced by the body; it is obtained from food such as fish.

Countries where the diet is high in fish have fewer cases of heart disease. Oily fish plays a central role in the diets of the Inuits (Eskimos) of Greenland, the Japanese, and many Mediterranean countries. Trials carried out in the UK have confirmed that the omega-3 oil in fish lowers blood fats by decreasing the chance of the blood vessels clogging with cholesterol. In turn this can reduce the risk of a heart attack. There is also evidence to suggest that people who eat fish twice a week are less likely to suffer a stroke. The British Heart Foundation recommends eating fish at least twice weekly, particularly fatty fish such as mackerel, lake trout, herring, sardines, tuna, and salmon.

Lack of omega-3

Symptoms of omega-3 fatty acid deficiency include fatigue, poor memory, dry skin, heart problems, mood swings or depression, and poor circulation.

Processing fish can destroy omega-3 content. Some brands of tuna, for example, may have the omega-3 removed during processing, so always check the label.

Vitamins

Oily fish contains useful amounts of important fat soluble vitamins A and D and is one of the best sources of these vitamins in the diet. Herring and canned oily fish, in particular, are good sources of vitamin D. White fish contain vitamins A and D in the liver oils, not in the flesh. Most fish contain a small amount of the B groups of vitamins. Some of the B vitamins are lost when fish is cooked because they are destroyed by heat.

Minerals

Fish offers a good source of calcium which the body needs for healthy bones and teeth. Sea fish is a good source of iodine and fluorine which are needed for growth and metabolism, as well as magnesium and zinc. Sodium, potassium and phosphorus are found in all fish.

The canning process softens fish bones so they can be eaten. This makes canned fish a rich source of calcium if the bones are eaten.

The calorific value of fish

White fish such as cod, haddock, plaice or sole can provide a tasty, low calorie meal option containing 81 kcal per 100g. Oil-rich fish such as mackerel, sardines and herring have around 190 kcal per 100g. These are still a healthy eating choice, particularly as they compare to meats such as:

lamb chops – 377 kcal per 100g

chicken with skin – 230 kcal per 100g

Key point

Canned fish is a very good source of calcium when the bones are eaten.

The omega-3 in fresh tuna is lost during canning.

Key point

Fish is easy to cook and to digest. This makes it an ideal food for young children, the elderly and people who are convalescing from illness.

Check it

1. Can you name the main nutrients in fish?
2. Can you name a nutrient which is not found in fish?

Activity

Compare the nutritional values of 100g quantities of some of the following protein foods:

haddock, herring, prawns, egg, chicken, beef mince, Cheddar cheese, haricot beans, lentils

Record the following nutritional value in a table:

protein, Kilocalories, fat, calcium, iron, vitamin A, vitamin D

Assess the value of fish in the diet in comparison with other foods.

Study tip

Discuss the importance of oily fish in the diet.

Key terms

Cholesterol – a fatty substance found in some foods and in human blood.

Omega-3 – essential fatty acids which are important for a healthy hear.

Unsaturated fatty acids – carbon is not attached to the hydrogen.

▲ Goose, duck, hen and quail eggs

EGGS

What will I learn?
- The choice of eggs available to the consumer
- Information to help the consumer make a choice when buying eggs

Where do eggs come from?
Most of the eggs we eat come from hens but eggs from other birds such as geese and ducks are also widely available. Egg consumption in the UK is estimated at 170 eggs a year per person.

EGG FARMING

- Barn – hens move freely inside the barn, but the light and feed are controlled.

- Battery or laying cage – hens are kept in cages indoors where the light, temperature and feed are controlled. This is the cheapest method of egg production.

- Free range – eggs come from hens that are allowed to roam in open air runs and live in hen houses at night to protect them from foxes.

- Organic – hens live on organic land and are fed an organic diet.

294 COMMODITIES

MEAT, POULTRY, FISH AND EGGS

Assurance schemes

Assurance schemes provide information to consumers on the conditions of production and origin of particular foods. They are voluntary organisations developed by the poultry industry to ensure that standards of welfare, traceability, husbandry, storage and other aspects of production are met to increase consumer confidence.

The British Lion quality mark on egg shells and boxes indicates that eggs are produced to a code of practice operated by the British Egg Industry Council. Around 85 per cent of UK eggs are stamped with the British Lion mark meaning that the eggs have been produced to the highest standards of food safety.

Laid in Britain Eggs is a consortium of independent egg producers and packers which markets locally and regionally. The label offers the guarantee that each egg can be traced to its origin.

EGG PRINTING EXPLAINED

Farming Method
- 0 = Organic
- 1 = Free Range
- 2 = Barn
- 3 = Cage

Country of Origin e.g. UK

Farm ID A specific code denoting the actual farm where your eggs were produced

Optional Information

Lion mark British eggs from hens vaccinated against salmonella and produced to a strict code of practice

Best before date

▲ Labelling information printed on an egg

Egg sizes

Stating egg size in a recipe is useful as using different sized eggs could lead to a difference in weight. For example, it is possible to buy a carton of large eggs all weighing 73g or, on the other hand, they could be 63g. If a recipe states 4 eggs, this could lead to a weight difference of 40g and this would explain why results may vary from time to time when using the same recipe.

Key point

The following information should appear on the egg box or be stamped directly on the eggs:
- the packing station number
- quality grade
- weight grade
- type of farming method
- best before date
- storage conditions

Key point

Eggs displaying the British Lion mark have been produced to the highest standard. The hens are tested for salmonella and hygiene is strictly controlled.

Check it

List factors which would influence your choice when shopping for eggs.

Study tip

Can you list the information found on egg boxes?

Activity

Carry out research on the price of barn, battery, free range and organic eggs. Note the results and explain any difference in price.

Complete the chart on eggs.

type of farming method	advantage	disadvantage
barn		
battery		
free range		
organic		

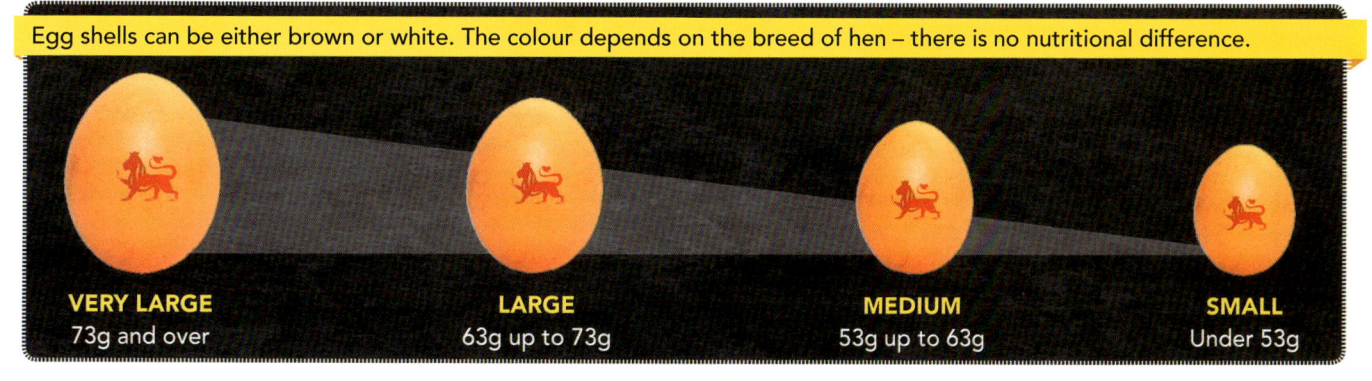

Egg shells can be either brown or white. The colour depends on the breed of hen – there is no nutritional difference.

VERY LARGE	LARGE	MEDIUM	SMALL
73g and over	63g up to 73g	53g up to 63g	Under 53g

▲ Size grading on hen's eggs

295

Egg quality

Under European law there are two classes of egg quality: A and B.
- Grade A eggs are the highest grade. They are naturally clean, fresh eggs, internally perfect with shells intact and the air sac not exceeding 6mm in depth. The yolk must not move away from the centre of the egg on rotation. Grade A eggs are sold as shell eggs.
- Grade B eggs are broken out and pasteurised.
- In addition, there is another class of eggs called industrial eggs which are for non-food use only and are used in products such as shampoo and soap.

Egg Structure

CHALAZAE
These are strands attached to the thick albumen which anchor the yolk in the middle of the egg.

WHITE OR ALBUMEN
When you crack an egg, you see two types of white – the thick white 'stands up' and the thin white runs towards the edge.

VITELLINE MEMBRANE
This holds the yolk together.

EGG CELL OR GERMINAL DISC
This is the part of the egg which would have developed into a chick if the egg had been fertilised. It is seen as a tiny speck on the surface of the egg

YOLK
This has a higher concentration of protein than the white.

SHELL MEMBRANES
There are two membranes – the outer and inner membranes. Their job is to as act as filters to help keep the egg in good condition.

AIR CELL
This is at the rounded end of the egg. As the egg ages, it loses water and air is drawn in to replace it so the air pocket gets bigger.

SHELL
Prevents damage to the egg and acts as a shield against bacteria.

The nutritional value of eggs (N)

Nutrition information

Typical values	Per medium size egg	Per 100g
Energy	277kJ 66kcal	547kJ 131kcal
Fat	4.6g	9.0g
of which saturates	1.3g	2.5g
monounsaturates	1.7g	3.4g
polyunsaturates	0.7g	1.4g
Carbohydrate of which sugars	trace	trace
Protein	6.4g	12.6g
Salt	0.2g	0.4g

Protein [N]

Eggs contain most of the nutrients needed by the body. They are an excellent source of high biological value protein. This is because they contain essential amino acids such as leucine.

Eggs are an excellent source of natural protein and are also relatively cheap when compared to other high-protein foods such as meat. On average, a medium-size egg contains around 6.2 grams of protein which makes up around 12.6% of the overall edible portion. Egg whites contain slightly more protein than egg yolks. One large egg white contains 3.6 grams of protein compared with 2.7 grams found in egg yolks.

Fat

Around 9% of the egg content is fat. It is found almost entirely in the yolk in the form of **lecithin**, in an emulsified state. The albumen contains less than 0.5% fat.

Most of an egg's total fatty acid composition is monounsaturated (approximately 38%). A further 16% is polyunsaturated and only 28% is saturated. An average medium size egg contains 177mg cholesterol, about 12% less than eggs contained twenty years ago as a result of improved feeding regimes for poultry.

Eggs are also rich in long chain omega-3 fatty acids, mainly in the form of DHA (docosahexaenoic acid). They therefore provide a useful alternative source of these important essential fatty acids, especially for people who do not consume oily fish. An average medium egg provides about 70mg of omega-3 fatty acids.

Until fairly recently, eating large quantities of eggs was thought to have a negative effect on a person's cholesterol levels. But recent scientific research by the British Heart Foundation has disproved this theory.

People used to think that the cholesterol levels in our bodies were directly influenced by the cholesterol in our food – but high cholesterol levels are usually caused by eating too much saturated fat, rather than eating too much cholesterol.

So, while eating lots of fried eggs might raise cholesterol levels, it is due to the fat used to fry the egg, not the egg itself. Poached, boiled, and scrambled eggs (without butter) will have no negative effects on cholesterol levels, and can be enjoyed as often as desired.

Vitamins

Eggs contain most vitamin groups with the exception of vitamin C. Eggs are a good source of fat soluble vitamin A and also provide useful amounts of vitamin D, as well as some vitamin E.

They are naturally rich in vitamin B2 (riboflavin), vitamin B12, a number of other B vitamins including folate, biotin, pantothenic acid and choline.

Minerals

Eggs contain most of the minerals that the human body requires for health.

In particular, eggs are an excellent source of iodine and phosphorus. They provide a significant amount of zinc, selenium and calcium. Research suggests that the iron in egg yolk is not fully absorbed unless it is eaten in conjunction with a vitamin C rich food. Egg yolk also contains a significant amount of iron, the vital ingredient of red blood cells, but the availability of this iron to the body is uncertain.

Carbohydrate and dietary fibre

Eggs contain only traces of carbohydrate and no dietary fibre.

Key point

- 1 egg is 12.6% protein
- 2 eggs = 1 portion of protein
- Eggs and egg dishes account for 3% of total protein source in the British diet.

Activity

Choose a selection of protein rich foods such as milk, meat, poultry, fish, soya beans, tofu, lentils, or nuts.

Compare the protein content of a 100g quantity of egg in comparison with 100g quantities of your chosen foods.

Find out the cost of each 100g amount of the chosen foods. Which protein food, in your opinion, gives best value for money? Give reasons to show your understanding of protein foods.

Check it

1 Name the nutrients which are found in eggs.
2 Which vitamin assists in the absorption of iron?
3 Suggest a suitable complementary food which would supply this vitamin in a breakfast consisting of boiled eggs.

The calorific value of an egg N

On average an egg yields between 55 and 80 calories depending on its size and how it is prepared. A small egg has 55 calories, a medium egg has 70 calories and a large egg has 80 calories.

Most of these calories come from the yolk, which is the most nutritious part of the egg and includes essential vitamins and minerals. Eggs are therefore very useful for people who are on a slimming diet as they are low in calories.

The way eggs are prepared will of course affect their nutritional value. For instance, an egg fried in fat will increase the overall number of calories but an egg poached in water will not. It is also important to eat eggs with other nutrient-rich foods, such as vegetables, salads and whole grains.

Egg allergy is common in children under 12 months. Few children are allergic to eggs after the age of six, although in some cases the allergy can persist.

▶ Calorific value: the fried egg in the top picture is higher in calories and fat than the poached egg below

Key point

The body only absorbs the iron in egg yolk if it is combined with a vitamin C rich food.

Study tip

Learn the nutritional value of eggs.
Explain why eggs are a good food to include in the diet.

Brown versus white eggs?

Brown and white eggs have the same nutritional value. The difference in shell colour is determined by the breed of hen laying the egg. White hens produce white eggs, and brown/red hens produce brown eggs. Generally, brown/red hens are larger and require more feed; therefore brown eggs may be more expensive.

MEAT, POULTRY, FISH AND EGGS

HOW DO WE USE EGGS?

What will I learn?

- The uses of eggs in dishes and meals
- The functions of eggs in food preparation and cooking

Eggs are used extensively as a main ingredient in a variety of dishes to add flavour, colour, tenderness, and richness.

They are also used on their own and can be cooked by the following cooking methods:

BAKING
Included in custard and flan recipes, eggs are used as a main protein ingredient and have the additional ability to set the filling.

FRYING
For frying it is essential to use high quality eggs and fat such as butter or sunflower oil and maintain a controlled low heat.

To make an omelette, whole eggs are whisked, seasoned and shallow fried in quality oil or butter.

BOILING
Boiled eggs can be served hot in shell, either soft or hard boiled. Hard boiled eggs are also used as a garnish, in a salad or as a sandwich filling. They can be combined with other ingredients to form dishes such as Scotch eggs.

POACHING
Poached eggs are cooked in gently boiling water with a little vinegar added. The acid in the vinegar helps to set the protein.

SCRAMBLING
Scrambled eggs is a dish made from egg whites and yolks of eggs that have been stirred as they cook, sometimes with butter, milk or cream and various other ingredients.

Eggs are a versatile cooking ingredient and perform many functions in the preparation and cooking of food. They are easily digested and a valuable food for convalescents and people on a light diet.

Eggs enrich, flavour, moisten, shorten, help form glazes and assist in the aeration of baked products. The colour in the yolk gives an attractive shade to cake crumb and helps to give structure to the finished product.

Whole eggs are amongst the most important of all the baker's raw ingredients and are used in the production of cakes, sponges, biscuits, pastries and some types of yeast mixtures. The combined characteristics of egg white and yolk provide all the qualities necessary to give a wide range of confectionery a good flavour, colour, texture, volume and keeping qualities.

Separating egg white and yolk

Many recipes require the egg white to be separated from the yolk.

The traditional method for separating is to break the egg over a bowl, first cracking the shell in two with a knife or the side of the bowl, then passing the contents from one shell to the other allowing the white to fall into the bowl whilst retaining the yolk in the shell.

The easiest method is to use an egg separator, a kitchen utensil designed to fit over a mixing bowl. It traps the yolk in a central reservoir while the white falls through slots and into the container below.

Using egg whites and yolk

Egg white is used mainly in the production of royal icing, meringues, macarons, marshmallows and rich sponge mixtures. It consists mainly of a solution of one part protein to seven parts water which is almost tasteless and when heated coagulates to a white, opaque solid. When whisked, egg white has the ability to produce a light foam consisting of millions of tiny air bubbles.

Egg yolk is used as an enriching agent in baked products, particularly sponges and cakes. It gives colour to the product and because it is high in fat and protein, it improves the nutritional value of the product. Egg yolk helps in the formation of smaller air cells and, as a result, give the goods a finer texture.

Nowadays, it is safer than ever to eat eggs – but eating them raw is less safe than cooking them first. This is because cooking kills any bacteria in eggs.

Many everyday foods and sauces (like mayonnaise, hollandaise sauce, ice cream and mousse) are made with raw eggs – but manufacturers will usually use pasteurised raw eggs, which means they are free of bacteria.

> **Study tip**
>
> Learn the functions of eggs in cooking. Can you give examples of each?

> **Activity**
>
> Research a range of dishes to illustrate the different functions of eggs.
>
> Either choose dishes suitable for:
>
> specific target groups such as children, lacto vegetarians, weight reduction, pregnant women
>
> or
>
> specific meals such as breakfast, snacks, main course, dessert

The functions of eggs

FUNCTION	DESCRIPTION	EXAMPLES
AERATION	Egg protein can stretch as it is whisked or beaten due to the ability of **ovalbumin** to stretch. Air becomes trapped within the eggs and this makes mixtures light and foamy. It can also act as a raising agent in cake making.	Mousses, cold soufflés, sponges, meringues
BINDING	Eggs **coagulate** (become solid) when heated.	Fish cakes, burgers, stuffing, meatloaf, rissoles, falafel
COATING	Before frying, foods are coated in raw egg then dipped into crumbs or flour. The egg protein coagulates on heating, sealing the food as it cooks forming a crispy coating and preventing the food from overcooking.	Scotch eggs, fish cakes, rissoles, fish in batter
GLAZING	Beaten egg, egg yolk or egg white is brushed over the surface of food to give a shine and a brown colour.	Savoury pastry dishes, bread, scones
EMULSIFYING	Egg yolk contains lecithin, which holds together oil and water and stops them from separating.	Mayonnaise, aioli, creaming mixture for cakes
THICKENING	Egg protein coagulates on heating and causes thickening.	Sauce, custards, soups
ENRICHING	Adding egg to a dish makes it richer in nutrients.	Sauces, custards, mashed potato, milk puddings, pasta dishes
GARNISH	Sliced boiled egg is used to add colour to a dish.	Salads

Check it

Give four guidelines on the safe storage and handling of eggs.

What happens to eggs during storage?

During storage the air space within an egg gets bigger. Water moves into the yolk from the white. The yolk increases in size and becomes less viscous. The skin surrounding the yolk becomes weaker which means that the yolk could break into the white. Moisture is lost and bacteria enter through the porous shell. The bad smell which develops in a rotten egg is caused by the reaction of the sulphur from the egg white and phosphoric acid in the yolk. The egg eventually decomposes.

What happens to eggs during preparation and cooking?

Whole eggs can be beaten to form a foam, but the volume will be less than when only egg whites are used. This type of foam is used in cake making, for example. It gives whisked sponge mixtures a light, open texture.

Egg whites can increase in volume by as much as eight times when beaten or whisked. This happens because egg white traps air when beaten, and produces a large mass of bubbles called a foam. A **foam** is a dispersion of gas (air) within a liquid (egg white).

The egg white protein forms a protective coating or network around the bubbles, which stops the liquid and air mixing. This stabilises the foam, but if it is left to stand it will collapse. When the foam is heated the air cells in the foam grow bigger. The egg white protein coagulates to make a solid network of bubbles, and the foam changes from a liquid to a solid and is made permanent, i.e. when baking a meringue.

Eggs which are a few days old produce a better foam than newly laid eggs. This is because egg white becomes thinner as the amount of egg white protein decreases.

▼ Stages in whisking egg white to a foam

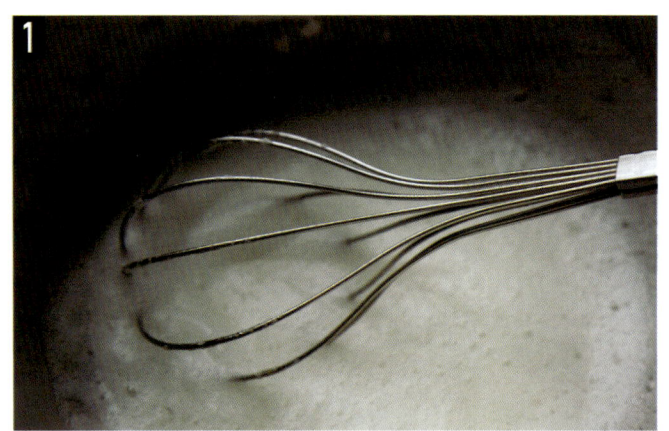

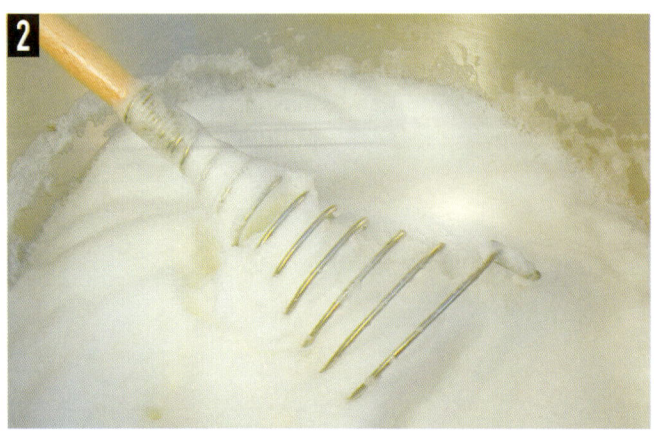

The pH rises because carbon dioxide is lost from the egg. This can affect some cooking processes. For example, when the pH has risen, the egg becomes less acid and more alkaline which can lengthen the time it takes to make a good foam.

When eggs are heated the proteins in both white and yolk coagulate. At about 60°C, egg white begins to coagulate. At 70°C, egg yolk begins to coagulate.

Certain ingredients affect the coagulation temperature of eggs, for example sugar increases the coagulation temperature and cooking times. Acids decrease the coagulation temperature and cooking time.

Overheating eggs

If an egg is boiled for longer than 10 minutes, a green/black ring of iron sulphide forms around the yolk. This is due to the reaction of sulphur in the egg white with iron in the egg yolk, particularly in eggs which are not very fresh. This reaction can be prevented by accurate timing and, to a certain extent, by cooling the egg rapidly as soon as it has been cooked.

If egg proteins are heated at too high a temperature, **syneresis** occurs. This is also known as curdling or weeping. When you cook an egg mixture such as a custard sauce too rapidly or for too long, the protein becomes over-coagulated and separates from the liquid, leaving a mixture resembling fine curds and whey. If the curdling in a custard sauce hasn't progressed too far, it can often be reversed by removing the mixture from the heat and stirring or beating it vigorously.

To prevent syneresis or curdling in a custard sauce, use a low temperature, stir (if appropriate for the recipe), cook until the custard just thickens, and cool quickly by setting the pan in a bowl of ice or cold water, stirring for a few minutes.

Certain ingredients affect the coagulation temperature of eggs, for example, sugar increases the coagulation temperature and cooking times and acids decrease the coagulation temperature and cooking time.

The term **curdling** is usually used in connection with a stirred mixture such as custard sauce, while weeping or syneresis are more often used with reference to pie meringues or baked custards.

Check it

1. Do you know what 'coagulation of egg' means?
2. A meringue is made by whisking egg whites. Can you explain the process?

▼ The green-black ring which appears when eggs are boiled for too long.

Study tip

Learn coagulation temperatures.

Check it

Curdling and syneresis are terms which apply to eggs in food preparation. Can you explain what they mean?

Key point

Temperature is important for eggs.

- To **emulsify** and stabilise successfully, yolks should be used at room temperature.
- If egg proteins are heated at too high a temperature, syneresis occurs, producing a hard, tough mass and making the proteins difficult to digest.

STORING EGGS

What will I learn?

- How to store eggs correctly
- The safe handling of eggs during food preparation and cooking
- What egg allergy and intolerance are

Be aware of the best before date on the eggs – this is not a legal requirement, but all British Lion eggs are date-stamped.

Store at a constant temperature below 20°C, or in the refrigerator away from strong smelling foods such as onions. Ideally place the eggs point down in their boxes or trays. For best results, take them out of the fridge half an hour before cooking.

Like any protein rich food, eggs need to be handled carefully.

Egg freshness

There are two ways to test the freshness of eggs:

1. Place the egg into a glass bowl full of cold water. Freshly laid eggs will sink to the bottom. Eggs which are approximately a week old will float slightly but still be usable. Eggs which are more than two weeks old may float. If so, they should not be used.

Key points

- Egg shells are porous and absorb smells. Store away from strong smelling foods.
- Wash hands before and after handling raw eggs.
- Check the use-by date. Use eggs in rotation, first in, first out.
- Never use dirty, cracked or broken eggs.
- Egg dishes should be consumed as soon as possible after preparation, or, if not for immediate use, refrigerated.

TESTING EGG FRESHNESS
An illustration of an egg freshness test

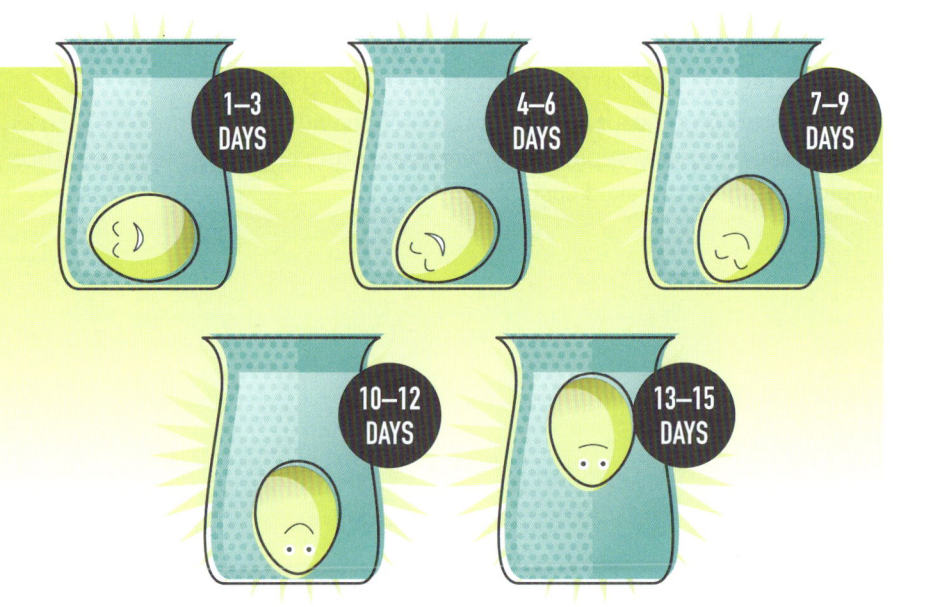

1–3 DAYS
4–6 DAYS
7–9 DAYS
10–12 DAYS
13–15 DAYS

Key point

A fresh egg will not float but a stale egg will not **sink**.

When you shell a hard-boiled egg you can see from the shape of the egg how big the air cell was and how old the egg is.

304 COMMODITIES

MEAT, POULTRY, FISH AND EGGS

2   Break the egg onto a plate. In a fresh egg, the yolk sits up high and the white is thick and closely surrounding the yolk. An older egg has a flat yolk that breaks easily, and a thin, watery white.

Salmonella

Hens can pass salmonella bacteria into their eggs and thus cause food poisoning. Since its introduction in 1998, however, the British Lion scheme has been successful in effectively eliminating salmonella in British eggs.

The British Lion mark means that the eggs have been laid by hens vaccinated against salmonella and have been produced to the highest standards of food safety. The safety record of the British Lion scheme means that babies, pregnant women and other vulnerable groups can now confidently eat runny eggs that bear the Lion mark.

Pasteurised egg

Pasteurised eggs are used extensively in the catering industry. The eggs are washed, sanitised and then broken into sterilised containers. After combining the yolks and whites, they are strained, pasteurised – heated to 63°C for 1 minute – then rapidly cooled. Pasteurised egg is available as whole, white or yolk and dried.

Egg allergy

Egg allergy is more common in young children than in adults. An egg allergy can be to all forms of egg or only to partly cooked or raw egg dishes.

Examples of partly cooked dishes include quiches, creme brulée, scotch eggs, omelette and poached egg. Examples of raw egg dishes include home made mayonnaise, mousse and some ice creams. Egg replacers are available from specialist health food shops; they have no nutritional value but are useful in food preparation.

▲ Some dishes to be avoided by people with egg allergy

Study tip
Learn about the safe handling and cooking of eggs.

Key point
When preparing food using raw eggs, it is always safer to used pasteurised eggs rather than normal raw eggs.

Activity
The sale of eggs increases during Easter season. Why do you think this is the case?

Do research into the important significance of eggs at Easter time.

Key terms
Ovalbumin – one of the main proteins in egg.

Coagulate – to become solid or to set.

Syneresis – when the proteins coagulate and shrink rapidly causing any liquid that the egg contains to be squeezed out.

Emulsify – to use an ingredient as a mediator in a mixture, enabling two ingredients to mix without the mixture separating.

Stabilise – a substance that allows fat or oil and water to mix.

Lecithin – the name of a fat in egg yolk which acts as an the emulsifier.

EXAM QUESTIONS

1. Complete the paragraph using words from the box.

   | myoglobin   gelatine   muscle proteins   collagen |
   | marinading   Maillard reaction |

   Myosin and actin are the ___ in meat. The red colour of meat is due to a pigment called ___. The red colour changes to brown during cooking. This is called the ___. Meat can be tenderised by ___ which allows the tougher ___ to be changed to ___. [6]

2. a Identify three types of offal. [3]
   b State the nutritional value of offal. [3]

3. The following cuts are popular choices by consumers:
   - boneless cuts
   - boneless, rolled joints
   - lean minced meat

   Give reasons for the popularity of these cuts and suggest ways in which they can be used for family meals. [6]

4. Meat is considered to be a 'high risk' food.
   Give advice on the storage and preparation of raw meat. [6]

5. Explain why marinades are used in food preparation. Give examples of ingredients used to prepare marinades. [6]

6. a Give advice to consumers on
      i   handling raw chicken
      ii storage of raw chicken
      ii cooking chicken. [6]
   b Evaluate the impact on health of handling and consuming contaminated chicken. [6]

7. Meat can be cooked by dry and moist methods of cooking.
   a Discuss the factors that influence the choice of method.
   b Suggest suitable cuts of meat which can be cooked using each method. [10]

8. Consumption of meat is influenced by different factors and consumer issues.
   Identify and discuss these factors and issues. [8]

9. Complete the sentences using words from the box:

   | omega-3   cod   canned   oily   iron   carbohydrate |
   | whiting |

   Two examples of white fish are ___ and ___.
   Salmon is a type of ___ and is a very good source of ___.
   An excellent source of calcium is ___ fish.
   Fish has a high nutritional value as it contains all the essential nutrients except ___. [6]

10. Match the type of fish to a suitable cooking method. [4]
    A = fried in breadcrumbs, B = barbequing, C = steaming, D = baking

Cooking method				
Type of fish	mackerel	haddock	whole salmon	goujons of cod

11. a List the quality and freshness signs to look for when buying a fresh salmon. [4]
    b Compare the nutritional value of oily and white fish. Give examples of each type of fish. [6]

12. a Name two different types of fish which can be: [4]
       i   smoked
       ii canned
    b Give reasons why frozen fish is so popular. [4]

13. Explain the importance of obtaining fish from a sustainable source. [6]

14. Despite promotions and recommendations, people in the UK do not include enough fish in their diet.
    a Evaluate why people in the UK are not including enough fish in their diet
    b Explain why it is beneficial to include fish in the diet
    c Suggest ways people can be encouraged to eat more fish. [12]

15. Fill in the missing words

    | coagulation   syneresis   lecithin   emulsifier |
    | salmonella   yolk   amino acids   white   standard |

    Eggs are a high biological value food and contain essential ___ ___

    Eggs which have a Lion mark stamp have been injected against ___ and have been produced to a high standard.
    The egg ___ contains ___ which acts as an ___ in the making of mayonnaise.
    When eggs are cooked, the ___ sets first. This setting is called ___
    If eggs are overcooked ___ occurs and this makes the egg tough. [8]

16 State two main nutrients found in:
   a egg yolk [2]
   b egg white [2]
17 Explain the function of eggs when making the following:
   a Fish cakes [2]
   b A whisked sponge [2]
   c Quiche [2]
18 An egg box contains information.
   a Explain the importance of the Lion Quality Mark. [3]
   b Evaluate the usefulness of all other information found on an egg box to the consumer. [5]
19 a Name two dishes which illustrate the following techniques:
       emulsification [2]
       coagulation of eggs [2]
       an egg white foam. [2]
   b Explain the scientific principles underlying each technique. [6]
20 Eggs are considered to be a 'high risk' food. Give advice on the safe handling of eggs during preparation and cooking. [8]
21 A wide choice of eggs is available to the consumer.
   a Describe the factors which would influence consumer choice when buying eggs. [6]
   b Use the information from the nutrition facts egg label to answer the following questions:

Typical values	Per medium size egg	Per 100g
Energy	277kJ 66kcal	547kJ 131kcal
Fat of which saturates monounsaturates polyunsaturates	4.6g 1.3g 1.7g 0.7g	9.0g 2.5g 3.4g 1.4g
Carbohydrate of which sugars	trace	trace
Protein	6.4g	12.6g
Salt	0.2g	0.4g

   i   The sodium (salt) content is approximately 3% of the reference intake. State the recommended daily sodium intake. [1]
   ii   Give one reason why egg has no dietary fibre. [1]
   iii Give one reason why eggs are a suitable choice for growing children. [1]
   iv   Give one reason why eggs are a suitable choice for a weight-reducing diet. [1]

22 Describe the changes that take place during the:
   a storage of eggs [2]
   b whisking of eggs [2]
   c cooking of eggs [4]
   Suggest suitable egg dishes for the following meals, giving reasons for your choice:
   a lunch for a toddler [2]
   b midday meal for an elderly person [2]
   c packed lunch for a teenager [2]
23 Eggs have been given good and bad press in recent years for several reasons.
   Identify these reasons and comment on any impact this has had on consumption of eggs [6]
24 Give reasons for the following: [8]
   a a black ring between the white and yolk of a boiled egg [2]
   b an egg custard which is weepy and full of air holes [2]
   c a meringue topping is runny and will not hold its shape for piping [2]
   d a custard sauce which looks like 'curds and whey' [2]

TOTAL: 198

FOOD INVESTIGATIONS

Food investigations for meat products

Investigation 1 Recipe adaptation
Take a basic beef burger recipe using:
- 225g good quality minced beef
- 1 small onion, minced or very finely chopped
- 1 small egg, beaten
- 1 tsp chopped parsley
- 2 tsp tomato paste
- salt and pepper

Investigate ways of bulking or extending meat to make a cheaper product. Use the following headings to compare results:
- ease of preparation
- time taken to prepare and cook
- tenderness/mouth feel
- flavour
- appearance
- unit cost

Variations to try:
- use pork or chicken or a combination of meats
- dishes which combine beef mince and soya mince e.g. cottage pie.

Investigation 2 Comparing cost
Compare the cost per kilo of different cuts of meat from different parts of the animal. For example: breast of lamb, leg of lamb and loin of lamb.
Present your findings in a table and comment on the difference in cost and amount of fat, lean meat etc.

Investigation 3
Comparing nutritional value of meat
Compare the nutritional value of red meat and poultry. Comment on your findings with reference to:
i protein
ii saturated fat
iii iron

Investigation 4
Commercially prepared products
Research into ready prepared meat and poultry food products to assess:
a) how the meat or poultry content has been prepared to make cooking easier
b) the range of meat and poultry products which are sold as meals and snacks in supermarkets.

Food investigations for egg products

You can carry out many experiments to better understand how eggs behave during food preparation and the effect of heat on eggs.
Remember:
- Use the same size egg each time.
- Keep temperatures constant.
- Keep equipment clean.
- Follow the same procedure every time.
- Accurate timing is important.
- Note all observations accurately.

Investigation 1 Egg white foams
Whisk an egg white at room temperature (about 21°C). Use a standard whisk for each experiment. Observe the four stages of stiffness.

Method
1. slightly beaten – large air bubbles, frothy appearance (uses: coating, thickening, emulsifying)
2. wet peak – stiff foam, smaller air cells, white moves when bowl is tipped, shiny and moist in appearance. Makes rounded peaks when beaters are lifted (uses: soft meringues, mousses, sponge cakes)
3. stiff – air cells very small and white (uses: hard meringues, soufflés)
4. overbeaten – dull white appearance, lumps/flakes separate out, liquid gradually leaks out.

Investigation 2 Adding to the egg white

Investigate the effect of adding each of the following to the egg white before beating. Make sure you observe the appearance each time:
- a little egg yolk
- ¼ tsp salt
- 1 level tsp sugar
- 1 tsp vinegar
- ¼ tsp cream of tartar

Whisk until a foam is obtained. Note:
- the time taken to reach this stage
- the volume of the foam
- the characteristics of the foam

Investigation 3 Coagulation temperatures

Place equal amounts of the following in different test tubes and heat in a water bath. Record the coagulation (setting) temperatures.
- whole egg
- egg yolk
- egg white

Investigation 4 Boiling eggs

- 3 whole eggs with their shell intact
1. Boil for 10 minutes then plunge directly into cold water; leave until cool.
2. Boil for 10 minutes then leave to cool in the hot water.
3. Boil for 10 minutes. Remove from the water, then leave to cool.

Cut in half and observe the difference where the white and the yolk meet. Account for the difference.

Investigation 5 Egg custards

Prepare five egg custards as follows:
- 200ml fresh milk
- 1 egg
- 25g sugar

Warm the milk to 60 °C. Do not boil. Beat the egg and sugar and add the warm milk.

Pour into a small ovenproof dish and bake as follows:

Method
1. Stand the dish in a tray of hot water and bake at gas mark 3 (160 °C) for about 40 minutes until set.
2. Repeat 1 but do not use a tray of water.
3. Repeat 1 but bake at gas mark 9 (240 °C).
4. Repeat 3 but do not use a tray of water.
5. Repeat 1 but boil the milk before adding it to the egg.

Compare the cooked custards for appearance, flavour and texture. Account for the differences. What difference does the tray of water make to the finished products?

Activities

1. Research the use of eggs as a main ingredient in international cuisine.
2. State the function of the eggs in the recipes you have chosen.

CHICKEN KIEV

Portion size: 2   Difficulty rating: ★★

INGREDIENTS:

100g unsalted butter	25g plain flour
1 clove garlic, peeled and crushed	50g breadcrumbs
2 tbsp flatleaf parsley, finely chopped	1 large egg, lightly beaten
vegetable oil for frying	cling film
2 skinless chicken breasts, wing bone in	kitchen paper

EQUIPMENT LIST:

weighing scales	mixing bowl	2 plates
bowl	tablespoon	deep fat fryer
chopping board	small bowl	serving dish
chopping knife	fork	

METHOD:

1. Mix together the butter, crushed garlic and chopped parsley. Add salt and pepper and mix.
2. Place a sheet of cling film on the work surface and spoon the garlic butter onto the cling film, pull the edge of the cling film on top of the butter and mould the butter into a log shape. Twist the ends of the cling film to seal and chill in the fridge for at last an hour.
3. Heat the oil in a deep fat fryer to 160°C.
   While the oil is heating, cut a deep pocket in each chicken breast, inserting the knife into the bone end, just under the bone.
4. Remove the cling film from the garlic butter and slice into 1cm slices. Stuff the chicken breasts with a few slices of garlic butter, pushing them into the chicken as far as possible.
5. Sprinkle the flour on to a plate, beat the egg in a bowl and place breadcrumbs on another plate. Dust each chicken breast with flour, then dip into the egg, then roll in breadcrumbs until completely coated.
6. Carefully lower the chicken kievs into the hot oil and fry 8-10 minutes until the breadcrumbs are a golden brown colour and the chicken is cooked through.
7. Drain on kitchen paper.

NUTRITION:	Recipe	100g	Portion	Reference Intake Men	Women	Children
Energy (kJ)	7854	1172	3927			
Energy (kcal)	1884	281	942	38%	47%	52%
Fat (g)	125	19	63	66%	89%	89%
Saturates (g)	59	9	30	98%	148%	148%
Carbohydrate (g)	61	9	31	10%	13%	14%
Sugars (g)	3	1	2	1%	2%	2%
Salt (g)	3	0	2	25%	25%	38%

EATWELL GUIDE:

SUCCESS CRITERIA
- Succulent moist chicken
- Golden brown appearance
- Crispy coating

SKILLS / TECHNIQUES
- Chopping herbs
- Preparation of chicken
- Coating with egg and breadcrumbs
- Frying as a cooking method

RECIPE MODIFICATION
- Use crushed cornflakes instead of breadcrumbs

SCIENCE INVOLVED
- Effect of cooking on meat proteins
- Coagulation of egg protein to set the coating
- Heat transfer - conduction

COOK'S TIPS
- Heat the oil in a heavy based saucepan and test the temperature by dropping a breadcrumb into the hot oil. It should sizzle and turn borwn in seconds.
- Test the chicken by piercing the thickest part with a skewer; the juices should run clear.
- Do not pierce too deeply or the butter will escape.

ALLERGENS
Plain flour, egg

COMMODITIES

MEATBALLS WITH PEPPERS AND TOMATOES

Portion size: 2–3   Difficulty rating: ★★★

MEAT, POULTRY, FISH AND EGGS

INGREDIENTS:

225g good quality minced beef
125g sausagemeat
½ a small green pepper, deseeded and finely chopped
1 small egg, beaten
1 small onion, minced or very finely chopped
1 clove garlic
1 dsp chopped parsley
1 slice bread, made into breadcrumbs
2 tsp tomato paste
salt and pepper
flour for coating
oil for frying

For the sauce:
225g tinned or fresh tomatoes
1 small onion, chopped
1 clove garlic, crushed
½ a small green pepper, deseeded and finely chopped
a few fresh basil leaves

EQUIPMENT LIST:

weighing scales	teaspoon	fork
large bowl	dessertspoon	small bowl
chopping board	tablespoon	large frying pan
chopping knife	plate	casserole dish

METHOD:

1. Place all the meatball ingredients into a bowl and mix together thoroughly with a fork.
2. Take about a tablespoonful of the mixture and roll into small rounds to give 8-9 meatballs. Coat each with flour. Set aside on a plate.
3. Heat the oil in a large pan and brown the meatballs evenly.
4. Pre heat the oven to 190°C/gas mark 5.
5. Transfer meatballs to a casserole dish.
6. In the juices remaining in the pan, gently fry the onion, garlic and peppers for about 5 minutes.
7. Add the tomatoes and basil and simmer for a few minutes, add seasoning then pour the sauce over the meatballs.
8. Cover with a lid and cook for about 30 minutes then remove the lid and cook for a further 10 minutes.
9. Serve with noodles or rice.

NUTRITION:	Recipe	100g	Portion	Reference Intake Men	Women	Children
Energy (kJ)	5465	464	1822			
Energy (kcal)	1309	111	436	17%	22%	24%
Fat (g)	80	7	27	28%	38%	38%
Saturates (g)	22	2	7	24%	37%	37%
Carbohydrate (g)	92	8	31	10%	13%	14%
Sugars (g)	33	3	11	9%	12%	13%
Salt (g)	11	1	4	61%	61%	92%

EATWELL GUIDE:

SUCCESS CRITERIA
- Evenly chopped onion
- Evenly shaped and sized meatballs
- Evenly browned meatballs
- Correct consistency sauce
- Appropriate and aesthetic garnishing
- Thoroughly cooked meatballs, served at correct temperature

SKILLS / TECHNIQUES
- Weighing and measuring
- Preparation of onion and garlic
- Shaping and moulding
- Frying, simmering

RECIPE MODIFICATION
- This meatball recipe can be used to make beef burgers by dividing into four and shaping into flat round burgers of equal thickness and size. They can be fried, grilled or baked.
- Additional ingredients may be added, for example grated carrot or finely chopped celery.
- Add other flavourings such as curry powder or chilli flakes for additional spiciness.

SCIENCE INVOLVED
- Effect of heat on meat proteins
- Coagulation of egg protein
- Heat transfer – conduction and convection

COOK'S TIPS
- Keep turning and moving the meatballs during frying

ALLERGENS
Flour, egg

SECTION 3

311

COD BAKE WITH A HERB CRUST

Portion size: 2   **Difficulty rating:** ★

INGREDIENTS:

- 2 x 180g pieces of cod loin
- 2 tbsp fresh white breadcrumbs
- 2 tbsp chopped fresh herbs (such as a mixture of chervil, chives, parsley, coriander) – optional
- 1 clove garlic, crushed finely
- 2 tbsp olive oil
- salt and freshly ground black pepper
- 140g even sized new potatoes
- 160g fresh or frozen peas

EQUIPMENT LIST:

weighing scales	chopping knife	tablespoon
bowl	garlic crusher	baking tray
chopping board	2 saucepans	

METHOD:

1. Heat the oven to 200°C/180°C Fan/gas mark 6.
2. Mix together the herbs (if using), garlic and oil. Stir in the breadcrumbs and season with salt and pepper. Put the fish on a baking sheet and spread the breadcrumb mixture over the fish. Bake in the oven for 10–15 minutes until the flesh becomes opaque and flakes easily.
3. Boil the potatoes in a large pan of water for 12–15 minutes, until cooked through. Boil the peas in a separate pan of water for a few minutes until just cooked. Take the cod out of the oven and serve with the potatoes and peas.

NUTRITION:

	Recipe	100g	Portion	Reference Intake Men	Women	Children
Energy (kJ)	4023	511	2012			
Energy (kcal)	958	122	479	19%	24%	27%
Fat (g)	36	5	18	19%	26%	26%
Saturates (g)	5	1	3	8%	13%	13%
Carbohydrate (g)	79	10	40	13%	17%	18%
Sugars (g)	8	1	4	3%	4%	5%
Salt (g)	6	1	3	50%	50%	75%

EATWELL GUIDE:

SUCCESS CRITERIA

- Fish should be moist
- Crispy herb crust
- Potatoes cooked but retaining a firm texture

SKILLS / TECHNIQUES

- Cooking fish
- Cooking potatoes and peas

RECIPE MODIFICATION

- Use othe type of white fish such as haddock or pollock.
- Additional ingredients may be added, for example grated carrot or finely chopped celery.
- Add other flavourings such as curry powder or chilli flakes for additional spiciness.

SCIENCE INVOLVED

- Effect of cooking on fish proteins

COOK'S TIPS

- Recipe works best with thick pieces of fish

ALLERGENS

Breadcrumbs

FISH PIE

Portion size: 4   Difficulty rating: ★★★

MEAT, POULTRY, FISH AND EGGS

INGREDIENTS:

- 450g potatoes, peeled and cut into chunks
- 150ml single cream
- 25g butter, plus extra for greasing
- salt and white pepper
- pinch freshly grated nutmeg
- 300g skinless, boneless fish
- squeeze lemon juice
- 2 hard-boiled eggs, shells removed, quartered

For the parsley sauce:
- 25g butter
- large bunch of parsley, leaves only, finely chopped
- 25g plain flour
- 250ml milk
- splash of single cream, to taste

EQUIPMENT LIST:

weighing scales	juicer	saucepan for the sauce
1 large pan	peeler	wooden spoon
chopping board	potato masher	spatula
chopping knife	measuring jug	ovenproof dish

METHOD:

1. Cook the potatoes in boiling salted water for 15-20 minutes until soft.
2. Pre heat the oven to 200°C/400°F/Gas 6 and generously butter a deep ovenproof dish.
3. To make the parsley sauce, heat the butter in a heavy-based pan over a very low heat then stir in the flour. Cook, stirring regularly, for about three minutes. Do not let the mixture brown.
4. Add the milk into the roux (the butter and flour mixture) a little at a time, whisking or beating after each addition until completely smooth. Whisk in single cream, to taste.
5. Bring the sauce to the boil, stirring continuously, then reduce the heat, add the chopped parsley and simmer over a low heat for 3-4 minutes.
6. Drain the potatoes well and mash. Add the cream and butter, season with salt and pepper and nutmeg. Mix well until smooth and creamy. Taste, adding more seasoning if required, then set to one side.
7. Cut the haddock and salmon into chunks, lay in the dish, season lightly and squeeze over a little lemon juice.
8. Pour the hot parsley sauce over the top, place the quartered eggs evenly over the sauce and spoon over the mashed potatoes.
9. Bake for 35-40 minutes, until the top is crisp and brown. Serve at once.

NUTRITION:	Recipe	100g	Portion	Reference Intake Men	Women	Children
Energy (kJ)	6977	501	1744			
Energy (kcal)	1672	120	418	17%	21%	23%
Fat (g)	96	7	24	25%	34%	34%
Saturates (g)	54	4	14	45%	68%	68%
Carbohydrate (g)	113	8	28	9%	12%	13%
Sugars (g)	19	1	5	4%	5%	6%
Salt (g)	7	1	2	29%	29%	44%

EATWELL GUIDE:

SUCCESS CRITERIA
- Good balance between fish, sauce and topping
- Smooth lump free sauce
- A well seasoned sauce
- Creamy, smooth potato topping

SKILLS / TECHNIQUES
- Weighing and measuring
- Knife skills
- Cooking and mashing potatoes
- Sauce making
- Assembling the dish

RECIPE MODIFICATION
- Add some cooked prawns to the recipe
- Add some grated cheese to the potato topping
- Substitute butter with low fat spread and omit the cream to reduce calorific value
- Use cornflakes instead of breadcrumbs

SCIENCE INVOLVED
- Heat transfer – conduction and convection
- Cooking potato – effect of heat on starch
- Sauce making – gelatinisation

COOK'S TIPS
- Choose a variety of potato suitable for boiling
- The milk will mix in more easily if it is heated before adding to the roux
- Piping the potato on top give a better appearance and adds another skill
- Dish could be topped with grated cheese for added protein, extra flavour and a crispier topping.

ALLERGENS
Plain flour, milk

PAELLA

Portion size: 4–6 **Difficulty rating:** ★ ★ ★

INGREDIENTS:

- 25ml olive oil
- 10 mussels (about 300g)
- 10 clams
- 125g boneless pork, diced
- 1 tsp minced garlic
- 1 onion, chopped fine
- 1 medium tomato, deseeded and chopped
- 1 small red pepper, deseeded and chopped
- 1 small green pepper, deseeded and chopped
- 1 small yellow pepper, deseeded and chopped
- 100g chicken breast
- ½ tsp paprika
- ¼ tsp dried rosemary
- ¼ tsp dried thyme
- ¼ tsp ground cumin
- 150g paella rice
- 500ml chicken stock
- ¼ tsp saffron
- 1 chorizo sausages
- 10 shrimps
- 30g frozen peas
- lemon wedges to garnish

EQUIPMENT LIST:

- weighing scales
- paella pan or wok
- chopping board
- small sharp knife
- chopping knife
- teaspoon
- large spoon/wooden spoon
- measuring jug

METHOD:

1. Scrub and debeard the mussels and clams, discarding any that do not close when tapped sharply. Set aside.
2. Heat half the olive oil in a paella pan or wok. Add the pork, and brown all sides. Mix in the garlic, onions, tomato, and peppers, stirring constantly until cooked. Remove from the pan and set aside.
3. In the same pan, heat the remaining olive oil and cook the chicken until browned on all sides. Season with salt, pepper, paprika, rosemary, thyme, and cumin. Transfer the chicken to a plate and set aside.
4. In the same pan, sauté the rice in the remaining oil until it is translucent. Pour in the chicken stock, and combine well. Add the pork mixture, stirring constantly. Sprinkle in the saffron and continue to stir until well mixed.
5. Mix in the chicken, chorizo sausages, mussels, clams, shrimp and peas combining well.
6. Cook, uncovered, for around 25 minutes, stirring occasionally, or until all the liquid has been absorbed.
7. Discard any mussels and clams that have failed to open. Serve the paella straight from the pan, garnished with lemon wedges.

NUTRITION:

	Recipe	100g	Portion	Reference Intake Men	Women	Children
Energy (kJ)	8045	428	1341			
Energy (kcal)	1914	102	319	13%	16%	18%
Fat (g)	77	4	13	14%	18%	18%
Saturates (g)	17	1	3	9%	14%	14%
Carbohydrate (g)	179	10	30	10%	13%	14%
Sugars (g)	29	2	5	4%	5%	6%
Salt (g)	28	2	5	78%	78%	117%

EATWELL GUIDE:

SUCCESS CRITERIA
- Rice which is cooked 'al dente'
- Outcome should have a creamy sauce consistency, not too dry

SKILLS / TECHNIQUES
- Weighing and measuring
- Chopping onion
- Cleaning and preparing clams and mussels

RECIPE MODIFICATION
- Add peeled shrimps and a few shrimps in their shells for effect

SCIENCE INVOLVED
- Heat transfer – conduction cooking to set the batter

COOK'S TIPS
- Stir frequently otherwise the rice will stick to the base of the pan

ALLERGENS
Mussels, clams

CHEESE SOUFFLÉ

Portion size: 2 as a main dish   Difficulty rating: ★ ★ ★

MEAT, POULTRY, FISH AND EGGS

INGREDIENTS:

- 20g butter
- 15g plain flour
- ½ tsp mustard
- pinch cayenne pepper
- 150ml whole milk
- 1 tbsp double cream
- 55g grated Cheddar cheese
- salt and freshly ground black pepper
- 2 large free range eggs, separated

EQUIPMENT LIST:

weighing scales	wooden spoon	mixing bowl
baking tray	measuring jug	whisk
2 ramekin dishes	grater	tablespoon
saucepan	teaspoon	spatula

METHOD:

1. Preheat oven to 220°C/Gas mark 7.
2. Brush the inside of two ramekin dishes with melted butter.
3. Place a baking sheet in the oven to heat up.
4. Make the roux sauce. Add the cream, mustard, cayenne and seasoning.
5. Remove from the heat, add the cheese and egg yolks. Allow to cool slightly.
6. Whisk the egg whites until stiff peaks form. Fold into the cheese mixture.
7. Spoon the mixture into the ramekins.
8. Place the ramekins onto the hot baking tray. Bake for 8-10 minutes until well risen and golden brown.

NUTRITION:

	Recipe	100g	Portion	Reference Intake Men	Women	Children
Energy (kJ)	3343	853	1672			
Energy (kcal)	806	206	403	16%	20%	22%
Fat (g)	66	17	33	35%	47%	47%
Saturates (g)	36	9	18	60%	90%	90%
Carbohydrate (g)	20	5	10	3%	4%	5%
Sugars (g)	8	2	4	3%	4%	5%
Salt (g)	7	2	4	58%	58%	88%

EATWELL GUIDE:

SUCCESS CRITERIA

- Golden brown appearance
- Well risen/good volume
- Smooth texture and consistency/no lumps
- Good cheesy flavour
- Well seasoned

SKILLS / TECHNIQUES

- Weighing and measuring
- Making a roux sauce
- Separating eggs
- Whisking egg whites
- Folding in
- Baking
- Appropriate serving

RECIPE MODIFICATION

- Substitute butter with low fat spread/polyunsaturated fat
- Substitute whole milk with semi-skimmed/skimmed
- Use soya milk/goat milk
- Remove the double cream
- Use an alternative type of cheese or reduce the quantity
- Additional ingredients may be added for flavour e.g. ham, chopped herbs

SCIENCE INVOLVED

- Gelatinisation of starch in thickening the sauce
- Use of a soft flour, low gluten content
- Heat transfer – conduction and convection

COOK'S TIPS

- Stir the sauce all the time whilst it is thickening.
- If lumps occur, try whisking to disperse them.
- Serve immediately as the soufflé will collapse on standing.

ALLERGENS

Plain flour, eggs

SECTION 3

SCOTCH EGGS

Portion size: 2   **Difficulty rating:** ★★★

INGREDIENTS:

3 eggs
100g sausage meat
50g fresh white breadcrumbs
cooking oil
25g plain flour

EQUIPMENT LIST:

saucepan
basin
fork
knife
brush
kitchen paper/plate
weighing scales
draining spoon

METHOD:

1. Place 2 eggs in a saucepan, cover with cold water and bring to the boil.
2. Boil for 5–8 minutes then plunge into cold water.
3. Turn on deep fat fryer, set at 170ºC.
4. Cool and shell eggs.
5. Beat raw egg in a basin, halve the sausage meat. Flatten each piece using floured hands.
6. Coat each egg evenly with sausage meat making sure there are no gaps.
7. Brush the eggs with egg and roll in breadcrumbs, shaking off any excess crumbs.
8. Gently lower the eggs into the fryer and cook for up to 8 minutes until golden brown, turning occasionally.
9. Drain on kitchen paper and cut into halves or quarters before serving.

NUTRITION:	Recipe	100g	Portion	Reference intake Men	Women	Children
Energy (kJ)	5319	1313	2660			
Energy (kcal)	1278	316	639	26%	32%	36%
Fat (g)	96	24	48	51%	69%	69%
Saturates (g)	20	5	10	33%	50%	50%
Carbohydrate (g)	68	17	34	11%	15%	15%
Sugars (g)	5	1	3	2%	3%	3%
Salt (g)	4	1	2	33%	33%	50%

EATWELL GUIDE:

SUCCESS CRITERIA

- Eggs boiled without any dark discolouration between yolk and white
- Even thickness of sausage meat
- Evenly browned appearance

SKILLS / TECHNIQUES

- Boiling eggs
- Coating with egg and breadcrumbs
- Frying

RECIPE MODIFICATION

- Add finely chopped onion or herbs to the sausage meat
- Use wholemeal breadcrumbs, different breads or crushed cornflakes

SCIENCE INVOLVED

- Plain, soft flour with low gluten content to give crumbly texture
- Coagulation of eggs
- Heat transfer – conduction

COOK'S TIPS

- Use eggs which are several days old as they are easier to shell.
- Roll each portion of sausage meat into a ball before flattening.
- Check temperature of the oil with a thermometer and do not leave the pan unattended.

ALLERGENS

Eggs, plain flour

RECIPES

COMMODITIES

SECTION 3
COMMODITIES

BEANS, NUTS AND SEEDS, SOYA, TOFU AND MYCOPROTEIN

- PULSES AND BEANS   318
- NUTS   321
- SEEDS   324
- ALTERNATIVE PROTEIN FOODS   326
- EXAM QUESTIONS   330
- FOOD INVESTIGATIONS   331
- RECIPES   332

SECTION 3
COMMODITIES

BEANS, NUTS AND SEEDS, SOYA, TOFU AND MYCOPROTEIN

What will I learn?
- What beans, nuts and seeds are
- The variety of beans, nuts and seeds available
- The importance of beans, nuts and seeds in the diet
- The nutritional value of beans, nuts and seeds
- Allergies and intolerances caused by beans, nuts and seeds

What are beans, nuts and seeds?

Beans are part of a group called **legumes** or **pulses** that also include lentils and peas. Nuts are fruit encased in a hard shell. They are generally edible but are an expensive commodity so they feature in small amounts in the diet. Seeds are the embryo of the plant. A seed is basically a miniature plant packaged up inside a protective coating, along with some food to nourish it and help it grow.

PULSES AND BEANS

What will I learn?
- The variety of pulses and beans that are available
- The nutritional value of pulses and beans
- How to prepare beans safely

There are many different types of pulse, but the definition of each is the same: an edible seed that grows in a pod. Pulses include all beans, peas and lentils, such as:

- baked beans
- red, green, yellow and brown lentils
- chick peas
- garden peas
- black-eyed peas
- runner beans
- broad beans
- kidney beans, butter beans, haricots, cannellini beans, flageolet beans, pinto beans and borlotti beans

318 COMMODITIES

BEANS, NUTS AND SEEDS, SOYA, TOFU AND MYCOPROTEIN

Some of the most popular types of pulses are ▼

Peas
Peas are native to northern Europe. The UK is the largest European producer of peas for freezing. Frozen peas are a popular choice as they are as nutritious as fresh peas. Peas provide a variety of nutrients including protein, carbohydrate and fibre. They are low in fat and provide vitamins A and C, folate and thiamin, iron and phosphorus.

Chick peas
These are the main pulse crop of India. They are used in salads and stews, and are also used to make the popular dish hummus.

Lentils
Lentils are indigenous to India, the Middle East and Mediterranean countries. There are many varieties of lentils, the most popular types being the red and green lentil, as well as various other types known as dhal in Indian cooking. Lentils are a good source of protein and iron.

Baked beans
These are haricot beans in a tomato sauce. They are a very popular food in the UK: we consume more baked beans than most other Western countries.
The overall contribution of beans and pulses to the UK diet is not as important as it is to the diet of Eastern countries.

The nutritional value of pulses N
Pulses are a cheap, low-fat source of protein, fibre, vitamins and minerals and they count towards the recommended five daily portions of fruit and vegetables. One portion is 80g, which is equivalent to around three heaped tablespoons of cooked pulses. However, if you eat more than three heaped tablespoons of beans and pulses in a day, this still only counts as one portion of your '5 a day'. This is because while pulses contain fibre, they don't give the same mixture of vitamins, minerals and other nutrients as fruit and vegetables. This excludes green beans, such as broad beans and runner beans, which count as a vegetable and not a bean or pulse for 5 a day.

Pulses contain more protein than any other vegetable and are therefore particularly important for people who do not get their protein from meat, fish or dairy products. Pulses can also be a healthy choice for meat-eaters, and can be added to soups, casseroles and meat sauces to add extra texture and flavour. This means you can use less meat, which makes the dish cheaper and lower in fat.

Pulses are a starchy food and add fibre to a meal. The fibre found in pulses may help lower blood cholesterol, so they are good for your heart. Pulses are also a good source of iron.

Using pulses in the diet
Pulses are typically bought either tinned or dried. Tinned pulses have already been soaked and cooked, so they are suitable to be used straight away, either cold or heated through. All dried pulses, except lentils, need to be soaked before cooking. They need to be soaked either in cold water overnight or for 2–3 hours when soaked in boiled water, and then drained before simmering gently in fresh water until soft.

Cooking times vary depending on the type of pulse and how old they are, so follow the instructions on the packet or a recipe.

Pulses can be included in meals in a variety of ways:

Soups and stews – to thicken and add extra protein

Salads – pulses can be cooked and served cold with a dressing or combined with other salad vegetables

Vegetable accompaniment – served in a sauce with meat or other vegetables

Vegetarian meals – as a main source of protein in vegetarian meals, e.g. bean burgers.

Check it
How should dried pulses be prepared before eating? Do you know how to prepare different types of pulses?

Cooking kidney beans safely

To ensure that kidney beans have been cooked properly before eating, follow these three steps:

1. Soak the dried beans in water for at least 12 hours.
2. Drain and rinse the beans, then cover them with fresh water.
3. Boil them vigorously for at least 10 minutes, then simmer for 45-60 minutes to make them tender.

Tinned kidney beans have already been cooked, so you can use them straight away.

Storing cooked pulses

If you cook pulses and you aren't going to eat them immediately, cool them as quickly as possible and then put them in the fridge or freeze them.

As with all cooked foods, don't leave cooked pulses at room temperature for more than an hour or two because this allows bacteria to multiply.

If you keep cooked pulses in the fridge, eat them within two days.

It should be safe to keep pulses frozen for a long time, as long as they stay frozen. However, keeping food frozen for too long can affect its taste and texture. Follow the freezer manufacturer's instructions on how long food can be kept frozen.

Key point

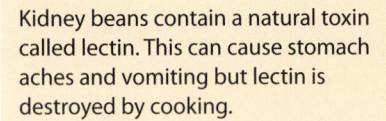

Kidney beans contain a natural toxin called lectin. This can cause stomach aches and vomiting but lectin is destroyed by cooking.

Study tip

Know the key nutrients provided by different pulses and beans.

Learn why these nutrients are needed in the body.

Activities

1. What nutritional contribution do pulses make to the diet? Explain the function of these nutrients.
2. Name 3 popular pulses and describe how they can be included in the diet.
3. How must dried kidney beans be prepared before eating? Explain why.

Bean Facts

Chickpeas

Chick peas have a distinctive shape which is not unlike a ram's head. Their Latin name, *cicer arietinum*, means 'small ram'.

Bean carbohydrates have been proven to drastically improve the stability of blood sugar levels in diabetics. Many adult-onset diabetics have been able to greatly reduce or eliminate their dependence on insulin through diets containing substantial amounts of beans.

Borlotti

The Borlotti is the most popular bean of northern Italy. It has a high iron content and is widely thought of as the best substitute for meat.

NUTS

BEANS, NUTS AND SEEDS, SOYA, TOFU AND MYCOPROTEIN

What will I learn?
- How nuts are included in the diet
- Allergic reactions caused by nuts
- The nutritional value of nuts N

The seed or fruit of a nut is contained within a hard shell that does not easily open to release it. This means nuts have a long shelf life and their outer shells prevent handling and contamination issues. Nuts have been a food source since prehistoric times, when prehistoric humans developed tools to be able to crack open the nut shell.

There are many different nuts available, examples include:

▲ Almond   ▲ Brazil   ▲ Cashew   ▲ Pecan

▲ Pistachio   ▲ Hazelnut   ▲ Walnut   ▲ Macadamia

▲ Variety of whole nuts in their shell

Peanuts are often considered a nut, however they are actually part of the legume family. They have similar properties to nuts, tend to be less expensive than nuts and are often mixed with foods to bring down the cost. Due to their high oil content peanuts are made into cooking oil and margarine. They can also be eaten raw, roasted and are especially popular when turned into peanut butter.

Using nuts in the diet

Shelled nuts can be eaten raw or prepared in a number of ways for cooking; e.g. blanched, chopped, slivered and ground. They can also be roasted and flavoured with salt or other seasonings and eaten as snacks.

Nuts can be used in sweet and savoury dishes to add flavour, texture and colour. They are useful in vegetarian meals, such as nut roast, and can be used in stuffing or sprinkled on salads. When ground, nuts are a thickener in dishes such as curry.

▲ Peanuts: a legume not a nut

321

Study tip

Know the key nutrients provided by different nuts and why they are needed in the body.

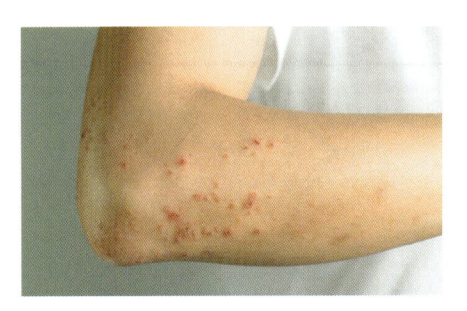

The nutritional value of nuts

Nuts aren't eaten in big amounts and make only a limited contribution to the diet because they are a fairly expensive commodity. That does not mean, however, that they do not contain a range of nutrients. Nuts are a good source of protein, but because they lack the amino acid lysine they are classed as being of low biological value.

Nuts can be a good alternative to snacks high in saturated fat. They are a good source of monounsaturated fat, which can help reduce the amount of cholesterol in our blood. They also contain essential fatty acids, another type of unsaturated fat which the body needs for good health.

Nuts are high in fat, so it's a good idea not to eat too many of them. Intake of salted nuts should be limited because they are very high in salt.

▲ Hives caused by a nut allergy

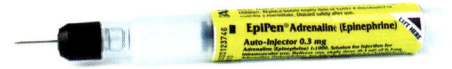

▲ The epi-pen is designed for emergency treatment of anaphylaxis

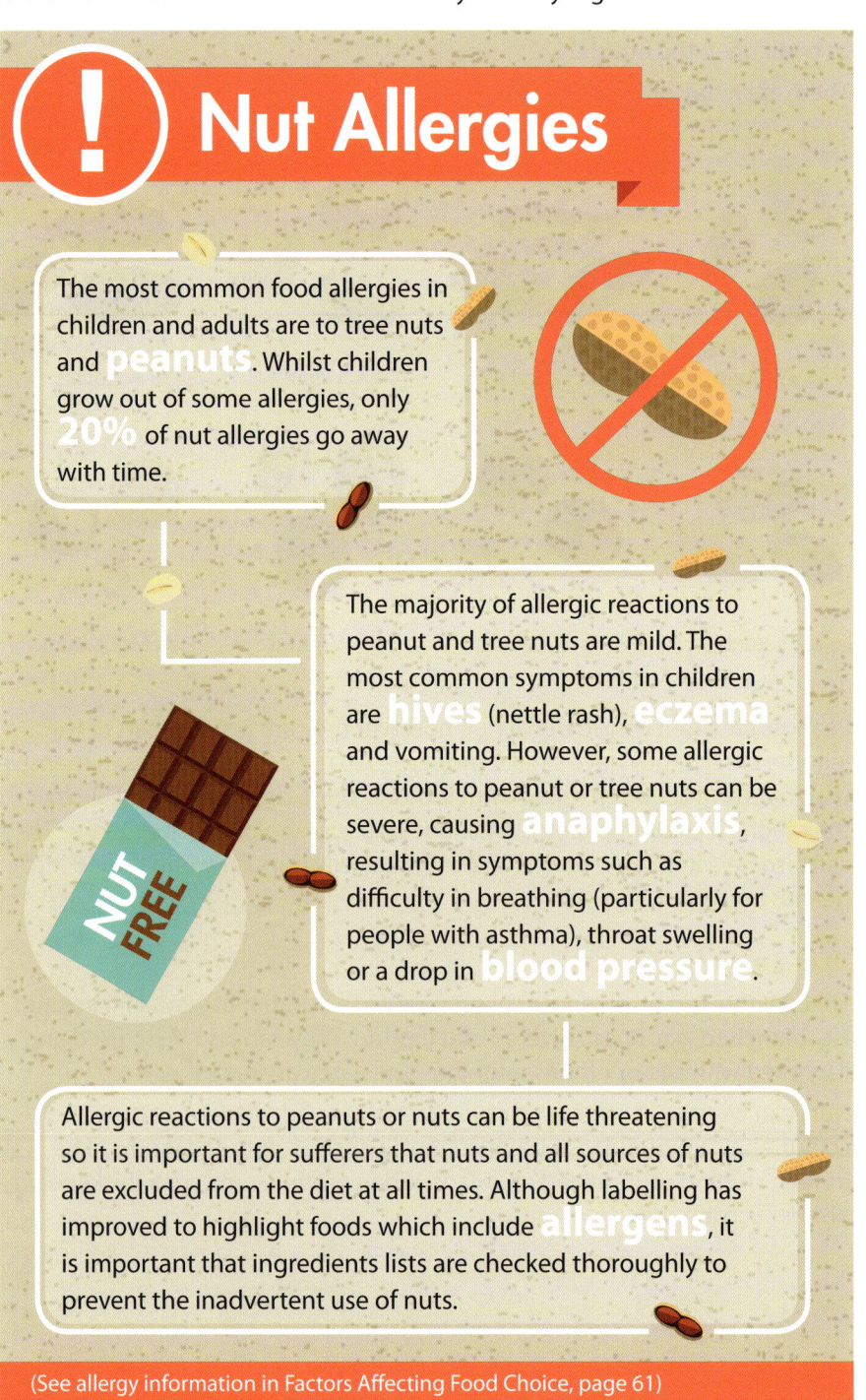

! Nut Allergies

The most common food allergies in children and adults are to tree nuts and **peanuts**. Whilst children grow out of some allergies, only **20%** of nut allergies go away with time.

The majority of allergic reactions to peanut and tree nuts are mild. The most common symptoms in children are **hives** (nettle rash), **eczema** and vomiting. However, some allergic reactions to peanut or tree nuts can be severe, causing **anaphylaxis**, resulting in symptoms such as difficulty in breathing (particularly for people with asthma), throat swelling or a drop in **blood pressure**.

Allergic reactions to peanuts or nuts can be life threatening so it is important for sufferers that nuts and all sources of nuts are excluded from the diet at all times. Although labelling has improved to highlight foods which include **allergens**, it is important that ingredients lists are checked thoroughly to prevent the inadvertent use of nuts.

(See allergy information in Factors Affecting Food Choice, page 61)

Activities

1. List 5 ways that we can include nuts in the diet.
2. Why is eating too many nuts not recommended?
3. What are the main nutrients provided by nuts? Why are they needed by the body?
4. Why is it important for someone with a nut allergy to avoid all products including nuts? How can they ensure they do this?

COMMODITIES — Principles of Nutrition: p8

BEANS, NUTS & SEEDS, SOYA, TOFU & MYCOPROTEIN

Nutrition of Nuts

Nuts provide a range of other nutrients that differs depending on the type of nut, as can be seen below.

Almond
Calcium – for bone health
Vitamin E – for healthy skin and to protect the body from disease
Almond skin provides flavonoids – beneficial to heart health

Brazil
Selenium – needed for an active thyroid hormone and for wounds to heal

Hazelnut
Folate – for the formation of red blood cells and the prevention of birth defects, e.g. spina bifida, a malformation of the spine
Vitamin E – to protect the body from disease and help the skin

Cashew
Iron – to help make haemoglobin in the red blood cells
Zinc – to help fight disease and infection
Magnesium – for bone growth and nerve function

Macadamia
Fibre – for a healthy digestive system
Magnesium – for bone growth and nerve function
Calcium – for bone health
Potassium – to balance body fluids

Pecan
Oleic acid – useful in reducing cholesterol levels and blood pressure
Vitamin B1 and B3 (thiamin and niacin) – to help release energy from carbohydrates

Pistachio
Vitamin B6 (pyridoxine) – needed for the metabolism of protein and the formation of red blood cells
Potassium – to balance body fluids
Fibre – for a healthy digestive system

Walnut
Omega-3 – to help prevent coronary heart disease and strokes
Vitamin E – to maintain the integrity of cell and mucus membranes and to protect the skin from harmful free radicals

SECTION 3

323

▲ Seeds can be used to add texture to bagels

> **Extension**
> Use the Internet to find out the range out more about using chia seeds as a replacement to eggs when cooking.

SEEDS

What will I learn?
- The uses of seeds in the diet
- The nutritional value of seeds [N]
- Processing of seeds into oil

Seeds are the part of the plant that contains the embryo from which future plants will grow. There are many seeds which we can include in our diet to add variety and nutritional value. Some of the most common seeds in food are:

- Sesame seeds
- Flax seeds
- Pumpkin seeds
- Sunflower seeds
- Poppy seeds
- Chia seeds

▲ Sesame seeds, flax seeds, pumpkin seeds, sunflower seeds

▲ Poppy seeds    ▲ Chia seeds

Using seeds in the diet
Seeds are mostly used as an additional ingredient in recipes to give texture, flavour and nutritional value. Seeds can be used in bread and cakes and can be added to breakfast cereal and salads. They are rich in oil, which makes them ideal as the main ingredient in oils for culinary use e.g. sunflower oil. Chia seeds, when soaked, create a gel-like substance which has proved a useful substitute for eggs in cooking.

Nutritional value of seeds [N]
Seeds are a good source of protein, B group vitamins, calcium, iron, zinc, magnesium and selenium. In addition, flax and sunflower seeds are high in vitamin E, pumpkin seeds and poppy seeds provide copper and manganese, and chia seeds provide phosphorous and omega-3 fatty acids.

324 COMMODITIES

BEANS, NUTS AND SEEDS, SOYA, TOFU AND MYCOPROTEIN

PRODUCTION OF SUNFLOWER OIL

THE MANUFACTURING PROCESS

Some vegetable oils, such as olive, peanut, and some coconut and sunflower oils, are cold-pressed. This method, which entails minimal processing, produces a light, flavourful oil suitable for some cooking needs.

CLEANING AND GRINDING

1. Magnets are passed over oil seeds to remove any trace metal before the outer layer of shell and husk are removed.

2. The stripped seeds or nuts are then ground into coarse meal to provide more surface area to be pressed.

PRESSING

3. The heated meal is then fed continuously into a press, the oil is squeezed out and collected.

4. The oil is refined to remove colour, odour, and bitterness.

REFINING THE OIL

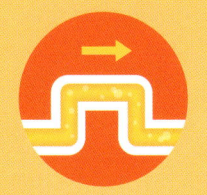

5. Oil that will be heated (for use in cooking) is then bleached by filtering it.

6. Finally, the oil is deodorised to give it the correct taste and aroma.

PACKAGING THE OIL

7. The processed oil is measured and poured into clean containers, usually plastic bottles for domestic oils to be sold in supermarkets.

Study tip

Know the key nutrients provided by different seeds and why they are important in the body.

Can you write a summary of how sunflower seeds are processed to make sunflower oil?

▲ A selection of seeded bread

▲ Poppy seed muffins

Activities

1. Why are seeds a good product to make into oil?
2. What are the nutritional value of seeds?
3. List 3 dishes that include seeds.

🔖 Key terms

Blanched – cooked to enable the skin to be removed.

Eczema – a medical condition where patches of skin become rough or inflamed which caused itching.

Anaphylaxis – a severe, potentially life threatening allergic reaction.

Allergens – substances that cause an allergic reaction.

Legumes – upright or climbing beans or plants.

Pulses – including beans and lentils, the seeds of legume plants

Cold-pressed – a production process where the temperature of the oil must not exceed 49°C when pressed and ground.

ALTERNATIVE PROTEIN FOODS

▲ Alternative proteins can be used to replace meat in a variety of dishes e.g. chilli

What will I learn?

- What alternative proteins are
- The variety of alternative protein foods available
- The use of alternative protein foods in the diet
- The nutritional value of alternative protein foods N

What are alternative protein foods?

'Alternative proteins' is a term that describes foods used as a replacement for meat in the diet. They can be used when someone is vegetarian or vegan or just wanting to include more variety in their diet. Also called **novel protein foods** (NPFs), these are products based on vegetable protein and micro-organisms. Novel protein foods were originally developed as a way to replace expensive animal protein but demand for them has increased in recent years as consumers seek healthy and tasty alternatives to meat.

The most popular alternative protein foods are tofu, textured vegetable protein and Quorn.

Key point
Alternative proteins are produced from vegetable proteins and micro-organisms.

▲ Tofu

▲ Soya mince

▲ Quorn

▲ Textured vegetable protein

Did you know that 30% of the Earth's entire land surface – a massive 70% of all agricultural land – is used for rearing farmed animals? It takes 2 to 15 kg of vegetable feed to produce 1 kg of animal protein. 40 to 50% of the world's cereal production is used to feed animals. Novel protein products made with plant-based proteins are therefore an essential component in feeding the growing global population and in reducing our carbon footprint.

Check it
What are alternative protein foods and why were they developed?

COMMODITIES

Soya

Soya beans have been cultivated in China for over 5000 years and they are native to Asia, but spread to the USA in the 1800s. Today North America is the largest producer of soya beans, with other major producers being Brazil and China. Soya beans grow in pods and grow best in countries with a warm climate. They reach maturity in four months.

▲ Soya beans growing in a pod (left) and dried

The nutritional value of soya [N]

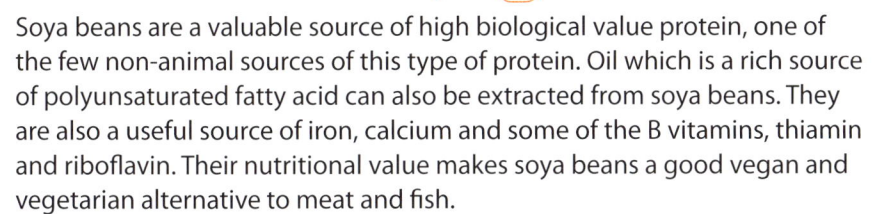

Soya beans are a valuable source of high biological value protein, one of the few non-animal sources of this type of protein. Oil which is a rich source of polyunsaturated fatty acid can also be extracted from soya beans. They are also a useful source of iron, calcium and some of the B vitamins, thiamin and riboflavin. Their nutritional value makes soya beans a good vegan and vegetarian alternative to meat and fish.

Products are made from soya

Soya beans have a variety of uses, they can be:

- used as a vegetable in salads
- fermented to produce soy sauce.
- ground into flour to make **textured vegetable protein** (TVP)
- soaked, heated and ground to make soya milk, which can be turned into another popular alternative protein, **tofu**.

Textured vegetable protein

Textured vegetable protein is a meat-like product made from soya flour. TVP is found primarily in vegetarian products, but is also used as an additive in meat products to add bulk and reduce the cost.

The nutritional value of textured vegetable protein

Textured vegetable protein is as the name suggests a very good source of protein, but it is also low in fat and provides dietary fibre. It is low in sodium but rich in potassium and provides calcium, iron and phosphorous. It is also a good source of vitamin B9 folate.

Textured vegetable protein production

Textured vegetable protein is made by first crushing soya beans and extracting the soya bean oil to produce defatted soya flour which is then blended to form a dough. The dough is heated under pressure to 100°C and then extruded into reduced pressure to allow the product to expand. When the desired texture is achieved the product is cut into pieces and dried. Colours and flavours can then be added to the dough so that the final product has a meaty colour and texture. Textured vegetable protein is generally produced as mince or chunks.

Check it

What are the uses of soya beans in the diet?

Extension

Investigate when and why textured vegetable protein was developed and its uses in the diet. Produce a presentation of your findings.

> **Key point**
>
> Soya bean products are a source of high biological value (HPV) protein, which means they contain all the essential amino acids.

> **Study tip**
>
> Know the ways that soya can be used as an alternative protein food.

Tofu

In Asian cuisine tofu is a very popular component in a variety of dishes. Tofu is a soya bean curd made by setting soya milk with calcium sulphate. There is a variety of types of tofu and tofu products, the main types being fresh tofu and processed tofu. Tofu has a different texture depending on the type; it can be soft or firm. Soft varieties can be used in place of dairy products and eggs in smoothies and desserts, whilst the firm variety is more commonly used cut into chunks in stir fries.

The nutritional value of tofu

Like soya beans, tofu is a good source of high biological value protein and is low in fat. It also provides some calcium and iron to the diet.

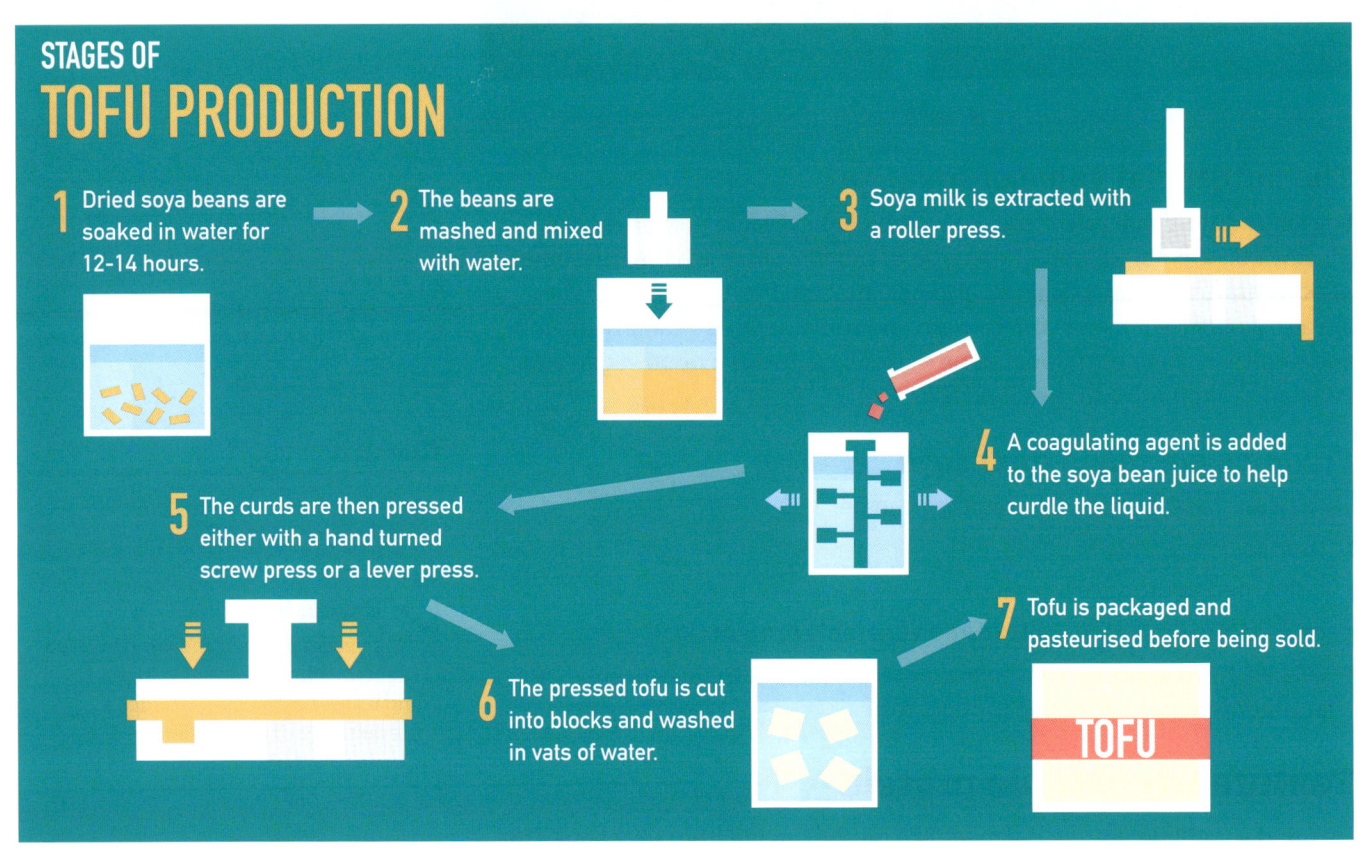

STAGES OF TOFU PRODUCTION

1 Dried soya beans are soaked in water for 12–14 hours.
2 The beans are mashed and mixed with water.
3 Soya milk is extracted with a roller press.
4 A coagulating agent is added to the soya bean juice to help curdle the liquid.
5 The curds are then pressed either with a hand turned screw press or a lever press.
6 The pressed tofu is cut into blocks and washed in vats of water.
7 Tofu is packaged and pasteurised before being sold.

▲ Tofu production

> **Activities**
>
> 1 What alternative protein foods are made from soya?
> 2 What are the nutritional benefits of eating soya products?
> 3 How is tofu produced?
> 4 Suggest 2 dishes that use the following:
>   a) Tofu
>   b) Textured vegetable protein

Quorn

Quorn is a **mycoprotein** made from a fungi called **fusarium venenatum** which was first discovered in Buckinghamshire growing near wheat fields. The product Quorn was first used in the UK in the 1980s. It has since been developed into more than 90 products and is now available in other countries such as the USA.

Mycoprotein is sold under the Quorn brand name. It can be processed into ready meals or products such as mince, fillets, burgers and sausages which can be used to create a variety of dishes. Quorn products are not all suitable for vegans due to the fact that they contain egg and sometimes milk. However, a new vegan range has recently been developed that uses potato to bind the product.

Quorn is made by adding nutrients to the mycoprotein and mixing it with egg white and seasoning.

> **Activities**
>
> 1 What is Quorn made from?
> 2 What processes in the production of Quorn ensure that it has a meat-like texture?

BEANS, NUTS AND SEEDS, SOYA, TOFU AND MYCOPROTEIN

A mycoprotein fermenter (40 metres high) runs continuously for five weeks at a time.

It is first sterilised and filled with a water and glucose solution. Then a batch of fusarium venenatum is introduced.

Once the fungus starts to grow, it is continuously fed nutrients, including potassium, magnesium and phosphate, as well as trace elements. The pH balance, temperature, nutrient concentration and oxygen are all constantly monitored to achieve optimum growth rate.

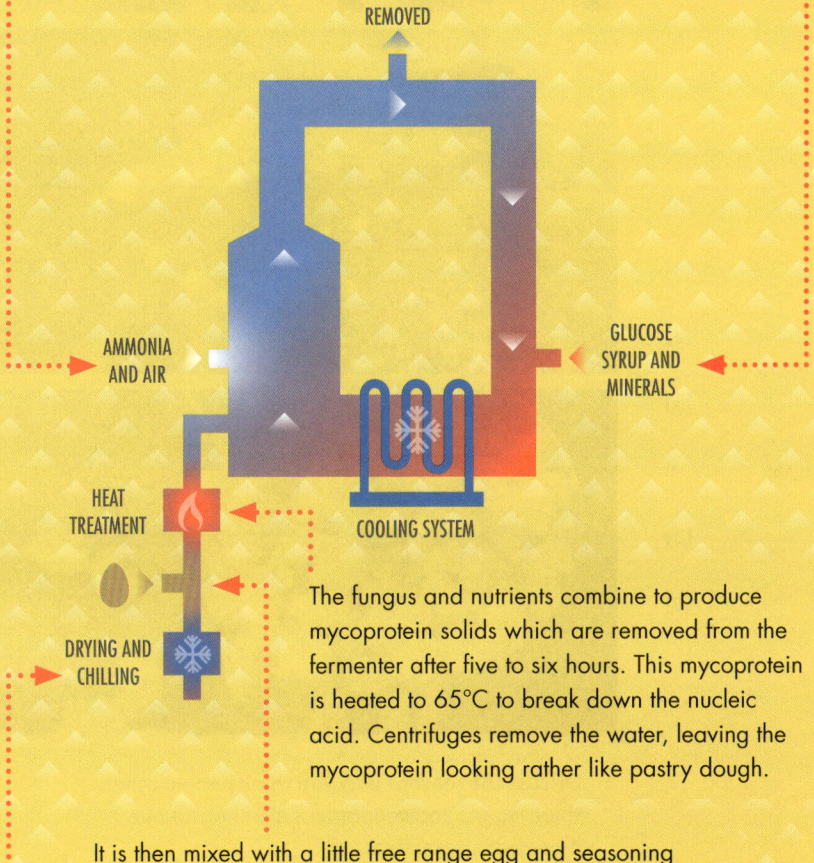

WASTE GASES REMOVED

AMMONIA AND AIR

GLUCOSE SYRUP AND MINERALS

HEAT TREATMENT

COOLING SYSTEM

DRYING AND CHILLING

The fungus and nutrients combine to produce mycoprotein solids which are removed from the fermenter after five to six hours. This mycoprotein is heated to 65°C to break down the nucleic acid. Centrifuges remove the water, leaving the mycoprotein looking rather like pastry dough.

It is then mixed with a little free range egg and seasoning to bind the mix and steam-cooked for about 30 minutes and then chilled before being chopped into pieces or mince.

Finally the product is frozen. This is an important step in the process: ice crystals push the fibres together, creating bundles that give mycoprotein its meat-like texture.

The nutritional benefits of mycoprotein [N]

- An excellent source of high quality protein and contains all the essential amino acids for adults.
- High in dietary fibre, this is important for the digestive system and sets it apart from meat protein which contains no fibre.
- Low in fat and saturated fats and contains no cholesterol or trans fats at all.
- Low in sodium.

Check it
What are the nutritional benefits of including mycoprotein/Quorn in the diet?

Study tip
You need to know the nutrients provided by alternative protein foods.

Extension
1 Using nutritional software or by searching nutritional data in books or online, complete the nutritional information in the following table:

Per 100g	Tofu	TVP	Quorn	Beef
Energy (kcal)				
Fat (g)				
Protein (g)				
Fibre (g)				

a) How do the alternative proteins compare in nutritional value to the beef?

b) Was the data what you expected? Why?

c) How can this information be used to advise people about choices they make in their diet?

Key terms

Novel protein foods – foods that have been produced by a method not previously used for food.

Textured vegetable protein – high protein meat substitute made from soy flour.

Tofu – a high protein food made by coagulating soy milk and pressing the resulting curds into soft white blocks.

Mycoprotein – protein derived from fungi, especially as produced for human consumption.

Fusarium Venenatum – the principal ingredient of mycoprotein is an ascomycota, one of the largest groups within the fungi family.

329

EXAM QUESTIONS

1. Beans and pulses are classed as a low biological value protein.
   a. Explain what is meant by the term low biological value. [4]
   b. Explain how a vegan could use alternative proteins, beans, nuts and seeds to ensure they include all the essential amino acids in their diet. [6]

2. a. What is meant by the term high biological value protein? [4]
   b. Name a vegetable source of high biological value protein. [1]

3. a. Discuss the nutritional value of pulses in the diet. [6]
   b. Explain why beans can only be counted as one portion of your '5 a day' fruit and vegetables?

4. Explain how kidney beans should be cooked to ensure they are safe to eat. [3]

5. List 3 ways that seeds can be included in diet. [3]

6. a. Name 3 nutrients provided by nuts. [3]
   b. Explain why nuts make only a limited contribution to the diet. [3]

7. The number of people suffering from food allergies has been steadily increasing.
   a. List 3 common food allergens [3]
   b. Explain how someone with a food allergy can avoid having an allergic reaction [5]

8. Name the alternative protein sources shown in each picture. [3]

9. Discuss the reasons why you think people other than vegans and vegetarians are choosing to buy meat alternatives. [8]

10. How do the commodities meat and alternative proteins compare in terms of:
    a. Nutritional value [4]
    b. Value for money [4]

TOTAL: 60

FOOD INVESTIGATIONS

BEANS, NUTS AND SEEDS, SOYA, TOFU AND MYCOPROTEIN

Investigation 1
Sensory attributes of alternative proteins

Conduct an experiment to find out the differences in taste, texture and nutritional value of tofu, Quorn and TVP (textured vegetable protein).

Method

Choose a recipe that would be suitable to cook with tofu, Quorn and TVP.

Cook the dishes according to the recipe and complete the following chart.

Alternative protein	Appearance	Texture	Taste	Nutritional value
Tofu				
Quorn				
Textured vegetable protein				

Ask yourself the following:

What was the most successful alternative protein to use in the recipe? Use your sensory comments and nutritional information to explain why.

What was the least successful alternative protein to use in the recipe? Why do you think this was?

Which dish had the best nutritional value? Did you expect this?

What have you learnt about alternative proteins from this investigational work?

Do you think that you could have improved your investigational work in any way? How?

Optional additional task

Do you think you chose a suitable dish to make? What dishes do you think would be suitable to make with each of the alternative proteins?

Investigation 2   Comparing mycoprotein and minced beef when making Bolognaise

Investigate the differences between Quorn mince and minced beef when making a bolognaise sauce:

125g minced beef	1 garlic clove
125g Quorn mince	50g mushrooms
Basic bolognaise recipe as follows:	1 tbsp tomato purée
	1 tin chopped tomatoes
1 tbsp oil	1 stock cube
1 onion	1 tsp mixed herbs

Method

1. Dice the onions and mushrooms and crush the garlic.
2. Take 2 small saucepans, add ½ tbsp oil to each pan.
3. Fry the onions and garlic over a medium heat until soft.
4. Add the beef to one saucepan and the Quorn to the other. Cook for 5 minutes until the beef has browned, and the Quorn has heated. Add the half the chopped mushrooms to each pan.
5. Add ½ tbsp tomato purée to each saucepan and stir.
6. Add half the tin of tomatoes to each saucepan.
7. Crumble in the stock cube and add the mixed herbs.
8. Bring to the boil and simmer for 20 minutes.

Comment on the taste, texture and appearance of each of the finished products.

Using the nutritional labels from the Quorn and beef packaging, compare the nutritional value of the two sauces. Compare the cost of the different protein sources.

Consider the value of using each type of protein when making a range of dishes.

Investigation 3   Comparing beans and pulses

Investigate the variety of cooked pulses when making bean burgers. Use a selection of the following or any other pulses of your choice:

- kidney beans
- butter beans
- borlotti beans
- chickpeas
- lentils

Basic recipe as follows:

1 can of beans or pulses

50g breadcrumbs

1 egg

½ tsp black pepper

1 tsp herbs or spices of your choice

Method

1. Drain the beans, reserving the liquid, and mash the beans in a small bowl.
2. Add the breadcrumbs, egg, pepper and herbs/spices.
3. Add some of the bean liquid until the mixture holds together but is not wet.
4. Divide the mixture into 3 patties.
5. Heat a tablespoon of oil in a frying pan and cook the patties until a crisp crust forms on both sides, this will take about 6 minutes.

Ask yourself the following:

Which type of pulses were the most successful in making the burgers? Comment on taste, texture and appearance.

Use the nutritional labelling or a nutritional analysis program to compare which burgers have the best nutritional value.

Compare the cost of using each type of pulse, which was the best value for money?

CHEESY BEAN BURGERS

Portion size: 4   **Difficulty rating:** ★★

INGREDIENTS:

400g can butter beans	75g Wensleydale cheese
3 tbsp olive oil	1 tbsp plain flour
1 small onion	1 egg beaten
1 garlic clove	50g fresh white breadcrumbs or dried breadcrumbs
salt and pepper for seasoning	

EQUIPMENT LIST:

green chopping board	small basin	plate x 2
vegetable knife	fork	shallow bowl
garlic crusher	frying pan	fish slice
sieve	metal spoon	

METHOD:

1. Dice the onion finely, and crush the garlic.
2. Drain the butter beans and tip into a bowl and mash with a fork to form a rough purée. Put to one side.
3. Heat 1 tbsp of oil in a small frying pan and add the onion and garlic. Cook over a gentle heat for 3-4 mins, until softened.
4. Stir the onion mixture into the butter beans, along with the cheese, then season. Shape the mixture into 4 patties, put onto a plate, cover and chill for 10 mins.
5. Put some flour onto a piece of greaseproof paper, roll the patties in the flour and dust off any excess.
6. Crack the egg into a shallow bowl and mix with a fork, carefully roll the patties in the egg.
7. Put the breadcrumbs onto a plate and coat the patties.
8. Heat remaining oil in a non-stick frying pan on a medium heat and add burgers. Cook for 8-10 mins, turning occasionally until golden.
9. Drain on kitchen paper to remove any excess oil and serve with a salad.

NUTRITION:	Recipe	100g	Portion	Reference Intake Men	Women	Children
Energy (kJ)	5808	759	1452			
Energy (kcal)	1389	182	347	14%	17%	19%
Fat (g)	79	10	20	21%	28%	28%
Saturates (g)	23	3	6	19%	29%	29%
Carbohydrate (g)	120	16	30	10%	13%	14%
Sugars (g)	12	2	3	3%	3%	4%
Salt (g)	6	1	2	25%	25%	38%

EATWELL GUIDE:

SUCCESS CRITERIA

- Divide the mixture evenly into 4 to ensure all the burgers are the same size.
- Do not leave the frying pan unattended when frying either the onions or burgers, ensure the heat is not too high so they do not burn.

SKILLS / TECHNIQUES

- Shaping, coating.
- Dicing, bridge hold, claw grip, mashing.

RECIPE MODIFICATION

- Change butter beans to any other type of bean
- Change Wensleydale to grated Cheddar cheese
- Optional extra ingredients:
- 1 tsp chilli powder, 1 tbsp chopped fresh herbs e.g. chives, parsley, 1 tsp paprika

SCIENCE INVOLVED

- Coagulation of egg allows the breadcrumbs to form a crispy coating and prevents the burgers overcooking

COOK'S TIPS

- To help shape the patties you could use a straight edged cutter and press the mixture into it, to ensure even sized and shaped burgers.

ALLERGENS

Egg, milk in cheese

THAI QUORN CURRY

Portion size: 4 **Difficulty rating:** ★★★

BEANS, NUTS AND SEEDS, SOYA, TOFU AND MYCOPROTEIN

INGREDIENTS:

- 300g pack Quorn Meat Free Chicken Pieces, defrosted
- 2 tbsp light soy sauce
- 1-2 tbsp vegetable oil
- 2 tbsp green Thai curry paste
- 1 small onion, finely chopped
- 1 green chilli, de-seeded and finely chopped
- 3 garlic cloves, crushed
- 400g tin coconut milk
- 125g baby corn, blanched
- 125g green beans, trimmed and blanched
- 1 red pepper, deseeded and cut into thin strips
- 125g pak choi, leaves separated and washed
- 1 tbsp lime juice
- Small bunch of fresh coriander, chopped

EQUIPMENT LIST:

mixing bowl	garlic crusher	wok
chopping board	small saucepan	wooden spoon
sharp knife	small basin	juicer

METHOD:

1. Marinate the Quorn Meat Free Chicken Pieces in the light soy sauce for up to 30 minutes.
2. Finely dice the onion on a green chopping board, deseed and finely chop the chilli and crush the garlic. Deseed and slice the red pepper.
3. Cut the baby corn in half and trim the green beans, put into a small saucepan, cover with boiling water and bring to the boil. Once boiling, remove from the heat and transfer the vegetables into a bowl of ice cold water to blanch.
4. Heat the oil in a wok, add the green Thai curry paste and cook for 2 minutes stirring frequently.
5. Add the onion, chilli and garlic and stir fry for 2 minutes. Stir in the marinated Quorn Pieces and fry for 1 minute.
6. Pour in the coconut milk and bring to a simmering point. Add the blanched baby corn, green beans and red pepper. Cook over a medium heat for 3-4 minutes, stirring continuously. Add the pak choi and cover with a lid for 1 minute to steam and wilt the leaves. Stir in the fresh lime juice and half the chopped coriander.
7. Serve sprinkled with the remaining coriander.

NUTRITION:

	Recipe	100g	Portion	Men	Women	Children
Energy (kJ)	3676	259	919			
Energy (kcal)	879	62	220	9%	11%	12%
Fat (g)	49	3	12	13%	18%	18%
Saturates (g)	6	0	2	5%	8%	8%
Carbohydrate (g)	54	4	14	5%	6%	6%
Sugars (g)	41	3	10	9%	11%	12%
Salt (g)	11	1	3	46%	46%	69%

EATWELL GUIDE:

SUCCESS CRITERIA
- Prepare all vegetables as the start of the recipe to ensure they are ready to be added during the recipe.

SKILLS / TECHNIQUES
- Marinating, blanching
- Bridge hold, claw grip, dicing

RECIPE MODIFICATION
- Quorn could be replaced with prawns, tofu, beef, chicken, pork or beef.

SCIENCE INVOLVED
- Blanching stops the cooking process so the vegetables retain their colour and texture.

COOK'S TIPS
- Serve with Jasmine rice for an authentic taste.

ALLERGENS
Soya in soy sauce

TOFU NOODLES

Portion size: 4   **Difficulty rating:** ★★

INGREDIENTS:

- 2 tbsp sesame oil
- 396g pack firm tofu
- 150g dried rice noodles
- 1 tbsp soy sauce
- 2 tsp Chinese five-spice powder
- 1 tbsp clear honey
- 1 red pepper
- 1 bunch spring onions, cut into fingers
- 2 heads pak choi

EQUIPMENT LIST:

- green chopping board
- vegetable knife
- tablespoon
- frying pan
- plate
- saucepan
- colander

METHOD:

1. Ensure the tofu is firm, if there is any excess liquid, put the tofu between two chopping boards and apply a heavy weight on top to remove the liquid whilst chopping the vegetables.
2. Deseed the pepper and slice thinly.
3. Remove the root of the spring onions and trim the top, cut on a diagonal into 3cm pieces.
4. Wash and separate the leaves of the pak choi.
5. Cut the tofu into strips of 1cm by 3cm, pat dry.
6. Heat half the oil in a frying pan over a **medium** heat. When hot, add the tofu and cook for 5 mins on one side. Turn, then fry for another 3 mins. Continue cooking for 10 mins more, turning regularly. Remove to a plate and keep warm.
7. Meanwhile, cook the noodles following pack instructions. Drain and set aside.
8. Make the dressing by mixing ½ tbsp oil, soy sauce, five-spice and honey.
9. Heat the remaining ½ tbsp sesame oil in the frying pan and cook the pepper for 1 min, then add the spring onions and pak choi. Toss together for 3 mins, until just wilted.
10. Add the noodles and half the dressing and mix well. Heat through and divide between 4 bowls. Top with the tofu and drizzle remaining dressing over.

NUTRITION:	Recipe	100g	Portion	Reference intake Men	Women	Children
Energy (kJ)	8353	665	2088			
Energy (kcal)	2007	160	502	20%	25%	28%
Fat (g)	103	8	26	27%	37%	37%
Saturates (g)	5	0	1	4%	6%	6%
Carbohydrate (g)	160	13	40	13%	17%	18%
Sugars (g)	32	3	8	7%	9%	9%
Salt (g)	3	0	1	13%	13%	19%

EATWELL GUIDE:

SUCCESS CRITERIA
- Make sure that the vegetables and tofu are prepared before you start cooking so you don't have to leave the pan unattended when cooking the tofu.

SKILLS / TECHNIQUES
- Stir-frying, making a dressing.
- Deseeding, slicing and dicing evenly.

RECIPE MODIFICATION
- Use different vegetables such as bean sprouts, baby sweetcorn or mange tout to add a variety of colours and flavours.

SCIENCE INVOLVED
- Effect of heat on cooking tofu changes the texture.
- Quick cooking method ensures colour and texture of vegetables are maintained.

COOK'S TIPS
- Don't worry if the tofu falls apart a little, these pieces become crispy and add a good texture to the dish.

ALLERGENS
Sesame oil, soya in tofu and soy sauce

SECTION 3
COMMODITIES

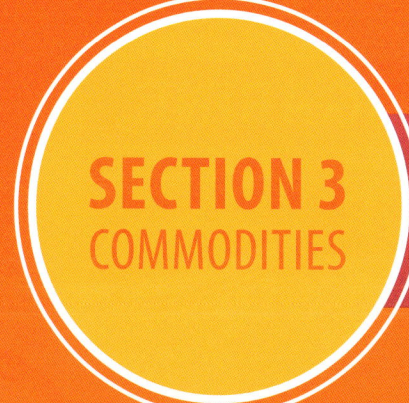

BUTTER, OIL, MARGARINE, SUGAR AND SYRUP

- TYPES OF FAT AND OILS   336
- OILS   340
- PROPERTIES OF FAT AND OILS   346
- SUGAR AND OTHER SWEETENERS   348
- EXAM QUESTIONS   360
- FOOD INVESTIGATIONS   361

SECTION 3
COMMODITIES

BUTTER, OIL, MARGARINE, SUGAR AND SYRUP

What will I learn?
- The choice of fats and oils available to the consumer
- The composition of fats and oils
- The nutritional value of fats and oils in the diet
- The properties of fats and oils
- The functions of fats and oils in food preparation

Key point

There are many different fats and oils available to the consumer.

Types of fat and oils

There are many different types of fat and oils.

FAT AND OIL

A general rule is that fats, for example butter, are solid or semi-solid at room temperature. Oils, for example olive oil, are liquid at room temperature. A small number of fats from plant sources are naturally solid or semi-solid at room temperature.

At room temperature (18°C)

Fats are solid

Fats mostly come from animal sources.

Oils are liquid

Oils mostly come from plant sources.

Animal
Vegetable
Fish

336 COMMODITIES

Fats

Butter

Butter is made from churning cream and is high in saturated fat.

Clarified butter is produced by melting regular butter over low heat and skimming off the milk solids that rise to the top. The golden yellow clarified layer is then strained off, leaving only sediments in the bottom of the pan.

Butter is one of the most popular cooking fats, providing rich flavour to foods, but it has a low smoke point (see page 346), so care must be taken not to burn it when using it for high heat sautéing and frying. For sautéing, many cooks combine butter with a type of oil that has a higher smoke point to prevent it from burning.

Butter is used as a topping for breads and rolls, is melted onto cooked vegetables, and is added to many types of sauces to provide a rich, smooth flavour. It is also used as an ingredient in baked goods such as bread, rolls, cakes, and pastries.

Butter is perishable so it should be stored in the refrigerator. It should be tightly wrapped because it will absorb odours and flavours quite easily.

Ghee

Ghee is a form of clarified butter that has had its milk solids removed, making it clear. As it is heated for a long time, ghee has a stronger, nuttier flavour and darker colour. Its higher smoke point means it is good for frying. It is used in Indian cookery as an ingredient in baked dishes and sauces and as a condiment.

Lard

Lard comes from pig fat that has been rendered and clarified to produce a firm and evenly textured product with a mild flavour. Lard that is not processed has a soft, greasy texture and a strong flavour. It is softer than butter and white in colour. In the past, lard was widely used as an all-purpose cooking fat and in baking. It has become much less popular because of the health problems associated with the overuse of saturated fat in the diet.

Suet

Suet is a white, solid fat obtained from the area surrounding the kidneys of beef and sheep. It is used for the creation of dumplings and for several traditional English steamed puddings, such as steak and kidney pudding and jam roly-poly. It was very popular at one time, but it has now fallen out of favour due to increased awareness of health problems associated with saturated fat. Suet is sold in large chunks or in shredded form in small packets.

> Suet and lard are used infrequently nowadays, mainly because of their high cholesterol and saturated fat content.

BUTTER, OIL, MARGARINE, SUGAR AND SYRUP

▲ Butter

▲ Ghee

▲ Lard

▲ Suet

Key point

Butter is made from churning cream.

Both butter and ghee are high in saturated fat and cholesterol.

▲ Buttery spreads (above) and margarine (below)

Solid vegetable fats or vegetable shortenings

Solid vegetable fats are made purely from vegetables.

Made from vegetable oils, vegetable **shortening** is fat that has undergone a process called **hydrogenation** (hydrogen is added to the oils). This changes the chemical characteristics of the oils, making them solid at room temperature.

Like lard, vegetable shortening is very useful in baking light and flaky pastries. Some varieties may have butter flavouring added, which enhances the flavour and gives the shortening a light golden colour.

Spreads

Soft spreads are blended from vegetable oils. The oil is hardened by adding hydrogen gas.

Reduced or low fat spreads contain 40–80% fat. Some low fat spreads can contain about half the fat of soft spreads and butter. They are an emulsion of fat and water and their high water content makes them unsuitable for frying and baking.

Margarine

Margarine has been a popular butter substitute for over a hundred years. Like butter, regular margarine must contain a minimum of 80% fat. It is made from various vegetable oils such as soya bean and corn.

In order to produce margarine in a solid form, the vegetable oil must undergo hydrogenation (see page 344).

Like butter, margarine can be used as a topping for bread, rolls, biscuits or vegetables. It is much more spreadable than butter when used straight from the refrigerator. Margarine is used in a variety of baked goods and can be used in any recipe requiring butter. It has a lower smoke point than many cooking oils and fats so it is usually not the first choice for sautéing or frying.

Check it

1. Name three fats obtained from animal sources.
2. Name three oils obtained from plant sources.
3. Name two types of margarine which are considered to be healthier options.
4. Name two types of margarine which are designed for easier spreading.

Activity

Consumer needs are influenced by factors such as diet or cost. Conduct a supermarket survey of vegetable fats, margarines and spreads available for people on special diets and record the price of each.

Study tip

Learn the different types of solid fats, their sources, properties and uses in food preparation.

OTHER TYPES OF MARGARINE INCLUDE:

SOFT MARGARINE: formulated to be easy to spread.

WHIPPED MARGARINE: beaten vigorously to add air to the mixture, which makes it very spreadable.

LIQUID MARGARINE: packaged in a squeezable bottle, making it easy to add to foods such as corn on the cob or for use as a basting liquid.

REDUCED FAT MARGARINE: with as much as 65% less fat than regular margarine, it is a healthier alternative. However its high water content means that it isn't as suitable for some baked goods as regular margarine and it isn't as useful for sautéing or frying.

FAT-FREE MARGARINE: a much healthier spread than regular margarine when used as a condiment. Its water content is much higher than regular margarine so it should not be used for sautéing, frying or baking.

BUTTER, OIL, MARGARINE, SUGAR AND SYRUP

Nutritional labelling

The fat content is displayed on food labels and some foods will also give figures for saturated fat, or 'saturates'.

Total fat content is labelled as either high or low. High is more than 20g fat per 100g. Low is 3g fat or less per 100g. If the amount of fat per 100g is in between these figures, then that is a medium level of fat.

Saturated fat content is also labelled as high or low. High is more than 5g saturates per 100g. Low is 1.5g saturates or less per 100g. Anything in between is considered a medium level of saturated fat.

Key point

Read the labels on packaged food to understand which type of fat they contain. Some contain 'hidden fat' too.

▼ Food labels displaying fat content

Each 30g serving contains of your Reference Intake
- Calories 120 — 6%
- Sugar 10.1g — 11%
- Fat 1.3g — 2%
- Saturates 0.3g — 2%
- Salt 0.2g — 3%

Each 200ml serving provides...
- cal 128
- fat 7.2g
- total sugars 9.4g
- sat fat 4.6g
- salt 0.28g

Krisp-es

NUTRITION FACTS

| Serving size | 25g |
| Calories: | 124 |

		% Daily Value*
Total fat	1.7g	3%
Saturated fat	1g	5%
Cholesterol	0mg	1%
Sodium	8g	8%
Total carbohydrate	12g	4%
Dietary Fibre	3g	9%
Sugar	14.4g	12%
Protein	4g	9%
Vitamin A	0%	Vitamin C 2%
Calcium	4%	Iron 25%

*Percent Daily Values are based on a 2,000 calorie diet. Your daily values may be higher or lower depending on your calorie needs.

SECTION 3

OILS

Oils are mostly obtained from plant sources. Vegetable oils are obtained from seeds such as sunflower seeds or from the flesh of fruit such as olives. They include corn, rapeseed, walnut, soya and olive.

ALMOND

FACTS Obtained from nuts, almond oil is very expensive so the demand for it is limited. It has a subtle toasted almond aroma and flavour.

USES It has a high smoke point so it may be used for high heat cooking. It is suitable for salad dressings and as an addition to sauces.

COMPOSITION Almond oil is a good source of monounsaturated fat and vitamins A and E.

AVOCADO

FACTS Avocado oil has a light, but unique flavour. It is usually produced from avocados that are damaged or not aesthetically pleasing.

USES Refined avocado oil has the highest smoke point of any plant oil, so it is useful for high heat cooking. It is an excellent choice for salad dressings or for use as a condiment.

COMPOSITION It is a good source of monounsaturated fat and vitamin E, which makes it nutritionally beneficial.

CANOLA / RAPESEED

FACTS This oil is popular in Japan, China, and India and it is the most widely used oil in Canada. It is cheap to produce.

USES It is an excellent choice for cooking or baking, or as an ingredient for salad dressings.

COMPOSITION It has the lowest level of saturated fat of any edible oil and one of the highest levels of monounsaturated fat. It also contains a high level of omega-3 fatty acids.

CHILLI

FACTS Chilli oil is derived from hot, red chillies that have been steeped in vegetable oil to extract the flavour and heat.

It is very popular in the creation of Chinese dishes.

USES It is most often used as a flavouring and should not be used as a cooking oil because the strong flavour will overpower the food.

COMPOSITION Chillies are regarded as a strong antioxidant and are claimed to lower blood glucose levels.

COCONUT

FACTS Coconut oil is extracted from the dried meat of the coconut and is very popular in India and Southeast Asia. It solidifies at room temperature and has a buttery texture.

USES In baking, stir fries and as a non dairy replacement for butter.

COMPOSITION Coconut oil contains a high level of saturated fat (92%).

CORN

FACTS Corn oil is produced from the germ of corn kernels. It is often used in the manufacture of margarine. It has a light golden colour and is almost tasteless and odourless.

USES Refined corn oil is one of the best oils for frying because it has a high smoke point. It is a good choice for baking. It can be used for salad dressings when oil with little or no taste is required.

COMPOSITION High in polyunsaturated fat.

FLAX SEED

FACTS Also known as linseed oil, it is obtained from flax seeds.

USES It has a buttery flavour, which makes it a good choice for salad dressings or as a topping for potatoes and vegetables.

COMPOSITION Flax seed oil has the highest level of polyunsaturated fat and omega-3 fatty acid. It is used more often as a nutritional supplement than for cooking.

BUTTER, OIL, MARGARINE, SUGAR AND SYRUP

OLIVE

FACTS Olive oil has been one of the staples of the Mediterranean diet for thousands of years and its popularity is growing rapidly in other parts of the world. It is one of the most frequently used food oils.

USES Its versatility as a cooking oil and its ability to enhance the flavour of many foods make it an excellent alternative to butter or margarine as a condiment or for use in food preparation.

COMPOSITION It has proven nutritional and health benefits.

SUNFLOWER

FACTS Sunflower seeds are popular as a snack, but oil can also be extracted from them. Sunflower seed oil is a light yellow colour and has a mild flavour.

USES It is suitable for use as a base for salad dressings or in combination with stronger-flavoured, more expensive oils that can be used more economically when combined with sunflower oil. It is also used for cooking because like most other refined oils, it has a fairly high smoke point.

COMPOSITION It is low in saturated fat and cholesterol.

SESAME

FACTS The only steps required to produce unrefined sesame seed oil are crushing the seeds and filtering the resulting oil. The oil is light and has a mild flavour. It is very popular in Middle-Eastern and Indian cooking.

USES The strong, rich flavour goes a long way, so only small quantities are necessary to liven up stir-fry dishes and marinades for meat or fish.

COMPOSITION It is low in saturated fat.

VEGETABLE

FACTS The label may or may not list the types of oil contained within the blend, so the consumer will often never know exactly what they are purchasing

USES The refining process usually results in oil that has a high smoke point and a colour ranging from almost clear to golden yellow, but with very little taste or aromaw. This makes vegetable oil a good all-purpose oil for sautéing, frying, and baking.

COMPOSITION Vegetable oil usually consists of a highly refined blend of various oils such as soya bean, corn and sunflower or it may consist of only one type of oil.

SOYA BEAN

FACTS Soya bean oil is one of the most widely used oils in the manufacture of margarine, vegetable oil, and shortening. In fact, in the United States, soya bean oil is used more than any other in the production of commercially prepared food items. It has long been a favourite for use in Chinese cooking.

Many brands of 'vegetable oil' are often 100% soya bean. Soya bean oil is inexpensive.

USES Soya bean oil is highly refined and has a high smoke point, making it a good all-purpose cooking oil.

COMPOSITION It has several healthy attributes, including high levels of polyunsaturated (including omega-3 fatty acid) and monounsaturated fats and it is fairly low in saturated fat.

WALNUT

FACTS Walnut oil, which is cold pressed from the meat of dried walnuts, has a strong and distinctive walnut flavour. Walnut oil is expensive.

USES It is generally used as a flavouring for baked goods and for some sauces. It can provide a bold flavour to salad dressings or it can be added to mildly flavoured oils to create a subtle taste. It can be used for sautéing and pan-frying, but the high heat will diminish the flavour of the oil and the unrefined version does not have a particularly high smoke point.

COMPOSITION It is very low in saturated fat and very high in polyunsaturated fat.

SECTION 3

341

Check it

1. Suggest two types of oil which can be used for a salad dressing. Give a reason for your choice.
2. Suggest two types of oil which are suitable for frying. Give a reason for your choice.
3. Which oil is associated with Mediterranean cooking?
4. Which oil is associated with Chinese style dishes?

Key point

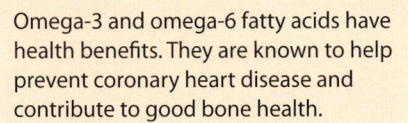

Omega-3 and omega-6 fatty acids have health benefits. They are known to help prevent coronary heart disease and contribute to good bone health.

Check it

What are essential fatty acids?

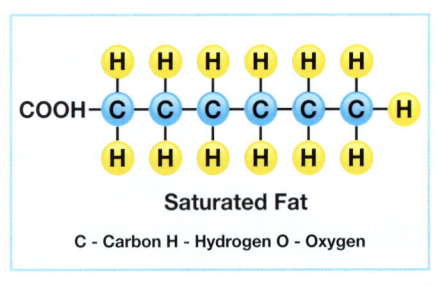

▲ Chemical composition of saturated fat

Nutritional value of fats and oils

Fat and oils provide energy and keep us warm. Edible fats and oils are 100% fat and provide a very concentrated source of energy along with essential fatty acids such as omega-3 and omega-6.

Fat also provides a protective layer around our internal organs such as our kidneys.

Fat is a carrier of fat soluble vitamins A, D, E and K and is necessary for their absorption by the body.

While some edible fats from plant sources, such as olive oil and flax seed oil, are considered very healthy, they are all high in calories. All plant oils have about 120 calories per tablespoon so they should be consumed in moderation as part of a balanced diet. Fats readily contribute to weight gain.

1 gram of fat provides 37 kJ (9 kcal).

Fats and oils are composed of the elements carbon, hydrogen and oxygen.

Fats and oils are made up of different types of fatty acids and glycerol. A fatty acid is made up of a chain of carbon atoms with a methyl group at one end and an acid group at the other. Each atom in between has either one or two atoms attached.

They combine to form fat molecules as one unit of glycerol to three units of fatty acids. The presence of specific fatty acids at different positions on the glycerol molecule will determine the characteristics of the fat or oil, for example melting point and digestibility.

Fatty acids are usually classified as saturated or unsaturated fat (monounsaturated or polyunsaturated) depending on their chemical structure.

Saturated fat

Animal fats, butter, cream, and whole milk are the primary sources of saturated fat, which is the least healthy type of fat. Saturated fat raises the level of LDL (bad) cholesterol, which can cause numerous health problems if consumed in large quantities. They have no double bonds. This means that some of the carbon atoms are joined to others and are not completely saturated with hydrogen atoms.

Cholesterol, a fatty substance known as a lipid, is vital for the normal functioning of the body and is found in some foods.

Cholesterol can build up in the artery wall, restricting the blood flow to the heart, brain and the rest of the body.

A high fat intake, and in particular a high intake of saturated fatty acids (saturates), has been associated with a raised blood cholesterol level, which is one of the risk factors for coronary heart disease (CHD).

Unsaturated fats and oils

Unsaturated fats are found mainly in vegetable oils e.g. cooking oils. Unsaturated fats contain less cholesterol. Unsaturated fats can be either monounsaturated or polyunsaturated depending on their chemical composition.

BUTTER, OIL, MARGARINE, SUGAR AND SYRUP

Monounsaturated fat FS N

Most animal and vegetable fats contain monounsaturated fat, but in varying quantities. It is in liquid form at room temperature, but it may begin to solidify when it is chilled. Monounsaturated fat is the most desirable type of fat in the diet because it helps to decrease the LDL (bad) cholesterol in the blood and increase the HDL (good) cholesterol.

Good sources of monounsaturated fat are nuts and oils such as macadamia nut oil, olive oil, canola oil and peanut oil. Macadamia nut oil has the highest percentage (about 83%) of monounsaturated fat of any edible oil, but it is expensive and it is not commonly used in cooking. Olive oil has the highest percentage (about 77%) of monounsaturated fat among the oils frequently used for that purpose.

Polyunsaturated fat

The main sources of polyunsaturated fats are seeds, nuts, grains, and vegetables. Polyunsaturated fat is liquid at room temperature and also when chilled. It lowers the overall cholesterol level, including the level of HDL (good) cholesterol. Reference Intakes of polyunsaturated fats should be part of a balanced diet. Sunflower oil has the highest percentage (about 77%) of polyunsaturated fat of any edible oil.

Omega-3 fatty acid is a type of polyunsaturated fat that is especially healthy. Omega-3 fatty acids help to reduce the risk of heart disease, lower blood pressure, guard against plaque build-up in the arteries, and aid in brain development. It is found in some plant oils and in the tissues of all sea creatures. Among the plant oils rich in **omega-3 fatty acids** are flaxseed, canola, and soya bean oil.

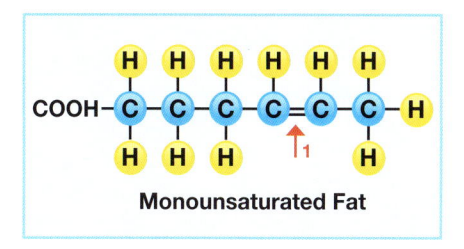

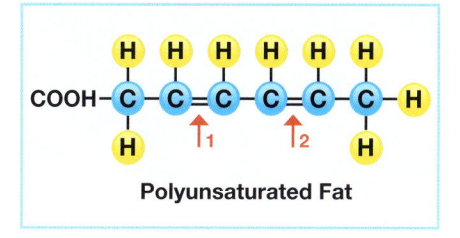

▲ Chemical composition of monounsaturated fat, polyunsaturated fat

Study tip

Learn the difference between a saturated fat and an unsaturated fat along with examples of each.

TYPE OF FAT	MONOUNSATURATED	POLYUNSATURATED	SATURATED
Almond Oil	73%	19%	8%
Avocado Oil	70%	10%	20%
Butter	30%	4%	66%
Canola Oil	62%	32%	6%
Cocoa Butter	35%	3%	62%
Coconut Oil	6% - Lowest	2% - Lowest (tie)	92% - Highest
Corn Oil	25%	62%	13%
Cottonseed Oil	26%	50%	24%
Grape Seed Oil	17%	71%	12%
Hazelnut Oil	76%	14%	10%
Lard	47%	12%	41%
Macadamia Nut Oil	83% - Highest	3%	14%
Margarine (Hard)	14%	16%	80%
Margarine (Soft)	47%	33%	20%
Mustard Oil	76%	23%	1% - Lowest
Olive Oil	77%	9%	14%
Palm Oil	38%	10%	52%
Palm Kernel Oil	12%	2% - Lowest (tie)	86%
Peanut Oil	49%	33%	18%
Rice Bran Oil	47%	33%	20%
Safflower Oil	13%	77% - Highest	10%
Sesame Oil	40%	46%	14%
Soya bean Oil	24%	61%	15%
Sunflower Oil	20%	69%	11%
Walnut Oil	19%	67%	14%
Wheat Germ Oil	30%	50%	20%

▲ Percentage of saturated and unsaturated fats in different fats and oils

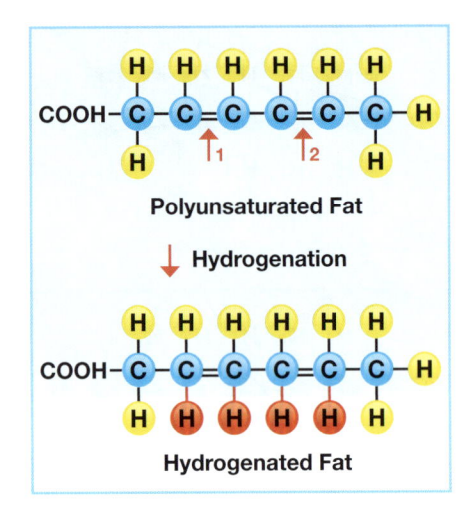

Hydrogenation of fats

Hydrogenation changes the chemical composition of vegetable oils so they become solid at room temperature. The hydrogenation process also produces trans-fatty acids, which converts the healthy unsaturated fats of the vegetable oils into solid saturated fats.

The primary advantage of hydrogenation is that hydrogenated fats are less likely to turn rancid, which is very beneficial to the commercial food industry in creating foods with a longer shelf life. As with any type of food containing saturated fat, foods containing hydrogenated or partially hydrogenated fat should be enjoyed in moderation in order to maintain a balanced and healthy diet.

There are concerns that trans-fatty acids are as bad, in terms of health-related issues, as naturally occurring saturated fats. Like saturated fat, trans-fat may raise blood cholesterol levels and increase the risk of heart related diseases. Many shortenings, margarines, and commercially baked goods are high in trans-fatty acids.

Tip for reducing fat in the diet

- Choose foods that are lower in fat, for example baked chips instead of fried.
- Use low fat Greek yogurt instead of cream.
- Reduce intake of processed meats like pork pies, sausage rolls and salami.
- Choose lean cuts of meat and trim off any visible fat.
- Grill, bake, poach or steam rather than frying and roasting so you don't need to add any extra fat.
- Choose lower fat versions of dairy foods whenever you can, such as semi-skimmed or skimmed milk, reduced fat yoghurt, low fat cheeses or very strong tasting cheese so you don't need to use as much.
- Try using yoghurt or fromage frais in recipes instead of cream or soured cream.

Polyunsaturated Fat → Hydrogenation → **Hydrogenated Fat**

Key point
Hydrogenation is the process of adding hydrogen to transform a liquid fat (or oil) into a solid one.

Study tip
Learn the meaning of hydrogenation and the arguments for and against hydrogenation.

Activity
Foods containing 'hidden' or 'invisible' fat include readymade foods such as pizzas, snack foods, biscuits, take away food and ready meals. Some foods such as doughnuts, samosas and fish cakes are cooked in fat which adds to fat content.

Investigate the foods in your kitchen at home. Check the labels for fat content and types of fat – saturated or unsaturated.

Key point
Fats and oils have a place in the diet but their intake must be controlled to avoid obesity and other diet related illnesses.

Study tip
Learn the importance of fats and oils in the diet. Suggest 6 ways of reducing fat in the diet.

WAYS TO REDUCE FAT IN YOUR DIET

344 COMMODITIES

FUNCTIONS OF FATS AND OILS

Required to **aerate** mixtures. When fat is creamed with sugar it helps trap air

Helps to **extend** the shelf life (makes the product last longer) of baked products. The fat helps the product keep its moisture, e.g. muffins

Gives shortening ability to a mixture and changes the texture. Fats give shortbread its characteristic crumbly and short texture

Acts as a **cooking medium** for roasting foods, e.g. chicken

Adds distinct **flavours** and aromas to food, e.g. biscuits

Prevents lumps of flour forming in sauce, e.g. parsley sauce

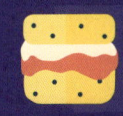

Oils form an **emulsion**, with liquids such as vinegar, e.g. salad dressings

Improves the **texture** of flaky and puff pastry. The fats help to separate layers by creating steam

Adds **colour** and shine to foods, e.g. scones

FS Fats are used for:

- Spreading on bread, toast, teacakes, for adding flavour, and to form a waterproof coating in sandwiches to prevent the filling from making the sandwich bread soggy.

- Creaming - when creamed with sugar, fats have the ability to trap tiny air bubbles which helps make mixtures rise.

- **Shortening** - a range of fats can be used in cake and pastry making. The fat coats the flour particles and this gives a waterproof coating to prevent the absorption of water and the gluten in the flour from developing layers between the strands of gluten. The pastry is shortened, giving a characteristic melt-in-the-mouth, crumbly, flaky texture. Fats give cakes a soft texture.

- Frying - oils are generally used for deep and shallow frying; butter and margarine are also suitable for shallow frying and stir frying depending on desired flavour and on personal choice.

- Making an **emulsion** - oils are specifically used in making salad dressings. The emulsification of fat occurs when the oil and vinegar (water based) are mixed with an emulsifying ingredient which stabilizes the mixture to form an emulsion.

Key point

All fats and oils have unique flavours and aromas.

Some are more suited for particular purposes than others.

Fats and oils contribute to the texture of food.

Check it

1 Explain the function of fat in the following recipes
   a Victoria sandwich cake
   b mayonnaise
   c short crust pastry
2 List the different functions of fats and oils in cooking.

Key point

The melting point and smoke point of fats and oils vary according to the composition of the fat and oil.

▲ Smoke point

▲ Flash point

Check it

What is the difference between the 'smoke point' and the 'flash point' when heating fats and oils?

Properties of fats and oils

Effect of heat on fats and oils

Fats and oils have different melting points. This explains why some are solid at room temperature. The melting point is determined by the type of fatty acid in the fat. The more saturated the fatty acid, the more solid the fat and the more unsaturated the fatty acid, the more liquid the fat.

Smoke point

When a fat is heated it melts and turns into a liquid oil. On further heating, it will give off smoke and eventually ignite (flash point). The temperature at which this occurs varies according to the type of fat or oil and is called the smoke point.

The **smoke point** of an oil or fat is the temperature at which it gives off a blue smoke. At this temperature the fat molecules start to split up and give the food being cooked an unpleasant flavour. The next stage is the **flash point**, where fat ignites and the food burns.

Cooking oil	Smoke point
Canola oil unrefined	107°c
Extra virgin olive oil	160°c
Canola oil refined	204°c
Grapeseed oil	204°c
Virgin olive oil	216°c
Peanut oil	231°c
Sesame oil refined	232°c
Soya bean oil	257°c
Corn oil	236°c
Avocado oil	271°c

Vegetable oils can generally be heated to higher temperatures because of their fatty acid content and their purity. Fats such as butter and margarine contain other substances such as water and emulsifiers and are not suitable for heating to high temperatures.

COMMODITIES

BUTTER, OIL, MARGARINE, SUGAR AND SYRUP

Rancidity [FS]

Foods containing a high proportion of fat such as cakes and biscuits are susceptible to rancidity. This happens when a fat starts to decompose and develops an unpleasant odour and 'off' flavour. It can be caused by the enzyme lipase in fat. The fat molecules break down and the resulting free fatty acids cause a bad odour and taste.

Exposure to oxygen can also cause rancidity. The oxygen is absorbed by the fat and it reacts with the fat molecules causing substances to be produced which give the bad taste and odour associated with fat which has 'gone off'.

Certain conditions such as light, impurities in the fat, enzymes and the presence of some polyunsaturated fatty acids can speed up this oxidation process.

Antioxidants are added to foods containing fat to prevent the process of rancidity.

Plasticity

All fats do not melt at the same temperature, but over a range of temperatures. This is called **plasticity**. It gives all fats their unique characteristics, such as the ability to spread easily when refrigerated, or a high melting point for cooking.

Aeration

Products such as creaming mixture for cakes need to have air incorporated into the mixture. This is achieved by creaming fat such as butter or margarine with caster sugar. Small bubbles of air are incorporated and form a stable foam which gives a well risen texture when cooked. **Aeration** is achieved by creaming a fat, such as butter or margarine with caster sugar. Small bubbles of air are incorporated and form a stable foam.

Check it

1. What causes fat to become rancid?
2. How should fats be stored?

Key point

The plasticity of fats is due to the mixture of triglycerides, each with its own melting point.

Study tip

Learn the meaning of flash point, smoke point, rancidity, plasticity and aeration. Explain the importance of each when using fats and oils in food preparation.

Activities

1. Comment on the appearance, softness, texture and consistency of different types of fats.
   a) Melt 25g of each fat and record the time it takes to melt completely, and whether it spits and smokes.
   b) Drop a 3cm cube of bread into each of the melted fats and record what happens immediately. Record the time it takes for the bread to turn golden brown and crisp.
2. Compare different fats for pastry making using the ratio half fat to flour.
3. Conduct a blindfold test for tasting and acceptability of different fats.

Key terms

Saturated fat – all of the carbon atoms in the fatty acid molecules are linked by single bonds.

Unsaturated fat – two or more of the carbon atoms are linked by a double bond.

Hydrogenation – the process of changing a liquid fat or oil to a solid one at room temperature by the addition of hydrogen.

Monounsaturated fat – containing only one double bond per molecule.

Polyunsaturated fat – containing more than one double bond per molecule.

Omega-3 and omega-6 – types of polyunsaturated fatty acid the body cannot make itself.

Cholesterol – a fatty substance known as a lipid which is found in blood and in food.

Sautéing – to fry quickly in a little hot fat or oil

Smoke point – the temperature at which it gives off a blue smoke. At this temperature the fat molecules start to split up and give the food being cooked an unpleasant flavour.

Nutritional supplement – adding dietary or nutritional value.

Condiments – substances added to give flavour or complement food.

Aeration – incorporating air into the mixture.

Shortening – a substance which gives a resulting characteristic crumbly texture in, for example, pastry, biscuits and shortbread.

Emulsion – when the oil and vinegar (water based) are mixed.

Plasticity – the ability of fat to hold its shape.

347

▲ Different types of sugar

SUGAR AND OTHER SWEETENERS

What will I learn?
- The types of sugar and other sweeteners available to the consumer
- The composition of sugar
- The nutritional value of sugar and other sweeteners in the diet
- The functions of sugar in food preparation and cooking
- Current issues with sugar consumption

Foods have been sweetened for thousands of years. The early sweeteners were natural ones such as honey. Sugar (sucrose) has been used for centuries as a preservative and flavouring in some parts of the world, such as India. It was only used in Europe from about 1200 onwards because it was an expensive item that only the very wealthy could afford. It did not really feature in the average person's diet until the late nineteenth century.

Since then sugar consumption in the UK has risen dramatically, and it is fast becoming one of the biggest dangers to public health. The World Health Organization now recommends that a person's daily calorie intake from sugar should not exceed 5%. However, the latest UK research figures suggest that adults are getting about 12% of their daily calories from sugar, and for teenagers it is an even higher 15%.

Other products which have sweetening properties include honey, molasses, the syrup family, for example barley malt, brown rice, cane, corn, maple, golden syrup (obtained from sugar cane or sugar beet), and sugar from the agave plant.

Artificial sweeteners were first developed in the late nineteenth century as low energy value substitutes for sucrose. Examples are saccharin, aspartame and sucralose. The use of these man-made sweeteners has not been without controversy. They have been linked to a range of health concerns including cancers and migraine.

Check it
Name three commonly used artificial sweeteners.

Many fizzy drinks contain large amounts of sugar – one 330ml can may have up to 9 teaspoons of sugar, or 35g! ▶

Sugar

Sugar is made from either sugar beet or sugar cane. Sugar beet is grown in countries with temperate climates, for example the UK. Sugar cane is grown in countries with a tropical climate, for example Brazil.

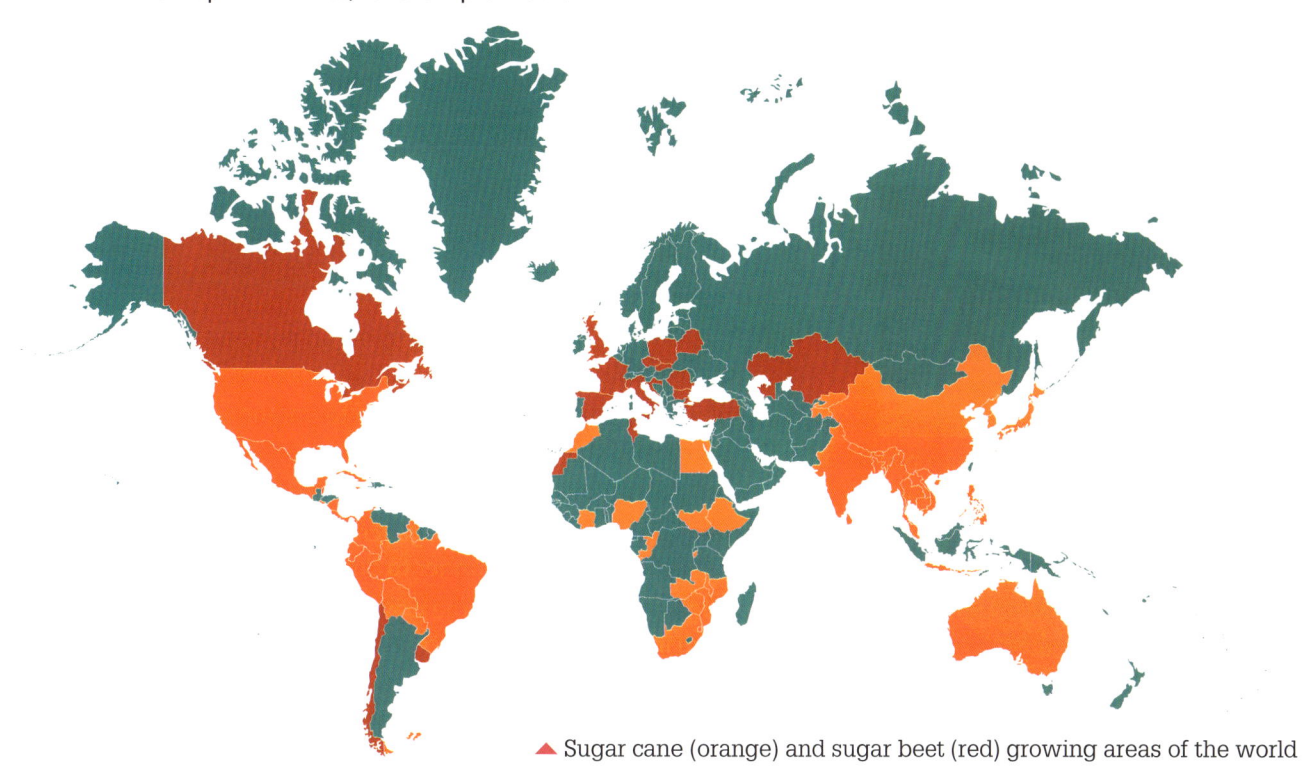

▲ Sugar cane (orange) and sugar beet (red) growing areas of the world

Extracting sugar

The sugar from cane is found in the soft fibres in the centre of the cane. To extract it, the fibres are first crushed then sprayed with water. This makes a solution containing sugar (sucrose), water and impurities. The impurities are removed until a clear, brown solution (molasses) is left. This contains a solution of sugar crystals and liquid. The liquid is spun off until what is left is raw sugar, brown in colour.

Beets store sugar in their root. To extract it, the beets are shredded and soaked in hot water. The solution obtained contains sugar, water and impurities. The impurities are removed and the water is evaporated to leave raw brown sugar.

Raw sugar contains sucrose in the form of sugar crystals and molasses. Sugar syrup is added to the raw sugar and the mixture is forced through a centrifuge. This process separates the crystals from the syrup, and they are then washed in water to remove impurities. The liquid is allowed to filter through bone charcoal to remove the colour, leaving a clear liquid.

The liquid is then evaporated to produce sugar crystals. The crystals are then washed again and centrifuged. The syrup that is spun off is used for the manufacture of golden syrup or soft brown sugar.

▲ Sugar cane

▲ Sugar beet

Check it

Describe granulated, caster and icing sugar.

Study tip

Can you name examples of white and brown sugars and, for each one, suggest uses in food preparation and cooking?

▲ Syrup being boiled in a pan

▲ Molasses

▲ Golden syrup

▲ Black treacle

▲ Sap being collected from a maple tree

Types of sugar

White sugar

- **Granulated sugar** is made following the process described above.
- **Caster sugar** is made in the same way but the process is modified to produce small, fine crystals.
- **Icing sugar** is made by pulverising granulated sugar into a very fine powder.

Brown sugar

Brown sugar is made by crystallising the syrup obtained at the end of the refining process. It is moister than white sugar. There are several types of brown sugar, including:

- **soft brown** (dark or light)
- **demerara** has larger crystals and is traditionally served with coffee and used for cake making
- **muscovado** is a type of partially refined to unrefined brown sugar with a strong molasses flavour.

Other types of sugar include:

- **Coffee sugar crystals** are large sugar crystals, sometimes sold in mixes of different colours. They take longer to dissolve than other sugars.
- **Lump sugar** is made in the same way as granulated sugar, but the crystals are poured into special moulds, cooled until solid and then cut into cubes or lumps.

Syrups

Black treacle is made from molasses. It is a thick, heavy and dark coloured syrup with a strong flavour.

Golden syrup is refined, light syrup with a gold colour. Some of the sugar it contains is **invert sugar**. This is produced when sugar is heated with water and weak acid. This splits the complex sugar (sucrose) into two simpler sugars (glucose and fructose) which, together, make invert sugar. Invert sugar is sweeter than sucrose, which is why golden syrup is very sweet.

The mixture is sold as a viscous liquid and is often referred to as trimoline or invert syrup. Compared to sucrose, the components in invert sugar (glucose and fructose) tend to retain moisture and are less prone to crystallization.

Invert sugar is automatically produced when making jams by combining the sugar with the acid in the fruit and heating. Most of the sugar in honey is also invert sugar. The food industry makes extensive use of it. It is hygroscopic – this means that it absorbs moisture from the surrounding environment – and consequently adds to the shelf life of the product.

Maple syrup is made from the sap (a sugary fluid) of maple trees. It is generally made using a natural process in which a hole is drilled in the maple tree which allows the sap to leak out. It is then collected into a container. The sap is boiled until most of the water evaporates, leaving a thick sugary syrup, which is then filtered to remove impurities. Over 80% of the world's supply is now produced in Canada.

Honey

Bees produce honey from the nectar they collect from various flowers. During its passage through the bee's body, enzymes convert the sugars into simple sugar, mainly glucose and fructose, which is stored in honeycombs.

Honey has been used for sweetening through the ages. It was valued as a natural sweetener long before sugar became widely available in the sixteenth century.

Honey is usually named after the flower from which the nectar was taken, for example clover, lavender or orange blossom.

The flavour, colour and consistency of honey varies: as a general rule, the darker the colour, the stronger the flavour. Honey colours range from golden to dark brown. It can be clear and runny or thick and opaque. It is sold in jars, in honeycomb form, or as a chunk of honeycomb suspended in runny honey.

Honey is slightly lower on the Glycaemic Index (GI) than sugar so it is absorbed into the body at a slightly slower rate. Honey is also higher in calories than regular refined cane sugar. A teaspoon of commercial natural honey contains about 22 calories, whereas a teaspoon of refined sugar has around 16 calories.

Honey has medical properties and it can be used as a cough mixture, as well as having antioxidant, antibacterial and antifungal properties. These make it ideal for treating some open wounds. Manuka honey is made with pollen gathered from the flowers of the Manuka tree (a medicinal plant found in Australia and New Zealand) and is said to be especially beneficial.

Check it
List four ways in which honey can be used in food preparation.

Key point
Invert sugar is produced when sugar is heated with water and acid – this process occurs in jam making.

▲ Honey can be thick and opaque (left) or very clear and runny and may have the honeycomb in the jar too (right)

THE USES OF Honey

- Honey is excellent spread on bread.

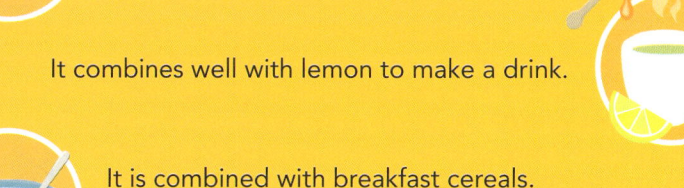

- It combines well with lemon to make a drink.

- It is combined with breakfast cereals, usually as a coating.

- It is used as the 'sweet' ingredient in sweet-sour mixtures for meat, fish or poultry.

- It combines with flour and fat to produce attractive baked goods such as Turkish baklava.

- It is used for curing ham. It can also be spread on the outside of ham, duck etc. before cooking to make a crispy coating.

> **Key point**
>
> There are many types of artificial sweeteners which provide a low/no calorie substitute for sugar.

> **Check it**
>
> Explain the benefits of using artificial sweeteners in food products. Can you think of any disadvantages to using them?

Artificial sweeteners

These are commonly known as low calorie sweeteners, no-calorie sweeteners, non-nutritive sweeteners, sugar replacers or artificial sweetener replacements.

Artificial sweeteners are synthetically produced food additives which offer sweetness without calories. They are so intensely sweet that they must be diluted with fillers like dextrose or maltodextrin to give a similar sweetness and bulk as sugar. They provide no energy and pass through the body undigested.

Almost all artificial sweeteners have a distinct aftertaste, but regular users find them to be good sugar substitutes in drinks. They may mimic the taste of sugar in a hot drink, but they are not suitable for food preparation and cooking because:

- they lack in bulk and, as a result, cakes sweetened with artificial sweeteners are very dense in comparison with cakes sweetened with ordinary sugar
- they don't melt like sugar, so the resulting cake texture is often dense, dry, and lumpy, more like that of a biscuit than cake.

Three of the most well-known brands are Sweet'N Low, Nutrasweet, and Splenda. Examples of other artificial sweeteners used in food production include:

NAME OF ARTIFICIAL SWEETENER	DESCRIPTION	USES
Acesulfame potassium or acesulfame K	A zero-calorie sweetener up to 200 times sweeter than sugar. It is often blended with sucralose and used to decrease the bitter aftertaste of aspartame.	A wide range of low-calorie foods and drinks contain acesulfame K, including table top sweeteners, chewing gum, jam, dairy products, frozen desserts, drinks and baked goods.
Aspartame	A combination of the two amino acids, aspartic acid and phenylalanine, it is 160–220 times sweeter than sugar and contains 4kcal per gram.	Cereals, sugar-free chewing gum, low-calorie (diet) soft drinks and table top sweeteners.
Saccharin, sold under the brand name Sweetex	The oldest artificial sweetener, it is calorie free and 300–400 times sweeter than sugar. Some people find it has a bitter or metallic aftertaste.	A wide variety of foods and drinks have saccharin added to them, including baked goods, chewing gum, drinks and table top sweeteners. It is also used in cosmetic products (such as toothpaste, mouthwash and lip gloss), as well as vitamins and medications.
Sucralose	Derived from sugar, it is calorie free and up to 650 times sweeter than sugar. It is valued for having no bitter aftertaste and is often mixed with other sweetening ingredients that are not calorie-free, such as dextrose or maltodextrin, in order to dilute its intense sweetness.	It is found in a broad range of low calorie foods, including table top sweeteners, fizzy drinks, chewing gum, baking mixes, breakfast cereals and salad dressings.

BUTTER, OIL, MARGARINE, SUGAR AND SYRUP

NAME OF ARTIFICIAL SWEETENER	DESCRIPTION	USES
Sorbitol	Chemically extracted from glucose, this low-calorie sweetener is available in powder and liquid form. It occurs naturally in certain fruit, such as apples and pears, stoned fruit, such as peaches and apricots, and dried fruit, such as prunes and raisins. Sorbitol is a **polyol** – a type of carbohydrate generally manufactured from sugars (such as dextrose). Sorbitol has the look and feel of sugar, but with 60% the sweetness and 30% fewer calories (2.6kcal/g, compared to 4kcal/g for sugar). It has a mouth-cooling sensation, with virtually no aftertaste.	Sorbitol helps food stay moist, making it a useful ingredient in the production of confectionery, baked goods and chocolate. The use of polyols in soft drinks is banned in the EU because of their laxative effect.
Stevia-based sweeteners, whose brand names include Truvia, PureVia, SweetLeaf, Rebiana, Sun Crystals	It is made from the purified extracts (steviol glycosides) of the leaves from the stevia plant, which is native to Paraguay. Stevia is a virtually calorie-free sweetener that is 200 times sweeter than sugar. Even though it is derived from a plant, some consider it artificial because it is so highly refined. Pure stevia can only be purchased from health-food retailers.	Used for baking, steviol glycosides are approved for use in sugar-free soft drinks, jams, flavoured milk and other dairy products, cakes, desserts and alcohol, among other things.
Tagatose, sold under the brand name PreSweet	It is a naturally occurring sweetener found in milk which has become used as a sweetener in recent years. Like some yogurt, it contains probiotics, which are claimed to help good bacteria. It is 92% as sweet as sugar, with only a third of the calories. It has a clean neutral taste, and browns very well when used in baked goods.	Used in baking, although it tends to have a gummy texture with a slightly sour finish.
Xylito Brand names include XyloSweet, XyloPure, Miracle Sweet, Nature's Provision	It is 5% less sweet than sugar, but has 40% fewer calories and a low Glycaemic Index. It is primarily extracted from corncobs and hardwoods. The bulk of xylitol is made from corn imported from China and is available in both powder and liquid form. A variety of fruits and vegetables such as plums, strawberries and cauliflower contain naturally occurring xylitol. The human body can produce a small amount.	Used in baking, Xylitol looks like sugar, tastes like sugar, responds like sugar and has no aftertaste.

The composition of sugar [FS]

Sugars are carbohydrates which provide fuel (energy). The term sugar covers the full range of mono and disaccharide molecules.

Monosaccharides

Monosaccharides are single molecules of sugar. The most common monosaccharides in the diet are: glucose, fructose and galactose.

Glucose – also known as dextrose – is a monosaccharide found naturally in fruit and vegetables. It is used in confectionery and baking as glucose syrups.

Fructose occurs naturally in fruits, vegetables and honey and is used in fruit preparations and dairy products.

Galactose is part of lactose which is the sugar found in milk.

Disaccharides

Disaccharides are two linked sugar molecules which are broken down into monosaccharides by digestion. Sucrose, lactose and maltose are disaccharides.

Sucrose is glucose + fructose, also known as table sugar (such as granulated, caster or demerara sugar). It is used in confectionery, cakes, biscuits, jams and preserves.

Lactose is glucose and galactose, and occurs naturally in milk and dairy products. It is used in dairy and dry mixes such as instant soups.

Maltose is glucose and glucose, and occurs naturally in germinating seeds such as barley. It is used in malted drinks and beers, and glucose syrups for confectionery and baking.

The nutritional value of sugar in the diet

Sugar is often described as having 'empty calories', meaning that it adds no nutrients to the diet. Yet in the UK the average person eats 38kg of sugar a year. Sugars are a source of energy to the body, and are digested and absorbed relatively quickly.

All sugars and starches are classed as carbohydrates. Starches have to be digested into sugars before their energy can be released. Energy from starches is released more slowly than from sugars. Eating more carbohydrates (or any sugar) than the body requires will lead to excess fat being stored in the body.

'Hidden sugar' can be found in readymade foods such as bread, soups, sauces, fruit-flavoured yoghurts and breakfast cereals. Hidden sugars are ingredients that are present in food and drink but may not be recognised as sugar because they do not taste sweet. Even so, they can contribute to excess calories and can cause tooth decay.

If you read the nutritional labels on food packaging you will see how much sugar there is in any food product. Remember that there are different names for 'sugar' such as glucose syrup, corn syrup or sucrose.

> **Study tip**
>
> Learn the difference between monosaccharides and disaccharides, then learn which types of sugar are monosaccharides and disaccharides.

BUTTER, OIL, MARGARINE, SUGAR AND SYRUP

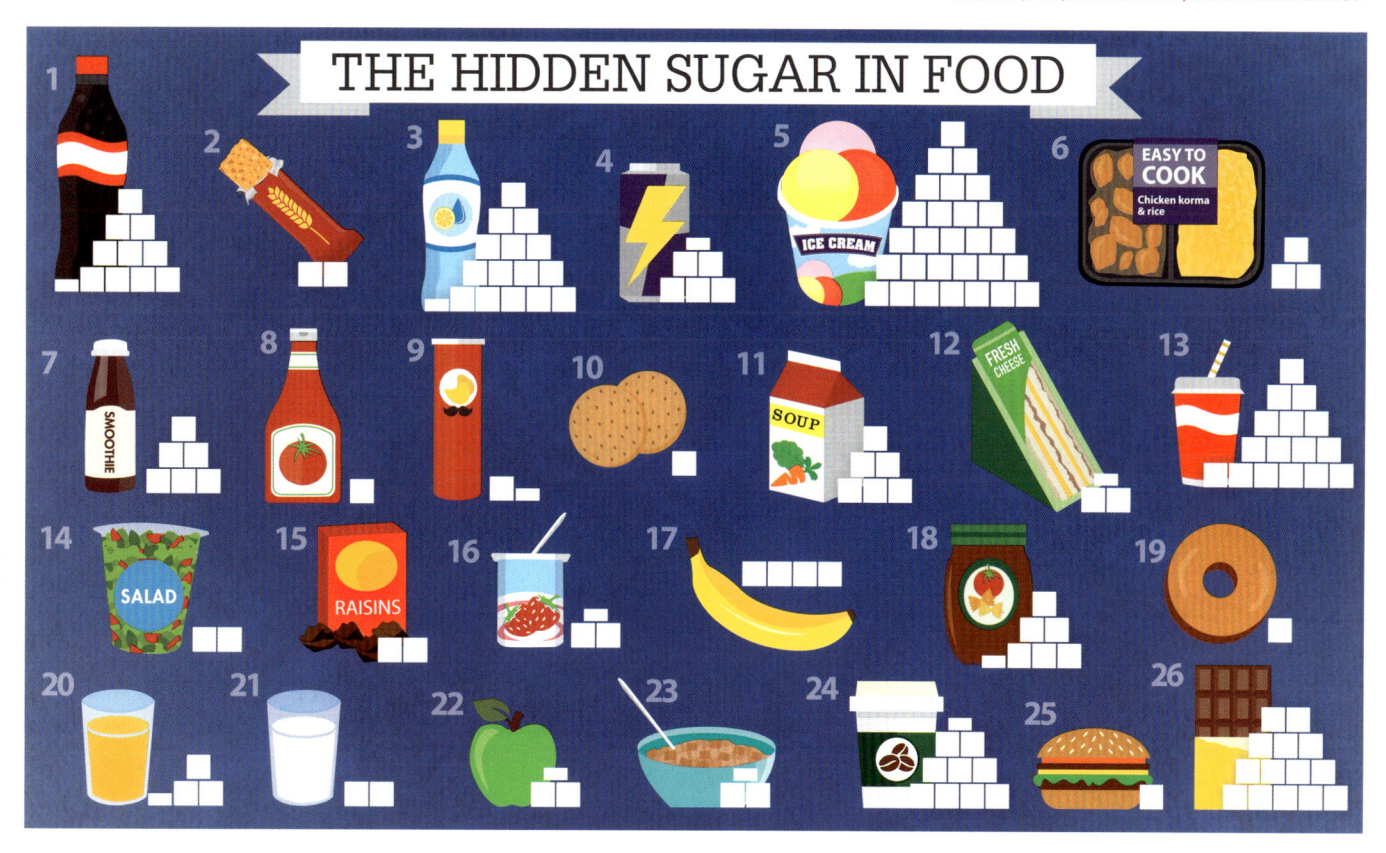

THE HIDDEN SUGAR IN FOOD

The Glycaemic Index (GI) measures how fast carbohydrate-containing foods cause the level of blood glucose (blood sugar) to rise. Foods that are absorbed slowly have a low GI rating, while foods that are more quickly absorbed have a higher rating.

Low GI diets have been associated with reducing the risk of health issues including cardiovascular disease, type 2 diabetes and strokes.

Low GI – <55   **Medium GI – 56 to 69**   **High GI – >70**

Recent figures show that, on average, a person in the UK obtains about 15% of their total energy from sugar. Health experts have been calling to halve the current recommendation for sugar consumption to 30g a day or just 5% of total energy. The widespread use of extrinsic sugars (free or added sugars, including milk sugars) is causing health concerns. These sugars are found typically in products such as sugar-sweetened drinks, sweets and cakes. They are also often found in many processed products such as ready made meals and fruit juices.

Clinical trials have shown links between free sugars and health problems such as type 2 diabetes, obesity and tooth decay and cavities, especially in children. Several options have been proposed to tackle these health issues, including:

- a reduction in the marketing of high sugar products
- a proposed tax on sugary drinks
- better labelling of sugar content on all food in order to help shoppers make a more informed choice.

Check it

What is meant by 'empty calories' and 'hidden calories'?

Extension

1 Many leading supermarkets are making an effort to encourage consumers to reduce sugar intake. Could they do more?

2 Should the Government regulate the sugar content of food products aimed at children and teenagers?

Key point

Sugar contains empty calories. It has no nutritional value.

Key point

Food labels contain useful nutritional information to assist consumers in planning healthy diets and balanced meals.

Study tip

List 10 ways to reduce the sugar intake in the diet.

▲ Sugar content, as specified on food label

Nutrition labelling N

Nutrition labels often tell you how much sugar a food contains. By comparing labels on your preferred food products you can choose foods that are lower in sugar.

Some labels list the information under different headings – for instance, look for the 'Carbohydrates (of which sugars)' figure in the nutrition label.

- high – over 22.5g of total sugars per 100g
- low – 5g of total sugars or less per 100g

If the amount of sugars per 100g is between these figures, that is regarded as a medium level.

Nutrition labels also use red, amber and green colour-coding and advice on reference intakes (RI) of some nutrients, which can include sugar. These allow you to see at a glance if the food is high, medium or low in sugars.

- **red** = high
- **amber** = medium
- **green** = low

NUTRITION LABELLING ON PACKAGING

Sugar free – this means less than 0.5 g sugar per serving

Reduced sugar – this means that the sugar content of the product has been reduced by at least 25%

No sugar added – as it suggests, no sugar or any other ingredient containing sugar has been added to the product

Low sugar – this means the product has less than 5g of sugar per 100g

356 COMMODITIES

BUTTER, OIL, MARGARINE, SUGAR AND SYRUP

Tips to help *reduce* sugar intake

Gradually reduce the amount added to drinks and breakfast cereals until sugar can be eliminated altogether.

Instead of sugary fizzy drinks or sugary squash, choose water, lower fat milks, or sugar free, diet and no added sugar drinks. Remember that even unsweetened fruit juice is sugary, so limit the amount you have to no more than 150ml a day.

Check nutrition labels for sugar content, or go for the low sugar version.

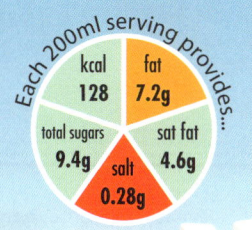

Each 200ml serving provides...
kcal 128 | fat 7.2g
total sugars 9.4g | sat fat 4.6g
salt 0.28g

Try diluting fruit juice with sparkling water for a low sugar fizzy option.

Choose tinned fruit in natural juice rather than syrup.

Swap cakes or biscuits for a currant bun, scone or some malt loaf with low-fat spread.

Try a lower-fat spread, sliced banana or low-fat cream cheese on toast instead of jam, marmalade or syrup.

Choose wholegrain breakfast cereals, not those coated with sugar or honey.

The function of sugar and other sweeteners in food preparation and cooking [FS]

Sugars occur naturally in fruit, vegetables and dairy foods, as well as being an ingredient used in a wide range of food and drinks.

Sugar and other sweeteners are used in food preparation and cooking for the following reasons:

Adding sweetness

Used in recipes, a sweetener such as sugar makes food products more acceptable to eat and drink.

The sweet flavour of sugar is used to:

- reduce the acidity/sharpness of food, for example when sprinkled on grapefruit or when added to stewed rhubarb
- improve the flavour of some foods, for example the natural flavour of fruit is enhanced by the addition of sugar
- sweeten a variety of drinks and products, including some manufactured products such as baked beans.

▲ Sugar is added to sweeten foods

Adding texture

Sugar softens the gluten in baked products when they are cooked and this adds a soft crumb with a moist texture. Sugar is attracted to water i.e. it is **hygroscopic**. This property means that sugar helps products stay moist. This keeps them in good condition for longer, so they have a longer shelf life and keep their texture and mouth feel longer. Bread and cakes are good examples of this.

▲ Sugar is one of the main ingredients in baked goods like biscuits. It is also used in decorating icing

SECTION 3

357

Alternatively, if treacle or a syrup is included in a recipe, the type of sugar they contain absorbs a lot of moisture from the atmosphere, i.e. it acts as a humectant. Honey is also a humectant. This is why products made with golden syrup, treacle or honey (such as gingerbread, parkin or honey cake) keep moist and in good condition for a long time.

The water-attracting property of sugar also helps to make baked products tender. This is because the sugar takes up some of the water that would otherwise be taken up by the protein in flour. Gluten development is reduced and a more tender, soft crumb is produced as a result.

Sugar also helps to tenderise meat. It can be added to a marinade in which the meat soaks or it may be sprinkled on its surface.

Adding colour

Sugar caramelises when heated and gives the brown colour associated with baked products such as cakes and pastries. Sugar helps to give products colour. When it is heated as a liquid it begins to turn brown when the temperature reaches 154°C. This is called caramelisation.

Another type of browning occurs when sugar and amino acids 'work' together in baked products. This is called non-enzymic browning or the Maillard reaction.

As a raising agent

When fat and sugar are creamed together, or eggs and sugar are whisked together to make cakes, the sugar aids in the aeration process by trapping air. For instance, when making meringues the sugar makes the egg white foam more stable.

Aeration makes mixtures light and risen. When sugar is added to fat and creamed, the crystals of sugar mix with the fat and the air which is beaten into the mixture sticks to the crystals. The fat surrounds the air bubbles and 'traps' them in the mixture. The large numbers of fine crystals in caster sugar give the best results because more crystals mean that more air bubbles are produced in the mixture.

For preservation

Sugar is a main ingredient in preservation. It gives jam, jelly, marmalade and chutney a longer shelf life – the sugar solution in each product actually acts as a preservative. Sugar is also used as a preservative in the bottling and freezing of fruit.

Very concentrated solutions of sugar in water can be produced. They are called heavy syrups. Organisms that spoil food such as yeast and moulds cannot live in these heavy syrups. This is why they are used to lengthen the shelf life of fruits.

Fermentation

Sugar helps to speed up the action of yeast during bread, wine or beer making. Sugar speeds up the production of carbon dioxide (the fermentation process in bread making). A small amount of sugar provides food for the yeast and gets it working quickly. The yeast attacks the sugar and carbon dioxide is produced more quickly. If too much sugar is added the process slows down.

▲ Sugar browns to produce a caramel

▲ Sugar has the ability to help aerate a mixture

▲ Sugar as a preservative

▲ Sugar speeds up fermentation of yeast

BUTTER, OIL, MARGARINE, SUGAR AND SYRUP

Coagulation

Sugar increases the coagulation temperature of eggs and gluten in a mixture. This means that the gas cells in a mixture have more time to expand before the mixture sets, thus achieving a more risen, lighter result.

Sugar helps to avoid curdling in products such as egg custards, because it raises the temperature at which the egg proteins coagulate.

Sugar can also decrease the thickness (viscosity) of starch based puddings and sauces. It raises the temperature at which thickening takes place. The product becomes thinner on cooling.

Foaming

Sugar helps foams such as meringues to remain stable. This means that the air beaten into the egg white is not easily lost. The foam is **stabilised** (strengthened) by the sugar, and can be piped or spread without the air bubbles bursting.

Enzymic browning

Adding sugar syrup to raw fruit prevents it turning brown. It protects the surface of the fruit from oxygen in the air and prevents enzymic browning occurring.

Some recipes involve heating sugar solutions to a very high temperature. The temperature plays an important part in the success of recipes.

▲ Coagulation in an egg custard

▲ Egg white and sugar foam

Boiling temperature	Properties	Uses
104°C	large gloss	jam, marmalade, jelly
107°C	thread	sugar syrups, some icings, Italian meringues
115°C	soft ball	fudge, fondants
118-121°C	hard ball	caramels, nougat, soft toffee
138°C	crack	toffee
143-149°C	hard crack	butterscotch, nut brittle, barley sugar
155-190°C	caramel	for lining dishes and moulds, for colouring sauces, soups

⌐ Key terms

Invert sugar – the process of converting sugar into simple sugars.
Glycaemic index – the impact of a carbohydrate food on blood sugar level.
Hygroscopic – attracted to water.
Tenderise – to make softer.
Caramelisation – a change in the molecular structure due to the removal of water.
Non-enzymic browning / Maillard reaction – when sugar and amino acids react to change the colour of a food.
Enzymic browning – colour change caused by the reaction between enzymes and oxygen.
Aeration – incorporating air into the mixture.
Coagulation – setting.
Yeasts - a microorganism belonging to the fungi family, made up of single oval cells that reproduce by budding. Yeast can ferment sugar in to alcohol and carbon dioxide and is also used as a raising agent when making bread.
Moulds – a type of fungi.
Polyols – a group of versatile, reduced-calorie carbohydrates that provide the taste and texture of sugar with about half the calories.

Check it

Sugar is an essential ingredient in many recipes.

Identify four recipes which use sugar and explain its role in each recipe.

Activities

Making sugar solutions

1. Mix 1 tablespoon sugar with 1 tablespoon water and gently heat without stirring until the sugar dissolves. Take great care as sugar solutions can burn!
2. Continue heating gently, noting any further changes to colour, consistency and aroma.
3. Repeat 1 but stir the solution while it is boiling.
4. Repeat 1 but add a little cream of tartar.
5. Repeat 1 but use 100g sugar and 50ml water. Drop small samples into a jug of water at 10°C intervals from 110°C to 180°C. Squeeze the samples and note the flavour and texture of each.

EXAM QUESTIONS

1. Describe the functions of fat in the body. [6]

2. a) State the difference between fats and oils. [2]
   b) Explain the factors which influence consumer choice when buying fats and oils [8]

3. a) Name two plant sources and two animal sources of fat

   Plant: 1

   2

   Animal: 1

   2 [4]

   b) Suggest a fat or oil for the following, giving a reason for each choice:

   (i) rubbing in

   choice of fat or oil _____

   reason _____

   (ii) creaming mixture cake

   choice of fat or oil _____

   reason _____

   (iii) deep fat frying

   choice of fat or oil _____

   reason _____

   (iv) stir frying

   choice of fat or oil _____

   reason _____ [8]

4. Describe the effect of heat on fat. [4]

5. Explain the function of sugar in the following basic recipes: [8]
   - crème caramel
   - Swiss Roll
   - meringues
   - jam making

6. Sugar is an example of a sweetener. Identify other types of sugars and sweeteners available to the consumer and suggest how each can be used in food preparation. [10]

7. Discuss the role of sugar in the diet. [8]

8. Give a different example of how each of the following types of sugar and sweeteners can be used in food preparation and cooking: [6]
   a) caster sugar
   b) soft brown sugar
   c) demerara sugar
   d) golden syrup
   e) honey
   f) maple syrup

9. Recent Government advice is to 'limit the consumption of fruit juice and smoothies to no more than a combined total of 150ml a day'.
   Assess this advice. [8]

TOTAL: 72

FOOD INVESTIGATIONS

The following investigative approach can be used as a group activity with any of the basic recipes suggested.

Comparison of different sugars and sweeteners used to make creamed cake mixtures, egg white foams, smoothies, biscuit making.

Compare different sugars and sweeteners in terms of their:
- appearance
- colour
- texture
- ability to aerate the mixture
- cost.

Produce a sensory profile, a taste test or preference test for each sample. Record your findings.

Investigation 1   Comparing how different sugars and sweeteners perform in a creaming mixture

For the control recipe you will need:

50g margarine
50g caster sugar
1 egg, beaten
50g self-raising flour, sieved
9 paper cases

Method

1. Pre-heat the oven to 190°C or gas mark 5.
2. Line a bun tray with 9 bun cases.
3. Place the margarine and sugar in a mixing bowl. Cream the mixture until light and fluffy.
4. Slowly add the beaten egg and mix thoroughly.
5. Add the flour and fold in.
6. Place a heaped tablespoonful of mixture into each paper case.
7. Bake for 15–20 minutes until the cakes are golden brown and well risen.

Follow the same recipe and process for the next 6 batches, but instead of using 50g sugar, use:

5g of Canderel
5g of Sucron
4 tbsp. of Splenda
50g of Stevia
50g of granulated sugar
50g of demerara sugar
50g of soft brown sugar

Investigation 2   Comparing sensory attributes of fats and the effect of heat on fats

Collect samples of different solid (block type) cooking fats.

Examine and comment on appearance, softness, texture (plasticity), ingredients added during manufacture.

Melt each type of fat and record
- the time it takes to melt completely
- whether it melts easily, spits, smokes.

Drop a 3cm cube of bread into each melted fat and record
- what happens immediately
- the time it takes for the bread to become crisp and brown

Investigation 3
Tasting test on different spreads

Choose four different spreads and label them A-D. Spread crackers with an even layer of each spread.

Carry out a blindfold test using a sample group of 6 to 8 tasters.

Each taster will rank the four spreads in order of preference and number them 1 – 4 (with 1 being the best).

Record the results in a chart.

Which spread do you like best?	A	B	C	D
Taster 1				
Taster 2				
Taster 3				
Taster 4				
(etc.)				

Investigation 4   Comparing the suitability of different cooking oils for frying

Choose a selection of cooking oils.

Heat each variety of oil in a pan until it reaches 180ºC. Record the time it takes for each variety of oil to reach this temperature.

Drop a 3cm cube of bread into the hot oil and note the time it takes for the bread to become brown and crispy.

Taste each sample and place in order of preference.

Which cooking oil would you recommend for frying and why?

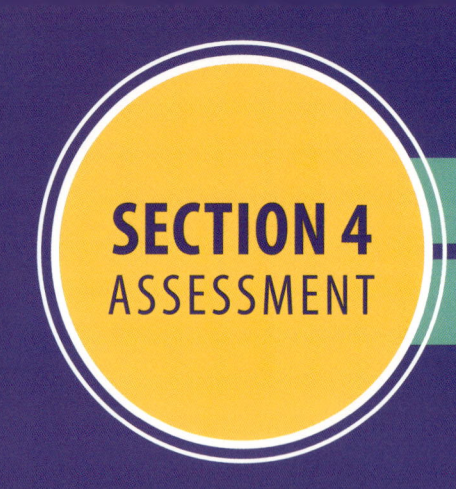

SECTION 4: ASSESSMENT

PART ONE: THE WRITTEN EXAM

What will I learn?
This chapter will guide you through how you will be assessed for your written examination.

Key point
This GCSE is a linear specification. This means that all assessments must be completed in your final academic year. For most students this will be in year 11, although in some schools this may be different – if you are not sure, ask your teacher.

Assessment overview – a reminder

Before we start, please note that students in Wales will be entered for the WJEC qualification which is called GCSE Food and Nutrition.

Two assessment components

1	Written examination	UNIT 1: wjec cbac Principles of Food and Nutrition 40% of the qualification
2	Two non-examination assessments (NEAs) These are the 2 assessed pieces of work you do in your final year of the course.	Unit 2: wjec cbac Food and Nutrition in Action (i) Assessment 1: The Food Investigation Assessment 20% of the qualification (ii) Assessment 2: The Food Preparation Assessment 40% of the qualification

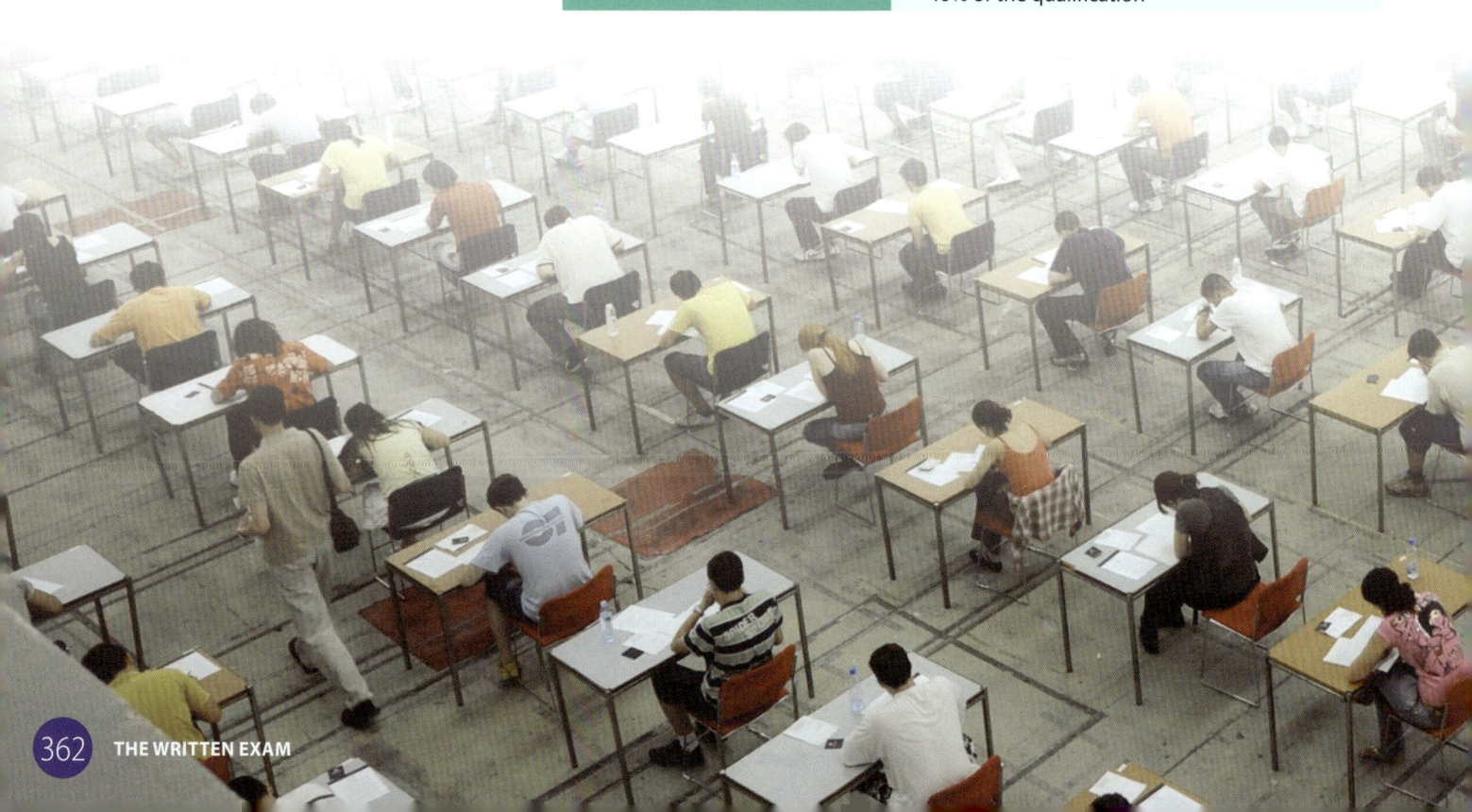

How will you be assessed?

Both the written exam and the two NEAs will be assessed using the following criteria:

	Assessment Objectives
AO1	Demonstrate knowledge and understanding of food, cooking and nutrition
AO2	Apply knowledge and understanding of food, cooking and nutrition
AO3	Plan, prepare, cook and present dishes, combining appropriate techniques
AO4	Analyse and evaluate different aspects of food, cooking and nutrition, including food made by yourself and others

Here is the percentage breakdown for each assessment for Wales:

Unit	Assessment				
	AO1	AO2	AO3	AO4	Total
Unit 1 Written examination	15%	15%	–	10%	40%
Unit 2 Assessment 1 (The Food Investigation Assessment)	–	15%	–	5%	20%
Unit 2 Assessment 2 (The Food Preparation Assessment)	–	–	35%	5%	40%
	15%	30%	35%	20%	100%

The written exam

UNIT 1: Principles of Food and Nutrition
1 hour 30 minutes
80 marks
40% of the qualification

Unit	Assessment				
	AO1	AO2	AO3	AO4	Total
Unit 1 Written examination	15%	15%	–	10%	40%

This unit will consist of **two** sections both containing **compulsory questions** and will assess the **six areas of content** listed below (and covered in this book).

Areas of content:
1 Food commodities
2 Principles of nutrition
3 Diet and good health
4 The science of food
5 Where food comes from
6 Cooking and food preparation

Section A (12 marks): questions based on stimulus materials.

Section B (68 marks): a range of question types to assess all content related to food and nutrition.

This textbook covers all the areas of content that you need for GCSE Food and Nutrition. We have included sample examination questions at the end of each main commodity in the book to help you. This chapter gives you worked examples and explains the examination and assessment requirements in more detail, as well as giving you lots of tips and pointers to help you through this process.

Understand the exam

Unit 1 **wjec cbac**

What will I learn?

- How the exam paper is structured, including sample exam questions and worked examples
- About the different styles of exam questions that will be included in the written exam
- The topic areas that you will be tested on during the written exam
- The relevance of Assessment Objectives (AOs) when exam questions are written and marked
- Useful hints and tips to maximise your exam success

The exam structure

The written exam is a compulsory element and you will be tested on the **six areas of content** listed in the introduction to this chapter.

The format of the paper will always be the same. **ALL QUESTIONS ARE COMPULSORY** and there are **two sections** called **Section A and Section B.**

The written exam will use the following assessment criteria:

	Assessment Objectives
AO1	Demonstrate knowledge and understanding of food, cooking and nutrition
AO2	Apply knowledge and understanding of food, cooking and nutrition
AO4	Analyse and evaluate different aspects of food, cooking and nutrition, including food made by yourself and others

Section A

Questions based on **stimulus materials** – the stimulus materials are a visual prompt. Examples could be pictures of stages during the making of a dish, such as for example, the making of a cake, or a mood board showing dishes made with shortcrust pastry.

SECTION A VISUAL STIMULI
Cake making

Section B

In Section B you will be asked a range of questions, some will ask you to write brief answers, other questions will require longer answers with more discussion and explanation within your answers.

Note however that you will find:

- Questions that ask for **extended writing** will take place throughout the paper
- When questions require extended writing the marks will be split across the assessment objectives (AOs), for example, an 8 mark question may be split as follows:
  - 4 marks for AO1 – demonstrate knowledge
  - 4 marks for AO2 – apply knowledge
- See pages 366 to 378 to show you examples of the types of questions that can be asked in Sections A and B.

UNDERSTAND THE EXAM

Types of questions

- **Data response questions** – these will have data or information that you have to respond to. You will be given some kind of information, for instance nutritional information from food packaging, a recipe or a graph. The questions will be linked to the data provided.
- **Structured questions** – there will be space given for you to write your answers and the marks allocated will be placed next to where you need to write your answer. The amount of space will give you a guide as to how much you are expected to write.
- **Graduated lead-in questions** – these will have a question worth 1 or 2 marks at the beginning, which then leads in to a longer marked question, often with 6 or 8 marks.
- **Free response questions** – these are usually the longer questions where the question often includes command words such as assess, describe, discuss, explain or evaluate. These are generally what are referred to as 'the mini essay style questions'.

We give you examples of all question types on pages 366–378.

What are examiners looking for when marking the paper?

There are clear guidelines for the examination system: these are freely available so that candidates, teachers and examiners know what is expected and how marks will be awarded. These can be seen on specimen assessment materials (SAMs) and on previous markschemes for past papers. The examiner wants you to write clearly and to the point.

- **Answer the question**

  Examiners are only allowed to credit answers that are relevant to the question. Don't be tempted to write down everything you know about a topic – you need to structure your writing to make sure what you are saying clearly answers the question.

- **Write a clear and logical response to the question or command**

  This means that your response has a structure; this should be absolutely clear to whoever reads it.

  When you are asked to:
  - list
  - state

  then you are able to write one word or short sentence answers.

  When you are asked to:
  - discuss
  - explain
  - evaluate

  your answer should be longer, you should be using full sentences and should be linking your discussion back to the question.

  The clue is in the mark allocation – the more marks linked to a question the more likelihood you will have to form a discussion, with suggestions or examples in your answers.

Guidance for the written examination

- Follow the instructions given on the front of the exam paper
  - Use black ink or black ball-point pen
  - Do not use pencil or gel pen
  - Do not use correction fluid.
- Read each question carefully and highlight or underline key words. Read each question several times before you start answering the question, make sure you understand the question
- Write as legibly as possible and do not use text speak
- Write clearly on any additional continuation pages which question you are continuing to answer. (Your paper is likely to be scanned for marking so it's important that any continuation sheets are clearly identifiable.)
- One word answers are only acceptable for question types that ask for this type of response, e.g. "name one type of pastry".
- Remember that there are different question types in Sections A and B. Many questions test understanding as well as knowledge; you are likely to be asked to assess or evaluate, rather than just list or explain a topic area. You should practise applying your knowledge in this style of question – try not to use bullet points. This can look the same as writing a list, therefore it is important that you expand your answers and give a fact or point, explanation or reason, and good examples.

  This might help:
  - make use of PEE for longer answers: (Point, Evidence, Explanation).
- For the longer answers, draft a brief plan in the margin – stick to the plan and don't go off on a tangent.
- Make good use of technical terms – as relevant.
- Keep an eye on the time. Allow yourself 5 minutes or so at the end to read through your answers, and check that facts (points), reasons or explanations and examples are given throughout.
- Check the number of marks available for each question and think carefully about how many points you have included in your answer; ask yourself whether you have included enough detail to be able to achieve near to full marks for the higher marked questions.
- Make sure you understand the following terms which are commonly used in examination papers:

Define	give the meaning of
List	make a list
State	write clearly but briefly
Describe	give an account of
Discuss	give important aspects of
	give advantages and disadvantages of
	give benefits and constraints of
Explain	make clear, giving reasons
Evaluate	give important aspects of; give your own opinion of
Assess	consider, weigh up, evaluate, make a judgement about

Sample questions

This section gives you a feel for the way the exam questions will look. We also give you the markscheme.

As a reminder, the assessment criteria for Wales follows:

Unit	AO1	AO2	AO3	AO4	Total
Unit 1 Written examination	15%	15%	–	10%	40%

	Assessment Objectives
AO1	Demonstrate knowledge and understanding of food, cooking and nutrition
AO2	Apply knowledge and understanding of food, cooking and nutrition
AO4	Analyse and evaluate different aspects of food, cooking and nutrition, including food made by yourself and others

Sample Section A question

Section A questions will be worth 12 marks

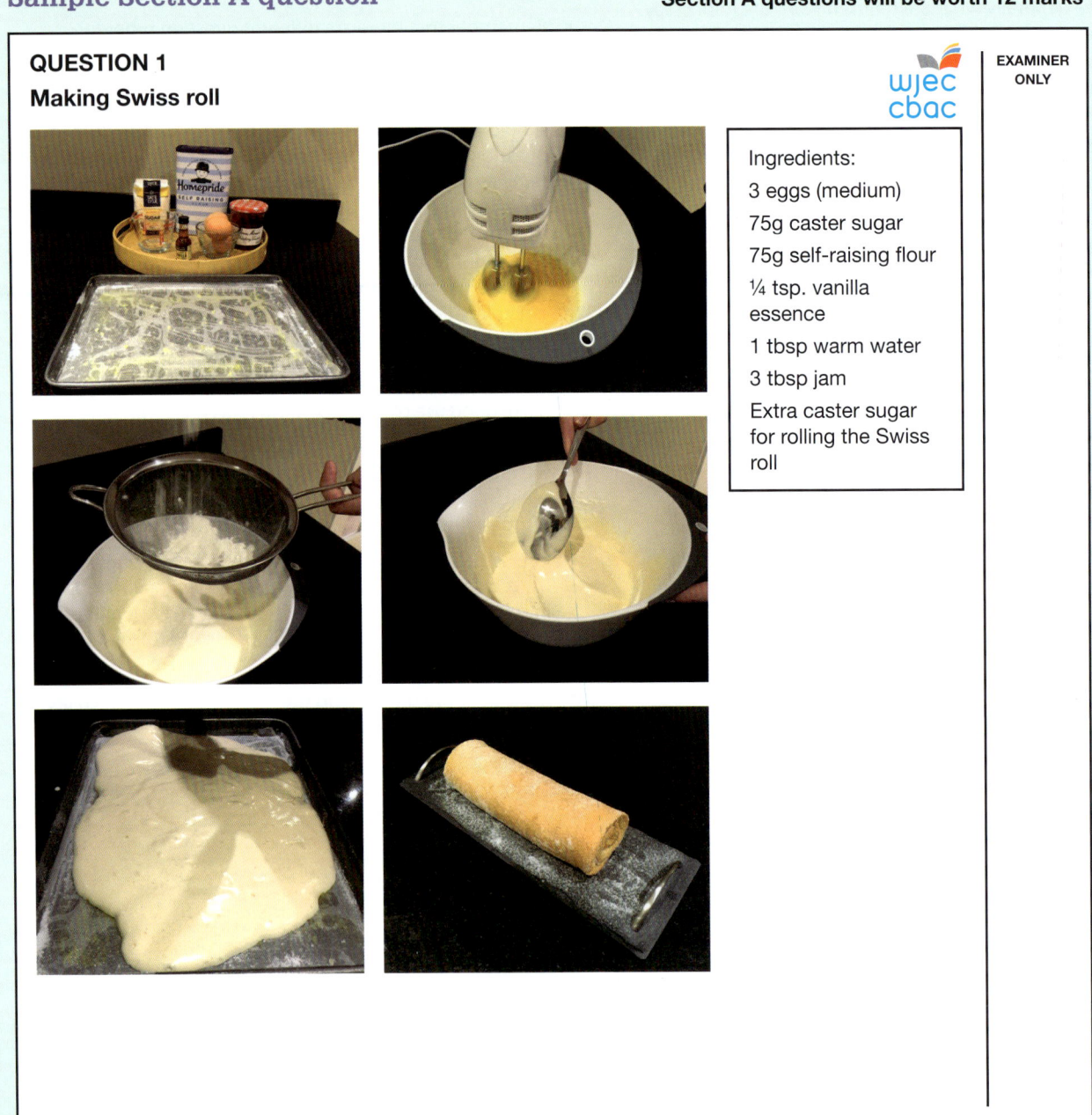

QUESTION 1
Making Swiss roll

Ingredients:
3 eggs (medium)
75g caster sugar
75g self-raising flour
¼ tsp. vanilla essence
1 tbsp warm water
3 tbsp jam
Extra caster sugar for rolling the Swiss roll

THE WRITTEN EXAM

1. (a) **Identify** the method of cake making shown in the images. [1]

　..

(b) Air is the main raising agent in the Swiss roll. **Explain** how air is incorporated during the making of the Swiss roll. [2]

　..
　..

(c) Describe **how** and **why** the flour is "folded" into the mixture when making a Swiss roll. [2]

　..
　..

(d) Accurate weighing and measuring of ingredients is essential when making a Swiss roll.
Explain what could happen if too much sugar was used when making a Swiss roll. [5]

　..
　..
　..
　..
　..
　..
　..

(e) **Suggest two** fillings other than jam that could be used in a Swiss roll. [2]

　(i) ....
　(ii) ....

Mark scheme

This is how the mark scheme is presented – it shows which Assessment Objective/s are used for each question.

Question		Section A	Mark	AO1	AO2	AO4	Total
1	(a)	**Award 1 mark** for the correct response Whisking	1	1			1
	(b)	**Award 1 mark** for each correct response up to a maximum of 2 marks Air is incorporated when • the eggs and sugar are being whisked/combined (air is trapped – "pale and fluffy") • When **sifting** flour into mixture • When **folding** flour into the mixture	2	2			2
	(c)	**Award 1 mark** for a point relating to a description of **how** up to a maximum of 1 mark • using a metal spoon, plastic spatula, not a wooden spoon, cut through the mixture with the edge of the spoon • use sieved flour to add air • use a figure of 8 action when folding in the flour **Award 1 mark** for one reason **why** • ensures that air is not lost from the mixture • air bubbles are maintained helps ensure the Swiss roll sponge has a light texture when cooked	2		2		2
	(d)	**Indicative content** Answers could include: • texture of the Swiss roll sponge will be gooey in the centre • crisp sugary crust will form a chewy, crunchy top • appearance of the Swiss roll sponge – will appear sunken as extra sugar softens the gluten so much it can't hold the risen shape • top of Swiss roll sponge will caramelise, sugary speckled crust • sugar syrup is produced which will cause Swiss roll sponge to stick to the tin • taste – the cake will taste too sweet	5		5		5

Band	AO2
3	**Award 4–5 marks** An excellent response with specific clear detailed application of knowledge relating to three or more factors within the indicative content, i.e. what would happen if too much sugar is used, when making a Swiss roll sponge.
2	**Award 2–3 marks** A good response with some application of knowledge and explanation of what would happen if too much sugar was used when making a Swiss roll sponge. At least 2 factors within the indicative content have been referred to.
1	**Award 1 mark** A limited response which gives a basic description (1 factor) of what would happen if too much sugar was used in a sponge mixture.
0	**Award 0 marks** Response not credit worthy or not attempted.

	(e)	**Award 1 mark** for **each** correct suggestion, up to a maximum of 2 marks • Cream　　　　　　　• Orange curd • Butter icing or butter cream　• Fresh fruit • Fromage frais　　　　• Marmalade • Lemon curd　　　　　• Peanut butter • Chocolate spread or nutella	2	2			2

THE WRITTEN EXAM

Sample Section B questions

QUESTION 1

The image below shows a ready-made Macaroni Cheese sold in supermarkets, it serves one portion. The ingredients are listed alongside.

Ingredients list:
Cooked Macaroni (43%) (Water, Durum **Wheat** Semolina, Rapeseed Oil), Water, Cows' **Milk**, Mature Cheddar Cheese (Cows' **Milk**) (13%), Single Cream (Cows' **Milk**), Mild Cheddar Cheese (Cows' **Milk**) (3.5%), Cornflour, Salt, **Mustard** Powder, White Pepper, Bay.

This is an example of a question which includes data response.

(a) **Study** the ingredients used in the product and answer the following questions:

   (i) name **one** ingredient which would thicken the sauce [1]

   (ii) name **one** ingredient which would provide a good source of calcium [1]

   (iii) name **one** ingredient which is used as seasoning [1]

(b) List **one** known **allergen** listed on the Ingredients list [1]

(c) The manufacturer wishes to change the existing Macaroni Cheese recipe to **reduce** the **fat** content. **Study** the ingredients list and identify **three** ingredients which contain the greatest amount of fat and for each one suggest a lower fat alternative [6]

High fat ingredient	Lower fat alternative ingredient

(d) The nutritional information for the Macaroni Cheese is shown below:

Typical values per portion	
Energy	602kcal
Protein	25.2g
Carbohydrates	65.2g
Fat	23.3g
Fibre	15.4g

   (i) **State** the total energy per portion

   (ii) The Macaroni Cheese contains 25.2g of protein. **State two** functions of protein in the diet [2]

Mark scheme

Question	Section B	Mark	AO1	AO2	AO4	Total
1 (a) (i)	**Award 1 mark** for the correct response Cornflour	1	1			1
(ii)	**Award 1 mark** from one of the following: • Cow's Milk • Mature Cheddar Cheese • Single Cream • Mild Cheddar Cheese	1	1			1
(iii)	**Award 1 mark** from one of the following: • Salt • Mustard Powder • White Pepper • Bay	1	1			1
(b)	**Award 1 mark** from one of the following: • Wheat • Semolina • Milk • Cheese • Mustard	1	1			1
(c)	**Award 1 mark** for each correct high fat ingredient. **Award 1 mark** for each lower fat alternative ingredient. 	High fat ingredient	Lower fat alternative ingredient
---	---
Cow's milk	• semi skimmed/skimmed milk (must be a named milk type) • soya milk accepted • (do not accept goat's milk unless say skimmed or semi skimmed)
Mature Cheddar cheese	• lower fat/half fat cheese or Edam, Feta, Ricotta, Cottage cheese
Single cream	• change to **reduced fat** / "lite" single cream • (do not accept low fat) • semi skimmed / skimmed milk • low fat / reduced fat yogurt • low fat / half fat crème fraîche		6		6		6
(d) (i)	602 kcal	1	1			1
(ii)	**Award 1 mark** for any of the following: • Growth • Repair / maintenance	1	1			1

QUESTION 2

This fruit salad contains apples, oranges, strawberries, grapes and bananas.

(a) Fruit salad is often served as a "healthy option" on a dessert menu.
List two reasons why fruit salad is a healthy option. [2]

(i) ....

(ii) ....

(b) Some fruits will go brown when exposed to oxygen. **Name** the scientific term for when fruits go brown? [1]

....

(c) **Name one** fruit included in the fruit salad shown above which could turn brown. [1]

....

(d) **Suggest one** method that can be used to slow down this browning. [1]

....

(e) The Eatwell Guide recommends we should have at least 5 portions of fruits and vegetables daily.
List two different ways you can increase the amounts of fruit and vegetables in your diet. [2]

An example has been done for you.

(i) Make a fruit smoothie drink

(ii) ....

(iii) ....

this is an example structured question

(f) The Government continues to promote its "5 a day" fruit and vegetable campaign.

Discuss the benefits of eating a diet rich in fresh fruit and vegetables. [8]

....

....

....

....

....

....

....

Mark scheme

Question	Section B	Mark	AO1	AO2	AO4	Total
2 (a) (i)	**Award 1 mark** for each correct response up to a maximum of 2 marks Contain: • Fibre which helps removal of waste products – helps you go to the toilet ("poo") • Anti-oxidants – helps your immune system / fights "free radicals" • Contain vitamins once (accept named vitamin also) • Contain minerals once (accept named mineral) • Low in fat	2	2			2
(b)	**Award 1 mark** for Enzymic browning (needs to contain both words – do not accept "browning" by itself)	1	1			1
(c)	**Award 1 mark** from one of the following: Apple Banana	1	1			1
(d)	**Award 1 mark** from one of the following: • Use of acid, e.g. vinegar, lemon juice • Use of sugar • Remove oxygen, e.g. submerge in water or juice • Blanching (kills enzyme responsible for browning)	1	1			1
(e) (ii and iii)	**Award 1 mark** for each correct response up to a maximum of 2 marks • Add vegetables into sauces, e.g. with pasta • Have snacks which include pieces of fruits or vegetables • Put vegetables on pizza for toppings • Include fruits in home baked cakes and desserts *Accept any sensible suggestions*	2	2			2
(f)	**Indicative content:** Answers could include: • Eating 5 a day fruit and vegetables links into the healthy eating guidelines (accept converse answers) • Eat more fibre – fruit and vegetables are high in fibre particularly when eaten raw • Eat less sugar – fruit (in particular) contain natural sugars • Eat less fat – fruit and vegetables are virtually fat free (avocados are an exception) • Fruit and vegetables contain ACE vitamins which are anti-oxidants • Eating the rainbow of fresh fruit and vegetables (i.e. all the colours of the rainbow) will provide the range of vitamins and minerals the body needs • Fruit in particular needs no preparation or cooking – they are ready to eat raw • Fruit and vegetables add colour, texture and flavour to dishes • Fruit and vegetables because of their fibre content help to keep the digestive system healthy (prevent constipation, said to prevent some colon cancers)	8	4	4		8

			8	4	4		8
	<ul><li>Fruit and vegetables can be cooked in many ways to add variety to the diet</li><li>Fruit and vegetables are naturally moist so prevent against dehydration - they are refreshing on a hot day</li><li>Fruits rich in vitamin C are said to prevent infection</li><li>Vitamin C found in citrus fruits help the body absorb iron</li><li>Eating fresh fruit and vegetables is said to improve skin</li><li>Fruit juices and smoothies are good ways of getting the nutrients from fruit and vegetables</li><li>Fruit and vegetables are cheap when in season – easy to obtain and quick to prepare – wide variety available</li></ul>*Accept any sensible suggestions*						

Band	AO1	AO2
3	**Award 4 marks** An excellent response which demonstrates clear knowledge understanding of the benefits of eating a diet rich in fresh fruit and vegetables. The candidate has used highly appropriate technical terminology confidently and accurately in relation to the indicative content	**Award 4 marks** An excellent response with specific clear detailed application of knowledge relating to three or more factors within the indicative content, i.e. the benefits of eating a diet rich in fresh fruit and vegetables. Benefits listed are realistic related to fruits and vegetables
2	**Award 2–3 marks** A good response that demonstrates an adequate level of knowledge and understanding of the benefits of eating a diet rich in fresh fruit and vegetables. The candidate has used appropriate technical terminology referring to the indicative content	**Award 2–3 marks** A good response demonstrating adequate application of knowledge of the benefits of eating a diet rich in fresh fruit and vegetables. At least two factors within the indicative content have been referred to. The majority of suggestions are realistic and achievable
1	**Award 1 mark** A limited response that demonstrates a basic level of knowledge and understanding of the benefits of eating a diet rich in fresh fruit and vegetables. A simple list or bullet points of with little or no explanation	**Award 1 mark** A limited response which gives a basic application of knowledge (1 factor) of the benefits of eating a diet rich in fresh fruit and vegetables. A simple list or bullet points of with little or no explanation
0	**Award 0 marks** Response not credit worthy or not attempted	**Award 0 marks** Response not credit worthy or not attempted

QUESTION 3

Many processed foods contain additives.

This is an example of a graduated lead-in question

(a) **Name two** categories of food additives. [2]

(i) ....

(ii) ....

(b) **Discuss** the benefits of additives in food products. [6]

....

....

....

....

....

....

....

....

QUESTION 4

(a) **Explain** what is meant by energy balance. [2]

....

....

....

This is an example of a free response question

(b) **Suggest** ways of encouraging children to eat a healthy diet. [6]

....

....

....

....

....

....

....

....

374 THE WRITTEN EXAM

Mark scheme

Question	Section B	Mark	AO1	AO2	AO4	Total
3 (a)	**Award 1 mark** for each correct response up to a maximum of 2 marks • Flavourings / flavour enhancers / flavour intensifiers • Preservatives • Colourings • Emulsifiers and stabilisers • Antioxidants • Sweeteners • Added nutrients (do not accept E numbers)	2	2			2
(b)	**Indicative content:** Answers could include reference to: • Eye appeal – linked to a range of additives including preservatives, colourings, anti-oxidants • Increasing shelf life • Addition of nutrients • Increases choice available • Enhances quality • Ensures product remains the same - what the customer expects • Prevents rancidity *Accept any sensible suggestions*	6		6		6

Band	AO2
3	**Award 5-6 marks** An excellent response which shows in depth knowledge and understanding of the benefits of additives in food products. At least three factors within the indicative content have been explained in full. Response is clearly expressed, and shows accurate use of technical terminology. Benefits listed are realistic related to additives in food
2	**Award 3-4 marks** A good response which shows clear knowledge and understanding of the benefits of additives in food products. At least two factors within the indicative content have been identified and discussed. Response is adequately expressed, and shows appropriate use of technical terminology. The majority of suggestions are realistic and achievable
1	**Award 1-2 mark** A limited response which shows some knowledge and understanding of the benefits of additives in food products. At least one factor within the indicative content has been identified and discussed. Response shows basic use of technical terminology. There may be a simple list or bullet points of with little or no explanation
0	**Award 0 marks** Response not credit worthy or not attempted

Mark scheme

Question		Section B		Mark	AO1	AO2	AO4	Total
4 (a)	Band	AO1	AO2	2	1	1		2
	1	**Award 1 mark** Candidate has identified that: Energy balance = amount of energy for our body needs	**Award 1 mark** Candidate can apply knowledge and understanding: • If we consume more food than we need, the excess is converted to fat • If we eat less than we need, and use up energy by taking exercise, fat stores burn and we may get thinner • Energy input and energy output should be the same					
	2	**Award 0 marks** Response not credit worthy or not attempted	**Award 0 marks** Response not credit worthy or not attempted					
(b)	**Indicative content:** Answer could refer to: • Children should be part of food making process • Avoid high salt and sugar foods • Include high fibre foods in meals and snacks • Include foods with variety • Fruit and vegetables - at least 5 a day • Adding hidden vegetables to meals • Making interesting dishes with fresh ingredients • Adding fresh foods to lunch boxes		• Eating as part of a family; not having separate meals • Avoid following "junk" trends • Children should be included in shopping • Setting good habits by parents • Attractive and colourful food • Making food fun • 3 a day campaign – dairy • Advertising techniques that support parents to promote healthy food.	6	3	3		6
	Band	AO1	AO2					
	3	**Award 3 marks** An excellent response which demonstrates clear knowledge and understanding of ways of encouraging children to eat a healthy diet. The candidate has used highly appropriate technical terminology confidently and accurately in relation to the indicative content	**Award 3 marks** An excellent response with specific clear detailed application of knowledge relating to three or more factors within the indicative content, i.e. ways of encouraging children to eat a healthy diet. Demonstration of depth of nutritional knowledge applicable to children. Suggestions listed are realistic related to encouraging children to eat a healthy diet					
	2	**Award 2 marks** A good response that demonstrates an adequate level of knowledge and understanding of the ways of encouraging children to eat a healthy diet. The candidate has used appropriate technical terminology referring to the indicative content	**Award 2 marks** A good response demonstrating adequate application of knowledge of the ways of encouraging children to eat a healthy diet. At least two factors within the indicative content have been referred to. The majority of suggestions are realistic and achievable					
	1	**Award 1 mark** A limited response that demonstrates a basic level of knowledge and understanding of ways of encouraging children to eat a healthy diet. A simple list or bullet points with little or no explanation	**Award 1 mark** A limited response which gives a basic application of knowledge (1 factor) of the ways of encouraging children to eat a healthy diet. A simple list or bullet points with little or no explanation					
	0	**Award 0 marks** Response not credit worthy or not attempted	**Award 0 marks** Response not credit worthy or not attempted					

QUESTION 5

The pictures below show some of the different stages involved when lining a tin with pastry.
Describe what is happening at each stage and explain why it is important.

(i) ....
....
.... [2]

(ii) ....
....
.... [2]

(iii) ....
....
....
.... [2]

(iv) **Explain** why some recipes require the pastry case to be baked blind. [2]

....
....

(v) **Name** a dish that makes use of baking blind. [1]

....

Mark scheme

Question	Section B	Mark	AO1	AO2	AO4	Total
5 (i)	**Award 1 mark** for each correct response up to a maximum of 2 marks	2	1	1		2
	Band — **AO1** — **AO2**					
	1 — **Award 1 mark** Pastry is being unrolled so that it fits/rests on the flan dish — **Award 1 mark** This makes it easier to line the dish accurately / neatly / prevents pastry from breaking					
	0 — **Award 0 marks** Response not credit worthy or not attempted. — **Award 0 marks** Response not credit worthy or not attempted.					
(ii)	**Band** — **AO1** — **AO2**	2	1	1		2
	1 — **Award 1 mark** The pastry is being lowered and guided into the base of the flan dish — **Award 1 mark** Possible answers: • This stops it from tearing/not being large enough to fit the dish • Carefully lowering pastry and pushing into base reduces risk of shrinkage in cooked pastry case					
	0 — **Award 0 marks** Response not credit worthy or not attempted. — **Award 0 marks** Response not credit worthy or not attempted.					
(iii)	**Band** — **AO1** — **AO2**					
	1 — **Award 1 mark** Greaseproof paper and baking beans / dried peas have been added to the pastry case — **Award 1 mark** Possible answers: • This gives the case its structure/shape • Helps to keep sides from collapsing • This stops it from rising / lets steam escape and prevents crust from bubbling					
	0 — **Award 0 marks** Response not credit worthy or not attempted — **Award 0 marks** Response not credit worthy or not attempted					
(iv)	**Award 1 mark** to a simple response, with one suggestion, e.g. to prevent a soggy base. **Award 2 marks** for a developed response, with two suggestions, e.g: to prevent a soggy base / to give a crisp pastry; as no further cooking is required after filling has been added	2	2			2
(v)	Award correct response: • Lemon meringue pie • Quiche • Egg custard, Pastry flan case / tartlets with fruit *Or other valid answer*	1	1			1

Worked Examples

Question 1 Low Mark Answer

These are examples of questions completed by two students. Compare the marks achieved by each one – do you see how you can achieve higher marks with just a little more attention to detail in your answer?

Candidate 1

5/9

(a) State **three** nutrients found in milk. [3]

(i) protein — 1
(ii) vitamin D — 1
(iii) calcium — 1

(b) Supermarkets sell a wide range of different milks. Discuss the reasons why such a wide range is now available. [6]

Because people want a range of milk. AO1
There is cows milk, goats milk, nut milk and soya milk. AO1

You can buy milk in cartons, cans and dried. AO1
You can make lots of dishes such as cauliflower cheese and lasagne with milk. AO1

2 Marks

This candidate has demonstrated knowledge and understanding but has not applied any.

Question 1 High Mark Answer

Candidate 2
9/9

(a) State **three** nutrients found in milk. [3]

(i) Protein — 1
(ii) Calcium — 1
(iii) Vitamin A — 1

(b) Supermarkets sell a wide range of different milks. Discuss the reasons why such a wide range is now available. [6]

Because there is consumer demand. [AO1] Some people have 'special dietary needs' such as an [AO1] allergy to lactose in cows milk - so they will use an alternative [AO2] such as goats milk or soya milk. Some people will buy skimmed to keep their fat [AO1] consumption down - this might be because they are watching their calorie intake, [AO2] or because they are watching their saturated fat intake. For some people, they buy UHT milk, [AO1] this is 'long life' milk, so you can store it at room temperature [AO2] until you open it (then chill it). Some people are vegan, so will buy soya or coconut or almond milk. [AO1]

This candidate has shown AO1 and AO2.

AO1 - 3 marks
AO2 - 3 marks

6 Marks

(4301-01)

Question 2 Low Mark Answer

Candidate 1

Children's menus are often boring and high in fat, sugar and salt.

(a) Explain the health implications of eating too much fat. [4]

- will get fat and possibly even obese.
- might cause heart problems & they could have a heart attack.

A basic answer is given.

2

A plan would help to structure each answer

(b) Discuss ways in which a caterer could make children's menus:

(i) Meet healthy eating guidelines; [6]

- Fat - use low fat ingredients when you can.

- Sugar - don't add it to foods.

- Grill rather than fry foods.

2

The candidate has made 3 points, these points are a list and are not well developed, no explanations are given.

(4732-01)

381

Candidate 1

(ii) Interesting and appealing. [6]

- Colours, flavours & textures in foods eg green pasta and a tomato sauce. ← *basic example*

- write a menu and that it appeals to kids eg give it a theme like Star Wars or maybe after a toy? ← *good response*

2

- Have lots of colar in the plates, napkins etc ← *need example*

The candidate has made 3 points, these points are in a list. It would have been relatively easy for this candidate to gain higher marks, they just needed to develop their answers a little more.

Question 2 High Mark Answer

Candidate 2

Children's menus are often boring and high in fat, sugar and salt.

(a) Explain the health implications of eating too much fat. [4]

Foods which are high in fat are also high in energy. If you put into your body more energy than you need you will become overweight & possibly obese. Obesity can lead to complications such as joints problems, high blood pressure (leading to strokes) and type 2 diabetes (circulation problems). If fats are saturated this can cause high blood cholesterol & lead to CHD (coronary heart disease). As a child becomes an adult this can cause NHS thousands of £.

Margin notes: Type 2 diabetes, overweight → obesity ↓ high blood pressure, fat → high energy, saturated ↓ cholesterol ↑ CHD — answer is planned

Examiner marks: AO2 × 4, mark: 4

(b) Discuss ways in which a caterer could make children's menus:

(i) Meet healthy eating guidelines; [6]

Firstly by planning dishes which are low in fat. Where possible use low in fat ingredients alternatives, e.g. skimmed or semi skimmed rather than full fat in a white sauce. Also buying leaner cuts of meat e.g. chicken breast instead of lamb chops. Cut/remove visible fat. Don't add salt to food — flavour with herbs & spices. Keep sugary foods to a minimum and when planning desserts use fresh fruits & natural sugar sources such as honey. Try to include high fibre ingredients, e.g. pulses, cereals & make sure you use wholemeal rather than white bread for toast & sandwiches. Make sure there is plenty of fruits & vegetables in the dishes selected, you can 'hide' lots of vegetables by pureeing soups & sauces. Avoid frying foods e.g. fish, poaching, grilling or baking are healthier cooking methods.

Margin notes: low fat, low salt, low sugar, high fibre, 5 a day (anti-oxidants), cooking methods

Examiner marks: AO2 × 6, mark: 6 — all suggestions are relevant and each point made is well explained

(4732-01)

383

[*could have given an example of a colourful plate, e.g. pink salmon, boiled potatoes tossed in parsley, green beans*]

Candidate 2

(ii) Interesting and appealing. [6]

The chef can make that he/she has menu items that have a range of colours, flavours & textures. Colour- a range of colourful foods - you don't want the white plate to look beige, say a range of flavours & textures e.g. crispy crumbed salmon fingers with new potatoes, oven baked & crunchy carrots & broccoli. **AO2** Shape is also important make sure the ingredients on the plate look interesting e.g. round fishcakes with spiralised courgettes **AO2** & carrots. The presentation of food is important, so he/she needs to think of garnishes e.g. carrot flowers & decorations e.g. fanned strawberries **AO2**. When you write up the menu, you could give it a theme & maybe introduce child friendly & colourful graphics. **AO2**

5

4 factors discussed. Well answered.

REVISION TIPS

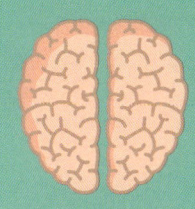

UNDERSTAND YOUR WORK

It is easier to learn if you understand your work rather than if you try and simply remember it. If you don't understand something talk to your teacher and ask for help. They will be very pleased that you have asked for help as the chances are if you don't understand something many of your peers won't either.

USE A RANGE OF REVISION TECHNIQUES

Different styles of learning suit different people, so find out which methods suit you best. Examples include using index cards, making notes, creating posters, watching videos, talking about and writing about work.

WORK INTENSIVELY FOR SHORT BURSTS

Your studying will be more effective if you take a short break to process your work before trying to learn more. Regular exercise, such as walking, can help you to recall more and will reduce stress, another barrier to effective learning.

DEVELOP YOUR EXAM WRITING SKILLS, ESPECIALLY FOR THE FREE RESPONSE QUESTIONS

Practise writing answers for the free response questions – these are likely to be the questions over four marks. Do so by highlighting key words, reading the question several times to check your understanding, writing a brief plan in the margin and ensuring you use PEE in your answer.

REVISIT WORK

Little and often works best for learning, so re-reading material on a regular basis will help you to retain it. Leaving revision to the last minute is a weak strategy. Creating index cards or posters and looking at them regularly is a stress-free and easy way of reminding yourself of key points.

BE WELL-PREPARED

Look for Specimen Assessment Material (SAM) on the exam board website, and past papers and past examiners' reports. This gives a clue as to the type of questions asked, the markschemes and how previous candidates have succeeded, or perhaps failed, to do as well as they might have done. Look at the banded markscheme to see how the marks are allocated.

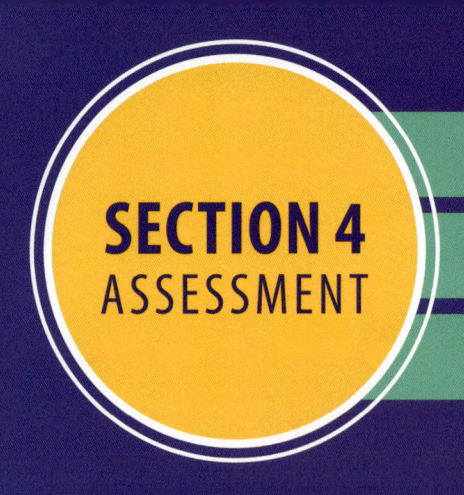

SECTION 4: ASSESSMENT

PART TWO: NON-EXAMINATION ASSESSMENTS (NEAs)

What will I learn?
- The percentage breakdowns and mark allocation for each NEA
- The recommended time allocated to each NEA and how much writing is involved
- How to approach each NEA. We give you:
  - examples and pointers for each section
  - lots of tips and advice in order to do well

There are two non-examination assessments (called NEAs) which you have to complete in your final year of the course.

These are:

Assessment 1: The Food Investigation Assessment
Assessment 2: The Food Preparation Assessment

Each one will now be discussed and we will give you some pointers on how to be successful, together with some annotated examples to give you guidance.

Assessment 1: The Food Investigation Assessment

The WJEC **specification** says:

this is a scientific food investigation which will assess your knowledge, skills and understanding in relation to scientific principles underlying the preparation and cooking of food.

This means that:

you will be asked to do a practical food science investigation and write up your findings.

Your teacher will have been preparing you for this assessment since the beginning of the course, so you will be familiar with how to conduct a food science-based investigation.

How does this assessment work?

Your teacher will give you a written brief and you will have a fixed amount of time to do this task in class. It is a **formal assessment** so once you start you will not be allowed any help. There is a recommended amount of time to complete this assessment: it is 10 hours.

Some key points for this assessment are as follows:

Assessment title	**The Food Investigation Assessment** 20% of the qualification
Recommended time for this assessment	10 hours
Word / page guidance	2,000–2,500 words (plus any charts, graphs and photographs) 6–7 pages when typed with a font size of 11/12 Documents over 2,500 words are not permitted Your work can be presented in electronic or hard copy

ASSESSMENT 1: THE FOOD INVESTIGATION ASSESSMENT

There are three sections to the Food Investigation Assessment, and they are as follows:

Section A (AO2)	Research and investigate the task: (maximum 10 marks) This is where you are expected to: • research the chosen task • produce a plan of experiments to be carried out • predict an outcome • apply knowledge and understanding to justify choices for experimental work/modifications
Section B (AO2)	Investigate and evaluate the working characteristics, functions and chemical properties of ingredients through practical experimentation: (maximum 20 marks) This is where you are expected to: • demonstrate your ability to review and make improvements to the investigation by amending the ingredients to include the most appropriate ingredients, process and cooking method • demonstrate an understanding of the working characteristics and functional and chemical properties of the ingredients selected • record in detail the outcomes of your investigation, the modification and adjustments made during the preparation and cooking process, and the sensory preference tests carried out to formulate the results
Section C (AO4)	Analyse and evaluate the task: (maximum 10 marks) This is where you are expected to: • analyse the data and results collected, draw conclusions • justify findings, the reasons for the success or failure of the ingredients selected to trial • evaluate the hypothesis and confirm if the prediction was proven

Tips before you start

If you follow these guidelines then you should produce a successful Food Investigation:

- Approach this task like a science experiment. It will help you get in the right frame of mind.
- Spend time deciding on your **hypothesis** – once you have decided on it, make sure your wording is clear when you write it up. Your hypothesis forms the basis of the whole task so give it lots of thought and set it out clearly.
- When you do your practical work make sure that you only change one thing at a time. It could be a specific ingredient such as changing plain flour to self-raising flour, or it could be a method such as switching from the creaming method to the all-in-one method of cake making. By only changing one part of the process each time, you are making sure the test is **fair**.
- Make sure you have a **control recipe** and method – you can then compare your results against this control.
- If you are in any doubt about your results, there is nothing wrong – providing you have time and resources – in deciding to repeat an experiment.
- Make sure that you record your method and results – it's easy to forget what happened if the experiments are not written up straight away.
- Be very precise with weighing, measuring and timings. Sloppy work will affect your results.
- Think about what sensory testing methods you will use, do this before you start to do your experiments and make sure you have sheets that your reviewers can fill in easily. These sheets can then be converted into tables or graphs.

Assessment criteria used

The **assessment criteria** are listed in the specification – make sure you are familiar with them. Within each Section (so that is Section A, Section B and Section C) there are bands – so you need to read the banding criteria for each section to work out which band your work fits into best.

If you want to find out how exactly you will be assessed take a look at the specification.

Factors affecting food choice: Sensory analysis and testing pp148–151

Practical things to think about

To Do List – Raising agent experiment with scones

I need the following equipment:

Digital scales
Mixing bowl
Sieve
Knife
Flour dredger
Rolling pin
Scone rolling guides
Scone cutter
Palette knife
Measuring jug
Pastry brush
Baking tray lined with greaseproof paper
Oven gloves
Cooling rack
Ruler
Digital timer
Serrated knife

I need the following ingredients:

3 x 115g plain flour
1 x 115g self-raising flour
4 x 15g butter
4 x 70ml fresh milk
4 x pinches of salt
5g baking powder
7.5g bicarbonate of soda
5g cream of tartar

- Make sure you know what equipment you need – write a list
- Make sure you know the ingredients and quantities you need – write another list
- Think about how you will take photographs. Make sure you have easy access to take photos of what you are doing.

Key point

This assessment is not testing you on how well you cook, it is testing you on your ability to conduct and evaluate a scientific food experiment.

Study tip

It is important to have clear photos in your finished written work – these photos will evidence the key points of your investigation.

How should the written work be presented?

You can write or type your work. To get the highest marks you are encouraged to create and format your own unique document. To do this you should read and understand the assessment criteria (ask your teacher for a copy).

A writing frame is allowed if this helps you to structure your work. These are the key headings you should think about using in your written work:

1. **Title of the task**
2. **Summary of the research methods**
3. **Hypothesis**
4. **Plan of action**
5. **Experiments**

(this should take up a significant proportion of your work and time)

6. **Conclusions**

What type of briefs will you be given?

Each year the briefs will be different. Your teacher will be given the brief from the exam board.

Once you have been given your brief you will quickly start the task, so it is important before this that you have had practice runs with some different briefs so that you know what is expected in the real assessment. There is no time to waste.

Here are some examples of the types of brief you may get but remember, it can be on ANY food science related aspect covered in the exam board specification.

Example Brief 1

The success of creamed sponge mixtures relies on a suitable raising agent.
Investigate the success of different raising agents when making a creamed sponge.
This task must be supported by investigational work.

Example Brief 2

Many commercial low calorie desserts rely on the use of artificial sweeteners.
Investigate the use of alternative sweeteners when making a fruit mousse.
This task must be supported by investigational work.

These example briefs have taken from the materials provided in the WJEC Sample Assessment Materials.
WJEC: http://www.wjec.co.uk/qualifications/food-and-nutrition/wjec-gcse-food-and-nutrition-sams-from-2016-e.pdf

EXAMPLE FOOD INVESTIGATION ASSESSMENT

To help you we have included an example for each section of the Food Investigation Assessment. These will show you the kind of processes that you have to follow and what a finished piece of work might look like.

Remember!

- The Food Investigation is a controlled task. As a student you have to do your work independently in the classroom under teacher supervision and without teacher feedback.
- These examples are only suggestions about how the task can be conducted and presented. They are not the only way – you may have a very different way of approaching the task and presenting your material and that is OK.
- Make sure you understand the assessment criteria as you go along and keep reviewing your work and reflecting on what you have done. Ask yourself how well you have met the assessment criteria – which banding do you think your work meets and is there anything you need to do to be able to get yourself into a higher banding?

Study tips

- Each section has 3 or 4 assessment bands. Study these carefully before you start your assessment so that you understand fully what you need to do to meet the assessment criteria.
- Be organised – you will be far more successful in this task if you are organised and plan ahead.

The remainder of this section shows you an example from each of the six headings we suggested earlier – **Title of the task, Summary of the research methods, Hypothesis, Plan of action, Experiments** and **Conclusions** – and gives you some pointers to tell you how well each section can be done.

1 Title of the task

Make sure you include the task details (that's the written brief) – so that the moderator can see clearly which task you are doing.

> **There are a number of ways to thicken a sauce.**
>
> Investigate the working characteristics and the functional and chemical properties (where appropriate) of the different methods used to thicken a sauce.

These resources have been adapted from the materials provided in the WJEC Teachers Guide. This is freely available at:
WJEC: http://www.wjec.co.uk/qualifications/food-and-nutrition/WJEC%20GCSE%20Food%20and%20nutrition%20-%20GFT.pdf

2 Summary of the research methods

The research you do will depend on the brief. Some useful sources you can consider include:

- Recipe books – think about finding a control recipe from a reliable source
- Magazines and newspapers – food magazines, including the free ones from supermarkets, newspaper articles
- Online sources – articles, videos, food bloggers
- Text books – including the food science chapters
- TV programmes

Think about summarising your research findings concisely. Avoid any waffle. How could you do this? A list, a table, a mind map or thought shower? It is up to you – whatever works best for you.

This student has developed the structure and headings for themself.
Writing frames / pro-formas have not been used.

Research methods:

The **first** thing I did was jot down the ways I could think of that you would thicken a sauce. These were my initial thoughts:

Using different ingredients: wheat flour, cornflour, arrowroot, potato starch and rice starch. These ingredients will thicken by a process called gelatinisation.

Using different methods: roux, all in one method, reduction and puréeing.

The **second** thing I did was to look through my textbook and cookbooks to see if I had missed anything – I wanted to make sure there weren't any other ways to thicken a sauce that I had missed. I then found out about beurre manié[1]. This is a mix made up of equal parts of soft butter and flour and is used to thicken soups and sauces. This is often added towards the end of the cooking process when a sauce needs thickening. So, I added this to my list of methods of making sauces.

The **third** thing I did was research online, by googling '*different ways to thicken a sauce*' to see if I had missed anything else. On the Jamie Oliver forum[2] I read one posting that said they thickened soups using bread. I then researched this some more and found that bread sauce (used on Christmas day as an accompaniment to roast turkey) and a chilled Spanish soup called gazpacho are thickened with bread[3]. Another website (http://www.wikihow.com/Thicken-Sauce[4]) told me that you can also use food gums as thickening agents such as xanthan gum, agar and guar gum. It also suggested using potato flakes. It also showed how to use eggs as a thickening agent e.g. egg yolks in custard.

Another website (http://www.cooksrecipes.com/tips/how-to-thicken-sauce.html[5]) also suggested boiling cream to make it thicker and then adding it to a sauce to help to thicken it. It also mentioned thickeners such as blood (like in black pudding) yogurt, fresh cheese and ground almonds.

I put all my ideas into a mind map, which I hand drew and photographed as it's much quicker for me. Here it is:

You can see this student has not wasted any time with long introductions; he has got straight to the point.

A good range of research has been done.

Food science term used.

DIFFERENT WAYS TO THICKEN A SAUCE

INGREDIENTS
- Starches: Wheat flour, Cornflour, Arrowroot, Potato Starch, Rice Starch
- Gums: Xanthan gum, Guar gum, Agar
- Proteins: Eggs, Cream, Yoghurt, Cheese, Blood, Nuts

METHODS
- Using starches: Roux, All in one, Cornflour (slurry), Beurre manié, Bread, Potato flakes
- Reduction
- Puree: Puree whole sauce OR Add a puree to a sauce to thicken

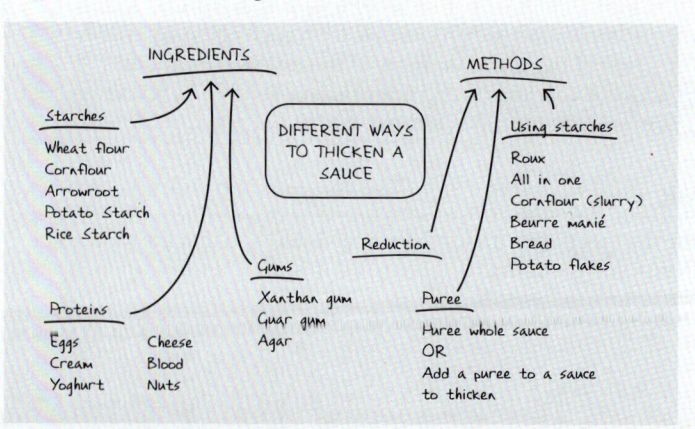

1 Davies, Jill (2005) *Hammond's Cooking Explained*, 4th edition. Longman: Pearson Education Limited
2 Jamie Oliver.com (2015) forum: Food & Drink http://www.jamieoliver.com/forum/viewtopic.php?pid=574032
3 The Telegraph online (2015) The Kitchen Thinker: Bread sauce http://www.telegraph.co.uk/foodanddrink/8194243/The-Kitchen-Thinker-Bread-sauce.ht
4 Wikihow: (2015) How to thicken sauce http://www.wikihow.com/Thicken-Sauce
5 cooksrecipes.com (2015) From The Cook's Bible: How to Thicken a Sauce (http://www.cooksrecipes.com/tips/how-to-thicken-sauce.html)

The student has referenced his sources well.

EXAMPLE FOOD INVESTIGATION ASSESSMENT

3 Hypothesis

In a sentence or two say what you are hoping to prove.

> My hypothesis is that the best way to thicken a tomato sauce suitable for a pizza topping is by using a cornflour slurry.

The hypothesis is clear and to the point.

4 Plan of action

This is where you explain what you are planning to do. Include a list of tasks or experiments you have decided to do and what you hope to find out.

Plan of action:

- I need to decide what my ideal pizza sauce is. What should the appearance, texture and thickness be like?
- I need to find a recipe for my ideal pizza sauce which I will use as a standard recipe.
- I need to decide on the ingredient variables I will include in my experiments. I also need to decide whether I will do experiments with different methods of thickening, like I showed in my mind map.
- I then need to conduct my experiments (and provide my teacher with a requisition list for each practical).
- I need to conduct sensory analysis to find out which is the preferred sample to use as a tomato sauce topping on a pizza.
- I need to analyse my results and draw conclusions.

Expanded plan of action	
I need to decide: what is my ideal pizza sauce?	My ideal pizza sauce will be smooth and quite thick. It should not flow too much. This is because that is what I have seen from other pizza sauces. I particularly like the pizza sauce that is used in Pizza Express but I can't buy that in the supermarket to use as a comparison, so I have found this own-brand product, which I am going to use as my **control** for the appearance, texture and thickness. I am not interested in the flavour (I think that is another experiment I could do if I had time).
I need to find a recipe for my ideal pizza sauce which I will use as a standard recipe.	I have decided to use the following base recipe and then I will add my different thickeners to this: 100ml passata (sieved tomatoes) 5g of thickener mixed with 20ml water into a slurry **I predict that cornflour will produce the most appealing thickened pizza sauce – as it will be smooth, glossy and lump free.** I predict some of the other starches might give me lumps in my sauce, especially wheat flour.
I need to decide on the variables I will include in my experiments.	The ingredients I will use are: 5g of each of the following: wheat flour, potato starch, rice flour, arrowroot, cornflour, cassava flour
I then need to conduct my experiments.	I will keep the method and quantities the same so that I have conducted a fair investigation.
I need to conduct sensory analysis to find out which is the preferred sample to use as a tomato sauce topping on a pizza.	I will do a range of sensory tests to ensure I record feedback on: • appearance • texture • thickness
I then need to decide if I would benefit from any other experiments.	If I have time I may repeat the experiments with different ratios of starch to passata. I may also look at different methods such as reduction and puréeing.
I need to analyse my results (measuring appearance, texture and thickness) and draw conclusions.	I will come up with recommendations and suggestions.

This is an example of an excellent plan of action. The student has started with a summary of the plan of action and then this is expanded on in greater detail in a table.

It is worth spending time on planning your investigation.

391

5 Experiments

This is where you show the experiments you did – it's a good idea to show how one experiment might lead to another depending on the results you get.

The number of experiments you decide to do will depend on your task and the hypothesis you have set yourself. Don't get trapped into thinking that the more experiments you do, the higher the marks you will get – it does not work like that. Read the assessment criteria to gain understanding.

For each experiment you do, record your findings and remember to take photographs.

You can provide a brief summary of the ingredients and method if you feel that is relevant – but do not use too much space or words, especially if it takes you over the word count. Remember it is the results of your experiments that are important; take photographs to include in your written work.

Make sure you evaluate each experiment and include a discussion on the food scientific changes that have taken place as well as results from sensory testing too.

Session 1:

Ingredients for each experiment:

100ml passata

5g of thickener mixed with 20ml water into a slurry

Thickeners are: 5g of each of the following:

wheat flour, potato starch, rice flour, arrowroot, cornflour, cassava flour

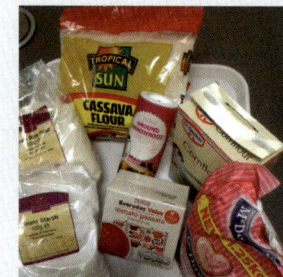

Method

Each method was the same:

- Weigh 100ml passata sauce into a measuring jug and transfer into a small saucepan. Place onto a gentle heat.
- While the passata is heating, measure 20ml of cold water into a measuring jug and put in the 5g starch. Mix into a slurry with a teaspoon. Make sure all the starch is mixed.
- As the passata sauce comes to the boil add the starch slurry and keep mixing until the starch thickens the sauce (called gelatinisation). Cook through for 60 seconds (use timer to be accurate).
- Using a plastic spatula, tip all the hot thickened sauce onto the viscosity mat and record how far it spreads.
- Repeat experiments with other starches. Compare appearance, texture and thickness of each sauce against the control (own-brand pizza sauce)

You can give a brief summary of the method for the experiment, but ensure it is BRIEF, remember you are on a strict page limit and word count.

Results:

Own-brand sauce	Wheat flour	Potato starch	Brown rice flour	Arrowroot	Cornflour	Cassava flour
Comments on appearance and texture						
Shiny, glossy, bright, lumpy (due to tomato and onion), flecks of green	Grainy, dull, few flecks of flour visible, pale	Dull, flat, cloudy, lacks lustre	Wet, grainy, looks like tomato purée	Shiny, glossy, mirror-like, smooth	Thick, dull, opaque, dark, flat	Dull, thick, flat, lacks shine
Did the sauce have lumps?						
Yes (but from onion and tomatoes, not due to the starch)	yes	no	no	no	no	no
How far did each sauce spread on the viscosity mat?						
5	5	3.5	4.5	4	3	4

The photos taken are clear.

The results are easy to read.

This student has used a viscosity mat to show how much each sauce has spread.

392 NON-EXAMINATION ASSESSMENTS

Analysis of results 1:

Thickness (viscosity):

Here is a summary from most thick to least thick:

most thick ────────────────────────────────► least thick

Cornflour   Potato starch   Arrowroot / Cassava flour   Brown rice flour   Own-brand sauce   Wheat flour

Appearance and texture:

I asked 6 of my classmates to complete a sensory table, so that I could find out which they preferred the look of, when considering the sauce as a pizza sauce. I used the following table[6]:

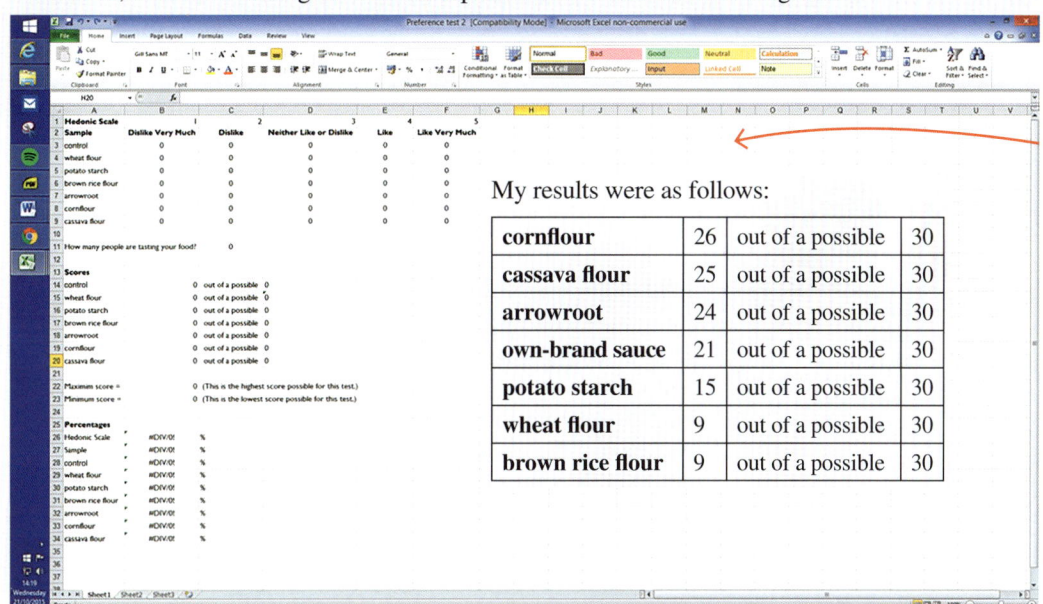

[screenshot of Excel spreadsheet titled "Preference test 2"]

My results were as follows:

cornflour	26	out of a possible	30
cassava flour	25	out of a possible	30
arrowroot	24	out of a possible	30
own-brand sauce	21	out of a possible	30
potato starch	15	out of a possible	30
wheat flour	9	out of a possible	30
brown rice flour	9	out of a possible	30

Margin note: This student has been very resourceful and reduced the word count and page quantity by providing a screen shot of their results table created in a spreadsheet. This student can see that the moderator is only interested in the types of sensory testing that took place and a summary of the results.

So, from the experiments conducted so far I have found out that:

- Using 5g starch in 20ml water and 100ml passata the thickest sauce using cornflour and the least thick sauces are using wheat flour and brown rice flour.
- I have also found out that from the 6 classmates tested, the most popular sauce (in terms of appearance and texture) was cornflour, followed very closely by cassava flour and arrowroot. The least popular were made with wheat flour and brown rice flour.

Margin note: Good summary paragraph of results here.

Conclusions:

Cornflour, cassava flour and arrowroot are all suitable thickeners that can be used to thicken a pizza sauce. They all provide a sauce which has an attractive gloss and sheen. They did not form lumps, like the wheat flour, in the method I used. I can also see that different starches have different concentrations – so I would like to experiment with different quantities of starch to see if I can improve on the viscosity and get a result nearer to the own-brand pizza sauce which I used as a control.

Science behind gelatinisation:

When you mix the starch with the water it forms a suspension. When this suspension is added to the hot passata liquid the starch granules start to swell as they absorb the liquid. As the heat increases, and over time, the starch granules keep swelling until they form a gel, this process is known as gelatinisation and is what happened in each of my experiments in Session 1 to thicken my passata.

Session 2:

I will repeat the experiment from Session 1 but this time use cornflour only.

I will use 2g, 3g and 4g of cornflour in 20ml of water to see if this improves the viscosity.

Here are my results;

2g cornflour	3g cornflour	4g cornflour
Comments on appearance and texture		
All 3 samples looked the same: thick, dull, opaque, dark, flat, smooth, no lumps or bubbles		
How far did each sauce spread on the viscosity mat?		
4.5	4.5	4

Analysis of results 2:

By adjusting the quantity of cornflour by a matter of 1g or 2g it does have an effect on the viscosity of the sauce. It also shows that how accurate I am when measuring the passata, water and cornflour will affect the final thickness of the sauce – as you can see 2g and 3g had approximately the same thickness. The 4g samples was a little firmer but not as firm as the 5g cornflour sample I used in session 1.

The student has made sure his report includes some food science terms and explanations relevant to his experiments.

6 Conclusions

You may have already written some conclusions after each experiment, but this is the place where you come to your final conclusions. Make sure you pull together the findings of all the experiments you did – AND THIS IS VERY IMPORTANT – make sure you relate your conclusions to your hypothesis.

It is fine if your conclusions do not prove your hypothesis to be right – just explain your findings.

References: Record any references that you use – books, magazines, websites etc.

Final Conclusions:

I can conclude that one of the best ways to thicken a tomato sauce suitable for topping on a pizza is by using a cornflour slurry. It is however not the only way as there are other starches that perform just as well. I can also conclude that it is really important to weigh and measure ingredients accurately, especially when making such small samples.

When I looked closely at the ingredient declaration on my own-brand pizza sauce (which I used as my control) I saw that they also used cornflour as the thickener. I did not know that until I had thought of my hypothesis and was well into my experiments. The cornflour also acts as a stabiliser.

Possible future developments:

If I had more time, I could experiment a little more, by looking at some other methods of thickening I have mentioned on my mind map – such as with eggs, gums, adding purées and reducing the sauce by heating further.

Word count:

A final conclusion has been drawn.

The student has given suggestions on how the experiment could be developed. This is not essential, but if you can think of suggestions to develop the investigation further you could mention it.

Check the word count and page quantity regularly as it is important you stick to the guidelines.

NON-EXAMINATION ASSESSMENTS

GENERAL NEA GUIDANCE

Whether you are doing research for the Food Investigation Assessment or the Food Preparation Assessment here are some basic tips to get you moving in the right direction.

Research is useful as it helps you to look in detail at your chosen area and gives you the chance to gather information that will help you to understand the topic better. It is important that you gather research from reliable sources and you allow yourself time to analyse your findings.

Primary research is when you collect the information yourself.

Examples of primary research include surveys and questionnaires, taste testings, supermarket or restaurant visits, interviews, recipe trialling, experimental work, mood board or mind map of ideas of dishes and skills.

How to write a questionnaire for your assessment

- First make sure you know the brief. Think about who might be your target group; this will help you to make sure that the questions you ask are appropriate to your target group.
- Decide how many people you want to ask, what age range you need to ask and whether you need all male / all female or a mix of male and female? Do you need to target a specific group of people – such as children, teenagers, athletes, etc?
- Write down a list of questions you want to ask and ask a friend to check the questions – do they make sense?
- Make sure your questions are clear and easy to understand. Try not to have too many 'open ended' questions as these are more difficult to analyse. Closed questions are more useful – this is when you will either get yes or no answers or when you give the interviewee choices of boxes to tick from.

Open question example:
What is your favourite dessert?
Closed question example:
If you have to choose only one, which one from the following dessert options would you prefer:
- Pastry based tarts
- Creamy mousses
- Fruit topped meringues
- Crumbles
- Set cheesecakes
- Steamed sponges (with custard)

In this question, if you ask 20 people you could potentially get 20 different answers; this will make analysing your findings more difficult.

If you ask your interviewees to select from a choice you provide, then this will make the information easier to convert to tables or graphs.

- When you have conducted your questionnaire think about how you will communicate your findings – graphs and tables are often a good visual form of presentation, like below:

If you have to choose only one, which one from the following dessert options would you prefer:

- PASTRY BASED TARTS: 8
- CREAMY MOUSSES: 2
- FRUIT TOPPED MERINGUES: 2
- CRUMBLES: 6
- SET CHEESECAKES: 7
- STEAMED SPONGES (WITH CUSTARD): 5

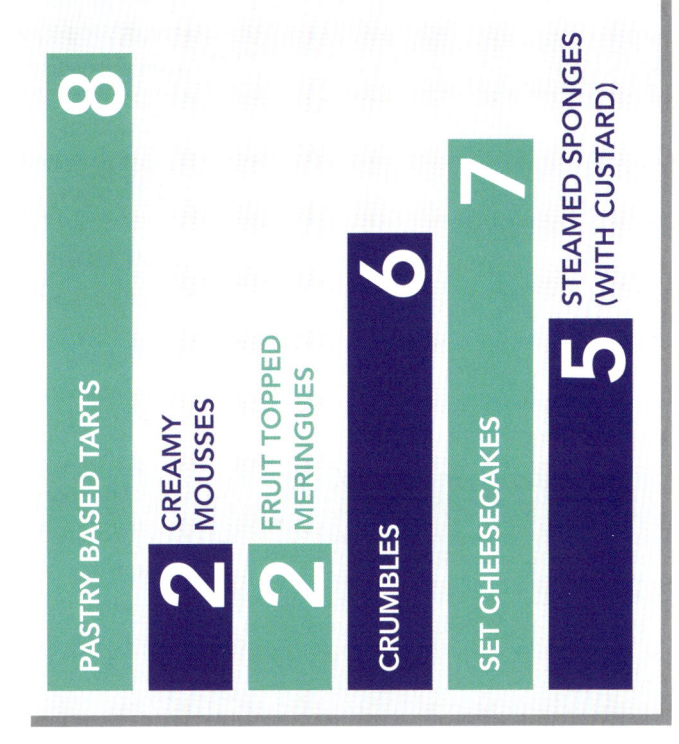

- Make sure you include some form of summary which says what you found out. Use your findings to help you decide and develop your ideas and opinions.

Questionnaires are a form of primary research.

Secondary research is when you look at information that has been collected or written by someone other than yourself.

Examples of secondary research include books, magazines, newspapers, online sources such as websites, online forums, magazines, food bloggers and vloggers.

Don't copy!

Whatever sources you use as part of your research it's important that you take the information, analyse it, and write up your findings in your own words. You must not copy and paste information as this is plagiarism.

Analysing your research findings

It's important that once you have conducted your research that you analyse it and give an opinion based on your findings. You should then use these findings to help you make a decision about the next stage of your task.

Assessment 2: The Food Preparation Assessment

The WJEC specification says:

The Food Preparation Assessment

assesses your knowledge, skills and understanding in relation to the planning, preparation, cooking and presentation of dishes to form a menu.

This means that: *you will be asked to plan, prepare, cook and serve 3 dishes (with appropriate accompaniments) that meet the needs of the brief.*

There will be lots of cooking you have to do to as part of trialling dishes and ideas, and there will also be written work that you have to provide which will support your practical work.

You will have been building up your practical skills since the beginning of the course and this is your chance to showcase your practical and written work.

How does this assessment work?

Your teacher will give you a written brief and you will have a fixed amount of time to do this task in class. This will happen over a period of weeks, so make sure you attend every lesson.

The recommended amount of time to complete this assessment is 15 hours and this includes a 3 hour practical task.

Assessment title	The Food Preparation Assessment
	40% of the qualification
Recommended time for this assessment	15 hours
Word / page guidance	A maximum of 15 pages (30 sides) of A4 (or A3 equivalent), which is to include all photographs, charts and graphs when typed with a font size of 11/12
	Documents over this size are not permitted
	Your work can be presented in electronic or hard copy

Assessment

The Assessment criteria is listed in the specification – make sure you are familiar with it. Within each Section (so that is Section A, Section B(i) and Section B(ii), Section C and Section D) there are bands so you need to read each banding criteria for each section to work out which band your work fits into best. This will give you an idea as to how well you are doing.

ASSESSMENT 2: THE FOOD PREPARATION ASSESSMENT

There are 3 sections to the assessment and they are as follows:

Section A (AO3) (maximum 10 marks)

Research and investigate the task:

You will be expected to:
- research and investigate the assessment using a range of resources
- trial suitable dishes with accompanying written evaluations and photographic evidence

Section B (AO3) (maximum 15 marks)

Section B (i)

Planning the task:

(i) You will be expected to select your menu and justify your choice of dishes

(maximum 6 marks for (i))

Reference should be made to:
- how the research has helped you decide on your dishes
- suitability of dishes chosen to the brief
- skills and cooking methods to be used
- ingredients to be used with awareness of food cost/waste, air miles, food provenance and seasonality

Section B (ii)

(ii) You will be expected to produce a detailed, dovetailed order of work

(maximum 9 marks for (ii))

Reference should be made to:
- timings and relevant health and safety points
- correct ingredients
- quantities and weights
- three clear sections should be included: mise en place, cooking and serving/finishing

Section C (AO4) (maximum 45 marks)

This is the practical 3 hour cooking task

Prepare, cook and present a menu of three dishes and accompaniments:

You will be expected to demonstrate a range of skills related to:
- selection and safe and competent use of a range of kitchen equipment (4)
- knife skills (4)
- accurate weighing and measuring (3)
- suitable preparation of fruits/vegetables/meat/poultry/fish as needed (8)
- production of the meal (15)
- tasting and seasoning (3)
- presentation of final dishes (8)

Section D (AO4) (maximum 10 marks)

Section D

Evaluate the selection, preparation, cooking and presentation of three dishes and accompaniments:

You will be expected to evaluate your work under the following headings:
- time management of the practical session (2)
- technical skills demonstrated in the practical (2)
- taste, texture, appearance and aroma of final dishes (4)
- modifications and improvements (2)

EXAMPLE FOOD PREPARATION ASSESSMENT

To help you, we have included an example for each section of the Food Preparation Assessment, and we will now guide you through each one. This will give you an idea of how your work might look and the detail needed to do well.

You should also look out for examples of work that the exam board will provide to your teachers.

1. Task description
2. Introduction
3. Research ideas
4. Plan of action
5. Results and analysis of research
6. Recipe trials
7. Listing your final dishes
8. Reasons for choice
9. Shopping list
10. Small and large equipment and serving dishes
11. Timeplan (including mise en place and order of work)
12. Evaluation
13. References and bibliography
14. Photographic images of final dishes

Remember!

Please note – the examples we have given in this section are only suggestions as to how the task can be conducted and presented. They are not the only way – you may have a very different way of approaching the task and presenting your material and that is OK. Just make sure you understand the assessment criteria as you go along and keep reviewing your work and reflecting on what you have done. Ask yourself how well you have met the assessment criteria – which banding do you think your work meets and is there anything you need to do to be able to get yourself into a higher banding?

What type of brief will you be given?

Each year the briefs given to your teacher from the exam board will be different. Once you have been given your brief you should start to research the task – your teacher will guide you through this.

Here are some examples of the types of brief you may get:

Example Brief 1

A local restaurant in your area is holding an international week. Research, prepare and cook **three dishes** *with accompaniments that could be served on a themed menu to promote the cuisine of a specific country or region.*

Example Brief 2

Celebrity chefs have been promoting the importance of a healthy diet for children.

Research, prepare and cook **three dishes** *with accompaniments that could be served on an open day menu to encourage new pupils to eat in the school canteen.*

The remainder of this section shows you an example from each of the suggested headings and gives you some pointers to help you understand how well each section can be done.

Guidelines for the Food Preparation Assessment

How can the written work be presented?

You can hand write or type your work. To get the highest marks you are encouraged to create and format your own unique document; to do this you should read and understand the assessment criteria (ask your teacher for a copy).

A writing frame is allowed if this helps you to structure your work. At the top of this page you will also see the key headers that are a good idea to include in your written work. They are all highlighted and numbered, and we will work through them one by one and show you an example of each – the examples are taken from different briefs so it's not one whole piece of coursework, but a collection of sections using different briefs.

1 Task description

Make sure you include the task details (that is the written brief) – so that the moderator can see clearly which task you are doing.

A local restaurant in your area is holding an **international week**. *Research, prepare and cook* **three dishes** *with* **accompaniments** *that could be served on a* **themed menu** *to promote the cuisine* *of a* **specific country** *or* **region.**

Set the scene by showing which task you are doing.

Highlight key words to help you focus on the task.

EXAMPLE FOOD PREPARATION ASSESSMENT

2 Introduction

Here is where you analyse the task.

> Before I start I am going to do some research on what international food and regional foods mean and then jot down the ideas I have that could form part of my research.
>
> **What does international food and regional food mean?**
>
> **International food** is food from all over the world. It can be English, Italian, African, Jamaican, French, American and so on.
>
> There has been an increase in the amount of internationally themed food available in the UK. Some reasons for this increase include the fact that the UK is a multi-cultural society, this influences our food choices as the availability of exotic ingredients and international restaurants increases. Foreign holiday travel, improvements to transport and the popularity of cookery programmes and celebrity chefs are important factors too.
>
> **Regional food** is food that is specific to a particular geographical area such as in the UK cheeses are often made in and named after an area e.g. Caerphilly, Cheddar, Stilton. Other foods are named after the area that they were first made such as Glamorgan sausage, Bakewell tart, Eccles cakes and Melton Mowbray pork pies.
>
> People's desire to try new foods and cuisines should all contribute to a successful International week in a local restaurant.

This is a good introduction, it is concise and relates to the brief.

3 Research ideas

This is where you can list research tasks you are going to do.

As part of your research, try to include a minimum of three recipe trials - include an evaluation of each recipe trial. Ensure each recipe trial evaluation includes a discussion on nutrition, skills, cooking methods and sensory qualities.

> **Research ideas for international foods:**
>
> I did a mind map to jot down ideas I had on the types of research I could do. This was really helpful as it made me think of different ways I could research information.
>
> For my research I have decided to:
>
> - do a survey to decide on my country
> - reflect on my personal strengths and weaknesses
> - compile a questionnaire
> - carry out a supermarket survey
> - create a mind map of ideas and skills
> - carry out recipe trials.
>
> QUESTIONNAIRE/SURVEY
> Find out which countries people like – how much will they pay?
> Do they have any specific dietary requirements etc?
>
> RESTAURANT VISIT
> e.g. Za Za Bazaar where I can taste as many food from different cultures as possible?
>
> INTERVIEW
> Interview a chef from my chosen country.
>
> BOOKS/MAGAZINES/WEBSITES
> Look through some to get more of an idea on dishes, presentation, ingredients etc.
>
> MENU RESEARCH
> Collect menus from restaurants and analyse – or do online survey. Get ideas on popular dishes.
>
> MY RESEARCH IDEAS FOR INTERNATIONAL FOODS
>
> MY OWN SKILLS
> Think about the skills I already have. How can I use these to show off & get good marks?
>
> SUPERMAKET VISIT
> This will help me to get more of an idea on dishes, types & availability of ingredients etc.
>
> IDEAS
> Create a mind map of ideas of dishes. Link this to skills.
>
> COOKING METHODS + EQUIPMENT
> Are there any special materials + pieces of equipment? e.g. China – wok or stir frying

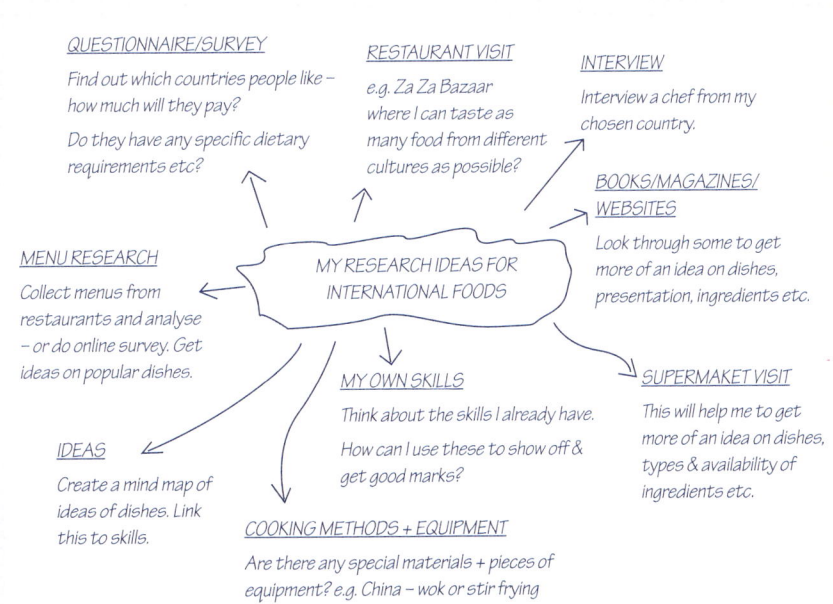

It's clear from this list the research this student plans to do. It is always helpful if you can think carefully about the research that you want to do before you start, but also be flexible – sometimes the findings from one research task will lead you on to another research task.

4 Plan of action

This is where you summarise what you plan to do.

Plan of action

Decide on the research I need to do:

FIRST THING TO DO:	HOW?
Survey people to decide which country is most popular.	I am going to do a quick survey of 20 people to find out what is their favourite cuisine when visiting restaurants – this will help me to decide on my country.
Review my personal strengths when it comes to cooking.	I am going to think about and write down my own personal strengths when it comes to cooking, so that I make sure I show off skills which I know I can do well.
SECOND THING TO DO:	**HOW?**
Decide on my final country.	Using the findings of my quick survey I will make a decision.
Do some primary research linked to my chosen country.	- do a more detailed questionnaire asking people more questions to help me decide on the types of dishes to make for my final country - visit a restaurant or do supermarket survey.
Do a mind map of dishes I could make, and link this to skills.	Look through cookbooks, food magazines, cooking websites and get ideas, then put this onto a mind map. I will use the skills table we have in class so that I make sure I think about the skill level of the dishes I might want to make.
Do some recipe trialling so that I can develop my practical skills.	Use the time in class to develop my skills and knowledge of dishes – I will aim to make at least three dishes that I can make in lesson time.
I will then write all this up and decide on my final three dishes and accompaniments.	Using Word for typing text and Excel for tables and graphs.

In this plan of action it is clear to see what the student wants to do and they have explained how they think they will achieve this.

This student is going to decide very quickly on their final country. This is a good thing as then they can make progress with the rest of the task.

It's really important when you do recipe trialling that the ideas you cook are not the exact final dishes. The recipe trials are a chance to try out ideas, methods, forms of presentation and so on that will help you come to a decision as to what you are going to cook in your 3 hour assessment.

5 Results and analysis of research

This is where you summarise each research task – make sure you list your key findings and give a brief analysis.

Once you have analysed your research, it might be helpful to list some key objectives that you would like to achieve – this can then be used as a starting point for your discussion during the evaluation.

Results and analysis of research:

1. **Survey people to decide which country is most popular**

   Analysis – the most popular countries were Italy with 10 votes, then India with 6 votes and thirdly USA with 4 votes. Before I decide which country I am going to think about what skills and dishes I am good at.

2. **Review my personal strengths when it comes to cooking skills:**

I am good at …	I am not so great at …
Knife skills – I can dice and slice fruits and vegetables neatly	Watching blades – I need to be careful as I have had a few cuts using the knife
I can bone a chicken neatly	Gutting and filleting fish – I find the smell and touching the fish unpleasant
Making cakes – they always rise well and taste great	Decorating cakes – I can pipe OK but I am not so good at making my cakes look professional
Making bread, I can knead and shape well	Pastry – I tend to be a bit heavy handed so my pastry often shrinks and tastes a bit tough

You will need to include a summary of what you found out when doing your research in here – so try to keep it well summarised so that you keep to the page allowance.

400 NON-EXAMINATION ASSESSMENTS

Roux sauces – my sauces tend to be smooth and I never get lumps	Custard – I always seem to over heat the egg yolk and end up with scrambled egg
Making pasta – I love making shapes too	Using gelatine – I always seem to get lumps of gelatine in my cheesecakes
Making quiche fillings	Hollandaise – however hard I try my hollandaise has split
Making meringues	Choux pastry – my éclairs were flat and disappointing
Shallow frying – when I made fish cakes they were evenly cooked	Putting food in and out of the oven – I need to be more careful as I have burnt myself a couple of times.
Shaping mixes into shapes – e.g. meatballs, dumplings and bread rolls. I am good at making these even	
I am neat and tidy when I work	
I am accurate at weighing and measuring ingredients	
I am good at matching flavours together	

Analysis – I need to decide on the skills I want to showcase in my final practical. On the one hand I want to push myself so that I get better at the skills I am not so great at, but on the other hand I don't want to get a bad mark because I made a dish I am not good at. So, what I will do is use my trial sessions to try to improve on some skills like pastry making, cake decorating if I can and then if I can get better at these I could maybe make dishes using these skills in my final assessment.

3. Decide on my final country

I have decided to choose **Italy** as my final country. **Why?** It got the most votes (10), I can research Italian restaurants quite easily as there are three on our high street, Italian ingredients are easy to get hold of in the supermarket. My family like Italian food so my mum will be happy to buy me the ingredients and all my family will give me feedback on my dishes, I am good at making pasta and would like to explore making pasta dishes some more, it gives me the opportunity to show lots of skills.

4. PRIMARY RESEARCH: Do a more detailed questionnaire asking people more questions to help me decide on the types of dishes to make for my final country.

I drafted up 12 questions to ask people and then asked a range of ages (the youngest was 12 and the oldest was 82). I have included my results and analysis here.

Here is a summary of my questions:

Are you male or female?

In a restaurant how much do you think is appropriate to spend on three dishes?

How old are you?

Do you suffer from diabetes?

Do you have any other allergies if so what are they?

Are you a vegetarian?

Do you prefer sweet or savoury dishes?

What is your favourite carbohydrate accompaniment with a main meal?

Which of the following types of pasta sauce would you prefer?

Would you prefer desserts to have a soft or crunchy texture?

Which fruits do you prefer to eat?

Which of the following types of animal proteins do you prefer?

Final analysis of questionnaire:

Here is a summary of what I found out having done my questionnaire, I should bear these points in mind when choosing my final dishes:

- My dishes need to appeal to both male and female customers
- My customers would be happy to spend up to £20 in a restaurant on my three dishes – which means I can spend £10 to £12 on ingredients if I want to make a profit in my restaurant.
- My dishes need to appeal to all age ranges – from 12 to 82 years.
- I do not have to consider customers with diabetes although I should be careful about obesity levels and not going overboard on unhealthy and especially sugary dishes.

Final analysis of questionnaire (contd)...
- I do not have any customers who have allergies, but again, should be considerate about allergies when planning my dishes.
- None of the people surveyed were vegetarian – so I can include meat in my dishes if I wish to.
- I can make both sweet and savoury dishes in my food preparation assessment.
- I should consider pasta, bread, potatoes and rice as possible carbohydrate accompaniments to a dish.
- If I decide to make pasta, both tomato and cream sauces were liked by those surveyed, but tomato was more popular than cream sauces.
- If I do a sweet dish, more people preferred a soft rather than a crunchy dessert so I should bear that in mind.
- Citrus fruits and bananas were the most popular types of fruits
- Chicken was the most preferred source of animal protein.

5. PRIMARY RESEARCH: visit a restaurant or do supermarket survey

I decided to visit my local supermarket to get some ideas on Italian foods and ingredients:

Here is a summary of my findings:

What did I look at?

I chose to research specific types of food like frozen foods, breads and cakes, different fruits and vegetables, ready meals, savoury snacks and speciality items like spices, herbs and oils.

What did I find out?

There were a lot of Italian **carbohydrates**. There were products like dried pasta (tagliatelle, fettuccine, spaghetti, penne, fusilli, lasagne, tortellini etc), bread (ciabatta, focaccia, garlic bread, bruschetta) and risotto rices (Arborio, and Carnaroli). This made me consider making a dish with pasta (I am thinking about ravioli) or rice (risotto) and or bread as part of an Italian dish.

There were also a lot of **pasta ready meals**: ravioli already filled, pasta already covered in sauce, carbonara and lots more. This made me realise that you need good skill to be able to cook Italian food properly so most people just settle for ready made meals. It also showed me that for my food preparation assessment if I do a pasta dish (which is quite likely) I need to practice it to perfection to make sure every component of it is perfect.

This visit opened my eyes to different **Italian ingredients** and not just the ones we use and eat day to day. I saw speciality oils, cheeses (Parmesan, Dolcelatta, Pecorino and Taleggio), capers, pestos (basil, red pepper, walnut), canned beans such as borlotti and cannellini and plum tomatoes (canned and fresh).

At the supermarket I also went down the frozen foods aisle. I looked at the ice cream to see what flavours were available, I saw coffee, chocolate, rum and raisin flavours, as well as the traditional vanilla ice cream. I also saw some sorbets (lemon, mango, raspberry) and had an idea that a sorbet would be a good accompaniment to a fruit tart (if I have time to make it).

There was a large variety of fruit and vegetables, many used in Italian cuisine. I will try and include vegetables to make my dishes healthy. The ones I think would work well in Italian dishes include: sweet potato, spinach, tomatoes, courgettes, peppers, garlic, speciality mushrooms, aubergine, fennel, artichoke and rocket.

Fruits I saw for sale which I can use include: Sicilian lemons, fresh raspberries, melons, apricots and peaches. There was a huge selection of fresh herbs such as basil, rosemary and parsley. These will help to add flavour to dishes.

I looked at the ready-prepared desserts; there were tarts such as pear and almond, Sicilian lemon, chocolate and coffee tart, mousse style dishes such as raspberry mousse and tiramisu. There were panna cottas and ricotta baked cheesecakes, so there is plenty of choice when thinking about sweet dishes I could make for my assessment.

Analysis: Doing this visit was very helpful – it has made me think about the types of Italian dishes which are popular with UK consumers. It has also made me think about skills as to get a good mark I need to show some high level skills in my dishes.

> This is great because the student is relating these dishes from the supermarket to the types of dishes she could consider, as well as the skills levels she needs to demonstrate for higher marks.

EXAMPLE FOOD PREPARATION ASSESSMENT

6 Recipe trials

You should try and do at least three recipe trials, and more if you can. Practice your dishes and make changes to them so that your final dishes will not be the same as your practice ones.

> In class we were given 4 hours of lesson time to do some recipe trialling.
>
> **Recipe trial 1:** Tagliatelle with tomato ragu
>
> On 4th December I made an Italian inspired pasta dish: tagliatelle with tomato ragu. I wanted to practice pasta making and making a simple tomato sauce. I believe that my tagliatelle with a tomato ragu came out successfully. Not bad for a first attempt. The overall taste was very satisfying as all the flavours complemented each other very well. The appearance was neat and had an array of colours which were balanced out to resemble the Italian flag. What I would have to improve on if I was going to do this dish as part of my assessment is to make the pasta more quickly, as I found that I was spending too much time on the stages of making the pasta than doing things like washing up and sanitising my work surfaces. To improve upon the appearance of my dish, if I was going to use it as my part of my final assessment, I would mix the pasta in with the sauce, which is known for being the traditional Italian way of presenting pasta with sauce. There were lots of skills when making this dish such as making fresh pasta, laminating, cutting into tagliatelle ribbons, using a pasta rolling machine, cooking the tagliatelle until al dente, making the ragu – gentle simmering, assembly and presentation. This dish will be a good source of starchy carbohydrate, which is needed for energy, the tomatoes will provide vitamin C and fibre and the dish is low in saturated fat. It's a healthy dish.

There are lots of ways you can write up recipe trials including tables, graphs, annotating photos.

Choose the way that works best for you.

Try to include a minimum of 3 recipe trials.

Include an evaluation of each recipe trial. Ensure each recipe trial evaluation includes a discussion on nutrition, skills, cooking methods and sensory qualities.

The student then went on to conduct three further recipe trials, written up in the same way as the example above.

> Having done all of this research I have set myself the following objectives.
>
> I would like to achieve the following:
> - Prepare dishes that really showcase a range of skills and that I am able to do really well.
> - Make a range of popular Italian dishes and accompaniments, appealing to all ages and both sexes, including a pasta dish and chicken as a source of animal protein.
> - Include citrus fruits as they were popular amongst those asked.
> - Use ingredients that cost me no more than roughly £12.
> - Try to be as healthy as possible with the ingredients and cooking methods I choose.

7 Listing your final dishes

List your final three dishes and accompaniments.

> Now that I have done all my recipe trialling I have been able to improve my practical skills when making fresh pasta, white- and tomato-based sauces, gelatine-set puddings, rubbing-in needed for shortcrust pastry.
>
> I have decided that my three final dishes and accompaniments will be:
>
> *Sweet potato and amaretti ravioli with tomato sauce, served with endive salad*
>
> *Calzone pizza filled with marinated spicy chicken, mushrooms, spinach and melted mozzarella, with a red pepper pesto*
>
> *Lemon tart with raspberry gelato and coulis*

It's important to make sure that its clear what the final dishes will be.

403

8 Reasons for choice

Write these in the future tense. Link why you chose your dishes (your reasons) back to the brief and your research findings.

Make sure your discussion includes:
- how the research has helped you decide on your dishes
- the suitability of your chosen dishes to the brief
- a summary of the skills and cooking methods you will be showing
- link the ingredients to be used with an awareness of food cost/waste, air miles, food provenance and seasonality.

Other factors you may discuss (depending on the brief):
- special diets
- nutritional content
- sensory expectations (appearance, flavour, texture, aroma, presentation)
- time management.

> *Try to keep your reasons for choice concise and relevant to the task.*
> *Likewise, the reasons should be linked in to your research findings.*
> *In this task there is no need to mention nutritional content as this is not a focus of the brief. The brief relates to International food, so the relevance of the 3 dishes should be linked to international cuisine.*
> *A different brief may be linked to a dietary consideration (such as needing iron-rich sources in your dishes or dishes low in saturated fat etc.) and in this instance you may have to include a discussion on nutrients in your dishes and the relevance to the diet you considering. You would also benefit from then including nutritional data, calculated using food tables or a nutrient analyser – your discussion would then be linked to this data.*

Reasons for choice:

I have chosen my three dishes and accompaniments as these are popular Italian inspired dishes that I am confident I can make in my three hour time allowance and if I do them well I can show a range of skills which I hope will get me good marks.

Sweet potato and amaretti ravioli with tomato sauce, served with endive salad

Calzone pizza filled with marinated spicy chicken, mushrooms, spinach and melted mozzarella, with a red pepper pesto

Lemon tart with raspberry gelato and coulis

I have summarised the skills that I will show in each dish as follows:

> *Skills and cooking methods covered here, this is very detailed, more than it needs to be.*

1. Sweet potato and amaretti ravioli with tomato sauce, served with endive salad
- *Baking sweet potatoes, making purée, crushing biscuits*
- *Making pasta dough: kneading, laminating, forming shapes (sealing and removing air to make sure the parcels do not burst when cooked). Cooking pasta until al dente (not mushy)*
- *Knife skills – onion dicing, crushing garlic*
- *Sautéing, simmering, blending, passing through a sieve*
- *Arranging leaves and ravioli parcels artistically*
- *Making a French dressing*

2. Calzone pizza filled with marinated spicy chicken, mushrooms, spinach and melted mozzarella, with a red pepper pesto
- *Making a bread dough from scratch: kneading, proving, knocking back, forming into a perfect round base*
- *Knife skills – sautéing mushrooms, onion and spinach*
- *Preparing and marinating raw chicken*
- *Forming calzone, baking, control of oven*
- *Roasting red peppers, making a pesto*

3. Lemon tart with raspberry gelato and coulis
- *Making shortcrust pastry – rubbing-in*
- *Lining tin, baking blind (without shrinking or burning)*
- *Making lemon custard, baking without cracking or splitting the custard*
- *Making ice cream (not custard recipe)*
- *Making a coulis*
- *Presenting artistically*

My dishes will look attractive as for the ravioli dish I will make sure that each ravioli pillow is evenly sized and filled. The ravioli will be presented with a drizzle of smooth, shiny tomato sauce; the endive salad will provide an eye catching colour contrast as well as providing a crunchy alternative to the soft ravioli pillows. The calzone pizza will have a rustic appearance. I will fold it and seal it carefully so that the filling doesn't escape and it will have a drizzle of my red pepper pesto over the surface to add interesting colour and texture. My lemon tart will be made as a whole tart (with paté sucrée and a baked blind pastry case) and I will cut it into a neat slice so that there is a generous ratio of smooth tart lemon filling to pastry. My raspberry gelato will be smooth and free from ice crystals and the raspberry coulis will be presented as small spheres in decreasing diameter.

Your reasons for choice are written in the future tense as they are written before the practical takes place.

I will take care to ensure I taste my dishes as I make them to ensure the flavours are well balanced from the sweetness of the sweet potato and amaretti ravioli filling to the sweet and acidic lemony custard filling.

There will be a contrast of textures from the al dente pasta to the soft and velvety sweet potato filling and the shiny and glossy tomato sauce accompanying the ravioli. The calzone pizza base, made with yeasted dough, will be rolled out thinly, there will be a generous filling and so that the pizza dough is not too overpowering. The dough will be crunchy and I will make sure that the base is well cooked and not soggy. For the lemon tart the shortcrust pastry base will be sweet and shortbread-like and the gelato will contrast well with the zingy lemon filling. I will keep back some fresh raspberries for added decoration and add a tiny fresh mint leaf for contrast against the creamy yellows and pinks.

I will make sure that I complete my tasks within the three hour time allowance by taking time and effort to write my time plan in detail and multi task as much as possible. I will tick off each task as I do it so that I don't forget anything and make sure I give myself enough time to wash up and present my dishes.

Because this brief is about making dishes for a restaurant I will do my best to present my dishes as you would expect to see in a restaurant, so I will try to get matching crockery and make good use of garnishes and decorations. I will try to make my food and table look as professional as possible.

I have taken on board some of the findings from my questionnaire, so for example, I would say that all three dishes would appeal to both men and women and all ages. To try to keep within a budget of £12 on food cost I will shop carefully and keep a careful eye on my spending. In terms of suitability for people with specific dietary needs, my dishes won't be suitable for coeliacs as all three contain wheat flour. Apart from the pizza (as it has chicken in the topping), they are suitable for lacto-ovo vegetarians and those with nut allergies. Diabetics would need to avoid the lemon tart due to the sugar content, but both the savoury dishes would be acceptable menu choices for those with diabetes.

I will do my best to shop locally and buy locally produced foods as well as those in season rather than imported foods, but this will depend on prices, as I also need to make sure I stick as close as possible to a £12 budget.

I have managed to include pasta and bread (pizza base) in my dishes which is what those people I surveyed said they preferred. My lemon filling for the tart together with the gelato are soft so that will please those who prefer a soft rather than a crunchy sweet dish. I will include spicy marinated chicken in my pizza filling so that will ensure those people who said they prefer chicken are happy.

My final dishes have included inspiration from my supermarket visit as they contain pasta which was a sold in large quantities and in many varieties, plus pesto, lemons for my tart and of course pizza. The gelato to go with the lemon tart was chosen because the supermarket visit made me see that gelato is an ideal Italian style accompaniment to a dessert menu item.

This student does not have to talk about costings or nutritional data in any detail as it is not part of the brief.

This student has included discussions on skills, appearance, flavour, texture, aroma, presentation, time management, special diets, applied reasons to results from various research tasks, mentioned local produce and seasonality and budgetary constraints.

9 Shopping list

It is important that you list all your ingredients and quantities and one way to do this is a shopping list.

Greengrocer
Vegetables
6 garlic cloves
4 shallots
4 button mushrooms
4 maris piper potatoes
1 small stick of celery
250g chantenay carrots
250g green beans
Fruit
250g fresh raspberries
3 lemons
Fresh herbs
1 sprig of thyme
3 tbsp of parsley
1 sprig of parsley

Grocer
1 cube of chicken stock
30ml sunflower oil
15ml extra-virgin olive oil
185g caster sugar
75g icing sugar
200g plain flour
Salt
7 eggs
1 can of chopped tomatoes

Dairy
200g butter
850g double cream
500ml milk

Butcher / Fishmonger
1 medium whole chicken
60g bacon lardons

10 Small and large equipment and serving dishes

It's a good idea to write a list of equipment that you need. You can have the list with you in your practical assessment, and take some time during the preparation session (mise en place) to make sure you have all the equipment that you need before you start cooking.

Small Equipment
(in addition to what I know I will already have in my cupboard and drawers)

Chef Knife	Frying pan	Rolling pin
Boning Knife	Vegetable knife	Red chopping board
Juicer	Mixing bowl	Measuring jug
Sieve	2 baking dishes	Piping bag and nozzle
Large pan	Baking tray	
Small pan	Green chopping board	
Flan tin	Wooden spoon	
Slotted spoon	Brown chopping board	

Large Equipment
Blast chiller
Oven
Mini food processor
Food processor
Hand held electric whisk
Oven
Hob

Display Equipment
2 large circular plates
2 large dish plates
2 glass small plates
4 forks
2 knives
Table runner
Flower in a vase
2 wine glasses
2 napkins

EXAMPLE FOOD PREPARATION ASSESSMENT

11 Timeplan

To give yourself the best chance of getting good marks in this section, make sure this plan is detailed enough so that someone else could follow it.

This example is just one way of doing it – it's useful to have a list for mise en place and then a separate timeplan for cooking time.

Make sure there is evidence of dovetailing in your timeplan – this means that you break down the tasks so that the ones that take the longest you will do first. For example if you were making a pizza you would make the yeasted dough at the beginning of the assessment so that you give as much time as possible for the dough to prove. Then if you were making macaroni cheese you could do that later on, as you know as soon as it comes out of the oven it's ready to serve.

This is quite a hard skill to master, but it will improve the more practice you have writing time plans.

This timeplan is for a French inspired menu. Note the colour coding the student has used in the plan – so that everything relating to each dish within the overall plan is really easy to see at a glance.

> **Key point**
>
> It's important that your timeplan could be followed by someone else – so ask yourself *'Do I have enough information on here so that someone else can make my dishes well?'* (i.e. you haven't missed off any key parts of making the dishes!)

Colour coding:

Poulet à la sauce tomate (chicken in a tomato sauce) with green beans and Vichy carrots
Moules marinieres with crusty baguette
Lemon tart with raspberry coulis and raspberry ice cream

Colour coding the dishes is a helpful way of being able to follow the timeplan easily.

I have 3 hrs total time, including mise en place time for my assessment. I have decided to allow myself 45 mins to do my mep and 2 hrs to cook, plus the final 15 mins to serve, and wash up any last minute equipment.

mep means mise en place.

I will arrive at my assessment with some of my ingredients pre-weighed out, I will use the scales at school to double-check the weights and weigh out the remaining ingredients – this is especially important for my pastry and baguette ingredients.

MISE EN PLACE (45 minutes)

Mise en place	Health and safety points
Prepare self – remove all jewellery, tie hair back, wash hands with anti-bacterial soap, and put on apron	Make sure water is hot and apron is clean
Sanitise work surfaces	Use anti-bacterial spray
Pre-heat oven to 180°C fan, for lemon tart pastry	
Collect and weigh all ingredients and place onto white trays. Place high risk ingredients into refrigerator	High risk ingredients are: double cream, clotted cream, whipping cream, milk, butter **near to the top of the fridge,** chicken and fresh mussels **at the bottom of fridge – all covered**
Collect all equipment and serving dishes and place to the side until needed	
Check weighed ingredients for pastry and baguette	Use digital scales for accuracy
Grease the baking tray and tart tin	
Top and tail green beans, wash and place into steamer tray for later	Place waste in compost bucket for all vegetable trimmings
Peel and tidy up carrots and place into a saucepan for later	
Peel small onions and place into small saucepan	
Wipe over baby mushrooms with damp cloth and trim as necessary with small vegetable knife. Store in small bowl and chill	
Crush the garlic	
Make bouquet garni	

You have 3 hours in total for your practical assessment – talk to your teacher about how long you should take for mise en place before you start cooking.

How to write your timeplan pp 419

Mise en place	Health and safety points
Clean the mussels by thoroughly scrubbing them under plenty of running water, pulling away the 'beards'. Discard any broken mussels along with the 'beards', and any mussels that don't close tightly when you tap them.	**HIGH RISK** **Make sure bought as fresh as possible and kept refrigerated (2 to 5°C). MUST NOT USE ANY MUSSELS THAT WILL NOT CLOSE WHEN TAPPED.**
Dice onion, chop garlic and parsley for moules.	
Butcher whole chicken into 2 breasts, 2 thighs, 2 wings and 2 drumsticks.	**HIGH RISK** **Back into fridge when prepared – base of fridge, well covered.**
Open the can of chopped tomatoes.	
Make up chicken stock with stock cube and boiling water.	
For bread: Sift the flour and salt into the mixing bowl. Add the quick action dried yeast and blend together.	
For pastry: Sift the flour into the mixing bowl. Cut the butter into small pieces and rub fat into flour until resembles coarse breadcrumbs. Add in caster sugar and stir. Cover with clingfilm and chill. Measure out water for pastry and chill.	
Separate egg yolks from whites.	
Zest and juice lemons for lemon tart, make the raw custard (egg yolks, lemon juice, cream, sugar), cover and chill. Keep one egg white back and lightly beat. Juice a lemon for the coulis.	Keep egg whites and freeze.
Lay the table: Place cloth on table, vase of flowers, cutlery and menu card. Also crockery – some will be placed into oven for warming later on. Make sure the plates are all circular.	Take time to get the presentation right.

ORDER OF WORK (allow 2 hrs to cook and 15 mins to serve and finish tidying up)

Time	Activity	Health and safety points / Food safety points	Food quality points
9 mins	**Make bread dough for baguette and prove** Make a well in the centre of the flour and yeast and add all the warm water and oil. Mix to a soft dough with a wooden spoon. Knead on a lightly floured surface for approximately 5 minutes until the dough is smooth and springy. Allow to prove in a lightly floured bowl, covered with a damp cloth.	Somewhere warm, so that bread will prove faster.	Additional water may be needed the dough is too dry. Need dough quite sticky. Until volume has increased and dough is light & spongy. The longer the dough can be allowed to prove the better.
5 mins	**Make pastry for lemon tart and rest.** Using a knife, stir in just enough of the cold water to bind the dough together. Wrap the dough in clingfilm and chill for 10-15 minutes.		Water, equipment and hands should be chilled to produce good quality shortcrust pastry.
5 mins	Wash up and let dishes drip dry.	Make sure water is hot	
1 min	**Start on chicken dish.** Place the small saucepan onto the hob, fill with water, bring the water to the boil, then blanch the onions.	Keep saucepan handles way from side of hob. Use oven gloves when draining and take care with the steam.	Drain in a colander and refresh under cold running water.
5 mins	Roll out pastry for tart, line with beans and blast chill.		Chill to ensure that the pastry case doesn't shrink. Roll pastry between clingfilm sheets if it's crumbly. Keep any leftover pastry and reuse.

An indication of time should be included in the timeplan.

This student has sensibly planned their practical so that all 3 dishes will be served towards the end of the practical. As this is not a meal the dishes do not have to be served in sequence (e.g. starter first, then main, then dessert) but to show dovetailing it would be expected that the dishes are served within a close time of each other.

EXAMPLE FOOD PREPARATION ASSESSMENT

Time	Activity	Health and safety points / Food safety points	Food quality points
1 min	Drain the onions and allow to cool.		
5 mins	Dry up then wash up again, drip dry.		Drip drying saves me time.
1 min	Bake lemon tart pastry blind.	Use oven gloves – avoid burns. Make sure the paper is trimmed so that it doesn't catch fire in the oven.	I want the pastry just cooked – I don't want to colour it.
5 mins	**Carry on with chicken dish** *Brown onions and soften lardons* Place the 15g butter and 1 tbsp sunflower oil into the base of the casserole dish and soften the diced bacon. Add the drained and cooled onions shaking the pan to brown them evenly all over. Remove the bacon and onions from the pan and place onto a plate until later.	Beware of the lardons spitting. Watch the butter doesn't burn. **DO NOT LEAVE THE PAN UNATTENDED.**	Use a frying pan if a casserole dish is not suitable for the hob. Use a slotted spoon to remove bacon and onions.
6 mins	**Pan fry chicken** Place the chicken pieces into the pan and brown the skin. Using tongs, turn the chicken over and do the same of the reverse side. When the chicken is evenly browned (it will not be cooked yet) remove from the pan.	**DO THIS QUICKLY TO REDUCE THE RISK OF FOOD POISONING AND BACTERIA MULTIPLYING.**	Put on chicken pieces skin side up. Add extra butter and oil if needed. Place onto the plate with the bacon and onions.
2 mins	**While the chicken is being browned** Check on pastry for lemon tart – remove baking beans – back in oven 5 mins to finish cooking (I don't want it brown).	Careful – beans will be hot.	Need to make sure all pastry is cooked – the centre of the tin will take the longest to cook.
5 mins	**Make roux** Keeping the pan on the heat, add the flour. Slowly add the chicken stock and stir with the magic whisk, then add chopped tomatoes, crushed garlic, bouquet garni, salt and freshly ground black pepper. Allow the sauce to come to the boil and gently add back the bacon, onions and chicken. Reduce to a simmer.		Add hot chicken stock gradually to avoid lumps. Transfer everything to ovenproof dish when ready to go in oven.
2 mins	Pastry case out of oven, brush with egg white and back in oven for 2 mins.	Will stop any 'leaks' of the lemon custard (due to coagulation of protein in egg white, forms a waterproof layer).	
5 mins	Dry up and wash up again, drip dry.		
5 mins	**During washing up** Pastry out of oven and chicken in oven temp down to 150°C. Sieve and pour on lemon topping and back in oven to bake.	On a tray in the oven Take care – use oven gloves.	Place tin on baking tray before it goes in the oven. Set timer for 30 mins to check on it so I don't forget.
8 mins	**Make ice cream and freeze** Blend the frozen raspberries, vanilla essence, icing sugar and clotted cream in a food processor for 5 seconds. With the motor running, pour in the whipping cream and continue to blend until smooth. Spoon the ice cream into a container and freeze.	**WATCH BLADE – VERY SHARP**	Make sure covered in freezer.
5 mins	**Back to bread dough for baguette** Knock back bread dough and shape into baguette – allow to prove on the greased baking tray.		Prove somewhere warm.
6 mins	**Back to the chicken** Pan-fry mushrooms for chicken dish and then add to casserole, transfer to hob to finish cooking.	Don't have the heat too fierce – needs to be on a steady simmer.	Add to poulet à la sauce tomate after 30 mins. Stir from time to time so that it doesn't catch on the bottom.

Washing up regularly is important – it avoids getting a huge pile of washing up at the end.

Time	Activity	Health and safety points / Food safety points	Food quality points
5 mins	At the same time: dry up then wash up		
2 mins	Remove lemon tart from oven – cool at room temperature then blast chill. Turn oven up to 230°C for baguette.	Use oven gloves.	Don't want it brown – needs to have a slight wobble in the centre. Also want to avoid any cracks in the lemon custard.
2 mins	Check on ice cream – beat to remove any ice crystals and carry on freezing.		
8 mins	**Make raspberry coulis and chill** Heat the sugar and water in a small saucepan over medium heat, stirring from time to time, until the sugar dissolves completely – about 5 minutes. Put the raspberries, lemon juice and the sugar syrup in a mini blender and purée. Strain through a fine mesh sieve to remove the seeds and chill until needed.		Needs to be strained to remove seeds; taste it – may need lemon juice or sugar to balance the flavour.
5 mins	Dry up then wash up again. Keep an eye on baguette dough proving.		
1 min	**Vegetables for chicken** Put kettle on to boil for water - needed to steam green beans and simmer carrots.	Avoid trailing wires from the kettle	
2 mins	**Back to bread dough for baguette** Make slits on surface of bread and place into oven to bake.	Set timer so I don't forget.	
2 mins	**Start to cook carrots** Place carrots in a large saucepan with the butter, sugar and a pinch of salt. Cover the carrots half way with water and bring to the boil. Reduce the heat to a simmer, then cover and cook for 10 mins until just tender.	Pan handles away from edge of hob.	
1 min	Place plates for moules and poulet à la sauce tomate into the oven to warm.		
5 mins	**Start doing moules** Heat the olive oil in a heavy pan with a tight-fitting lid. Add the onions and garlic and cook over a medium heat until softened, but not coloured.		Pay attention – don't want to burn onion or garlic.
	At same time: **Start to steam green beans** **Carry on cooking carrots** *Carrots:* Turn up the heat and cook until the water has evaporated and I am left with a buttery glaze. This will take 5-10 minutes.	Lift lid away from myself if I need to lift lid.	
5 mins	**Back to the moules** Add the stock and turn up to a high heat. As the stock starts to boil, add the cleaned mussels and thyme to the pan. Turn the heat down to low. Put the lid on the pan and allow the mussels to steam. Cook for about 4-5 minutes, lifting the lid from time to time to check.	I will know they are cooked when the shells have opened. Discard any mussels that remain closed. **FOOD SAFETY ISSUE – MUST NOT FORCE OPEN ANY UNOPENED SHELLS.**	
	At the same time as moules is cooking Dry up and put equipment away.		
1 min	**Bread out of oven** Onto cooling rack.	Use oven gloves.	I will know the bread is done when it is a good golden brown colour, and when tapped on the underside it will sound hollow.
1 min	Add the double cream and cook for a further minute. Scatter with the chopped parsley.		

Time	Activity	Health and safety points / Food safety points	Food quality points
	Start serving (allow 15 mins)		
	Serve Moules Mariniere straightaway with crusty bread	Probe and ensure mussels are at a minimum of 75°C. Use anti bacterial wipes.	Present attractively
	Serve poulet à la sauce tomate with Vichy carrots and steamed green beans	Probe and ensure chicken is at a minimum of 75°C. Use anti bacterial wipes.	Present attractively
	Slice lemon tart, serve with raspberry ice cream and raspberry coulis		If ice cream is a little soft treat it like whipped cream, don't get it out of the freezer until just before serving.
	Wash up any remaining dishes.		
	Dry and put away draining dishes, wash up and dry up remaining dishes. Resanitise area for final time.		
	Ensure cooker is switched off, and that all equipment is returned to the correct storage areas.		

The cooking assessment

Since studying food at school, you will have been learning about how to work well in your practical lessons – you will have been learning about different skills and cooking methods, how to cook with specific ingredients, the importance of working safely and hygienically, ways to present foods attractively and so on. You will also be working on your organisation and be getting a feel for how long tasks take.

The practical task for this assessment has a maximum of 45 marks and is done in a three-hour slot. You will be expected to cook your chosen three dishes and accompaniments independently in one session.

In this section we give you some pointers to help you get it right.

The 45 marks for this three hour cooking assessment are broken down as follows:

- selection and safe and competent use of a range of kitchen equipment (4 marks)
- knife skills (4 marks)
- accurate weighing and measuring (3 marks)
- suitable preparation of fruit/vegetables/meat/poultry/fish as needed (8 marks)
- production of the meal (15 marks)
- tasting and seasoning (3 marks)
- presentation of final dishes (8 marks).

If you want to find out in more detail how each of these points is assessed take a look at the specification.

Deciding on your dishes

- Make sure that the dishes and accompaniments that you have chosen are achievable in the time that you have. Don't pick dishes that you know you just cannot manage in the three hour time or that take a long time to set or cook.
- Choose dishes that can show a range of skills – you do not want three dishes and accompaniments which include the same skill. For example, it would not be appropriate to make three pastry dishes, or three dishes using a roux sauce, as then you would be repeating the skills across all three dishes, and missing the chance to showcase additional skills.
- Pick skills that you know you are good at – so if for example you know you are excellent at making fresh pasta, select an appropriate dish which shows this off; or if you know you are well experienced and can fillet fish confidently, chose a dish that requires you to do this – on the proviso that this fits well with the brief of course!
- Choose dishes that will work well together in terms of the equipment that you have – so don't choose three dishes that all need the oven at three different temperatures or that mean your will need six saucepans on the hob at the same time.
- Make sure you use both the oven and the hob.
- Make sure your three dishes and accompaniments have a contrast of colours, textures and flavours – so, you don't want three dishes to be the same, e.g. beige, soft and tasting of vanilla!
- Use recipe sources that you know can be trusted – do not use a recipe from a random website which you have never used before.
- Try to choose three dishes that will take you roughly the same amount of time – do not pick one dish that you know will take up most of your time and energy.
- Do not pick expensive ingredients – there really is no need.
- Do not plan to cook large quantities of each dish, this will take you longer to prepare and cook. Aim for approximately two portions for each dish – some dishes may be larger such as a whole cake or whole quiche, others may be smaller such as a bowl of soup or a plate of pasta and sauce.
- Look at the skills table and make sure you pick dishes that have suitable skills that you can achieve based on your ability.

Before the practical

- If you are providing your own ingredients, try to pack them up into separate boxes so that you know which box relates to which dish. Don't let someone else do this for you as you might get ingredients muddled up (plain and self-raising flour for instance). Make sure each ingredient is clearly labelled.
- Have your timeplan printed out, also your ingredients and equipment list (these can be really useful to refer to during the assessment).

- Get a good night's sleep.
- Make sure any ingredients that are in the refrigerator or freezer are not left at home!
- Eat breakfast and take some water into school – as you will need to keep hydrated during the assessment. Depending on the time of the day that your assessment takes place, you might want to take a snack or packed lunch.
- Go to the toilet before you go to your food room to start the assessment.
- Make sure you know which part of the kitchen you are working in, this will help to make your feel settled and calm.

Good use of the mise en place time

In your mise en place time (also called preparation time) you can get yourself ready so that when you start cooking, you will be ready to start and all your basic preparation will be done.

The types of tasks you can do include:

- laying your table (if there is a table free for you to do so)
- greasing and lining tins
- vegetable and fruit prep: washing, peeling, slicing, dicing, grating etc.
- butchering meat, chicken, fish
- rubbing in fat to flour
- beating eggs
- opening cans
- juicing citrus fruits

Do not cook anything – if you are not sure ask your teacher when you are writing your timeplan and not on the day of your assessment!

During the practical

- Do not chat – stay focused all the time.
- Use your timeplan to help keep you on track and make regular time checks or use timers so that you don't forget about any foods cooking.
- Lay out all your ingredients on trays. If there are enough trays try to have a separate tray for each dish – this will help you to stay well organised.
- Work neatly and clean down your area regularly.
- Drink small sips of water often to keep you hydrated.
- Do your mise en place first – this is why a detailed timeplan is important, so that you don't forget to prepare something. Cooking will be much quicker if you don't have to stop to dice an onion or grate some carrot – so mise en place is key to this.
- Make sure you work carefully and safely – show that you know how to handle knives, electrical equipment and so on sensibly and safely.
- Use the right tool for the job.
- Make sensible use of the refrigerator – do not leave high risk ingredients such as raw fish, meat, and cream out at room temperature. Also make sure you keep the risk of cross contamination of foods to a minimum.
- Work hygienically, wash up as you go along. Let your dishes drip dry – it will save you time.
- Do not get out more equipment than you need, it takes up room.
- Allow enough time to present your food at the end and give thought to the style of display dishes and garnishes and decorations you use on the finished dishes.
- When you are finished, tell your teacher so that they can mark your work.
- Serve food at the correct temperature; hot food should be hot (not lukewarm) and cold food should be cold (not room temperature).
- Make sure that your food is photographed.

After the practical

- Leave your work area as you found it – the equipment should be returned washed and dried, your work surfaces should be cleaned. Make sure there are not any nasty surprises lurking in the plughole. This is many a teacher's pet hate!
- Check the floor and give it a quick sweep if necessary.
- Make sure all your food is put away and stored appropriately until it is time for you to go home.
- Get feedback – do not leave this too long as you will forget – ask your peers or adults for their opinion as to how your food looks and tastes. Make notes on this – you can use these opinions when you do your evaluation.

12 Evaluation

This is where you talk about whether the dishes you chose and then made met the brief. You will evaluate the selection, preparation, cooking and presentation of the three dishes and accompaniments.

In your discussion, make sure you include:

- time management of the practical session (2 marks)
- technical skills demonstrated in the practical – how suitable were they? How did you carry them out? (2 marks)
- taste, texture, appearance and aroma of final dishes (use specialist terminology) (4 marks)
- suggestions for modifications and improvements (2 marks)

Did my meal meet the brief?

Earlier I wrote a list of the key points I wanted my three dishes to include. I will now evaluate my practical against these key points:

I have made three traditional French dishes:

My first savoury dish was poulet à la sauce tomate with steamed green beans and Vichy carrots, my second savoury dish was moules marinieres with crusty baguette and my sweet dish was lemon tart with raspberry coulis and raspberry ice cream. All three dishes are popular menu items in French restaurants, both in France and the UK. The final recipes were obtained from French inspired cookbooks and websites and were popular suggestions given to me during the questionnaire I conducted.

Feedback I received from both adults and my peers all indicted that my three dishes were French in name and in content, so I believe that I definitely met the brief well.

Some other key points that came out when I carried out my research were:

- To include a poultry product
- To ensure that the dishes were nut free
- That I should consider using seafood
- That I should consider in season and local produce
- That citrus fruits should be included as they were popular amongst the people surveyed.

I made sure that I included all these aspects in my final menu. I used chicken in the poulet à la sauce tomate and to demonstrate higher skills I portioned a whole chicken. I chose dishes that I knew would be nut free. The moules mariniere contained fresh mussels which are actually from the south coast (near to where I live) and are also a regional speciality in French coastal towns. I used seasonal and local ingredients wherever possible, which I know is also an ethos of French chefs – so I used local onions, carrots, chicken, cream and green beans. The lemon tart contains a significant amount of lemons (both the juice and the rind) so I ensured that one of my dishes contained citrus fruits.

[Skills mentioned here]

How skilful were my final dishes?

In my reasons for choice I summarised the skills that would be needed for each dish.

As you will see if you refer to the reasons for choice section, there are a wide range of skills demonstrated in theory – the question is did I manage to do all these skills and did I do them well?

[Skills listed in reasons for choice – so credit given]

The feedback from Mr Jones, Deputy Head, who came and saw all our dishes after the assessment, was positive. He commented on the presentation of my dishes and said he particularly liked the way that I had arranged the breast on the plate for the poulet à la sauce tomate (sliced and fanned). I must admit that I found the butchering of the chicken quite tricky – I had done this two or three times before – both as a class task and also as a trial, when I trialled chicken in a cream sauce. But I think nerves got the better of me and I left more meat on the carcass than I would have liked. I think if I could do this again I would practise this technique some more.

[Skills mentioned here]

I also found the making of the paté sucrée for the tart challenging. I think this was because the room was really warm, which meant that the dough was soft, as the butter was really soft. My hands were hot too, and the key to successful shortcrust-style pastry is to ensure that all the ingredients and equipment are cool. I got over this by popping the pastry in the fridge to cool it down. I am glad

[The student has discussed improvement here]

I managed to do that as I was pleased that the pastry didn't shrink when I baked it blind. If there was a next time, I would do this earlier on, before the room gets too hot.

Cleaning and de-bearding the mussels took me longer than I had planned. This meant that I got behind in my mise en place time so I had to work really hard to get myself back on track. At one point I felt overwhelmed by how much I had to do, but because I had done my timeplan in good detail I could keep referring to it and ticking off each task when it was done, this really helped me to stay focused and organised, and kept me sticking to my plan. I am so glad I took the effort to write my timeplan to the detail I did.

If you look at the presentation of my three dishes in the photographs you will see I did my best to try to make them look as attractive as possible. I used similar shaped crockery, all white, and used garnishes and decorations to add colour to the presentation, the fresh raspberries on the tart, and the fresh parsley on the mussels.

Sensory evaluation of my final dishes

Poulet à la sauce tomate with steamed green beans and Vichy carrots

From looking at the poulet à la sauce tomate I can clearly see that the chicken is tender and strongly coloured by the rich maroon roux. The beans have a deep forest green colour retained by the steaming process and they are neatly stacked. As the star diagram shows, the Vichy carrots got a 4/5 score meaning that they were well glazed. The mushrooms look tender and soft, contrasting well with the other textures in the dish. The range of colours used in the dish compliment it and makes it stand out. The stock used infuses the dish with an enriching, warming flavour. To improve the presentation of the dish I would add more flour to the roux to make it thicker; I might also put some extra jus in a little pouring pot in order to give the customer accessibility to more if they want it. The plate looks full; this is a great appearance to have in a restaurant as it shows skill and good presentation skills and also helps to make the dish look more professional. Looking at the finished table the portion sizes are very well controlled as I counted the Vichy carrots and green beans. I also used a slotted spoon to remove the chicken from the baking tin so that the sauce did not spill over the plate, and then after I put the sauce on the plate I wiped it down, to prevent greasy finger marks or drips from the sauce ruining the presentation of the dish. Mr Jones is said this dish was 'superb'. My friend, Sophie, found the Vichy carrots 'addictive' as she really enjoyed the buttery taste.

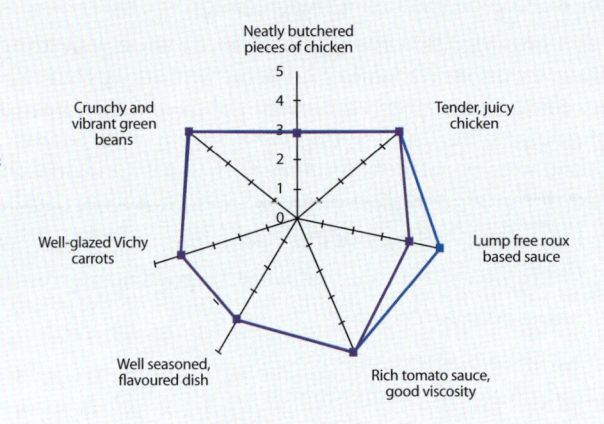

EXAMPLE FOOD PREPARATION ASSESSMENT

Moules marinieres with crusty baguette

The feedback I got from my tasters for this dish was really positive. They all really enjoyed the tender cooked mussels and all my hard work when cleaning them paid off as they did not have any grit or sand in them. The aroma was pretty strong, as you would expect. The sauce was creamy and velvety and had the garlic-enhanced flavour. The crusty bread was well shaped (it did look like a baguette, which I was worried it wouldn't do) and it was light and fluffy inside. The lowest scoring attribute was the colour. I did add a leaf of parsley and also added a lemon wedge for colour but my taster scored this a 3, which was the lowest score. Maybe next time, I could put it in a more colourful serving dish, as I am not sure how else I could make it more colourful.

Lemon tart

As you can see from the full picture of the lemon tart the filling has a delightfully creamy looking pale, pastel-yellow filling achieving a 5/5 and a 4/5 on the star diagram. The pastry case has an evenly spread golden appearance and looks almost full to the brim with the lemon filling. I used the raspberries on the lemon tart to show the strong contrast in colour from the raspberries – which achieved a 4/5 on the star diagram. As shown from the picture of the presented slice, the filling has held its shape well and the pastry is very thin in comparison to the size of the filling; the fact that the filling has held well shows that the timing was very good in order to get the tart from the oven to the blast chiller to leave me enough time to present it well. Clearly from the picture, I have paid attention to detail whilst presenting the coulis on the tart and ended up using a coulis dropper to help me. I used a scoop for the ice cream to make sure that each scoop was the same size and tried to make it look like a quenelle but as you can see from the picture that worked quite well.

As the star diagram shows, the pastry was a 5/5 when described as golden, buttery, melt-in-the-mouth pastry, meaning that it was blind baked well as it ended up at that texture. My parents really enjoyed this dessert saying it was 'delightful' as it is one of their favourite desserts and they loved the presentation of the dish; Mr Harris loved how thin the pastry was and also the creamy lemon filling, finding it 'divine'. A large tart made 8 portions, which were evenly sliced to make sure that the dish was evenly portioned for each person.

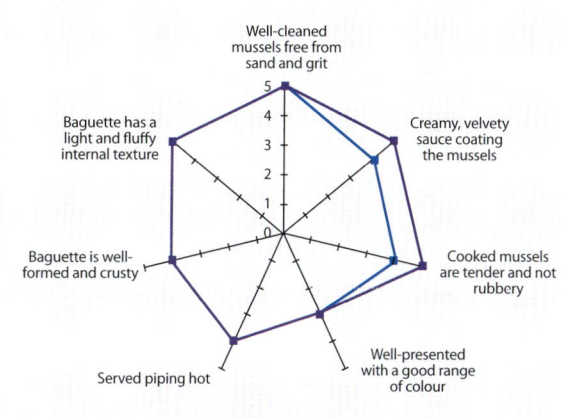

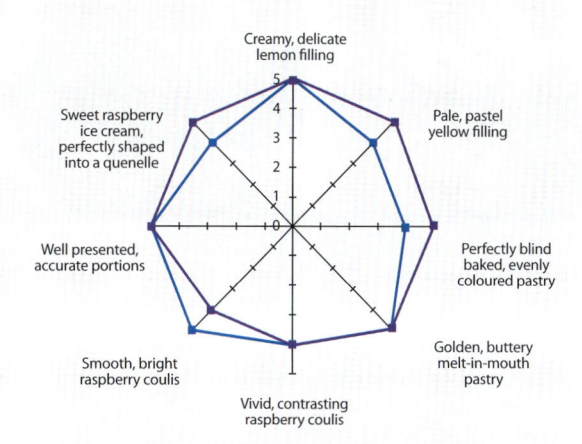

Improvements
- If I was given the same task again I would try to make the roux thicker in the Poulet à la sauce tomate and provide some in a little pouring pot with the dish.
- I would also practise portioning chicken until I was more skilled and more importantly confident.
- If I had more time, I could have done a trio of desserts instead of just one, with a range of pastries to show off the finesse of the cuisine, I also would have done this as it would give a little taste of the range of desserts from the cuisine as a whole.

13 References and bibliography

Here is where you include any resources you used e.g. books, internet, magazines, video clips, etc.

14 Photographs of the final dishes

Make sure that your work is submitted with clear photographic images of your final dishes. Here are some finished dishes from a task based on foods from a specific country to show you.

> **Study tip**
>
> Make sure all your pages have (in either the header or the footer on every page):
> - your name, candidate number and centre number
> - page number

French inspired dishes

Poulet à la sauce tomate with green beans and Vichy carrots

Fruit tartlets (a sweet pastry shell, filled with crème patissière, topped with freshly prepared fruits and glazed with apricot)

Floating Islands (strawberry compote, topped with custard and poached meringue)

Italian inspired dishes

Arancini (rice balls in a crispy coating, deep fried) filled with mozzarella cheese and rosemary served with homemade mayonnaise

Stuffed chicken breast served with gnocchi (Italian potato dumplings) and a tomato sauce

Panna cotta, with raspberry coulis and shortbread biscuit

SKILLS

In order to do well in your Food Preparation Assessment it is important that the dishes you choose showcase your practical skills.

We often talk about dishes being:
- high skill
- medium skill
- low skill.

In reality, nothing is that black and white. A student could choose a high skill dish, say, a lemon meringue pie, but if there are parts of the dish that did not go as well as they should have, then this may no longer be thought of as a high skill dish.

So – what could go wrong to reduce the skill level of this lemon meringue pie?

Things that could go wrong include:
- the pastry may have shrunk when it was baked blind
- the pastry may be raw on the base
- the pastry could be tough when tasted
- the lemon filling may be lumpy or scrambled
- the meringue may be flat
- the meringue may be burnt
- the presentation may be untidy

Therefore it is important to realise that in order for a dish to be considered high skill, not only should the skills shown by the student reflect the high skill criteria, but the practical work should also be conducted in a highly skilled manner.

Here are some examples of named dishes and the skills that can be shown in these dishes. This gives you an idea of the skills and skill levels that can be shown in a range of different dishes.

Name of dish	Specific skills involved (remember that high skills have to be done in a skilful way to be recognised as high skill!)	Skill level criteria (high, medium or low)
Savoury		
Beef lasagne	**Meat sauce** Knife skills – dicing vegetables, crushing garlic Sautéing, simmering **Fresh pasta** Making a pasta dough Laminating and cutting to shape **White sauce** Making a roux Thickening without lumps – sauce should be smooth and velvety (if adding cheese – ensuring cheese is melted and not stringy) **Assembly** Assembling layers of meat sauce, pasta and white sauce evenly Ensuring evenly baked and well gratinated	High (medium if using dried pasta)
Lamb burgers	Dicing onion Binding and forming meat patty rounds – ensuring they are equally sized Cooking evenly and thoroughly (minimum core temperature 75°C achieved)	Medium
Leek and cheese tart	**Shortcrust pastry** Rubbing-in Mixing Forming dough of correct consistency, resting dough Rolling out and lining tin Baking blind **Filling** Knife skills – dicing and slicing vegetables and other ingredients Sautéing Grating cheese Making egg custard – ensuring white and yolk of egg well blended Baking	Medium / high (for high skill - pastry must not have shrunk and must be 'short' and tender Filling must be well baked and not overcooked)
Vegetable samosas (*making samosa pastry from scratch*)	Making samosa pastry from scratch Making curry paste from scratch Knife skills – dicing and slicing vegetables Sautéing Rolling out samosa dough Sealing one side of samosa dough by dry frying Forming cone shape and filling and sealing Use of deep fat fryer	Medium / high

Name of dish	Specific skills involved *(remember that high skills have to be done in a skilful way to be recognised as high skill!)*	Skill level criteria *(high, medium or low)*
Sweet		
Sultana and cranberry muffins	Folding/mixing Dividing mix evenly between paper cases Minimal drips on paper cases Baking	Low
Cheesecake (gelatine set)	**Base** Crushing biscuits Melting butter Forming base **Filling** Beating/whisking cream Flavouring Melting gelatine and using appropriate quantities of gelatine so that cheesecake has the required texture Setting **Finishing** Applying decorative finishes	Medium/high *(for high skill – biscuit base could be made from scratch, cheesecake should have elaborate decorative finishes e.g. a coulis or fruit glaze, piped cream, segmented orange slices, spun sugar etc.)*
Fruit filled Swiss roll	Whisking method of cake making Even baking, well risen and not burnt Rolled neatly, free from cracks Filled appropriately (more than solely jam) Well assembled with decorative finishes	Medium
Chocolate éclairs (choux pastry)	Ensuring fat and water mix come to a rolling boil before adding sifted flour Producing raw choux pastry to the correct consistency (not too stiff nor too runny) Piping into even éclair shapes Baking – need to be golden brown and well risen Filled with appropriate filling e.g. crème patissière / crème Chantilly Finishing technique used e.g. glacé icing, chocolate topping	High *(for high skill – finished product must be well baked and have elaborate and well-presented decorative finishes*

Here is an example of a simple dish – Leek, potato and onion soup.

The column on the left shows what a student would need to do to make sure that this was produced as a medium skill dish, the column on the right shows what the student actually managed – which meant that their medium skilled soup became a low skilled soup.

Skills which can be included in most of the recipes above, and skills that your teacher will be looking for in all your cooking include:

- weighing and measuring accurately
- appropriate knife skills (slicing, dicing, chopping etc.)
- control of oven / hob / grill and small scale electrical equipment
- greasing and lining tins and trays *(when relevant)*
- working hygienically and cooking food thoroughly
- working safely – to avoid accidents
- ability to manage time and **dovetail** (and **multi-task**)
- appropriate presentation of dishes with garnishing and decorative techniques used to enhance the presentation
- consideration as to seasoning and flavours of finished dish.

Leek, potato and onion soup	
Criteria for dish to be a MEDIUM SKILL	**Skills actually demonstrated by learner**
Onions and potato finely diced	Onions and potato diced unevenly, some pieces of peel and skin in the pan when being sautéed
Leeks sliced thinly, and free from grit/soil	Leeks sliced unevenly and unwashed
Vegetables are gently sautéed, very little colour achieved (definitely no burnt bits)	Vegetables were sautéed, but student did not control the heat well, so there are too many burnt bits of onion, potato and leek
Vegetables are gently simmered in stock	Student had trouble controlling the hob, and the soup was boiling rather than simmering
Final soup is velvety, smooth, well blended, no grainy bits or missed pieces of onion, potato or leek	Final soup looked and felt grainy (potatoes needed longer cooking), there were too many pieces of vegetables which missed being blended (this is supposed to be a smooth soup)
The soup is well seasoned	The soup has not been tasted and is bland.
Soup has been presented attractively – evenly coloured and sized croutons or cream drizzled or thin slices of sautéed leek.	Little thought given to presentation – the bowl had greasy finger-marks over it, and there was no thought given to garnishing it.

These resources have been adapted from the materials provided in the WJEC Teachers Guide:
WJEC: http://www.wjec.co.uk/qualifications/food-and-nutrition/WJEC%20GCSE%20Food%20and%20nutrition%20-%20GFT.pdf

HOW TO WRITE YOUR TIMEPLAN

This section explains how to put together your timeplan – it is really important that you do your best to create a well-organised and detailed written timeplan as this will contribute to marks in both the Planning and Practical sections of the assessment criteria.

The timeplan will be very helpful to guide you through the 3 hour practical task.

Doing a brilliant timeplan!

Here are some step-by-step instructions to help you create your timeplan. You can do this by hand or on a computer (word processing is the easiest software, although you could also do this on a spreadsheet).

Step 1

Get each of your chosen recipes on separate sheets of paper (this task works really well if you are typing up your work).

You may have five or six recipes depending on how many accompaniments you are making alongside your main dishes.

Colour code the written instructions for each recipe – so that each recipe has a different coloured font (use highlighters if doing by hand).

Step 2

Read and understand each recipe and make sure you really know how to make each dish and accompaniment.

Step 3

Jot down on a separate sheet the names of your dishes and accompaniments and then jot down a rough order of making – at this point you don't need any detail. Here is an example of what this rough order may look like.

I am making:

Poulet à la sauce tomate (chicken in a tomato sauce) with green beans and Vichy carrots
Moules marinieres with crusty baguette
Lemon tart with raspberry coulis and raspberry ice cream

Rough order of making will be:
- Make bread dough for baguette and prove
- Make pastry for lemon tart and rest
- Blanch onions for chicken dish
- Roll out pastry for tart, line with beans and chill
- Drain the onions and allow to cool
- Bake lemon tart pastry blind
- Carry on with chicken dish
- Brown onions and soften lardons
- Pan fry chicken
- While the chicken is being browned:
- Check on pastry for lemon tart
- Make roux
- Pastry case out of oven, brush with egg white and back in oven for 2 mins
- Pastry case out of oven and chicken in oven temp down to 150°C
- Sieve and pour on lemon topping and back in oven to bake
- Make ice cream and freeze
- Back to bread dough for baguette – knock back, shape, prove
- Back to the chicken
- Remove lemon tart from oven – cool at room temperature and then chill
- Turn oven up to 230°C for baguette
- Check on ice cream
- Make raspberry coulis and chill
- Vegetables for chicken
- Back to bread dough for baguette – put in oven
- Start doing moules
- Start to steam green beans and carry on cooking carrots
- Back to the moules
- Bread out of oven
- Finish moules
- Serve

Start with the dishes / tasks that take the longest first. So, for example, if you are making a bread dough you would need to make that early on so that the dough has time to prove; if you are making a cauliflower cheese, you can make this later so that it's served as soon as it comes out of the oven.

Ice cream or dishes that need to set such as panna cotta would need to be made near the beginning of the 3 hour practical – so that you give them enough time to set.

NON-EXAMINATION ASSESSMENTS

Step 4

Create a table (we give you suggested headers here).

Order of work:

Time	Activity	Health and safety points / Food safety points	Food quality points

Add or delete rows as needed

Step 5

Now roughly add in each task – again, at this point don't add the detail in.
Add in when you want to wash up.
Here is an example:

Activity
Make bread dough for baguette and prove
Make pastry for lemon tart and rest
Wash up and let dishes drip dry
Start on chicken dish
Blanch onions
Roll out pastry for tart, line with beans and chill
Drain the onions and allow to cool
Bake lemon tart pastry blind
Carry on with chicken dish
Brown onions and soften lardons
Pan fry chicken
While the chicken is being browned:
Check on pastry for lemon tart
Make roux
Pastry case out of oven, brush with egg white and back in oven for 2 mins
Dry up and wash up again, drip dry
During washing up:
Pastry out of oven and chicken in oven, temp down to 150°C
Sieve and pour on lemon topping and back in oven to bake
Make ice cream and freeze
Back to bread dough for baguette – knock back, shape & prove
Back to the chicken
At the same time dry up then wash up
Remove lemon tart from oven – cool at room temperature and then chill
Turn oven up to 230°C for baguette
Check on ice cream
Make raspberry coulis and chill
Dry up and wash up again
Vegetables for chicken
Back to bread dough for baguette – place in oven
Start to cook carrots
Start doing moules
At the same time:
Start to steam green beans and carry on cooking carrots
Back to the moules
At the same time as moules is cooking:
Dry up and put equipment away
Bread out of oven
Finish moules
Serve

> Break down the tasks in recipes and reorder the sequence that you make them in to make best use of your time. This is called **dovetailing** (and multitasking).

Read over this and check you have the order right – and if you want to move the order around a little do so.

422 NON-EXAMINATION ASSESSMENTS

Step 6

When you are happy with the order that you are going to make your dishes in, you can start to add in the detail.

Use the detail from your recipes sheets and copy them into the rows so that you add enough detail.

Activity
Make bread dough for baguette and prove Make a well in the centre of the flour and yeast and add all the warm water and oil Mix to a soft dough with a wooden spoon. Knead on a lightly floured surface for approximately 5 minutes until the dough is smooth and springy Allow to prove in a lightly floured bowl, covered with a damp cloth
Make pastry for lemon tart and rest Using a knife, stir in just enough of the cold water to bind the dough together Wrap the dough in cling film and chill for 10-–15 minutes
Wash up and let dishes drip dry
Start on chicken dish Blanch onions Place the small saucepan on the hob, fill with water, bring the water to the boil, then blanch the onions
Roll out pastry for tart, line with beans and chill
Drain the onions and allow to cool
Bake lemon tart pastry blind
Carry on with chicken dish Brown onions and soften lardons Place the 15g butter and 1 tbsp sunflower oil into the base of the casserole dish and soften the diced bacon Add the drained and cooled onions shaking the pan to brown them evenly all over Remove the bacon and onions from the pan and place onto a plate until later
Pan fry chicken Place the chicken pieces into the pan and brown the skin. Using tongs, turn the chicken over and do the same on the reverse side When the chicken is evenly browned (it will not be cooked yet) remove from the pan
While the chicken is being browned: Check on pastry for lemon tart – remove baking beans – back in oven for 5 mins to finish cooking (I don't want it brown)
Make roux Keeping pan on the heat, add the flour Slowly add the chicken stock and stir with the magic whisk, then add chopped tomatoes, crushed garlic, bouquet garni, salt and freshly ground black pepper. Allow the sauce to come to the boil and gently add back the bacon, onions and chicken. Reduce to a simmer
Pastry case out of oven, brush with egg white and back in oven for 2 mins
Dry up and wash up again, drip dry
During washing up: Pastry out of oven and chicken in oven temp down to 150°C Sieve and pour on lemon topping and back in oven to bake
Make ice cream and freeze Blend the frozen raspberries, vanilla essence, icing sugar and clotted cream in a food processor for five seconds. With the motor running, pour in the whipping cream and continue to blend until smooth Spoon the ice cream into a container and freeze
Back to bread dough for baguette Knock back bread dough and shape into baguette – allow to prove on the greased baking tray

Back to the chicken   Pan fry the mushrooms for chicken dish and then add to the casserole, transfer to hob to finish cooking
At the same time dry up then wash up
Remove lemon tart from oven – cool at room temperature and then chill
Turn oven up to 230°C for baguette
Check on ice cream – beat to remove any ice crystals and carry on freezing
Make raspberry coulis and chill   Heat the sugar and water in a small saucepan over medium heat, stirring from time to time, until the sugar dissolves completely, about 5 minutes.   Put the raspberries, lemon juice and the sugar syrup in a mini blender and purée.   Strain through a fine mesh seive to remove the seeds and chill until needed
Dry up and wash up again   Keep an eye on the bread dough proving
Vegetables for chicken   Put kettle on to boil for water – needed to steam green beans and simmer carrots
Back to bread dough for baguette   Make slits on surface of bread and place into oven to bake
Start to cook carrots   Place carrots in a large saucepan with the butter, sugar and a pinch of salt. Cover the carrots half way with water and bring to the boil. Reduce the heat to a simmer, then cover and cook for 10 minutes until just tender
Place plates for moules and poulet à la sauce tomate into the oven to warm
Start doing moules   Heat the olive oil in a heavy pan with a tight-fitting lid. Add the onions and garlic and cook over a medium heat until softened, but not coloured.
At the same time: Start to steam green beans and carry on cooking carrots   Carrots: turn up the heat and cook until the water has evaporated and you're left with a buttery glaze. This will take 5–10 minutes.
Back to the moules   Add the stock and turn up to a high heat. As the stock starts to boil, add the cleaned mussels and thyme to the pan. Turn the heat down to low.   Put the lid on the pan and allow the mussels to steam. Cook for about 4–5 minutes, lifting the lid from time to time to check.
At the same time as moules is cooking: Dry up and put equipment away
Bread out of oven – onto cooling rack
Finish moules – add the double cream and cook for a further minute.   Scatter with the chopped parsley
Serve Moules Mariniere straight away with crusty bread
Serve Poulet à la Sauce Tomate with Vichy carrots and steamed green beans
Slice Lemon tart, serve with raspberry ice cream and raspberry coulis
Wash up remaining dishes
Dry and put away draining dishes, wash up and dry remaining dishes. Re-sanitise area for final time
Ensure cooker is switched off, and that all equipment is returned to the correct storage areas

It is important that your timeplan could be followed by someone else – so ask yourself "Do I have enough information on here so that someone else can make my dishes well?"
(i.e. you haven't missed off any key parts of making!).

Step 7

As you are doing this, anything that you think you should be doing as part of your mise en place you should add to the mise en place sheet.
Here is what a finished mise en place sheet (preparation sheet) can look like:

Mise en place (45 minutes)

Activity	Health and safety points
Prepare self – remove all jewellery, wash hands with anti-bacterial soap and put on apron	Make sure water is hot and apron is clean
Sanitise work surfaces	Use anti-bacterial spray
Pre-heat oven to 180°C fan, for lemon tart pastry	
Collect and weigh all ingredients and place onto white trays. Place high risk ingredients into refrigerator.	High risk ingredients are double cream, clotted cream, whipping cream, milk, butter, store near to the top of the fridge Chicken and fresh mussels stored at the bottom of the fridge
Collect all equipment and serving dishes and place to the side until needed	
Check weigh ingredients for pastry and baguette	Use digital scales for accuracy
Grease the baking tray and tart tin	
Top and tail green beans, wash and place into steamer stray for later	Place waste in compost bucket for all vegetable trimmings
Peel and tidy up carrots and place into a saucepan for later	
Peel small onions and place into small saucepan	
Wipe over baby mushrooms with damp cloth and trim as necessary with small vegetable knife. Store in a small bowl and chill	
Crush the garlic	
Make bouquet garni	
Clean the mussels by thoughroughly scrubbing them under plenty of running water, pulling away the 'beards', discard any broken mussels along with the beards, and any mussels that don't close tightly when you tap them	HIGH RISK make sure bought as fresh as possible and kept refrigerated (2–5°C) MUST NOT USE ANY MUSSELS THAT WILL NOT CLOSE WHEN TAPPED
Dice onion, chop garlic and parsley for moules	
Butcher whole chicken into two breasts, two thighs, two wings and two drumsticks	HIGH RISK back into fridge when prepared – base of fridge well-covered
Open the can of chopped tomatoes	
Make up chicken stock with stock cube and boiling water	
For bread: Sift the flour and salt into the mixing bowl. Add the quick-action dried yeast and blend together	
For pastry: Sift the flour into the mixing bowl. Cut the butter into small pieces and rub fat into flour until resembles coarse breadcrumbs. Add in caster sugar and stir. Cover with cling film and chill. Measure out water for pastry and chill	
Separate egg yolks from whites	

Activity	Health and safety points
Zest and juice lemons for lemon tart, make the raw custard (egg yolks, lemon juice, cream, sugar), cover and chill. Keep one egg white back and lightly beat. Juice a lemon for the coulis.	Keep egg whites and freeze
Lay the table: Place cloth on table, vase of flowers, cutlery and menu card. Also crockery – some will be placed into oven for warming later on (make sure the plates are all circular)	Take time to get the presentation right

Once you have got the activity column completed in your timeplan then move on and add in relevant information to the following columns:
- Health and safety points (this means tips to prevent accidents)
- Food safety points (this means tips to prevent food poisoning)
- Food quality points (this means tips to make sure the food is served at its best in terms of quality)

If you need tips on this, look at the example we have given you below.

Step 8

Now add in approximate timings – this is the first column on the left.
You can chose to add the length of time you expect each task to take or you can put the actual time that it will be on the clock.
Whichever you find easiest for you.

> **Study tip**
>
> Having a colour coded timeplan will help to make it easier to refer to and don't forget to have it with you on the day of your practical assessment.

Time	Activity	Health and safety points / Food safety points	Food quality points
9 mins	Make bread dough for baguette and prove Make a well in the centre of the flour and yeast and add all the warm water and oil. Mix to a soft dough with a wooden spoon. Knead on a lightly floured surface for approximately 5 minutes until the dough is smooth and springy. Allow to prove in a lightly floured bowl, covered with a damp cloth	Somewhere warm, so that bread will prove faster	Additional water may be needed if the dough is too dry. I need the dough quite sticky Until volume has increased and dough is light & spongy. The longer the dough can be allowed to prove the better
5 mins	Make pastry for lemon tart and rest Using a knife, stir in just enough of the cold water to bind the dough together. Wrap the dough in clingfilm and chill		Water, equipment, hands should be chilled to produce good quality short crust pastry.
5 mins	Wash up and let dishes drip dry	Make sure water is hot	
1 min	Start on with chicken dish Blanch onions Place the small saucepan onto the hob, fill with water, bring the water to the boil, then blanch the onions	Keep saucepan handles way from side of hob Use oven gloves when draining and take care with the steam	Drain in a colander and refresh under cold running water
5 mins	Roll out pastry for tart, line with beans and blast chill		Chill to ensure that the pastry case doesn't shrink. Roll pastry between

Once you have completed this main timeplan go over the mise en place sheet and make sure you have included all the tasks you want to do in your mise en place.

NON-EXAMINATION ASSESSMENTS

Key terms

Areas of content – the topics in the specification that have to be covered as part of this GCSE.

Assessment criteria – the key points you will be marked on.

Control recipe – a standard recipe and method with which you compare your other results.

Dovetail – this refers to when you are making two or more dishes. It is when you split the tasks within the recipes to make the best use of your time, e.g. if making a cake and soup – the sponge mix for the cake could be made while the vegetables for the soup are sautéing, and once the cake is in the oven, the soup could have the stock added and then be brought to a simmer. Then the butter icing for the cake should be made while the soup is simmering and the cake is baking.

Extended writing – where you have to write a more detailed answer. It's a good idea when you make a point to develop it with a detailed explanation and where possible an example to show what you mean.

Fair testing – where you only change one thing at a time in each experiment so that it is clear to see what has happened in each test.

Formal assessment – counts towards your final GCSE and your teacher cannot help you.

Hypothesis – a statement of what you think is likely to happen.

Mise en place – preparation; the tasks you do before you start cooking.

Multi-task – when you can perform two or more tasks at the same time.

Specification – a detailed description of the areas to study and the assessment requirements.

Stimulus materials – an image or selection of images or other visual prompt such as a flow diagram to help your understanding of a topic.

Timeplan – written instructions that break down the practical tasks with an indication of timing.

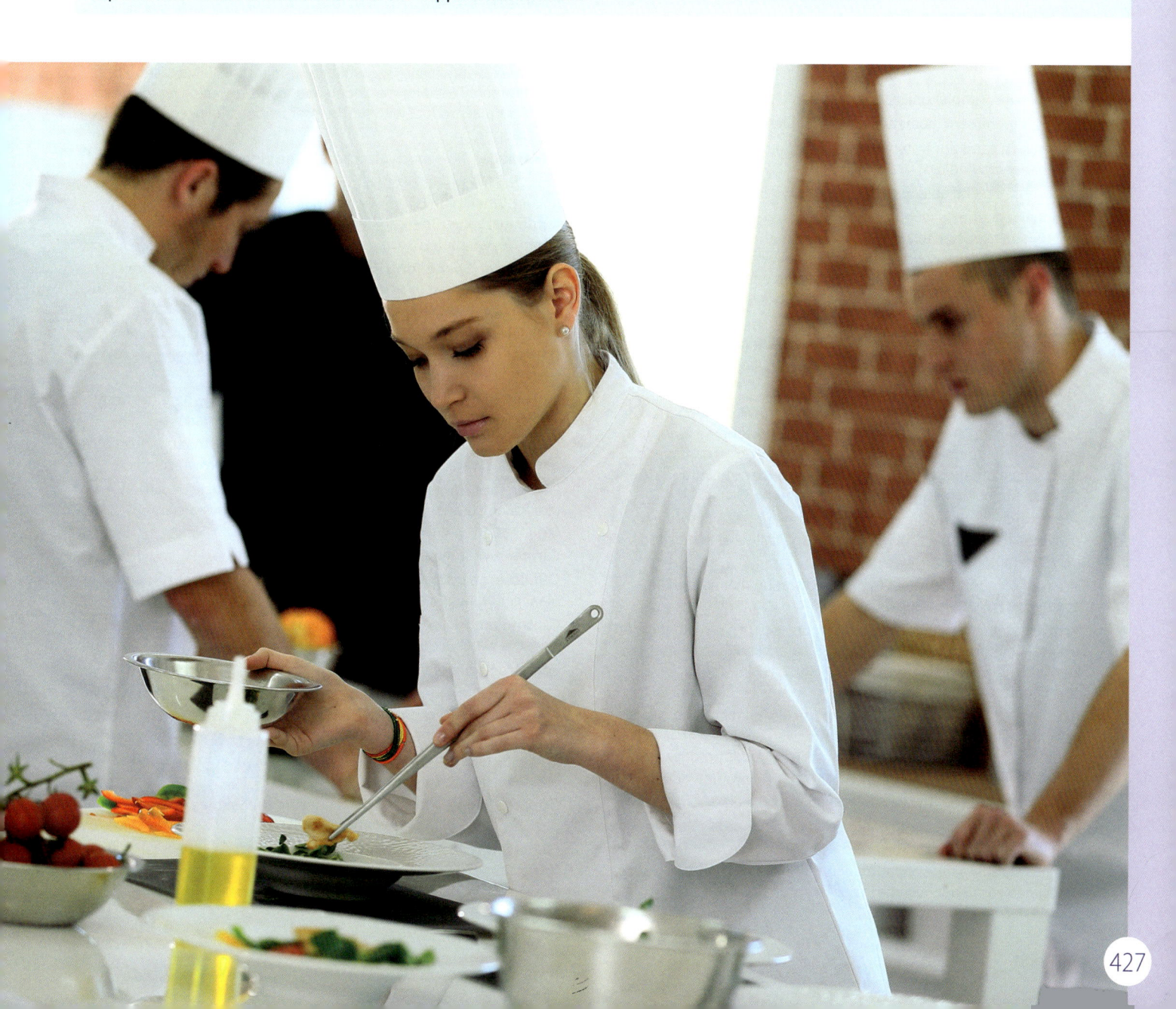

GLOSSARY

Accompaniments things that accompany something else in a complementary way, for example, table sauces, or foods that work well with other foods or drinks.

Acidic when something has a PH level of below 7, it has acidic properties or contains acid. Examples of foods with a high acidic content include milk, blueberries and squash.

Adipose tissue cells that store energy in the form of fat.

Advertising providing information to consumers about a product or service.

Aeration incorporating air into the mixture.

Agitate to stir, shake or disturb a liquid.

Air mainly a combination of oxygen and nitrogen and is an invisible gas surrounding the earth.

Alkaline when something has a PH level of above 7, it has alkaline properties or contains alkaline. Examples of foods with a high alkaline content include spinach, almonds and watermelon.

Allergens substances that cause an allergic reaction.

Allergies an immune system reaction that occurs soon after eating a certain food.

Ambient foods foods that can be stored, at room temperature, in a sealed container. All foods found on supermarket shelves are ambient foods.

Amino acids simpler units of protein, made up of long chains.

an accompaniment something that complements or adds to a dish

Anaemia a condition where the body lacks enough healthy red blood cells or haemoglobin.

Anaerobic – being able to exist without oxygen.

Anaphylactic shock when a person suffers an extreme allergic reaction on exposure to an antigen to which the body has become hypersensitive. It causes swelling, hives, low blood pressure and dilated blood pressure and when not treated effectively, can be fatal. Food is a common cause of anaphylactic shock and typical trigger foods include nuts, shellfish, diary and eggs.

Anaphylaxis a severe, potentially life threatening allergic reaction.

Anthocyanins water soluble pigment or colour found in red, purple or blue plants.

Antioxidant a molecule that is able to stop the oxidisation process in other molecules and therefore can be useful in stopping foods from deteriorating. Antioxidants can prevent or slow down damage to our body which otherwise can lead to diseases such as heart disease and cancers. Antioxidants also improve our immune system.

Application (app) a self-contained program or piece of software designed to fulfil a particular purpose, especially as downloaded by a user to a mobile device.

Areas of content the topics in the specification that have to be covered as part of this GCSE.

Arrowroot a starch extract taken from the root of the maranta, a tropical plant traditionally found in the Americas. When heated, the starch turns into a clear and tasteless jelly so is ideal for thickening sauces, juices or similar.

Artisan a skilled worker, expert in a particular craft or trade, usually carried out by hand, for example, handwoven textiles. With reference to food and drink, this would typically refer to foods produced or prepared in a traditional way and using high-quality ingredients.

Assessment criteria the key points you will be marked on.

Atherosclerosis a build-up of fatty deposits in the arteries, sometimes called 'furring of the arteries'.

Bacillus cereus a type of pathogenic bacteria that produces toxins, associated with poor hygiene in cooked rice.

Balanced diet a diet which provides all the necessary nutrients in the correct amount to meet the body's needs.

Barcode a small image of lines (bars) and spaces on retail store items, identification cards and postal mail to identify a particular product number, person, or location.

Basic Metabolic Rate (BMR) the number of kilojoules the body uses to stay alive each day.

Basted when fats or juices are poured over something (usually meat) while cooking in order to keep it moist and to add flavour. For example, roasting meats.

Beri beri a muscle wasting disease due to a lack of vitamin B1 (thiamin) in the diet

Beta-glucan – a form of soluble fibre

Binary fission the reproduction of one cell splitting into two genetically identical cells.

Biodegradeable decomposed by bacteria or other living organisms.

Biotechnology the manipulation (as through genetic engineering) of living organisms or their components to produce useful usually commercial products, e.g. pest resistant crops.

Blanched cook to enable the skin to be removed.

Blind tasting test a test where a food or drink is tasted without the consumer being able to see what they are tasting. Blind tasting tests are commonly used for marketing and market research, to test the response to a product without the user being influenced by brand perceptions.

Blood sugar how much glucose is in the blood.

Bran the fragments of grain husk that are separated from flour after milling. When bran is removed from grains, there is a reduction in nutritional value. Bran can be milled from any cereal grain and can be found, for example, in rice, wheat, barley and corn.

BSE (Bovine Spongiform Encephalopathy) commonly referred to as mad cow disease, a slow developing disease affecting the nervous system of cattle. It is often fatal.

Bulk fermentation also known as primary fermentation, the first stage of fermentation when baking bread (which typically has two fermentation stages).

Calcium deficiency also known as hypocalcaemia, where the body suffers from not having enough calcium for its needs.

Caramelisation a change in the food's molecular structure due to the removal of water resulting in a nutty flavour and brown colour.

Carbon footprint a carbon footprint measures the total carbon dioxide emissions caused directly and indirectly by a person, organisation, event or product.

Carotenoids pigment or colour found in plants.

Cellulose an insoluble substance which is the main constituent of plant cell walls. It is a polysaccharide.

Centrifugation the separation of two liquids such as the fatty cream from the watery liquid of the milk.

Cereal an edible grass.

Chlorophyll the substance responsible for the green colour of plants and also for the process of absorbing sunlight in order to perform photosynthesis.

Cholesterol a fatty substance known as a lipid which is found in blood and in food.

Climate change a large-scale, long-term shift in the planet's weather patterns or average temperatures.

Climate the weather conditions typical to an area in general or at any specific time.

Coagulate to become solid or to set.

Coagulation an irreversible change to proteins from a liquid or semi-liquid state to a solid state.
Coeliac disease a chronic intestinal disorder caused by sensitivity to the protein gliadin contained in the gluten of cereals.
Cold-pressed a production process where the temperature of the oil must not exceed 49°C when pressed and ground.
Collagen protein in the connective tissue which holds cells together.
Composition the different parts or substances that make up something.
Condiments substances added to give flavour or complement food.
Conduction heat is transferred between two surfaces by direct contact, and molecules in each surface pass heat to each other.
Connective tissue the tissue that connects, supports, bonds, or divides other tissues or organs in the body, for example, cartilage or bone.
Consistency thickness or viscosity
Control recipe a standard recipe and method with which you compare your other results.
Convection heat is transferred by the circulation of either a heated liquid or gas.
Convenience food food that needs little preparation, especially food that has been pre-prepared and preserved for long-term storage.
Coronary heart disease (CHD) a narrowing of the arteries that supply your heart with oxygen-rich blood, due to the build-up of fatty material within their walls
Creaming when sugar is combined with a solid fat, typically butter, margarine or shortening.
Cross-contamination the transfer of bacteria from one food to another, from humans, animals, other food or equipment.
Cuisine a style of cooking.
Culture the way of life, the general customs and beliefs of a particular group of people at a particular time.
Curds a soft, white substance formed when milk sours, used as the basis for cheese.
Dairy intolerance usually a condition caused by the body being unable to process lactose, a natural sugar found in milk and dairy products.
Danger zone the temperature range within which bacteria multiply rapidly.
Decalcification gradual removal of calcium from bones and teeth.
Deficiencies a state of lacking or incompleteness. For example, deficiencies in the consumption of certain vitamins can cause health issues.
Dehydration when water is lost or removed. For the body, losing too much water can be very dangerous to health and ultimately fatal.
Demographics the statistical data on a population.
Denaturation the process of altering a protein's molecular characteristics or properties by heat, enzyme action, or chemicals.
Dextrinisation –the browning that occurs when foods containing starch are cooked, or exposed to an alkali, acid or enzyme.
Diabetic a person who suffers from diabetes, a condition that occurs when the body can't use glucose normally.
Dies machinery attachments used to make special pasta shapes that cannot be made by hand.
Diet the type of food we eat or drink.
Dietary guidelines advice on diet.
Dietary Reference Values (DRVs) an estimate of the nutritional requirements of a healthy population.
Digestion the process where food is broken down by mechanical and enzymic activity into more simple chemical compounds that can be absorbed and used by the body.
Disaccharide a carbohydrate made from two sugar molecules ('di' means two).

Disposable income the portion of income that a household or individual has left after tax has been deducted and that they are able to spend as they please.
Dovetail this refers to when you are making two or more dishes. It is when you split the tasks within the recipes to make the best use of your time, e.g. if making a cake and soup – the sponge mix for the cake could be made while the vegetables for the soup are sautéing, and once the cake is in the oven, the soup could have the stock added and then be brought to a simmer. Then the butter icing for the cake should be made while the soup is simmering and the cake is baking.
Durum wheat high protein wheat used to make pasta.
Eczema a medical condition where patches of skin become rough or inflamed which cause itching.
Elastin a highly elastic protein that allows our connective tissues to stretch and then resume their original shape. Found mostly in the dermis of the skin but also other parts of the body that require some flexibility, such as the arteries and lungs.
Empty calories calories that are present in foods that have very little or no nutritive value.
Emulsify to use an ingredient as a mediator in a mixture, enabling two ingredients to mix without the mixture separating.
Emulsion a fine dispersion of minute droplets of one liquid in another.
Endosperm the main part of the grain, a starch and protein supply.
Energy the strength that the body needs to function and sustain physical and mental activity.
Environmental factors the impact of human activities on the natural environment.
Enzymes biological catalysts which speed up biochemical reactions without being used up themselves. Digestive enzymes are important for the process of breaking down food so that the body can absorb its nutrients.
Enzymic browning a chemical process where oxygen and enzymes in the food react to cause the surface to become brown. This process cannot be reversed.
Estimate Average Requirement (EAR) a useful indication of how much energy the average person needs.
Extended writing where you have to write a more detailed answer. It's a good idea when you make a point to develop it with a detailed explanation and where possible an example to show what you mean.
Extraction rate how much of the original wheat grain is in the flour. 100% means that it contains all the grain.
Extrinsic sugar added sugar.
Extruded pasta is forced through a die to achieve a special pasta shape, e.g. spaghetti, macaroni.
Factory farming where animals are bred and fattened using modern industrial methods.
Fair testing where you only change one thing at a time in each experiment so that it is clear to see what has happened in each test.
Fairtrade a partnership between producers and consumers; selling on Fairtrade terms provides farmers with a better deal and more income. This allows them the opportunity to improve their lives and plan for their future.
Farm assured a British organisation that promotes and regulates food quality.
Fat the fatty portion of cream or milk.
Fat soluble vitamins these vitamins (the A, D, E, and K groups) dissolve in fat.
Fermentation the chemical breakdown of sugar to acid, gas or alcohol by bacteria, yeasts or other microorganisms.
Ferment where bacteria produces lactic acid, which acts on the milk protein to give yoghurt its texture and characteristic tang.
Fertile land or soil that is able to produce plentiful crops.

Foam when bubbles form on the surface of a liquid as a result of a chemical reaction.
Food banks a place where food is given, free of charge, to individuals in need.
Food chain a series of processes by which food is grown, produced, and eventually consumed.
Food miles the distance that a food has been transported from its point of production to its consumer. This measure is also used to consider the environmental impact of a food's production.
Food miles the distance the food travels from field to plate.
Food poverty when a household or individual does not have access to healthy food of satisfactory nutritional benefit, often due to a low financial income or a lack of suitable shops or outlets nearby.
Food safety a scientific expertise in the safest methods of handling, preparing and storing of food to ensure any hazard to health is avoided.
Foraging the process of searching an area for wild food resources, for example edible vegetation.
Formal assessment counts towards your final GCSE and your teacher cannot help you with this assessment.
Fortification adding vitamins and minerals to foods.
Fortified food a food product in which a nutrient is added to increase its nutritional value.
Free radicals chemicals which can cause us harm. Antioxidants will protect the body from these harmful free radicals.
Free range a method of farming, where for at least part of the day, animals can roam freely outdoors.
Free sugars extrinsic sugars not from milk.
Friction the action of one surface or object rubbing against another.
Functional foods foods that have a positive effect beyond basic nutrition, such as boosting optimal health or reducing the risk of disease.
Function what something does, or why it is needed.
Fusarium Venenatum the principal ingredient of mycoprotein is an ascomycota, one of the largest groups within the fungi family.
Fusion combining two or more very different regional ingredients or techniques.
Gelatine a natural protein substance present in the tendon, ligaments and tissues of animals. It is translucent and colourless.
Gelatinisation the thickening of a mixture, in the presence of heat, due to swelling of starch grains.
Gel liquid which is dispersed in a solid.
Genetically modified food (GMF) foods derived from organisms whose genetic material has been modified.
Genetically modified organisms (GMO) organisms whose genetic material (DNA) has been altered by mating and/or natural recombination.
Germ source of fat and B vitamins, it is where the new plant grows.
Giblets the edible offal of poultry, typically including gizzard, heart and liver.
Gliadin and Glutenin the core proteins of the gluten part of wheat seeds. Gliadin and glutenin are known to be a cause of coeliac disease, a digestive disorder where gluten must be avoided in the diet as it causes destructive immune responses in the small intestine.
Gluten formed from the two wheat proteins gliadin and glutenin, in presence of water. Gluten is developed by kneading.
Glycaemic index the impact of a carbohydrate food on blood sugar level.
GM food genetically modified food.
Goitre an enlargement of the thyroid gland seen as a neck swelling, from insufficient intake of iodine.
Grain the edible part of the cereal.
Haem iron from animal sources

Haemoglobin the part of blood that contains iron, carries oxygen through the body, and gives blood its red colour
Halal when the choice of food or way in which food is prepared complies with the requirements of Muslim law. For example, animals must be slaughtered and prepared using specific methods and techniques and the process carried out by a Muslim.
Hard wheat a type of wheat that has a hard grain with a high gluten content.
Harvesting the process of gathering or reaping crops.
Health claims when a claim is made about a food and its relationship with or impact on health.
Heat transfer the way heat moves from one area to another through conduction, convection and radiation.
High biological value (HBV) protein foods containing all the essential amino acids.
High fat foods that contain a high fat content. Examples of high fat foods include cheese, butter, lard, fatty meats (saturated fats), olive oil, nuts and avocados (unsaturated fats).
High Pressure Processing (HPP) a processing method that subjects food to elevated pressures (with or without the addition of heat) to render bacteria inactive.
Homogenisation the breaking down of large milk fat globules into much smaller fat globules.
Homogenised when milk is processed so that the fatty portion of the milk is fused with the rest of the milk content, meaning that the cream does not separate.
Humectant any substance that helps another substance retain moisture.
Humid when there is a high level of moisture, or water vapour, present in the atmosphere.
Hydrogenation the process of changing a liquid fat or oil to a solid one at room temperature by the addition of hydrogen
Hydroponics the growing of plants in a soil-less medium, or an aquatic based environment.
Hygroscopic attracted to water.
Hypercalcaemia an abnormally high level of calcium in the blood.
Hypothesis a statement of what you think is likely to happen.
Ingredients the foods or substances needed to make a particular dish.
Insect any small arthropod animal that has six legs and generally one or two pairs of wings.
Insoluble fibre fibre which the body cannot absorb.
Insulin a hormone which controls blood sugar level.
Intensive farming farming that aims to produce as much as possible, usually with the use of chemicals.
Intolerances individual elements of certain foods cannot be properly processed and absorbed by our digestive system.
Intrinsic sugar natural sugar.
Invert sugar the process of converting sugar into simple sugars.
Irish cuisine the style of cooking originating from Ireland and/or Irish people.
Iron deficiency anaemia a condition where lack of iron in the body leads to a reduction in the number of red blood cells.
Knock back to re-knead the dough which knocks out some of the carbon dioxide allowing the yeast to produce more carbon dioxide.
Kosher when food or where food is cooked, eaten or sold complies with the requirements of Jewish law. For example, animals must be slaughtered and prepared using specific methods and techniques, meat and milk cannot be cooked or consumed together and certain meat and shellfish is forbidden.
Kwashiorkor a form of malnutrition linked to protein deficiency.
Lactic acid an acid formed in sour milk.
Lactose the natural sugar found in milk.

Lactose intolerant when a person is unable to digest lactose, a sugar found in milk and some other dairy products. This condition can cause bloating and cramps in the stomach, nausea, flatulence and diarrhoea.

Laminating rolling out pasta into thin sheets.

Lamination a method of making pastry where alternate layers of dough and butter are pressed together. Examples of laminated pastry include croissant pastry and Danish pastry.

Lecithin a fat in egg yolk which acts as an the emulsifier.

Legumes upright or climbing beans or plants.

Low biological value (LBV) protein foods lacking in one or more of the essential amino acids.

Lower economically developed countries (LEDC) countries that have the lowest levels of socioeconomic development based on United Nations developed criteria that measures poverty, nutrition, health, education and economic vulnerability.

Macronutrients a class of chemical compounds which humans consume in the largest quantities.

Magnetron the part of the microwave oven that generates the microwave radiation.

Maillard reaction (or non-enzymic browning) a chemical reaction between a protein and a carbohydrate in the presence of dry heat.

Malnutrition imperfect nutrition.

Marinading a process of soaking foods in a liquid mixture, usually wine, vinegar or lemon juice with various spices and herbs, prior to cooking.

Marketing the activities involved in encouraging consumers to buy a product or service.

Market research the gathering and studying of data relating to consumer opinions and preferences, purchasing power, etc., especially prior to introducing a product to the market.

Masa harina finely ground corn flour treated with slaked lime; main ingredient in corn tortillas.

Megaloblastic anaemia a type of anaemic blood disorder, often caused by a Vitamin B-12 and folic acid deficiency, causing the number of blood cells to be lower than normal. Metabolism – all the chemical processes in the body, especially those that cause food to be used for energy and growth.

Metabolism the chemical processes that occur within the body in order to maintain life.

Micronutrients nutrients required in small quantities to facilitate a range of physiological functions.

Microorganism usually single cell microscopic organisms such as bacteria, moulds and fungi.

Migrate when people or animals move from one geographical area to another.

Mirepoix a mixture of sautéed chopped vegetables.

Mise en place preparation; the tasks you do before you start cooking.

Modified Atmospheric Packaging (MAP) food packaging that changes the internal atmosphere of the packet, normally reducing the amount of oxygen present to slow down food decay.

Molecular gastronomy the scientific study of the physical and chemical processes that occur while cooking.

Monosaccharide a simple carbohydrate (mono means one; saccharide means sugar).

Monounsaturated fats Fats that contain one double bond in the molecule. These fats are associated with keeping cholesterol levels low. Examples of foods containing monounsaturated fats include red meats and avocado.

Mould a fungus that grows in filaments creating a fuzzy appearance on food. It is a soft, green or grey growth that develops on old food. May give some cheeses their characteristic colours and flavours.

Multitask when you can perform two or more tasks at the same time.

Mycoprotein a food made from the fungi family which contains all the essential amino acids needed by the body. Suitable for lacto-ovo vegetarians

Mycotoxins extremely dangerous toxins produced by fungi that can even cause death.

Myoglobin a protein that stores oxygen in the muscle cells of animals.

Nanotechnology the science of manipulating materials on an atomic or molecular scale.

Night blindness also known as nyctalopia, an inability to see in poor light or at night time, commonly caused by a vitamin A deficiency.

Non haem iron from vegetable sources.

Non-Milk Extrinsic Sugars (NMES) added sugar from non-milk sources.

Non starch polysaccharide (NSP) More commonly known as dietary fibre (insoluble fibre and soluble fibre), NSP is a form of complex carbohydrate that is not digested in the small intestine. NSP is found in foods such as wholegrain cereals, fruits and vegetables and is important for maintaining the health of the colon.

Novel protein foods foods that have been produced by a method not previously used for food.

Nut allergies a common form of allergic reaction to any form of nut that is used in food preparation.

Nutrients the properties found in food and drinks that give the nourishment vital for growth and the maintenance of life. The main nutrients needed by the human body are carbohydrates, proteins, fats, vitamins and minerals.

Nutritional claims when a claim is made that a food has particular nutritional properties.

Nutritional requirements estimates of energy and nutrients needed by individuals or groups of people.

Nutritional supplement adding dietary or nutritional value.

Nutritional value the nutrients in food and how they impact on the body.

Obesity when a person is carrying around so much extra weight that it is dangerous for their health.

Olfactory receptors the receptors found in the back of the nasal cavity that are responsible for our sense of smell.

Omega-3 and omega-6 types of essential fatty acid the body cannot make itself which are important for a healthy heart..

Onset time the time it takes for the pathogenic bacteria to produce symptoms.

Organically produced grown using natural fertilizers and pesticides.

Organic farming farming that produces food without the use of chemicals, fertilizers and pesticides.

Organic food any food that is grown or made without the use of chemicals.

Origin the place from which something is derived.

Osteomalacia a softening of the bones, through deficiency from calcium or vitamin D.

Osteoporosis a medical condition in which the bones become brittle and fragile.

Ovalbumin one of the main proteins in egg.

Over-worked gluten the dough has been over handled/rolled/beaten.

Overnutrition a condition where the body gets too much of a particular nutrient or nutrients.

Oxalic acid a naturally occurring component of plants, particularly dark green vegetables.

Oxidation exposure to the oxygen in the air.

Oxidise to undergo a chemical reaction with oxygen resulting in food losing freshness and colour.

Paddies the term given to rice when it is still in the husk, as in growing in a paddy field.

Pasteurisation the process of heating a food to a specific temperature for a specific period of time in order to kill microorganisms that could cause disease, spoilage or undesired fermentation.

Pathogenic bacteria bacteria that causes disease, unlike many bacteria which are harmless and often even beneficial to health. Common foodborne bacteria include shigella, campylobacter and salmonella.

Peak bone mass refers to the largest amount of bone tissue that a person has at any point in life. Most people reach their peak bone mass by the age of 30.

Pectin a soluble polysaccharide which is present in ripe fruits and used as a setting agent in jams and jellies.

Pellagra a deficiency disease due to a lack of vitamin B3 (niacin) in the diet. Causes skin, nerve and mental health problems plus diarrhoea. Often occurs where maize is a staple food.

Percentage of fat the ratio of fat found in food and drinks.

Perishable foods foods that will decay or 'go bad' quickly.

Pernicious anaemia a type of anaemia caused by a lack of vitamin B12 (cobalamin).

Pester power the ability of a child to nag a parent relentlessly until the parent succumbs and agrees to buy something they would not usually buy.

Photosynthesis the chemical change that occurs in plants when sunlight is absorbed by the leaves. Water and carbon dioxide are converted to create oxygen and glucose, creating food for the plant itself and the environment in general.

pH value the measure of the acidity or alkalinity of a liquid substance.

Physical Activity Level (PAL) the number of kilojoules the body uses to fuel physical activity.

Phytic acid a form of phosphorous which limits absorption of calcium and iron in the body.

Phytochemicals a group of plant-derived compounds supposedly responsible for disease protection.

Plasticity the ability of fat to hold its shape.

Polyols a group of versatile, reduced-calorie carbohydrates that provide the taste and texture of sugar with about half the calories.

Polysaccharide a complex carbohydrate (poly means many).

Polyunsaturated fats Fats that contain several double or even triple bonds in the molecule. Examples of foods that contain polyunsaturated fats include salmon, flaxseeds and walnuts.

Portion size and/or weight of a typical amount of food.

Prebiotics promote the growth of particular bacteria in the large intestine that are beneficial to intestinal health and also inhibit the growth of bacteria that are potentially harmful to intestinal health.

Preservation keeping something in its present state or preventing it from being damaged.

Primary dentition first set of teeth, 20 in all.

Primary processing the conversion of raw materials into food commodities e.g. milling of wheat grain into flour.

Probiotics live microorganisms which when taken in adequate amounts confer a health benefit.

Product placement placing a product in a prominent position to encourage people to buy it.

Proportion a part or amount to be considered in relation to the whole

Protein content the ratio of protein found in food or drink. Eggs, milk, chicken, pork, fish and seafood are all examples of foods with high protein content.

Provenance the place where food originates, i.e. where is it grown, raised or reared.

Prove refers to a specific rest period during fermentation.

Pulses including beans and lentils, the seeds of legume plants.

Pungent when something has a sharp or strong taste or smell. Examples of things with a pungent taste or smell might be onions, ginger and many spices.

Purification the cleaning of wheat grains before milling.

Quenelle soft food formed into a rugby ball shape between two spoons.

Quick response code (QR Code) a two-dimensional barcode that can be read by smartphones and links directly to text, emails, websites, or phone numbers.

Radiant heat in the form of infra-red waves, can be applied above or below the food with the heat transferring to the surface of the food.

Radiation the transfer of heat energy by particles or waves.

Raising agent a substance added to a food product that makes it rise when cooked.

Rancidity the unpleasant taste or odour that fats and oils develop over time.

Rancid refers to foods which develop an unpleasant flavour or smell as a result of decomposition or chemical change to the fat or oil within the food.

Reconstituted dried food that is restored to its original form by adding water.

Reference Nutrient Intake (RNIs) an estimate of the amount of proteins, vitamins and minerals that should meet the needs of most of the group to which they apply.

Regional foods dishes or foods that are uniquely associated with a particular area of a country and come to be identifiable with that area.

Rennet an enzyme that used to be taken from calves' stomachs, but is mostly now produced from vegetarian sources.

Respires when yeast aerobically respires, or breathes, during bread making, producing water and carbon dioxide which is what causes the dough to rise.

Reticulin a protein that forms a network of fibres in the body in order to provide a supporting meshwork for some connective tissues, for example, bone marrow, the lymphatic system and some organs.

Retrogradation when a gel 'leaks' liquid after solidifying.

Rickets a disease caused by lack of calcium and vitamin D. The bones become soft and weak, leading to bone deformities.

Rubbing a technique where flour is rubbed into a fat, typically to make shortcrust pastry, crumbles or doughs.

Sago a starch extract taken from the pith of the sago palm, traditionally found in the swamps of South East Asia and New Guinea. When processed into sago flour, it can be used to make puddings or as a thickener.

Salamander a high intensity grill used in the catering industry.

Salmonella pathogenic bacteria found in raw egg.

Satiety when someone or something is sated, or satisfied.

Saturated fat all of the carbon atoms in the fatty acid molecules are linked by single bonds. This type of fat is mostly from animal sources and can be bad for our health.

Sautéing to fry quickly in a little hot fat or oil.

Scurvy a disease caused by a deficiency of vitamin C. It causes gums to become swollen and bleed and can also cause previously healed wounds to open again.

Sear to scorch the surface of food with a sudden, intense heat.

Seaweeds large algae growing in the sea or on rocks below the high-water mark.

Secondary processing converting primary processed foods into other food products, e.g. flour into biscuits.

Shelf life the length of time that a commodity may be stored without becoming unfit for use, consumption, or sale.

Shortening Butter, lard or other fat that remains solid at room temperature, used for making pastry or bread.

Sieving the process of passing food through a sieve, typically to separate larger or coarser particles from smaller or fine particles, or to remove solids from liquids, or to reduce soft solids to a pulp.

Signature dishes a dish or food that is identified with a particular restaurant or chef.

GLOSSARY

Silage grass grown in the summer and preserved to feed cattle in the winter months.

Smoke point the temperature at which a fat gives off a blue smoke. At this temperature the fat molecules start to split up and give the food being cooked an unpleasant flavour.

Soft flour flour with a slightly lower level of gluten.

Soluble fibre fibre that attracts and dissolves in water, so is easier to digest than insoluble fibre but still slows and improves the digestion process. Examples of foods that contain high proportions of soluble fibre include barley, beans, nuts, seeds, lentils, peas and some fruits and vegetables.

Source a place, person or thing from where something originates. For example, animal source foods include meat, milk, cheese and eggs and plants are an important source of vitamins and minerals.

Sowing the process of planting or scattering seed in order to grow crops.

Soya bean an Asian bean plant.

Specification a detailed description of the areas to study and the assessment requirements.

Spina bifida this congenital condition causes a defect where part of the spinal cord is exposed through an opening in the backbone. It often causes paralysis in the lower limbs and can also cause learning difficulties.

Spore a bacterium that has formed a strong, protective outer coating.

Stabilise a substance that allows fat or oil and water to mix.

Standard of living the measure of wealth, comfort and material goods typical of people in a community or region.

Stanols a chemical compound found naturally in plants and known to reduce cholesterol levels in blood.

Staple food food that forms a large part of the diet, usually from starchy foods

Starch a polysaccharide, a complex carbohydrate

Starter culture a bacteria mix used to ripen milk and help start the cheese making process.

Steam a gentle method of cooking where food is cooked by steam from water boiling beneath it but is kept separate from the water itself. Steaming is a popular method for cooking seafood and vegetables.

Sterilise to use boiling water or a very hot oven to kill bacteria that may be on the surface of equipment.

Sterols naturally occurring steroid alcohols found in plants and animals.

Stimulus materials an image or selection of images or other visual prompt such as a flow diagram to help your understanding of a topic.

Strong flour flour with a higher level of gluten, e.g. durum wheat flour.

Sugar a monosaccharide or disaccharide, a simple carbohydrate.

Sustainability describes human activity that is not harmful to the environment and does not deplete natural resources, thereby supporting long-term ecological balance.

Sustainable source when food or ingredients originate from a continuing or renewable source. An example would be fishing either from farms or other sources that are able to sustain reproduction without a negative impact on the species or environment.

Sustenance food or drink that provides nourishment to sustain the body and life.

Syneresis the sudden release of moisture from protein molecules.

Tapioca a starch extract taken from the root of the cassva, traditionally found in the South Americas. It can be used to make puddings or as a thickener.

Tenderise to make softer.

Terrain a stretch of land, typically referred to in reference to the characteristics of that land. For example, rough terrain.

Textured Vegetable Protein (TVP) vegetable protein, especially from soya beans, that is used as a substitute for meat, or is added to it.

Timeplan written instructions that break down the practical tasks with an indication of timing.

Tipo '00' flour a flour milled from hard wheats that contain a slightly lower level of protein than standard bread flours. Typically used to make pizza dough, or pasta.

Tofu a high protein food made by coagulating soya milk and pressing the resulting curds into soft white blocks.

Toxins bacterial poisons.

Traceability the ability to track any food through all stages of production, processing and distribution.

Traditional products foods made in a specific way according to their gastronomic heritage and transmitted from one generation to the next. Food is associated with a certain local area, region or country.

Traditions customs, ways of living or beliefs that are recognised as very long established and typically passed from one generation to another over time.

Trans-fats unsaturated fatty acids formed by the partial hydrogenation of vegetable oil, believed to raise blood cholesterol level.

Tuberculosis a serious bacterial infection found in cattle.

Undernutrition eating too little food to meet the body's needs.

Unleavened refers to bread, cake and biscuits made without raising agent.

Unsaturated fats fats that contain a high ratio of fatty acid molecules with at least one double bond. Unsaturated fats are considered to be healthier than saturated fats. Examples of foods containing unsaturated fats are rape seed oil and olive oil.

Unsaturated fatty acids carbon is not attached to the hydrogen.

Use-by date indicates the date after which there is no guarantee that the food is safe to eat.

Vacuum packing/packaging a preservation method that removes all the air from a food container or package before sealing, particularly oxygen which causes degradation.

Vegans people who do not use or eat any animal products, such as leather, meat or dairy.

Viscous when a liquid is thick and sticky.

Water soluble vitamins these vitamins (the B group and vitamin C) dissolve in water

Whey the watery part of milk that remains after the formation of curds.

Whisking a method of beating or stirring a food substance using light, rapid movements.

White flour contains just the endosperm; the bran and germ have been removed.

Whole grain 100% of the grain, nothing has been removed.

Yeast a microorganism belonging to the fungi family, made up of single oval cells that reproduce by budding. Yeast can ferment sugar in to alcohol and carbon dioxide and is also used as a raising agent when making bread.

ANSWERS TO EXAM QUESTIONS

Principles of nutrition (p 43)

Q1. i) True; ii) False; iii) True. **Q2.** a) i) Pasta. ii) To fight infection. iii) Liver. b) Any two from growth/muscle strength, repair or secondary source of energy/provides energy/more energy. **Q3.** i) Food sources can include Retinol (animal sources), dairy, egg yolk, oily fish, liver, beta-carotene (plant sources), fortified margarines, yellow/red/green leafy vegetables, carrots, sweet potatoes, red peppers, yellow fruit such as mango or papaya. ii) Vitamin C. iii) Strong bones and/ or teeth, or calcification of bones. **Q4.** a) growth of cells, repair or maintenance of cells, secondary source of energy/calories, regulation of enzymes. b) refer to HBV (animal source contains essential amino acids like meat, fish, milk, cheese or eggs; refer to LBV (vegetable or plant source but does not contain all essential amino acids like cereals, pulses or nuts); refer to specific examples of foods like beans on toast, lentil soup with bread roll; refer to soya and mycoprotein, Quorn. **Q5.** a) correct answers include links between salt and high blood pressure, risk factors in coronary heart disease, government reports highlighting need to reduce salt intake, Eatwell Guide, high levels of salt in processed foods which easily exceed 6g per day limit, stomach cancer risks, strain on kidneys. b) i) – iii) Correct answers include not adding salt to meals, not using salt during cooking, avoiding ready meals/convenience foods or take-aways, not using stock cubes or components high salt, reducing visits to fast food outlets, choosing foods low in sodium, substitution with spices/flavourings, use of 'LoSalt', switching to low salt versions of everyday foods, e.g. breakfast cereals/named spreads, e.g. Flora, tinned foods/reduced salt options, avoiding/limiting salty foods from diet such as nuts, crisps, cheese, ham, pretzels, bacon, smoked fish, read labels when choosing meals or to check for hidden salt. c) a basic definition might be "salt you can't see", a better answer would be a definition plus example: used in ready meals, savoury snacks, soy sauce, sauces, or as a preservative, or In cakes, biscuits, pastries and puddings in the form of sodium bicarbonate (raising agent). Hidden sodium in foods – monosodium glutamate (MSG) **Q6.** a) fruits and vegetables (can be named fruits and vegetables (e.g., carrots, bananas, apples etc) or the generic phrase of fruits and vegetables). Wholegrain cereals and flours – e.g. wholemeal flour, brown rices. b) insoluble fibre – not easily broken down by the digestive system; most passes through the body unchanged. Helps to keep bowels healthy and helps prevent digestive problems such as constipation and haemorrhoids (piles). Found in plant-based foods, including fruit, vegetables (especially the skins), whole and unprocessed grains, nuts, corn, oats, fruit and vegetables. soluble fibre – broken down by bacteria in your large bowel and can be digested by the body. Helps to reduce the amount of cholesterol in the blood; can protect against coronary heart disease (CHD). Oats lower cholesterol due to the presence of soluble fibre called oat beta-glucan. Soluble fibre sources include: oats, barley, rye, most beans and peas, fruit, such as bananas and apples, root vegetables, such as carrots. Discussion can include any of the following points: dietary fibre intake for adults should be 30g each day. High fibre foods in diet. Help you feel fuller for longer (so will prevent snacking); help people maintain a healthy weight, reduce chances of weight gain and obesity). Make your faeces softer and easier to pass through your bowel. Will prevent constipation, haemorrhoids (piles), diverticulitis, type 2 diabetes, some cancers (such as cancer of the colon) and lower the risk of coronary heart disease (CHD). Fibre will slow down the absorption of carbohydrates in the blood, which can help to keep your blood sugar level constant. This can be useful for those who have diabetes.

Diet and good health (p 67)

Q1. True, False, True. **Q2.** In vertical order down the table: PAL, DRVs and RIs. **Q3.** a) any two from the following: age, sex, height, weight, and level of activity. b) Energy input must equal energy output. If energy input is less than output, there could be possible weight loss. If energy input is more than energy output, there could be weight gain leading to obesity. Obesity can contribute towards diet related illnesses such as Coronary Heart Disease, type 2 diabetes and hypertension. **Q4.** a) Answer should include some of the following points, with reasons cut down on calorie intake, a calorie-controlled diet is essential when trying to lose weight; avoid foods high in fat and sugar because these are high in calories. Beware of 'hidden fat and sugar' in food products – read labels for information; choose low in fat and sugar options – there is a wide variety available and they can contribute to a calorie controlled diet; eat breakfast – a good start to the day and helps prevent the temptation to snack mid morning; use cooking methods which do not require addition of fat or oil e.g. grilling, steaming. Use herbs and spices to flavour food instead of fat or oil; plenty of exercise – tones the body and muscles. b) Breakfast – unsweetened fruit juice or fresh or dried fruit with or without a sugar free breakfast cereal or porridge. Skimmed milk, no added sugar. Eggs cooked without any additional fat with wholemeal bread or alternative yeast product. Yoghurts (plain) or sweetened with artificial sweeteners / honey. Midday meal – any balanced food choice such as a soup and bread roll, salad, and pasta dish. Choice should be based on low fat, low sugar, low calorie option that is nutritionally balanced, with a variety in colour, flavour and texture. Snacks – choice based on some carbohydrate food but otherwise low in fat and sugar. Suggestions could include unsalted nuts, fresh fruit, vegetable sticks, low fat crisps. Filled pitta bread, plain biscuits with cottage cheese. Drinks – unsweetened juices, water, skimmed milk, and smoothies. Evening meal – should include a dish containing a high protein food such as chicken or fish, some carbohydrate such as boiled rice, pasta, couscous or jacket potato and plenty of steamed vegetables or salad. Include unlimited fresh fruit and / or vegetables daily. **Q5.** Fruit and vegetables / 5–6 portions needed daily / vitamins, dietary fibre, some carbohydrate; Milk and alternative / 3–4 portions / protein, calcium, vitamins A and D, fat; Beans, pulses, fish, eggs / 5–6 portions / protein, iron, vitamins, calcium. **Q6.** a) dietary Reference Value, Estimated, Average Requirements, Guideline Daily Amounts. b) RIs (previously Guideline Daily Amounts) give a benchmark for the amounts of energy and nutrients needed by adults. They are recommendations for an average person to maintain a healthy diet. Labels give information on the energy provides by 100g amounts of the food as well as % RI for fat saturates, sugars and salt. It is useful for consumers for making informed decisions and choices when planning for special diets. **Q7.** a) benefits include: prevention of obesity and related illnesses, brain functions at its optimum, a fitter body to take part in activities, it lays down a good foundation, forms good eating habits for later years, a healthy child is usually a happier child, psychological benefits. b) Recent measures include: advice on healthy eating – the Eatwell Guide. Emphasis on the importance of choosing unsaturated fats and oils, plant proteins that are more environmentally sustainable. Energy requirements have been added to reinforce the fact that all food and drink contribute to total energy intake. The Scientific Advisory Committee on Nutrition advice on 'free sugars' (sugars added to food by manufacturers, cook or consumer). Recommended intake for sugar has changed to a recommended 5% of total dietary intake. Welsh Assembly Government Food and Fitness plan to improve access to food and drink. Change for Life is a campaign aimed to help people make lifestyle changes through improved nutrition and exercise. Appetite for Life and Healthy Eating in Schools are both measures aimed to improve the nutritional standards of food and drink in schools. **Q8.** A nutrition claim relates to the nutrients that food product does or does not contain, for example sugar, fat, fibre – a health claim related to any health benefit that a food product may have, for example plant sterols lower blood cholesterol. **Q9.** a) protein – growth of body cells, maintenance and repair of body cells, a source of energy if other sources are lacking. Protein needs at birth are required for growth. Additional protein is required during growth spurts through to adolescence to coping with increase in body size and for the maintenance of increasing body cells. b) calcium – formation and development of the skeleton, normal clotting of blood, normal functioning of nerves and muscles. Calcium requirements increase with age. Babies and children's needs are high, in order to develop good bone density. Vitamin D promotes the absorption of calcium. c) iron – formation of haemoglobin that carries oxygen to the body tissues. Iron requirements increase with age reaching a peak at adolescence. Girls need more than boys to replace the loss during menstruation. **Q10.** Lifestyle includes religion and beliefs that dictate people's food choice. Examples are all types of vegetarianism – vegans, lacto vegetarians, lacto-ovo vegetarians. Vegetarians do not eat meat of any kind. They choose not to eat meat for a variety of reasons that include the cruelty of killing animals, environmental issues, medical reasons and a possible dislike to the texture of flesh. Some vegetarians do not eat fish as well as meat and there are others who do not eat animal products that include eggs and milk. Lacto ovo eat both dairy products and eggs. Lacto vegetarians eat dairy but avoid eggs. Vegans do not eat dairy products, eggs or anything derived from animals, which includes honey. Religious beliefs include: Buddhists who follow a strict vegetarian diet; Hindus who also follow a strict vegetarian diet; Jews and Muslims do not eat pork or products form a pig, birds of prey and shellfish. Jewish meat must be slaughtered according to Kosher (Jewish) and halal (Muslim) laws. Rastafarians are also vegetarians and only eat a food deemed to be 'natural', that is without artificial colours, flavourings and preservatives.

The science of cooking food (p 83)

Q1. Conduction, convection, radiation. **Q2.** a) denaturing is where proteins are irreversibly changed due to heat, acids or enzymes. b) any from: boiled egg, meringue, skin on hot milk, melted and stringy cheese. **Q3.** Roasting uses fat/oil during cooking whereas boiling uses water. Roasting takes place in a hot oven whereas boiling takes place in a saucepan of boiling water. **Q4.** Chicken, eggs, shellfish. **Q5.** A barbeque creates extreme heat so the surface of the meat is browned (Maillard reaction) and then easily burnt due to a lack of heat control. The surface cooks very quickly and will burn before the heat is able to permeate to the centre of the steak. However, rare steak is safe to eat. **Q6.** Advantage – it is fast / creates a crunchy surface. Disadvantage – the food is submerged in oil/fat which is absorbed by the food making it unhealthy. Only small pieces of food can be cooked this way e.g. chips, sausages. **Q7.** This is particularly important when the dish needs to be risen e.g. cakes and Yorkshire pudding. A burst of hot air is needed to create steam from the water in the food. The steam assists raising the dish. When bread is placed into a hot oven the yeast is killed and the gluten structure is set. **Q8.** Energy can be reduced by: using a steamer to cook several items of food or a whole meal at once; if using the oven cook more than one item in it. Ovens use a lot of energy so it is a waste to cook just one or two jacket potatoes. The extra food can be oven cooked and frozen for a later time or for the next day's meal. Switch off the hob, oven, grill as soon as you have finished cooking; put lids on saucepans – the water comes to the boil more quickly and there is minimal heat loss meaning less fuel is needed to maintain a simmer; use a microwave oven to cook foods e.g. a jacket potato takes about 10 mins to cook in the microwave oven but an hour in a traditional oven. **Q9.** Any from: roasting, baking, braising, casseroling. **Q10.** Boiled: hot water convection currents will soften the potato starch – soft potatoes that are 'mashable'. Roasted: the hot air convection currents with very hot fat will create a fairly dry, crunchy surface to the potato. The moisture inside the potato will soften the internal potato. Microwaved jacket potatoes: the microwaves penetrate the potato causing the molecules to agitate creating friction. The heat formed will cook and soften potato. Potatoes cooked in a casserole: the moist convection currents will soften the potato. Chips: the very hot oil seals the surface of the potato pieces creating a crispy finish. The heat of the oil is transferred to the middle of each chip and the moisture in the potato cooks the potato through. **Q11.** a) convection and conduction; b) radiant heat (infrared radiation); c) convection; d) microwave (radiation). **Q12.** a) Roasting requires fat/oil so the potato will absorb some of this increasing the energy value of the potatoes. Jacket potato is a 'sealed' food and the convection current of hot air transfers through the potato skin making the inside of the potato hot cooking the potato starch. The nutritional values remain similar to the raw, whole potato. There are no added Kcals. b) Steamed broccoli: because the broccoli is cooked in the steam from boiling water-soluble vitamins are not lost. Boiled broccoli loses water-soluble vitamins because the broccoli is immersed in the water resulting in the vitamins 'dissolving' into the water. **Q13.** a) advantage; quick method of cooking. Disadvantage: loss of water-soluble vitamins /soft texture. b) advantage: added/improved flavour. b) disadvantage: takes a long time to cook. c) advantage: water-soluble vitamins not lost/added flavour. Disadvantage: vegetables can burn easily. **Q14.**

Description	Method of heat transference	Example of cooking method
The saucepan is heated which heats the water inside the pan. The heat from the hot water transfers to the food.	Convection	Rice cooked in hot water – simmering/boiling.
The food container is heated directly by the gas flame/electric element and the heat transfers to the surface of the food.	Conduction	Metal pan on a hob – frying, boiling etc. Baking tins, trays etc in oven, baking/roasting.
Heat travels directly onto the food by infra-red rays	Radiation	Food being grilled.

Q15. a) proteins are coagulated at 71c-85c. Coagulation is where the proteins become firm and harden. e.g. fried egg, grilled cheese. b) caramelisation occurs when sugar is exposed to high heat causing the food to brown, sweeten and become crispy e.g. ginger biscuits, topping of a crème brulee. c) dextrinisation- golden brown dextrins are formed when starchy food is heated. e.g. toast, cake surface. **Q16.** 1. Liquid + starch+heat causes the flour to gelatinise. 2. Gelatinisation is where starch granules when heated, soften and absorb the liquid cause the liquid to thicken. 3. Gelatinisation occurs at about 66c and above. **Q17.** Top to bottom: baked products – cakes, biscuits; bread; roasted meat. Next row: ready-made meals; jacket potatoes; defrosting frozen food; reheating foods. Bottom row: steamed vegetables; chicken breast; suet puddings; cake puddings e.g. sticky toffee pudding. **Q18.** Add tomatoes/drop of vinegar to the meat; marinade the meat; 'hammer' the meat to break up the fibres; cook tough cuts long and slow. **Q19.** Carbon dioxide, steam. **Q20.** Plain flour might have been used; no added raising agent in the recipe; scone dough rolled too thin; uncooked scones not put straight into the hot oven (left hanging around); scones put into a cold oven. **Q21.** Advantages: i) very quick cooking method. ii) gives the food a golden brown colour. iii) food develops a crispy surface. iv) adds flavour to the food. Disadvantages: i) fat is absorbed by the food increasing the energy values & makes the food relatively unhealthy. ii) the food cooking must be supervised at all times. iii) unsupervised frying can be a fire hazard.

Food spoilage (p 95)

Q1. Milk stored in fridge door; raw chicken on bottom shelf; cheesecake on top shelf. **Q2.** a) red = raw meat, blue = raw fish, green = fruit, salad & vegetables. b) The benefit of using different coloured boards is that cross contamination of foods is minimised. For example; use only a red board when preparing raw meat. This will prevent campylobacter or salmonella pathogenic bacteria from being passed onto other foods such as bread or cheese. A cheese sandwich should be made on a general purpose / white board where only low risk foods are prepared. By adhering to the rule of using different coloured boards for specific foods the risk of contracting food poisoning is reduced. c) correct answer could include: washing hands using hot, soapy water; do not cough or splutter over food; do not allow pets in the kitchen; spoons used for tasting food must be washed between tastings. **Q3.** From top down: boiling point of water, core temperature for cooked food, minimum temperature for "hot-held" foods e.g. carvery buffet, maximum core temperature for chilled food, temperature at which food freezes, minimum core temperature of frozen foods. **Q4.** Any two of the following: Salmonella, Campylobacter, E. Coli, Staphylococcus Aurous , Listeria, and Bacillus Cereus. **Q5.** The date after which food may not be safe to consume and hence risking food poisoning. **Q6.** Any four of the following: store all raw meat covered and on the bottom shelf of a fridge at 5c; always use a red board when preparing raw meat; wash hands after handling raw meat; never wash raw meat; cooked meat should have a core temperature of 75c; cooked chicken juices must run clear and not pink; unused cooked meat must be cooled quickly and stored, wrapped in a fridge. **Q7.** a) freezing i) & ii) raw meat, vegetables, ready meals, fresh milk, soups and gravies. b) pickling, iii) and iv) eggs, vegetables eg onions, cabbage. **Q8.** Hazard Analysis Critical Control Point. **Q9.** Cod, roast chicken and rice salad. **Q10.** Food safety – all food safety regulations must be followed eg date checking of food, correct storage of food such as raw meat on the bottom shelf of the fridge and ambient foods placed in sealed containers or cupboards; fresh eggshells must be clean and dirt free. The freezer, fridge, hot serving counters must all be operating at correct temperatures. The core temperature of all cooked foods must be at a minimum of 75c. Foods should never be left 'hanging around' a kitchen. Hygiene – all surfaces in the kitchen must be cleaned regularly. Fridges must be washed out once a week and best practice is to use a sanitiser after washing all surfaces. Spillages and dropped food must be cleaned up immediately to prevent any pest infestations. Personal hygiene is critical. Daily showers and regular hand washing is key to minimise body bacteria (staph A). Hair must be tied back and jewellery should not be worn. All cuts must be clean and covered whilst preparing food. Spitting and coughing near food should not happen

Food provenance and food waste (p 105)

Q1. Food provenance refers to where food comes from – where is it grown, raised or reared. **Q2.** Correct answers could include: using biodegradable packaging which will decompose; producing refill packs for products so consumers can reuse the original container; remove unnecessary layers of packaging and use only that which is essential. **Q3.** Biodegradable packaging is packaging that can completely decompose with the aid of micro-organisms. **Q4.** Correct answers would include: EU food protection marks can help protect against imitation as it ensures that consumers know only genuine products will carry the logo. It prevents companies calling a food by a certain name if it has not followed the traditional, approved processes. **Q5.** Correct answers from the following: buy local – choosing locally produced food can make the biggest impact on food miles; grow your own vegetables; eat food that is in season; pick your own; walk or cycle to the shop, shop less frequently. **Q6.** Plan your food shopping – this helps to avoid buying food already in the house, or being tempted to buy too much. Store food in the correct place at the correct temperature – a cool cupboard, the fridge or the freezer – to avoid it going off prematurely. Be waste-free by using up leftovers, for example in soups and smoothies. Understand the difference between 'use by' and 'best before' dates. Food that is eaten after the 'best before' date will not be of such good quality but will not be harmful to eat. Compost food that cannot be eaten such as vegetable peelings and teabags. **Q7.**

	Advantages	Disadvantages
Plastic	Can be recycled.	A litter problem as it does not biodegrade easily.
Paper/Cardboard	Easily recycled and biodegradable.	Recycled paper and card cannot be used with food products.
Metal	Steel and aluminium can be separated and both can be recycled.	A lot of energy used in extraction.

Q8. a) 'Food loss' is unintentional waste caused by poor equipment, transportation and infrastructure. 'Food waste' is caused by consumers over-buying and companies rejecting food that does not meet specific aesthetic standards. b) The issue of food loss can be addressed by providing support to developing countries to ensure water supplies, obtain better equipment and introduce more productive crops. People should also be encouraged to form co-operatives to work together to get the most out of the land that they have. Food waste could be addressed by applying less rigorous aesthetic standards on food, such as allowing 'ugly fruit and vegetables' to be sold, this means that fruit and vegetables will not be wasted. Consumers can also address food waste in their own homes by planning shopping so as not to over-buy, causing some food to be thrown away. They can also ensure they store food correctly to prevent it going off, using up leftovers and composting inedible food waste. **Q9.** a) food packaging is used as a marketing tool for the company and to make the product look more attractive to customers. It also preserves the freshness of the product, this ensures that when a customer eats it, it has the best possible taste. Packaging also helps to prevent contamination of the product, either from bacterial, chemical or physical sources and prevents the product being tampered with. Some packaging is used to protect the product from damage e.g. an egg box and to make the product easier to transport. b) Food packaging produces a large amount of waste, but in recent years there have been attempts to reduce its impact on the environment. One change is the use of biodegradable packaging, which will break down completely reducing the amount of packaging going into landfill. Recycling options is a second change, making food packaging from plastic, paper and cardboard, metal and glass is better for the environment as they are able to be recycled. Food packaging has been redesigned to reduce the amount of unnecessary packaging, including just what is needed to be functional, rather than having additional aesthetic packaging layers. Many products are now available in refill packs such as cleaning products and coffee. Glass milk bottles are returnable and jars can be reused for storage or home preservation e.g. pickled onions. **Q10.** Benefit delays, low income and benefit changes are the primary reasons why people are currently being referred to foodbanks for emergency food. Food poverty can be addressed in several ways – food co-ops, (food distribution outlets organised by the local community where decisions regarding the production and distribution of its food is chosen by its members.) Gives the community control over the prices they charge and by forming a co-op they are able to buy food at a lower price. Another way is community cafés – businesses that are run by the community for the community, money that is made is reinvested into the café, and prices of products are not as high as other outlets. Ready meals and pre-prepared food can be expensive, but due to a lack of food knowledge and skills some people rely on them, however cooking and nutrition programmes and courses allow people to be hands-on with food preparation skills, and show them that making healthy meals can be economical and improve their diet, which can help them get out of food poverty. Breakfast or lunch clubs offer the opportunity to have an affordably priced meal in a social setting and can be for the community in general or specific groups, e.g. older people. Children are affected by food poverty so many school tuck shops provide fruit and vegetables to children, important for children from low income families who may not otherwise have access to fresh fruit and vegetables.

Technological developments (p 133)

Q1. a) probiotic yoghurts/margarines/spreads/drinks. b) Functional foods deliver additional or enhanced benefits over and above their basic nutritional value. Some functional foods are generated around a particular functional ingredient, for example foods containing probiotics, prebiotics, or plant stanols and sterols. Functional foods and drinks may provide benefits in health terms, but should not be seen as an alternative to a varied and balanced diet and a healthy lifestyle. Examples of functional foods include: probiotics are live bacteria and yeasts promoted as having various health benefits and are often described as 'good' or 'friendly' bacteria. **Q2.** Technological developments – population increase (higher demand for different food sources); transport and travel (products from different areas being able to be transported, people visiting different areas and trying different foods); preservation methods (improvements so foods can be preserved for longer to help with transportation); media (people are more aware of new products available); environmental factors (people are more aware of environmental issues and demand new products that damage the environment less); economic understanding and trade (companies offer more lines to gain more market share); scientific advancements (in developing new products/preservation/transportation); consumer demand (demand is the mother of invention, if customers want it someone will make it); wider understanding of nutrition, diet and health. Health awareness pressures – wider understanding of nutrition, diet and health – through media, travel etc, more understanding of food and what it is required for and what is does to the body and environment. Government initiatives explaining about health. Cost of unhealthy foods – food tax makes people want healthier foods. Education in school. Better packaging and labelling. More people with allergies. **Q3.** One from: transport – better transportation to help food last longer; preservation methods – improved preservation methods and new methods helping food last longer MAP HPP pasteurisation vacuum packaging intelligent packaging new plastics; environmental factors – grow at home and pick when you want the food; scientific advancements – pesticides/ packaging/seeds development / transportation /preservation/ hydroponics / gm/ automation to speed up production. **Q4.** a) functional foods deliver additional or enhanced benefits over and above their basic nutritional value. b) Examples could be yoghurts /drinks/spread/fats/cereals/ breads / fruit drinks. **Q5.** a) advantages could be: maintain natural colour/flavour/ texture, improves nutrient retention, environmentally friendly and extends the shelf life of products. b) correct answers would be: sliced meat/ soup/ hummus / guacamole / cheese / milk. **Q6.** Margarine: A Flora Light or B proactive. Why? Lower in fat, more polyunsaturated, lower in calories but proactive is slightly higher in fat but is better to lower cholesterol. If Alison was a vegetarian, could you give her the same advice? Why or why not?Fat spreads can contain animal fats so she would need to read the label to see if she could have the spread. If Alison was a vegan then she should also need to check if it contains milk products also as vegans cannot eat milk products derived from cow's milk.

Factors affecting food choice (p 156)

Q1. Any four from: availability, cost, culture, religious beliefs, ethical food choices, seasonal food, medical conditions, marketing and advertising, labelling. **Q2.** Correct answers include: increase in global population, increase in agricultural costs, increase in fuel costs, affecting production and transport, political unrest, e.g. wars, change in the weather and climate, change in buying habits. **Q3.** Coeliac disease is an autoimmune disorder that affects the lining of the gastrointestinal tract, it can cause the villi in lining of the small intestine to be damaged and prevent nutrients being absorbed. It is important that someone who is coeliac avoids eating the protein gluten that is found in wheat, and some other cereals like rye and barley. Iron-deficiency anaemia is a condition where a lack of iron in the body leads to a reduced number of red blood cells. Having fewer red blood cells than is normal can lead to symptoms such as tiredness, pale complexion and shortness of breath. Including the following foods in the diet can be helpful in boosting iron levels in the body; dark-green leafy vegetables, iron-fortified cereals or bread, brown rice, pulses and beans, red meat, eggs and dried fruit, such as dried apricots, prunes and raisins. Dairy intolerance can be caused by either the protein in dairy products or specifically the milk sugar (lactose). People with lactose intolerance don't produce enough lactase, so lactose stays in the digestive system, it causes symptoms such as a bloated stomach and diarrhoea. Someone suffering from a dairy intolerance should avoid milk and milk products and choose alternative dairy products like soya milk. **Q4.**

Islam	Food must be halal, which means that animals have been slaughtered in the Islamic way. Muslims are not permitted to eat pork, pork products, lard or gelatine. Muslims are forbidden from drinking alcohol or eating food that contains alcohol.
Judaism	In order to meet Jewish dietary laws, food must be kosher, meaning 'clean' or 'proper'. Kosher rules ensure that: · Meat and poultry has been slaughtered in a special way. · Pork and shellfish are forbidden. · Meat and dairy products must not be prepared or eaten together. Separate cooking equipment should also be used.
Hinduism	Beef is a forbidden food, as Hindus believe the cow is sacred. Many Hindus follow a vegetarian diet. Alcohol is also forbidden. Strict Hindus will avoid onions, mushrooms, garlic, tea and coffee.

Q5. Red Tractor logo / Red Tractor assurance – Foods display the Red Tractor logo as a sign of farm assurance, it shows the product has met strict standards through the whole of the food chain products can be traced back to the farms they came from. Fairtrade mark – This logo is used on products sourced from developing countries and shows that products meet international Fairtrade standards such as ensuring producers receive a fair price for their products, have greater control over the trading process and help invest in projects that are sustainable for communities. Soil Association Organic symbol – Foods displaying this logo shows the food has been produced with higher levels of animal welfare, lower levels of pesticides and no manufactured herbicides or artificial fertilisers. **Q6.** An answer could include: people choose to buy food products for ethical reasons. Ethical issues are wide ranging and are of increasing importance to consumers. Can include the way food is produced/where the food comes from. Can include food production methods, for example, some consumers choose to buy free-range eggs. Consumers will also look for food labels that show their food has been produced to meet strict standards, both in animal welfare and the quality of the product produced. This could be the Red Tractor logo that shows food is produced in the UK to strict standards, and also informs them they are buying a British product. Other ethical considerations include organic food production, as some people believe they are choosing a more sustainable product that has less environmental impact and that the products are more ethical as they are produced without the use of artificial fertilisers and pesticides. Genetically modified food is also an issue that concerns some consumers. There is increasing concern over the environmental impact of food choice, especially the amount of miles food travels. The final ethical issue to consider is Fairtrade, and foods displaying the Fairtrade logo show that the food has been produced by workers in developing countries who are getting a fair wage for their products, it also shows that they haven't used child labour to produce the products and that the workers are benefitting from improved working conditions. **Q7.** a) marketing and advertising is designed to make people want to choose a particular product. It has an important role in affecting food choice for example within shops product placement ensures that certain products catch our attention and make us want to buy them. Attention is also attracted through the use of colourful packaging and displays. Consumers can be encouraged to try new products by stores offering free tasting sessions, this may cause them to deviate from their usual buying habits. Likewise special offers, money off vouchers and loyalty points also encourage people to buy different foods. Marketing or advertising can also focus on seasonal products e.g. low fat or health products in January to kick-start a healthy new year. b) Food labelling can be an important source of information to consumers when making food choices. Important for someone with a food allergy. Ingredients lists and allergen information will ensure they are able to choose foods that won't cause an allergic reaction. They can also be helpful for people following a special diet e.g. low fat. Ethical logos can also help consumers choose the products that they would prefer to buy, for example they may want to choose a Fairtrade produce or organic foods. Other information that could be useful to consumers is the place of origin, this can help people who are concerned about the amount of miles their food travels or who would prefer to buy British products. **Q8.** a) ways that families can save money when shopping for food include: comparing food prices on the Internet; shopping at low-cost supermarkets like Aldi and Lidl or choose supermarket own brands or value lines; use 'special offers' in the shops, e.g. buy one get one free or half price and also save them money but care is needed so they don't buy products they don't need, or more than can be consumed before the use-by date or they will be wasted; incentives like coupons, vouchers or cards to collect loyalty points from shops; plan meals before going shopping, and stick to the list and avoid buying more food than is needed; check dates on food and eat by the 'use buy' or 'best before' date to avoid waste; buy foods that are in season locally. b) When preparing and cooking food careful planning can help save money, for example using leftovers from one meal to make another; consider the type of product being bought e.g. using cheaper cuts of meat and offal; save money by using quick methods of cooking, e.g. microwave, to reduce the amount of energy used; make food in large batches to avoid ingredients being wasted and then freeze for use at a later date; save money by making meals at home rather than buying takeaway foods and ready meals.**Q9.** a) Food choice has been increased by a number of developments. People are now concerned about the ways their food is produced, this had led to a range of ethical foods being produced and labelled. They can include Fairtrade products, which ensure workers in developing countries have a fair price for their products. Environmental considerations have also seen products labelled with Rainforest Alliance logos and British flag logos to show that food hasn't had to travel so far. Other ethical considerations include animal welfare with products such as free range and outdoor reared meat. Organic food has increased in popularity as people want to buy more natural products that do not include artificial or chemical substances, there is now a wide range of organic products available from fruit and vegetables, to meat, tea and eggs. Other developments in food products include the introduction of functional foods, these are foods which have been modified to benefit either the nutritional qualities or the use of the product for example, smart starches which thicken instantly e.g. instant soup or cholesterol lowering spreads. Genetically modified foods have allowed products to be altered to improve them, this has included developing crops with a quicker growth or less resistant to disease e.g. tomatoes. b) Despite the developments there are many factors that could influence whether they are used in family meals, some consumers may have concerns about genetically modified foods, especially as there are worries that not enough is known about them and that they are not always clearly labelled. Ethical concerns may also mean that people are worried about the fact that nature is being tampered with that could affect the balance of nature. However it is a useful way of producing crops that will be less resistant to disease and help to feed a growing population and could help reduce the cost of products which could be beneficial for families. Food choice is also influenced by moral values, this could mean that some families would rather choose organic products as they feel the food is more natural or Fairtrade food as they feel that they are supporting workers in developing countries. Animals products that have been reared with welfare in mind may also be more appealing to families than intensively farmed products. Functional products could be helpful for consumers who want to be able to prepare food quickly e.g. instant desserts and for consumers with health issues like high cholesterol who could buy spreads and yogurt products that can combat this.

Commodities:
Cereals (p 208)

Q1. a) i) white bread. Ii) wholemeal bread. iii) it contains the bran and the germ, which is where fibre is found. b) i) & ii) can use flour with a lower protein content, and it is faster than the bulk fermentation method. b) reasons to include: the more you knead the more elastic the dough will be. The more you knead the more gluten (protein) will be developed, which gives bread the structure. If bread dough is not kneaded enough, it will not be able to hold the tiny pockets of gas (CO2) created by the leavening agent (such as yeast), and will collapse, leaving a heavy and dense loaf. c) answers could include: yeast is not active or not enough CO2 production; not enough liquid to assist the softening of gluten; proving time too short, needs to prove for longer; protein content in flour too low, must use a high protein flour. **Q2.** i) durum wheat. ii) from top down, fusilli, farfalle and tagliatelle. iii) to the tooth / with a slight bite. iv) Roux consists of equal quantities of fat and flour. When the fat has melted the flour is added. The melted fat (butter / margarine) coats the starch granules. The fat and flour mixture (called the roux) are cooked over a low heat. Some starch will gelatinise, but most will remain uncooked. This is because at this point there is not enough liquid to complete the gelatinisation process. The liquid (infused milk) is added gradually and carefully stirred into the roux. The starch will form a suspension until the sauce is returned to the heat the sauce is stirred continuously whilst heating to keep the starch granules dispersed. This constant stirring is important to avoid lumps forming. As the temperature rises the fat melts and is absorbed by the starch. The starch granules swell as they take up the milk. As the sauce comes to boiling point the starch gelatinises causing the mixture to thicken and produce a smooth, glossy and lump free sauce. A gel is formed. **Q3.** a) from top down: self-raising flour, strong plain white flour, plain flour. b) i) 13%. ii) Ham. iii) 6g. iv) wholemeal bread or similar high fibre bread suggestion / add salad / vegetables such as peppers, spinach, sliced tomatoes, cucumber, onion. v) Correct answers include: rotate stock – FIFO (first in, first out); make sure all stock is clearly labeled with use by dates; food operators must have high standard of personal hygiene – hair covered, protective clothing, all clean clothing, no chewing, washing hands regularly (after breaks, loo visits, blowing nose etc) and each time task is started, no eating, chewing, coughing etc, wearing disposable gloves is optional – emphasis is on clean hands rather than glove wearing; separate equipment and utensils for different foods – eg coloured tongs, knives, chopping boards; wash all fresh salad ingredients; make sure ingredients are pre-chilled; check each ingredient is free form pest contamination; avoid cross-contamination during sandwich assembly and storage; all food contact surface and equipment must be cleaned and sanitized; store and transport sandwiches safely. c) Correct answers include: freeze the bread and use it as you need to from freezer; make breadcrumbs from stale bread and freeze them until needed; use breadcrumbs in recipes such as bread pudding, treacle tart, as a crumb for fishcakes, goujons, mixed with cheese for an au-grain topping; use leftover or stale bread to make into other dishes (bread and butter pudding, Summer pudding, croutons (can be kept in an airtight container), make toasted sandwiches; make a salad such as panzanella; brown bread ice cream

Fruit and Vegetables (p 236)

Q1. Clockwise, from top right – cherry, lemon, kiwi fruit, pineapple, peach, melon. **Q2.** a) i) grapefruit, lemon, lime, orange, tangerine, clementine. ii) potatoes, carrots, beetroot, parsnips, turnips, swedes, sweet potatoes. iii) fruit rich in vitamin C – oranges, grapefruit, lemons, limes, blackcurrants, raspberries, rowanberries. iv) leafy green vegetables – spinach, cabbage, pak choi, kale, sprouting broccoli, brussels sprouts. b) Any four from: they contain natural or intrinsic sugars; vitamins A, C, E which are important for maintaining healthy tissue, normal vision and have antioxidant properties; folate for the nervous system and the formation of healthy blood cells. Spinach an excellent source; potassium for the functioning of a healthy nervous system; magnesium to help maintain healthy bones and teeth; dietary fibre, found in the pith, skin and fibrous part of the plant cells in variable amounts; low in fat and calorific value; some fruit, for example avocado, rich in vitamin E; pulse vegetables are a good source of Low Biological value protein; fruit and vegetables can be included in every meal, are useful as snacks and are refreshing because of their high water content, for example melon; eating fruit and vegetables should be encouraged from a young age to set good eating habits **Q3.** Stages to include: require careful cooking otherwise nutritional content is reduced; prepare just before cooking otherwise the enzymatic action of oxygen will destroy vitamin C content; shred finely immediately before cooking; add to fast boiling water if boiling is chosen method of cooking; boil in minimum water with lid on to retain heat; minimum cooking time to retain texture and colour; serve immediately; use cooking liquid as stock for gravy or sauce. **Q4.** a) any two from steaming, boiling, microwaving and stir-frying. b) i) some methods enhance the overall colour of the vegetables more than others, for example stir frying gives a golden brown appearance. Colour is retained in steaming but boiling can alter the colour because of volatile acids reacting on the chlorophyll (green colour). The vegetables turn bright green to olive green to grey-green quite quickly. ii) cooking softens the walls of the cells in plant tissue, which releases the water inside the cells and makes the texture softer. This makes the vegetable lose a lot of bulk – applies to green leafy vegetables, such as spinach, in particular. Crispness is retained in steaming, texture is firmer with more 'bite'. Boiling on the other hand can soften the cells in plant tissue to such an extent that the resulting texture is soft and mushy. iii) Some vitamin loss depending on methods of cooking. Vitamins B and C are water-soluble and leach into the cooking liquid. Methods of cooking such as steaming, where the vegetables do not come into contact with water, retain most vitamins. **Q5.** a) cooking food in the steam from boiling water. Steamers are available with perforated base which fit over a pan of water. Steam enters through the perforations. Steamers can be tiered allowing several foods to be cooked at the same time. Electric steamers are also available with automatic cooking timing devices. b) answer to include: retention of colour- colour does not leach into cooking water; retention of texture – cooking in water breaks down fibrous plant cells more than steaming; retention of flavour – flavour keeps in the plant cells; retention of water soluble vitamins B and C – they do not leach into cooking water; can be more economical method on fuel if electric steamer used (with timing device) **Q6.** a) Reasons may include: aim for at least 5 a day (which can include one portion fruit juice). Canned fruit and vegetables, frozen varieties, dried fruit all contribute towards the 5 a day; they contain natural or intrinsic sugars; vitamins A, C, E which are important for maintaining healthy tissue, normal vision and have antioxidant properties; folate for the nervous system and the formation of healthy blood cells. Spinach an excellent source; potassium for the functioning of a healthy nervous system; magnesium to help maintain healthy bones and teeth; dietary fibre, found in the pith, skin and fibrous part of the plant cells in variable amounts; low in fat and calorific value; some fruit, for example avocado, rich in vitamin E; pulse vegetables are a good source of Low Biological value protein; fruit and vegetables can be included in every meal, are useful as snacks and are refreshing because of their high water content, for example melon; eating fruit and vegetables should be encouraged from a young age to set good eating habits. b) Ways might include: serve fruit and vegetables in interesting ways; include in packed lunches as prepared sticks, cherry tomatoes; add fresh and dried fruit to breakfast cereals; add additional chopped vegetables to Bolognese and stews; stuffed baked vegetables with interesting fillings; fruit packs as snacks; smoothies, juices and fruit syrups are refreshing and packed with antioxidants. **Q7.** Describe methods of cooking + example: Boiling – carrots, beetroot, parsnips, potatoes. Example – cooking vegetables in water. The vegetables should be covered with cold water, brought to the boil and simmered until tender. Green vegetable are plunged into boiling water and boiled for minimum time. Lid should cover the pan. Roasting – peppers, sweet potatoes, butternut squash, artichokes. Example – a roasting tray containing oil or fat is heated before adding the prepared vegetables. The vegetables are often parboiled first. Braising – celery, leeks, onions, red cabbage. Example – prepared vegetables are cooked on a bed of fried root vegetables (a mirepoix) with enough stock to cover the mirepoix. The food is basted at intervals with the stock and a lid kept on the pan. The liquid is used as a sauce. Steaming – Brussels sprouts, broccoli, spinach, cauliflower. Example – cooking food in the steam from boiling water. Steamers are available with perforated bottoms that fit over a pan of water. Steam enters through the perforations. Steamers can be tiered allowing several foods to be cooked at the same time. Electric steamers are also available with automatic cooking timing devices. **Q8.** Preserving fruit can save money when homegrown fruit is plentiful and in season. Fruit has a short shelf life and when in glut and plentiful, can be preserved for later use. There are many methods of preservation which can be used to avoid waste and save money. Fruit preserved by these methods last for six months to a year under correct storage conditions. Fruits can be preserved in many ways. Preserving fruit to save money. How can a family save money and minimise waste Methods of preserving fruit include: Jam making – fruit is first softened to break down the cellulose, sugar added and the jam boiled to a high temperature to enable the jam to gel and set; jelly making – the same principles are followed as for jam making but the cooked fruit is strained through muslin so that a clear jelly is obtained; bottling – fruit is place in sterile jars, a syrup added and the jars sealed and heated to a high temperature to seal and sterilise the content. This will destroy micro-organisms; freezing – fruit in peak condition is placed on trays to open freeze and afterwards placed in plastic bags. Alternatively the fruit in placed in plastic bags or containers and then frozen quickly; fruit syrups – fruit is simmered with sugar and water until the fruit is soft. It is strained and the liquid stored in bottles or jars; chutney – fruit used as an ingredient in chutney making with vegetables, spices and vinegar. The mixture is cooked until it becomes soft and pulpy and then placed into jars. **Q9.** a) i) fresh. ii) dried. iii) 40mg for adults. iv) two from: formation of connective tissue, absorption of iron, an antioxidant which helps to protect the body, helps wound healing. b) there has been vitamin C loss during the drying process; the high temperatures involved with some drying processes accelerate the loss; ascorbic acid (vitamin C) is readily oxidised; vitamin C is water soluble, when water is driven off, this causes reduction in vitamin content. **Q10.** Storage: use as soon as possible after purchase or there will be deterioration of flavour, colour and texture. Store in cool dark place to reduce loss of vitamin C. Oxidation of vitamin C is increased by light and heat. Preparation: prepare just before required or cooking to reduce the loss of vitamin C. Once cut, ascorbic acid oxidase is released. Remove any soil or dirt, avoid soaking in cold water as vitamin C is water-soluble. Use a sharp knife for cutting to avoid rupturing the plant cells as much as possible. Blunt knives cause more cells to be disrupted with further losses of vitamin C through oxidation. Tearing prevents disruption of cells and prevents release of ascorbic acid oxidase. Acids such as lemon juice prevent the loss of vitamin C by oxidation and prevents susceptible fruit such as apples and pears from browning. Cooking – use minimum amount of water to prevent loss of vitamin C, thiamine, riboflavin and nicotinic acid. Green vegetables should be plunged into boiling water to reduce the loss of vitamin C. The high temperature denatures the enzyme ascorbic acid oxidase. Cook quickly for the minimum time to retain nutritive value, texture and colour. Never add bicarbonate of soda to the cooking liquid. The rate of oxidation is increased by alkali and this destroys the vitamin C content.

Milk, Cheese and Yoghurt (p 256)

Q1. Any from: milk, cheese, yoghurt, butter, crème fraiche, fromage frais, cream. **Q2.** Any four from: a good source of HBV protein for growth and repair of cells; a good source of calcium for the formation of strong bones and teeth; whole milk is a good source of essential fatty acids; all fresh milk is classed as 'low fat' so can be useful in a low-fat diet; it is easily digested which is good for babies, toddlers and people who are unwell. **Q3.** Moulds are introduced into firm cheese to form the 'blue' in cheeses such as Stilton or Roquefort. The 'blue' adds flavour to the cheese. **Q4.** As cheese is heated the proteins denature causing the cheese to soften and melt releasing the fat. If cheese is over-heated the proteins harden and go tough. **Q5.** Pasteurising – fresh milk is heated to 75c and rapidly cooled to below 5c. Homogenising – pasteurised milk is forced under pressure through a very fine mesh. This action breaks up the large fat (cream) globules into smaller particles so that the cream is evenly distributed throughout the milk. This gives a uniform consistency and 'creaminess.' Curds – an acid is added to fresh milk which creates solid or firm clumps which go on to form cheese. The solid clumps are the curds. Whey – is the liquid 'squeezed' or pressed from the curds creating a firmer more solid curd. **Q6.** Possible answer: different milks have different characteristics which need to be considered when choosing a milk to use when cooking. Skimmed milk will successfully make a béchamel sauce but it will lack the creaminess given by full fat milk. Jersey or Guernsey milk will add richness to a béchamel sauce, custard or rice pudding due to the richer cream content. Condensed milk needs to be used when making a milk-based caramel or fudge because it lacks liquid volume and has a concentrated, thick texture. Evaporated milk used in custard or milk puddings adds a sweeter, slightly caramel flavour which cannot be achieved by using 'ordinary' fresh milk. **Q7.** Milk, butter, cream, cheese and yoghurt are all products from intense dairy farming. Vegans do not eat these dairy products because they disagree with how the animals are reared, how females are 'forced' to give birth to calves, one after the other, in order to continually produce milk and how male calves are slaughtered soon after birth because there is no use for them. **Q8.** Any two from: soya, goat's, almond, and rice. **Q9.** a) to prevent it from spoiling, stop if from going off or from developing bacterial growth. b) to enable the consumer to know that the yoghurt is safe to eat. If eaten after this date the food may be unsafe and cause food poisoning. **Q10.** From top down: soya/almond/rice milk; whole milk; skimmed milk. **Q11.** Any two from: condensed milk, evaporated milk, dried milk, and UHT/long-life milk. **Q12.** Whole milk – used to be very popular because it was the only milk known about and people were less health conscious. More people are trying to lose weight now and are therefore switching to lower fat milk which helps reduce calorie intake. Semi-skimmed milk – it has a lower fat profile so considered to be healthier. Great push by the government to reduce intake of fat and/or Kcals. There is a vogue for "low fat" diets. Increase in the number of people trying to lose weight. People think by using semi-skimmed milk it is a healthy option. Greater advertising of this product. Skimmed milk – skimmed has fewer Kcals and fat so choose this as a healthy option. **Q13.** Points would include: milk can be used in many dishes such as soups, roux/béchamel sauces, batters, milk puddings, baked products such as cakes and tea, coffee and smoothies. Milk used will determine creaminess. Butter has a number of uses e.g. spreading on bread, toast and crackers, as a base for roux sauces and soups, cakes and in shortcrust, pate sucree, puff and flaky pastries. Butter gives a richer flavour and colour. Many uses for cheese include sauces, sandwich fillings, toppings on pasta, dips and spreads, baked products such as cheese pastry and bread, soufflés, cheesecakes and fondues. Many different cheeses available so choose according to flavour and texture (need to name at least one & its use). Yoghurt can be used in drinks, desserts (cheesecake), salad dressings and used as a cream alternative for toppings on desserts and curries. Different textures /set will determine use. Processed milks such as evaporated / condensed can be used in sweet tart fillings. Benefit is that these have a long shelf life. [For top marks the answer should include all four milk types stating benefits and give examples]. **Q14.** Answer could include: there are many different types of cream available and all vary in terms of their fat content. For a cream to be whipped successfully it needs to be transformed from a liquid into a foam by air bubbles being introduced into the cream. For cream to be whipped it must have a fat content of 38–42%. If the fat content is too low, there will not be enough fat to enclose the air bubbles and form a foam. Single cream is unsuitable for whipping and should be used for pouring or stirring into a dish. If the fat content is too high, the fat globules come into contact with each other too easily and instead butter granules are formed. Clotted cream is unsuitable for whipping and should only be spooned on to the top of desserts

Meat, Poultry, Fish and Eggs (p 306–307)

Meat

Q1. Myosin and actin are the muscle proteins in meat. The red colour of meat is due to a pigment called myoglobin. The red colour of meat changes to brown during cooking. This is called the Maillard reaction. Meat can be tenderised by marinading which allows the tougher collagen to be changed to gelatine. **Q2.** a) Any three from: kidney, tripe, heart, liver, brains, and sweetbread. b) Offal is rich in protein, iron, vitamin A and D. **Q3.** Reasons for popularity: they have been prepared and are ready to use or cook. There is less waste and they cook more quickly than joints on the bone. They are easier to carve or slice when cooked. Rolled joints can be stuffed and the joint stays intact during cooking. Lean implies that there is very little fat for people who are health conscious or following a low fat diet. Suggestions for family meals: boneless cuts can be served as a traditional roast dinner, for example a boned leg of lamb can be roasted with garlic and rosemary and served with boiled new potatoes, glazed carrots and green vegetables with a gravy. Boneless rolled joints such as hand of pork can be pot roasted on a bed of root vegetables and served with braised red cabbage and roast potatoes. Lean minced beef can be made into spicy meatballs with a rich tomato sauce and served with boiled noodles. **Q4.** Storage advice: meat and poultry are high risk foods and should be stored a below 5°C; raw meat should be stored away from cooked meat; bottom of the refrigerator, covered; remove any plastic packaging and/or giblets; pre-packed offal should remain in its packaging; check date; use offal on the day of purchase. Preparation advice: use of different coloured or colour-coded chopping boards and knives; thorough washing of hands before and after handling; thorough defrosting of meat and poultry in particular before cooking. **Q5.** Marinades are used to tenderise meat before cooking. The tougher collage is changed to gelatine, which allows the meat to hold more liquid and become more tender during cooking. The ingredients used are an acid such as lemon juice, tomatoes, wine or vinegar and aromatic herbs and spices. The acids helps to break down the connective tissue and the herbs and spice give additional flavour. **Q6.** a) i) thorough washing of hands before and after handling; use of different coloured or colour coded chopping boards and knives; do not wash the chicken, the splashing can cause cross contamination. ii) poultry is a high risk food and should be stored a below 5°C; raw poultry should be stored away from cooked poultry; store at the bottom of the refrigerator, covered; remove any plastic packaging and / or giblets; check date on pre-packed poultry. iii) thorough cooking; temperature check with food probe ⌧ core temperature of 75°C; juices should run clear when pierced with a skewer between thigh and drumstick. b) cross contamination as bacteria spreads from raw chicken to other foods; possible bacteria in chicken include salmonella, listeria and campylobacter. All these bacteria can cause food poisoning. **Q7.** a) factors which influence choice: dry methods of cooking are suitable for the more expensive, tender cuts of meat. These cuts are obtained from the rear end of the animal carcass that has less connective tissue and muscle than the front end. Examples of methods of cooking include grilling and roasting. Moist methods of cooking are more suitable for the cheaper, tougher cuts of meat. These cuts are obtained from the front end of the carcass of meat which has more connective tissue and muscle. Examples of methods of cooking are stewing, braising and casseroling. Cost would influence choice. Some methods do not need a lot of attention, for example, casseroling in a slow cooker needs no attention. b) suitable cuts which can be cooked by each method include: grilling – steaks, chops (lamb and pork); roasting – shoulder of lamb, leg of lamb, sirloin of beef, topside of beef, leg of pork, loin of pork; braising – neck of lamb, brisket of beef, belly pork; stewing – neck of lamb, chuck steak, flank of beef; casseroling – shank of lamb, ribs of beef, shoulder of pork. **Q8.** Factors and consumer issues influencing consumption of meat: family likes and dislikes, religious beliefs and lifestyle. For example some people choose not to eat meat or eat very little meat because of health issues, cost and environmental concerns. Saturated fat and cholesterol content of red meat has had publicity and people are advised by health experts not to consume too much red meat. Meat is an expensive item in the household budget and many people are choosing cheaper options of protein food. Environmental issues include the cost of rearing animals for meat, land resources and the fact that it is cheaper and more sustainable to raise crops than it is to rear animals for slaughter. Health scares and other issues such as BSE, Mad cow disease and cancer scares linked with eating red meat and processed meat. Poultry has had recent bad press with claims that supermarket bought poultry has a high bacterial content.

Fish

Q9. Two examples of white fish are cod and whiting. Salmon is a type of oily fish and is a very good source of omega-3. An excellent source of calcium is canned fish. Fish has a high nutritional value as it contains all the essential nutrients except carbohydrate. **Q10.** mackerel – barbequing; haddock – baking / steaming; whole salmon – baking / steaming; goujons of cod – fried in breadcrumbs. **Q11.** a) bright and shiny appearance; bright scales; pleasant sea smell; plenty of scales; firm to touch; clear, shiny eyes. b) Oily fish has protein, fat (more than 5%) in the flesh, vitamins A and D, omega-3 fatty acids, iodine, B vitamins and vitamin E. Examples are salmon, tune, herring, mackerel, sardines. White fish has protein, vitamins A and D, iodine. Examples are cod, haddock, whiting, halibut, coley. **Q12.** a) smoked haddock and smoked mackerel; canned tuna and canned sardines. b) frozen fish is popular because it has been prepared and is ready to use. It is fresh because it has been caught at sea, gutted, prepared and usually frozen at its best before it is brought to shore. It is widely available and reasonably priced. It reduces the smell associated with fresh fish when prepared in the kitchen at home. It is also available whole, cut into fillets, cutlets, steaks or goujons and coated with batter or breadcrumbs. Available with a sauce in boil in the bag and microwavable options. **Q13.** Answer could include: fish stocks are reducing because of over-fishing; many fish are injured or die because of pollution in the seas and rivers. Fish also caught in illegal nets and are killed; many dead fish are thrown back into the seas because they cannot be sold commercially. Sustainable fish means that our fish supplies will last longer. Some of the world's poorest population rely on fish as their main source of protein food. Fish farms have boomed in recent years which provide sustainable sources of fish. **Q14.** a) possible reasons: people do not like cleaning and cooking fish; it cannot be prepared in advance and; needs attention when cooking; cooking smell. b) benefits of eating fish: high Biological Value protein; low in fat; low in calories; oily fish high in Omega-3; contains valuable B vitamins and iodine; can be cooked in a variety of ways; very digestible. c) smoked fish suitable for making into patés; barbequing fish and serving with a spicy sauce; fish goujons served with a named dip; baked fish with a herb crust; shellfish added to risotto; fish pies using a variety of white, oily and shellfish; fishcakes made with fresh or canned fish.

Eggs

Q15. Eggs are a HBV food and contain essential amino acids. Eggs which have a Lion Mark stamp have been injected against salmonella and have been produced to a high standard. The egg yolk contains lecithin which acts as an emulsifier in the making of mayonnaise. When eggs are cooked, the white sets first. This setting is called coagulation. If eggs are overcooked syneresis occurs and this makes the egg tough. **Q16.** Egg yolk – fat, vitamin A, vitamin D, protein, iron. Egg white – vitamin, protein, calcium, water. **Q17.** Fish cakes – coating where the eggs coagulate on heating, sealing the food to form a crisp coating and preventing the food from overcooking. Whisked sponge – raising agent where the whole eggs are whisked with sugar to aerate. When eggs are whisked the ovalbumin in the egg white stretch and trap air. This makes the mixture light and foamy. Quiche – egg proteins coagulate on heating to set the mixture. Eggs enrich and add nutritional value to the quiche. **Q18.** a) the Quality mark means that the eggs have been produced to a high standard of quality and the hens have been inoculated against salmonella. b) gives the consumer an informed choice on: provenance (barn, free range, organic, battery); size of egg which is useful information when following recipes; quality of eggs; date stamp to determine freshness; country of origin; farm ID for traceability. All this information ensures that eggs are suitable for purpose, at their best to prevent any food poisoning and the information is useful for traceability. **Q19.** Emulsification – mayonnaise, salad dressing. Coagulation – egg custard, Quiche. Egg white foam – meringue, pavlova. Emulsification is the ability of the lecithin in the egg yolk to stabilise an oil and water mixture and stop them from separating. Coagulation is the ability of whole egg to become solid or set when heated. Egg white foam is the ability of egg whites to stretch when whisked due to the ability of the albumen to stretch and trap air. **Q20.** Advice on safe handling of eggs: raw eggs carry salmonella bacteria; high risk food, potential food poisoning; possible cross contamination during food preparation; example of cross contamination – cracking raw egg, not washing hands afterwards; Lion mark stamp denotes hens have been injected against salmonella; using before best before date recommended; store at below 20°C away from strong smelling foods. **Q21.** Factors influencing choice of eggs when buying: type of egg required – provenance: free range, barn, organic, battery; size and quantity of egg required; pasteurised for commercial use. Amount of sodium: no more than 6g daily. Why egg has no fibre – fibre present in plant sources only; eggs are foods sourced from animals. **Q22.** a) storage – air space between the shell and membrane gets bigger as it absorbs air. Water from the egg white moves into the yolk. The yolk becomes more watery and less thick. With increased storage, the skin surrounding the yolk becomes weaker and some yolk enters the white. Bacteria enters the egg through the shell and a bad smell develops caused by the reaction between the sulphur in the white and phosphoric acid in the yolk. b) whisking – increased volume during whisking – as much as eight times the original. The egg white traps air; ovalbumin in the white has the ability to stretch and create a foam (a dispersion of gas within a liquid). c) cooking – egg proteins coagulate on heating. The yolk starts to coagulate at around 60°C and the white at around 70°C. Boiling for longer than 10 minutes gives a black ring between the yolk and white. This is caused by a reaction between the sulphur in the white and the iron in the yolk. Egg dishes for: lunch for a toddler • scrambled egg on toast; midday meal elderly person • a Spanish omelette; packed lunch teenager • Scotch egg.

Q23.
- Salmonella outbreak
- Scares such as bird 'flu
- Reports and bad press on the welfare of egg producing hens
- Benefits of eating eggs which contain 'good' cholesterol
- Happy hens image as a promotion campaign
- Versatility of eggs in food preparation and cooking

Q24. Explain the following: a) Black ring between egg white and yolk of boiled egg – boiling for longer than 10 minutes gives a black ring between the yolk and white. This is caused by a reaction between the sulphur in the white and the iron in the yolk. b) Egg custard which is weepy – cooking at too high a temperature causes the proteins to over coagulate and separate from the liquid. c) Meringue which is runny – the bowl for whisking may have had traces of fat or egg yolk or the egg white were too stale. These would prevent a stable foam from forming. White could have been over whisked, over stretching the albumin with loss of stability. Foam left to stand too long before use. d) Egg custard sauce curds and whey texture – cooking the sauce too rapidly or for too long. Egg proteins become over stretched and the proteins separate from the liquid.

Beans, Nuts and Seeds, Soya, Tofu and Mycoprotein (p 330)

Q1. a) Low biological value (LBV) is a term applied to proteins that do not contain all of the essential amino acids that the body must get from the foods we eat. Vegetable sources of protein such as beans, rice and lentil are classed as LBV protein. b) Soya products such as tofu and textured vegetable protein are sources of HBV protein which is suitable for a vegan diet. They can also have protein from quinoa which is also a source of essential amino acids. Protein complementation can also be used e.g. beans on toast or dhal and rice, this ensures that the essential amino acids absent in one food source are present in the other. **Q2.** a) High biological value (HBV) protein foods contain all the essential amino acids needed by the body. The body can make some amino acids, but essential amino acids are the ones the body must get from the foods we eat. Different foods contain different amounts of amino acids, and animal products (such as chicken, pork, beef, fish, etc.) contain all the essential amino acids. b) Any from: soya, tofu, textured vegetable protein, quinoa, and amaranth. **Q3.** a) pulses are a cheap, low-fat source of protein, fibre, vitamins and minerals and they count towards the recommended five daily portions of fruit and vegetables. Pulses contain more protein than any other vegetable, and are therefore particularly important for people who do not get their protein from meat, fish or dairy products. Pulses are a starchy food and add fibre to a meal. The fibre found in pulses may help lower blood cholesterol, so they are good for your heart. Pulses are also a good source of iron. b) Beans can only count as one of your 5 a day because even though pulses contain fibre, they don't give the same mixture of vitamins, minerals and other nutrients as fruit and vegetables. **Q4.** Step 1 – soak the dried beans in water for at least 12 hours. Step 2 – drain and rinse the beans, then cover them with fresh water. Step 3 – boil them vigorously for at least 10 minutes, then simmer the beans for around 45–60 minutes to make them tender. **Q5.** Any from: to produce oil, in salads, in cakes and baking or in breakfast cereals. **Q6.** a) protein, fat (monounsaturated), Vitamin E, fibre. b) they are an expensive commodity so we eat them in such small amounts. They can also be high in fat if we eat too many of them so this is another reason their intake is restricted. **Q7.** a) any from: nuts, peanuts, shellfish, celery, cereals containing gluten, eggs, fish, and sesame seeds. b) check all food packaging to see if the product contains potential allergens or has been produced in a factory containing them. Avoid eating products in restaurants where they are not sure of the ingredients in the dishes and whether there has been any cross contamination from another source. **Q8.** Left to right: tofu, Quorn, textured vegetable protein. **Q9.** Reasons could include: alternative protein foods were developed to meet the need for a cheaper alternative to meat. They provide an excellent source of protein to vegetarians and vegans and are now popular with a wide market. Meat alternatives are a healthier option, as they are lower in fat and saturated fat, whilst still providing a range of the nutrients found in meat. They are also a source of fibre. A wide range of meat alternatives gives consumers more choice and allows a range of meals to be produced. Some people believe that choosing meat alternatives is better for the environment as there is no need for crops to be used to feed animals and there is a low carbon footprint. **Q10.** a) nutritional value: meat and alternative protein foods are both sources of high biological value protein, which ensures that whichever product is chosen, the consumer will be eating all of the essential amino acids. Meat has a higher fat content than alternative proteins and alternative protein also provides fibre which meat does not. Alternative proteins are also lower in sodium. b) value for money: now less to choose in price between them. Meat remains more expensive per 100g to buy than vegetable protein due to the following reasons: animals need to be fed, protected against diseases and provided with shelter during their rearing. It also takes a lot of space to rear animals for meat production. If the same amount of space was given to producing crops for vegetable sources of protein, they would be produced more quickly, needing less production costs and therefore be less expensive to buy. However cuts of meat cost different prices, so choosing a stewing steak or offal would be less expensive than a fillet steak. This reduces the price gap between meat and alternative protein further.

Butter, Oil, Margarine, Sugar and Syrup (p 360)

Q1. Functions of fat: concentrated source of energy- 1g fat yields 9kcals; acts as an insulating layer under the skin; helps protect body organs such as kidneys and heart; helps the absorption of fat soluble vitamin A, d, E and K; contain essential fatty acids, omega-3 and 6 which are important for the maintaining the functioning of body cells. **Q2.** a) a fat is solid at room temperature; an oil is solid at room temperature. b) Factors which influence consumer choice: type of fat which is mainly dependant on cost, health issues, family like / dislike and use; some fats e.g. butter, walnut oil, sesame oil are more expensive than others; many fats are low in cholesterol, have plant sterols, are low in saturates which have health benefits; spreads are chosen for their plasticity, able to spread straight from the refrigerator, shortness. Some have advantages for use in particular culinary techniques; flavour of fats and oils for culinary purposes such as butter for spreading on toast, olive oil for stir frying, sesame oil for salad dressings; trans fats have been given bad press and many people avoid these. **Q3.** a) plant sources – olive, sunflower, walnut, sesame, linseed, corn, chilli, rapeseed, almond, soya. Animal source – butter, ghee, lard, suet. b) rubbing in – butter, lard, block margarine have good shortening properties, flavour and are firm in consistency. Creaming mixture – soft margarines have the plasticity enabling them to trap air. Deep fat frying – a soya bean or sunflower oil which has a high smoke point. Stir frying – olive oil, rapeseed oil which have good flavour. **Q4.** Fats and oils have different melting points which are determined by the fatty acid content of the fat or oil. A fat or oil has its specific smoke temperature which is the temperature at which a blue smoke is given off. This varies between different fats and oils. At this temperature the fat molecules start to split up giving the food being cooked an unpleasant flavour. The next stage is the flash point where the fat ignites and the food burns. **Q5.** Crème caramel: the sugar adds colour. When heated the sugar turns brown at a temperature of 154°C. This is called caramelisation. Swiss roll: when sugar and eggs are whisked together as in the making of a Swiss Roll, the sugar aids aeration. Aeration makers a mixture light and foamy. Meringue; sugar helps to make a foam which enables the egg whites to trap air. The sugar acts as a stabiliser which strengthens the mixture. Jam making: sugar gives the jam a longer shelf life because the sugar solution acts as a preservative. Organisms that spoil food cannot grow in a sugar solution. **Q6.** Sugars include caster, used mainly for cooking; Icing sugar, used for icings and cake toppings; cube sugar for sweetening drinks; demerara sugar is served with coffee and used to make flapjacks; honey has its own distinct flavour and is a popular alternative to syrup and treacle as well as being used as a sweetener; soft brown, dark brown and muscovado are all used mainly in making cakes and biscuits where a rich flavour and deep colour is required; treacle is an ingredient used in making Parkin or a recipe where the distinct flavour is required to disguise other bitter flavours; golden syrup is used in cake and biscuit recipes; maple syrup is served as a dessert topping for pancakes and ice cream. Artificial sweeteners are used instead of sugar and other sweeteners because they have no calorific value and can be used as sugar substitutes in diets, food preparation and cooking. There are numerous artificial sweeteners each with different properties and uses. Examples include Sorbitol, Splenda and Sucralose. **Q7.** Sugar belongs to the group of nutrients known as carbohydrates which release energy in the body. Sugar has sweetening properties and is released quickly to provide energy. It supplies the body with calories but has very little other nutritional benefit. Natural sugars are found in fruit and vegetables. These are known as intrinsic sugars. Sugars which are added by the consumer either to food or in cooking or by the manufacturer may have a negative effect on health. These are known as free sugars. Consumption of sugar is claimed to be too high in the UK. Many children are overweight as a result of a diet too high in sugary foods. Tooth decay is also a problem amongst children. It is claimed that sugar consumption has risen in recent years because of 'hidden sugars' in manufactured foods. Sugar content has to be stated on nutrition labels and consumers need to read this information in order to make informed choices when planning healthy, balanced diets.

INDEX

additives 138, 152–154, 327, 354
adipose tissue 13, 25
advertising 144–145
aeration 79–80, 255, 299, 301, 345, 347, 358, 361
allergies 61, 142, 146, 305
ambient foods 85, 89, 94
amino acids 19–21, 26, 29, 63, 206, 234, 243, 270, 275, 297, 322, 328–329, 352, 358
antioxidants 27, 32, 37–38, 126, 153, 219, 226, 270–271, 340, 347, 351
anaemia 21, 30–31, 34, 37, 48, 58, 142, 181
animal welfare 262–263
apples, stuffed baked, making 238
arrowroot 206, 209
arteries 23, 25, 59, 142, 181, 342–343
artificial sweeteners 348, 352–353
assurance schemes 128, 138, 295
automation 128–129
avocado 9, 24, 30, 113–114, 117, 119, 215–216, 340, 343, 346

bacillus cereus 88, 207
bacon 24, 27, 35, 41, 47, 68–70, 84, 107–110, 113, 127, 153, 211, 231, 264, 273, 278
bacteria reproduction 87–88
batter 77, 79, 107, 115, 117, 164, 184, 246, 289–290, 301
    making 164
baking/baked 69–70, 72, 74, 77–81, 93, 107–108, 110–111, 113–114, 117, 167, 180, 184–188, 191, 224–226, 228, 232, 235, 237–238, 240, 260, 289–290, 299–300, 302–303, 309, 311–313, 315, 338, 340–341, 344–345, 351–354, 358, 361
baked beans 318–319, 357
balanced diet 26, 28, 32, 44–45, 48, 53–54, 56, 59–60, 126, 147, 181, 342–343
barbequed food 69, 226, 277
barcodes 122–123
barley 12, 17, 58, 61, 79, 108, 110–112, 118, 142, 176, 181, 203–204, 206, 348, 354, 359
    nutritional value of 204
    using 204
Basic Metabolic Rate (BMR) 51
bean burgers, cheesy, making 332
beans 10–12, 17, 18, 21, 29–30, 33–35, 37, 45–46, 58, 61, 63, 68, 71, 76, 110–111, 113–119, 125–126, 141–142, 146, 215–217, 221, 234–235, 246, 318–320, 327–328, 331–333, 338, 341, 343, 346, 357
    soya 11–12, 30, 61, 76, 116–117, 125–126, 146, 234, 246, 327–328, 338, 341, 343, 346
beef 24, 29, 34–35, 41, 64–66, 69, 76, 90, 98, 107–118, 126, 136–137, 230–231, 263–265, 267, 269–275, 278, 308, 311, 331, 337
beri beri 29, 31, 199
beta-glucan 16, 203
biotechnology 124–125, 128
biotin 10, 30, 297
biscuits 9, 13, 23, 41, 47, 58, 70, 78–80, 109–110, 135, 142, 151, 164, 174, 177, 181–184, 203, 299, 338, 345, 347, 352, 354, 357, 361
    making 164
blanching/blanched 71, 235, 321, 333
boiling/boiled 68–71, 75, 81, 110, 113–114, 116, 163, 166, 182, 194, 211, 224–226, 228, 235, 237, 239–240, 266, 269, 277, 290, 297, 299, 301, 303–304, 309, 312–313, 316, 319–320, 331, 333, 350, 359
bread 9–11, 15–17, 21, 29, 33–34, 37, 41, 45, 47, 53–54, 57–58, 62–63, 70, 72, 74, 76, 78–80, 90, 107–119, 142, 152, 159, 164, 177, 181–192, 205–206, 209, 217, 228, 231, 233, 278, 301, 311, 316, 324–325, 337–338, 345, 347, 351, 354, 357–358, 361
    fibre content 17
    ingredients used 185–187
    making 78, 168–169, 185–189, 191
    nutritional value of 185
    white 15–16
    whole grain 10–11

blood pressure 32, 34–35, 47–48, 59, 61, 203, 219, 322–323, 343
blood sugar (blood glucose) 13–17, 32, 59, 142, 320, 340, 355
braising 69, 71, 224–226, 268–269, 277, 279
breadcrumbs 107–108, 110–111, 117, 170–171, 212, 289, 291, 310–313, 316, 331–332
broccoli 10–11, 29–31, 33–34, 46, 62, 117, 215, 220, 250
brown rice 11, 15–16, 29, 34, 58, 142, 197–198
Buddhist diet 64, 66, 137
butter, making 337
cakes 9, 13, 23, 41, 47, 58–59, 68, 70, 74, 77–81, 90, 107, 111, 113, 142, 151, 158–159, 177, 181–184, 203, 230, 232–233, 250, 253, 255, 299–302, 308, 324, 337, 345, 347, 350, 352–355, 357–358, 361
    making 158–159
calcium 11, 13, 16–17, 28, 33–34, 36, 40, 45, 52–57, 60–61, 63, 143, 179–182, 185, 218, 234, 243, 247, 251, 254, 290, 293, 297, 323–324, 327–328
    deficiency 143
calories 13, , 38, 47, 51, 57, 60, 216, 219, 293, 298, 342, 348, 351–355; also see kcal
campylobacter 86–87, 89, 280
cancer 13, 16, 24, 32, 38, 48, 56, 103, 135, 181, 216, 348
caramelisation 73–74, 225, 238, 358
carbohydrates 8–9, 12–16, 22, 29, 45, 49, 51–52, 54, 59, 73, 118, 142, 147, 176, 181–182, 185–186, 192, 199, 201, 203–205, 210–212, 218, 220, 238–240, 243, 258–260, 296–297, 310–316, 319–320, 323, 332–334, 353–356; also see starch
    complex 12, 16
    effect of cooking on 73–74
    fast release 14
    slow release 14
carbon footprint 96, 98, 140, 326
cardiovascular disease (CVD) 32, 58–60, 355
cellulose 12, 16, 218, 235
cereals 8–10, 17–18, 21, 24, 27–30, 33–37, 41, 45, 47, 49, 54, 56–58, 61–63, 76, 106, 108, 110, 126–127, 135, 142, 146, 164, 175–212, 217, 253, 324, 326, 351–352, 354, 357
    definition of 176
    fibre content 17
    nutritional value of 176
    storing 195
    whole grain 10, 17, 29–30, 33–37, 56, 176, 195, 357
cheese 10, 18, 24, 27, 30, 36, 41, 45, 47, 54, 57–59, 61–64, 69, 75–76, 86, 88, 91–94, 97, 107–115, 143, 146, 163, 211, 230–231, 233, 242, 246–250, 257, 260, 313, 315, 332, 344
    effect of heat on 250
    making 248–249
    nutritional value of 247
    storage of 250
    uses of 250
cheese soufflé, making 315
cheesy bean burgers, making 332
chicken see poultry
chicken kiev, making 310
chick peas 18, 63, 112, 115, 118–119, 234, 318–320, 331
chocolate orange mousse, making 258
cholesterol 16, 23–25, 52, 59, 125–126, 142, 176, 203–204, 206, 254, 265, 267, 293, 297, 319, 322–323, 329, 337, 341–344
Chorleywood bread making process 187
choux, making 166–167
Christian diet 64, 66, 137
climate 106, 121, 123, 134–135
climate change 121, 123, 135
coagulation 72, 75, 184, 188, 240, 247, 249, 253, 279, 300–303, 309–311, 316, 328, 359
cobalamin 10, 30, 40
cod bake with a herb crust, making 312
coeliac disease 33, 58, 142, 181, 204
conduction 69, 72, 310–311, 313–316
convection 69, 72, 311, 313, 315
convenience foods 23, 99, 131, 152, 192

cooking mistakes 81
corn see maize
coronary heart disease (CHD) 16, 23, 25, 48, 52, 56, 59, 103, 142, 203, 254, 323, 342
cream
    nutritional value of 254
    storage of 255
    uses of 255
creaming 77–78, 159, 164, 301, 345, 347, 361
critical control point 89–90
cross-contamination 88–90, 280
culture 106–119, 137
custard, making 259

decalcification 56
deep frying 69–70, 110, 115, 117, 119, 289–290
deficiency 8, 21, 25, 27–38, 48, 55–56, 58, 60–61, 66, 127, 142–143, 181, 199, 201, 293
defrosting 69, 85, 89, 91, 184, 209, 250, 281–282
dehydration 29, 32, 38, 47, 56, 278
denature 72, 75, 79, 250, 279
diabetes 13, 15–16, 22, 24, 32, 48, 55–56, 58–60, 103, 135, 142, 176, 355
diet, definition of 44
dietary guidelines 44–51
Dietary Reference Values (DRVs) 49–50
digestion 12
disaccharides 12, 49, 354
dried fruit 10, 29–30, 33–34, 56, 58, 60, 62–63, 107–108, 112, 118–119, 142, 158, 185, 195, 212, 215, 217, 221, 226, 232–233, 235, 238, 353
dry frying 69, 271
dry heat methods of cooking 70
durum wheat 182, 192

E coli 86–87, 280
Eatwell Guide 44–45, 47, 50, 54, 63, 131, 217
egg freshness, testing 304
egg white 30, 72, 77, 79, 258, 297, 299–303, 308–309, 315, 328, 358–359, 361
egg yolk 27, 30, 79–80, 258, 296–303, 305, 309, 315
eggs 9–10, 18, 24, 26–30, 37, 41, 45, 47, 53–54, 56–58, 60–66, 68–69, 71–72, 74–75, 77, 79–80, 86–87, 93, 97, 100, 107–108, 110, 112–113, 116–117, 119, 127, 138, 142, 146, 158–159, 161, 164, 166, 185, 193–194, 207, 210, 212, 217, 231–233, 240, 258–259, 266, 285, 289–291, 293–305, 308–311, 313, 315–316, 324, 328–329, 331–332, 358–359, 361
    effects of cooking on 302–303
    farming 294–295
    functions of 301
    nutritional value of 296–298, 300, 305
    preparation of 302
    printing 295
    quality 296
    separating 300
    sizes 295
    storing 302, 304–305
    structure of 296–297
    uses of 299–301
empty calories 13, 354–355
emulsion 79, 162–163, 243, 338, 345
energy 9–15, 18, 21–22, 25–26, 29–30, 33–35, 38, 40, 45, 47–49, 51–57, 59–60, 63, 66, 69, 72, 98, 102, 121, 136, 140, 147, 181, 187, 201, 210–212, 238–240, 258–260, 270–272, 290, 296, 310–316, 323, 332–334, 342, 348, 352, 354–355
environment 102, 120, 123–124, 138, 140, 283
enzymic browning 75, 359
essential amino acids 63, 206, 234, 297, 328–329
Estimate Average Requirement (EAR) 51
exercise 47–48, 59–60
enzymes, effect on food 76

factory farming see intensive farming
Fairtrade 96, 102, 128, 139

443

Farm Assured 128, 138
fat 8–9, 12–13, 22–30, 32, 36, 38, 41, 45, 47, 49–52, 54–55, 59–60, 63–64, 69–72, 75–77, 79–81, 102, 108, 112–113, 125, 129, 131, 136, 138, 142, 144–145, 147, 152, 158–161, 163–164, 166, 170–171, 173, 176, 185, 187, 190, 195, 199, 203, 206, 210–212, 217–219, 228, 238–240, 242–245, 247–248, 250–251, 254–255, 258–260, 263–267, 269–275, 277–279, 285, 289–290, 292–293, 297–300, 308, 310–316, 319, 322, 327–329, 332–334, 336–347, 351, 354, 357–358, 361
   content of foods, average 42
   effect of cooking on 73
   effect of heat on 346
   functions of 346–347
   monounsaturated 22, 24, 216, 264, 270, 297, 322, 339–343
   nutritional value of 342
   polyunsaturated 22, 24, 27, 41, 142, 270, 297, 315, 327, 339–344, 347
   properties of 345
   recommended daily intake 25
   saturated 22–23, 25, 47, 55, 59, 142, 152, 254, 270, 297, 308, 322, 329, 337, 339–344, 346
   unsaturated 22, 24, 27, 41, 45, 59, 142, 216, 264, 270, 293, 297, 315, 322, 327, 339–344, 346–347
fat soluble vitamins 26–28, 32, 54, 271, 293, 342
fermentation 37, 61, 76, 78, 111, 116–117, 143, 186–190, 249, 252–253, 257, 278, 327, 329, 358
fibre (dietary) 16–17, 38, 45, 47, 49, 52, 56–57, 59, 126, 127, 142, 145, 152, 176, 178, 180–182, 185, 192, 198–199, 203–206, 217–219, 221, 243, 247, 297, 319, 323, 327, 329
   insoluble 16–17, 203–204
   recommended daily intake 17
   soluble 16–17, 203–204
fish 9–11, 18, 20, 24, 26–28, 30, 33–37, 45, 47, 53–54, 56–66, 68–71, 75–76, 85–86, 91–93, 97, 102, 107–118, 135, 137, 140, 142–143, 146, 164, 217, 228–232, 234–235, 281, 283–293, 297, 301, 312–313, 319, 327, 336, 341, 351
   buying/selecting 286–287
   composition of 292
   cooking 289–290
   oily 9–10, 24, 26–28, 47, 53–54, 57, 59–60, 63, 234, 285, 287, 290, 292–293, 297
   filleting 288
   nutritional value of 292–293
   preparing 286, 288
   preserving 291
   processing 291
   removing bones 288
   shellfish 11, 34, 37, 61, 65–66, 86, 110, 113–117, 137, 284–285, 287, 289, 291
   skinning 288
   smoked 91, 110, 112, 118, 230, 291
   storing 286
   types of 284–285
   white 285, 290, 292–293, 312
fish cakes 136, 228, 301, 344
fish fingers 291
fish pie 228, 313
fish pie, making 313
fish stocks 283
five-a-day 44, 46, 59, 130, 216–217, 226
flour 11, 33–34, 58, 62–63, 74, 77–80, 107, 109–111, 116, 158–164, 166, 168, 170–171, 173, 177–192, 194, 199, 201, 204–206, 209–210, 212, 228, 240, 289–290, 301, 310–311, 313, 315–316, 327, 332, 345, 351, 358, 361; also see wheat
   protein content of 181
fluoride 11, 36–37
foam 79, 190, 258, 300, 302–303, 308–309, 347, 358–359, 361
folic acid 10, 30–31, 40, 56, 57, 127
food banks 103, 135
food chain 96, 125, 138, 280
food contamination, sources of 86, 96, 207
food cost 103–104, 135–136
food cultures/cuisines 106–119
food, effects of
   cooking/heat on 73, 228, 250, 302–303, 346
   enzymes on 76
   oxygen on 75

food labelling 52, 145–147, 222, 339, 356
food miles 98–99, 122, 128, 140
food origins 97
food packaging 92–94, 100–101, 128–131, 140, 222, 280
food, pH of 75, 87–88, 90–91, 220, 237, 303, 329
food poisoning 57, 86, 207, 280, 282, 305
food poverty 103–104, 135
food preparation/cooking
   methods of cooking 69–72
   reasons for cooking 68
   vitamin loss 32
food preservation 90–91, 120, 122, 128, 234–235, 291, 358
food provenance 96–99, 128
food safety 84–94
food security 104
food spoilage 84–94
food storage 85, 128, 194–195, 220, 222, 228, 246, 250, 255, 280–281, 286, 302, 304–305, 320
food technology 120–131
food trade 128
food waste 90–91, 99, 102–103, 140
fortified food/drink 10–11, 25, 27–30, 34, 54, 56, 58, 62–63, 126–127, 143, 179–181, 186, 195, 246
   breakfast cereal 10, 28–30, 34, 54, 56, 58, 62–63, 195
   flour 30, 34, 179–181, 186
free radicals 32, 323
free range 97, 138, 265–266, 294–295, 329
free sugars 14–15, 49–50, 217, 355
fructose 12, 14, 50, 220, 223, 350–351, 354
fruit
   contents of 218–219
   cooking 225–226
   five-a-day portion 46, 216–217, 226
   preparation of 223
   preservation 234–235
   processing 221–222
   storing 220
   types of 214–216
   using 217, 219, 226
fruit juice 38, 45, 49–50, 135, 153, 216–217, 355, 357
frying/fried 68–70, 81, 108–111, 113, 115–119, 126, 129, 164, 172, 224–226, 228, 233, 237, 240, 267–269, 271–272, 289–290, 297–299, 301, 310–311, 316, 331–334, 337–338, 340–341, 344–345, 361
functional foods 126–127

galactose 12, 354
gammon 107, 264, 273
gelatine 137, 174, 269, 275, 279, 292
gelatinisation 73–74, 80, 173–174, 184, 188, 211, 228, 313, 315
genetically modified 124–125, 139
ghee 337
glucose 12–15, 50, 59, 61, 220, 223, 329, 340, 350–351, 353–355; also see blood sugar
gluten 58, 61, 72, 78–79, 81, 142, 146, 160, 181, 184, 186–189, 203–206, 209–210, 315–316, 345, 357–359
Glycaemic Index (GI) 15, 70, 351, 353, 355
goat 64, 66, 109, 112–115, 118–119, 242, 246–247, 250, 265, 269
goitre 36–37
government guidelines for healthy eating 47
grilling/grilled 68–70, 81, 109, 111–112, 116, 118–119, 162, 224–225, 268–269, 271–272, 277–279, 289–290, 292, 311, 344

haemoglobin 30, 34, 270, 274, 323
ham 35, 41, 76, 107–109, 111, 153, 232, 264, 273, 278, 251
healthy diet see balanced diet
herbs 229–231
high biological value (HBV) protein 18–20, 328
high-density lipoproteins (HDL) 23–25, 343
Hindu diet 64, 66, 137
homogenisation 79, 244–245, 252
honey 12, 14, 49, 62, 110, 112, 119, 195, 238, 334, 348, 350–351, 354, 357–358
   uses of 351
horsemeat 265
humectant 358

hydration 38, 45, 47
hydrogenation 23, 338, 344
hydroponics 124
hypercalcaemia 28
hypocalcaemia 61

immigration 121–122
immune system 10–11, 27, 37, 47–48, 58–59, 61–63, 76, 216, 270
indispensable amino acids see essential amino acids
insect protein 126
insoluble fibre 16–17, 203–204
insulin 12, 59, 142, 320
intensive farming 138, 265
invert sugar 350–351
iodine 11, 36–37, 234, 293, 297
irritable bowel syndrome (IBS) 17
iron 11, 13, 16–17, 21, 31, 33–34, 36, 40, 45, 53–58, 62–63, 126, 142, 179–182, 185, 199, 204, 217–219, 234, 243, 265, 267–268, 270–271, 297–298, 303, 319–320, 323–324, 327–328
iron deficiency anaemia 31, 34, 58, 142, 181
irradiation 91

Jewish diet 64, 66, 137

kidney beans 46, 68, 115, 118, 234, 318, 320, 331
   cooking safely 320
kilocalorie (kcal) 12, 22, 51, 293; also see calories
kilojoule (kj) 12, 22, 51
kwashiorkor 21, 34

labelling of food 52, 145–147, 222, 339, 356
lactation 57
lactose 12, 14, 33, 49–50, 58, 61, 125, 143, 243, 246, 249, 252, 354
lactose intolerant 58, 61, 125, 143, 246
lamb 41, 64–65, 69, 97–98, 107–110, 112, 114–115, 117–119, 136, 231, 264, 268–276, 278, 293, 308
lard 9, 23–24, 41, 113, 116, 137, 161, 337, 343
leavened bread 190
legumes see beans; pulses
lentils 18, 36, 58, 63, 114–116, 118–119, 215, 218, 234–235, 318–320
listeria 57, 207, 248, 208
liver (body) 13, 22, 25–29, 86, 142, 270–271
liver (food) 10, 26–30, 34, 54, 56–57, 107, 110, 136, 268–269, 271, 278, 282, 285, 293
low biological value (LBV) protein 18–20
low fat products 23, 27, 36, 41, 49–50, 52, 130, 217, 251, 338, 344, 357
low-density lipoproteins (LDL) 23, 25, 126, 342–343

macronutrients 8, 18, 22
magnesium 11, 35, 45, 55, 219, 270, 293, 323–324, 329
Maillard reaction 73, 275, 358
maize 29, 31, 58, 63, 114, 118, 139, 176, 181, 195, 200–201, 206, 243
   processing of 201
malnutrition 21, 34, 48, 135
maltose 12, 354
margarine 9–10, 23–24, 28, 54, 57, 73, 161, 321, 338, 340–341, 343–347, 361
marketing 144
measuring ingredients 80
meat 9–10, 18, 21, 23–24, 27, 29–30, 33–37, 41, 45, 47, 52, 54, 56–59, 62–66, 68, 70–76, 85–88, 90–94, 96, 102, 106–119, 123, 135–138, 140, 142, 150, 153, 163, 217, 226, 228–233, 235, 243, 262–282, 292–293, 297, 301, 308, 310–311, 316, 319–320, 326–327, 329, 341, 344, 351, 358
   buying 280
   choosing 272–273
   composition of 274
   cooking 275–277, 279, 282
   effect of cooking on 279
   freezing 281
   nutritional value of 270–271
   portion size 271
   preparation of 276, 281
   red 11, 29–30, 34, 37, 54, 56–57, 75, 270–271
   storage of 280–281
   white 75, 266

meat products 278
meatballs 108, 112, 118, 311
meatballs with peppers and tomatoes, making 311
media 122–123
megaloblastic anaemia 30
metabolism 10, 30, 37–38, 56, 128, 293, 323
micronutrients 8, 26, 33, 36, 48, 126
microorganisms 76, 84–85, 91, 101, 124, 126
microwave cooking 69, 72, 120, 130, 136, 145, 163, 226, 281, 290
migration 106, 121–122
milk 10, 12, 14, 18, 20, 24–28, 30, 33, 36, 38, 41–42, 45, 49–50, 53–54, 56–58, 60–64, 66, 72, 74–76, 79, 86 88, 91, 93, 107, 109–110, 112–117, 119, 125–126, 135, 143, 146–147, 163–164, 173, 182, 185, 199, 217, 232–233, 242–249, 251–255, 257, 259–260, 263, 269, 290, 299, 309, 313, 315, 327–328, 337, 342, 344, 353–355, 357
    nutritional value of 243
    processing of 243–245
    soya 20, 56, 63, 125, 143, 257, 315, 328
    storage of 246
    types of 244–246
    uses of 246
minerals 8, 11, 16, 33–36, 47, 50–51, 54–56, 60, 63, 71, 124, 126, 135, 138, 179, 181, 186, 195, 198–199, 205, 217, 219, 223, 225, 243, 246, 270–271, 274, 277, 279, 292–293, 297–298, 319, 329
    deficiencies 33–35
moist heat methods of cooking 71
monosaccharides 12, 49, 354
monounsaturated fat 22, 24, 216, 264, 270, 297, 322, 339–343
mousse, chocolate orange, making 258
mushroom risotto, making 211
Muslim diet 65–66, 137
mycoprotein 18, 63, 125, 328–329
    nutritional benefits of 329
myoglobin 75, 274–275

nanotechnology 125, 128
nervous system 10, 29–30, 35, 57, 63, 219
niacin 10, 29, 40, 179–180, 201, 204, 323
non starch polysaccharide (NSP) 16, 180–181
non-enzymic browning see Maillard reaction
Non-Milk Extrinsic Sugars (NMES) 14
nutrients 8–10, 13, , 17–18, 21–22, 26, 32–33, 36, 38, 40–41, 44–45, 47–57, 60, 62–63, 75–76, 84, 86, 88, 120, 122, 124–128, 131, 139, 142, 147, 176, 179–180, 186, 201, 216–217, 219, 224, 234, 243, 247, 251, 270, 272, 297–298, 301, 319–320, 322–323, 325, 328–329, 354, 356
    complementary 36
    reference intake per person per day 40
nutritional requirements 40, 49, 53–57
    adulthood 56
    babies 53
    children 54
    old age 56
    teenagers 55
nutritional supplements 32, 340
nutritional value 13, 20, 72, 124–127, 162–163, 176, 181, 185, 192, 195, 199, 201, 203–205, 218, 225–226, 237, 243–244, 246, 247, 251, 254, 270–271, 275, 283, 289, 292–293, 297–298, 300, 305, 308, 319, 322, 324–328, 331, 342, 254–355
    of barley 204
    of bread 185
    of cereal 176
    of cheese 247
    of cream 254
    changes in 226
    of eggs 296–298, 300, 305
    of fat 342
    of fish 292–293
    of meat 270–271
    of milk 243
    of nuts 322, 324
    of oats 203
    of oils 342
    of pasta 192
    of poultry 270–271
    of pulses 319
    of rice 199
    of rye 205
    of seeds 324
    of soya 327
    of sugar 354
    of textured vegetable protein (TVP) 327
    of tofu 328
    of wheat 181
    of yoghurt 251
nuts 9–11, 17–18, 24, 27, 29–30, 33–37, 53, 56, 58–59, 61–63, 70, 109, 112–113, 115–119, 126, 142–143, 146, 195, 215–216, 233–234, 238, 251, 258, 318, 321–323, 325, 340–341, 343
    allergy 58, 61, 142, 322
    nutritional value of 322, 324
    types of 321, 323
    uses of 321

oats 15–18, 29, 34, 41, 47, 108, 110–111, 176, 181, 195, 202–203, 246
    nutritional value of 203
    processing of 202–203
obesity 13, 22, 24–25, 32, 48–49, 54–55, 58–60, 102–103, 123, 135, 144, 203, 344, 355
offal 10, 34, 107–108, 110–111, 119, 136, 262, 268–269, 271, 280, 282
oils
    effect of heat on 346
    functions of 345
    nutritional value of 342
    properties of 346–347
    types of 340–341
oily fish 9–10, 24, 26–28, 47, 53–54, 57, 59–60, 63, 234, 285, 287, 290, 292–293, 297
omega-3 24, 47, 62–63, 234, 264–265, 283, 293, 297, 323–324, 340–343
olive oil 9, 27, 59, 79, 111–112, 118–119, 341–343, 346
organic food 58, 124, 130, 138, 180, 214, 263, 266, 294–295
osteomalacia 28, 33, 61
osteoporosis 33, 55, 60, 143, 181
overnutrition 48
oxalic acid 36, 218
oxidation 31, 153, 347
oxygen, effect on food 75

packaging of food 92–94, 100–101, 128–131, 140, 222, 280
packaging waste 94
paella, making 314
pantothenic acid 10, 297
pasta 9, 15, 45, 47, 52–54, 58, 79, 81, 86, 88, 94, 108, 111, 113, 135, 162, 182–183, 192–194, 207, 210, 217, 226, 230, 301
    cooking 194
    making 193–194, 210
    nutritional value of 192
    storing 194
pastry making 160–161, 170–171
pâté 28, 57, 110, 268–269, 271, 278
pathogenic bacteria 68, 86–89, 207, 244
peak bone mass 28
pectin 12, 16, 154, 235
pellagra 29, 31, 201
perishable food 85, 94, 146, 280, 337
pernicious anaemia 30
pH of food 75, 87–88, 90–91, 220, 237, 303, 329
phosphorous 11, 34, 36, 181–182, 243, 247, 268, 293, 297, 319, 324, 327
Physical Activity Level (PAL) 51
phytic acid 16, 36, 181
plant sterols/stanols 25, 52, 126
plasticity 73, 347, 361
poaching/poached 68–69, 71, 109, 116, 277, 289–290, 297–299, 305, 344
polysaccharides 12, 16, 180–181, 234
polyunsaturated fat 22, 24, 27, 41, 142, 270, 297, 315, 327, 339–344, 347
population increase 121
pork 30, 41, 64–66, 107, 109–111, 113–118, 136–137, 226, 231, 264, 270–275, 278, 314, 344

potassium 11, 34, 36, 217, 219, 234, 243, 270, 293, 323, 327, 329, 352
potato Dauphinoise, making 260
potatoes 9–10, 12, 27, 29, 31, 34, 41, 45, 47, 54, 58, 69, 71, 75, 98, 107–118, 129, 135–136, 141–142, 181, 192, 211, 215, 217–218, 220, 223–228, 231, 237, 240, 260, 301, 312–313, 328, 340
    changes during cooking 228
    storing 228
poultry 18, 24, 34, 54, 56–57, 62, 75, 86–88, 107–110, 113, 137, 229–231, 262–263, 266–267, 270, 272, 274, 276–282, 295, 297, 308, 351
    buying 280
    choosing 272
    cooking 277, 282
    nutritional value of 270–271
    preparation of 281
    storage of 280–281
pregnancy 27–28, 30–32, 34, 36–37, 40, 42, 49, 57, 60, 248, 271, 305
pressure cooking 69, 71, 224
primary processing 178, 182, 197, 202, 243
protein 8–9, 10, 12–13, 18–22, 25, 30, 40, 45, 47, 49, 51–52, 54, 57–58, 63, 68–69, 71–73, 75–77, 79, 86, 88, 116, 125–126, 142–143, 147, 176–178, 181–182, 184–189, 192, 194, 199, 201, 203, 205–206, 209–210, 217, 234, 243, 246–248, 250–251, 253–254, 265, 267–271, 274–275, 279, 290, 292, 296–297, 299–305, 308, 310–313, 319, 322–324, 326–329, 331, 358–359
    alternative/novel protein foods 326–329
    complementary 21
    effect of cooking on 72–73, 279, 301–303, 310–311, 359
    high biological value (HBV) 18–20, 328
    low biological value (LBV) 18–20
    recommended daily intake 21
    sources of 18
pulses 9, 11–12, 34, 37, 45, 53, 56, 58–59, 62–63, 71, 91, 102, 111, 115, 119, 142, 217–218, 234, 318–320, 325, 331
    nutritional value of 319
    storing when cooked 320
    uses of 319
pyridoxine 10, 204, 323

quick response (QR) codes 123
quinoa 18–20, 47, 63, 114, 142, 176, 206
Quorn™ 18–19, 63, 326, 328–329, 331, 333
    thai curry, making 333

rabbit 107, 111, 113, 262, 265
radiation 69, 72, 91
raising agents 68, 77–81, 110, 158, 179–181, 187–191, 212, 301, 358
    types of 77–79
rancid 75, 85, 153, 263, 344, 347
Rastafarian diet 65–66, 137
ratatouille, making 239
ready meals 35, 56–57, 69, 100, 120, 136, 152, 226, 235, 328
recycling food packaging 92–94, 100–102, 140
red meat 11, 29–30, 34, 37, 54, 56–57, 75, 270–271
Reference Intake (RI) 51–52, 147
Reference Nutrient Intake (RNI) 21, 40, 50–51, 53, 55
religious diets 62, 64–66, 106, 137
retrogradation 184
riboflavin 10, 40, 55, 218, 297, 327
rice 10–12, 15–16, 21, 29, 31, 34, 45, 47, 53–54, 58, 61, 63, 71, 81, 86, 88, 106, 111–119, 135, 139, 142–143, 176, 181, 192, 195–200, 204, 206–207, 209, 211, 217, 229, 230, 232–233, 246, 314, 343, 348
    brown 11, 15–16, 29, 34, 58, 142, 197–198
    nutritional value of 199
    processing of 196–197
    types of 198–199, 348
    white 15–16, 198
    whole grain 198–199
rickets 28, 33
risotto, making 211
roasting/roast 68–70, 73, 107, 109, 119, 224–226, 271, 273, 276–279, 321, 344–345
rosti cakes, making 240
roux sauce, making 173

rye 17, 58, 79, 106, 111–112, 142, 176, 181, 185, 203, 205, 209
   nutritional value of 205
   using 205

sago 206
salmonella 57, 87, 89, 207, 280, 295, 305
salt 35, 40, 47, 49, 51–55, 59, 63, 76, 78, 91, 97, 102, 108–111, 113–114, 116, 118, 122, 129, 137, 144–145, 147–149, 152, 160, 164, 168, 170–171, 173, 185, 187, 190, 193–195, 210, 219, 221, 224, 239, 249, 257, 264, 273–274, 278–279, 291, 296, 309, 321–322
saturated fat 22–23, 25, 47, 55, 59, 142, 152, 254, 270, 297, 308, 322, 329, 337, 339–344, 346
saturated fatty acids 55, 270, 342, 346
sauces, making 162–163, 172–173
sausages 9, 23, 35, 41, 47, 69–70, 76, 107–111, 113, 118–119, 265, 268–269, 271, 278, 314, 328
Scotch eggs, making 316
scrambling 68–69, 297, 299
scurvy 31
searing/seared 69, 71
seasonal food 99, 102, 109, 134, 140–141, 214, 219
secondary processing 183, 199, 201, 203, 244
seeds 9–11, 18, 20, 24, 27, 29–30, 33–35, 58–59, 61, 63, 70, 111–117, 119, 126, 142, 146, 178–179, 205–206, 214–216, 218, 229–230, 232–234, 318, 321, 324–325, 340–343, 346, 354
   nutritional value of 324
   uses of 324
selenium 11, 37, 62–63, 234, 268, 270–271, 297, 323–324
sensory analysis 150–151
sensory perception 148–149
Seventh Day Adventist diet 65–66
shelf life 23, 76, 92–94, 120, 122, 124, 127–129, 139, 146, 152–153, 187, 193–194, 205, 221, 228–229, 234, 244–246, 250, 253, 255, 269, 280, 321, 344–345, 350, 357–358
shellfish 11, 34, 37, 61, 65–66, 86, 110, 113–117, 137, 284–285, 287, 289, 291
shortening 23, 187, 316, 338, 341, 344–345
Sikh diet 65–66, 137
simmering 26, 69, 71, 118, 211, 224, 237, 239, 258–259, 269, 311, 313, 319–320, 331, 333
smoke point 346
smoked fish 91, 110, 112, 118, 230, 291
smoked bacon/pork 264, 273
sodium 11, 34–35, 38, 40, 47, 75, 131, 243, 293, 327
soluble fibre 16–17, 203–204
sorghum 118, 176, 206
soufflé, making 315
sourdough 79, 112, 118, 185, 191
sous vide 71
soy sauce 35, 76, , 116–117, 327, 333–334
soya 11–12, 18–20, 24, 27, 30, 33, 37, 45, 54, 56–58, 61, 63, 76, 116–117, 125–126, 143, 146, 234, 246, 257, 308, 315, 327–328, 333–334, 338, 340–341, 343, 346
   beans 11–12, 30, 61, 76, 116–117, 125–126, 146, 234, 246, 327–328, 338, 341, 343, 346
      milk 20, 56, 63, 125, 143, 257, 315, 328
      mince 308
      nutritional value of 327
      oil 341, 343, 346
spreads 338
spices 229, 232–233
spina biffida 10, 30–31, 57, 323
spinach 10, 27, 30, 33, 35–36, 111–112, 114–115, 117, 194, 210, 215, 218, 220, 226
Staphylococcus Aureus 87, 280
staple foods 29, 106, 127, 176, 185, 192, 196, 199–201, 206, 218, 227
starch 12–16, 45, 47, 54, 57–60, 68–69, 71–74, 76, 81, 118, 142, 173, 176–178, 180–182, 184–186, 188, 190, 192, 194, 198–199, 201, 203–206, 209, 211, 217–218, 220, 223, 225–226, 228, 250, 313, 315, 319, 354, 359
starter (bread making) 191
starter culture (cheese making) 249, 252
steaming/steamed 26, 69–71, 114, 116–118, 182, 203, 224–226, 277, 289–290, 329, 333, 337, 344
sterilisation 221, 235, 244, 246, 255, 305, 329

stewing/stew 41, 63, 68–69, 71, 110, 112–114, 118–119, 206, 217, 225–226, 228, 230–231, 235, 269, 271–272, 277, 279, 319, 357
stir frying 70, 116–117, 224, 226, 233, 268–269, 271–272, 328, 333–334, 340–345
stuffed baked apples, making 238
sucrose 12, 14, 50, 220, 223, 348–350, 354
suet 110, 160–161, 337
sugar 12–17, 32, 38, 45, 47, 49–55, 60–61, 69, 73–74, 77–78, 80, 91, 102, 107, 110–115, 117–118, 123, 129, 131, 135–136, 139, 142–145, 147, 152, 158–159, 161, 164, 168, 174, 184–185, 187–188, 190, 195, 212, 216–219, 221, 225–226, 230, 234–235, 238, 245–246, 251–253, 259, 275, 278, 303, 309, 320, 345, 347–359, 361
   cane/beet 12, 14, 348–349
   composition of 354
   extracting 349
   extrinsic 14, 55, 355
   function of 357–358
   intrinsic 14
   nutritional value of 354
   types of 350
sunflower oil, production of 325
sustainability of food 102, 123–124, 138, 283
sweet potatoes 12, 27, 113–114, 116, 118, 211, 215
syneresis 94, 249, 303
syrups 350

tapioca 206
tenderising 68, 71, 268, 276, 279, 292, 358
textured vegetable protein (TVP) 18, 20, 125, 327, 331
   production of 327
   nutritional value of 327
Thai Quorn curry, making 333
thiamine 10, 40, 54, 179–180, 199, 205, 218, 271, 319, 323, 327
thickening agents 154, 163, 184, 204, 206, 209, 211, 228, 255, 301, 308, 315, 321, 359
toasting 69–70, 180
tofu 18, 20, 58, 60, 63, 116–117, 125, 142, 326–328, 331, 334
   noodles, making 334
   nutritional value of 328
tomato sauce, making 172
tooth decay 11, 13, 36–37, 61, 354–355
traceability 96, 128, 262, 295
trace elements 8, 11, 36–38, 329
trans-fats 22–23, 138, 344
type 2 diabetes 13, 16, 22, 24, 48, 55–56, 58–59, 176, 355

ultra heat treated (UHT) 135, 245–246, 255
undernutrition 48
unleavened bread 190
unsaturated 22, 24, 27, 41, 45, 59, 142, 216, 264, 270, 293, 297, 315, 322, 327, 339–344, 346–347
unsaturated fatty acids 293, 327, 346–347
use-by date 85, 90, 92, 94, 128, 136, 146, 194, 280–281, 304

veal 111, 264
vegan 30, 37, 58, 62–65, 137, 234, 326–328
vegetable oil 10, 23–24, 26–27, 41, 126, 325, 338, 340–342, 344, 346
vegetable rosti cakes, making 234
vegetables
   choosing 220
   contents of 218–219
   cooking 224–226
   five-a-day portion 46, 216–217, 226
   preparation of 223
   preservation 234–235
   processing 221–222
   storing 220
   types of 214–216
   using 217, 219, 226
vegetarian 62–65, 106, 108, 115, 137, 150, 226, 234, 246, 249, 319, 321, 326–327
venison 107, 109, 265

vitamins 8, 10, 13, 22, 24–34, 36, 40, 45, 47, 49–52, 54–57, 60–63, 70–71, 75, 126, 135, 138, 176, 179–181, 185–187, 192, 195, 198–199, 201, 204–205, 216–219, 221, 223–227, 243–244, 246–247, 251, 254, 268, 271, 275, 277, 279, 290, 293, 297–298, 319, 323–324, 327, 340, 342, 352
   A 10, 22, 25–27, 32, 40, 45, 54–55, 57, 201, 218–219, 226, 243, 247, 251, 254, 268, 271, 290, 293, 297, 319, 340, 342
   B 13, 26, 29–30, 32, 40, 45, 49, 56, 62–63, 176, 179–181, 185, 192, 199, 201, 204–205, 243–244, 247, 251, 271, 293, 297, 323–324, 327
   C 10, 26, 31–32, 34, 36, 40, 45, 49, 54, 56–57, 63, 75, 187, 217–219, 224, 226–227, 243–244, 247, 297, 319
   D 22, 24–26, 28, 32–33, 36, 45, 52, 54, 56–57, 60–61, 63, 243, 247, 251, 254, 271, 290, 293, 297, 342
   deficiencies 27–31
   E 10, 22, 25–27, 32, 54, 176, 218, 297, 323–324, 340, 342
   fat soluble 26–28, 32, 54, 271, 293, 342
   K 10, 22, 25–27, 32, 54, 216, 218, 342
   water soluble 26, 29–32, 71, 226, 243–244, 279

wagyu 263–264
water
   drinking 38, 42, 47–48
   effect of cooking on 74
water soluble vitamins 26, 29–32, 71, 226, 243–244, 279
Welsh cakes, making 212
wheat 10, 12, 15–18, 27, 29, 34, 47, 58, 61, 63, 72, 79, 106, 108, 110–113, 116–119, 142, 176–187, 192–193, 195–197, 200, 203–206, 209, 328, 343
   nutritional value of 181
   processing of 178–180, 182–183
wheat flour
   properties of 184
   types of 180
whipped cream, making 165, 254
white fish 285, 290, 292–293, 312
white meat 75, 266
whole grains 10–12, 17, 24, 29–30, 33–37, 47, 56–57, 59, 62, 176, 195, 198–199, 204, 206, 298
   bread 10–11
   cereals 10, 17, 29–30, 33–37, 56, 176, 195, 357
   rice 198–199

yeast 10, 29–30, 35, 63, 76, 78–80, 84–85, 107, 110, 112, 126, 168, 185–191, 207, 209, 234, 299, 358
yoghurt 18, 25, 27, 50, 57–58, 76, 93–94, 100, 109, 112, 115, 119, 126–127, 145, 182, 242, 251–253, 257, 344, 354
   making 252–253
   nutritional value of 251
   types of 251

zinc 11, 37, 45, 57, 126, 247, 268, 270, 293, 297, 323–324

Image credits:

©Alamy: p31(TR): Custom Medical Stock Photo; p46(kidney beans): FoodCollection; p70(toasting): The Picture Pantry; p71(poaching): Photography Viages; p94(CL): BWAC Images; p96(meat label): Oliver Ring; p97(cheese): DGB; p101(bags): BWAC Images; p101(coffee): Carolyn Jenkins; p101(recycling bins): PhotoEdit; p114(Papian): Cultura RM; p121(TL): Mary Evans Picture Library; p121(BL): Steve Vidler; p122(BL): Ian Dagnall; p123(CR): Chris Ridley – Internet Stock; p126(probiotic yoghurt): Helen Sessions; p127: Peter Titmuss; p128(soil association logo): Shaun Finch – Coyote-Photography.co.uk, Soil Association, Waitrose; p129(CR): Xinhua; p133(TL): Mediablitzimages; p133(CL): Mediablitzimages; p133(CL): studiomode; p144(TL): Jeff Morgan 03; p144(TC): RosaBetancourt 0 people images; p145: RosaBetancourt 0 people images; p154(CR): studiomode; p181(BR): Tim Gainey; p187: Richard Levine; p192(BL): studiomode; p195: Carolyn Jenkins; p223(Fanning): Joris Luyten; p224(braising): Kramp & Gölling, AgencyFood Centrale Hamburg GmbH; p242(yoghurt): Ashley Cooper; p248(cheshire): YAY Media AS; p252(pro-biotic yoghurt): Helen Sessions; p252(live yoghurt): Mediablitzimages; p252(bio-yoghurt): MediaforMedical/Michel Cardoso / Universal Images Group; p262: Libby Welch; p269(sweetbread): Bonisolli, Barbara; p291: epa european pressphoto agency b.v.; p299(poaching): Photography Viages; p302(CL): migstock; p306: Libby Welch; p319(TR): Heinze, Winfried; p320(TL): Radius Images; p322(epi-pen): eye35.pix; p326(soy mince): foodfolio; p344(milk): Robert Morris; p350(syrup): S. Vincent; p352: ACORN 9; p356(CL): Alex Segre; p356(BL): Libby Welch; p377(TC): Food and Drink Photos; p389: MBI; p417(samosas): Jon Arnold Images.

©Coeliac UK: p181(C).

©emc design ltd: p224(Background); p371; p268–269(background).

©European Food Council: p97(EU logo).

©Daniel Gray: p107–108(England and Wales maps).

©Fairtrade Austria: p128(fairtrade logo); p139(fairtrade bananas logo); p156(fairtrade logo).

©Fotolia: p198(pudding): ajbstudio; p200(TL): chamillew; p200(TC): chamillew; p202(TC): hjpix; p206(BR): axway; p206(BL): Unclesam; p223(Sheds): Francesco83; p233(cumin): Viktor; p242(goat milking): Maslov Dmitry; p251(natural yoghurt): cook_inspire; p254(TC): NorGal; p268(ox liver): alain wacquier; p289(egg): superfood; p295(C): superfood; p337(ghee): Marek; p340(linseed): NorGal; p341(sunflower): tashka2000; p344(yoghurt): Peredniankina.

©Getty: p18(Quorn): Bloomberg; p19(Quorn): Keith Getter ; p21: Graeme Robertson ; p46(peas): garysludden; p46(broccoli): Tetra Images; p65(B): Hindustan Times; p114(Jerk Pork): Bob Carey; p115(tandoor oven): Boaz Rottem; p292(T): Steven Kazlowski; p326(Quorn): Bloomberg; p330(Quorn): Bloomberg; p350(tracle): Rachel Husband.

©Halen Mon: p97(salt).

©Illuminate publishing: p73(flour and butter, forming sauce, completed sauce); p74(Brulee, Caramelisation, carrots, onions): Jayne Hill; p75(CR, CL); p81(TR); p170(1–8); p171(1–8): Peter Burton; p172(1–6); p173(1–6); p174(1–8): Peter Burton; p288; p337(suet): Bethan Jones; p366(ingredients, whisking, sieving, folding, baking, final product): Eliscia & Saskia Santos; p369; p392(Ingredients, measuring jugs, brand, wheat flour, potato starch, brown rice flour, Arrowroot, Cornflour, Cassava flour): Fiona Dowling; p393: Fiona Dowling; p394(2g cornflour, 3g cornflour, 4g cornflour): Fiona Dowling; p403: Fiona Dowling; p414: Fiona Dowling; p415(moules, tart): Fiona Dowling; p416(chicken, fruit, panna cotta, floating islands, gnocchi, arancini): Fiona Dowling.

©iStock: p16(BL): ttsz; p18(grains): egal; p18(dairy): intraprese; p18(beands): ValentynVolkov; p23(CL): elenaleonova; p23(TR): oculo; p24(oily fish): vuk8691; p34: ttsz; p36(fruit): yasuhiroamano; p36(bread): Photosiber; p70(roasting): tirc83; p71(braising): vicuschka; p94(BL): onebluelight; p98: luoman; p101(recycling): FlairImages; p111(crostini): Rus32; p112(baklava): Images_of_Beauty; p118(biltong): HandmadePictures; p118(couscous): vertmedia; p124(TL): selimaksan; p129(CL): CristiNistor; p159(3): foodandwinephotography; p163(souffle): bonchan; p178(TR): Grafissimo; p186(BC): Ioan Florin Cnejevici; p191(BR): BackyardProduction; p192(TC): Photology1971; p193(BL): Syldavia; p198(basmati): eelnosiva; p201(cornmeal): sf_foodphoto; p202(BL): Bonga1965; p204(TL): Sascha Burkard; p205: melkon_lv; p227(TL): Ivan Vojnic; p228(boiling): Ivan Vojnic; p228(mashed): StockSolutions; p230(chives): Avalon_Studio; p230(coriander): li jingwang; p230(angelica): sommail; p230(dill): Tomboy2290; p231(mint): anna1311; p231(sage): Avalon_Studio; p231(rosemary): clubfoto; p231(marjoram): Floortje; p231(tarragon): Floortje; p231(thyme): Floortje; p231(parsley): Tomboy2290; p242(milking): zmeel; p250(CC): Moncherie; p263(calf): JMichl; p266(CL): JohnGollop; p266(CC): Richard Griffin; p266(CR): Richard Griffin; p268(heart): Alexandra Thompson; p269(calf tounge): bonchan; p272(thin strips): bgsmith; p280(TC): Eraxion; p281: sturti; p282(storing): sturti; p289(batter): Difydave; p294(free range hens): George Clerk; p298(poached eggs): JoeGough; p299(scrambling): merc67; p301(whisked egg): gourmetphotography; p301(thickening): Magone; p302(BR): Acronycal; p304(TL): themosse; p312: SabinaS; p313: StockSolutions; p318(CC): sara35mm; p320(BR): sara35mm; p324(bagels): littleny; p338(margarine): JoLin; p341(sesame): ChamilleWhite; p344(bacon): Peter Burnett; p346(flash point): TARIK KIZILKAYA; p353: NoDerog; p356(TL): BrianAJackson; p418(Muffins): juliannafunk.

©LIDL: p136(TL).

©Marine Stewardship Council: p283(CR).

©Red Tractor Assurance: p128(red tractor logo); p138(BL); p156(red tractor assurance); p263(red tractor logo).

©RSPCA Assured: p128(RSPCA logo); p263(RSPCA assured logo).

©Science Photo Library: p69(BR): Science Stock Photography; p69(CR): Tony Mcconnell; p126(fortified spread): Steve Horrell.

©Shoutout: p73(starch); p73(starch softening); p73(starch swelling); p165(1–7); p166(–8); p167(9–16); p168(1–8); p169(9–15); p228(starch, starch softening, starch swelling).

©Shutterstock: p7: S-F; p8: marilyn barbone; p9(avocado): Africa Studio; p9(chicken): Magdanatka; p9(spaghetti): Viktor1; p10(Wallnuts): Ajakor; p10(Milk): AS Food studio; p10(Oranges): el lobo; p10(Salmon): Evgeny Karandaev; p10(liver): freeskyline; p10(Eggs): Mamuka Gotsiridze; p10(spinach): Nataliya Arzamasova; p10(Almonds): Sea Wave; p10(Cereal): sss615; p10(mushrooms): Steve Cukrov; p10(Asparagus): vm2002; p10(rice): warlord76; p10(Broccoli): Yuliya Gontar; p11(Brown rice): DONOT6_STUDIO; p11(Brazil nuts): HandmadePictures; p11(Yogurt): Sea Wave; p11(scampi): Shaiith; p11(Steak): stockcreations; p11(eggs and bacon): Tatiana Volgutova; p11(beans): Timolina; p11(seabass): Timolina; p11(Salmon): Tiramisu Studio; p11(tea): Yuliya Gontar; p13(diabetes): designer491; p13(Lollipops): Elena Schweitzer; p13(tarts): Elenadesign; p13(obesity): kurhan; p13(Cans): Oleksiy Mark; p13(tooth decay): PhotoHouse; p14(CR): Marcos Mesa Sam Wordley; p14(B): Nitr; p14(CC): S-F; p15: JFunk; p16(TL): marilyn barbone; p17(B): Juliar Studio; p18(meat): alexpro9500; p18(seeds): marekuliasz; p18(eggs): Pakhnyushchy; p18(soy): Patty Orly; p19(eggs): Jiri Hera; p19(steak): Lisovskaya Natalia; p19(oats): MaraZe; p19(cannelini beans): marilyn barbone; p19(amino acid): molekuul_be; p19(Wholemeal bread): Natali Zakharova; p19(Almonds): Sea Wave; p19(cheese): Viktor1; p22: multiart; p23(BL): James W Copeland; p24(tuna can): Anna.zabella; p24(dairy): Evgeny Karandaev; p24(meat): Isantilli; p24(avocado): Nataliya Arzamasova; p24(nuts): neil langan; p25(TR): hywards; p25(TC): Juan Gaertner; p26: Patty Orly; p27(TR): charnsitr; p27(TL): Nataliya Arzamasova; p27(CL): Sea Wave; p27(BL): Yuliya Gontar; p28(CL): Evgeny Karandaev; p28(TR): joshya; p29(liver): freeskyline; p29(creal): sss615; p29(mushrooms): Steve Cukrov; p29(rice): warlord76; p30(walnuts): Ajakor; p30(milk): AS Food studio; p30(eggs): Mamuka Gotsiridze; p30(aparagus): vm2002; p31(BR): el lobo; p31(CR): Lighthunter; p31(TL): Riccardo Mayer; p31(CL): Syda Productions; p32(BR): Pisit Rapitpunt; p32(CC): Viktar Malyshchyts; p33(x-ray): Praisaeng; p33(yoghurt): Sea Wave; p36(toothpaste): Kenishirotie; p36(pills): Tashatuvango; p44: MaraZe; p45: tacar; p46(orange juice): Africa Studio; p46(strawberries): Aleksandra Zaitseva; p46(strawberries): Aleksandra Zaitseva; p46(grapes): BITOEYpixx; p46(apricots): Maxsol; p46(orange): Melpomene; p46(pear): mythja; p46(raisins): Ulada; p48(CL): akturer; p48(TL): Lestertair; p52: Brent Hofacker; p53: Annasunny24; p55: Annasunny24; p57: Wavebreakmedia; p62(BL): Lucky Team Studio; p62(TC): Stefanina Hill; p64(CR): Aleksandar Todorovic; p64(BR): ChameleonsEye; p64(T): Mivr; p65(TR): ChameleonsEye; p65(CR): rj lerich; p68: Jackthumm; p70(stir frying): Blinka; p70(shallow frying): Joel O'Brien; p70(grilling): Monkey Business Images; p70(deep frying): seksan kingwatcharapong; p70(baking): wsf-s; p71(pressure cooking): Carlos Restrepo; p71(sous vide): Gulsina; p71(stewing): istetiana; p71(blanching): Kondor83; p71(steaming): StudioSmart; p71(boiling): timages; p71(simmering): vvoe; p73(steak): hlphoto; p74(Toast): Jiri Hera; p75(TR): Sebastian Studio; p77(CR): AS Food studio; p77(TR): Chalermsak; p77(TL): Jiri Hera; p77(BR): Vania Georgieva; p78(fermenting yeast): ChameleonsEye; p78(fresh yeast): Jiri Hera; p79(CR): vanillaechoes; p79(BR): Maly Designer; p81(CR): nikkytok; p83(Microwave): MrGarry; p83(Oven): ppart; p83(Steamer): Shai_Halud; p84: O'SHI; p85(bread): Ariene Studio; p85(strawberries): Jeeranan Thongpan; p85(apples): StepanPopov; p86(Biological): Horoscope; p86(Chemical): Sebastian Duda; p86(Physical): Tiago M Nunes; p90(rubbish bags): 1000 Words; p90(rubbish bin): SpeedKingz; p93(paprboard): Africa Studio; p93(glass): Angel Simon; p93(plastic): IriGri; p93(metal): JL-Pfeifer; p93(paper bags): symbiot; p94(TL): jannoon028; p95: FuzzBones; p96(pigs): 2xSamara.com; p96(farmers market): Christian Mueller; p96(butchers): Monkey Business Images; p97(pigs): Mike Charles; p99: 06photo; p100: Fotos593; p102: PANYA KUANUN; p104: De Visu; p111(wurst): Viktor1; p112(dolmades): Craevschii Family; p114(ceviche): Foodio; p115(dhal): Eve's Food Photography; p115(samosa): highviews; p115(poppadoms): Paul Cowan; p116(satay): bonchan; p116(pho close-up): LA the Crocodile; p116(pho): Marina Nabatova; p116(som tum): Preto Perola; p117(sushi): Lisovskaya Natalia; p117(gyoza): Nickola_Che; p117(peking duck): Paul_Brighton; p118(kefta): Ramon grosso dolarea; p118(kunafa): Tanya Stolyarevskaya; p120(CL): jordache; p120(T): 06photo; p121(TR): monkeybusinessimages; p122(TL): Paula Cobleigh; p123(TR): Bloomua; p124(CR): BallBall14; p125: AlikeYou; p126(blueberries): Arina P Habich; p126(prebiotic foods): Pixelbliss; p126(Fried-bamboo-caterpillar): wasanajai; p128(strawberry punnets): GUNDAM_Ai; p129(BR): Kaesler Media; p130: Everett Collection; p134(T): 1000 Words; p134(CL): SpeedKingz; p135: kazoka; p136(BL): goodluz; p136(CL): Pictoores; p138(TR): Antonova Anna; p138(TL): Matee Nuserm; p139(TR): Graphic Compressor; p140: hddigital; p141(kale): Binh Thanh Bui; p141(leeks): Binh Thanh Bui; p141(brussel sprouts): Edward Westmacott; p141(cauliflower): Egor Rodynchenko; p141(Strawberries): EsHanPhot; p141(Aparagus): Hong Vo; p141(cabbage): lidante; p141(cucumber slice): Martins Vanags; p141(blackberries): Nata-Lia; p141(cucumber): S1001; p141(rasperries): saras66; p141(fresh corn): Shaiith; p141(red cabbage): Viktar Malyshchyts; p142(BL): images72; p142(TL): xuanhuongho; p148(TL): Fotovika; p148(TC): Ruth Black; p149: Arisa_J; p150: Lilyana Vynogradova; p151: Ruth Black; p152(TC): Sirapob; p152(TL): Sorbis; p152(BL): Tobik; p153(CR): Kvini; p153(TL): Alena Haurylik; p153(CL): Joe Gough; p153(BR): Julie Clopper; p154(BL): Alena Haurylik; p154(BR): Anna-Mari West; p154(TL): Ti Santi; p157: Pinkyone; p158: Antonio Danna; p159(1): MaraZe; p159(4): Marie C Fields; p159(2): ninikas; p159(5): Pinkyone; p160(sieving): Chehova; p160(resting): ffolas; p160(mixing): ninikas; p160(adding liquid): PeterG; p160(cooking): Soloviova Liudmyla; p160(rolling out): spass; p161(6): Elena Demyanko; p161(1): Marie C Fields; p161(3,4,5): Paul Broadbent; p161(2): Paul Cowan; p162(fish): Alena

Ozerova; p162(spaghetti): Piotr Krzeslak; p162(ham): stockcreations; p163(mayonnaise): MaraZe; p163(chicken): Monkey Business Images; p163(gazpacho): Stanjoman; p164(tempura asparagus): ARENA Creative; p164(Toad in the hole): AS Food studio; p164(grilled enchiladas): Daniel Anohin; p164(Shortbread): Jiri Hera; p164(Chocolate shortbread): Lesya Dolyuk; p164(Oat bars): MShev; p164(sugar finger biscuits): Olaf Speier; p164(Fish and chips): Pixelbliss; p164(fried bananas): Raihana Asral; p164(pancakes): Yulia Davidovich; p175: Elena Schweitzer; p176(wheat): aristoteles; p176(oats): Brent Hofacker; p176(T): Elena Schweitzer; p176(maize): focal point; p176(barley): id-art; p176(rice): perfectlab; p177(B): Aleksandar Kamasi; p177(TC): aristoteles; p178(BL): Gilmanshin; p178(TL): rsooll; p180(CR): Oksana Shufrych; p182(burghul): Ariene Studio; p182(kibbled wheat): Heike Rau; p182(couscous): joannawnuk; p182(wheat bran): kazmulka; p182(puffed wheat): MichelleSC; p182(semolina): White78; p183(sauces): AlenKadr; p183(muffins): bonchan; p183(pies): Brent Hofacker; p183(biscuits): chrisdorney; p183(crisp breads): chrisdorney; p183(pastries): Cio; p183(pizza): Jag_cz; p183(bread): Joe Gough; p183(cake): Lesya Dolyuk; p183(doughnuts): MaraZe; p183(crackers): Nuttapong; p183(waffles): Oleksandra Naumenko; p183(crumpets): Paul Michael Hughes; p183(cereal bars): Piotr Rzeszutek; p183(noodles): Sanit Fuangnakhon; p183(pancakes): Suto Norbert Zsolt; p183(pasta): Timolina; p183(ice cream): unpict; p183(cereal): www.BillionPhotos.com; p185(bakery items): Crepesoles; p185(breads): Moving Moment; p185(BL): Shaiith; p185(TL): Whytock; p186(C): Whytock; p189: KucherAV; p190: Antonova Anna; p191(TL): Arina P Habich; p191(TC): BarryTuck; p192(BR): al1962; p192(TL): Volodymyr Krasyuk; p193(BR): Africa Studio; p193(TR): foodlove; p193(BC): Tyler Olson; p194: Africa Studio; p195: Artush; p195: Sony Ho; p196(TC): HamsterMan; p196(BR): TippaPatt; p197(BL): Chatrawee Wiratgasem; p197(CR): Guitar photographer; p197(TR): inlovepai; p198(white long): HamsterMan; p198(brown long): Imageman; p198(arborio): Jiri Hera; p198(glutinous): MAHATHIR MOHD YASIN; p198(sushi): Mariemily Photos; p198(wild): Oliver Hoffmann; p198(jasmine): Valentin Valkov; p200(B): EMJAY SMITH; p201(CR): Antonio Gravante; p201(popcorn): Brent Hofacker; p201(corn oil): Evan Lorne; p201(cornflour): Gayvoronskaya_Yana; p201(corn syrup): PR Image Factory; p201(cornflakes): Tomophafan; p202(TL): dymax; p202(TL): Roman Samokhin; p203(CL): alina_danilova; p203(CC): Anna Kurzaeva; p203(TL): milosducati; p203(TC): MShev; p204(BL): Azdora; p204(TC): Iakov Kalinin; p206(CR): Brent Hofacker; p206(BC): koosen; p206(CC): matin; p206(CL): picturepartners; p206(TL): Sayanjo65; p206(TC): Sayanjo65; p207(BL): Kateryna Kon; p207(TL): pathdoc; p208(orzo): B Calkins; p208(shells): bioraven; p208(bows): Maryna Burnatna; p208(fusilli): Sebastian Studio; p208(tagliatelle): Volodymyr Krasyuk; p210: S_Photo; p211: Lisovskaya Natalia; p212: Paul Cowan; p213: leonori; p214(T): Aleksandar Mijatovic; p214(BL): DenisNata; p215(artichokes): Binh Thanh Bui; p215(beetroot): Egor Rodynchenko; p215(cauliflower): Egor Rodynchenko; p215(lemon): Jag_cz; p215(mushroom): jhy; p215(quince): M. Unal Ozmen; p215(figs): Maks Narodenko; p215(hazelnut): Maks Narodenko; p215(leek): merc67; p215(spinach): Nataliya Arzamasova; p215(gooseberry): neil langan; p215(mange tout): Robyn Mackenzie; p215(kelp): Still AB; p215(cherries): Tim UR; p215(pomegranate): Tim UR; p215(rhubarb): Valentyn Volkov; p215(passion fruit): Viktar Malyshchyts; p215(courgette): Viktor1; p216(avocado): Africa Studio; p216(baked beans): AS Food studio; p216(peppers): Dream79; p216(grapes): Olha Afanasieva; p216(lolly): Teri Virbickis; p218(brocolli): akiyoko; p218(green vegetables): Brent Hofacker; p218(lentils): cooperr; p218(pulses): Esin Deniz; p218(citrus fruits): Marina Yesina; p218(root vegetables): Phish Photography; p218(potatoes): tok anas; p219: leonori; p220(TC): Arina P Habich; p220(TL): leonori; p220(BL): Somporn Wongvichienkul; p221(juice cartons): Kvini; p221(salad): aerogondo2; p221(dried fruit): aerogondo2; p221(frozen vegetables): Evikka; p221(packed fruit): littleny; p221(canned fruit): villorejo; p221(jarred fruit): Zigzag Mountain Art; p223(Segmenting): Ina Ts; p223(Diced): Vladislav Nosik; p223(Strips): warrengoldswain; p224(roasting): alely; p224(baking): Irina Bg; p224(frying): Lisovskaya Natalia; p224(grilling): Maminau Mikalai; p224(boiling): Nitr; p224(steaming): StudioSmart; p225(CR): Arina P Habich; p225(BR): Olha Afanasieva; p226: M. Unal Ozmen; p227(B): Andriano; p227(TR): James Peragine; p228(baking): ken6345; p228(frying): Mariya Siyanko; p228(salad): paulbrighton76; p229(BR): Fotografiche; p229(TL): marilyn barbone; p229(TR): marilyn barbone; p229(BL): matka_Wariatka; p230(bay leaf): Dionisvera; p230(basil): Dionisvera; p230(horseradish): Kuttelvaserova Stuchelova; p231(lemongrass): Sombat S; p232(cardamom): Anna Kurzaeva; p232(allspice): B.and E. Dudziscy; p232(cayenne): bolsher; p232(caraway): Charlotte Lake; p232(cinnamon): Nata-Lia; p232(anise pepper): Nattika; p232(chili): ploedfisch; p232(cloves): Sea Wave; p232(chinese five spice): topnatthapon; p233(fenugreek): Dipak Shelare; p233(saffron): Evgeny Karandaev; p233(poppy seeds): Iasmina Calinciuc; p233(sesame seeds): Iasmina Calinciuc; p233(mustard seed): Lovely Bird; p233(pepper): MAHATHIR MOHD YASIN; p233(ginger): Nata-Lia; p233(paprika): ploedfisch; p233(mace or nutmeg): popovaphoto; p233(turmeric): yingthun; p234(frozen vegetables): Africa Studio; p234(herbs): Gts; p234(quince): hlphoto; p234(pickled vegetables): monticello; p236(peach): Africa Studio; p236(lemons): Jag_cz; p236(kiwi fruit): Nataliya Arzamasova; p236(melon): Phonlawat_51; p236(pineapple): Phonlawat_51; p236(Cherries): Vorobyeva; p238: margouillat photo; p239: Civil; p240: maryskin; p241: Evgeny Karandaev; p242(whipping cream): goodluz; p242(butter): Sea Wave; p242(cheese): Sea Wave; p242(cows): symbiot; p244(BR): Andrey Ezhov; p244(C): Lakeview Images; p245(BR): Africa Studio; p245(TR): Ana Photo; p245(CR): MaraZe; p247(BL): Anna Shepulova; p247(TR): Goode Imaging; p247(BR): Joshua Resnick; p247(TL): Olena Kaminetska; p248(mascapone): Bruno D'Andrea; p248(feta): cristi180884; p248(cheddar): ffolas; p248(edam): Jiri Hera; p248(parmesan): Joe Gough; p248(brie): Moving Moment; p248(blue stilton): NatashaPhoto; p248(cottage cheese): Sea Wave; p248(background): stockphoto mania; p248(ricotta): Sunny Forest; p248(mozzerella): Teodora D; p248(fromage frais): wsf-s; p250(CR): Stepanek Photography; p251(fat free yoghurt): areeya_ann; p251(set yoghurt): Gayvoronskaya_Yana; p251(yoghurt icon): Gyorgy Barna; p251(luxury yoghurt): Gyorgy Barna; p251(yoghurt in glass): Meg Wallace Photography; p254(T): 54613; p258: Gaus Nataliya; p259: maryskin; p260: iuliia_n; p261: Elena Schweitzer; p263(stag): Alex Helin; p263(sheep): Eric Isselee; p263(organic logo): Jason Winter; p263(rabbit): JIANG HONGYAN; p263(cow): photomaster; p263(pig): photomaster; p263(horse): photomaster; p263(goat): photomaster; p264(bacon): denio109; p264(gammon): hlphoto; p264(wagyu): Kondor83; p264(lamb): Lisovskaya Natalia; p264(veal): Shebeko; p265(goat): Azdora; p265(venison): hlphoto; p265(rabbit): natalia bulatova; p267(quail): ADA_photo; p267(ostrich): Andrey_Kuzmin; p267(wood pigeon): chris2766; p267(goose): Eric Isselee; p267(guinea fowl): Eric Isselee; p267(turkey): photomaster; p267(pheasant): photomaster; p267(duck): Rosa Jay; p268(lamb liver): n7atal7i; p268(kidney): Oleksandr Lysenko; p269(tripe): bonchan; p269(oxtail): casanisa; p270(TL): Nataliia Pyzhova; p270(CL): Nataliia Pyzhova; p270(BL): Nataliia Pyzhova; p272(boneless cut): cozyta; p272(rolled joint): Edward Westmacott; p272(lean mince): Joe Gough; p272(cubes): margouillat photo; p272(butchers shop): racorn; p272(lean cut): Valery121283; p274(lamb chops): Christian Jung; p274(pork chops): Diana Taliun; p274(beef steak): serg_dibrova; p274(marbled steak): smuay; p275(B): maggee; p275(TL): Mariemily Photos; p276(batting): Ivan Mateev; p276(boning): janecat; p276(tying): janecat; p276(tenderising): yingko; p278(BL): Jiri Hera; p278(TL): Yulia Kozlova; p279(TR): Brent Hofacker; p279(CR): Mariemily Photos; p280(BL): Angela Bragato; p280(CC): ducu59us; p280(TL): www.BillionPhotos.com; p282(washing): Anetlanda; p282(cutting meat): Iakov Filimonov; p283(TL): Andrey Armyagov; p283(TR): jordache; p283(BL): racorn; p284(background): Bejim; p284(herring): bonchan; p284(plaice): Edward Westmacott; p284(crab): Hong Vo; p284(cod): Krasowit; p284(lemon slices): Linda Hughes; p284(lobster): Isantilli; p284(salmon): Olgysha; p284(haddock): picturepartners; p284(prawn): prapat1120; p284(trout): RACOBOVT; p285(octopus): Alexander Raths; p285(crayfish): D7INAMI7S; p285(turbot): JIANG HONGYAN; p285(hake): picturepartners; p285(cockles): sarawutnirothon; p286: Andrey Armyagov; p287: Dani Vincek; p289(flour): Coprid; p289(breadcrumbs): Coprid; p290(TL): kazoka; p290(BL): Shahril KHMD; p290(CL): showcake; p292(B): ernstc; p294(barn hens): branislavpudar; p294(eggs): CatMicroStock; p294(caged hens): Fotos593; p294(organic hens): sylv1rob1; p294(fried egg): Tossapol; p295(B): PIMPUN TAWAKOON; p298(fried eggs): Nitr; p299(icon): ffolas; p299(boiling): gosphotodesign; p299(baking): Irantzu Arbaizagoitia; p299(frying): Tossapol; p300(TL): ffolas; p300(TC): ffolas; p300(TR): ffolas; p300(CC): mates; p301(coating): Anetlanda; p301(mixture): Destinyweddingstudio; p301(glazing): ffolas; p301(emulsifying): ffolas; p301(souffle): Magdanatka; p301(enriching): margouillat photo; p301(binding): Timolina; p301(garnishing): vanillaechoes; p302(CR): Africa Studio; p302(BL): kubais; p303(boild eggs): Africa Studio; p303(curdled eggs): Dariya Angelova; p304(TC): vanillaechoes; p305(BC): Dasha Petrenko; p305(BR): Elena Veselova; p305(BL): minadezhda; p308: Lisovskaya Natalia; p310: Joe Gough; p311: Timolina; p314: stockcreations; p315: sarsmis; p316: Magdanatka; p317: Be Good; p318(T): Elena Schweitzer; p318(CL): StepanPopov; p319(CL): Jessmine; p319(CR): Jiri Hera; p319(TL): marlee; p320(CC): oksana2010; p321(TL): Christopher Boswell; p321(TR): Elena Veselova; p321(CL): Macrovector; p321(BR): Moving Moment; p322(hives): PANYA KUANUN; p323(background): Christopher Boswell; p323(walnut): Dionisvera; p323(almonds): Lepas; p323(cashews): mayakova; p323(pistachio): NinaM; p323(pecan): Olga Popova; p323(macadamia nut): PhilipYb Studio; p323(brazil nut): Tim UR; p323(hazelnut): Tim UR; p324(poppy seeds): Alexandra Lande; p324(icon): Ekaterina Garyuk; p324(seed variety): Elena Schweitzer; p324(chia seed): Toni Genes; p325(seeded bread): Moving Moment; p325(muffins): N K; p326(icon): HandmadePictures; p326(tofu): HandmadePictures; p326(tofu dish): Koyjira; p327(soya bean pod): MAKSYM SUKHENKO; p327(soya bean jar): showcake; p330(tofu): HandmadePictures; p332: Nataliya Arzamasova; p333: Foto2rich; p334: Jacques PALUT; p335: Christian-Fischer; p336: 6493866629; p337(lard): JPC-PROD; p337(butter): Sea Wave; p338(butter): Ari N; p338(shelves): defotoberg; p340(avocado): Africa Studio; p340(coconut): Africa Studio; p340(corn): ddsign; p340(chilli): FabioBalbi; p340(almond): Iryna Denysova; p340(rapeseed): verca; p341(walnut): 5PH; p341(vegetable): Aleksandrs Samuilovs; p341(soya bean): Amarita; p341(olive): DUSAN ZIDAR; p344(chips): MarinaP; p345(creaming): Africa Studio; p345(spreading butter): ALEXSTAND; p345(bacon): Anna Hoychuk; p345(cake): Monkey Business Images; p345(salad): Patty Orly; p346(smoke background): art studio; p346(smoke point): Ruggiero Scardigno; p347: Mariontxa; p348(TC): Nitr; p348(BR): Radu Bercan; p348(TL): Sunny Forest; p349(sugar bees): Gelia; p349: NoRegret; p349(sugar cane): smart.art; p350(golden syrup): Elena Elisseeva; p350(sap): Marc Bruxelle; p350(molasses): Murat Ileten; p351(clear honey): Pakorn Amonstian; p351(cloudy honey): Volodymyr Herasymchuk; p357(CR): Irina Zavyalova; p357(BR): Kenneth Dedeu; p358(raising agent): Dalton Dingelstad; p358(fermentation): Grom Art; p358(preservative): kostasgr; p359(CR): Adriana Nikolova; p359(TR): Jamie Rogers; p374: graphixmania; p377(CC): ffolas; p377(BC): Sarah Marchant; p391: pogonici; p396: michaeljung; p412: ruigsantos; p417(tart): kostrez; p417(lasagne): margouillat photo; p417(burgers): Strannik_fox; p418(roll): AS Food studio; p418(cheesecake): Bahadir Yeniceri; p418(eclairs): bernashafo; p427: goodluz; p230–231(background): Krivosheev Vitaly; p232–233(background): stockphoto mania; p362–363: bibiphoto.

©**Soil Association** : p156(soil association logo): Soil Association; p180(CL): Soil Association .

©**Superstock**: p301(aeration): Paul D. Van Hoy II / age fotostock; p326(vegetable protein): Westend61; p330(vegetable protein): Westend61; p358(colour): Food and Drink.

©**Trussell Trust:** p103

©**Vegetarian Society:** p62(TL)

©**WJEC and NUTRITION Sample Assessment Materials 6:** p364: WJEC CBAC Ltd.